A·N·N·U·A·L E·D·I·T·I·O·N·S

American History
Volume I

15th Edition

Pre-Colonial through Reconstruction

EDITOR

Robert James Maddox
Pennsylvania State University
University Park

Robert James Maddox, distinguished historian and professor of American history at
Pennsylvania State University, received a B.S. from Fairleigh Dickinson University in
1957, an M.S. from the University of Wisconsin in 1958, and a Ph.D. from Rutgers
in 1964. He has written, reviewed, and lectured extensively, and is widely respected
for his interpretations of presidential character and policy.

Dushkin/McGraw-Hill
Sluice Dock, Guilford, Connecticut 06437

Visit us on the Internet
http://www.dushkin.com/annualeditions/

Credits

1. The New Land
Facing overview—Illustration by Mike Eagle.
2. Revolutionary America
Facing overview—Painting of sailing boats at historic James Towne courtesy of Virginia State Library.
3. National Consolidation and Expansion
Facing overview—Drawing of "Emigrants' Noonday Halt," by Sol Eytinge, courtesy of the Library of Congress.
4. The Civil War and Reconstruction
Facing overview—Drawing of Union and Confederate soldiers trading, by Edwin Forbes, courtesy of the Library of Congress.

Cataloging in Publication Data
Main entry under title: Annual Editions: American history, vol. one: Pre-Colonial through reconstruction. 15/E.
   1. United States—History—Periodicals. 2. United States—Historiography—Periodicals. 3. United States—Civilization—Periodicals. I. Title: American history, vol. one: Pre-Colonial through reconstruction.
E171.A75   973'.5   74—187540
ISBN 0-697-39380-1

Copyright

Members of the Advisory Board are instrumental in the final selection of articles for each edition of ANNUAL EDITIONS. Their review of articles for content, level, currentness, and appropriateness provides critical direction to the editor and staff. We think that you will find their careful consideration well reflected in this volume.

EDITORS

Robert James Maddox
Pennsylvania State University
University Park

ADVISORY BOARD

Arthur H. Auten
University of Hartford

Edward H. Beardsley
University of South Carolina

Neal A. Brooks
Essex Community College

Douglas M. Dinwiddie
New Mexico State University
Carlsbad

Nancy Gentile-Ford
Bloomsburg University

Celia Hall-Thur
Wenatchee Valley College

Melvin G. Holli
University of Illinois

Harry Russell Huebel
Texas A & M University

Wilma King
Michigan State University

Bryan F. LeBeau
Creighton University

Larry Madaras
Howard Community College

Joseph G. Mannard
Indiana University of Pennsylvania

Ronald McCoy
Emporia State University

Randall M. Miller
St. Joseph's University

Rameth Owens
Clemson University

Robert C. Pierce
Foothill College

Barbara Reinfeld
New York Institute of Technology

Irvin D. Solomon
Florida Gulf Coast University

James R. Sweeney
Old Dominion University

EDITORIAL STAFF

Ian A. Nielsen, Publisher
Roberta Monaco, Senior Developmental Editor
Dorothy Fink, Associate Developmental Editor
Addie Raucci, Senior Administrative Editor
Cheryl Greenleaf, Permissions Editor
Joseph Offredi, Permissions/Editorial Assistant
Diane Barker, Proofreader
Lisa Holmes-Doebrick, Program Coordinator

PRODUCTION STAFF

Brenda S. Filley, Production Manager
Charles Vitelli, Designer
Lara M. Johnson, Design/
Advertising Coordinator
Laura Levine, Graphics
Mike Campbell, Graphics
Tom Goddard, Graphics
Juliana Arbo, Typesetting Supervisor
Jane Jaegersen, Typesetter
Marie Lazauskas, Word Processor
Kathleen D'Amico, Word Processor
Larry Killian, Copier Coordinator

Editors/Advisory Board

Staff

To the Reader

In publishing ANNUAL EDITIONS we recognize the enormous role played by the magazines, newspapers, and journals of the public press in providing current, first-rate educational information in a broad spectrum of interest areas. Many of these articles are appropriate for students, researchers, and professionals seeking accurate, current material to help bridge the gap between principles and theories and the real world. These articles, however, become more useful for study when those of lasting value are carefully collected, organized, indexed, and reproduced in a low-cost format, which provides easy and permanent access when the material is needed. That is the role played by ANNUAL EDITIONS.

New to ANNUAL EDITIONS is the inclusion of related World Wide Web sites. These sites have been selected by our editorial staff to represent some of the best resources found on the World Wide Web today. Through our carefully developed topic guide, we have linked these Web resources to the articles covered in this ANNUAL EDITIONS reader. We think that you will find this volume useful, and we hope that you will take a moment to visit us on the Web at *http://www.dushkin.com/* to tell us what you think.

Not that long ago, most historical writing fell into identifiable categories: political, economic, diplomatic, and military history, among others. There was, moreover, a tendency to focus on notable leaders and how they helped shape the course of history. Presidents, titans of industry, and generals and admirals who won or lost great battles were interpreted and reinterpreted. This is not surprising. The lives of such men (women did not figure much in traditional accounts, except for a few lines devoted to prominent writers and reformers) seemed inherently more significant and interesting than those of ordinary people. Although attention continues to be paid to such figures, there has been, over the past 30 years, a veritable explosion of interest in individuals and groups that were previously ignored or mentioned only in passing. The roles of women, Native Americans, Hispanics, Asians, and other groups are now introduced and analyzed in an ever-increasing number of books and articles.

These "new" histories can only be applauded for enriching our understanding of the past and for interpreting events through a variety of viewpoints. America's western movement, for example, no longer is presented solely as the "conquering of a continent" by white settlers, but also as a series of tragedies that were experienced by those who stood in its path. Unfortunately, the new historians and the traditionalists all too often push their own agendas, while denouncing the other side's as irrelevant or wrongheaded, at the expense of synthesis. Unfortunately, too, much recent work that appears in professional journals is written in an impenetrable jargon that renders it inaccessible to most readers. The fifteenth edition of *Annual Editions: American History, Volume I,* attempts to present a fair sampling of articles that represent different approaches and that are intelligible.

Annual Editions: American History, Volume I, contains a number of features designed to aid students, researchers, and professionals. These include a *topic guide* for locating articles on specific subjects; the *table of contents* abstracts that summarize each essay, with key concepts in bold italics; and a comprehensive *index*. Articles are organized into four units, each preceded by an overview that provides a background for informed reading of the articles, emphasizes critical issues, and presents *key points to consider.*

New to this edition are *World Wide Web* sites that can be used to further explore the topics. Additionally, these sites are cross-referenced by number in the *topic guide.*

Every revision of *Annual Editions: American History, Volume I,* replaces about 50 percent of the previous articles with new ones. We try to update and improve the quality of the sections, and we would like to consider alternatives that we may have missed. If you find an article that you think merits inclusion in the next edition, please send it to us (or at least send us the citation, so that the editor can track it down for consideration). We welcome your comments about the readings in this volume, and a postage-paid reader response card is included in the back of the book for your convenience. Your suggestions will be carefully considered and greatly appreciated.

Robert James Maddox

Robert James Maddox
Editor

Contents

To the Reader   iv
Topic Guide   2
◎ Selected World Wide Web Sites   4

Overview   6

1. **Mighty Cahokia,** William R. Iseminger, *Archaeology,*   8
   May/June 1996.
   Located 8 miles east of what is today St. Louis, Missouri, Cahokia
   was **an important Native American trading center** whose
   influence extended through a large portion of the continent during
   the period 1050–1150 A.D. Archaeology has revealed much of
   what the settlement looked like and how it functioned.

2. **Columbus Meets Pocahontas in the American**   15
   South, Theda Perdue, *Southern Cultures,* Volume 3, Number 1, 1997.
   In the popular mind, Christopher Columbus represents European
   discovery and conquest, while Pocahontas has become the embodiment of New World hospitality and opportunity. The two never
   actually met, but Theda Perdue argues that their "symbolic encounter involved a sexual dynamic that was inherent to **the whole
   process of European colonization,** particularly of the American South."

3. **A "Newfounde Lande,"** Alan Williams, *American His-*   21
   tory, September/October 1997.
   For Europeans, 1992 marked the 500th anniversary of Columbus's
   "discovery" of the New World. Columbus first explored islands in
   the Caribbean, then the coast of South America. The year 1997
   saw the quincentennial of what is generally regarded as **the first
   European expedition to land in North America.** Author
   Alan Williams tells what is known of John Cabot's explorations.

4. **Laboring in the Fields of the Lord,** Jerald T. Mi-   26
   lanich, *Archaeology,* January/February 1996.
   Beginning in the late sixteenth century, Spanish Franciscan friars
   established dozens of missions in what is now southern Georgia
   and northern Florida. By the time Spain ceded the area to Great
   Britain in 1763, only two missions remained. Although many of
   the friars acted from the highest motives, the net effect of **the
   Spanish presence among native peoples** was catastrophic.

5. **Journey to Jamestown,** Audrey J. Horning, *Archaeol-*   33
   ogy, March/April 1998.
   British colonists founded **the village of Jamestown** in 1607.
   The settlement evolved into a town that served as capital of the
   Virginia colony for 92 years, then was abandoned. Audrey Horning describes what historical and archaeological research has revealed about the rise and fall of this community.

UNIT 1

The New Land

Eight selections discuss the
beginnings of America, the new
land, from pre-Columbian times,
early life of the colonists, and
religious intolerance, to the stirrings
of liberty and independence.

---

6. Squanto and the Pilgrims, Lynn Ceci, *Society,*   **39**
May/June 1990.
Legend has it that Squanto taught the Pilgrims how to
grow corn as the Native Americans did. However, this "invented"
Squanto, Lynn Ceci shows, "stands in contrast to the real, very
interesting historical Squanto," who probably learned his farming
techniques from other Europeans.

7. Bearing the Burden? Puritan Wives, Martha Sax-   **44**
ton, *History Today,* October 1994.
Puritan women were expected to view their husbands as "God's
representative in the family" and defer to their authority. Martha
Saxton describes how women attained moral and spiritual authority
despite their subordination to men in secular matters.

8. America's First Experiment in Toleration, John Hart-   **49**
sock, *History Today,* January 1993.
King Charles I granted George Calvert, a Catholic, the portion of
the American coast that became Maryland. Although Calvert died
before receiving the charter, his son organized an expedition that
landed in 1634. The Calvert family established ***religious toleration*** for the colony until a 1689 rebellion by Protestants denied
Catholics the right to worship publicly.

Overview   **54**

9. Making Sense of the Fourth of July, Pauline Maier,   **56**
American Heritage, July/August 1997.
On July 2, 1776, the Second Continental Congress resolved that
"these United Colonies are, and, of right ought to be" independent
of Great Britain. Two days later, the Congress adopted the Declaration of Independence. ***Celebrating the Fourth of July,***
Pauline Maier writes, "makes no sense at all"—unless we celebrate
not just independence but the Declaration of Independence. She
explains how the meaning and function of the Declaration have
changed over time.

10. The *Radical* Revolution, Fredric Smoler, *American*   **64**
Heritage, December 1992.
The French Revolution was "radical," according to conventional
wisdom, while its American counterpart was largely a war for
independence that resulted in only moderate social and political
change. In this interview, Gordon Wood, author of *The Radicalism
of the American Revolution,* argues against this view, claiming that
the revolutionary heritage helped produce the "most democratic culture on the face of the earth."

UNIT 2

Revolutionary America

Six articles examine the start of the
American Revolution. The new land
offered opportunities for new ideas
that led to the creation of an
independent nation.

The concepts in bold italics are developed in the article. For further expansion please refer to the Topic Guide and the Index.

11. **"Pvt. Robert Shurtleff": An Unusual Revolutionary War Soldier,** Kathleen Doyle, *American History Illustrated,* October 1988.   **70**
During the Revolutionary War, Private Robert Shurtleff reported on sick call with a high fever. Doctors were astonished to discover that the soldier actually was Deborah Sampson, who had enlisted in a Massachusetts regiment in disguise.

12. **'It Is Not a Union,'** Peter Onuf, *The Wilson Quarterly,* Spring 1987.   **72**
When the Revolutionary War ended, Americans looked ahead to a future of unparalleled prosperity that would be free of British interference. Within a few years there were territorial disputes among states, economic problems, and a host of other divisive issues culminating in Shays's Rebellion during the summer of 1786.

13. **. . . by the Unanimous Consent of the States,** Ezra Bowen, *Smithsonian,* July 1987.   **76**
The Founders avoided collapse of the Constitutional Convention by accepting numerous compromises. Tight security was enforced to keep the proceedings secret. "If the debates had been public," James Madison later wrote, "no constitution would ever have been adopted."

14. **The Founding Fathers, Conditional Antislavery, and the Nonradicalism of the American Revolution,** William W. Freehling, from *The Reintegration of American History: Slavery and the Civil War,* Oxford University Press, 1994.   **82**
In a revision of his earlier views on *the Founding Fathers and slavery,* William Freehling argues that although they did not intend to bring about a true social revolution, they did "a most nonrevolutionary something to weaken slaveholders' defenses." Their actions set this nation on its "meandering" path toward emancipation.

The concepts in bold italics are developed in the article. For further expansion please refer to the Topic Guide and the Index.

UNIT 3

National Consolidation and Expansion

Twelve selections examine the developing United States, the westward movement of people seeking a new life, and the realities of living in early nineteenth-century America.

Overview   **92**

15. The Greatness of George Washington, Gordon S. Wood, *Virginia Quarterly Review,* Spring 1992.   **94**
George Washington virtually created the American presidency, for which there was no precedent. He also established the standard by which subsequent presidents have ultimately been regarded—"their moral character."

16. 1796: The First Real Election, John Ferling, *American History,* December 1996.   **101**
George Washington was elected twice to the presidency without opposition. When he refused a third term, he set the stage for the first two-party election. The campaign was vicious, with much behind-the-scenes maneuvering. *The orderly transferal of power* from George Washington to John Adams marked the end of an era and also "represented a triumph for the republic."

17. Lewis and Clark: Trailblazers Who Opened the Continent, Gerald F. Kreyche, *USA Today Magazine (Society for the Advancement of Education),* January 1998.   **106**
By 1800 Americans knew little about what lay west of the Mississippi River. *Meriwether Lewis and William Clark* changed all that in 1804 when they led an expedition that eventually reached the Pacific Ocean. Gerald Kreyche describes the explorations of these two intrepid men and the group they led, designated the Corps of Discovery.

18. Indians in the Land, William Cronon and Richard White, *American Heritage,* August/September 1986.   **110**
Environmental historians William Cronon and Richard White discuss the enormous *differences between Native American and white cultures* that made each group's assumptions about nature incomprehensible to the other.

19. Jefferson's Retreat, Joseph J. Ellis, *Civilization,* December 1996/January 1997.   **116**
Thomas Jefferson still owned nearly 200 slaves when he died on July 4, 1826. Historian Joseph Ellis analyzes the paradox of Jefferson as a "fervent believer in human freedom who lived his entire life as a slave owner." *Jefferson's dilemma* was emblematic of the larger disjunction in American society "between the promise of liberty and the fact of racial discrimination."

The concepts in bold italics are developed in the article. For further expansion please refer to the Topic Guide and the Index.

20. **Before the "Trail of Tears,"** Teresa Amott and Julie Matthaei, *Ms.*, November/December 1990. **122**
Recent research indicates that **Indian women enjoyed a "degree of sexual freedom and equality** unknown by and hence unrecognizable to European colonists." The "European invasion" undermined much of this equality and independence.

21. **"All We Want Is Make Us Free!"** Howard Jones, *American History*, February 1998. **124**
Recently the subject of a popular motion picture, **a slave mutiny on board the Spanish ship Amistad** on July 2, 1839, set in motion a remarkable series of events that ultimately led to the case being heard by the Supreme Court of the United States. Howard Jones describes the individuals and groups that worked to bring the issue before the American people and government.

22. **Mountain Legend,** Michael Martin, *American History*, September/October 1996. **131**
Jim Beckwourth was a hunter and trapper who mixed as easily with Indians as he did with other "mountain men." Unfortunately, his penchant for telling tall tales resulted in his autobiography being received as "a self-serving fantasy." Michael Martin shows that, despite his exaggerations, Beckwourth's daring exploits "helped to conquer the wilderness and open up the American West."

23. **James K. Polk and the Expansionist Spirit,** Harlan Hague, *Journal of the West*, July 1992. **136**
During the election of 1844, Polk had campaigned calling for **the annexation of Texas and the Oregon country.** As president he compromised with the British over Oregon but went to war with Mexico over Texas. He left to his successors the question of slavery in the newly acquired territories.

24. **All That Glittered,** Richard Reinhardt, *American Heritage*, February/March 1998. **141**
In January 1848, a carpenter named Jim Marshall spotted a metallic twinkle in the freshly dug earth and allegedly shouted, "Boys, I believe I've found a gold mine!" What followed, **the California gold rush,** still resonates in American history. Richard Reinhardt separates fact from fiction about the "forty-niners."

The concepts in bold italics are developed in the article. For further expansion please refer to the Topic Guide and the Index.

25. The Lives of Slave Women, Deborah Gray White, **147**
Southern Exposure, November/December 1984.
Slave women in the American South were worked as hard as men. They did the same field work, either with men or in segregated gangs. Deborah Gray White examines some of the social dynamics of **Southern slave women.**

26. Eden Ravished, Harlan Hague, *The American West,* **153**
May/June 1977.
The threat of **exhausting our natural resources** has become obvious in recent decades. Harlan Hague shows that some voices were raised on this issue even before the Civil War. Despite these warnings, however, the belief in the inexhaustibility of resources in the West generated the unique American acceptance of waste as the fundamental tenet of a lifestyle.

UNIT 4

The Civil War and Reconstruction

Nine articles discuss the tremendous effects of the Civil War on America. With the abolishment of slavery, the United States had to reconstruct society.

Overview **160**

27. "The Doom of Slavery": Ulysses S. Grant, War Aims, and Emancipation, 1861–1863, Brooks D. Simpson, *Civil War History,* March 1990. **162**
The nature of the Civil War changed in 1863 from a limited conflict to total war against Southern morale and resources as well as manpower. General U. S. Grant, Union army, realized that at bottom the dispute was about slavery.

28. Lee's Greatest Victory, Robert K. Krick, *American Heritage,* March 1990. **171**
During 3 days in May 1863, **General Robert E. Lee conducted a risky and skillful battle** that ended in victory. The cost was high, as his able subordinate General "Stonewall" Jackson was killed by his own men while returning to the Confederate lines.

29. Gallantry under Fire, John E. Aliyetti, *Civil War Times,* October 1996. **183**
More than 186,000 black men served in the Union army during the Civil War. Of the 16 Medals of Honor awarded to blacks, 14 were bestowed for the battle of New Market Heights. John Aliyetti describes this heroic and bloody engagement.

30. The Struggle for Black Freedom before Emancipation, Wayne K. Durrill, *OAH Magazine of History,* Fall 1993. **188**
In most accounts of the Civil War, black Americans received their freedom by way of the Emancipation Proclamation and advancing Northern troops. Wayne Durrill emphasizes **the role black people played in gaining their own emancipation.**

The concepts in bold italics are developed in the article. For further expansion please refer to the Topic Guide and the Index.

31. The Northern Front, Dara Horn, *American Heritage,*   **192**
April 1998.
Boston's association with the Revolutionary War is so great that its role in the Civil War often is overlooked. "No battle was fought near the city," Dara Horn writes, "but Boston was the center of some of the most ***vocal protests against slavery*** and of the most enthusiastic support for the Union cause."

32. The Man at the White House Window, Stephen B.   **198**
Oates, *Civil War Times,* November/December 1995.
Abraham Lincoln claimed he was fighting the Civil War to preserve the Union. His opponents charged that he was trying to abolish slavery. Stephen Oates explores ***Lincoln's motives*** and concludes that "as the war grew and changed, so Lincoln grew and changed."

33. Why the South Lost the Civil War, Carl Zebrowski,   **208**
American History, October 1995.
Ten Civil War experts explain ***why they think the South lost*** the war. Reasons range from inferior leadership to lack of a spiritual core.

34. A War That Never Goes Away, James M. McPherson, *American Heritage,* March 1990.   **213**
More than 50,000 books and pamphlets have been written about ***the Civil War,*** and a 1991 television special series attracted millions of viewers. James McPherson explains the war's enduring interest and significance for Americans.

35. The New View of Reconstruction, Eric Foner, *American Heritage,* October/November 1983.   **218**
Prior to the 1960s, according to Eric Foner, ***Reconstruction*** was portrayed in history books as "just about the darkest page in the American saga." He presents a balanced view of the era and suggests that, even though Reconstruction failed to achieve its objectives, its "animating vision" still has relevance.

Index   **225**
Article Review Form   **228**
Article Rating Form   **229**

The concepts in bold italics are developed in the article. For further expansion please refer to the Topic Guide and the Index.

Topic Guide

This topic guide suggests how the selections and World Wide Web sites found in the next section of this book relate to topics of traditional concern to American history students and professionals. It is useful for locating interrelated articles and Web sites for reading and research. The guide is arranged alphabetically according to topic.

The relevant Web sites, which are numbered and annotated on pages 4 and 5, are easily identified by the Web icon (◎) under the topic articles. By linking the articles and the Web sites by topic, this ANNUAL EDITIONS reader becomes a powerful learning and research tool.

TOPIC AREA	TREATED IN	TOPIC AREA	TREATED IN
Adams, John	16. 1796: The First Real Election ◎ *(1, 3, 4, 11, 16, 17)*		34. War That Never Goes Away ◎ *(1, 2, 4, 5, 17, 22, 27, 28, 29, 30, 31)*
African Americans	14. Founding Fathers, Conditional Antislavery, and the Nonradicalism of the American Revolution 19. Jefferson's Retreat 20. Before the "Trail of Tears" 21. "All We Want Is Make Us Free!" 25. Lives of Slave Women 27. "Doom of Slavery" 29. Gallantry under Fire 30. Struggle for Black Freedom before Emancipation 31. Northern Front 32. Man at the White House Window 35. New View of Reconstruction ◎ *(1, 2, 4, 6, 15, 16, 22, 27, 28, 29, 30, 31)*	**Colonial America**	4. Laboring in the Fields of the Lord 5. Journey to Jamestown 6. Squanto and the Pilgrims 7. Bearing the Burden? Puritan Wives 8. America's First Experiment in Toleration ◎ *(1, 2, 4, 6, 9, 11, 16, 17, 18)*
		Constitution	13. . . . by the Unanimous Consent of the States 14. Founding Fathers, Conditional Antislavery, and the Nonradicalism of the American Revolution ◎ *(1, 4, 5, 15, 16)*
American Revolution	9. Making Sense of the Fourth of July 10. *Radical* Revolution 11. "Pvt. Robert Shurtleff" ◎ *(1, 2, 3, 4, 5, 6, 11, 16, 17, 18)*	**Culture**	1. Mighty Cahokia 2. Columbus Meets Pocahontas 4. Laboring in the Fields of the Lord 6. Squanto and the Pilgrims 20. Before the "Trail of Tears" 31. Northern Front ◎ *(1, 2, 4, 5, 6, 8, 9, 10, 11, 18, 23, 25, 26, 27)*
Articles of Confederation	12. "It Is Not a Union" ◎ *(1, 4, 5, 11, 16)*		
Civil War	27. "Doom of Slavery" 28. Lee's Greatest Victory 29. Gallantry under Fire 30. Struggle for Black Freedom before Emancipation 31. Northern Front 32. Man at the White House Window 33. Why the South Lost the Civil War	**Declaration of Independence**	9. Making Sense of the Fourth of July ◎ *(1, 4, 5, 15, 16)*
		Environment	17. Lewis and Clark 18. Indians in the Land 26. Eden Ravished ◎ *(2, 6, 7, 11, 12, 13, 14, 15, 16, 17, 24)*
		Exploration	2. Columbus Meets Pocahontas 3. "Newfounde Lande" 17. Lewis and Clark ◎ *(8, 21, 24)*

TOPIC AREA	TREATED IN	TOPIC AREA	TREATED IN
Government	8. America's First Experiment in Toleration 9. Making Sense of the Fourth of July 10. *Radical Revolution* 12. "It Is Not a Union" 13. . . . by the Unanimous Consent of the States 14. Founding Fathers, Conditional Antislavery, and the Nonradicalism of the American Revolution 15. Greatness of George Washington 16. 1796: The First Real Election 23. James K. Polk and the Expansionist Spirit 32. Man at the White House Window 35. New View of Reconstruction *(1, 2, 3, 4, 7, 12, 13, 14, 15, 16, 17, 18, 19, 20, 28)*	**Polk, James K.**	23. James K. Polk and the Expansionist Spirit *(1, 4, 17, 21, 26)*
		Reconstruction	35. New View of Reconstruction *(1, 4, 19, 27, 29, 30)*
		Religion	8. America's First Experiment in Toleration *(1, 2, 4)*
		Slavery	14. Founding Fathers, Conditional Antislavery, and the Nonradicalism of the American Revolution 19. Jefferson's Retreat 21. "All We Want Is Make Us Free!" 25. Lives of Slave Women 27. "Doom of Slavery" 30. Struggle for Black Freedom before Emancipation 31. Northern Front 32. Man at the White House Window *(1, 2, 4, 5, 6, 16, 22, 27, 28, 29, 30)*
Hispanics	2. Columbus Meets Pocahontas 4. Laboring in the Fields of the Lord *(21)*		
Jefferson, Thomas	9. Making Sense of the Fourth of July 19. Jefferson's Retreat *(1, 2, 4, 5, 11, 15, 16, 17, 18)*	**Western Expansion**	17. Lewis and Clark 18. Indians in the Land 22. Mountain legend 23. James K. Polk and the Expansionist Spirit 24. All That Glittered 26. Eden Ravished *(21, 24)*
Labor	24. All That Glittered 25. Lives of Slave Women *(1, 4, 6, 27, 30)*	**Women**	2. Columbus Meets Pocahontas 7. Bearing the Burden? Puritan Wives 11. "Pvt. Robert Shurtleff" 20. Before the "Trail of Tears" 25. Lives of Slave Women *(1, 2, 4, 6, 25, 26, 27)*
Lee, Robert E.	28. Lee's Greatest Victory *(1, 4, 6, 28, 29)*		
Lincoln, Abraham	32. Man at the White House Window *(1, 4, 6, 17, 19, 28, 29, 30)*		
Native Americans	1. Mighty Cahokia 6. Squanto and the Pilgrims 18. Indians in the Land 20. Before the "Trail of Tears" *(1, 2, 4, 5, 6, 8, 9, 10, 11)*		

○ AE: American History, Volume I

The following World Wide Web sites have been carefully researched and selected to support the articles found in this reader. If you are interested in learning more about specific topics found in this book, these Web sites are a good place to start. The sites are cross-referenced by number and appear in the topic guide on the previous two pages. Also, you can link to these Web sites through our DUSHKIN ONLINE support site at *http://www.dushkin.com/online/*.

The following sites were available at the time of publication. Visit our Web site—we update DUSHKIN ONLINE regularly to reflect any changes.

General Sources

1. American Historical Association
http://chnm.gmu.edu/aha/
This is the logical first visitation site for someone interested in virtually any topic in American history. All affiliated societies and publications are noted, and AHA and its links on this site present material related to myriad fields of history and having to do with different levels of education.

2. American Studies Web
http://www.georgetown.edu/crossroads/asw/
Links to a wealth of Internet resources for research in American studies, from agriculture and rural development, to government, to race and ethnicity, are provided on this eclectic site.

3. Harvard University/John F. Kennedy School of Government
http://www.ksg.harvard.edu/
Starting from this home page, you will be able to click on a huge variety of links to information about American history, politics, and government, including material related to debates of enduring issues.

4. History Net
http://www.thehistorynet.com/THNarchives/American History/
Supported by the National Historical Society, this site provides information on a wide range of topics. The articles are of excellent quality, and the site has book reviews and even special interviews. It is also frequently updated.

5. Library of Congress
http://www.loc.gov/
Examine this extensive Web site to learn about the extensive resource tools, library services/resources, exhibitions, and databases available through the Library of Congress in many different subfields of government studies.

6. Smithsonian Institution
http://www.si.edu/
This site provides access to the enormous resources of the Smithsonian, which holds some 140 million artifacts and specimens for "the increase and diffusion of knowledge." Here you can learn about American social, cultural, economic, and political history from a variety of viewpoints.

7. U.S. Information Agency
http://www.usia.gov/usis.html
An interesting and wide-ranging home page of the USIA, it provides definitions, related documentation, and a discussion of topics of concern to students of American history. It addresses today's "Hot Topics" as well as ongoing issues that form the foundation of the field. Many Web links are provided.

The New Land

8. 1492: An Ongoing Voyage/Library of Congress
http://lcweb.loc.gov/exhibits/1492/
Displays examining the causes and effects of Columbus's voyages to the Americas can be accessed on this Web site. "An Ongoing Voyage" explores the rich mixture of societies coexisting in five areas of this hemisphere before the European arrival. It then surveys the polyglot Mediterranean world at a dynamic turning point in its development.

9. The Mayflower Web Page
http://members.aol.com/calebj/
The Mayflower Web Page represents thousands of hours of research, organization, and typing; it grows daily. Visitors include everyone from kindergarten students to history professors, from beginning genealogists to some of the most noted genealogists in the nation. The site is a merger of two fields: genealogy and history.

10. University of California at Santa Barbara/Department of Anthropology
http://www.anth.ucsb.edu/projects/index.html
Visit this interesting site to learn about different facets of pre-Columbian Americas. Click on the Web link for the Great Kiva project, which offers a virtual-reality tour of a major structure of the Anasazi culture of the American southwest. The three-dimensional model provides extraordinary detail.

Revolutionary America

11. The Early America Review
http://www.earlyamerica.com/review/
Explore this Web site of *The Early America Review*, an electronic journal of fact and opinion on the people, issues, and events of eighteenth-century America. The quarterly is of excellent quality.

12. House of Representatives
http://www.house.gov/
This home page of the House of Representatives will lead you to information about current and past House members and agendas, the legislative process, and so on.

13. National Center for Policy Analysis
http://www.public-policy.org/~ncpa/pd/pdindex.html
Through this site, you can click onto links to read discussions of an array of topics that are of major interest in the study of American history, from regulatory policy and privatization to economy and income.

14. Senate
http://www.senate.gov/
This home page of the Senate will lead you to information about current and past Senate members and agendas, legislative activities, committees, and so on.

15. Supreme Court/Legal Information Institute
http://supct.law.cornell.edu/supct/index.html

Open this site for current and historical information about the Supreme Court. The archive contains a collection of nearly 600 of the most historical decisions of the Court.

16. U.S. Founding Documents/Emory University
http://www.law.emory.edu/FEDERAL/
Through this site you can view scanned originals of the Declaration of Independence, the Constitution, and the Bill of Rights. The transcribed texts are also available, as are *The Federalist Papers.*

17. The White House
http://www.whitehouse.gov/WH/Welcome.html
Visit the home page of the White House for direct access to information about commonly requested federal services, the White House Briefing Room, and all of the presidents and vice presidents. The "Virtual Library" allows you to search White House documents, listen to speeches, and view photos.

18. The World of Benjamin Franklin
http://www.fi.edu/franklin/
Presented by the Franklin Institute Science Museum, "Benjamin Franklin: Glimpses of the Man," is an excellent multimedia site that lends insight into Revolutionary America.

National Consolidation and Expansion

19. Consortium for Political and Social Research
http://icg.fas.harvard.edu/~census/
At this site, the inter-university Consortium for Political and Social Research offers materials in various categories of historical, social, economic, and demographic data. Check it out for a statistical overview of the United States beginning in the late eighteenth century.

20. Department of State
http://www.state.gov/
View this site for understanding into the workings of what has become a major U.S. executive branch department. Links explain what the Department does, what services it provides, what it says about U.S. interests around the world, and much more information.

21. The Mexican-American War Memorial Homepage
http://sunsite.unam.mx/revistas/1847/
For a change of pace and culture, visit this site from Mexico's Universidad Nacional Autonoma. It describes, from a Mexican perspective, the Mexican-American War.

22. Mystic Seaport
http://amistad.mysticseaport.org/main/welcome.html
The complex *Amistad* case is explored in a clear and informative manner on this online educational site. It places the event in the context of the issues of the 1830s and 1840s.

23. Social Influence Website
http://www.public.asu.edu/~kelton/
The nature of persuasion, compliance, and propaganda is the focus of this Web site, with many practical examples and applications. Students of such topics as the roles of public opinion and media influence in policy making should find these discussions of interest.

24. University of Virginia Library
http://www.lib.virginia.edu/exhibits/lewis_clark/
Created by the University of Virginia Library, this site examines the famous Lewis and Clark exploration of the trans-Mississippi west.

25. Women in America
http://xroads.virginia.edu/~HYPER/DETOC/FEM/
Providing the views of foreign women travelers from the British Isles, France, and Germany on the lives of American women, this exceptionally valuable site covers the years between 1820 and 1842 and is informative, stimulating, and highly original.

26. Women in the West
ftp://history.cc.ukans.edu/pub/history/general/articles/prater1.art/
For something out of the ordinary, open this site to read Donna C. Prater's article "Sabers and Soapsuds: Dragoon Women on the Frontier, 1833–1861." It provides a different perspective and a joining of the history of the West with women's history.

The Civil War and Reconstruction

27. Anacostia Museum/Smithsonian Institution
http://www.si.edu/organiza/museums/anacost/
This is the home page of the Center for African American History and Culture of the Smithsonian Institution, which is expected to become a major repository of information. Explore its many avenues.

28. Abraham Lincoln Online
http://www.netins.net/showcase/creative/lincoln.html
A well-organized, high-quality site that will lead you to substantial material about Lincoln and his era. Discussions among Lincoln scholars can be accessed in the Mailbag section.

29. Civil War
http://www.access.digex.net/~bdboyle/cw.html
Dozens of links to Civil War sites on the Internet are provided on this useful site.

30. Gilder Lehrman Institute of American History
http://vi.uh.edu/pages/mintz/gilder.htm
Click on the links to the various articles presented through this Web site to read outstanding, first-hand accounts of slavery in America through the period of Reconstruction.

31. Secession Era Editorials Project
http://history.furman.edu/benson/docs/
Newspaper editorials of the 1800s regarding events leading up to secession are presented on this Furman University site. When complete, this distinctive project will offer additional features that include mapping, statistical tools, and text analysis.

We highly recommend that you review our Web site for expanded information and our other product lines. We are continually updating and adding links to our Web site in order to offer you the most usable and useful information that will support and expand the value of your Annual Editions. You can reach us at: *http://www.dushkin.com/annualeditions/.*

www.dushkin.com/online/

Unit Selections

1. **Mighty Cahokia,** William R. Iseminger
2. **Columbus Meets Pocahontas in the American South,** Theda Perdue
3. **A "Newfounde Lande,"** Alan Williams
4. **Laboring in the Fields of the Lord,** Jerald T. Milanich
5. **Journey to Jamestown,** Audrey J. Horning
6. **Squanto and the Pilgrims,** Lynn Ceci
7. **Bearing the Burden? Puritan Wives,** Martha Saxton
8. **America's First Experiment in Toleration,** John Hartsock

Key Points to Consider

❖ A common perception of Native Americans in the lands north of Mexico is that they lived in relatively small groups that survived independently of one another and had self-sustaining, primitive economies based on hunting, fishing, and gathering. In what ways does the article on Cahokia contradict this perception?

❖ Evaluate the essay on Columbus and Pocahontas. Is it misleading to use an event that did not and could not have taken place to evaluate attitudes and ideas of a bygone era? Or can such a device shed light on cultural contrasts?

❖ What purposes did the legend of Squanto, as opposed to a more realistic appraisal of the man, serve for white settlers and for Americans ever since?

❖ In what ways did Puritan men justify the subordination of women? How could women achieve moral authority and influence under such circumstances?

 **Links** | **www.dushkin.com/online/**

8. **1492: An Ongoing Voyage/Library of Congress**
   http://lcweb.loc.gov/exhibits/1492/
9. **The Mayflower Web Page**
   http://members.aol.com/calebj/
10. **University of California at Santa Barbara/Department of Anthropology**
    http://www.anth.ucsb.edu/projects/index.html

These sites are annotated on pages 4 and 5.

In 1492, when Columbus "discovered" (for Europeans) the New World, there already were between 80 to 100 million inhabitants. Most of them were concentrated in Mexico, Central America, and a few other places. Between 2 and 10 million lived north of Mexico, widely scattered between the Pacific and the Atlantic coasts. The Norse had landed in the New World as early as the tenth century, but they established no permanent settlements and had no lasting effect. Spanish expeditions and expeditions by the French and English that followed would have profound and often catastrophic consequences for the native peoples. Partly this was due to the military operations that were conducted by the invaders; partly it was because of the many communicable diseases that the Europeans brought with them, against which indigenous groups had no immunity.

Those whom we call "native" Americans first came from Asia tens of thousands of years ago across an ancient land bridge to Alaska. Although those who settled in what is now the United States never established powerful empires such as the Aztecs did in Mexico or the Incas did in Peru, some developed sophisticated social and economic organizations. In "Mighty Cahokia," the first selection in this unit, William Iseminger describes a town that was established near present-day St. Louis, Missouri. At its heyday, about 1050 to 1150 A.D., it was a central trading community for a large region. In "Columbus Meets Pocahontas in the American South," author Theda Perdue uses a symbolic encounter to discuss the ways that men and women crossed racial and cultural boundaries, and how such relationships reveal European views of female sexuality. "A 'Newfounde Lande,'" by Alan Williams, tells what is known of the Italian explorer, John Cabot, who headed the first European expedition known to have landed in North America. In "Laboring in the Fields of the Lord," Jerald Milanich examines the establishment of Spanish missions in what is now Georgia and Florida and the disastrous results that followed the highly motivated acts of many of the friars.

The English came relatively late to the New World. Some of them were searching for gold, silver, and jewels, as had their predecessors. Others came to settle permanently, either to escape religious persecution or simply to build new lives for themselves. In "Journey to Jamestown," Audrey Horning tells what is known

about the fate of this community that was founded by English colonists in 1607. Capital of the Virginia colony for nearly 100 years, it declined and subsequently was abandoned. Lynn Ceci, in "Squanto and the Pilgrims," argues that the Squanto of legend—the kindly Native American who taught settlers the Indian methods of agriculture—was created to help justify English expansion. The real Squanto was a far more complicated figure who straddled two cultures.

Women in the English colonies were subordinate to men legally and in a variety of other ways. "Bearing the Burden? Puritan Wives," by Martha Saxton, describes the changing roles of women in Puritan communities and tells how women were able to attain moral and spiritual authority despite their unequal status. Finally, in "America's First Experiment in Toleration," John Hartsock examines the founding of Maryland by the Calverts, a Catholic family that received its charter from King Charles I. The Calverts established religious toleration in an age of intolerance until Protestants rebelled in 1689 and denied Catholics the right to practice their faith in public.

Mighty Cahokia

A major trading center whose influence extended throughout much of North America, Cahokia was in its day the greatest settlement north of Mexico.

William R. Iseminger

William R. Iseminger is an archaeologist and curator at Cahokia Mounds State Historic Site.

I t is the time of the annual harvest festival celebrating the fall equinox. Traders from distant territories have brought precious offerings for the lords of Cahokia. Ramadas have been erected everywhere to shelter the merchants and their goods: beads and other ornaments shaped from native copper; drinking vessels and gorgets cut from large whelk and conch shells, many engraved with symbolic designs; baskets of tiny marginella shells; bangles cut from sheets of mica; quivers of arrows tipped with gem-like points; galena, hematite, and ocher from which to make pigments for pottery, clothing and body paint; and salt from springs and seeps to the south. In exchange the Cahokians offer their own goods: feathered capes; freshwater pearls; finely woven fabrics; fur garments made from otter, mink, and beaver; chert hoes and axes; and corn, dried squash, pumpkin, and seeds from many other plants. These will be taken back to distant places, some in polished black ceramic vessels bearing incised designs of interlocking scrolls, forked eyes, and nested chevrons, symbols of power and prestige because of their place of origin—mighty Cahokia.

This fanciful yet fairly accurate description of Cahokia's harvest celebration is drawn from archaeological studies and early historical accounts of remnant Mississippian cultures in the Southeast. Eight miles east of St. Louis, Cahokia was in its day the largest and most influential settlement north of Mexico. Its merchants traded with cultures from the Gulf Coast to the Great Lakes, from the Atlantic coast to Oklahoma, and they helped spread Mississippian culture across much of that vast area. Some 120 earthen mounds supporting civic buildings and the residences of Cahokia's elite were spread over more than five square miles—perhaps six times as many earthen platforms as the great Mississippian site of Moundville, south of Tuscaloosa, Alabama. At its core, within a log stockade ten to 12 feet tall, was the 200-acre Sa-

COURTESY CAHOKIA MOUNDS STATE HISTORIC SITE

Today Collinsville Road passes in front of Monks Mound, which is 100 feet high, covers 14 acres at its base, and contains 22 million cubic feet of earth.

WILLIAM R. ISEMINGER, COURTESY CAHOKIA MOUNDS STATE HISTORIC SITE

Reconstruction of Cahokia at its apex shows (1) the 40-acre Grand Plaza, surrounded by temples and elite residences, within (2) a wooden stockade. Bordering the plaza are (3) Monks Mound and (4) the Twin Mounds. Outside the stockade is (5) the Woodhenge, where Cahokia's priests may have observed solstice and equinox sunrises, as well as houses of elite and less well-to-do inhabitants.

cred Precinct where the ruling elite lived and were buried. Atop a massive earthen mound stood a pole-framed temple more than 100 feet long, its grass roof possibly decorated with carved wooden animal figures festooned with glimmering beads, feathers, and cloth. Here Cahokia's rulers performed the political and religious rituals that united the realm. Estimates of the city's population at its zenith, ca. A.D. 1050–1150, range from 8,000 to more than 40,000, though most fall between 10,000 and 20,000. Around A.D. 1200, perhaps having exhausted its natural resources, Cahokia went into a decline that left it virtually empty by 1400.

In 1810 the lawyer and journalist Henry Marie Brackenridge, while surveying the Mississippi and Missouri valleys, visited the site and marveled at the "stupendous pile of earth" at its center. At the time a colony of Trappist monks was growing wheat and fruit trees on the earthen structure, soon to be known as

Monks Mound. Their plans to build a monastery atop it were abandoned when fever and a shortage of money forced them to leave the site in 1813. The first archaeological excavations at Cahokia took place in the 1920s under the direction of Warren K. Moorehead of the R. S. Peabody Museum in Andover, Massachusetts. Moorehead's work confirmed that the mounds were neither natural hills nor the work of a mysterious race of Mound Builders or Precolumbian colonists from Europe—as imagined by nineteenth-century amateur historians but had been built by American Indians. In the 1940s and 1950s archaeologists from the University of Michigan, the Illinois State Museum, the Gilcrease Institute of Tulsa, and elsewhere conducted scattered excavations at the site, but the most intensive work began in the early 1960s when Interstate 55–70 was routed through it. Over the years many of Cahokia's mounds have been lost to the bulldozer and the plow,

to subdivisions, highways, and discount stores. Today fewer than 80 remain, 68 of which are preserved within the 2,200-acre Cahokia Mounds State Historic Site, managed by the Illinois Historic Preservation Agency.

Cahokia owed its existence to a floodplain 80 miles long at the confluence of the Mississippi and Missouri rivers. Known as the American Bottom, the plain was interlaced with creeks, sloughs, lakes, and marshes. With fertile soil, extensive forests, and plentiful fish and game, the region was an ideal place to settle. During the Palaeoindian (ca. 9500–8000 B.C.) and Archaic (ca. 8000–600 B.C.) periods transient hunter-gatherers set up temporary camps or seasonal villages here. During the Woodland period (ca. 600 B.C.–A.D. 800) the population grew, cultivation of native crops began, and larger and more settled communities, including Cahokia, were established. Settlements spread slowly and grew in size throughout the

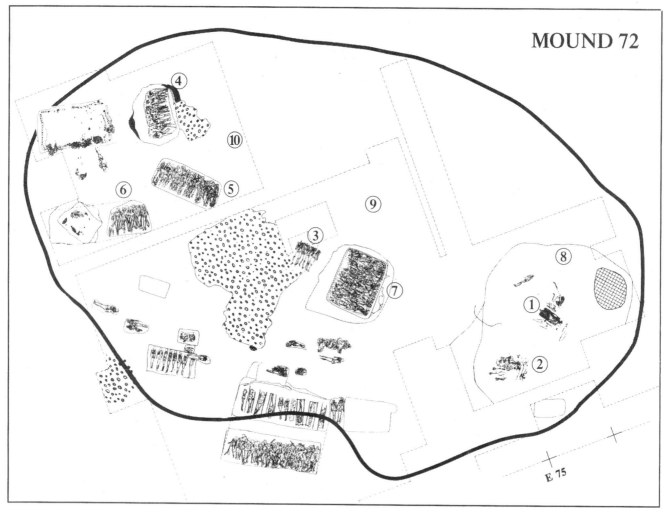

MOUND 72

Excavated between 1967 and 1971, Mound 72 contained the burials of about 280 people, including an elite male laid on a bed of some 20,000 shells (1). Nearby six people were interred with hundreds of arrowheads, beads, and other items (2). Four men buried without their heads and hands (3) and four mass graves of women (4–7) suggest human sacrifice. Mound 72 was originally three separate smaller mounds (8–10) that were later incorporated into a single structure about 140 feet long, 70 feet wide, and six feet tall.

Emergent Mississippian period (ca. A.D. 800–1000), then expanded rapidly in the Mississippian (ca. A.D. 1000–1400) as more intense farming, especially of corn, made fast population growth possible. Cahokia reached its apex during this period, when it was surrounded by dozens of satellite settlements (see box, "East St. Louis Yields a Satellite Settlement") and scores of smaller villages.

In time, Cahokia's influence spread far beyond the American Bottom. Artifacts made there, including Ramey Incised pottery and hoes of Mill Creek chert from southern Illinois, have been found at sites as far north as Minnesota, as far west as eastern Kansas and Oklahoma, and as far south as the lower Ohio River Valley, Arkansas, and Mississippi.

Local imitations of Cahokia's wares, especially pottery, have also been unearthed in these regions. At Cahokia itself we have found copper from the area of Lake Superior; mica from the southern Appalachian Mountains; shells from the Atlantic and Gulf coasts; and galena, ocher, hematite, chert, fluorite, and quartz from throughout the Midwest. Finely made ceramics from the lower Mississippi Valley, perhaps used to carry exotic commodities such as shells from that area, have also been discovered at Cahokia, along with local copies of many of these forms.

The most visible remains of the ancient city are its mounds. Most are rectangular with flat tops (platform mounds) that supported civic buildings

and the homes of the elite. Somewhat rarer are conical mounds that may have contained elite burials, as they did in the earlier Woodland period. During the 1920s Moorehead excavated several such burials, but it is often difficult to tell from his records whether they were found in the mounds themselves or in earlier layers. Rarest of all are rectangular ridgetop mounds that may have marked important locations such as community boundaries or mortuary complexes. The destruction of one such mound by farmers in 1931 revealed mass burials laid upon platforms of shell beads and cedar bark.

Monks Mound stands at the center of the site, on the northern edge of the 40-acre Grand Plaza. Covering 14 acres at the base and rising in four terraces to a height of 100 feet, it is the largest prehistoric earthen structure in the New World. Some 19 million man-hours of labor would have been required to excavate, carry, and deposit the estimated 22 million cubic feet of earth needed for this project. Excavations and soil cores indicate that it was built in stages between ca. A.D. 900 and 1200, each possibly related to the accession of a new leader. Probes on the summit have revealed wall trenches for a wooden building 104 feet long and 48 feet wide. Here the leader of Cahokia governed his domain, performed ceremonies, consulted with the spirit world, and may have resided as well. The bones of deceased chiefs may also have been stored here, as was the custom among some historical tribes in the Southeast.

One of the most fascinating discoveries at Cahokia came during the 1967–1971 excavation of Mound 72, a ridgetop one-half mile south of Monks Mound. Measuring 140 feet long, 70 feet wide, and barely six feet high, Mound 72 is oriented along a northwest-southeast axis, one end pointing toward the winter solstice sunrise and the other toward the summer solstice sunset. Excavations revealed that it had originally been three separate, smaller mounds, two platforms and one conical. Around and beneath these three mounds were some 280 burials dating to Cahokia's in-

itial development between ca. A.D. 1000 and 1050. Some of the dead had been borne to their graves on litters or wrapped in mats or blankets, while others had simply been tossed into pits, suggesting that people of different statuses were buried at the same place. Soon after the burials the three mounds were fused into a single ridgetop mound with a final mantle of earth.

In one opulent burial a man about 40 years old, perhaps one of Cahokia's early leaders, was laid upon a bird-shaped platform of nearly 20,000 marine-shell beads. Around him were several other bodies, perhaps of retainers or relatives, some interred for the first time and others reburied from elsewhere. Heaped atop six nearby burials were two caches of more than 800 newly made arrowheads, whose Midwestern cherts and hafting styles suggest possible origins in Wisconsin, Illinois, Missouri, Tennessee, Arkansas, and Oklahoma. One cache included 15 large concave ground-stone discs, sometimes known as "chunkey" stones, after a game played with similar stones by historical tribes in the Southeast. Also found were a large pile of unprocessed mica from the southern Appalachian Mountains, a three-foot-long roll of copper (possibly a ceremonial staff) hammered from Lake Superior nuggets, and more marine-shell beads.

Further excavations under Mound 72 revealed several mass burials, most of females between 15 and 25 years old, suggesting human sacrifice. The largest pit held more than 50 women laid out in two rows and stacked two and three deep; two others contained 22 and 24 women. A fourth pit, with 19 women, had been partially redug, and more than 36,000 marine-shell beads, another cache of unused arrowheads (more than 400 of chert and a few hundred more of bone and antler), and several broken ceramic vessels had been deposited there. Another burial, of four males whose heads and hands had been removed, may represent the ritual sacrifice of vassals or retainers, perhaps to accompany their leader in death. How and why these people were sacrificed remain mysteries, but there may be parallels with rituals performed by the Natchez Indians of seventeenth- and eighteenth-century Mississippi, where individuals often volunteered to be sacrificed upon a leader's death to raise their own or their family's status.

In the early 1960s archaeologists working in the remains of a residential area outside the stockade, to the west of Monks Mound, discovered a number of postholes at regular intervals along the circumferences of at least five circles of different diameters. Four of these constructions are thought to have been complete circles, with 24, 36, 48, and 60 posts, respectively. The fifth seems only to have had 12 posts standing along a portion of the circle; if complete it would have had 72. Why all five circles were formed of multiples of twelve posts is unknown, though some scholars have speculated that the number may have been related to lunar cycles. Because of their resemblance to the famous English megalithic monument of Stonehenge, Cahokia's circles of standing wooden posts became known as "woodhenges." One, with a large center post and 48 evenly spaced perimeter posts, was 410 feet in diameter and dates to just after A.D. 1100. It is the most completely excavated of the woodhenges and has been reconstructed in its original location. From a platform atop the central post a priest might have observed sunrises along the eastern hori-

COURTESY CAHOKIA MOUNDS STATE HISTORIC SITE

Archaeologists excavate Mound 72, whose ends point to the winter solstice sunrise and the summer solstice sunset.

East St. Louis Yields a Satellite Settlement

John E. Kelly

Once a thriving industrial city, East St. Louis had by the 1970s been abandoned by many of the companies that had long sustained it, becoming a wasteland of worn-out factories and vacant lots. Today a general cleanup is under way as part of a long-term effort to attract new business. In 1987 historical archaeologist Bonnie Gums and I began excavations in advance of the widening of Interstate 55–70, which runs through the city. Beneath one to two feet of historical trash we uncovered traces of earthen mounds and small wooden buildings—remains of a satellite of Cahokia. Many of the mounds had supported wooden temples and elite residences, but by the end of the twelfth century the site lay abandoned. One hundred years later Cahokia, too, was empty.

Some 45 mounds still stood in 1810 when the lawyer and journalist Henry Marie Brackenridge visited the site. Brackenridge climbed 40 feet to the top of the largest mound, about 200 by 300 feet at its base, later known as Cemetery Mound for the graveyard atop it used by settlers. From here he looked out over an ancient plaza and across the Mississippi to another group of mounds, remnants of another satellite settlement where St. Louis now stands. East St. Louis' mounds remained largely undisturbed for another 40 or 50 years until many were mined to build levees or demolished to make way for railroad tracks. When local dentist John Patrick mapped the site after the Civil War, only 15 mounds remained. A century later they had been buried beneath factories and Interstate 55–70.

In what was once an alley next to the highway we found remnants of small mounds. Soil stains atop them indicated where wooden structures had stood. Excavations nearby revealed the corner of a small, rectangular platform mound two feet tall linked to a long, low natural ridge.

JOHN E. KELLY

Excavations in East St. Louis have yielded remains of a satellite settlement of Cahokia.

Stains left in the ground by wooden posts indicated that a structure atop this mound had been rebuilt at least ten times. Later a wooden post three feet in diameter had been driven ten feet into the top of the mound, a practice also known from two mounds at Cahokia, perhaps to mark the end of its life as a ritual structure. At its base were the remains of other large wooden buildings. These extended east toward Cemetery Mound, which had been demolished in 1870 by contractors using its earth in construction projects. On its site we uncovered remains of a low platform that had served as a foundation for Cemetery Mound. Atop this we found traces of a sequence of buildings and an unusual elliptical enclosure of square wooden posts unlike anything at Cahokia. On three occasions the platform had been renovated with a new coat of earth six to 12 inches thick, and each time the posts had been replaced. These rejuvenations of platform and el-

lipse may have symbolically linked earthly rituals of fertility, purification, and renewal with the cosmic cycles of the stars and planets.

Buildings and fences had marked the southeastern corner of the plaza, now along the highway shoulder. In a clayey depression, once a shallow marsh, we found broken ceramics, animal bones, and carbonized plant remains. Flood deposits lay above the trash, and atop these stood a twelfth-century mound. Although we only exposed one corner, several constructions and reconstructions were visible, perhaps symbols of renewal like the layers of soil applied to other mounds. Later small, tightly packed houses had been built on the mound's edges. Here we found celts, knives, hoes, and ceramic vessels, some largely intact. Just beyond the last group of structures, two parallel rows of postholes marked where a palisade, similar to that at Cahokia, had stood alongside a moat. The palisade stretched north, but we were unable to find its extension on the other side of the highway. We did, however, discover another area in which small huts had been built amid the remains of earlier, grander buildings about the same time as the first building of the stockade at Cahokia. Clearly something happened across the region that forced people to take refuge in crowded enclaves behind defensive walls, and eventually to desert the settlement altogether.

As East St. Louis' abandoned factories give way to new businesses, its residents can take pride in the emergence of an ancient city in their midst.

JOHN E. KELLY *is the American Bottom survey coordinator for the Illinois Transportation Archaeological Research Program at the University of Illinois, Urbana-Champaign.*

zon aligning with particular perimeter posts at the equinoxes and solstices. On the equinoxes the sun would have risen over the front of Monks Mound, perhaps symbolizing the bond between earthly ruler and solar deity. Other posts may have marked other important dates, such

as harvest festivals or moon and star alignments.

Most of the work at Cahokia has dealt with the everyday life of its people, many of whom lived outside the stockade in small, rectangular one-family pole-and-thatch dwellings with walls

covered with mats or sometimes daub. Compounds of these dwellings grouped around small courtyards may have housed kinfolk. Each compound also included buildings used for storage, food processing, and cooking. Excavation of refuse pits around the houses has re-

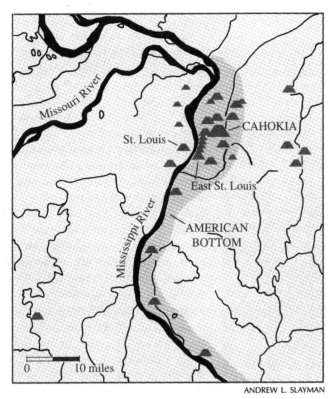

ANDREW L. SLAYMAN

Map shows regional settlements with mounds; not included are scores of smaller villages without mounds.

who lived there, probably members of the ruling lineage, with the general population admitted only for ceremonial occasions or markets, or in times of war.

The stockade was a monumental construction, built at a great cost of time, labor, and materials. Much of my own fieldwork at Cahokia has involved excavations along the lines of the stockade east of Monks Mound. Based on that work I have estimated that builders would have used nearly 20,000 logs each time the wall was built, and conservatively 130,000 man-hours to fell, trim, debark, transport, and place the posts in excavated trenches. Construction of the stockade, itself designed to protect the city center, may have contributed to Cahokia's decline beginning ca. A.D. 1200. The demands for wood would have been staggering, even for such a renewable resource. Wood was also needed for fires and construction, and people from nearby communities would have been competing for the same resources. The forests around Cahokia, and the animals and plants living there, would have been affected. Soil eroding from deforested slopes may have clogged streams and lakes with silt, increasing localized flooding of valuable farmland.

Beginning in the thirteenth century, a cooling of the climate and concomitant floods, droughts, and early and late frosts may have led to more crop failures and reduced yields. As food and other natural resources became scarce, economic disruption and social unrest could have become problems, perhaps even leading to wars between Cahokia and its neighbors. Eventually its political and economic power base eroded as nearby groups became more autonomous. Although increases in contagious diseases and nutritional deficiencies caused by a heavily corn-based diet may have affected Cahokia's population, more data are needed to determine the role of such health problems in Cahokia's decline.

Where the people of Cahokia went is one of the site's many mysteries. There is no evidence that the city was destroyed in a single catastrophe. It appears that its people slowly dispersed, breaking up into smaller groups, some

vealed that the Cahokians ate mainly cultivated corn, squash, and pumpkin, as well as the seeds of cultivated sunflower, lambs' quarters, marsh elder, little barley, and may grass. This diet was supplemented by hundreds of different wild plants and mammals, birds, fish, reptiles, and amphibians.

Household groups were in turn arranged around larger communal plazas that may have defined neighborhoods. Other structures found in each neighborhood included small circular sweat lodges, where water sprinkled upon heated rocks produced steam for ritual cleansing of the body and spirit; community meeting lodges, granaries, and storage buildings; and possibly huts to which women would have been restricted during menstruation.

Ceremonial structures, special-use buildings, and the dwellings of the elite were generally larger versions of the basic house. Many of the elite must have lived within the stockade, but so far none of their residences has been excavated. Elite areas outside the wall in-

clude a plaza mound group to the west; another group to the east; Rattlesnake Mound (named for the snakes in the area) to the south; and the North Plaza and Kunnemann (named after a family that once owned the land) groups to the north. We do not know whether the elite living outside the stockade differed from those living inside, although relationship to the leader by lineage or clan affiliation may have been a factor.

Evidence for warfare at Cahokia remains largely circumstantial. A stockade was erected around the Sacred Precinct ca. A.D. 1150 and rebuilt at least three times during the next hundred years. The defensive nature of the wall is suggested by the regular spacing of bastions at 85-foot intervals along its length. From elevated platforms in these projections, warriors could launch arrows at attackers and protect the narrow L-shaped entryways between some bastions. The everyday function of the wall may have been more social, to isolate and protect the Sacred Precinct. Free access may have been limited to the elites establishing new communities and perhaps new ways of life elsewhere. Many small Late Mississippian villages and hamlets have been found in the uplands surrounding the American Bottom and at higher elevations in the bottomlands themselves. Other people may have been absorbed into existing groups elsewhere, possibly where kinship ties already existed. In any event Cahokia was abandoned by 1400, and no positive ties have been established between the great city and any historical tribe.

Because of limited funding and the site's enormous size, only a small percentage of Cahokia has been excavated. Research continues through small field-school programs that include nondestructive remote-sensing projects using electromagnetic conductivity, electrical resistivity, and magnetometry, as well as soil coring. These efforts help locate man-made features underground, providing direction for future small-scale excavations. Detailed mapping projects, combined with soil-core studies, are helping identify the original forms of mounds that have suffered from heavy plowing or erosion. Unpublished data from earlier excavations are being analyzed or reexamined and the results published. In addition, salvage projects at contemporary sites in the American Bottom such as East St. Louis, are providing insight into Cahokia's interactions with these outlying sites.

Though I have worked at Cahokia for 25 years, I still marvel at what I see. It is an awesome site, massive and mysterious, especially in the predawn hours as I drive past the dark shapes of mounds poking through ground-hugging mist on my way to greet modern-day solstice and equinox observers at the reconstructed woodhenge. Cahokia, the largest prehistoric community north of Mexico, was one of the crowning achievements of the American Indians. Here they established a complex social, political, religious, and economic system and influenced a large portion of the midcontinent. Today, as then, the climb to the top of Monks Mound is breathtaking, literally as well as figuratively, and looking out from the summit one can only imagine what this truly extraordinary place must have been like.

Columbus Meets Pocahontas in the American South

by Theda Perdue

As icons of the European colonization of the Americas, Columbus and Pocahontas represent opposite sides of the experience—European and Native, invader and defender, man and woman. Biographies and other scholarly writings document their lives and deeds, but these feats pale in comparison to the encounter these two legendary figures symbolize. Columbus embodies European discovery, invasion, and conquest while Pocahontas has become the "mother of us all," a nurturing, beckoning, seductive symbol of New World hospitality and opportunity.[1] The two never actually met in the American South, of course, except metaphorically, but this symbolic encounter involved a sexual dynamic that was inherent to the whole process of European colonization, particularly that of the American South.

John Smith's tale of succor and salvation fixed the Pocahontas image forever in the American mind, and his autobiographical account of peaceful relations with her people, the Powhatans, has exempted Englishmen from the tarring Columbus has received as an international symbol of aggression. The Columbian encounter with Native women seemed, in fact, to be radically different from Smith's. On his initial voyage of discovery, Columbus had relatively little to report about Native women except that they, like men, went "naked as the day they were born." The loss of one of his ships on this voyage forced Columbus to leave about a third of his crew on Hispaniola. When he returned, he found the burned ruins of his settlement and the decomposing corpses of his men. Local Natives related that "soon after the Admiral's departure those men began to quarrel among themselves, each taking as many women and as much gold as he could." They dispersed throughout the island, and local caciques killed them. The men on Columbus's expedition had their revenge: "Incapable of moderation in their acts of injustice, they carried off the women of the islanders under the very eyes of their brothers and their husbands." Columbus personally presented a young woman to one of his men, Michele de Cuneo, who later wrote that when she resisted him with her fingernails, he "thrashed her well, for which she raised such unheard of screams that you would not have believed your ears." In the accounts of the conquistadores, Spaniards seized women as they seized other spoils of war.[2] Such violence contributed to the "black legend" of Spanish inhumanity to Native peoples and stands in stark contrast to early English descriptions of their encounters with Native women.

John Smith, according to his own account, did not face the kind of resistance from Pocahontas and other Native women of the Virginia tidewater that the Spanish had met in the Caribbean. When Smith and a delegation from Jamestown called at the primary town of Powhatan, Pocahontas's father, they discovered that he was away, but the chief's daughter and other women invited the Englishmen to a "mascarado." "Thirtie young women," Smith wrote, "came naked out of the woods, only covered behind and before with a few green leaves, their bodies all painted." They sang and danced with "infernal passions" and then invited Smith to their lodgings. By his account, written with uncharacteristic modesty in the third person, "he was no sooner in the house, but all these Nymphes more tormented him then ever, with crowding, pressing, and hanging about him, most tediously crying, Love you not me? Love you not me?"[3]

The Spanish supposedly raped and pillaged while the English nobly resisted seduction.

The contrast is obvious—the Spanish supposedly raped and pillaged while the English nobly resisted seduction. By focusing merely on the colonizing Europeans, however, we lose sight of the Na-

Originally appeared in *Southern Cultures*, Vol. 3, No. 1, 1997, pp. 4-21, a quarterly journal published for the University of North Carolina Center for the Study of the American South. © 1997 by the University of North Carolina Press. Reprinted by permission.

tive women who are central actors in this drama: they are, after all, both the victims of Columbus's barbarity and the seductive sirens luring Smith's party. Despite differences in the ways these women are portrayed in historical sources, their experiences suggest that conquest and colonization had their own sexual dynamic. One of the facts of

---

Nudity ensured that Native women were never far from the conscious thought of European men.

---

colonization that rarely surfaces in polite conversation or scholarly writing is sex, yet we know from the written records left by Europeans and from the more obscure cultural traditions of Native people that European men had sexual relations with native American women. What can the Columbian voyages, the Jamestown colonists, and the experiences of subsequent European immigrants to the American South tell us about the ways in which men and women crossed cultural and racial bounds in their sexual relations? What do these relationships reveal about European views of female sexuality? And how did these views shape European expansion?

THE EUROPEAN VIEW OF NATIVE SEXUALITY

One thing seems fairly certain: Native women were never far from the conscious thought of European men, be they Spanish or English. Nudity insured that this was so. Accustomed to enveloping clothes, Europeans marveled at the remarkably scant clothing of the Natives. De Cuneo described the Carib woman whom he raped as "naked according to their custom," and Smith noted that except for a few strategically placed leaves, his hostesses were "naked." De Cuneo and Smith were not alone in commenting on Native women's lack of clothing. The Lord Admiral himself noticed not only that the Caribbean women he encountered wore

little but that they had "very pretty bodies." The Jamestown colonists first encountered the prepubescent Pocahontas frolicking naked with the cabin boys. The combination of her youthful enthusiasm as well as her nudity led William Strachey, official chronicler of the colony, to describe Pocahontas as "a well featured, but wanton young girl." Other Europeans also tended to link the absence of clothing to sexuality: Amerigo Vespucci, for whom America was named, noted that "the women . . . go about naked and are very libidinous."[4]

While Native women frequently exposed breasts, particularly in warm weather, they normally kept pudenda covered. When women did bare all, Europeans had another shock in store: Native women in many societies plucked their pubic hair. While some evidence points to female singeing of pubic hair in ancient Greece and even early modern Spain, most Europeans recoiled from hairless female genitalia. Thomas Jefferson, whose interests extended far beyond politics, attempted to explain hair-plucking among Native Americans: "With them it is disgraceful to be hairy in the body. They say it likens them to hogs. They therefore pluck the hair as fast as it appears." Jefferson revealed both the reaction of non-Native men and the artificiality of the practice: "The traders who marry their women, and prevail on them to discontinue this practice say, that nature is the same with them as with whites."[5] However comfortable Euro-American men may have been with visible penises, depilation left female genitalia far more exposed than most could bear. Because women revealed their private parts intentionally, they seemed to be flaunting their sexuality.

Another cultural modification to the female physique also provoked comment. Among many Native peoples, women as well as men wore tattoos. While some Euro-Americans became so enamored of the practice that they adopted it, others regarded tattooing in the same light as make-up applied to make one more physically attractive. The late eighteenth-century Philadelphia physician Benjamin Rush, for example, compared the body markings of Native peoples to cosmetics used by the

French, a people whom he described as "strangers to what is called delicacy in the intercourse of the sexes with each other."[6] Unnatural markings on the body, to Europeans, signaled an enhanced sexuality.

As contact between Native peoples and Europeans grew, women gave up tattooing and hair plucking, and they adopted the blouses and long skirts common among non-Native women along the colonial frontier. Other features of Native culture, however, perpetuated the view of Native women as sexually uninhibited. Some Europeans found the humor of Native women to be terribly bawdy. Most women enjoyed teasing and joking, and pranks and jokes with sexual overtones were not necessarily taboo. The teasing Smith endured—"Love you not me? Love you not me?"—provides a good example. One Native woman even managed to shock a Frenchman. Louis-Philippe made a tour of the American West at the end of the eighteenth century, and during his visit to the Cherokees, his guide made sexual advances to several women. "They were so little embarrassed," wrote the future French king, "that one of them who was lying on a bed put her hand on his trousers before my very eyes and said scornfully, *Ah sick*."[7]

Directness characterized courtship as well as rejection. Smith clearly expressed amazement at the forwardness of the "thirtie young women." In *Notes on the State of Virginia*, Thomas Jefferson compared the "frigidity" of Native men with the assertiveness of women: "A celebrated warrior is oftener courted by the females, than he has occasion to court: and this is a point of honor which the men aim at. . . . Custom and manners reconcile them to modes of acting, which, judged by Europeans would be deemed inconsistent with the rules of female decorum and propriety."[8] When the epitome of the American Enlightenment attributed Native women with a more active libido than Native men, who could doubt that it was so?

The arrangement and use of domestic space seemed to confirm a lack of modesty on the part of Native women. Native housing afforded little privacy for bathing, changing what little clothes women did wear, or engaging in sexual intercourse. Several generations, as well as visitors, usually slept in the same lodge. The essayist Samuel Stanhope Smith admitted that Indians were unjustly "represented as licentious because they are seen to lie promiscuously in the same wigwam." Nevertheless, few Natives allowed the lack of privacy in their homes to become a barrier to sexual fulfillment. During early eighteenth-century explorations in Carolina, one of John Lawson's companions took a Native "wife" for the night, and the newlyweds consummated their "marriage" in the same room in which other members of the expedition feasted and slept: "Our happy Couple went to Bed together before us all and with as little Blushing, as if they had been Man and Wife for 7 Years."[9]

Most European accounts of Native women in the South commented on their sexual freedom, particularly before they married. In the late eighteenth century, naturalist Bernard Romans observed: "Their women are handsome, well made, only wanting the colour and cleanliness of our ladies, to make them appear lovely in every eye; . . . they are lascivious, and have no idea of chastity in a girl, but in married women, incontinence is severely punished; a savage never forgives that crime." John Lawson suggested that even married women "sometimes bestow their Favours also to some or others in their Husbands Absence." And the trader James Adair maintained that "the Cherokees are an exception to all civilized or savage nations in having no law against adultery; they have been a considerable while under a petti-coat government, and allow their women full liberty to plant their brows with horns as oft as they please, without fear of punishment."[10]

Women in the Southeast sometimes openly solicited sex from Euro-Americans because sex gave women an opportunity to participate in the emerging market economy. Unlike men, who exchanged deerskins, beaver pelts, and buffalo hides with Europeans for manufactured goods, women often had to rely on "the soft passion" to obtain clothing, kettles, knives, hoes, and trinkets. Among some Native peoples a kind of

specialization developed according to John Lawson, who claimed that coastal Carolina peoples designated "trading girls." Sometimes prostitution was more widespread. Louis-Philippe insisted that "all Cherokee women are public women in the full meaning of the phrase: dollars never fail to melt their hearts."[11]

Selling sex was one thing; the apparent gift of women by their husbands and fathers was quite another. To Europeans, sex was a kind of commodity, purchased from prostitutes with money and from respectable women with marriage. An honorable man protected the chastity of his wife and daughters as he would other property. Native men in many societies, however, seemed to condone or even encourage sexual relations between Europeans and women presumably "belonging" to them. Even husbands who might object to "secret infidelities" sometimes offered their wives to visitors.[12]

Europeans also viewed the widespread practice of polygyny, or a man taking more than one wife, as adulterous because they recognized only the first as the "real" wife. Many Native people favored sororal polygyny, the marriage of sisters to the same man, and the groom often took sisters as brides at the same time. Since this meant, in European terms, that a man married his sister-in-law, sororal polygamy was incest as well as adultery. Jedidiah Morse, in his *Universal Geography,* wrote: "When a man loves his wife, it is considered his duty to marry her sister, if she has one. Incest and bestiality are common among them."[13] Morse apparently regarded marriage to sisters as serious a violation of European sexual mores as human intercourse with animals; in his mind, both constituted perversion.

Polygynous, adulterous, and incestuous or not, marriage meant little to Indians in the estimation of many Euro-Americans. Lawson, for example, described the ease with which the Native peoples of coastal Carolina altered their marital status: "The marriages of these Indians are no further binding than the man and woman agree together. Either of them has the liberty to leave the other upon any frivolous excuse they can make." The trader Alexander Longe relayed a Cherokee priest's view of his people's

lax attitude toward marriage: "They had better be asunder than together if they do not love one another but live for strife and confusion."[14] Europeans would have preferred that they stay together and, despite domestic turmoil, raise their children in an appropriately patriarchal household.[15]

When husband and wife parted, children normally remained with their mothers because Native peoples of the southeast were matrilineal, that is, they traced kinship solely through women. John Lawson attributed this very odd way of reckoning kin, in his view, to "fear of Impostors; the Savages knowing well, how much Frailty posseses *Indian* women, betwixt the Garters and the Girdle." While paternity might be questioned, maternity could not be. Despite the logic of such a system, Europeans had both intellectual and practical objections. Matrilineality seemed too close to the relationship between a cow and calf or a bitch and puppies: it was, the Iroquois historian Cadwallader Colden asserted, "according to the natural course of all animals." "Civilized" man presumably had moved beyond this "natural course" and had adopted laws, civil and religious, that bound fathers to children and husbands to wives. Europeans who married Native women of matrilineal societies nevertheless had difficulty exercising any control over their children and often abandoned them to their mothers' kin because men had no proprietary interest in their offspring. Thomas Nairne wrote of the Creeks: "A Girles Father has not the least hand or concern in matching her. . . . Sons never enjoy their fathers place and dignity."[16]

European men thought that they had stepped through the looking glass into a sexual wonderland.

Blatant disregard of marital vows and paternal prerogatives was shocking enough, but many Native peoples exhibited little concern for the chastity of their daughters. Jean-Bernard Bossu reported that among Native peoples on the lower Mississippi, "when an unmarried brave passes through a village, he hires a girl for a night or two, as he pleases, and her parents find nothing wrong with this. They are not at all worried about their daughter and explain that her body is hers to do with as she wishes." Furthermore, according to Lawson, "multiplicity of Gallants never [gave] . . . a Stain to a Female's reputation, or the least Hindrance of her Advancement . . . the more *Whorish*, the more *Honourable*."[17]

THE REALITIES OF NATIVE SEXUALITY

European men who traveled through the Native Southeast thought that they had stepped through the looking glass into a sexual wonderland. Actually, they had encountered only a fractured reflection of their own assumptions about appropriate sexual behavior. Native women were not as uninhibited as most whites thought. Europeans failed to realize that Native peoples did have rules regulating marriage and sexual intercourse, although the rules were sometimes quite different from their own. In the Southeast, unmarried people could engage freely in sex, but many factors other than marital status regulated and limited sexuality. A warrior preparing for or returning from battle (sometimes much of the summer), a ball player getting ready for a game, a man on the winter hunt (which could last three to four months), a pregnant woman, or a woman during her menstrual period abstained from sex. In other words, Native southerners had to forego sexual intercourse for a far greater percentage of their lives than Europeans.

Furthermore, there were inappropriate venues for sex. Although a Native couple might engage in sex in a room occupied by others, there were places, such as agricultural fields, where amorous encounters were forbidden. Violation of this rule could have serious consequences. According to the trader James Adair, the Cherokees blamed a devastating smallpox epidemic in 1738 on "the adulterous intercourses of their young married people, who the past year, had in a most notorious manner,

violated their ancient laws of marriage in every thicket, and broke down and polluted many of their honest neighbours bean-plots, by their heinous crimes, which would cost a great deal of trouble to purify again."[18] For many Native southerners, therefore, a "toss in the hay" would have been a very serious offense.

For any given Cherokee, almost one third of all Cherokees were off-limits as sexual partners.

Native peoples also had rules against incest, but they did not define incest in the same way Euro-Americans did. Intercourse or marriage with a member of a person's own clan, for example, was prohibited, and the penalty could be death. Clan membership, which included all individuals who could trace their ancestry back to a remote, perhaps mythical figure, often ran into the thousands and included many people whom Europeans would not have regarded as relatives. Consequently, the number of forbidden partners was far greater than the number under the European definition of incest. The Cherokees, for example, had seven clans. No one could marry into his or her own clan, nor was the father's clan an acceptable marriage pool. The result was that, for any given Cherokee, almost one third of all Cherokees were off-limits as sexual partners.

Each Native people had particular rules regarding marriage and incest. Many societies permitted men to have more than one wife and to marry sisters. The effect was not necessarily the devaluation of women, as European observers often claimed. Some cultural anthropologists suggest, in fact, that sororal polygamy correlates positively with high female status.[19] In the Southeast where husbands lived with their wives, the marriage of sisters to the same man reduced the number of men in the household and strengthened the control of the women over domestic life. As Morse suggested,

sisters often wanted to share a husband just as they shared a house, fields, labor, and children.

Ignorant of Native rules, southern colonials tended to view Native women as wanton woodland nymphs over whose sexuality fathers, brothers, and husbands could exercise little control. Many colonists took full advantage of the situation as they perceived it. Some evidence, however, suggests that southeastern Native women were not as amenable to sexual encounters as Europeans suggested. Louis-Philippe's anecdote reveals a woman, however bold and uninhibited, rejecting a sexual advance. When women did engage in sexual activity, many of them probably succumbed to pressure or force rather than charm.

European culture at this time countenanced considerable violence against women. William Byrd's confidential account of surveying the boundary line between North Carolina and Virginia, for example, describes several episodes of sexual aggression. One young woman, he wrote, "wou'd certainly have been ravish't, if her timely consent had not prevented the violence." This cavalier attitude toward a woman's right to refuse sex characterized much interaction between Native women and Europeans. Race almost certainly exacerbated the situation. The records of the South Carolina Indian trade are replete with Native complaints of sexual abuse at the

---

Some Native peoples came to regard sexual misbehavior as the most distinguishing feature of European cultures.

---

hands of Europeans. One trader "took a young Indian against her Will for his Wife," another severely beat three women including his pregnant wife whom he killed, and a third provided enough rum to a woman to get her drunk and then "used her ill."[20] Obviously, the women in these incidents were not the ones who were lascivious.

Some Native peoples came to regard sexual misbehavior as the most distinguishing feature of European culture. The Cherokee Booger Dance, in which participants imitated various peoples, portrayed Europeans as sexually aggressive, and the men playing that role chased screaming young women around the dance ground. As it turns out, from the Native perspective, the British colonists of the American South may not have been so terribly different from Columbus's men after all.

The people who do stand in stark contrast are Native men. James Adair, a resident of the Chickasaw Nation and a trader throughout the Southeast, perhaps knew the region's Native cultures better than any other European in the eighteenth century. As the husband of a Chickasaw women and an occasional member of Chickasaw war parties against the Choctaws, he wrote with authority that "the Indians will not cohabitate with women while they are out at war; they religiously abstain from every kind of intercourse, even with their own wives." While Adair believed, perhaps correctly, that the reason for a period of abstinence was religious, the implications for female captives was clear. "The French Indians," he wrote, "are said not to have deflowered any of our young women they captivated, while at war with us." Even the most bloodthirsty Native warrior, according to Adair, "did not attempt the virtue of his female captives," although he did not hesitate to torture and kill them. Even the Choctaws, whom Adair described as "libidinous," had taken "several female prisoners without offering the least violence to their virtue, till the time of purgation was expired." Adair could not, however, resist the temptation to slander the Choctaws, the Chickasaws' traditional enemy: "Then some of them forced their captives, notwithstanding their pressing entreaties and tears."[21]

Captivity narratives suggest Indian men raped very few, if any, women victims of colonial wars—"a very agreeable disappointment" in one woman's words.[22] Rules prohibiting intercourse immediately before and after going to war may have contributed to the absence of documented sexual violence, but Native views on female sexuality and autonomy may have been equally responsible. Indians apparently did not view sex as property or as one of the spoils of war.

Columbus's men do seem to have equated sex and material plunder. The accounts of the destruction of the Hispaniola settlement link his men's desire for women with a desire for gold. In perhaps a more subtle way, British colonists also considered women to be a form of property and found the Native men's lack of proprietary interest in their wives and daughters incomprehensible. It called into question the Indians' concept of property in general and paved the way for Europeans to challenge Native people's ownership of land. From the second decade of colonization in the South, wealth depended on the cultivation of land, and southerners found the argument that Indians had no notion of absolute ownership particularly compelling.

People who objectified both land and sex had encountered people who did not.

While Native southerners forcefully maintained their right to inhabit the land of their fathers, they did not, in fact, regard land ownership in quite the same way as the Europeans who challenged their rights to it. They fought for revenge rather than for territory, they held land in common, and they permitted any tribal member to clear and cultivate unused tracts. Land did not represent an investment of capital, and Native southerners did not sell out and move on when other opportunities beckoned. Indeed, the land held such significance for most of them that they suffered severe economic, social, and political disruption rather than part with it. In the 1820s and 1830s, frontiersmen, land speculators, and politicians joined forces to divest Native peoples of their land, and southern state governments and ultimately the federal government took up the aggressors' cause. White southerners made a concerted effort to force their Indian neighbors to surrender their lands and move west of the Mississippi to new territory. What difference did it make, many whites asked, which lands the Indians occupied? With squatters encroaching on them, shysters defrauding them at every turn, and federal and state authorities unwilling to protect them, Native peoples in the South struggled desperately to retain their homelands. They did so for reasons as incomprehensible to Euro-Americans as the sexual behavior of Native women. People who objected both land and sex had encountered people who did not.

Ultimately, Native southerners lost. Representatives of the large southern tribes—the Cherokees, Chickasaws, Choctaws, Creeks, and Seminoles—signed treaties in which they agreed to move west to what is today eastern Oklahoma. Remnants of some of those tribes as well as other isolated Native communities simply retreated into the shadows and eked out a living on marginal land while the cotton kingdom expanded onto the rich soil that Native peoples had surrendered. In the cotton kingdom, land was saleable rather than sacred, and power not parity characterized sexual relationships.

In recent years we have come to admire Native sensitivity to the natural world and to compare ourselves unfavorably to Indians on environmental issues and attitudes toward the land. Columbus and Pocahontas probably thought about sex at least as often as they did ecology, but we seem incapable of recognizing that their views on sex might have been as different as their ideas about land use. Disney's recent movie, *Pocahontas,* merely perpetuates the notion that romantic love is a universal concept that transcends cultural bounds and has little connection with specific aspects of a culture. The film depicts Pocahontas not as the autonomous person she probably was, but as a subservient young woman submissive to her father, betrothed to the warrior Kocoum, and won by Smith. Pocahontas's love for Smith (and vice versa) resolves conflicts with the Indians, and the English presumably set about the task at hand. "Oh, with all ya got in ya, boys,"

Governor Ratclife sings, "dig up Virginia, boys." True love, of course, characterized neither the real relationship between Pocahontas and John Smith nor the dealings of Native women and European men. Instead of Disney's John Smith, most Native women really met Columbus. Perhaps in the American South, where Columbus and Pocahontas metaphorically collided so forcefully, we should expand our comparison of Native Americans and Europeans beyond environmental issues and consider the interactions between men and women. Then we might begin to make connections between the materialism and exploitation that have characterized so much of southern history and sexual violence against women.

NOTES

1. Samuel Eliot Morison, *Admiral of the Ocean Sea* (Little Brown and Company, 1942); Grace Steele Woodward, *Pocahontas* (University of Oklahoma Press, 1969); J. A. Leo Lemay, *Did Pocahontas Save Captain John Smith?* (University of Georgia Press, 1993); Philip Young, "The Mother of Us All," *Kenyon Review* 24 (1962): 391–441. See also Rayna Green, "The Pocahontas Perplex: The Image of Indian Women in American Culture," *Massachusetts Review* 16 (1975): 698–714.

2. Marvin Lunenfeld, ed., *1492: Discovery, Invasion, Encounter* (D. C. Heath and Company, 1991), 133, 161–64; S. E. Morison, ed., *Journals and Other Documents in the Life and Voyages of Christopher Columbus* (The Heritage Press, 1963), 212.

3. John Smith, *The Generall Historie of Virginia, New England and the Summer Isles . . .* (London, 1624), Book 3: 67.

4. Woodward, 5; Robert F. Berkhofer, *The White Man's Indian: The History of an Idea from Columbus to the Present* (Knopf, 1978), 7–9.

5. Paul Leicester Ford, ed., *The Writings of Thomas Jefferson,* 10 vols. (G. P. Putnam's Sons, 1892–99), 3: 154–55.

6. George W. Corner, ed., *The Autobiography of Benjamin Rush: His Travels Through Life, Together with His Commonplace Book* [1789–1813], *Memoirs of the American Philosophical Society,* vol. 25 (Princeton University Press, 1948), 71.

7. Louis-Philippe, *Diary of My Travels in America,* tr. Stephen Becker (Delacorte Press, 1977), 84–85.

8. Thomas Jefferson, *Notes on the State of Virginia,* (1787; reprt. Matthew Carey, 1794), 299.

9. Samuel Stanhope Smith, *An Essay on the Causes of the Variety of Complexion and Figure in the Human Species,* ed. Winthrop D. Jordan (1810; reprt. Harvard University Press, 1965), 128; John Lawson, *A New Voyage to Carolina,* ed. Hugh T. Lefler (University of North Carolina Press, 1967), 37–38.

10. Bernard Romans, *A Concise History of East and West Florida* (1775; reprt. University of Florida Press, 1962), 40–43; Lawson, 194; James Adair, *Adair's History of the North American Indians,* ed. Samuel Cole Williams (The Watauga Press, 1930), 1522–53.

11. Lawson, 41; Louis-Philippe, 72.

12. Romans, 40–43.

13. Jedidiah Morse, *The American Universal Geography; or a View of the Present State of All the Kingdoms, States, and Colonies in the Known World* (Thomas and Andrews, 1812), 105.

14. Lawson, 193; Alexander Longe, "A Small Postscript of the Ways and Manners of the Indians Called Charikees," ed. D. H. Corkran, *Southern Indian Studies* 21 (1969): 30.

15. Morse, 575–76; Albert Gallatin, "Synopsis of the Indian Tribes Within the United States East of the Rocky Mountains," vol. 2 of *Archaeologia Americana; Transactions and Collections of the American Antiquarian Society,* (Folson, Wells, and Thurston, 1836), 112–13.

16. Lawson, 57; Cadwallader Colden, *History of the Five Indian Nations of Canada which are Dependent on the Provinces of New York,* 2 vols. (1747; reprt. Allerton Brooks, 1922), 1: xxxiii; Alexander Moore, ed., *Nairne's Muskogean Journals; The 1708 Expedition to the Mississippi River* (University of Mississippi Press, 1988), 33, 45.

17. Seymour Feiler, ed., *Jean-Bernard Bossu's Travels in the Interior of North America, 1751–1762* (University of Oklahoma Press, 1962), 131–32; Lawson, 40.

18. Adair, 244.

19. Alice Schlegel, *Male Dominance and Female Autonomy: Domestic Authority in Matrilineal Societies* (Yale University Press, 1972), 87–88.

20. William K. Boyd, ed., *William Byrd's Histories of the Dividing Line Betwixt Virginia and North Carolina* (The North Carolina Historical Commission, 1929), 147–48; William L. McDowell, ed., *Journals of the Commissioners of the Indian Trade, Sept. 20, 1710–Aug. 29, 1718* (South Carolina Archives Department, 1955), 4, 37; McDowell, *Documents Relating to Indian Affairs, 1754–1765* (University of South Carolina Press, 1970), 231.

21. Adair, 171–72.

22. James Axtell, *The European and the Indian,* (Oxford University Press), 183.

A "Newfounde Lande"

BY ALAN WILLIAMS *Five hundred years after John Cabot's 1497 voyage brought word of the North American continent to Europe, scholars still hotly debate the exact location of his landfall.*

In 1992, THE AMERICAS marked the five-hundredth anniversary of the European discovery of the lands of the Western Hemisphere by Christopher Columbus, a Genoese navigator sailing in the service of Spain's King Ferdinand and Queen Isabella. Considerable controversy surrounded the commemoration of that event, as some disputed the notion that lands already occupied could be "discovered" and others pointed to earlier claims by Europeans of having crossed the Atlantic and visited the Americas long before the arrival of Columbus.

This year the world marks another important quincentennial, and again there is controversy, especially surrounding the exact landfall of the explorer, John Cabot. While the precise location of Columbus's initial landfall has been questioned, it is generally conceded that his discoveries involved first the islands of the Caribbean and later, the mainland of South America. Cabot is honored, especially in England and in Atlantic Canada, as the man who forged the way from Europe to the North American continent, but where in North America remains at issue.

Legends about Atlantic crossings by Carthaginians, Jews, Chinese, and the Welsh place visitors from the Old World in the Western Hemisphere as early as the fifth century B.C. The Irish tell of St. Brendan island-hopping the northern North Atlantic a thousand years later. And the exploits of the Vikings in North America between A.D. 800–1400 are not only recorded in oral Norse sagas, but have been substantiated through modern archaeological investigations in northern Newfoundland, particularly at the Norse settlement uncovered at L'Anse aux Meadows, now recognized as a World Heritage site.

Columbus's four voyages to the New World are well documented. His initial visit to the Caribbean region in 1492–93 was followed the next year by his exploration of the southern coast of Cuba, which he was convinced was the territory of the Grand Khan of China, and Haiti, which he named Hispaniola because it resembled Spain. In 1498, Columbus cruised the Venezuelan coast, believing it to be the coast of Asia. And on his fourth and final voyage to the New World in 1502, Columbus touched what is now known as Central America.

While the "Admiral of the Ocean Sea" was so engaged, John Cabot set sail in 1497 to test his own theories on an all-water route to the Indies and returned to England with the first certain news of the coast of North America. Unlike Columbus, however, Cabot left little documentary information about himself or his voyages to help today's scholars reconstruct his achievements.

It is generally believed that Cabot was really Giovanni Caboto, a native of Gaeta, near Naples, in Italy. Born in or before 1455, he grew up in Genoa and is thus of the same generation and city as Columbus. Cabot later moved to Venice and became a citizen of that city in 1476. He married a Venetian named Mattea, with whom he had three sons, Ludovico, Sancio, and the most famous, Sebestiano.

Cabot made his living as a merchant, trading with Alexandria, in North Africa, from where he acquired Asian spices, dyes, and silks for markets in Europe. Like other seafaring European merchants, Cabot wished for a way to avoid dealing with the Arab "middlemen" who controlled practically all of the land that surrounded the Mediterranean Sea.

An experienced mapmaker and navigator, Cabot believed that it was possible to sail west in order to reach Asia. Hoping to win financial backing that would enable him to prove his theories, Cabot moved to Spain in 1490 and soon after approached officials in Seville with plans for a westward voyage to Cathay (China). When word reached him of the triumph of Christopher Columbus, Cabot knew that there would be little chance of his gaining the patronage of Spain's royalty for his own scheme.

By now obsessed with the idea of finding a western route to Asia, Cabot turned to England for help in his quest. He counted on King Henry VII's desire to outdo his Spanish rival, King Ferdinand II, in the possible acquisition of new territories and the opportunity to tap the wealth that would presumably come to the first nation to reach the shores of Cathay.

In England, Cabot settled with his family in the western port of Bristol, one

From *American History,* September/October 1997, pp. 16-20, 65-66. © 1997 by Cowles Magazines, Inc. Reprinted through the courtesy of Cowles Magazines, publishers of *American History.*

COWLES ARCHIVE

CORBIS-BETTMANN

Originally intending to seek Spanish backing to test his theory on an all-water route to Asia, Cabot realized the futility of that course when Christopher Columbus returned from his first voyage to the New World in 1493 (above, right). The Italian-born explorer then moved his family from Spain to England, where he proposed his plan—to sail west as Columbus had, but at more northerly latitudes—to the merchants of Bristol and to King Henry VII (above, left).

of the nation's wealthiest cities. The Bristol merchants were a cosmopolitan group, fond of civic pomp, whose city, adorned with fine churches, mimicked London. Their trade in wool, cloth, hides, wine, and fish took their vessels to Iceland, Norway, Iberia, and the Mediterranean. The merchants, like the Norse before them, also sent seamen westward in search of fish and wood. Now Cabot approached them with a new and tantalizing objective.

Confidently asserting that he could reach the East by sailing west, as Columbus had done, Cabot promised to bring back the riches of Asia directly by sea, by-passing the Moslem traders of the eastern Mediterranean. He knew how far Columbus had sailed in southern latitudes without reaching Cathay and he cogently argued that, starting from England's more northerly latitude, he could reach the northeastern part of Cathay by traveling half the distance, just as German cartographer Martin Behaim had indicated on his globe in 1492.* Once they reached land, all that was necessary Cabot told the Englishmen, was to sail southwestward to the

warmer, populated regions of the East, such as Cipango (Japan) and India.

Probably on the basis of his skill as an advanced navigator, Cabot persuaded the merchants of his capability to captain such an expedition. Some of the instruments and charts that he carried were by far the most modern that the merchants had seen. Most of the instruments measured the angle between the stars or the sun and the horizon, so that the ship's position could be calculated. The cross-staff measured the angle of a star in relation to the horizon; the nocturnal figured the position of Ursa Major or Minor in relation to the Pole star; and the indispensable astrolabe determined latitude, the distance north or south of the equator.

After successfully securing the financial backing of the merchants of Bristol, Cabot petitioned the king for permission

---

*Behaim, using the academic geography available at the end of the fifteenth century, produced a terrestrial globe that showed only islands separating Europe from Asia. He grossly underestimated the actual circumference of the earth as well as the distance between Europe and Asia when sailing west.

to sail. He realized that he would not be able to claim any discoveries for England without royal assent, leaving his finds free for the taking by any European country. On March 5, 1496, Cabot and his sons, who do not seem to have accompanied him on his voyage, received letters patent (royal grants of right) from Henry VII authorizing them "to seek out, discover, and find whatsoever isles, countries, regions, or provinces of the heathen and infidels, whatsoever they be, and in what part of the world soever they be. . . ."

A letter written by John Day, an English merchant—"rather a slippery character with many irons in the fire"—who was reporting to Christopher Columbus on John Cabot's voyage, does not indicate exactly when or from where Cabot made his first attempt to cross the ocean, but it appears to have been in 1496, soon after he won his first letters patent from the English king. Day simply noted that Cabot "went with one ship, had a disagreement with his crew, he was short of supplies and ran into weather, and he decided to turn back."

Trying again in 1497, Cabot left Bristol, probably early in May in the *Matthew*, most likely named after his wife, Mattea. He struck out westwards for Cathay somewhere off the Atlantic coast of Ireland. Fifty-three days later, the *Matthew* reached land.

Cabot and his crew went ashore, the first Englishmen, although led by an Italian, to set foot on North American soil. They erected a cross and the banners of England and Venice, claiming all the country for the king. His party being small—Day wrote in a letter soon after Cabot returned home—Cabot "did not dare advance inland beyond the shooting distance of a crossbow and after taking fresh water he returned to his ship." Although they met no inhabitants, Cabot was certain that he had reached the northeastern extremity of Asia. Like Columbus when he coasted Cuba, Cabot expected that populous cities with roofs of gold and sources of silk and spices could not be too far off.

The exact point of Cabot's landing has been the subject of weighty argument. Scholars have so differently reconstructed Cabot's voyage, his known coasting, and his return journey that his North American landfall could have been anywhere between Labrador and Maine, perhaps even the Carolinas, with at least one historian taking him as far south as Florida.

Since no journal kept by Cabot or his crew has survived to indicate precisely where they went, historians have had to rely for documentation on a handful of letters sent from England to Spain and Italy by foreign diplomats. Even the fragmentary information contained in existing chronicles and maps made in the succeeding years, allegedly from Cabot's own globe and charts, may not be reliable.

The problem is further complicated by the fact that Cabot lost his life in 1498, either at sea or in the New World. The great Cabot scholar J. A. William-

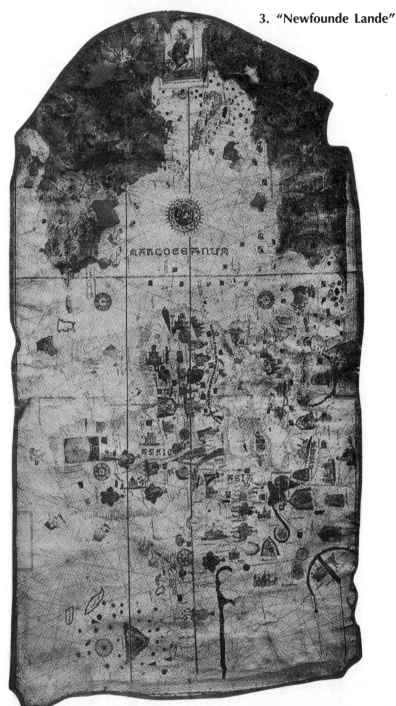

MUSEO NAVAL, MADRID

Dating from around 1500, the planisphere of the whole known world drawn by Juan de la Cosa, is the earliest cartographic representation of any part of the North American continent. La Cosa depicted that section of the map (top, right) on a larger scale than the Old World and included references to both Columbus's and Cabot's New World discoveries. Five English flags, thought by some to represent places claimed by Cabot for King Henry VII of England, appear along the northwest Atlantic coast. Because there exists scant documentary information about Cabot's voyage, scholars have for centuries debated exactly what route his ship, the *Matthew*, followed and where in North America he landed. One suggested route takes Cabot directly to the coast of the island of Newfoundland, while the other has him missing Newfoundland on his outbound journey, landing instead on the northern tip of Cape Breton Island (bottom, right).

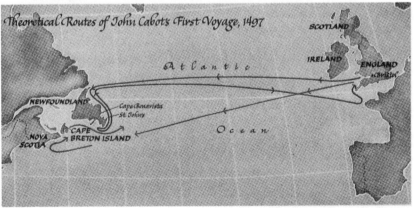

MAP BY JOAN PENNINGTON

son explained the reason why so little of Cabot's discovery is known, saying that while "Columbus had a faithful friend, the Bishop Las Casas [his biographer], and a son who revered his father's memory and saved it from being forgotten, John Cabot . . . had a son Sebastian, who seems to have been jealous of his father's fame and to have done his best to destroy the memory of his achievements."

Nineteenth-century American historiographer Henry Harrisse declared that Sebastian was one of the greatest liars in the history of discovery who, despite his long and generally successful career as a navigator and mapmaker in England and Spain, nevertheless wanted credit for his father's 1497 discovery. Thanks to the younger Cabot's efforts at distortion, the earliest chroniclers referred only to "a Venetian," and if they mentioned a name, it was that of Sebastian, not John.

The "Sebastian supremacy" lasted until the records were carefully searched by a Bristol librarian named Nicholls and an American Cabot scholar, Richard Biddle, in the first half of the nineteenth century. The investigations led historians on both sides of the Atlantic to eventually restore John Cabot to his rightful place in time for the four-hundredth anniversary of the landing in 1897, which saw a flurry of writing on the subject of his voyages.

Discussions concerning Cabot's right to be known as the "first discoverer of North America" and renewed debate on his likely route received added impetus with the uncovering of early cartographic evidence. The earliest find was a world map, made about the year 1500 by Juan de la Cosa, a skilled Biscayan navigator who had sailed with Columbus. Found in 1832, this was the first map to represent any part of the North American continent* and indicates both Columbus's "Indies" and Cabot's "northeastern part of Asia," which forms the western border of the Atlantic Ocean. La Cosa lined these lands with five English

flags, possibly indicating spots at which Cabot claimed territory for the Crown. La Cosa also identifies "Cauo de ynglaterra" (Cape of England) and "mar de descubierta por inglese" (sea discovered by the English).

William Ganong, a great cartographic scholar from New Brunswick, Canada, performed an analysis of the La Cosa map, which has been called "one of the most brilliant 'old map' expositions ever written." Ganong concluded that the La Cosa map could be a simplification of Cabot's own map, the result of successive re-drawings. He further theorized that Cabot missed Newfoundland on the outward voyage, landed on Cape Breton Island, off Nova Scotia, and returned along the southern coast of Newfoundland.

The case can be made that the land below the English flags, heading southward, represents the *whole* coast of North America, from Labrador to the Gulf of Mexico, but with part of the latter hidden by a depiction of St. Christopher. The distinguished historical cartographer R. A. Skelton considered the Cosa map "the only map which unambiguously illustrates John Cabot's voyage of 1497 and—with less certainty—his voyage of 1498."

Ganong's contention that Cabot could have missed Newfoundland on the outward voyage and reached Cape Breton is, naturally enough, disputed by Newfoundlanders, who maintain that it is highly unlikely he would not have sighted the coast of that large island, which is in such close proximity to the eastern shores of Cape Breton Island. However, given the fog-shrouded conditions often existing in that part of the North Atlantic, it is entirely possible that Cabot and his men could have missed observing Newfoundland as they sailed west.

The so-called "Sebastian Cabot" map of 1544, discovered in Germany in 1856, backs Cape Breton as the likely landfall. The words "Prima Tierra Vista" (land first seen) against a promontory obviously meant for Cape North, at the northernmost tip of Cape Breton Island, would seem to indicate that this was the point of land that first met the eyes of Cabot's crew as they looked from the sea.

The notion that Cabot landed on Newfoundland's Bonavista Peninsula

seems to go back only to the 1620s, when Captain John Mason's map of the island included the words "Bona Vista Caboto primum reperta." Many believe that Mason, a governor of the London and Bristol Company who resided in Newfoundland for three years, had either privileged information from an older chart now lost or knew fishermen whose fathers or grandfathers had sailed with Cabot.

But if Sebastian Cabot's claim for Cape Breton was personal, perhaps Mason's was political. Newfoundland author W. A. Munn suggested that Mason printed the Cabot discovery claim over Cape Bonavista in Latin because he wanted every mapmaker in Spain, Portugal, France, and Italy to interpret the meaning clearly: the English "got here first in 1497."

During the quatrocentennial celebrations of Cabot's voyages in 1897, a great rivalry developed between Newfoundlanders and residents of Canada's Maritime provinces, particularly in view of the fact that Newfoundland was not yet a part of Canada.** Both groups celebrated discovery with representatives from Bristol joining the Canadians in Halifax, Nova Scotia, while the Newfoundlanders laid the foundation stone of Cabot Tower, which now sits brooding over The Narrows, at the entrance to the harbor at its capital of St. John's.

The debate continued into the twentieth century. In 1936, Munn scathingly dismissed the "Cape Breton theorists," complaining that the efforts made by L. J. Burpee, editor of the *Canadian Geographical Journal,* and subsequent celebrations in Cape Breton and mainland Nova Scotia in 1934 "created a resentment from Newfoundlanders that Canadians have over-stepped the bounds of courtesy by asserting what they cannot prove."

Great mystery surrounds John Cabot's third and last voyage, undertaken in 1498. Henry VII authorized six ships for Cabot's new venture, but the mariner departed England with five, well-victualed and stocked with trade goods. The expedition encountered a fierce storm that forced one

---

*In 1965, Yale University Press published a privately owned medieval map of the world that included Vinland, a Norse or Viking settlement on the east coast of North America, as detailed by Icelandic navigator Leif Ericson, who visited and named the site in the early eleventh century. However, the authenticity of the New World sections of the Yale map have been sharply disputed.

**The Canadian province of Newfoundland and Labrador was admitted to confederation in March 1949.

of the ships to seek shelter in an Irish port, but "the Genoese kept on his way."

Although one contemporary wrote that it was believed that Cabot "found the new lands nowhere but on the very bottom of the sea," it is generally assumed that Cabot or at least some of his captains reached distant shores, or how else can the unflagged coasts on the La Cosa map be explained? "[W]e know what they found," Williamson commented, "primeval tracts and Indian tribes, no great state or government, no cities, no seaports, ships of trade, no spices and silks for barter—in a word, no Asia. Did any of them come back to tell this? The change in English outlook suggests that they did."

But Cabot was never seen again. Explorer Gaspar Côrte-Real's new world expedition of 1501 obtained a broken gilt sword of Italian manufacture and a pair of silver earrings of Venetian type from Indians somewhere in North America, which could suggest Cabot's fate. But while one story sinks Cabot at Grates Cove on Newfoundland's Avalon Peninsula, another suggests that some of his ships sailed southwestward to Florida and into the Caribbean, where Spaniards, resentful of the encroachment on lands and seas reserved for them by the Treaty of Tordesillas,* overcame and killed him.

---

*The Treaty of Tordesillas, signed on July 7, 1494, settled differences between Spain and Portugal that were brought about after Columbus's first voyage. The treaty divided the lands of the New World between the two Iberian nations.

While Christopher Columbus must be given credit for paving Europe's way to the New World, it does seem safe to say that John Cabot, the uncertainty surrounding his landfall notwithstanding, was the European "discoverer" of North America. The controversy is likely to remain unsettled, at least for the time being, and both Newfoundland and Cape Breton can commemorate this significant anniversary in the history of the "Age of Explorers" without fear of concrete contradiction.

Alan Williams has headed the Department of American and Canadian Studies in the School of History at England's University of Birmingham since 1987.

Laboring in the Fields of the Lord

The Franciscan missions of seventeenth-century Florida enabled Spain to harness the energies of tens of thousands of native people.

Jerald T. Milanich

Jerald T. Milanich is curator of archaeology in the department of anthropology at the Florida Museum of Natural History, Gainesville.

Beginning in the 1590s Franciscan friars established dozens of missions in what is today southern Georgia and northern Florida, but by the time Spain relinquished its Florida colony to Great Britain in 1763 only two missions remained. Spain regained control of the colony in 1783, only to cede it to the United States 38 years later. With the Spaniards gone, memories of

J. T. MILANICH

This Guale Indian grasping a cross was interred in a shallow grave on the floor of the church at mission Santa Catalina on Amelia Island, Florida. The piety of the Christian Indians was, in the eyes of the mission friars, extraordinary.

FLORIDA DIVISION OF HISTORICAL RESOURCES

This quartz pendant, nearly three inches long, was found at San Luís, a late seventeenth-century Apalachee mission.

their missions faded. Their wood-and-thatch buildings, like the native peoples they had served, simply disappeared from the landscape.

In the late 1940s archaeologists began searching for the north Florida missions. By the end of the 1970s fieldwork and historical research had, it was thought, closed the book on the history of the settlements. My own research and that of my colleagues has reopened that book, adding new chapters to the history of the Spanish colony.

The missions of La Florida were an integral part of Pedro Menéndez de Avilés' master plan for his colony, whose first town, St. Augustine, was established in 1565. By converting the native peoples to Catholicism, as required by contract between him and his sovereign, Philip II, Menéndez hoped to insure loyal, obedient subjects. He initially arranged for Jesuit friars to establish a handful of missions along the Atlantic and Gulf coasts. The Jesuits, however, failed to build support among the native peoples and returned to Spain in 1572. They were replaced by Franciscans subsidized by the Spanish Crown. At first the hardships of mission work—the rigors of travel, climate, and lack of supplies—sent them packing as well. By 1592 only two friars and one lay brother remained, but three years later 12 new friars arrived, and missionary efforts began in earnest. The friars were assigned to *doctrinas,* missions with churches where native people were instructed in religious doctrine.

The first Franciscan missions were established along the Atlantic coast, from St. Augustine north to Santa Elena on Parris Island, South Carolina. In 1587, however, raids by unfriendly Indians forced the abandonment of Santa Elena, and the chain of coastal missions serving the Timucuas and their northern neighbors, the Guale, stopped just short of present-day South Carolina. During the next 35 years a second chain of missions was established on the *camino real,* or royal road, that led westward about 350 miles from St. Augustine through the provinces of Timucua and Apalachee in northwestern Florida. Over time, these missions were moved or abandoned and

Reprinted with permission from *Archaeology* magazine, Vol. 49, No. 1, January/February 1996, pp. 60-67. © 1996 by the Archaeological Institute of America.

In this pencil drawing by Edward Jonas, the mission church at San Luís, in modern Tallahassee, Florida, faces a central plaza. Size and construction details—the walls, thatched roof, position of the front door, and presence of two bells—are based on data from excavations by Bonnie McEwan, an archaeologist with the San Luís project, Florida Division of Historic Resources.

new ones founded. Historian John Hann of the Florida Bureau of Archaeological Research estimates that as many as 140 existed at one time or another.

After the British settled Charleston in 1670—in territory that had once been under Spanish control—they began to challenge Spain's hold on La Florida. Through its Carolinian colonists, the British began to chip away at the Spanish presence. One effective way was to destroy the Franciscan missions. In the 1680s Carolinian militia and their native allies raided several missions in north Florida and the Georgia coast. Timucuas and Guale were captured and taken to Charleston where they were sold into slavery to work plantations in the Carolinas and the West Indies. The raids on the Georgia coastal missions grew so intense that by the late 1680s all of the missions north of Amelia Island were abandoned.

In 1702 and 1704 Carolinian raids on the Apalachee and Timucuan missions in northern Florida effectively destroyed the mission system west of the St. Johns River. Churches were burned and their contents smashed. Villagers were scattered, tortured, and killed. Nearly 5,000 Indians were sold into slavery, while others fled west to the Gulf of Mexico. Of some 12,000 original mission Indians fewer than 1,000 remained, and they fled to refugee villages that grew up around St. Augustine. When Spain turned La Florida over to Britain in 1763, only 63 Christian Indians remained, and the retreating Spanish took them to Cuba.

By the early 1980s archaeologists had found the remains of perhaps a dozen missions. In doing so, they had relied on an important document written by a seventeenth-century bishop of Cuba, Gabriel Díaz Vara Calderón. The bishop had vis-

ited La Florida from 1674 to 1675 to witness firsthand what the Franciscan friars had accomplished. His report lists 24 missions along the camino real and provides the distances between them:

Ten leagues [1 league = 3.5 miles] from the city of Saint Augustine, on the bank of the river Corrientes [the St. Johns], is the village and mission of San Diego de Salamototo. It [the river] is very turbulent and almost a league and a half in width. From there to the village and mission of Santa Fe there are some 20 uninhabited leagues. Santa Fe is the principal mission of this province. Off to the side [from Santa Fe] toward the southern border, at a distance of 3 leagues, is the deserted mission and village of San Francisco. Twelve leagues from Santa Fe is the mission of Santa Catalina, with Ajohica 3 leagues away and Santa Cruz de Tarihica 2. Seven leagues away, on

Missions before 1656 Rebellion

BETTE DUKE

Beginning in 1595 Franciscan missions were built along the Atlantic coast from St. Augustine to just short of present-day South Carolina. In 1606 a second chain of missions was started north and south of the camino real, or royal road, that led westward about 350 miles from St. Augustine through the provinces of Timucua and Apalachee in northwestern Florida.

lages, but they also discovered two seventeenth-century Spanish missions, both north of the camino real. Again, neither was listed by Bishop Calderón. The good news was that we had an excellent idea of de Soto's route; the bad news was that something was terribly wrong with our understanding of the history and geography of the missions.

I needed dates for the three mysterious sites. One way to get them was to study Spanish majolica pottery, a tin-glazed tableware that is common at Spanish colonial sites in the Americas and abundant at all three missions. Majolicas can be divided into types based on differences in vessel shapes, colors of glazes, and glazed designs. Because some types were popular mainly before ca. 1650 and others mainly after that date, we can date collections to the early or late seventeenth century. Analysis of majolicas from the mystery missions showed that all three were occupied only before 1650. Had something occurred in the mid-seventeenth century that led to their abandonment two decades before Bishop Calderón's visit?

Since the 1930s historians have known of Spanish accounts document-

the bank of the large river Guacara [the Suwannee], is the mission of San Juan of the same name. Ten [further on] is that of San Pedro de Potohiriba, 2 that of Santa Helena de Machaba, 4, that of San Matheo, 2, that of San Miguel de Asyle, last in this . . . province.

What made this guide especially valuable was the discovery and publication in 1938 of a map of the camino real drawn by a British surveyor in 1778, when the road was still a major route across northern Florida. Some names of Spanish missions appear on the map. It seemed that it would only be a matter of time until we had discovered all of the sites.

The first clue that the accepted history of the missions needed a major overhaul came in 1976. Excavating a seventeenth-century Spanish-Indian site in north Florida, I had uncovered the burnt remains of a small wooden church and an earth-floored friars' quarters, both adjacent to a Timucuan village. The evidence suggested that the site was one of the missions along the camino real. But which mission was it? Its position on the road did not match any of the locations mentioned in Bishop Calderón's account. It was too far east to be mission San Juan and too far west to be Santa Cruz.

More questions about the geography of the missions surfaced in the late

1980s when I was looking for archaeological traces of the Spanish conquistador Hernando de Soto's 1539 march across northern Florida (see ARCHAEOLOGY, May/June 1989). My field crews did indeed find de Soto-era native villages, but they also discovered two sev-

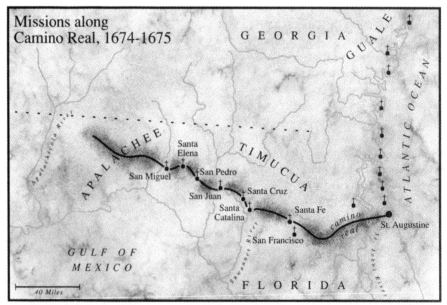

Missions along Camino Real, 1674-1675

BETTE DUKE

After the Timucuan rebellion of 1656, Governor Rebolledo relocated the Timucuan missions along the camino real, roughly a day's travel apart, where they functioned as way stations between Apalachee province and St. Augustine. The relocation also reflected the demographic devastation caused by epidemics, especially smallpox and measles.

FLORIDA DIVISION OF HISTORICAL RESOURCES

These native ceramics from Apalachee are typical of the mission period. Each Indian culture had its own style of pottery.

FLORIDA DIVISION OF HISTORICAL RESOURCES

Villagers were paid in glass beads and trinkets, which were exchanged for hides and furs for trading back to the Spanish.

ing a 1656 Indian rebellion at the Timucuan missions. The governor of Spanish Florida, Diego de Rebolledo, sent troops to put down the rebellion. Ten native leaders were rounded up and hanged. The governor was subsequently charged with having displayed great cruelty and was slated to answer for his actions, but he died before a hearing could be held.

What was not known until the early 1990s was that an investigation took place after Rebolledo's death. In the Archivo General de Indias in Seville, Spain, John Worth, then a doctoral student at the University of Florida, found lengthy testimony taken at the hearing and related documents that described the rebellion and its aftermath. They also rewrote what we had known about mission geography.

The documents recount how the rebellion began in the spring of 1656, when Lúcas Menéndez, one of the major chiefs in Timucua, and other chiefs defied Governor Rebolledo's orders. Hearing a report that the British were planning a raid on St. Augustine, the governor had commanded the chiefs of Apalachee and Timucua to assemble 500 men and march to St. Augustine. The Indians were ordered to carry food for a stay of at least a month. Because construction of fortifications was still under way and the number of soldiers stationed in the colony was well below its full complement, the town was poorly prepared to withstand an attack. The governor wanted to reinforce its defenses with Indian warriors.

But the chiefs of Timucua refused to go, a decision that grew out of dissatisfaction with treatment they had received from the governor on previous visits to St. Augustine. Rebolledo had not properly feasted the chiefs, nor had he given them gifts, as was customary. The chiefs also refused to carry their own food and supplies or to provide warriors to defend the town without compensation. The power of native leaders in Timucua had already been threatened by nearly a century of Spanish colonization, and Rebolledo's 1656 order was seen by the Timucuan chiefs as demeaning and an attempt to undercut their authority.

Chief Lúcas Menéndez told his followers and the other chiefs to kill Spaniards, though not the mission friars. The

FLORIDA DIVISION OF HISTORICAL RESOURCES

Painting by John LoCastro depicts the Apalachee Indian council house at San Luís. The 120-foot diameter building was at one end of a central plaza which served as a field for a game in which teams tried to kick a ball into an eagle-nest target atop a pole.

J. T. MILANICH

Remains of 59 villagers buried in a corner of Amelia Island's Santa Catalina church attest the decimation of native people. A 1659 report states that 10,000 people died in one measles epidemic.

first deaths occurred at San Miguel and San Pedro in western Timucua. At each site a Spanish soldier, part of the small military presence in the province, was slain. A Spanish servant and a Mexican Indian who by chance had camped in Timucua while traveling the camino real were the next to die. Warriors led by Lúcas Menéndez then raided a Spanish cattle ranch near modern Gainesville, killing a third Spanish soldier and two African workers. All across northern Florida Timucuas abandoned their missions.

Knowing the Spanish would retaliate, some of the rebellious Timucuas gathered at mission Santa Elena, which they converted into a palisaded fort. Rebolledo sent 60 Spanish infantry and several hundred Apalachee Indians to capture the rebels. After extended negotiations the Timucuas came out. Their leaders were seized along with several Timucuas who had participated in the murders. One man confessed almost immediately and was executed, probably by hanging. Other prisoners were taken to Apalachee and held while word was sent to the governor.

In late November Rebolledo and a small entourage marched from St. Augustine, capturing several chiefs along the way. A trial was held in Apalachee. Ten of the prisoners were sentenced to

forced labor in St. Augustine, while ten others, most of whom were chiefs, were sentenced to death. Rebolledo ordered the men hanged at various places along the camino real as grim reminders of the power of the Spaniards and the fate that awaited those who rebelled against the Crown.

Rebolledo also seized the opportunity to reorganize the province and its missions so they would better serve the needs of the colony and its Spanish overlords. Missions were relocated roughly a day's travel apart so they could function as way stations between Apalachee province and St. Augustine. This arrangement of missions was what Bishop Calderón had observed in 1674 and 1675. That explained two of our three mystery sites. One of the northern two was the pre-1656 mission of Santa Cruz, which was moved south to the camino real after the rebellion. The site we had excavated in 1976 was the mission of San Juan which, after the rebellion, was moved six miles west to a point on the camino real that intersected the Suwannee River. The identity of our third mission remains a mystery, although it seems certain it too was abandoned after the rebellion.

Worth's research led us to believe there were two mission systems in Timucua, one before and one after 1656. What made it necessary for the governor

to reorganize the missions? To answer that question we began to reexamine other Spanish documents discovered by Hann and Worth. They indicated that by 1656 epidemics had devastated the population of Timucua province. Although the occurrence of epidemics—especially smallpox and measles—had long been recognized by scholars, we had no inkling that demographic devastation had occurred so quickly in Timucua. The Spanish sources indicate that by the 1620s Timucuan mission villages had been hard hit, some so reduced in population that their chiefs could not send men to St. Augustine to provide labor for the Spaniards. The documents also indicate that epidemics struck soon after the first missions were founded. In 1595 an unknown epidemic hit the coastal missions. Between 1612 and late 1616 epidemics killed as many as 10,000 mission Indians. Another epidemic struck in 1649–1650, and in 1655 smallpox ravaged Timucua and Guale. In 1657, following the rebellion, Governor Rebolledo wrote that the Indians of Guale and Timucua were few in number "because they have been wiped out with the sickness of the plague [*peste*] and smallpox which have overtaken them in the past years." Two years later a new governor, Francisco de Corcoles y Martínez, reported that 10,000 mission Indians had died in a measles epidemic.

The decimation of mission Indians is grimly reflected in the archaeological record. The remains of hundreds of native villagers have been found in shallow graves under the floors of more than ten mission churches excavated in Apalachee, Guale, and Timucua. At some churches bodies were found stacked in layers three deep. Many older burials had been pushed aside to make room for new ones. The depopulation of Timucua is what apparently led Rebolledo to convert the missions into way stations on the camino real. With its larger native population, Apalachee province would be the focus of Spanish farming and ranching efforts, the colony's breadbasket, and the main source of labor.

The severity of the epidemics and the geographical reorganization of the Timucuan missions has provided a basis for reinterpreting the role of the missions in

T. DE BRY, BREVIS NARRATIO EORUM QUAE IN FLORIDA AMERICAE, 1591

Sick and dying Timucuas are depicted in this sixteenth-century etching by the Flemish engraver Theodor de Bry.

Spanish Florida. Now more than ever we see that missions and colonization were integrally related. Christianized Indians enabled the colony to function. In return for providing religious education for native people, the Spanish could harness them as workers in support of colonial interests. Religious instruction converted villagers to Catholicism and made them obedient, productive members of Spain's empire. One should not underestimate the hold the new beliefs and customs had on these people. The piety of converted Indians was, even in the eyes of the friars, extraordinary. In 1614 Father Francisco Pareja, a Franciscan friar at mission San Juan (north of modern-day Jacksonville), described the intensity of that devotion:

> Among them are Indian men who have sufficient knowledge to give instructions while there are Indian women who catechize other Indian women, preparing them for the recep-

tion of Christianity. They assist at Masses of obligation on Sundays and feastdays in which they take part and sing; in some districts that have their confraternities and the procession of Holy Thursday, and from the mission stations they come to the principal mission to hear the Salve [the Salve Regina] which is sung on Saturdays. . . . They take holy water and recite their prayers in the morning and evening. They come together in the community house to teach one another singing and reading. . . . Do they confess as Christians? I answer yes. . . . Many persons are found, men and women, who confess and who receive [Holy Communion] with tears, and who show up advantageously with many Spaniards. And I shall make bold and say and sustain my contention by what I have learned by experience that with regard to the mysteries of the faith, many of them answer better than the Spaniards.

Father Pareja also noted the effectiveness of conversion, writing that Catholicism had vanquished many of

the native superstitions so effectively that the mission Indians "do not even remember them . . . so much so that the younger generation which has been nourished by the milk of the Gospel derides and laughs at some old men and women. . . ."

Faith was an efficient tool for organizing native people who, now laboring in the fields of the Lord, performed a variety of tasks for the Spaniards. Adult males carried corn from Apalachee and Timucua to the Gulf Coast, where it was shipped to St. Augustine or exported to Cuba or other nearby Spanish colonies. Villagers also drove cattle over the camino real to St. Augustine. Supplies for the missions—lamp and cooking oil for the friars and construction hardware for repairing buildings—were shouldered from St. Augustine back to the missions. Indians tended fields and harvested crops for the soldiers stationed at St. Augustine. They helped build forts

31

CONDE DE REVILLA GIGEDO AND UNIVERSITY PRESS OF FLORIDA.

Pedro Menéndez de Avilés, founder of La Florida, believed converting natives to Catholicism would ensure loyal subjects.

FLORIDA DIVISION OF HISTORICAL RESOURCES

Spanish ceramics, made throughout the seventeenth century, are useful in dating mission sites across northern Florida.

and other fortifications; they cut and transported logs used for lumber; and they quarried coquina stone on Anastasia Island to build the town gates and the massive castillo that still dominates St. Augustine's waterfront. As many as 300 Christian Indians were involved in the construction of the castillo when it was begun in the 1670s.

Native laborers were paid in hawks' bells, knives, colorful glass beads, pieces of sheet brass, razors, cloth, and scissors. Some of these items were then traded to non-mission Indians to the north who did not have access to the much sought-after European imports. Mission Indians received deer hides and, perhaps, furs in exchange. These could be traded back to the Spaniards for more trinkets. The Spaniards, in turn, exported these hides, which were far more valuable than the trinkets they handed out.

Native people also labored for the Spaniards in the mission provinces. They maintained the camino real, clearing brush, repairing creek crossings, and even building bridges. Where roads crossed rivers too deep to ford, they operated ferries, probably little more than rafts or canoes lashed together. At the missions men, women, and children labored in support of the friars. They cooked, tended gardens, looked after farm animals, did household chores, hunted and fished, collected firewood, made charcoal, carried burdens, and paddled canoes when the friars traveled. Cornfields were planted, hoed, and harvested; the corn husked, shelled, ground into meal, and stored. Any surplus was sold by the friars to St. Augustine when times were hard in town, a clever way to generate credit against which Franciscans, who had taken vows of poverty, could charge items needed to maintain the missions. In Spanish Florida corn was money, whether it was taken to St. Augustine for use there or shipped out of the colony. Mission Indians were encouraged to increase production, aided by iron tools such as the hoes found at several missions. Increased production of corn for export resulted in huge numbers of ears being shelled, producing an equally large number of cobs that were used as fuel. Hundreds of charred corncobs have been found at every Spanish mission excavated thus far.

Lifetimes of labor in support of the Spaniards are reflected in bioanthropological analyses of the mission Indians themselves. The native workers enjoyed better living conditions than did their Precolumbian ancestors, but the stresses of labor resulted in more broken bones and injuries. Was this a benign system that improved the lot of the native people of Apalachee, Guale, and Timucua? Hardly. Although individual friars went to La Florida to bring a better life to the native people, in reality the missions provided the means for compelling the Indians to serve the Spanish Empire. In the end the process proved catastrophic. Tens of thousands of Apalachee, Guale, and Timucuas were destroyed by disease and war. By the time the British took over the territory, they had ceased to exist. Archaeology and history are now giving voice to that forgotten past.

Journey to JAMESTOWN

After nearly 40 years, archaeologists have returned to the site of the first permanent English settlement in the New World, looking for new clues to life in the ill-fated seventeenth-century Virginia capital.

by Audrey J. Horning

In May 1607, driven from their first landing site on the Chesapeake Bay by members of the powerful Powhatan chiefdom, 104 British colonists sailed their three small ships upriver, landing on a small, defensible, and uninhabited island whose principal village would become known as Jamestown, after the reigning English monarch. Despite initial hardships, the settlement evolved into a town that would serve as the capital of the Virginia colony for 92 years. Why it was abandoned, its farmlands and orchards given over to weeds, its brick row houses deserted, has intrigued historians and preservationists for more than a century.

In 1893 the Association for the Preservation of Virginia Antiquities (APVA) received as a donation a symbolic 22.5-acre piece of the island on the banks of the James River, which it sought to preserve as "the mecca of all true worshippers of a free government." The historical importance of the settlement led the federal government to buy the remainder of the island in 1934. Excavations began, using laborers from the Civilian Conservation Corps. Initially supervised by separate teams of architectural historians and archaeologists, the work was directed from 1936 to 1941 by Jean C. Harrington, who would become known for his pioneering work as the "dean of American historical archaeology." The early work plus Harrington's efforts, halted by World War II, yielded 52 brick foundations; 17 wells; a series of brick, pottery, and lime kilns; and a host of landscape features including paved walks, drains, boundary ditches, fence lines, and road traces. A second major project, directed by John L. Cotter, was begun in 1954 in preparation for the 350th anniversary of the Jamestown landing in 1957. Six miles of trenches were excavated across previously unexplored areas of the town site, revealing brick buildings, slight frame cottages, seven more wells, areas of manufacturing activity, and additional landscape features. The discovery of substantial brick row houses and the recovery of impressive quantities of expensive imported goods such as Venetian glass and porcelain added to the mystery surrounding the town's abandonment.

The quadricentennial celebration of 2007 has spurred a third ambitious project known as the Jamestown Archaeological Assessment, sponsored by the National Park Service (NPS) in cooperation with the Colonial Williamsburg Foundation and the College of William and Mary. Directed by Cary Carson and Marley Brown of Colonial Williamsburg, the assessment is focusing on the 1,500-acre portion of Jamestown Island owned and administered by the NPS. Reevaluation of excavated material coupled with painstaking historical research, careful and limited excavation

Reprinted with permission from *Archaeology* Magazine, March/April 1998, pp. 56-63. © 1998 by the Archaeological Institute of America.

in the town site, an extensive survey of the rest of the island, environmental studies, and geophysical prospecting has already given us a better understanding of the history of the island. A separate project, sponsored by the APVA and directed by William M. Kelso, has uncovered evidence for the 1607 James Fort (see box "Fortifying Jamestown").

From its inception, the assessment has differed from the earlier federally funded initiatives. There has been no massive excavation, no push to unearth new features. When the project began in 1992, the NPS storage cabinets were already bursting with artifacts from Jamestown, some of them not even cataloged. A primary goal of the assessment was to capitalize on this vast legacy, spending the time to analyze it carefully.

THE NEW SURVEY OF THE ISLAND, carried out by College of William and Mary archaeologists in 1994 and 1995, has located 58 sites representing 10,500 years of human presence on the island. While evidence of Paleoindian activity is relatively rare in eastern Virginia, the recovery of two fluted points on the island indicate it was used during the late Pleistocene (9500–8000 B.C.). At that time, the James River, now two miles wide, was a mere stream, and the island a low-lying peninsula with broad upland terraces and springs. Survey results indicate that Native American use of the island increased throughout the Archaic period (7000–2000 B.C.), when subsistence ranged from seasonal hunting to an increased reliance on shellfish and other marine resources, but slowly declined from the Middle Woodland (1000 B.C.–A.D. 700) to the Late Woodland (1000–1500), into the Protohistoric or Contact period (sixteenth century). As sea level rose and freshwater turned brackish, habitable areas became scarce. By the time the English arrived, the island was used only seasonally by the native population, who were by then living in permanent villages in more salubrious locations on the mainland.

The discovery of a series of outlying seventeenth-century English sites, ranging from small farmsteads to large plantations, will allow future investigators to examine the relationship between the town and its immediate frontier. A clearer understanding of the capital's impact on the island will help scholars evaluate its effect on more scattered settlements throughout the region. The remains of two extensive antebellum tobacco plantations present the opportunity to trace the development of the plantation system; the presence of a series of Civil War fortifications reflects the island's strategic position, first recognized by the English in 1607.

The study of environmental change on the island has been a key focus of the assessment. Since the English arrival, sea level has risen nearly three feet. Geologic cores extracted from swamps have revealed buried agricultural fields, suggesting a drier environment more conducive to settlement than the marshy, pest-infested island that exists today. An examination of cypress tree rings by the University of Arkansas has identified periods of drought during the past 1,000 years. Study of pollen, seed, and phytoliths from both geologic cores and sealed archaeological features such as refuse pits has allowed researchers to reconstruct plant life immediately preceding and during the colonial occupation, indicating how the early settlers used and altered the landscape. Wax myrtle seeds found in a refuse-filled clay borrow pit near an apothecary dating to the 1630s point to an interest in experimenting with the medicinal uses of New World plants. In 1609 Jamestown physician Lawrence Bohun recommended the indigenous plant as an ideal cure for "dissenterical fluxes."

The assessment has employed geophysical prospecting at the 13-acre town site to identify remains below the surface. Ground-penetrating radar, magneto-

Audrey J. Horning, Colonial Williamsburg Foundation

Drawing based on archaeological and documentary evidence shows the remains of structure 115, a row of brick houses destroyed during Bacon's Rebellion. Before the rebellion, one unit served as a jail. The remains of a drawn and quartered criminal were found in a nearby well.

metry, and soil resistivity and conductivity meters were all tested to determine the most effective and efficient remote-sensing instrument for Jamestown. Ground-penetrating radar and magnetometry worked well and in one case located a cluster of brick kilns in a previously unexplored field. Excavations have been designed to address specific research questions concerning the preservation of botanical remains, the reanalysis of particular buildings, and the surveying of documented activity areas. Since the early excavations at Jamestown, new methods have been developed to recover even the smallest of artifacts and plant and animal remains. Samples of backfilled soil have been reexcavated, screened, and analyzed to determine what types and quantities of such material were missed during the original investigations.

Rather than focusing on any single period in the town's history, the assessment has tried to determine what the settlement was like at 25-year intervals throughout the seventeenth century. We know now, for example, that beginning around 1618 the settlement outside the fort had scattered manufacturing and commercial activities and few residences. At the end of the century, by contrast, the town was filled with a variety of residences, colonial offices, and quite a few taverns, and had abandoned its earlier manufacturing role.

Archival research into the appearance and ownership of properties has been hampered by the destruction of official county records during the Civil War. Ironically, they were sent to Richmond for safekeeping, only to be burned in 1865 when the Confederates torched the city to keep it out of enemy hands. Our research has culled data from private family papers, English records, military data, personal narratives, and maps. Using a computerized drafting program, we have been able to draw property lines atop maps showing archaeological features, allowing for the first time ever a reliable association of known structures with their owners. The simplest case is that of William Sherwood, whose house was sketched on a surviving plan from 1686. When this plan was aligned with an archaeological map using a computer, Sherwood's residence overlaid a well-appointed brick home excavated in 1935.

Spatial analysis of a multitude of artifacts has also been crucial to understanding Jamestown's development and collapse. Confronted after his excavations with thousands of broken stems of clay tobacco pipes, Harrington hit upon one of the most useful dating tools available to archaeologists examining British colonial sites. As manufacturing techniques changed, the diameter of pipestems decreased, permitting them to be sorted into periods of roughly 25 years. While other artifacts such as coins and pottery can provide more exact dates for individual sites, the ubiquitous pipestems at colonial sites allow for comparative analysis. Early in the assessment, pipestem dates from features across the settlement were reexamined and plotted on a map, allowing us to group buildings and activities into 25-year periods. Immediately evident was the haphazard nature of the town's development; the pipestem distributions revealed that few structures or areas enjoyed continual occupation or use throughout the century. Intense periods of construction and occupation took place during the 1620s and 1630s, in the 1660s, and in the 1680s. Each occurred in a different section.

WITH SUCH APPARENTLY HAPHAZard development, was Jamestown ever "the metropolis of his majesties countrie," as claimed by one early chronicler? Standard explanations of the town's collapse emphasize either economic or environmental factors. Before the first decade of settlement had passed, Virginians had become economically dependent on tobacco. Its cultivation required large tracts of land, which led to the establishment of a plantation system that resulted in dispersed settlements. The easily navigable rivers throughout the Chesapeake region allowed each plantation to maintain its own storehouses and docks. The presence of expensive imported goods and sizable brick houses suggests that Jamestown struggled along as a town long after the plantation system had become entrenched.

Examination of each period has illuminated the economic forces and individuals behind Jamestown's evolution. Lots were laid out in what became New Towne in the early 1620s, with land near the river slated for warehouses. Manufacturing activity was centered in three distinct areas. One in the northwest, excavated by Cotters team in the 1950s and further tested between 1993 and 1996, had evidence of metalworking and the production of brick, tile, lime, and pottery; a brewhouse; and an apothecary. This manufacturing enclave and another property at the eastern end of town, which incorporated a brickmaking operation, were owned by Virginia governor John Harvey, who served during the 1630s. As governor, Harvey apparently sought to reduce the colony's reliance on England for manufactured goods, including tools, clothing, building materials, and household items. Concerned with economic diversification and the town's growth, Harvey passed laws that designated Jamestown the colony's sole port of entry and required artisans to settle in the town. The governor clearly backed up his beliefs with his own investments, supporting manufacturing on his properties and investing in glassmaking and iron production elsewhere. Harvey was forced out of office by enemies in the colony who lobbied the Crown for his removal, and he went bankrupt shortly thereafter, in 1639. Analysis of datable artifacts in Harvey's manufacturing enclave and the microstratigraphic analysis of a thin section of soil from a refuse-filled clay borrow pit indicate that all activity in the area ceased abruptly following his ouster.

That craftworking ended shortly after Harvey's departure from office illustrates the extent to which development relied on individual enterprise. Entrepreneurs like Harvey hoped not only to produce goods for use within the colony, reducing reliance upon imports, but also to export finished goods. Within England, a number of towns with specialized manufacturing were being successfully expanded and developed, funded in large part by speculative investors. Harvey and his contem-

Fortifying Jamestown

**Fearful of an invasion by the Spanish, the English settlers at James Fort
had only to withstand the onslaught of the Powhatan Chiefdom.**

BY WILLIAM M. KELSO AND NICHOLAS M. LUCCKETTI

IN MAY 1607, a determined group of English gentlemen, craftsmen, and peasants arrived at Jamestown Island and set about building gun platforms and a triangular, palisaded fort to protect their hastily built homes. The swampy, mosquito-infested island, lack of fresh water, Indian attacks, and the destruction of the fort by fire in 1608 all but annihilated the infant colony. But periodic fresh supplies from home and from friendly Indians, more settlers from England, and more vigorous leadership among the survivors resulted in an enlarged town within a five-sided fort. For the next 100 years Jamestown grew eastward, becoming the capital of Virginia until the seat of government was moved to Williamsburg in 1699. The town was abandoned and turned into farmland. Mid-nineteenth-century visitors to the island saw the ravages of river erosion near church ruins and concluded that the original settlement was either completely gone or eroding into the James River.

Excavations by the Association for the Preservation of Virginia Antiquities began in 1994. Removal of a foot of plowed earth south of the church uncovered a number of soil disturbances in the deeper clay that proved beyond a reasonable doubt to be the remnants of James Fort. These included marks left by sections of two fort walls and part of a projecting corner defensive bulwark, interior timber buildings, three backfilled pits, a series of ditches and postholes, and a grave. The soil and fill held more than 160,000 artifacts, most of which date to the first quarter of the 1600s and include arms, armor, ammunition, pottery, coins, and political tokens, as well as remnants of the manufacture of copper jewelry for the Indian trade.

Why was James Fort built? The English knew that sooner or later they would clash with the Indians living along the James River. But the colonists' archenemy was Spain. English settlement in the New World was a continuing source of irritation to the Spanish. Don Pedro de Zuñiga, Spain's ambassador to London from July 1605 to May 1610, consistently urged Philip II to destroy the fledgling Virginia Colony, and, indeed, the Spanish Council of War planned to attack Jamestown every year from 1607 to 1617. It never did.

Instructions from the Virginia Company of London to the Jamestown adventurers to be opened when they arrived in Virginia read in part:

When it shall please God to send you on the Coast of Virginia you shall Do your best endeavor to find out a Safe port in the Entrance of Some navigable River making Choose of Such a one as runt furthest into the Land. [Choose] Some Island that is Strong by nature from both sides of your River where it is Narrowest. . . . First Erect a little Sconce at the Mouth of the River that may Lodge Some ten men With Whom you Shall Leave a boat that when any fleet shall be in Sight they may Come with Speed to Give You Warning. . . . In the mouth of this River there Ys a place so fortified by nature, That If The Spaniard who will start upon this alarm, Recover this place before Vs, yhis actions Ys utterly overthrown.

It did not take long for the colonists to place a garrison at the entrance to the James River that could provide ample warning of a Spanish attack.

Jamestown Island, low, marshy, and bug-infested, would seem the worst possible place for a fort, but to the military

poraries promoted a similar development of Jamestown in anticipation of like profits.

THE NEXT MAJOR PERIOD OF ACTIVITY was the 1660s. An act passed by the Virginia Assembly, meeting at Jamestown in December 1662, echoed the king's recent orders to the colonial government to "build a towne" at Jamestown, the most convenient place in James River." The act itself suggests that Jamestown did not yet qualify as a town. One disgruntled visitor of 1660, in fact, complained that there were only "scarce but a dozen families in residence, all of them keeping ordinaries [taverns] at extraordinary rates."

With instructions to build 32 brick houses backed by government subsidies, investors decided to construct rows of adjoining houses. The required number was apparently never achieved, however, and the act was soon revoked by the Crown. Excavation in 1993 at one row of three houses, now known as structure 17, uncovered a foundation for another building, never completed, that would have forced neighbors to skirt a yawning, garbage-filled cellar hole. Similar instances of failed speculation are evident elsewhere in the town. Houses that were finished did not always serve their intended purposes. Shortly after the construction of structure 115, a row of four brick houses, one unit was converted into a jail, suggesting that tenants were both hard to find and not necessarily members of the colonial elite. A gruesome reminder of the nature of seventeenth-century justice was found in a well behind the row by Cotter's team: one-quarter of a drawn and quartered criminal. Structure 115 was destroyed in 1676 during Bacon's Rebellion, an attempt by disgruntled settlers to overthrow the colonial government, and only its eastern end was ever rebuilt. Leases were sold and resold on the western units, but there is no archaeological evidence to support their reconstruction or use after 1676.

The presence of large brick buildings at Jamestown, in a region where wooden mind of the Elizabethan-Jacobean period it made perfect sense. There are a number of natural positions between the island and the open sea that protect it from an attack coming upriver. Beside Point Comfort, Hog Island, about three miles downstream from Jamestown Island, offered opportunity for advance warning. The colonists took advantage of this position, fortifying Hog Island with a blockhouse sometime before 1609 "to give us notice of any shipping." Additionally, Jamestown Island is screened from any ships coming upriver by Hog Island, which in turn has a clear line of sight to the mouth of the James River. Indeed, a lookout perched in a 20-foot-high blockhouse could see the tall masts of even a relatively small ship 16 miles away. In 1607, Jamestown Island itself was connected to the mainland by a narrow neck easily protected by a blockhouse, which in fact was built in 1608. Furthermore, the island consists of a series of marshes and ridges, and one ridge on the western end was well suited for fortification, being the highest piece of ground on the river side, and protected from approaching enemies by low ground and marshes on the landward sides.

Although the James River is wide, navigation is limited to a narrow channel

that meanders as it moves upriver. The channel is closer to shore at the western end of Jamestown Island than at any other point downriver; settler George Percy wrote in 1607 that this was the deciding factor in establishing the town there. While the channel allowed convenient an-

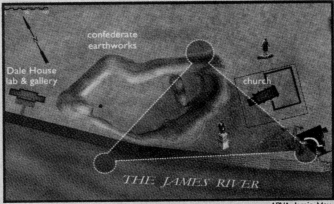

APVA, Jamie May

Dotted outline indicates the position of the 1607 James Fort. Excavations have yielded evidence of a palisade and a dry moat, solid lines, lower right.

chorage for ships at the western end of the island, elsewhere it kept enemy vessels offshore. The distance from the western end of the island to the south shore of the river is little more than a mile, and it is the narrowest point along the river from Jamestown to Hampton Roads. As a last line of defense, the channel would force any enemy ships that managed to make it upriver to sail within range of the town's

artillery. John Smith reports that Jamestown had "four and twentie peeces of Ordnance of Culvering, Demiculvering, Sacar, and Falcon, and most well mounted upon convenient platforms." At that time, a culverin had an extreme range of roughly 6,750 feet, well beyond the limits of the James River channel from the island's western ridge. Thus, even if an enemy ship with heavier guns reached the island, it could not escape Jamestown's culverin, nor could it get close enough to the western ridge to fire point-blank at the fort.

So the expedition leaders, it can be argued, made the best decision given the circumstances and resources. They built enough of a fort to protect them from guerrilla-type Virginia Indian warfare. They did not and could not build a state-of-the-art fortress capable of repelling the Spanish, who might or might not show up, but they could control the river with their artillery. The triangular fort's walls of small posts in narrow trenches were more than sufficient to ward off Powhatan arrows. In fact, the proof of its success is that James Fort never fell to any enemy.

WILLIAM M. KELSO *is director of archaeology for Jamestown Rediscovery.* NICHOLAS M. LUCCKETTI *is the project's field director.*

post-in-ground construction was the norm, has been interpreted as evidence of the presence of wealthy colonists. The use of brick, however, may have had more to do with fire prevention. Town planning in England had already begun to require the replacement of flammable timber buildings with sturdier fire-resistant brick structures.

Property research has also allowed us to focus on the activities of two of Jamestown's most active housing speculators from 1660 through the 1680s, Governor William Berkeley and Philip Ludwell, who continued buying and selling houses until their investments became "decayed and ruinous," as one of Ludwell's houses was described in a

deed. Both hailed from Bruton in Somerset, England, a village near Frome, one of the seventeenth century's fastest growing cloth-manufacturing centers. Described by the English novelist Daniel Defoe as one of the greatest and wealthiest inland towns in England, Frome proved a gold mine for speculators investing in worker housing. Berkeley and Ludwell followed this pattern of speculation at Jamestown. They and earlier investors might have succeeded had not the Crown blocked economic diversification by disallowing acts that sought to develop Jamestown. While Britain ostensibly supported town building efforts, the economic independence of the Virginia colony was

simply not in its interest while it could reap the profits of the tobacco trade. Tobacco production relied on plantations, not towns, and ensured that colonists remained dependent upon Britain for manufactured goods.

The Crown forbade an act, drafted in 1680, that sought to spur the development of Jamestown following the ravages of Bacon's Rebellion. While this act inspired the last burst of archaeologically traceable building activity in the town, the settlement soon faltered. All evidence of Jamestown's urban pretensions faded after a devastating fire in 1698, which occasioned the transfer of the capital to nearby Williamsburg the following year. Despite the move, Vir-

Only a fraction of the enormous archaeological potential of Jamestown has been realized.

Top: Audrey J. Horning. Bottom: Andrew Edwards, Colonial Williamsburg Foundation

Excavation at a row of three brick houses, above, now known as structure 17, uncovered a foundation for another building that was never completed, far left. Once thought to be evidence of wealthy colonists, brick was probably used to prevent fires. Portions of mid-eighteenth-century Ambler House, below, named for its owner, Richard Ambler, still stand.

ginia did not witness significant growth in towns for another half century, By that time, the region was no longer economically dependent on Britain. Despite Jamestown's ultimate failure, its archaeology encapsulates the speculative dreams and desires of investors throughout the century, dreams fueled not by a New World frontier experience, but by an intimate awareness of the nature of town building and profit making in England.

"Only a fraction of the enormous archaeological potential of Jamestown has been realized," lamented Harrington in 1984. The approach of the Jamestown Archaeological Assessment project has been to evaluate that potential, in order to guide future investigations not only of the seventeenth-century remains, a mere fraction of cultural time on the island, but of its entire 10,500-year record of human history, Although heavily excavated, the seventeenth-century town site continues to reveal tantalizing information that augments, challenges, and alters our understanding of early settlement and town development in the Chesapeake area. As the quadricentennial approaches, the symbolic appeal of Jamestown will continue to lure scholars and students of American culture. A sound framework and footing, built by interdisciplinary teamwork, is now in place that will support, broaden, and contextualize future research at the site.

AUDREY J. HORNING *is a research fellow in the department of archaeological research at the Colonial Williamsburg Foundation.*

Squanto and the Pilgrims

Lynn Ceci

On March 22, 1621, a New England native named Squanto strode into the Pilgrims' new establishment at Plymouth and offered the greeting, "Welcome Englishmen." According to Pilgrim William Bradford, that spring Squanto "directed them how to set their corn, when to take fish, and to procure other comodities," an act which gained him a prominent place in American history and folklore.

The Plymouth settlers, primarily artisans such as printers, weavers, watchmakers, and carpenters with little farming experience, readily accepted Squanto's advice. A letter written by E. W. (Edward Winslow?) from Plymouth on December 11, 1621, reports: "We set the last Spring some twentie Acres of *Indian* Corne, and sowed some six Acres of Barly & Pease, and according to the manner of the *Indians,* we manured our ground with Herings or rather Shadds, which we have in great abundance, and rake with great ease at our doores."

Winslow's logical deduction that fish manuring was a "manner" of all Indians appears to be a syllogistic extension of Squanto's particular knowledge to Indi-

ans in general. It was written, it should be noted, before he or any other Pilgrim actually witnessed Indians planting anywhere. By the spring of 1621, the cultivation practices of Squanto's own Algonquian tribe were no longer observable because of a recent plague; Squanto was then the "only native of Patuxet," the area the Pilgrims renamed Plymouth. When native planting was observed in the years following, reporters seemed surprised that Indians employed neither fish nor any other fertilizer.

Nonetheless, the original and, as I hope to demonstrate, unfounded conclusion that fish fertilizer was a "manner" of all Indians has long been accepted. It gained support in this century in 1916 when Clark Wissler proposed that the "aboriginal maize culture complex" included the trait of fertilizing with fish where available "everywhere in the Mississippi Valley and eastward." A year later, he expanded his theory further by stating—still without evidence—that the method of "placing a fish in the maize hill" was widely distributed in both continents. Here, Wissler has apparently linked Squanto's local advice at Ply-

mouth to coastal Peru, the only other confirmed location in the New World where the use of guano and fish fertilizer (actually fish heads) was demonstrably an indigenous practice. In the following decades, the notion that American Indians in general knew about or used fish fertilizer became entrenched in anthropological and botanical literature. It appears repeatedly in popular publications, often annexed to corn recipes, and is reinforced annually when countless numbers of schoolchildren reenact Squanto's contribution to the Pilgrims in pageants celebrating America's first Thanksgiving. The figure of Squanto now stands immortalized in a diorama at the Plymouth National Wax Museum, where is he shown burying fish before the Pilgrims.

That the evidence for Indian fish fertilizer in North America is poor was first noted in 1880 by G. B. Goode who, citing the South American data, inferred agricultural fertilizers must be indigenous throughout the Americas. The first scholarly challenge appeared in Regina Flannery's 1939 research on coastal Algonquian culture traits. Unable to find ethnohistoric or ethnographic sources confirming the practice anywhere along the eastern seaboard, she concluded, "The aboriginality of the trait is questionable." The second challenge came in 1957 when Erhard Rostlund discussed problems such as the seasonal availability of fish species in coastal zones, vagaries in the original citations, and the curious uniqueness of the practice. He concluded that the use of fish fertilizer was not a "common and widespread practice in any part of native North America."

This essay presents new evidence from an ethnohistoric, anthropological, and archaeological perspective. This evidence substantiates the conclusions of Flannery and Rostlund, and suggests further that Squanto learned about fish fertilizers in European settlements, not in those of his own or neighboring tribesmen.

Since Squanto's actions remain the single basis for the claim that the use of fish fertilizers was a native practice, let us first examine the possible sources of Squanto's agronomical knowledge. His rather remarkable history, often uncited, indicates that he had ample opportunity to learn the European "manner" of planting, which included fertilizing with marine debris and cultivating the New World crop, maize.

SQUANTO THE TRAVELER

In 1614, Captain Thomas Hunt, master of a vessel with Captain John Smith, kidnapped Squanto (and other Indians) and sold him into slavery at Malaga, Spain. This may have been Squanto's second kidnapping experience because Gorges claimed in 1658 that Captain George Weymouth had kidnapped a "Tasquantum" before, in 1605, from Maine. However, this name or other variations thereof (Tisquantum) do not appear on crewman Rosier's 1605 list of Indians Weymouth kidnapped that year in Maine. Since Gorges wrote his account 53 years after the event (and Maine was not Squanto's home), its accuracy is questionable. Similarly, it is unclear whether the native "Tantum" brought from England to Cape Cod in 1615 by Captain John Smith was the same Indian, Squanto.

Somewhat better documentation indicates that Squanto was smuggled from Malaga after a few years by a captain of a ship belonging to the Guy Colony in Newfoundland; he was brought to a place (ironically) named "Cornhill" in London where he resided for about two years with John Slanie, treasurer of the Newfoundland Company. The "savage Tasquantum" was next sent to "The Cupids" settlement in Newfoundland, where he served Captain John Mason, "governour there for the undertakers of that planation." Captain Thomas Dermer next took Squanto with him back to England in 1618, then used this well-traveled Indian the following spring as pilot and guide along the stretch of coast between Monhegan and Virginia.

Squanto left ship at some point and returned to Patuxet prior to greeting the Pilgrims in clear English, one of at least three languages he then spoke. He quickly became advisor to the Pilgrims in provisioning and planting "corne." More critical to their survival, he also served as interpreter and guide, advising them on how to trade with local Indians for furs, especially the unfamiliar beaver that European ship captains would accept in exchange for supplies they badly needed. Squanto's advantageous dealings with the English led to jealousy among local Indians. He received desirable goods, for example as noted in an account by Bradford, a "suite of cloathes ... a horsemans coate ... [and] other things." And as a seasoned trader, he also "sought his owne ends ... by putting the Indians in fear, and drawing gifts from them to enrich him selfe; making them believe he could stir up warr against whom he would ... [and that the English] kept the plague buried in the ground, and could send it amongs whom they would." In late September 1622, Squanto "fell sick of an Indian feavor, bleeding much at ye nose and ... dyed," after bequeathing his goods to English friends.

In the years immediately preceding his advice to the Pilgrims, Squanto had learned "foreign" ways by residing with Europeans in both the Old and New World. In Europe, use of fertilizer was a feature of farming technology since the Roman expansion, if not the ear-

lier Celtics. The particular use of marine waste was famous since the medieval period in France, where the fertility of the zone in which it was employed earned it the name "gold belt." Fish fertilizer was cited in a 1620 English publication, suggesting the practice was also known in England before Squanto—or the Pilgrims—departed for the New World. One might also note that Indian corn or maize had been cultivated in Spain since 1530, nearly a century before Squanto's arrival in Malaga; from there its cultivation with appropriate terracing and irrigation techniques quickly spread to several Mediterranean countries.

Europeans creating gardens in the New World before 1621 may have also used fertilizer with their Old World seeds, for example, in Newfoundland in 1583, the Cape Cod area in 1602 and 1603, and Maine in 1605, 1607, and 1614. According to an account by Lescarbot, the 1605 and 1614 gardens in Maine were planted by crewmen of Weymouth and Smith, two possible contacts of Squanto. In the 1604–1605 French colony in Maine and Nova Scotia, established for trafficking with New England Indians, fertilizer usage was specified: the gardens were "improved" with "hogs' dung, or the sweepings of the kitchen, or the shells of fish." So, too, the English used "manures" in 1611 and 1614 in the Virginia colony to the south.

A key location for Squanto was the John Guy and "Bristol's Hope" colonies located along "The Cupids" inlet on Conception Bay, Newfoundland, where agriculture was practiced and domesticated animals kept since 1610. In 1615, Guy was replaced by Captain John Mason, Squanto's "governour." In his 1620 book entitled *A Briefe Discourse of the Newfoundland*, Mason noted that "June has Capline a fish much resembling smeltes in forme and eating and such aboundance dry on shoare as to lade cartes." Looking to promote immigration, Mason continued with glowing accounts of the local harvests, attributing their success to the use of these fish as manure.

Since Squanto served in the very settlement described by Mason, he most probably observed these same scenes of surplus fish advantageously converted to manure. Given this and the other opportunities to learn the value of fertilizer, I suggest the intelligent and enterprising Squanto acquired his knowledge from European examples. Then, on his 1621 visit to Plymouth, Squanto merely passed along the practical advice he knew to be successful from his most recent experience in European, *not* Indian, settlements.

INSUBSTANTIAL EVIDENCE

The possibility that Squanto learned about fertilizer at his mother's knee is substantially reduced by the considerable negative evidence for the practice anywhere along the eastern coast of North America. It is only in this zone that sufficient numbers of anadromous fish ascending the rivers to spawn would have been available in the critical spring corn-planting months. Corn was not grown by Indians along the western coast of North America.

Along the south Atlantic Coast from Florida to Virginia, sixteenth and seventeenth-century French and English colonists described the native cultivation techniques; none mentions the use of fertilizer. In Virginia, where corn planting and fish trapping by Algonquians were carefully detailed and illustrated, fertilizer use was emphatically denied: "The ground they never fatten with mucke, dounge, or any other thing, neither plow nor digge it as we in England."

Further north, along the mid-Atlantic coast, the Dutch of New Netherlands (New Jersey to southern New England), also described native cultivation techniques. Again, the evidence for native fertilizers is negative, even in areas where fish were caught in great numbers each spring. Adriaen Van der Donck claimed in 1653, after residing near Indians of the upper Hudson River Valley and coastal New York for eight years, that he had "never seen land manured" by Indians and that "of manuring . . . they know nothing."

From New Netherlands north to the northernmost limit of maize cultivation, except for two Pilgrim statements, it is only the English who are identified as the users of fish fertilizer. In April 1622,

the spring after the Pilgrims were warned that "It would come to nothing" if they did not set seed with fish, visitor Richard Whitbourne reported that an "Incredible" abundance of herring-like fish had been taken that month and used for "manure." In 1627, Isaack DeRasieres, the Dutch Secretary at New Netherlands, also visited Plymouth and detailed how the English took 10,000 to 12,000 fish, carried them to their fields, and placed three or four in each cornhill; his comments imply that he found the procedure unusual and noteworthy, that is, unknown among Dutch or Indian cultivators elsewhere. The absence of a single line describing an Indian actually seen planting fish in any of the reliable ethnohistoric sources seems nothing short of remarkable, that is, *if* the practice was in fact current!

In short, the extant documentary evidence presents a consistent, uniform cultural pattern: no support for the use of any fertilizing agent as a "manner of the Indians" in the New England "homeland" of Squanto, among Algonquians and others along the Atlantic Coast, or in North America at large. The failure to employ fertilizers even after years of exposure to European farming technology suggests some cultural resistance or, as we shall see, a better alternate strategy. Let us examine the implications of planting corn with fish.

The type Indian corn grown "throughout the eastern United States" in the prehistoric and early historic periods was a race of Northern Flint called Maiz-de-Ocho. This short eight-rowed race with dented kernels, adapted to northern growing conditions, arrived in New England about 1400 and was described in 1678. Like its modern hybrid descendants, its productivity must have depended on a set of growing conditions such as soil type and fertility, total sunlight, length of the frost-free season, and moisture. The availability of particular nutrients, especially nitrogen, phosphorous, potassium, calcium, and lime directly affects corn's maturation rate and final size, hence its yields.

Soils in which maize is planted, except naturally rich river alluvia, loess deposits, and old lakebeds, are annually depleted of critical nutrients. The result-

ing problem of lower yields is commonly resolved by either of two solutions: shifting cultivation—move the planting to new, still naturally fertile fields or older "fallowed," temporarily "rested" fields; or fertilizing—restore the lost nutrients. The first solution was characteristic of early horticulturalists experimenting with cultigens and of later agriculturalists farming fields in marginally productive soil zones. Recent documentary and archaeological evidence indicates that this was also the practice of Indians cultivating maize races throughout the Eastern Woodlands including the Mississippi River Valley. Indians planting maize along fertile riverbanks further west also "knew nothing of the value of manuring."

In the interior Northeast, groups known as successful maize growers moved their settlements every eight to twelve years, in part because of soil depletion. Northeastern archaeologists recognize the role of shifting cultivation and soil depletion when interpreting sites occupied by Indian corn cultivators; soil fertility appears to correlate with site location and duration, and may influence population size as well as the development of social, political, and economic complexity.

The second remedy for decreasing yields, the use of fertilizer, is thought to be historically a relatively late practice throughout the world, one associated with the establishment of permanent villages and fields. This technological advance is based on recognition of the cause and effect relationship between soil improvement and subsequent productivity, a process observable, for example, where domesticated animals are penned or organic waste accumulates. In North America there were no penned domesticated fauna in pre-contact times for natives to observe, although the value of planting in old midden soils may have been recognized by some.

The most likely fertilizing agent American Indians might have used were the ashes created naturally wherever fields were cleared by burning. Yet documents raise doubts as to whether the specific value of ashes as a fertilizer—a modest source of phosphorous—was recognized or intended. In Virginia, Indians burned "weedes, grasse, & old stubbes of corn stalkes" but neither dispersed the ash "heapes" to "better the grounde" nor "set their corn where the ashes lie," according to an account by Quinn. Further north, New Netherlands Indians recognized that annual "bush burning" brought better grasses, but they, like those in New England, confined the burning to wild areas where they hoped to attract game and improve hunting. The concept of ash-improved growth was apparently not transferred to their gardens, and the beneficial effects of ashes on the soil were incidental.

The use of fish as fertilizer raises other more serious problems. The seasonal availability and quantities needed restrict the practice to areas near the northeastern rivers where runs of alewife, shad, and herring species coincide with the mid-to-late April beginning of the frost-free season, the earliest time to plant corn. Though collecting sufficient quantities was easy enough for natives or colonials, even without weirs, it is the intensified labor afterward that suggests good reasons why the practice would not be attractive to any planter. Given cornhill spacings of six, five, four, three, and two and one-half feet apart, the single acre would contain 1208, 1710, 2719, 4834, and 6961 cornhills respectively. If, as reported two to four whole fish were placed in each hill, the single acre would then require 2416 to 27,844 fish. If each fish weighed as little as one pound, then tons as well as quantities of fresh and rotting fish had to be gathered, transported to the fields, and buried one by one in each cornhill. The practice then generated the chore of guarding against night raiders attracted to the smelly fish in the 14-day rotting period.

And for all this labor, one must apply the critical test: was the effort worth it? There is first the news that despite their labors, the Pilgrims starved in the first few years. Their estimated rate of corn productivity—18 bushels per acre, was no greater than that for Indians not using fish, and less than the 20 bushels per acre raised in Plymouth County two centuries later without ground improvement.

INDIAN RESISTANCE

As a cultural strategy, it is not difficult to understand why experienced and observant Indians might resist the practice of using fish to "improve" their crops in any period and why English farmers, in particular, abandoned the practice in favor of animal manures by about 1640. From the Indians' perspective, there was also the allocation of huge fish supplies into the ground during the hungriest season, the traditional lean spring. Records indicate instead that northeastern natives took the more predictable course of action by feasting on spring supplies of fresh protein and converting surplus fish into future food supplies by smoking or drying. English farmers, by contrast, represent an alternate cultural strategy. The huge quantities obtained in one day—10,000 to 12,000 fish at "one tide"—must have resulted in surpluses far beyond the amount the Pilgrims could immediately consume or process; such a surplus, perhaps grown spoiled and odoriferous, would then be used for fertilizer or even fed to the pigs. That these farmers used fish as fertilizer only when or even because there was a surplus is suggested by both the Mason data from Newfoundland cited above and the New England comment, "the plenty of fish which they have for little or nothing, is better to be used, than cast away." If Indians were to resolve the problem of declining corn harvests, it seems unlikely that they would choose to gather thousands (and tons) of fish beyond their immediate needs and processing capabilities to reach that same point of surplus gathered by English settlers.

The tools and workforce needed to carry out this "solution" introduces additional considerations. While Indians possessed simple sacks, carrying baskets, crude stone, wood, bone, or shell hoes, and wooden digging sticks, the Pilgrim farmers had more efficient metal shovels, hoes, dung forks, and carts drawn by domesticated animals. Because the division of labor among northeastern Indians reflected the value system of societies still largely dependent on wild foods, the less prestigious planting chores were the work of fe-

males. At estimated yields of 18 bushels per acre, women working fields of 1.3 to 3.3 acres would have had to obtain, carry, and bury at least 3148 to 7973 fish (thousands more if cornhills were closer than six feet apart). Even if Indian males had recognized the value of the farming methods used by male colonists and their indentured servants, they would not have easily changed their traditional roles to help with the heavy fieldwork fish fertilizer entailed.

The many lines of evidence strongly suggest that the invention and use of fish fertilizer by northeastern Indians would have been maladaptive, a burdensome land-tethered chore of questionable value for improving corn yields. More adaptive was the well-documented fallowing technology, especially where beans were planted to "grow up with and against the maize," as Jameson describes. In this way, nitrogen became more available to the corn roots and the weed area was reduced. The combined bean/corn diet is also higher in available protein and a balance of amino acids, so helps prevent deficiencies caused by corn alone. Given these strategies, might one not argue that the experienced Indians were *too wise* to adopt the onerous fish fertilizer "solution" taken by the early Pilgrims?

The belief that fish fertilizer originated among North American Indians, and was communicated by Squanto to the Plymouth settlers, has achieved the status of an unquestioned legend and is difficult to challenge. That the fish fertilizer "manner of the Indians" was and remains so strongly defended despite the weak evidence raises questions about the folklorification process. Confabulated histories in several juvenile works make it clear that the Squanto figure is currently drawn as a "noble savage," a friendly, benign, almost childlike Indian who unhesitatingly shares native food, technology, and land with Europeans; he even welcomes their coming and suggests the Thanksgiving feast. This "invented" Squanto stands in contrast to the real, very interesting historical Squanto, an intriguing, enterprising survivor and culture-broker who facilitated the meshing of disparate cultures on a new frontier. More importantly, the invented

Squanto masks the more threatening and numerous Indians of the frontier period who, objecting to the usurpation and invasion of their lands, attacked and killed settlers—a more accurate representation but a history too uncomfortable for popular American consumption.

The noble savage movement of the last century is rooted in romantic reconstructions of Indians as uncorrupted natural beings—who were becoming extinct—in contrast to rising industrial and urban mobs. An Indian Head coin was struck in 1859 to commemorate their passing, and again (backed by the disappearing buffalo) in 1913–1938, the period when the Squanto/fish fertilizer story was revived. Thanksgiving is also a nineteenth-century invented tradition, a Protestant festival of Anglo-Saxon origins resurrected in 1863 by President Abraham Lincoln to promote a sense of national history and social cohesion in a country divided by the Civil War and waves of new immigrants.

As folklore, then, the Squanto-fish fertilizer story contains elements that touch American national and religious values, as well as the feelings of guilt or anger many hold about true Indian history. To challenge any aspect of the popular story, for non-Indians and Indians alike, would seem incredible, if not an attack on personal beliefs.

Nevertheless, while Squanto was unquestionably an important historic figure and did contribute substantially to the Pilgrims' survival, the belief that fish fertilizer was a "manner of the Indians" because Squanto knew about it should be revised. The current evidence indicates that his advice at Plymouth is best viewed as a special example of culture contact dynamics, one in which a native culture-bearer conveyed a technological idea from one group of Europeans to another.

READINGS SUGGESTED BY THE AUTHOR

Bradford, William and H. Wish, eds. *Of Plymouth Plantation.* New York: Capricorn Books, 1962.
Quinn, D. B., ed. The Roanoke Voyages, 1584–1590. London: Hakluyt Society Works 1 (Series 2), 1955.

Lynn Ceci was an avid teacher and writer of anthropology. An associate professor of anthropology at Queens College, New York, she authored and co-edited two books and is represented as a contributor to several others.

Bearing the Burden? Puritan Wives

Obedience, modesty, taciturnity—all hallmarks of the archetypal 'good woman' in colonial New England. But did suffering in silence invert tradition and give the weaker sex a new moral authority in the community? Martha Saxton investigates, in the first piece from a mini series examining women's social experience in the New World.

Martha Saxton

Martha Saxton teaches Colonial History at Columbia University. She is author of Louisa May Alcott *(Andre Deutsch, 1977) and is currently working on a study of American women's moral standards—those prescribed for them and those they fashioned for themselves.*

Seventeenth-century American Puritans subordinated female to male, wife to husband, and mother to father, insisting on obedience, modesty, and taciturnity for women. They justified this arrangement by emphasising woman's descent from Eve and her innate irrationality, both of which made her more vulnerable to error and corruption than man. Because of this she was to view her husband as God's representative in the family. He would mediate her religious existence and direct her temporal one. She would produce children and care for them, but he would have the ultimate authority over them.

At the same time, the experience of Puritans of both sexes in the second half of the seventeenth century undermined this clearly defined system of authority in which the allocation of secular power flowed from a presumed moral and spiritual hierarchy. After 1660, women began outnumbering men in the churches, and by the end of the century the numerical difference was sufficient to prompt Cotton Mather to attempt to account for the demonstrated female proclivity for spirituality. Mather ascribed enhanced female religiosity precisely to that subordination that Puritan men insisted upon as well as mothers' suffering during childbirth.

Long before Mather published his conclusions at the end of the seventeenth century, other Puritan men anticipated his thinking about female virtue, and many identified its sources in female suffering. Men praised the patient endurance of wives with abusive husbands. Others granted to childbirth pain the power to enhance goodness. Some saw the sacrifices of mothering, rather than childbirth *per se,* as a source of virtue and testified to the moral significance of their mothers in the conduct of their lives. And still others simply acknowledged their mothers, wives, or other female relatives as inspirational or spiritually influential to them.

In the Puritan world then, women could and did earn respect for their moral stature in the family, and this was meaningful to women deprived of public recognition in a society run by men. It would be an important heritage to women of a later era. Pious women would pass on the idea that their principled expressions of conscience could shape morally, both family and society.

Before looking at the way women achieved moral authority, let us look at how Puritan men elaborated beliefs about the propriety of subordinating women to men. John Winthrop, Governor of Massachusetts, who was happily married to three submissive women, writing in the mid-seventeenth century put the ideal case:

A true wife accounts her subjection her honor and freedom and would not think her condition safe and free but in her subjection to her husband's authority. Such is the liberty of the church under the authority of Christ, her king and husband; his yoke is so easy and sweet to her as a bride's ornaments; and if through forwardness or wantonness, etc., she shakes it off at any time, she is at no rest in her spirit until she take it up again; and whether her lord smiles upon her and embraceth her in his arms, or whether he frowns and rebukes her, or smites her, she comprehends the sweetness of his love in all, and is refreshed, and instructed by every such dispensation of his authority over her.

While not all American Puritans saw female obedience in such a cheerful light as Winthrop did, all agreed that it was essential to marital satisfaction and should exist regardless of the husband's comportment. John Cotton compared wifely obedience to the excellence and inevitability of the universe, the air we breathe, and the clouds that shower rain upon the earth. Benjamin Wadsworth, in a book published in 1712, wrote that a woman should 'reverence' her husband, as the bible commanded. He was God's representative in the family, and even if he should 'pass the bounds of wisdom and kindness; yet must not she shake off the bond of submission but must bear patiently the burden, which God hath laid upon the daughters of Eve'. And Cotton Mather, writing before his final, tempestuous marriage to Lydia Lee George would give these words a wistful ring, insisted that though the husband be 'ever so much a Churl, yet she treats him considerately'.

An important facet of this unanimous male insistence on female submission was the envy and fascination Puritan men felt for womanly meekness and obedience. Salvation demanded that men, as well as women, submit to God's will in all things. For women, submission to God's will and the will of the men around them made their lives, ideally, a continuum of obedience.

Men, however, enjoyed considerable social power during their lifetime as husbands and, depending upon their status, as community leaders. Submission and the self-suppression that it required, was, therefore, a more prickly and intractable issue for men than for women. Furthermore, as husbands, men determined how heavily or lightly the yoke of marriage would rest on their wives' shoulders. Men's direct responsibility for the suffering that their domination might cause women was likely to make them particularly alive to the issue.

Cotton Mather, who had openly linked woman's tendency to spiritual excellence with her subordination and suffering, wrote 'But if thou hast an Husband that will do so, [beat his wife] bear it patiently; and know thou shalt have—Rewards—hereafter for it, as well as *Praises* here...'. And Puritan men since the settlement of Plymouth had praised women for remaining uncomplainingly with husbands who were violent and/or unfaithful. Mrs Lyford, of Plymouth endured—and sometimes witnessed—her husband's sexual escapades for years in silence. Eventually, she testified against him. But, wrote the governor of the colony, William Bradford, approvingly, 'being a grave matron, and of good carriage... spoke of those things out of the sorrow of her harte, sparingly'.

The wife of Jared Davis submitted to years of her husband's cruelty, drunkenness, lies, scandalous behaviour, and indolence. He had, according to John Winthrop, neither compassion nor humanity toward his wife, insisted on sex with her when she was pregnant (which Puritans regarded as dangerous) and did not provide for her. The governor admired Mrs Davis who, under all these provocations, continued to try to help her husband. As Winthrop had written elsewhere, Mrs Davis was able to find in her husband's blows, God's love and correction. Winthrop and Bradford believed that the Christlike acceptance of lengthy, undeserved abuse endowed women with a unique moral vantage point from which they might even venture to criticise their victimisers.

Men were also fascinated by—and implicated in—the crisis of child labour and delivery, which combined submission to physical suffering as well as the more difficult task: resignation to the possibility of death. Husbands were awed by their wives' apparent conquest of mortal fear. Puritans believed that pregnancy rendered women more fearful than usual. The Reverend Peter Thacher wrote in his diary in February 1680, that his wife had fallen on a chair, and was 'soe frighted with it that shee had like to have fainted away' because she feared she had hurt the child in her womb. When normally timid women, rendered even more so by pregnancy, triumphed over the terror of death, they reassured the whole community of its ability to conquer its fear of the hereafter through submission to God. As Mather said at the funeral of seventeen-year-old Mrs Rebeckah Burnel in 1724:

But when it pleases Him, to take *children,* and those of that *Sex* which *Fear* is most incident and enslaving to; and make such *Babes and Sucklings* to triumph over the *Enemy,*—Oh! The *Wondrous Power* of our God!...

Thirteen years earlier, Cotton Mather's sister, Jerusha, decided when she was five months pregnant that it was time to get herself ready for death. She acknowledged that she was a fearful creature, and especially so because of her pregnancy, and wished to give herself up completely to God. She vowed that if God gave her an easy and short labour that she would dedicate herself to bringing up her child in fear of Him. She petitioned for a 'resigned will' and to be made fit for whatever God demanded for her. When her labour approached she prayed to be delivered from the sin of fear. As it happened, her labour was easy, but she and her baby died a short time later.

Mather, in recording his sister's death, assured his readers that Jerusha, while exceptionally joyous, said 'nothing that look'd at all Delirious', lest they discount the God-given courage with which she had faced her end. He quoted her as saying that when she was healthy 'Death was a Terror to me. But now I know, I shall Dy, I am not at *all afraid of it. This* is a Wonderful *Work of God!* I know *that I am* going to Christ...*I see things that are Unutterable!*'. Her father, Increase Mather, asked her if she were not afraid of death. 'She replied with great Earnestness; "Not in the least! Not in the least! Not in the least!"' Mather ended his memoir with what he said were her last words, 'Eye has not seen, Ear has not heard, neither entered into the Heart of Man, the things which

God has prepared for them that Love Him!' Mather's text pointed out in many ways that if a frail, sickly and frightened (i.e. womanly) woman lived as a Puritan woman should, she would die blissfully; hence, ran the implicit parallel, how much easier would it be for a strong man to do the same.

Similarly, Barbara Ruggles, an inhabitant of Roxburg, was able, according to the Roxburg Church records, to 'shine in her life & death' because of the way she dealt with her afflictions, including a fatal delivery. She had a 'stone chollik in which sicknesse she manifested much patiens, and faith; she dyed in childbed . . . & left a godly savor behind her'.

When a woman lost the mortal battle of birth graciously, she acquired unhesitating male praise. When she won, her husband's admiration might be muted by feelings of competition or guilty ambivalence about the pleasure in which such suffering originated. In journal accounts, husbands often expropriated the religious significance of their wives' brushes with death to themselves. They mingled their admiration with a vision of their *own* sins as the origin of their wives' agonies.

When, in the late 1660s, God visited upon the wife of the Reverend Joseph Thompson of Billerica such a weakness as made the couple fear her pregnancy might end badly, Thompson took a lesson in submission to the Lord's will from his wife's peril. He acknowledged that nothing could happen without God's intervention. The Lord further let him see that he had not been sufficiently grateful for the health, companionship, and work of his wife. He therefore feared that God might punish him by taking her away—although one can imagine that Mrs Thompson probably saw the punishment as hers. He prayed that the Lord would restore his wife's health and vowed perpetual gratitude for her. When his wife recovered, he charged himself with a return to indifference toward his blessings in her and a 'vile hart'. Mrs Thompson's near-death underlined to Thompson the sinful contrast between his unthankful acceptance of his spouse and his brief, divinely-inspired awareness of her value.

And uncertainty and fear gave Thompson an all-too-brief reminder of the level of active, spiritual struggle on which he should be conducting more of his life.

The Reverend Thomas Shepard, in ruminating about the imminent birth of his child in the 1640s, wondered what would happen if the labour did not go well 'and her pains be long and [the] Lord remember my sin? And I began to trouble my heart with fear of the worst'. When he learned that his wife had delivered a baby safely, ' . . . I saw the Lord's mercy and my own folly, to disquiet my heart with fear of what never shall be nor will be, and not rather to submit unto the Lord's will, and, come what can come, to be quiet there'. Like Thompson, Shepard's wife's mortal risk made him acutely conscious of his own sins. When his fears went unrealised he attempted to learn the lesson of peaceful resignation to God's will. He could not avoid seeing that his wife, in giving herself up to the miseries and uncertain outcome of travail, embodied this lesson.

In the same period the Reverend Michael Wigglesworth described his intimate involvement in his wife's labour. When she had pain, he:

> lay sighing, sweating, praying, almost fainting through weakness before morning. The next day, the spleen much enfeebled me, and setting in with grief took away my strength, my heart was smitten within me, and as sleep departed from myne eyes my stomach abhored meat, I was brought very low and knew not how to pass away another night.

He then described feeling hasty and impatient', presumably with the excessive duration of their labour, and he prayed that the Lord make him want to 'stoop to his will'. His wife's endurance taunted him with the patience and submission he lacked. And although he portrayed his wife's labour as his own, it was she who demonstrated uncomplaining fortitude in the face of pains which he likened to 'the pangs of eternal death'.

If women who were courageous in childbirth accrued complicated, competitive admiration from men, energeti-

cally religious mothering produced more straightforward praise. Sons whose mothers had toiled over their salvation knew from their own deep experience of maternal force what such efforts entailed. Unlike husbands who had impregnated their wives but been excluded from the redemptive suffering of labour, sons had been the object of mothers' strenuous efforts and sacrifices. Cotton Mather described a good mother 'travail[ing] for her children more than once' to save them from the abominable sinfulness with which human birth had infected them. She was to work as hard as she could, instilling the principles of religion in her babies and catechising them as soon as they could speak.

Perhaps the most fearsome aspect of a righteous mother was that she would rather see her children dead than living outside the grace of God. In Michael Wigglesworth's famous epic, *The Day of Doom,* (1662) 'The tender mother will own no other/of all her numerous brood/But such as stand at Christ's right hand/acquitted through his blood'. Mothers with this unique spiritual ferocity, who gave more importance to their children's salvation than to their physical lives, were exhibiting the highest form of human love a Puritan could imagine. And yet, it could engender the starkest fear.

Of all imagery pertaining to females, Puritans had the most positive associations with the lactating breast. In sermons, ministers used metaphors giving God, the father, the capacity to nurse his children. This potent symbol of security, warmth and joy—the union of loving mother and nursing infant stood in stark contrast to the mother who would repudiate her unsaved offspring. In the eyes of a small child, the mother's immense power to give peace and happiness was paired with her ability to destroy forever the ease and hope of the unrepentant child.

These contrasting childhood images of perfect love and total terror persisted in the imaginations of children of such fervent mothers. In childbirth husbands saw wives resigned to God's will to sacrifice their own lives to create life. But the sons of deeply pious women remembered their mothers' seeming willingness to sacrifice *them* if their wickedness demanded it. Such fearsome, Janus-faced mothers undoubtedly contributed to men's admiration for female virtue at the same time that they implanted an abiding fear of powerful women.

Thomas Shepard recalled admiringly that his second wife cried and prayed in secret for her son, requesting that 'if the Lord did not intend to glorify himself by thee, that he would cut thee off by death rather than to live to dishonour him by sin'. His first wife, on the other hand, displayed the other ultimate motherly virtue. In explaining to his son his mother's death, Shepard said that she 'died in the Lord, departing out of this world to another, who did lose her life by being careful to preserve thine, for in the ship thou wert so feeble and froward both in the day and night that hereby she lost her strength and at last her life'. The first Mrs Shepard had sacrificed her life so that her child could live, and the second Mrs Shepard was willing to sacrifice her *son* if his soul became corrupt. A mighty Puritan mother elicited both veneration and terror.

The sons of other spiritually influential women came up with more tranquil memories, formed from less terrifying maternal images. These men recalled prayerful women to whom love meant hawklike watchfulness for their sons' salvation. Thomas Shepard remembered that his own mother, who died when he was still young, bore 'exceeding great love to me and made many prayers for me'. In Increase Mather's *Autobiography* he called his mother, Cotton's grandmother, 'a very Holy, praying woman. She desired two things for him, he remembered: grace and learning. As a boy he learned to read from his mother. His father taught him to write, 'who also instructed me in grammar learning' in Latin and Greek. But, as Cotton later remembered, Increase's mother taught her son, his father, 'all that was Good . . . among her Instructions . . . she mightily Inculcated the lesson of *Diligence*'.

Mather had often heard about his grandmother's potent combination of love and exhortation. He proudly recounted family lore: when Increase was very little his mother told him, that he

was 'very much her *Darling*', and that all she wished for him was to be a good Christian and a good scholar. She pleaded successfully on her deathbed that her fifteen-year-old son go into the ministry. She had been most 'honourable . . . for her *Vertue*, . . . that for which a *Woman* is most of all *to be Praised*'. She was Mather's model for his twice-travailing mother. He wrote, 'She was a Woman of Uncommon Devotion, and in her Importunate Prayers for this her son, she . . . became *Twice a Mother* to him'. Mather's own mother had similar moral structure, challenging the family to live up to her example. Mather remembered her as 'a Godly, an Humble, and a Praying Woman, and one that often set apart *Whole Days* for prayer and Secret Interviews with Heaven'.

Frances Boland arrived in America from Scotland in 1682. In his journal he gave special thanks for the 'pious nurture and example of my godly mother. . . . She was a praying woman and prayed much for her children'. He went on to say what a blessing it was for the young to have parents such as his.

John Dane, a surgeon in Ipswich, Massachusetts, remembered with respect that his mother had been a 'serious woman'. He recalled that she had once had a dream in which she heard a certain minister deliver a sermon; according to Dane's account she accurately foresaw the date, the place, and the text of that preacher's talk. Dane prudently did not praise his mother as a seer and mystic, which would have unsettled New World Puritans. Instead, he portrayed her as a sober student, indifferent to her gift of prophecy and desirous only to make 'good improvement of that sermon', which, thanks to her vision, she was able to enjoy twice.

The zealous mother was an exacting conscience to her children and, by extension, to the community. Embedded in the Puritan notion of community was mutual moral responsibility and the notion that the sin of one member stained the whole society. Boys and girls both grew up cultivating the ability to spot a sin in themselves and others. Cotton Mather wrote approvingly that his sister, Jerusha, recorded in her journal judg-

ments on the activities and behaviour of people in the community. He wrote that in her journal:

> She Remarks on the Dealings of God with Others; Especially if anything either Good or Bad were observable in the condition of the Town; But most of all what occur'd Joyful or Grievous, unto her nearest *Relatives,* and their Families; and she employes agreeable *Meditations* and *Supplications* there-upon.

Wives, in particular, were supposed to watch their husbands' spiritual state. Benjamin Wadsworth had written that 'If Husbands that call themselves Christian, are vain, wicked, ungodly; their pious Wives (if such they have) should by a meek winning Conversation, indeavour their spiritual & eternal Good'. Christopher Lawson sued his wife for divorce in 1669, accusing her of failing in her duty as a converted Puritan to attend to the spiritual needs of her unconverted husband. 'The unbelieving husband', he wrote, 'should be wonn by the good conversation of the believing wife . . .'.

The Reverend John Ward praised his wife for being an 'accusing conscience' and letting him know when he was acting in an ungodly manner. Mather extolled Ward's wife who had lived happily with her husband for forty years:

> Although she would so faithfully tell him of everything that might seem amendable in him . . . yet she ever pleased him wonderfully. And she would oft put him upon the duties of secret fasts, and when she met with anything in reading that she counted singularly agreeable, she would still impart it unto him.

The marriage of the Wards was an active spiritual partnership in which Mrs Ward not infrequently gave her husband direction.

Women often achieved the role of conscience by becoming shadow ministers, absorbing, sometimes writing down (as Jerusha Mather did), and acting upon the weekly sermons of their husbands and/or pastors. Thomas Shepard commended his wife for her 'excellency to reprove for sin and discern the evils of men'. He went on to say that she loved the words of the Lord exceedingly and was, therefore, glad to read his notes for his sermons every week and ponder the thoughts therein.

Cotton Mather memorialised the second Mrs Whiting for her 'singular piety and gravity', who prayed in her closet every day to God. He commended her for writing down the sermons that she heard 'on the Lord's days with much dexterity', while living by their messages all week.

Although Puritan traditions cast doubt on women's capacity for goodness and prohibited them from exercising concrete authority, Puritan women did achieve moral stature from quietly enduring suffering, intense dedication to the salvation of their children, and gentle correction of the behaviour of their spouses and neighbours. The blessing Puritan men bestowed on notably virtuous women registered the conflict in which it was born. Women had to criticise, suggest, and direct others—particularly men—with extreme caution as Puritan men were deeply alarmed when women presumed to judge them. Nonetheless, Puritan women, inclined to religious depth, would find respect and deference in their communities, no small treasures in a male-dominated world. And they would bequeath to later generations of women a tradition of moral criticism and the conviction that zealous effort on behalf of the salvation of others was part of their human responsibility. This belief would empower women to turn their moral energies upon their husbands, families, and, in time, the world around them.

FOR FURTHER READING

Laurel Thacher Ulrich, *Goodwives: Image and Reality in the Lives of Women of Northern New England, 1650–1750* (Knopt, 1982); Carol Karlsen, *The Devil in the Shape of a Woman* (Norton, 1987; David Leverenz, *The Language of Puritan Feeling* (Rutgers University Press, 1980); Perry Miller, *The American Puritan* (Doubleday/Anchor, 1956); Lyle Koehler, *A Search for Power, The "Weaker Sex" in Seventeenth Century New England* (University of Illinois Press, 1980); Kenneth Silverman, *The Life and Times of Cotton Mather* (Harper & Row, 1970).

America's First Experiment in Toleration

John Hartsock *details the rise and fall of noble tolerance of religious freedom in 17th-century Maryland.*

Like the sudden thunderstorms that can roll swiftly up the Chesapeake Bay in summer, turning the normally tranquil waterway into a storm-tossed sea, an equally intolerant and dark spirit had descended on the hardscrabble tobacco plantations dotting the lush shoreline of that tidewater region some 300 years ago, in what was Lord Baltimore's former palatinate of Maryland.

In 1692, three years after a Protestant revolution had ousted a Catholic government in Maryland, the arrival of a royal governor appointed by William III confirmed its results and effectively spelled the end of the first experiment in England's Thirteen Colonies of the practice of religious toleration as a fundamental principle of civil governance. Three centuries later we can only marvel that the experiment lasted as long as it did.

Lord Baltimore's experiment in religious toleration is worth recalling not only for its novelty. At a time when

Americans have just completed observance of the bicentennial of their Bill of Rights, with its guarantee of religious freedom, the events that happened 300 years ago in Maryland are a reminder of the vulnerability of a principle now taken for granted. Considering the religious temper of the seventeenth century, Maryland's social experiment can only elicit admiration for the courage of an enlightened family who for more than half a century practised religious toleration as a guiding principle.

The groundwork for this novel experiment in religious freedom was laid in February 1632 when George Calvert, the first Lord Baltimore and a former secretary of state to James I, began lobbying the court for a grant creating the colony of Maryland. The request took courage on Calvert's part: as a matter of conscience he had openly avowed his Catholicism in 1625, this at a time when English Catholics were persecuted and proscribed from participation in govern-

ment affairs. Indeed, going public with his faith precipitated Calvert's resignation as a secretary of state.

That his petition was favourably received by Charles I is remarkable, but is a testament to the regard Calvert commanded in the kingdom for the circumspect and sober-minded service he is credited with having rendered to Charles' father, James I.

George Calvert's ambitions were cut short when he died on April 15th, 1632. Instead, a charter for the colony was granted to his son Cecil, the 2nd Lord Baltimore, on June 20th of that year. The document carved the Maryland colony (named in honour of Charles' queen, Henrietta Maria) from the Virginia grant and nominally called for the establishment of the Church of England as the state church in the new colony. But the ambiguous wording of the charter has left historians speculating that a quiet conspiracy existed between the king and the Calverts effectively giving

From *History Today*, January 1993, pp. 22-26, 28. © 1993 by History Today, Ltd., 20 Old Compton Street, London W1V 5PE, England. Reprinted by permission.

the ruling Lord Baltimore, designated the colony's 'Proprietor', an authority sufficiently independent of the crown to permit English Catholics a refuge where they could worship freely. Legally the new colony was a palatinate, a medieval form of political entity semi-autonomous from the crown.

In November 1633 between 130 and 150 colonists set sail from England aboard the two vessels the *Ark* and the *Dove*. Although no precise figures exist on just how many were Catholics, it is clear that the denomination was in the minority and they remained so throughout the history of the early colony. Some historians place their figures at as little as 10 per cent of the population. Cecil's brother, Leonard Calvert, accompanied the settlers as the colony's first governor.

The earliest evidence that the Calverts intended to practice a policy of toleration is contained in Cecil's instructions to his co-religionists 'to be silent' on matters of religion in the company of Protestant settlers. In addition, Cecil advised his brother to be 'very careful' to preserve 'unity and peace' between Catholics and Protestants. And he guaranteed Protestants that they would be treated with 'mildness and favour.' The implication was clear: Religion was not to play a role in the civil life of the community.

After a three-month passage the settlers landed in Maryland on March 25th, 1634, near where the Potomac River enters the Chesapeake Bay. The new colony was a thickly forested country, with towering trees that a carriage drawn by a team-of-four could drive between, according to the contemporary account of Father Andrew White, a Jesuit priest who accompanied the settlers. Within a few days of arrival, Governor Calvert bought a primitive village from local Yaocomaco Indians and it was here the settlers founded their first shelter. The village was named St Mary's and became the first capital of Maryland. Within two years the Indian shelters would be replaced by primitive clapboard structures.

The colony soon became a haven not only for English Catholics but also persecuted Puritans, Quakers, Anabaptists, Presbyterians and other groups. History is abundant with examples of the broad-minded toleration practiced by the Calverts. For example, in 1638 a court found a Catholic overseer guilty of interfering in the worship of two Protestants who worked as indentured servants on the plantation of a Jesuit mission near St Mary's City. The non-clerical overseer had discovered them reading a Protestant religious tract and prohibited them from continuing to do so. What makes the trial and verdict extraordinary is that a Jesuit priest testified against the overseer—his co-religionist—and that the court consisted of Governor Leonard Calvert and two other Catholics. By most accounts Leonard Calvert shared his father's and brother's spirit of toleration.

Nor was it the first time the Calverts had to suppress the zeal of their co-religionists. Early in the colony's history Jesuit missionaries demonstrated an eagerness to establish a firm Catholic presence by creating large plantation missions through direct purchase of land from Indians instead of from the proprietary government. Fearful the activity could jeopardise his proprietorship in the eyes of the home government, Cecil Calvert in 1641 prohibited additional acquisitions.

Religious toleration was perhaps at its most magnanimous when in 1648 Cecil invited 500 persecuted Puritans, a sect not likely to have much sympathy for a Catholic ruler, from nearby Virginia to settle in Maryland. Initially 300 accepted the offer. Calvert then appointed one of their number as his colonial governor to replace Leonard who had died the year before. Most of the group settled sixty-five miles to the north of St Mary's City in what would become Annapolis and the future capital of the colony.

The spirit of toleration extended beyond religion, however. In 1642 at the annual gathering of the Maryland General Assembly, Mathias de Sousa became the first African-American to cast a vote in a colonial legislature. Then in 1647 Margaret Brent, a major landholder who had been appointed by Leonard Calvert on his deathbed to handle his private affairs, voted in the General Assembly on behalf of the proprietary family in what was the first recorded vote of a woman in a colonial legislature. Finally, unlike policies elsewhere in the early colonies, Maryland's Indians had equal rights under Maryland law.

The culmination of the spirit of toleration came in 1649 when the Maryland General Assembly codified what had been official policy since the settlers' landing fifteen years earlier, the first official act of religious toleration in the Thirteen Colonies, the 'Act Concerning Religion'.

The work of both Cecil Calvert and the General Assembly under the guidance of Puritan Governor William Stone, the Act not only guaranteed freedom of worship, but prohibited the use of religious epithets such as 'papist' and 'antinomian'. The punishment for sectarian name-calling was potentially harsh or magnanimous: offenders could choose between a public whipping or a public apology. The Act acknowledged:

> The enforcing of conscience in matters of religion hath frequently fallen out to be of dangerous consequences in those commonwealths where it hath been practised.

According to the Act, no Christian would 'bee any wais troubled, molested or discountenanced for or in respect of his or her religion nor in the free exercise thereof'. Even though the 'Act Concerning Religion' excluded non-Christians from its guarantees, the tolerant spirit eventually extended to them as well, as Jacob Lumbrozo, a Jewish physician, discovered when in 1658 he was charged with blasphemy for, according to one historian, declaring in public that Christ's resurrection amounted to magicianship. Christian colonists were incensed. Nevertheless, Lord Baltimore dismissed the charges and Lumbrozo eventually attained full citizenship in the colony.

What emerges then is a picture of a family committed, and perhaps eager at any cost, to keep the peace among sects not particularly disposed at the time to forbearance. Not until 1689 did the British Parliament pass, and William III approve, the Toleration Act for Dissenting Protestants, considered the seminal guarantee of religious liberties in England. Pointedly, it excluded Catholics.

To be sure, Maryland did not have a monopoly on religious toleration. Rhode

Island under the guidance of Roger Williams is the other notable experiment in religious toleration in England's early North American colonies. In January 1636 Williams fled the Massachusetts Bay Colony because of his dissenting views. He settled in the wilderness that would evolve into the Rhode Island colony where in 1644 he made public his vision of religious toleration.

In Maryland, it was admittedly an imperfect toleration. Notwithstanding Mathias de Sousa's voting in the General Assembly, the Calverts encouraged the introduction of black slaves into the colony. And when Margaret Brent lobbied the General Assembly for the right to vote on her own behalf, her request was denied. That effort has earned her the sobriquet 'America's first woman suffragette'.

Nor did Indians always receive equal justice under the law. In a 1637 court case presided over by Leonard Calvert, a white colonist admitted in a signed confession to killing an Indian. Despite the confession, an all-white jury refused to find their fellow colonist guilty because the Indian was a heathen. Governor Calvert refused to accept the jury's verdict and directed it to reconsider. The second time the jury found the white colonist guilty of murder in his own defence. An 'infuriated' Calvert, as one historian described him, dismissed the jury and fined its members for returning an unreasonable verdict. Clearly the colonists had displayed their moral double standard. Later, a second jury found the colonist guilty of manslaughter.

But if toleration was imperfect, it was no less so in Rhode Island. Under that colony's first constitution, which was approved in 1664, Catholics were forbidden public worship. And Williams' personal sense of toleration had its limits. His impulse to establish religious toleration in Rhode Island was based more on a desire to protect his own dissenting Puritan views from the state. Finally, after Rhode Island was well established, he engaged in a public and acrimonious debate with Quakers, reviling the sect and lumping them together with Catholics as guilty of 'spitting and belching out fire from one fire of Hell'.

Yet if imperfect from a twentieth-century perspective, the toleration practiced in Maryland—as well as in Rhode Island—is still remarkable considering the age. In 1650, Maryland's Protestant Governor Stone, his Protestant councillors and burgesses, and thirty-eight Protestant freemen, signed and sent a 'Protestant Declaration' to the Cromwellian Parliament in which they defended the Calvert administration and declared that they had complete 'freedom and liberty in the exercises of our religion'.

Bearing in mind the religious climate of the time, what then inspired the magnanimous toleration of the Calvert family? Was it simply that they, like Roger Williams, had tasted the bitterness of religious persecution? After all, George Calvert had had to resign his position at court having revealed his faith, and there is reason to believe that Cecil never matriculated at Oxford because of his Catholicism.

Some historians have belittled the Calvert contribution to religious toleration. As recently as 1986, the toleration in Maryland was described as only 'grudging', the result of 'force of circumstance'. The Calverts, the argument goes, were forced by necessity to attract settlers regardless of faith if the colony was to prove viable.

And then there is the matter of the medieval palatine authority granted the Calverts, cited as evidence that they were hardly democrats. Calvert defenders counter that the stipulation in the colony's charter calling on the proprietor to rule with the 'advice, assent and approbation' of the colony's freeman provided the basis for what became the annual meeting of the Maryland General Assembly.

There is reason to believe that the Calverts' encouragement of toleration was more than just pragmatic. First, there is evidence that the family was strongly influenced by the humanist spirit of the age. Not the least of those influences was Sir Thomas More, whose *Utopia* was a treatise about a perfect society where 'every man might be of what religion he pleased'. One of the chief advisers to the Calverts was Father Henry More, a Jesuit priest and the great-grandson of Thomas More.

Whatever the direct influence of the martyr's views on the Calverts, beyond it was the intellectual spirit of the time that they as educated men were likely to be familiar with. Even though Europeans engaged in bloody religious persecutions in the Sixteenth and Seventeenth centuries, there were still voices of moderation in both Catholic and Protestant camps, not the least of whom was Erasmus. A friend and correspondent of Thomas More, he openly condemned religious persecution by his Catholic church while refusing to break with it.

On the Protestant side, men of moderation such as Sebastian Castellio (who was strongly influenced by Erasmus) openly opposed punishment of heretics. In what has been called 'the sixteenth century's most courageous and most noble plea for tolerance' Castellio protested when dissenter Michael Servetus was burned at the stake in 1553 by John Calvin.

The devastation of the Thirty Years' War could only make toleration more attractive and we see its almost simultaneous expression in Maryland and Rhode Island.

But it is recent archeological discoveries at the first colonial capital of St Mary's City that provide some of the most compelling evidence that the Calverts were social visionaries and not merely venture capitalists. In 1986 archeologists found evidence that the town was designed according to Italian baroque urban planning principles in the shape of a pair of outstretched wings. At the end of one wing stood the State House, while at the end of the second wing, exactly half a mile away, stood a Catholic church. Precisely in the middle lay the town square. The governor's house, the seat of everyday civil administration, overlooked the square, the place of everyday civil affairs.

The physical separation of the church and State House in such a plan represented an attempt at separation of church and state, concludes archeologist Henry Miller, research director at the site. 'The importance is not so much that St Mary's City was planned,' he says. 'Rather, it shows an interest in attempting to develop a new kind of society.

'Economic pragmatists', he adds, 'do not go to the trouble of planning cities'.

It is one of those disquieting historic ironies then that religious intolerance extinguished the first experiment in religious freedom in English North America. In the 1680s an extreme Protestant faction chafed away the proprietary rule of the very family that had provided them safe haven, in part because that family was Catholic.

The 1689 rebellion that lead to the downfall of the Calvert government was not the first uprising by disaffected Protestants. They had instigated several throughout the history of the early colony. Among them, a Protestant supporter of Parliament, one Richard Ingle, attacked St Mary's City in 1645 in one of the few instances—and probably the most violent—of the English Civil War reaching across the Atlantic to Britain's North American colonies. This was followed by a temporary takeover of the colony's government by Protestants in the early 1650s. The Calverts reasserted their authority but they were to lose the colony again in 1689.

The 1689 rebellion has been called, variously, the Maryland Revolution, the Glorious Revolution in Maryland, and Coode's Rebellion, the latter in honour of one of its leaders, John Coode, a sometime Anglican clergyman. It was, on the face of it, an extension of the Glorious Revolution of 1688 in England which saw the Catholic James II ousted. But unlike the event in the mother country which is celebrated as one of the watersheds in the development of individual liberties in the English-speaking world, the Maryland event took a darker turn.

When William of Orange ascended the throne, Charles Calvert, who succeeded as Lord Baltimore on his father Cecil's death in 1675, sent an emissary to Maryland directing the colony to swear allegiance to the new king. (Ironically, Cecil Calvert never visited his colony despite his strong guiding hand.) The emissary died *en route* and Charles was not notified of his death. Thus Maryland colonists never received official notice of their proprietor's charge. When word of the royal change reached Maryland from other colonies, Protes-

tant hotheads interpreted Charles Calvert's silence as an act of disloyalty to William. The group, nominally lead by Coode, organised themselves as the 'Protestant Association'. Besides accusing Calvert of disloyalty, they charged in a declaration that the Catholic family had not adequately provided for the establishment of the Church of England in the colony.

They had other longstanding grievances as well. Although Charles Calvert remained firmly committed to a policy of religious toleration, he did not seem to possess the wisdom and circumspection of his father, Cecil, and uncle, Leonard. Among his sins in the eyes of the Protestants was that he packed the upper chamber of the General Assembly with relatives and friends, and had appointed a governor, William Joseph, who was widely regarded as arrogant.

Also, under the terms of the colony's charter settlers paid a feudal quit rent to the Calverts for the land they built on and farmed, instead of owning the land outright and paying a property tax. The feudal nature of the legal arrangement suggested that the colonists were something less than freeman and property owners. Additionally, during the colony's fifty-year existence, its tobacco-based economy was buffeted by periodic slumps. The colonial administration of the Calverts was often cited as a scapegoat. Finally, demographics were against the Calverts. By the 1680s the colony was being flooded by new immigrants, mostly Protestant with little affinity for a Catholic proprietor. Clearly, the days of proprietary rule were numbered.

On July 16th, 1689, the aroused Protestant Association, interpreting Charles Calvert's silence on the succession in the mother country as treasonous, assembled above St Mary's City near the Potomac River. Drawing followers from St Mary's, Calvert and Charles counties, they began a march on the capital, picking up recruits along the way. Charles Calvert was in England at the time defending his proprietary rule before the crown.

The rebels numbered at least 250 and some estimates of the poorly armed militia's size go as high as 750. Not all

Protestants supported the rebellion, however. In Providence, which would be renamed Annapolis after the 1689 revolution and become the new state capital, the rebels found little support among the Puritans who were perhaps fearful that the Anglican faction would gain too much the upper hand in the revolt. In Charles County several prominent Protestants refused to join, declaring the rebellion without cause. Later they were jailed by the victorious rebels for failing to support the revolt.

There is no contemporary description of the confrontation that occurred in St Mary's City on July 27th of that year. At best all that is known is that when the rebels appeared before the State House, William Digges, a kinsman of the Calverts but also a Protestant, barricaded himself in the building with between eighty and 100 supporters. Governor William Joseph was absent at the time, staying at Lord Baltimore's estate in Mattapany about eight miles away.

Digges apparently planned to make a stand. Certainly he was well-equipped to do so because the province's armoury was stored in the attic of the State House. However, Digges' troops refused to fight. Many of them were Protestants not keen to fire on their own. Instead, the leaders of the two sides held a parley. In an anticlimax, Digges capitulated, peacefully surrendering the public records and seat of government to the association. Not a shot had been fired.

A week later the Protestant Association, armed with two cannon taken from a merchant ship, descended on Mattapany and confronted Governor Joseph, his ruling council, and about 150 supporters of proprietary rule. The Protestant Association, its numbers further swelled, demanded surrender. Confronted by overwhelming numbers, Joseph and his advisers agreed. The rebels provided for what have been called liberal terms: 'safe conduct of the proprietary party to their homes, guaranty of their just rights, with the sole requirement that all papists should be excluded from office'. Governor Joseph and some of his advisers took advantage of the liberal terms and fled to Virginia.

By any standard it was a modest revolution. But for the colony its consequences were profound. While the terms of the surrender at Mattapany were liberal, the clause prohibiting Catholics from holding public office was ominous. For two years Charles Calvert unsuccessfully lobbied the new Protestant king for the colony's return while the Protestant faction sought direct royal rule. Then in June 1691, the crown confirmed the revolution's results and appointed the first royal governor, Lionel Copley, who would arrive to take up his duties a year later in 1692.

Also in 1692, the Protestant-dominated General Assembly passed legislation establishing the Church of England as the official church of Maryland. The legislation was vetoed by the crown, as was subsequent legislation, on technicalities. Nonetheless, the tendency was clear and in 1702 the assembly succeeded in passing legislation acceptable to the crown which established the Anglican Church as the official state church. The legislation was tolerant—in a fashion. It permitted freedom of worship for dissenting Protestants. But like the law on religious liberty approved by Parliament in 1689, it excluded freedom of worship for Catholics and Jews.

Thus in the end the co-religionists of a family that sought to create a new kind of society out of the Maryland wilderness where everyone could worship freely now found themselves denied the opportunity to worship publicly. Protestants would continue efforts during the eighteenth century to further disenfranchise Catholics. The ignominy of the repression was reinforced in 1704 in an act important as much for its symbolism when a sheriff, directed by the royal governor, padlocked the door of the Catholic church in St Mary's City. The structure would never be worshipped in again, and was demolished a few years later.

Not until the American Revolution would Maryland's Catholics be permitted to worship in public again. Today, in the tobacco country of Southern Maryland, one can still find attached to old manor houses small chapels where Catholic plantation owners worshipped privately.

There is an ironic postscript. The law establishing a state church must have been a bitter pill to swallow for non-Anglican Protestants who participated in the revolt to eliminate Catholic rule: they were required to pay taxes to support the state church.

FOR FURTHER READING:

Patricia U. Bonomi, *Under the Cope of Heaven: Religion, Society and Politics in Colonial America* (Oxford University Press, 1988); Robert J. Brugger, *Maryland: A Middle Temperament: 1634–1980* (The Johns Hopkins University Press, 1988); Lois Green Carr and David Williams Jordan, *Maryland's Revolution of Government: 1689–1692* (Cornell University Press, 1974); J. Moss Ives *The Ark and the Dove: The Beginnings of Civil and Religious Liberties in America* (Cooper Square Publishers Inc., 1969 rpt: 1936); Aubrey C. Land, *Colonial Maryland: A History* from the series: *A History of the American Colonies in Thirteen Volumes* (KTO Press, 1981);

John Hartsock is Assistant Professor of Journalism at Marist College, New York and a freelance journalist.

Unit 2

Unit Selections

9. **Making Sense of the Fourth of July,** Pauline Maier
10. **The *Radical* Revolution,** Fredric Smoler
11. **"Pvt. Robert Shurtleff": An Unusual Revolutionary War Soldier,** Kathleen Doyle
12. **'It Is Not a Union,'** Peter Onuf
13. **. . . by the Unanimous Consent of the States,** Ezra Bowen
14. **The Founding Fathers, Conditional Antislavery, and the Nonradicalism of the American Revolution,** William W. Freehling

Key Points to Consider

❖ What purpose was the Declaration of Independence created to serve? How have perceptions of this document changed over the years?

❖ What changes did those who led the Revolution hope to bring about? What unintended changes resulted? In a broad sense, is it accurate to call the Revolution "radical"?

❖ Although many people agreed that the government formed under the Articles of Confederation had weaknesses and needed revision, why was it abandoned in favor of a new government?

❖ Discuss the most significant compromises made at the Constitutional Convention of 1787.

❖ How did secrecy help smooth the way for these compromises?

❖ What is meant by "conditional" antislavery? Given the situation at the time, would it have been possible to abolish slavery without splitting the union?

 **Links**   **www.dushkin.com/online/**

11. **The Early America Review**
    http://www.earlyamerica.com/review/
12. **House of Representatives**
    http://www.house.gov/
13. **National Center for Policy Analysis**
    http://www.public-policy.org/~ncpa/pd/pdindex.html
14. **Senate**
    http://www.senate.gov/
15. **Supreme Court/Legal Information Institute**
    http://supct.law.cornell.edu/supct/index.html
16. **U.S. Founding Documents/Emory University**
    http://www.law.emory.edu/FEDERAL/
17. **The White House**
    http://www.whitehouse.gov/WH/Welcome.html
18. **The World of Benjamin Franklin**
    http://www.fi.edu/franklin/

These sites are annotated on pages 4 and 5.

The British empire was based on the theory of mercantilism. According to this theory, the mother country should regulate economic activities for the purpose of enriching and strengthening the empire as a whole. In practice this meant that the American colonies should provide mostly raw materials to England and, in return, purchase finished goods. Such exchanges not only would help ensure a favorable balance of trade between the empire and other nations, but would enhance the British military position by enabling England to attain self-sufficiency with regard to strategic materials, such as lumber for ship masts and spars. Whatever benefited the empire, in theory, benefited the colonists as well.

Mercantilism had mixed consequences for the American colonies. Southern producers of rice and corn, for instance, had the advantages of selling in a protected market and of purchasing manufactured goods on British credit. New Englanders gained from selling lumber and from building ships—one of the few industries the British government encouraged for economic and strategic reasons. But others, in the middle colonies especially, often chafed at regulations that restricted their ability to buy goods at the best price and prevented these colonies from producing items that competed with British manufacturers. Generally speaking, the British government, preoccupied with the numerous problems of managing a huge empire, treated the colonies with a light hand and often failed to enforce its own regulations. This "benign neglect" meant that in day-to-day affairs the colonies enjoyed a great deal of independence within the system.

Decades of benign neglect, the passage of time, and the distance from England brought changes in colonists' attitudes. Although most regarded themselves as British subjects, they came to assume that the autonomy they enjoyed was the natural state of affairs. Few of them had ever visited the mother country; some spent their lives without seeing any visible trappings of the government to which they owed their loyalty. In short, many colonists regarded themselves as "American" as well as subjects of the Crown.

The end of what the colonists called the French and Indian War in 1763 brought dramatic changes in the relationship. The war had virtually bankrupted England, and extremely heavy taxes were levied on the British people. The government understandably concluded that the colonists should pay their share for a conflict in which they had been involved. After all, one settlement of the war had been the removal of the French from North America, which meant that they no longer presented a threat to the colonists.

The new taxes and regulations, along with much more vigorous enforcement efforts, were perceived by the colonists as an unwarranted intrusion on the rights and privileges they had come to take for granted. These burdens were imposed, moreover, at

a time when removal of the French threat made the colonists less dependent upon the Crown's protection. Economic disputes quickly spilled over into other areas, such as religion and politics. What seemed to the colonists as outrageous behavior by the British government caused more and more of them to conclude that the colonies would be best off if they cut ties with the empire and struck out alone. The British, of course, were determined to hold on to their possessions. Efforts by the government to enforce its will led to armed clashes and then to the Revolutionary War.

In "Making Sense of the Fourth of July," Pauline Maier analyzes the Declaration of Independence. Maier discusses how the meaning and function of the Declaration has changed over the course of time. "The *Radical* Revolution," as its title indicates, denies that the American Revolution was essentially a conservative movement, as some scholars have claimed. Fredric Smoler's essay is based on an interview with noted historian Gordon Wood, who points out the many deep and lasting changes that resulted. American women contributed to the war effort in a number of ways. Some served as nurses on or near battlefields. Deborah Sampson went a step further. She enlisted in the army as "Pvt. Robert Shurtleff" and served until she was found out, as Kathleen Doyle reports.

Americans, with French help, defeated the British and finally gained independence. The first experiment in self-government, the Articles of Confederation, succeeded in some areas but failed in others. In " 'It Is Not a Union,' " Peter Onuf discusses how dissatisfaction with the Articles led to the demand for serious revision or for an entirely new form of government. Ezra Bowen, in ". . . by the Unanimous Consent of the States," analyzes the numerous compromises that were made at the Constitutional Convention of 1787. Tight security over the proceedings permitted individuals to take positions that they would have found difficult to defend in public. In "The Founding Fathers, Conditional Antislavery, and the Nonradicalism of the American Revolution," William Freehling argues that, although the founders did not intend to destroy the institution of slavery, they took steps that led to its ultimate demise.

Making Sense of the Fourth of July

The DECLARATION OF INDEPENDENCE is not what Thomas Jefferson thought it was when he wrote it—and that is why we celebrate it

By Pauline Maier

JOHN ADAMS THOUGHT AMERICANS would commemorate their Independence Day on the second of July. Future generations, he confidently predicted, would remember July 2, 1776, as "the most memorable Epocha, in the History of America" and celebrate it as their "Day of Deliverance by solemn Acts of Devotion to God Almighty. It ought to be solemnized with Pomp and Parade, with Shews, Games, Sports, Guns, Bells, Bonfires and Illuminations from one End of this Continent to the other from this Time forward forever more."

His proposal, however odd it seems today, was perfectly reasonable when he made it in a letter to his wife, Abigail. On the previous day, July 2, 1776, the Second Continental Congress had finally resolved "That these United Colonies are, and of right ought to be, free and independent States, that they are absolved from all allegiance to the British Crown, and that all political connection between them and the State of Great Britain is, and ought to be, totally dissolved." The thought that Americans might instead commemorate July 4, the day Congress adopted a "Declaration on Independency" that he had helped prepare, did not apparently occur to Adams in 1776. The Declaration of Inde-

pendence was one of those congressional statements that he later described as "dress and ornament rather than Body, Soul, or Substance," a way of announcing to the world the fact of American independence, which was for Adams the thing worth celebrating.

In fact, holding our great national festival on the Fourth makes no sense at all—unless we are actually celebrating not just independence but the Declaration of Independence. And the declaration we celebrate, what Abraham Lincoln called "the charter of our liberties," is a document whose meaning and function today are different from what they were in 1776. In short, during the nineteenth century the Declaration of Independence became not just a way of announcing and justifying the end of Britain's power over the Thirteen Colonies and the emergence of the United States as an independent nation but a statement of principles to guide stable, established governments. Indeed, it came to usurp in fact if not in law a role that Americans normally delegated to bills of rights. How did that happen? And why?

According to notes kept by Thomas Jefferson, the Second Continental Congress did not discuss the resolution on

independence when it was first proposed by Virginia's Richard Henry Lee, on Friday, June 7, 1776, because it was "obliged to attend at that time to some other business." However, on the eighth, Congress resolved itself into a Committee of the Whole and "passed that day & Monday the 10th in debating on the subject." By then all contenders admitted that it had become impossible for the colonies ever again to be united with Britain. The issue was one of timing.

John and Samuel Adams, along with others such as Virginia's George Wythe, wanted Congress to declare independence right away and start negotiating foreign alliances and forming a more lasting confederation (which Lee also proposed). Others, including Pennsylvania's James Wilson, Edward Rutledge of South Carolina, and Robert R. Livingston of New York, argued for delay. They noted that the delegates of several colonies, including Maryland, Pennsylvania, Delaware, New Jersey, and New York, had not been "impowered" by their home governments to vote for independence. If a vote was taken immediately, those delegates would have to "retire" from Congress, and their states might secede from the union, which would seriously weaken the Americans'

This article originally appeared in *American Heritage,* July/August 1997, pp. 54-65. Adapted from *American Scripture: Making the Declaration of Independence,* by Pauline Maier. © 1998 by Alfred A. Knopf, Inc. Reprinted by permission.

chance of realizing their independence. In the past, they said, members of Congress had followed the "wise & proper" policy of putting off major decisions "till the voice of the people drove us into it," since "they were our power, & without them our declarations could not be carried into effect." Moreover, opinion on independence in the critical middle colonies was "fast ripening & in a short time," they predicted, the people there would "join in the general voice of America."

CONGRESS DECIDED TO GIVE THE LAGgard colonies time and so delayed its decision for three weeks. But it also appointed a Committee of Five to draft a declaration of independence so that such a document could be issued quickly once Lee's motion passed. The committee's members included Jefferson, Livingston, John Adams, Roger Sherman of Connecticut, and Pennsylvania's Benjamin Franklin. The drafting committee met, decided what the declaration should say and how it would be organized, then asked Jefferson to prepare a draft.

Meanwhile, Adams—who did more to win Congress's consent to independence than any other delegate—worked feverishly to bring popular pressure on the governments of recalcitrant colonies so they would change the instructions issued to their congressional delegates. By June 28, when the Committee of Five submitted to Congress a draft declaration, only Maryland and New York had failed to allow their delegates to vote for independence. That night Maryland fell into line.

Even so, when the Committee of the Whole again took up Lee's resolution, on July 1, only nine colonies voted in favor (the four New England states, New Jersey, Maryland, Virginia, North Carolina, and Georgia). South Carolina and Pennsylvania opposed the proposition, Delaware's two delegates split, and New York's abstained because their twelve-month-old instructions precluded them from approving anything that impeded reconciliation with the mother country. Edward Rutledge now asked that Congress put off its decision until the next day, since he thought that the South

Carolina delegation would then vote in favor "for the sake of unanimity." When Congress took its final tally on July 2, the nine affirmative votes of the day before had grown to twelve: Not only South Carolina voted in favor, but so did Delaware—the arrival of Caesar Rodney broke the tie in that delegation's vote—and Pennsylvania. Only New York held out. Then on July 9 it, too, allowed its delegates to add their approval to that of delegates from the other twelve colonies, lamenting still the "cruel necessity" that made independence "unavoidable."

Once independence had been adopted, Congress again formed itself into a Committee of the Whole. It then spent the better part of two days editing the draft declaration submitted by its Committee of Five, rewriting or chopping off large sections of text. Finally, on July 4, Congress approved the revised Declaration and ordered it to be printed and sent to the several states and to the commanding officers of the Continental Army. By formally announcing and justifying the end of British rule, that document, as letters from Congress's president, John Hancock, explained, laid "the Ground & Foundation" of American self-government. As a result, it had to be proclaimed not only before American troops in the hope that it would inspire them to fight more ardently for what was now the cause of both liberty and national independence but throughout the country, and "in such a Manner, that the People may be universally informed of it."

Not until four days later did a committee of Congress—not Congress itself—get around to sending a copy of the Declaration to its emissary in Paris, Silas Deane, with orders to present it to the court of France and send copies to "the other Courts of Europe." Unfortunately the original letter was lost, and the next failed to reach Deane until November, when news of American independence had circulated for months. To make matters worse, it arrived with only a brief note from the committee and in an envelope that lacked a seal, an unfortunately slipshod way, complained Deane, to announce the arrival of the United States among the powers of the

earth to "old and powerfull states." Despite the Declaration's reference to the "opinions of mankind," it was obviously meant first and foremost for a home audience.

As copies of the Declaration spread through the states and were publicly read at town meetings, religious services, court days, or wherever else people assembled, Americans marked the occasion with appropriate rituals. They lit great bonfires, "illuminated" their windows with candles, fired guns, rang bells, tore down and destroyed the symbols of monarchy on public buildings, churches, or tavern signs, and "fixed up" on the walls of their homes broadside or newspaper copies of the Declaration of Independence.

BUT WHAT EXACTLY WERE THEY CELEbrating? The news, not the vehicle that brought it; independence and the assumption of self-government, not the document that announced Congress's decision to break with Britain. Considering how revered a position the Declaration of Independence later won in the minds and hearts of the people, Americans' disregard for it in the first years of the new nation verges on the unbelievable. One colonial newspaper dismissed the Declaration's extensive charges against the king as just another "recapitulation of injuries," one, it seems, in a series, and not particularly remarkable compared with earlier "catalogues of grievances." Citations of the Declaration were usually drawn from its final paragraph, which said that the united colonies "are and of Right ought to be Free and Independent states" and were "Absolved of all Allegiance to the British Crown"—words from the Lee resolution that Congress had inserted into the committee draft. Independence was new; the rest of the Declaration seemed all too familiar to Americans, a restatement of what they and their representatives had already said time and again.

The adoption of independence was, however, from the beginning confused with its declaration. Differences in the meaning of the word *declare* contributed to the confusion. Before the Declaration of Independence was issued—while, in fact, Congress was still editing Jefferson's draft—Pennsylvania newspapers announced that on July 2 the Continental Congress had "declared the United Colonies Free and Independent States," by which it meant simply that it had officially accepted that status. Newspapers in other colonies repeated the story. In later years the "Anniversary of the United States of America" came to be celebrated on the date Congress had approved the Declaration of Independence. That began, it seems, by accident. In 1777 no member of Congress thought of marking the anniversary of independence at all until July 3, when it was too late to honor July 2. As a result, the celebration took place on the Fourth, and that became the tradition. At least one delegate spoke of "celebrating the Anniversary of the Declaration of Independence," but over the next few years references to the anniversary of independence and of the Declaration seem to have been virtually interchangeable.

The Fourth of July was rarely celebrated during the Revolution and seems actually to have declined in popularity once the war was over.

Accounts of the events at Philadelphia on July 4, 1777, say quite a bit about the music played by a band of Hessian soldiers who had been captured at the Battle of Trenton the previous December, and the "splendid illumination" of houses, but little about the Declaration. Thereafter, in the late 1770s and 1780s, the Fourth of July was not regularly celebrated; indeed, the holiday seems to have declined in popularity once the Revolutionary War ended. When it was remembered, however, festivities seldom, if ever—to judge by newspaper accounts—involved a public reading of the Declaration of Independence. It was as if that document had done its work in carrying news of independence to the people, and it neither needed nor deserved further commemoration. No mention was made of Thomas Jefferson's role in composing the document, since that was not yet public knowledge, and no suggestion appeared that the Declaration itself was, as posterity would have it, unusually eloquent or powerful.

IN FACT, ONE OF THE VERY FEW PUBLIC comments on the document's literary qualities came in a Virginia newspaper's account of a 1777 speech by John Wilkes, an English radical and a long-time supporter of the Americans, in the House of Commons. Wilkes set out to answer a fellow member of Parliament who had attacked the Declaration of Independence as "a wretched composition, very ill written, drawn up with a view to captivate the people." Curiously, Wilkes seemed to agree with that description. The purpose of the document, he said, was indeed to captivate the American people, who were not much impressed by "the polished periods, the harmonious, happy expressions, with all the grace, ease, and elegance of a beautiful diction" that Englishmen valued. What they liked was "manly, nervous sense . . . even in the most awkward and uncouth dress of language."

ALL THAT BEGAN TO CHANGE IN THE 1790s, when, in the midst of bitter partisan conflict, the modern understanding and reputation of the Declaration of Independence first emerged. Until that time celebrations of the Fourth were controlled by nationalists who found a home in the Federalist party, and their earlier inattention to the Declaration hardened into a rigid hostility after 1790. The document's anti-British character was an embarrassment to Federalists who sought economic and diplomatic rapprochement with Britain. The language of equality and rights in the Declaration was different from that of the Declaration of the Rights of Man issued by the French National Assembly in 1789, but it still seemed too "French" for the comfort of Federalists, who, after the execution of Louis XVI and the onset of the Terror, lost whatever sympathy for the French Revolution they had once felt. Moreover, they understandably found it best to say as little as possible about a fundamental American text that had been drafted by a leader of the opposing Republican party.

It was, then, the Republicans who began to celebrate the Declaration of Independence as a "deathless instrument" written by "the immortal Jefferson." The Republicans saw themselves as the defenders of the American Republic of 1776 against subversion by pro-British "monarchists," and they hoped that by recalling the causes of independence, they would make their countrymen wary of further dealings with Great Britain. They were also delighted to identify the founding principles of the American Revolution with those of America's sister republic in France. At their Fourth of July celebrations, Republicans read the Declaration of Independence, and their newspapers reprinted it. Moreover, in their hands the attention that had at first focused on the last part of the Declaration shifted toward its opening paragraphs and the "self-evident truths" they stated. The Declaration, as a Republican newspaper said on July 7, 1792, was not to be celebrated merely "as affecting the separation of one country from the jurisdiction of another"; it had an enduring significance for established governments because it provided a "definition of the rights of man, and the end of civil government."

The Federalists responded that Jefferson had not written the Declaration alone. The drafting committee—including John Adams, a Federalist—had also contributed to its creation. And Jefferson's role as "the scribe who penned the declaration" had not been so distinguished as his followers suggested. Federalists rediscovered similarities between the Declaration and Locke's *Second Treatise of Government* that Richard Henry Lee had noticed long before and used them to argue that even the "small part of that memorable instrument" that could be attributed to Jefferson "he stole from *Locke's Essays.*" But after the War of 1812, the Federalist party slipped from sight, and with it, efforts to disparage the Declaration of Independence.

When a new party system formed in the late 1820s and 1830s, both Whigs and Jacksonians claimed descent from Jefferson and his party and so accepted the old Republican position on the Declaration and Jefferson's glorious role in its creation. By then, too, a new generation of Americans had come of age and made preservation of the nation's revolutionary history its particular mission. Its efforts, and its reverential attitude toward the revolutionaries and their works, also helped establish the Declaration of Independence as an important icon of American identity.

THE CHANGE CAME SUDDENLY. As late as January 1817 John Adams said that his country had no interest in its past. "I see no disposition to celebrate or remember, or even Curiosity to enquire into the Characters, Actions, or Events of the Revolution," he wrote the artist John Trumbull. But a little more than a month later Congress commissioned Trumbull to produce four large paintings commemorating the Revolution, which were to hang in the rotunda of the new American Capitol. For Trumbull, the most important of the series, and the one to which he first turned, was the Declaration of Independence. He based that work on a smaller painting he had done between 1786 and 1793 that showed the drafting committee presenting its work to Congress. When the new twelve-by-eighteen-foot canvas was completed in 1818, Trumbull exhibited it to large crowds in Boston, Philadelphia, and Baltimore before delivering it to Washington; indeed, *The Declaration of Independence* was the most popular of all the paintings Trumbull did for the Capitol.

Soon copies of the document were being published and sold briskly, which perhaps was what inspired Secretary of State John Quincy Adams to have an exact facsimile of the Declaration, the only one ever produced, made in 1823. Congress had it distributed throughout the country. Books also started to appear: the collected biographies of those who signed the Declaration in nine volumes by Joseph M. Sanderson (1823–27) or one

volume by Charles A. Goodrich (1831), full biographies of individual revolutionaries that were often written by descendants who used family papers, and collections of revolutionary documents edited by such notable figures as Hezekiah Niles, Jared Sparks, and Peter Force.

Jefferson forgot, as the years went by, how substantial a role other members of the committee had played in framing the Declaration's text.

Postwar efforts to preserve the memories and records of the Revolution were undertaken in a mood of near panic. Many documents remained in private hands, where they were gradually separated from one another and lost. Even worse, many revolutionaries had died, taking with them precious memories that were gone forever. The presence of living remnants of the revolutionary generation seemed so important in preserving its tradition that Americans watched anxiously as their numbers declined. These attitudes first appeared in the decade before 1826, the fiftieth anniversary of independence, but they persisted on into the Civil War. In 1864 the Reverend Elias Brewster Hillard noted that only seven of those who had fought in the Revolutionary War still survived, and he hurried to interview and photograph those "venerable and now sacred men" for the benefit of posterity. "The present is the last generation that will be connected by living link with the great period in which our national independence was achieved," he wrote in the introduction to his book *The Last Men of the Revolution.* "Our own are the last eyes that will look on men who looked on Washington; our ears the last that will hear the living voices of those who heard his words. Henceforth the American Revolution

will be known among men by the silent record of history alone."

Most of the men Hillard interviewed had played modest roles in the Revolution. In the early 1820s, however, John Adams and Thomas Jefferson were still alive, and as the only surviving members of the committee that had drafted the Declaration of Independence, they attracted an extraordinary outpouring of attention. Pilgrims, invited and uninvited, flocked particularly to Monticello, hoping to catch a glimpse of the author of the Declaration and making nuisances of themselves. One woman, it is said, even smashed a window to get a better view of the old man. As a eulogist noted after the deaths of both Adams and Jefferson on, miraculously, July 4, 1826, the world had not waited for death to "sanctify" their names. Even while they remained alive, their homes became "shrines" to which lovers of liberty and admirers of genius flocked "from every land."

ADAMS, IN TRUTH, WAS MIFFED BY Jefferson's celebrity as the penman of Independence. The drafting of the Declaration of Independence, he thought, had assumed an exaggerated importance. Jefferson perhaps agreed; he, too, cautioned a correspondent against giving too much emphasis to "mere composition." The Declaration, he said, had not and had not been meant to be an original or novel creation; his assignment had been to produce "an expression of the American mind, and to give that expression the proper tone and spirit called for by the occasion."

Jefferson, however, played an important role in rescuing the Declaration from obscurity and making it a defining event of the revolutionary "heroic age." It was he who first suggested that the young John Trumbull paint *The Declaration of Independence.* And Trumbull's first sketch of his famous painting shares a piece of drawing paper with a sketch by Jefferson, executed in Paris sometime in 1786, of the assembly room in the Old Pennsylvania State House, now known as Independence Hall. Trumbull's painting of the scene carefully followed Jefferson's sketch, which unfortunately included architectural in-accuracies, as Trumbull later learned to his dismay.

Jefferson also spent hour after hour answering, in longhand, letters that he said numbered 1,267 in 1820, many of which asked questions about the Decla-ration and its creation. Unfortunately, his responses, like the sketch he made for Trumbull, were inaccurate in many details. Even his account of the drafting process, retold in an important letter to James Madi-son of 1823 that has been accepted by one authority after another, conflicts with a note he sent Benjamin Franklin in June 1776. Jefferson forgot, in short, how substantial a role other members of the drafting commit-tee had played in framing the Declaration and adjusting its text before it was submit-ted to Congress.

INDEED, IN OLD AGE JEFFERSON FOUND enormous consolation in the fact that he was, as he ordered inscribed on his tomb, "Author of the Declaration of American Independence." More than anything else he had done, that role came to justify his life. It saved him from a despair that he suffered at the time of the Missouri crisis, when every-thing the Revolution had accomplished seemed to him in jeopardy, and that was later fed by problems at the University of Virginia, his own deteriorating health, and personal financial troubles so severe that he feared the loss of his beloved home, Monticello (those troubles, inci-dentally, virtually precluded him from freeing more than a handful of slaves at his death). The Declaration, as he told Madison, was "the fundamental act of union of these States," a document that should be recalled "to cherish the principles of the instrument in the bosoms of our own citizens." Again in 1824 he interpreted the government's re-publication of the Decla-ration as "a pledge of adhesion to its prin-ciples and of a sacred determination to maintain and perpetuate them," which he described as a "holy purpose."

But just which principles did he mean? Those in the Declaration's sec-ond paragraph, which he understood ex-actly as they had been understood in 1776—as an assertion primarily of the right of revolution. Jefferson composed the long sentence beginning "We hold these truths to be self-evident" in a well-known eighteenth-century rhetorical style by which one phrase was piled on another and the meaning of the whole became clear only at the end. The se-quence ended with an assertion of the "Right of the People to alter or to abol-ish" any government that failed to se-cure their inalienable rights and to institute a new form of government more likely "to effect their Safety and Happiness." That was the right Ameri-cans were exercising in July 1776, and it seemed no less relevant in the 1820s, when revolutionary movements were sweeping through Europe and Latin Amer-ica. The American example would be, as Jefferson said in the last letter of his life, a "signal arousing men to burst the chains under which monkish ignorance and super-stition had persuaded them to bind them-selves, and to assume the blessings and security of self-government."

Others, however, emphasized the opening phrases of the sentence that be-gan the Declaration's second paragraph, particularly "the memorable assertion, that 'all men are created equal, that they are endowed by their Creator with cer-tain unalienable rights, and that to se-cure these rights, governments are instituted among men, deriving their just powers from the consent of the gov-erned.' " That passage, the eulogist John Sergeant said at Philadelphia in July 1826, was the "text of the revolution," the "ruling vital principle" that had in-spired the men of the 1770s, who "looked forward through succeeding generations, and saw stamped upon all their institutions, the great principles set forth in the Declaration of Inde-pendence." In Hallowell, Maine, another eulogist, Peleg Sprague, similarly de-scribed the Declaration of Independence as an assertion *by a whole people, of . . . the native equality of the human race,* as the true foundation of all politi-cal, of all human institutions."

AND SO AN INTERPRETATION OF THE declaration that had emerged in the 1790s became ever more widely repeated. The equality that Ser-geant and Sprague emphasized was not, however, asserted for the first time in the Declaration of Independence. Even before Congress published its Declara-tion, one revolutionary document after another had associated equality with a new American republic and suggested enough different meanings of that term—equal rights, equal access to of-fice, equal voting power—to keep Americans busy sorting them out and fighting over inegalitarian practices far into the future. Jefferson, in fact, adapted those most remembered open-ing lines of the Declaration's second paragraph from a draft Declaration of Rights for Virginia, written by George Mason and revised by a committee of the Virginia convention, which appeared in the *Pennsylvania Gazette* on June 12, 1776, the day after the Committee of Five was appointed and perhaps the day it first met. Whether on his own inspi-ration or under instructions from the committee, Jefferson began with the Mason draft, which he gradually tight-ened into a more compressed and elo-quent statement. He took, for example, Mason's statement that "all men are born equally free and independent," re-wrote it to say they were "created equal & independent," and then cut out the "& independent."

Jefferson was not alone in adapting the Mason text for his purposes. The Virginia convention revised the Mason draft before enacting Virginia's Declaration of Rights, which said that all men were "by nature" equally free and independent. Several other states—including Pennsylvania (1776), Vermont (1777), Massachusetts (1780), and New Hampshire (1784)—re-mained closer to Mason's wording, in-cluding in their state bill of rights the assertions that men were "born free and equal" or "born equally free and inde-pendent." Unlike the Declaration of Inde-pendence, moreover, the state bills or "declarations" of rights became (after an initial period of confusion) legally bind-ing. Americans' first efforts to work out the meaning of the equality written into their founding documents therefore oc-curred on the state level.

IN MASSACHUSETTS, FOR EXAMPLE, SEV-eral slaves won their freedom in the 1780s by arguing before the state's Supreme Judicial Court that the provi-sion in the state's bill of rights that all men were born free and equal made slavery unlawful. Later, in the famous case of *Commonwealth* v. *Aves* (1836), Justice Lemuel Shaw ruled that those words were sufficient to end slavery in Massachusetts, indeed that it would be difficult to find others "more precisely adapted to the abolition of negro slavery." White Americans also found the equality provisions in their state bills of rights useful. In the Virginia constitutional convention of 1829–30, for example, a delegate from the trans-Appalachian West, John R. Cooke, cited that "sacred instrument" the Virginia Declaration of Rights against the state's system of representing all counties equally in the legislature regardless of their populations and its imposition of a property qualification for the vote, both of which gave disproportional power to men in the eastern part of the state. The framers of Virginia's 1776 constitution allowed those practices to persist despite their violation of the equality affirmed in the Declaration of Rights, Cooke said, because there were limits on how much they dared change "in the midst of war." They therefore left it for posterity to resolve the inconsistency "as soon as leisure should be afforded them." In the hands of men like Cooke, the Virginia Declaration of Rights became a practical program of reform to be realized over time, as the Declaration of Independence would later be for Abraham Lincoln.

But why, if the states had legally binding statements of men's equality, should anyone turn to the Declaration of Independence? Because not all states had bills of rights, and not all the bills of rights that did exist included statements on equality. Moreover, neither the federal Constitution nor the federal Bill of Rights asserted men's natural equality or their possession of inalienable rights or the right of the people to reject or change their government. As a result, contenders in national politics who found those old revolutionary principles useful had to cite the Declaration of Independence. It was all they had.

T HE SACRED STATURE GIVEN THE DECLaration after 1815 made it extremely useful for causes attempting to seize the moral high ground in public debate. Beginning about 1820, workers, farmers, women's rights advocates, and other groups persistently used the Declaration of Independence to justify their quest for equality and their opposition to the "tyranny" of factory owners or railroads or great corporations or the male power structure. It remained, however, especially easy for the opponents of slavery to cite the Declaration on behalf of their cause. Eighteenth-century statements of equality referred to men in a state of nature, before governments were created, and asserted that no persons acquired legitimate authority over others without their consent. If so, a system of slavery in which men were born the subjects and indeed the property of others was profoundly wrong. In short, the same principle that denied kings a right to rule by inheritance alone undercut the right of masters to own slaves whose status was determined by birth, not consent. The kinship of the Declaration of Independence with the cause of antislavery was understood from the beginning— which explains why gradual emancipation acts, such as those in New York and New Jersey, took effect on July 4 in 1799 and 1804 and why Nat Turner's rebellion was originally planned for July 4, 1831.

Even in the eighteenth century, however, assertions of men's equal birth provoked dissent. As slavery became an increasingly divisive issue, denials that men were naturally equal multiplied. Men were not created equal in Virginia, John Tyler insisted during the Missouri debates of 1820: "No, sir, the principle, although lovely and beautiful, cannot obliterate those distinctions in society which society itself engenders and gives birth to." Six years later the acerbic, self-styled Virginia aristocrat John Randolph called the notion of man's equal creation "a falsehood, and a most pernicious falsehood, even though I find it in the Declaration of Independence." Man was born in a state of "perfect helplessness and ignorance" and so was from the start dependent on others. There was "not a word of truth" in the notion that men were created equal, repeated South Carolina's John C. Calhoun in 1848. Men could not survive, much less de-

velop their talents, alone; the political state, in which some exercised authority and others obeyed, was in fact man's "natural state," that in which he "is born, lives and dies." For a long time the "false and dangerous" doctrine that men were created equal had lain "dormant," but by the late 1840s Americans had begun "to experience the danger of admitting so great an error . . . in the Declaration of Independence," where it had been inserted needlessly, Calhoun said, since separation from Britain could have been justified without it.

F IVE YEARS LATER, IN SENATE debates over the Kansas-Nebraska Act, Indiana's John Pettit pronounced his widely quoted statement that the supposed "self-evident truth" of man's equal creation was in fact "a self-evident lie." Ohio's senator Benjamin Franklin Wade, an outspoken opponent of slavery known for his vituperative style and intense patriotism, rose to reply. Perhaps Wade's first and middle names gave him a special bond with the Declaration and its creators. The "great declaration cost our forefathers too dear," he said, to be so "lightly thrown away by their children." Without its inspiring principles the Americans could not have won their independence; for the revolutionary generation the "great truths" in that "immortal instrument," the Declaration of Independence, were "worth the sacrifice of all else on earth, even life itself." How, then, were men equal? Not, surely, in physical power or intellect. The "good old Declaration" said "that all men are equal, and have inalienable rights; that is, [they are] equal in point of right; that no man has a right to trample on another." Where those rights were wrested from men through force or fraud, justice demanded that they be "restored without delay."

Abraham Lincoln, a little-known forty-four-year-old lawyer in Springfield, Illinois, who had served one term in Congress before being turned out of office, read these debates, was aroused as by nothing before, and began to pick up the dropped threads of his political career. Like Wade, Lincoln idealized the men of the American Revolution, who were for him "a forest of giant oaks," "a fortress of strength," "iron men." He also shared the deep concern of his contemporaries as the "silent artillery of time" removed them and the *"living history"* they embodied from this world. Before the 1850s, however, Lincoln seems to have had relatively little interest in the Declaration of Independence. Then, suddenly, that document and its assertion that all men were created equal became his "ancient faith," the "father of all moral principles," an "axiom" of free society. He was provoked by the attacks of men such as Pettit and Calhoun. And he made the arguments of those who defended the Declaration his own, much as Jefferson had done with Mason's text, reworking the ideas from speech to speech, pushing their logic, and eventually, at Gettysburg in 1863, arriving at a simple statement of profound eloquence. In time his understanding of the Declaration of Independence would become that of the nation.

Lincoln believed the Declaration "contemplated the progressive improvement in the condition of all men everywhere." Otherwise, it was "mere rubbish."

Lincoln's position emerged fully and powerfully during his debates with Illinois's senator Stephen Douglas, a Democrat who had proposed the Kansas-Nebraska Act and whose seat Lincoln sought in 1858. They were an odd couple, Douglas and Lincoln, as different physically—at full height Douglas came only to Lincoln's shoulders—as they were in style. Douglas wore well-tailored clothes; Lincoln's barely covered his limbs. Douglas was in general the more polished speaker; Lincoln sometimes rambled on, losing his point and his audience, although he could also, especially with a prepared text, be

a powerful orator. The greatest difference between them was, however, in the positions they took on the future of slavery and the meaning of the Declaration of Independence.

Douglas defended the Kansas-Nebraska Act, which allowed the people of those states to permit slavery within their borders, as consistent with the revolutionary heritage. After all, in instructing their delegates to vote for independence, one state after another had explicitly retained the exclusive right of defining its domestic institutions. Moreover, the Declaration of Independence carried no implications for slavery, since its statement on equality referred to white men only. In fact, Douglas said, it simply meant that American colonists of European descent had equal rights with the King's subjects in Great Britain. The signers were not thinking of "the negro or . . . savage Indians, or the Feejee, or the Malay, or any other inferior or degraded race." Otherwise they would have been honor bound to free their own slaves, which not even Thomas Jefferson did. The Declaration had only one purpose: to explain and justify American independence.

To LINCOLN, DOUGLAS'S ARGUMENT left only a "mangled ruin" of the Declaration of Independence, whose "plain, unmistakable language" said *"all"* men were created equal. In affirming that government derived its "just powers from the consent of the governed," the Declaration also said that no man could rightly govern others without their consent. If, then, "the negro is a man," was it not a "total destruction of self-government, to say that he too shall not govern *himself?"* To govern a man without his consent was "despotism." Moreover, to confine the Declaration's significance to the British peoples of 1776 denied its meaning, Lincoln charged, not only for Douglas's "inferior races" but for the French, Irish, German, Scandinavian, and other immigrants who had come to America after the Revolution. For them the promise of equality linked new Americans with the founding generation; it was an "electric cord" that bound them into the nation

"as though they were blood of the blood, and flesh of the flesh of the men who wrote that Declaration," and so made one people out of many. Lincoln believed that the Declaration "contemplated the progressive improvement in the condition of all men everywhere." If instead it was only a justification of independence "without the *germ,* or even the *suggestion* of the individual rights of man in it," the document was "of no practical use now—mere rubbish—old wadding left to rot on the battlefield after the victory is won," an "interesting memorial of the dead past . . . shorn of its vitality, and practical value."

LIKE WADE, LINCOLN DENIED THAT THE signers meant that men were equal in *"all respects,"* including "color, size, intellect, moral developments, or social capacity." He, too, made sense of the Declaration's assertion of man's equal creation by eliding it with the next, separate statement on rights. The signers, he insisted, said men were equal in having " 'certain inalienable rights. . . .' This they said, and this they meant." Like John Cooke in Virginia three decades before, Lincoln thought the Founders allowed the persistence of practices at odds with their principles for reasons of necessity: to establish the Constitution demanded that slavery continue in those original states that chose to keep it. "We could not secure the good we did if we grasped for more," but that did not "destroy the principle that is the charter of our liberties." Nor did it mean that slavery had to be allowed in states not yet organized in 1776, such as Kansas and Nebraska.

Again like Cooke, Lincoln claimed that the authors of the Declaration understood its second paragraph as setting a standard for free men whose principles should be realized "as fast as circumstances . . . permit." They wanted that standard to be "familiar to all, and revered by all; constantly looked to, and constantly labored for, and even though never perfectly attained, constantly approximated and thereby constantly spreading and deepening its influence, and augmenting the happiness and value of life to all people of all colors everywhere." And if, as Calhoun said, American independence could have been declared without any assertion of human equality and inalienable rights, that made its inclusion all the more wonderful. "All honor to Jefferson," Lincoln said in a letter of 1859, "to the man who . . . had the coolness, forecast, and capacity to introduce into a merely revolutionary document, an abstract truth, applicable to all men and all times, and to embalm it there," where it would remain "a rebuke and a stumbling-block to the very harbingers of re-appearing tyranny and oppression."

JEFFERSON AND THE MEMBERS OF THE SECond continental Congress did not understand what they were doing in quite that way on July 4, 1776. For them, it was enough for the Declaration to be "merely revolutionary." But if Douglas's history was more accurate, Lincoln's reading of the Declaration was better suited to the needs of the Republic in the mid-nineteenth century, when the standard of revolution had passed to Southern secessionists and to radical abolitionists who also called for disunion. In his hands the Declaration became first and foremost a living document for an established society, a set of goals to be realized over time, the dream of "something better, than a mere change of masters" that explained why "our fathers" fought and endured until they won the Revolutionary War. In the Civil War, too, Lincoln told Congress on July 4, 1861, the North fought not only to save the Union but to preserve a form of government "whose leading object is to elevate the condition of men—to lift artificial weights from all shoulders—to clear the paths of laudable pursuit for all." The rebellion it opposed was at base an effort "to overthrow the princi-

ple that all men were created equal." And so the Union victory at Gettysburg in 1863 became for him a vindication of that proposition, to which the nation's fathers had committed it in 1776, and a challenge to complete the "unfinished work" of the Union dead and bring to "this nation, under God, a new birth of freedom."

The Declaration Lincoln left was not Jefferson's Declaration, although Jefferson and other revolutionaries shared the values Lincoln stressed.

Lincoln's Gettysburg Address stated briefly and eloquently convictions he had developed over the previous decade, convictions that on point after point echoed earlier Americans: Republicans of the 1790s, the eulogists Peleg Sprague and John Sergeant in 1826, John Cooke in the Virginia convention a few years later, Benjamin Wade in 1853. Some of those men he knew; others were unfamiliar to him, but they had also struggled to understand the practical implications of their revolutionary heritage and followed the same logic to the same conclusions. The Declaration of Independence Lincoln left was not Jefferson's Declaration, although Jefferson and other revolutionaries shared the values Lincoln and others stressed: equality, human rights, government by consent. Nor was Lincoln's Declaration of Independence solely his creation. It remained an "expression of the American mind," not, of course, what all

Americans thought but what many had come to accept. And its implications continued to evolve after Lincoln's death. In 1858 he had written a correspondent that the language of the Declaration of Independence was at odds with slavery but did not require political and social equality for free black Americans. Few disagreed then. How many would agree today?

The Declaration of Independence is in fact a curious document. After the Civil War members of Lincoln's party tried to write its principles into the Constitution by enacting the Thirteenth, Fourteenth, and Fifteenth Amendments, which is why issues of racial or age or gender equality are now so often fought out in the courts. But the Declaration of Independence itself is not and has never been legally binding. Its power comes from its capacity to inspire and move the hearts of living Americans, and its meaning lies in what they choose to make of it. It has been at once a cause of controversy, pushing as it does against established habits and conventions, and a unifying national icon, a legacy and a new creation that binds the revolutionaries to descendants who confronted and continue to confront issues the Founders did not know or failed to resolve. On Independence Day, then, Americans celebrate not simply the birth of their nation or the legacy of a few great men. They also commemorate a Declaration of Independence that is their own collective work now and through time. And that, finally, makes sense of the Fourth of July.

Pauline Maier is William Rand Kenan, Jr., Professor of American History at the Massachusetts Institute of Technology.

The *Radical* Revolution

*For years people have argued that France had the **real** revolution and that ours was mild by comparison. But now a powerful new book says the American Revolution was the most sweeping in all history. It alone established a pure commercial culture—a culture that makes America the universal society we are today.*

An Interview with Gordon Wood by Fredric Smoler

Fredric Smoler's discussion with Arthur Schlesinger, Jr., on multi-culturalism appeared in the February/March issue.

The French Revolution followed American independence by six years, but it was the later event that went into the books as "the Great Revolution" and became the revolutionary archetype. It is not only the contrast of the conspicuously greater political violence of the French Revolution that has led historians to play down the comparative radicalism of its American counterpart but the fact that the French Revolution swiftly became the model for radical political transformation. For more than a century successful revolutionaries no sooner took power than they designed tricolors and located themselves to the "left" or "right," terms that originally denoted where the delegates sat in the French Convention; the French taught succeeding generations the revolutionary drill. Until the Russian Revolution displaced it, the French Revolution formed the dominant modern political myth, the distorting mirror in which posterity located its dreams and dreads.

The American Revolution, on the other hand, was distinguished by its alleged conservatism; historians have generally held that we didn't kill enough people, engender enough proto-Bolsheviks, or produce a sufficient social upheaval to achieve true revolutionary significance—a failure lamented in some quarters and celebrated in others.

The revolutionaries not only destroyed the old ties but were unable to establish the kind of new ties they would have liked. They wound up with a very different society from the one they anticipated.

Gordon Wood's impressive new book *The Radicalism of the American Revolution* takes sharp issue with this consensus. American society is generally thought to embody cultural extremes of both egalitarian idealism and materialist vulgarity. Professor Wood thinks that these cultural characteristics are the direct—and thoroughly unintended—consequence of the Revolution, which made us for good and ill the most democratic culture on the planet. Thus our revolution was the most radical one imaginable, for it entirely discredited the older forms of paternalistic authority that everywhere else delayed the coming of capitalist modernity, and resulted in the construction of the first and so far the most completely commercial society the world has seen. If the measure of radicalism is the totality of the destruction of the old order, we are for Professor Wood's money the heirs of the most radical revolution in history.

I spoke with Gordon Wood in his office at Brown University in Providence, Rhode Island, where he is University Professor and Professor of History.

• **You argue that our Revolution's true radicalism lies in its destruction of an older hierarchical order. But just what was that order?**

It was a society characterized by a particular kind of hierarchy, a monarchy. This meant certain kinds of social relationships, mainly ones of dependency, with people tied together by patronage, blood, and kinship. Our revolution destroyed these kinds of monarchical relationships; that's what it was designed to do. But what makes it even more radical is the fact that the revolutionaries not only destroyed these ties but were unable to establish the kinds of ties they would have liked. They wound up in a very different society from the one they anticipated.

• **And you believe that one of the things they hadn't taken into account was religion.**

Yes. The old order was at the top rationalist, but ordinary people in the eighteenth century were still very much engaged with religion. It was the way they made fundamental sense of the world. What happens in the Revolution is that with the rise of ordinary people into dominance—which I suppose is a one-sentence summary of what the book is saying—they bring their religiosity with them. These people make sense of the world through religion, as ordinary people have done for centuries. People like Jefferson and Franklin were simply not religious in that sense; they did not use religion to explain the world, any more than most educated people today use religion to explain the world. But ordinary people did, and when they emerged into cultural, social, and political dominance in the early nineteenth century, they brought that religiosity with them, and that's what gives the nineteenth century such striking religious coloration.

• **You've quoted the Founders on their distress at the decline of secularism and rationalism.**
The ones who saw what was happening. Jefferson, for example, was very optimistic, as late as 1820 he thought that every person alive would eventually die a Unitarian. He saw the society becoming more like him, and he couldn't have been more wrong. The Founding Fathers were at most deists—they believed God created the world, then left it alone to run—but they were a very thin veneer on their society, and I think they misinterpreted what was going to happen. They certainly never intended to create the kind of evangelical Protestant world that emerged by the 1820s in the Second Great Awakening. This is true, I think, even for those who are always associated with Puritanism, like John Adams, for whom the Second Great Awakening was an unanticipated consequence, and for someone like Jefferson, for whom, when he finally caught on to what was happening, it was absolutely a horror show. It was just unbelievable; he could only blame the New England Puritan Federalists, who he decided had caused it all. This of course didn't help him explain the rise of evangelical Protestantism in Virginia.

• **And we're still the most religious of the industrial societies.**
I think that's because we are a society in which ordinary people continue to dominate the culture to a greater extent than in the societies of Western Europe. Our religiosity is a function of the democratic cast of our culture, which is, of course, the source of our vulgarity, our materialism, and all the other things that lots of people don't like about America.

• **No gentlemen, right?**
No gentlemen. And that's important. The whole phenomenon of the gentleman is important because it's about a lot more than just manners. The gentleman was not only somebody who knew how to behave but also somebody who knew how to rule. I think the idea of the gentleman and what happened to it is a fantastically interesting subject. The eighteenth century was the high point of the Anglo-American culture of the gentleman. It was a concept of increasing importance from the Renaissance on, and in the eighteenth century people were really wrestling with it. Jane Austen was fascinated with the subject; all her novels consider the definition of a proper gentleman. I think this examination was also occurring in the Colonies, where there was less and less emphasis on blood, family, wealth as being the proper measure of a gentleman and more on moral behavior, which made it possible for the Founders, who had by English aristocratic standards very little wealth and who could make very little appeal to the criterion of blood, to aspire to gentility.

• **What made someone qualify as a gentleman?**
A certain amount of wealth, giving one independence, was a prerequisite. Jane Austen, along with many other people, thought of a gentleman as someone who had, at a minimum, so many hundred pounds of income; Darcy had ten thousand pounds a year. Such an income would certainly constitute independence. Of course, you could not be a shopkeeper or manual laborer, but the more controversial question was, What is the relation of the professions to gentility? This was a period of transition in the ideal of gentility and the conception of the professions, but members of the professions were for the most part still regarded as primarily gentlemen, not as professionals. This is, of course, very confusing for historians, because we look at the period and notice growing numbers of lawyers and doctors, and we assume they're like modern professionals, but it's a mistake to anticipate the future.

Someone like Benjamin Rush was a doctor, but first he's a gentleman, then he practices medicine, and he doesn't practice the way a modern practitioner would. He's not at the hospital ten or twelve hours a day; he has a lot of time for doing the kinds of things that people in Jane Austen's world did, which is to visit and be genteel. And the same is true of lawyers. They're not working so many billable hours to get their salaries from their law firms; they are much more independent and leisured than that.

• **And you believe that the purpose of such leisure is to allow a gentleman to specialize in the art of ruling?**
That's the traditional view. Jefferson took it very seriously; so did Franklin. They felt they had a responsibility to devote themselves to philosophy, the arts, or public service. Now in the old order people were deferred to because they had power; they could command those who were in a condition of dependence and reward them with patronage, or wealth, or whatever. The Founding Fathers, despite their reputation for hardheaded realism, were naive enough to believe that the people would follow and obey them simply because they were more talented, and because they had been elected. They had tremendous confidence in elections; the people, having chosen them, would naturally follow their leadership.

We are indeed a materialistic capitalist society. That can be seen pejoratively, or it can be seen as a sign of equality. There's something peculiarly egalitarian about the cash nexus.

Those who doubted this became the Federalists as they emerged in the 1790s. John Adams is the archetype; his famous exchange with Jefferson late in

In a business allegory from an 1808 map of Philadelphia, the goddess Minerva, seated on Trade, instructs youth in navigation and commerce.

his life explored this issue. And I think Adams has the better of the argument. Jefferson remained a Pollyanna, naive about the sociology of democracy. Adams in effect said: "Don't kid yourself, Mr. Jefferson, the people who get elected aren't going to be the best and most talented. They're going to be the prettiest, the most handsome, the wealthiest, the people who can attract the attention of a television audience with the best sound bite." Jefferson remained committed to the revolutionary dream that talent would win out.

• **You talk about America as the first commercial society, a political order sustained by the new idea that men's calculations of their own economic interest constitute the sole social bond.**
That's why I think our revolution was so radical. Obviously commerce had existed from the beginning of history, and

so one gets into all kinds of arguments with people who will say, "Well, look, there was commerce already." But a commercial society doesn't mean merely one in which commerce occurs. In the North—the South remained closer to the eighteenth century, and I think this helps explain the sectional split—you have a society that increasingly comes to regard the business of America as business, buying and selling, with exchange for monetary gain as the basic adhesive of society. And it's that preoccupation that startled Tocqueville and everybody else who came here. Observers with traditional attitudes came and condemned, because the cash nexus is not supposed to be a nice way to tie people together. We are indeed a materialistic capitalist society.

That can be seen pejoratively, or it can be seen in another way, as a sign of

equality. There's something peculiarly egalitarian about the cash nexus. From the nineteenth century up to the present, we have come to regard the cash nexus as an unjust and wicked way to tie people together. But in the context of the old order the cash nexus was regarded as an egalitarian achievement, as a better way to connect people than through blood or patronage, who your father was or whom you married. It seemed better for a person to be assessed in terms of "What can I buy?" or "What can my money buy for me?"

• **Well, it certainly wasn't Jefferson's intent. How did the Revolution produce such a pure, expansive, inclusive commercial regime?**
It destroyed the older ties and discredited them in a way that has simply never happened in England. The Revolution made blood and patronage ties dishon-

orable in this new world. There were attempts made to construct new utopian arrangements, with varying degrees of success, but ultimately they weren't sufficient. What emerged to fill the vacuum, to tie people together, was commercial exchange, and this came about because this was what ordinary people were doing, and they thrived in this kind of environment. They didn't need justifications for relationships that the Founding Fathers might have needed. They certainly didn't feel the need for old-fashioned republican virtue; they simply wanted to get ahead, and pursue happiness. They took Jefferson's pursuit of happiness quite literally.

The way you do that is by making money. In that sense a commercial society is a victory for those very ordinary, self-interested people, the kinds of people who political philosophers from the beginning of time have said are ill equipped to run any government. They're too self-interested, too preoccupied with the pursuit of their private interests.

• **Interestedness plays a very big role in your book, and this brings us back to the gentleman. Gentlemen are by definition disinterested, and their disinterestedness is the justification for their political authority. The gentlemen remained a powerful force in every other European society; the old order survived. The American victory over the gentlemen was the least savage—we weren't guillotining them—but in some sense it's the most complete.**

Yes. Except in the South there was no traditional aristocracy left. And that's why there has never been a real working-class movement in America. Everybody claimed to work; everybody was saying, "Yes, I'm a workingman too." It was very difficult for a separate group of workingmen to establish their autonomy. There's no labor party that can develop when everybody says, "I'm a laborer." No socialist movement or workingman's movement can develop without the aristocracy at the other end to act as a foil. Now, obviously, the notion of disinterestedness doesn't die out entirely, and in fact it re-emerges later in the century, with members of the professions and academics and scientists coming to claim some of the disinterested qualities of gentlemen.

But the ideal was much diminished when compared with what had existed earlier. Interest seems to conquer all. That's what Tocqueville saw and that's what any outside observer would have seen, this dominance of interest in the culture. Many Americans would not have accepted this description of their society and would have been horrified by the notion that they were concerned only with interest.

But there was a realization that this was what democracy meant: the emergence of ordinary people who by definition have economic interest; that's what it means to have an occupation. To be a shoemaker or a businessman or a shopkeeper is to have an interest, and it's precisely because they aren't independent of the marketplace that they have these interests. In a democratic society these people are running the show, and they're bringing their interests with them; they can't shed them, they are inherent in their being businessmen. Nobody doubted that. Adam Smith understood it as well as anyone: These kinds of people do not make good legislators because they have private interests. That is why Smith always accepted the landed gentry's dominance in the House of Commons. They alone could be free of these kinds of interests.

Gentlemen don't have to exert themselves for their income. But anybody who worked for a living was going to have interests and was going to bring them into the political arena. Some sought to resist this by denying the reality. But others, like Madison, accepted the reality of interests. He said, in effect, "Well, that's the way it is, but we're going to deal with it by trying to keep these people out of political leadership by elevating and extending the national government." That was his solution, and it failed.

• **You're rather harsh on Madison. You certainly don't think much of his prophetic powers as a political theorist.**

Madison still conceived of public interest that transcends private interest, and in his Federalist Paper number ten he said, in effect, "Look, there are interests everywhere in society; I understand that. What we'd like to do is devise a political structure that will keep these interests from getting into government, or at least dominating government, and the way to do that is to expand the sphere of government so that these interests counteract one another and allow disinterested gentlemen to rule." His model was always religion; he understood that the secret of America's success in creating religious liberty and separating church and state, which is what allowed him and Jefferson and those other secular humanists or deists to run the show, was the fact that there were so many religious groups competing with one another that they negated one another, neutralized the state in religious matters, and allowed rationalist thinkers to predominate.

I think the intriguing person in all of this is Aaron Burr. Burr was the one aristocrat among the Founding Fathers who never made any claims for virtue. He was just a real American politician.

He hoped the same thing would happen in the larger sphere of interest-group politics. Let the interests collide and compete with one another in the society; let's erect a government on a national level that will be dominated by the likes of James Madison and Thomas Jefferson, people who were free of interest. I think he really saw himself as a disinterested person, capable of rising above narrow marketplace interests, and hoped to create a government that would be more or less dominated by his kind of person. Now it didn't work out quite like that, and I think that was part of the problem of the Federalists in the 1790s. There weren't enough James Madisons or Alexander Hamiltons or George Washingtons. There were too many Federalists who had interests to promote, even though they were presumably an aristocracy. They were an aristocracy caught up in interests.

I think the intriguing and revealing person in all of this is Aaron Burr. Burr was the one aristocrat among the Founding Fathers who never made any claims for virtue and had no visions of an America based on virtue and republican idealism. The explanation may be that he was a more authentic aristocrat who never needed to justify himself; his father was the second president of Princeton. He had as much aristocratic lineage as anybody in New England.

Burr never had the insecurity of the rest of the Founding Fathers, many of whom had to justify themselves in terms of achievement. In New York and even when he was Vice President, his behavior was very different from that of someone like Jefferson or John Adams. He was always writing letters to people promoting some kind of interest, trying to make money. He was an aristocrat, but he never had enough money to bring it off, and his correspondence is very revealing; it's full of "See if you can get a job for so-and-so. I owe him something. Burn this letter." You never find Thomas Jefferson saying, "Burn this letter." Burr sounds like a ward politician of the 1880s.

As a consequence he comes to be feared by both ends of the political spectrum. Both Hamilton and Jefferson fear Burr long before his ventures in the West. He's frightening to them because he's supposed to be the kind of person the Republic will need as a leader. He's a natural aristocrat, he has a Princeton education, he's got money, he's got all the pose and status of a gentleman, yet he's behaving in this interested way, conniving at land deals and banking deals in New York and persisting even when he gets to be Vice President. He had the gall to wonder if it would be possible for him to continue to practice law while he was Vice President. People talked about Hillary Clinton's continuing to practice law when her husband became President. Burr was actually hoping to practice law while Vice President. One of his confidants had to say to him, No, it's improper, you can't have the Vice President walking into court as an attorney; you would overawe the court.

What really scared his contemporaries, the real treason of Aaron Burr, is that he was a traitor to his class. They expected more from him. He had all the promise

of leadership, which is why he got elevated so quickly, first to the Senate and then to the Vice Presidency at a time when you had to be somebody to be Vice President. Think of who his predecessors were: Jefferson and Adams. Then there's Burr. He was expected to be one of the shining lights of the new Republic. He had a distinguished war record, he had everything going for him—looks, charm, extraordinary abilities—but he failed the test of disinterested leadership, and he scared the bejesus out of the other Founding Fathers.

And what was Burr? He was just an anticipation of a real American politician. Gore Vidal in his novel *Burr* makes him the natural father of Martin Van Buren. That's one of the invented sections of the book; there's no real evidence of that at all, though it was a scurrilous rumor at the time. But Vidal's

choice is interesting because Van Buren does emerge as the first great modern politician, still a gentleman, but a nineteenth-century version, a type simply unanticipated by the Founding Fathers, a victorious candidate who had done nothing notable to deserve office. He had written no great documents, he had won no battles, he had no great distinctions. But he had built the best political machine the country had ever seen. He was the most astute politician of his era and a great champion of the legitimacy of parties and interest groups in politics. There is a kind of spiritual tie between Burr and Van Buren, which Vidal hit upon.

• **You seem to suggest that self-interest is unchallengeable in American politics, that government can never stand above it but must merely accommodate as many interests as pos-**

LIBRARY COMPANY OF PHILADELPHIA

The apotheosis of commerce: a Philadelphia store ablaze with incentives, 1850s.

sible. And yet our politicians are always decrying "special interests."

Sure. That's our conventional rhetoric, and we continue to hope against hope that there is somebody out there who might stand above interests. One of the appeals of Perot is that he had so much money he would not be beholden to special interests. Perot in this sense has that independence that gentleman are supposed to possess in classical political theory. But when you get down to it, everybody has interests. Press them, and people say, "Well, I mean special interest . . . that other interest, not this one." There's a certain amount of fiction and incoherence that is involved in our rhetoric of "special interests."

• **But surely there is a persisting sense that the use of political power for economic purposes is illegitimate.**

I do agree that there is a dream of a leader out there who stands above interest. That persists in American life, and it accounts for our periodic election of military heroes and accounts as well for our anti-partyism, which continues right up to the present. We're seeing an indication of it in our systematic destruction of our political parties, most conspicuously in the weakening of the Democratic party over the last thirty years.

The liberal Republican movement, the Mugwump movement, and the Progressive movement were all anti-party. A party necessarily suggests interests; the term *party* does, after all, mean just that: taking a partial view. So despite our so-called acceptance of interests and parties, there's always been, perhaps as a consequence of the republican emphasis in the Founding Fathers' dream, a high level of rhetoric that condemns parties and interests, whether special or not.

• **Later in your book you argue that in the world created by the Revolution great disparities of wealth are not considered antithetical to a democratic order. But didn't the successive waves of American populism have a** strong and recurring hostility to concentrations of wealth—take the New Deal term *economic royalists,* for instance?

Sure. But what's extraordinary is the extent to which Americans have put up with and continue to put up with great disparities of wealth as long as they see the wealth as achieved. There's very little resentment of rich ballplayers and rock stars. In any event, I'm less concerned with what happened later than with explaining the 1820s and 1830s. Americans then clearly accepted—at least for a while—unprecedented disparities of wealth, disparities far greater than those of the eighteenth century, and nonetheless called their era the age of equality. This has led some historians to think that the first post-revolutionary generations misunderstood their own culture, that theirs was the age of the uncommon man, not the common man. I think the historians are wrong and the contemporaries were right when they called it the age of the common man, because differences of wealth are the least mortifying and least humiliating of the various ways in which people on top have made those on the bottom feel their inferiority. If you think about it a bit, that's true even today; if you're told that the reason you're inferior is your race or your bloodline or your father's ethnicity, that's not something you can do anything about. But if you're told that you're inferior because you haven't got as much money as someone else, that's something that you *can* theoretically do something about. To have wealth become the only source of distinction is to place only a weak social barrier between classes. That gave a lot of encouragement to a lot of ambitious people.

• **One of the great nineteenth-century hopes—it was John Stuart Mill's—is that people who are not used to exercising political power will get better at it by doing so; they will become** more rational. You don't put much stock in that, do you?

I suppose there may be some evidence here and there, but I don't have much confidence. I suppose you can work at educating people to be more disinterested; that's what a liberal arts education is supposed to be about. But I don't think it's working all that well, except perhaps in environmental matters. Not much suggests that we are becoming more disinterested.

Everybody's here. No race or nationality hasn't got somebody in the United States living as a citizen. It's extraordinary, and it's the product of our being so pure a commercial society.

• **Your book seems to say, Look, this is what we've got. This is a very stable commercial culture in its political habits, and there are some very lovely things and some rather nasty things about it.**

I think that's true. That's how I feel. I think we need to see all of the sides of what we've got. There are tawdry and unattractive sides, but American society is an extraordinary thing, now more than ever. We have a truly universal society; everybody's here. No race, nationality, or ethnic group hasn't got somebody in the United States living as a citizen. It's an extraordinary thing, and it is a product of our being so pure a commercial society without any particular claims of ethnicity or race. I think that every once in a while we ought to acknowledge that this democratic inclusiveness remains immensely impressive.

"Pvt. Robert Shurtleff": An Unusual Revolutionary War Soldier

by Kathleen Doyle

PRIVATE ROBERT SHURTLEFF HAD ALREADY survived two wounds while fighting in the War for Independence. Now serving in Philadelphia as a general's orderly, the Continental Army soldier had fallen victim to an epidemic of "malignant fever" that raged through the city.

At the hospital, Dr. Barnabas Binney, fearing Shurtleff dead, put his hand on the private's chest to check for a heartbeat. He discovered beneath the uniform a tightly wound bandage—and the reason for it: Robert Shurtleff was a woman!

"He" was actually Deborah Sampson, a nearly five-foot eight-inch, blue-eyed blonde with muscles hardened by years of farm work, who had created a *nom de guerre,* taking as a last name one that was common in her hometown of Plympton, Massachusetts.

Sampson ("Samson" was the original family name, with a "p" added later) was born December 17, 1760, from an ancestral line that included pilgrims John Alden, Priscilla Mullins, Miles Standish, Peter Hobart, and Governor William Bradford. Despite this admirable heritage, Jonathan Sampson, Jr., was a poor provider for his wife and seven children. Sampson's financial problems worsened as his family grew, and, when he found that his inheritance from his father's estate was smaller than expected, he turned to alcohol. Eventually he abandoned his family, never to be heard from again.

Poverty forced Sampson's deserted wife to send five-year-old Deborah to live with an elderly relative named Miss Fuller. Three years later Fuller died, and Deborah was placed in another home before being indentured at age ten to the family of Jeremiah Thomas, a deacon and farmer in Middleboro, Massachusetts.

Deborah worked the deacon's farm, but Thomas also gave her the opportunity to attend school. When her chores caused her to miss classes, the deacon's sons tutored her.

Deborah's indentured service ended in 1778. She remained with the Thomases for a while longer, supporting herself by raising some livestock, selling cloth she had spun and woven, and by teaching at the Middleboro school.

Apparently Deborah did not find such a life fulfilling. Nor did she look forward to the prospect of marriage to the man her mother had chosen for her. "I did not ... escape the addresses of a young man, of whom my mother, I believe, was passionately fond, and seemed struck with wonder that I was not," Deborah later wrote. " ... I had not her eyes to see such perfection in this lump of a man...."

So one night in the spring of 1781 or 1782 (historians debate the date), Deborah disappeared from Middleboro after changing into some men's clothes she'd made. She walked until she reached Bellingham, a town just north of the Rhode Island border. There, beardless, but with breasts bound and her hair pulled back in male fashion, she enlisted for a three-year term in the Fourth Massachusetts Regiment. After being mustered into service in Worcester, Massachusetts, Deborah and other recruits marched to West Point, New York, where they were issued arms and equipment.

Deborah served the Continental Army well. Among other battles, she fought in a skirmish with Tories along the Hudson River, receiving a sword cut to the left side of her head. The young woman soldier also incurred a bullet wound in the thigh when Tories ambushed part of her detachment at Eastchester, New York. Rather than risk discovery, Deborah cared for the wound herself until it healed. The injury troubled her for the rest of her life.

Deborah later swore she had been at the Battle of Yorktown in October 1791. But state records place her enlistment at

From *American History Illustrated,* October 1988, pp. 30-31. © 1988 by Cowles Magazines, Inc. Reprinted through the courtesy of Cowles Magazines, publishers of *American History Illustrated.*

a later date. Because federal records were lost in 1814 when the British burned several public buildings in Washington, D.C., historians may never know the facts.

Deborah's army days ended, however, after Dr. Binney discovered "Robert's" true identity. The physician kept the secret at first, but eventually exposed the deception and arranged for Sampson's honorable discharge in the autumn of 1783.

Deborah then headed for Stoughton, Massachusetts, where her uncle Zebulon Waters employed her on his farm. The former soldier continued to wear men's clothing until 1784 when she shifted to skirts, presumably because of her romance with farmer Benjamin Gannet. The couple married in early 1785.

Deborah and her husband settled in Sharon, Massachusetts, where they raised—with financial difficulty—three children. Partly because of poverty, Deborah in January 1792 petitioned Massachusetts for back pay for her service in the American Revolution. She declared that "being a Female, and not knowing the proper steps to be taken to get pay for her services, [she] has hitherto not receiv'd one farthing." Later

that month Massachusetts passed a resolution granting Deborah thirty-four pounds (then about $150), bearing interest from the day she was discharged.

Still in need of money, in 1797 Deborah worked with Herbert Mann on his fanciful biography of her, *The Female Review, or Memoirs of an American Young Lady*. Mann also encouraged her to lecture throughout New England and New York, which she did in 1802. She wore her soldier's uniform to each lecture and performed the manual of arms with her musket. Her speeches tended to moralize, but people went to see rather than hear her.

Additional assistance came in March 1805 when the former soldier was placed on the Massachusetts Invalid Pension Rolls under her married name, Deborah Gannet, at $48 a year. She later petitioned for and received benefits under a Congressional Act of 1818 that granted $8-per-month pensions to veterans who had served continuously for at least nine months and who relinquished all rights to state pensions.

Nevertheless, Deborah's financial situation remained pathetic. A few years before her April 29, 1827, death, the for-

mer soldier was asked to estimate the value of her possessions; she said all she owned was about $20 worth of clothes.

Infirm and poor, Benjamin Gannet found it necessary in 1831 to apply to have his late wife's pension continued. Six years later, on December 22, 1837, the Committee on Revolutionary Pensions recommended Gannet "be paid . . . the sum of eighty dollars per annum, commencing on the fourth day of March, one thousand eight hundred and thirty-one, for and during his natural life." But Gannet had already died in January of that year. So, in July 1838, Congress passed a Special Act for the relief of Deborah Gannet's heirs, awarding $466.66 to her three children.

In a final role reversal, the husband of the soldier-turned-wife-and-mother had set a precedent, becoming the first man granted a pension by the U.S. government for military service performed by his wife.

Kathleen Doyle is articles editor for American History Illustrated. *Her article about the centennial of golf in the U.S. appeared in the Summer 1988 issue.*

'It Is Not a Union'

Peter Onuf

Peter Onuf, 40, is associate professor of history at Worcester Polytechnic Institute. Born in New Haven, Connecticut, he received an A.B. (1967) and a Ph.D. (1973) from Johns Hopkins University. He is the Author of The Origins of the Federal Republic: Jurisdictional Controversies in the United States 1775–87 *(1983), and* Statehood and Union: A History of the Northwest Ordinance *(1987).*

When news of the Peace of Paris reached the United States in the spring of 1783, war-weary Americans marked the event with jubilant parades. In Philadelphia, a writer in the *Pennsylvania Gazette* pleaded with his fellow citizens to restrain their revels during the celebratory "illumination of the city." It was the end of seven long years of deprivation and sacrifice, and an occasion for much pride: The United States (with crucial help from France) had just bested the mightiest power on earth.

Patriots looked forward to a new epoch of prosperity and growth. In a Fourth of July oration in 1785, a prominent Boston minister named John Gardiner declared that "if we make a right use of our natural advantages, we soon must be a truly great and happy people." The hinterland would become "a world within ourselves, sufficient to produce whatever can contribute to the necessities and even the superfluities of life."

Many Americans shared Gardiner's optimism. Their land was inherently rich in natural resources, still barely exploited. Virtually all of its three million inhabitants (including some 600,000 black slaves) still lived within 100 miles of the Atlantic Ocean, in a band of settlement stretching some 1,200 miles from Maine to Georgia. In 1790, the first U.S. census would establish the nation's demographic center at a point 25 miles *east* of Baltimore. At the time of the Revolution, that Maryland city with a population of some 6,000, was the nation's fifth largest, behind Philadelphia (30,000), New York (22,000), Boston (16,000), and Charleston (14,000).

Directly or indirectly, city folk depended upon trade for their livelihood. Merchant ships set sail for Europe bearing wheat, corn, fur pelts, dried fish—or headed down the coast to pick up cargoes of tobacco, indigo, and rice from Southern plantations before crossing the Atlantic. They returned carrying calico, velvet, furniture, brandy, machinery, and often with new immigrants. Labor shortages in the cities pushed wages for servants, stevedores, and carpenters far higher than those prevailing in the cities of Europe. Many foreign visitors remarked on the new nation's general good fortune. "Nor have the rich the power of oppressing the less rich," said Thomas Cooper, a British scientist, "for poverty such as in Great Britain is almost unknown." (Such reports were not always reliable. One traveler wrote home about the amazing American Wakwak tree, with fruit that grew in the shape of a young woman.)

A CHRISTIAN SPARTA?

But the overwhelming majority of Americans—more than 90 percent—lived on farms. On a tract of 90 to 160 acres, the typical American farmer grew corn and other staples for home consumption, and raised chickens, pigs, and a dairy cow or two for his family with perhaps a few extra animals to be bartered in the village market. Visits to town were weekly events at best; anyone who journeyed more than 50 miles from home was probably heading west, leaving for good. People and news traveled slowly. It took about a month for a Philadelphia newspaper to reach Pittsburgh, then a crude frontier outpost 250 miles inland.

Despite the general sparsity of population, local crowding and worn-out cropland in New England produced growing numbers of migrants. They crossed the Appalachians over rough wagon trails to the frontier in western Pennsylvania and Virginia, or to the future states of Kentucky, Tennessee, and Ohio. Other settlers moved South, to Georgia and the Carolinas. And all during the 1780s modest numbers of new immigrants from Europe continued to arrive at East Coast ports, chiefly from Ireland, Scotland, and Germany.

And yet, despite the outward signs of economic vitality during the mid-1780s, there was a growing alarm among many of the new nation's leaders—men such as George Washington, John Jay, and Alexander Hamilton. The states, only loosely bound together under the Articles of Confederation of 1781, were constantly bickering over conflicting territorial claims beyond the Appalachians, and Congress was powerless to mediate. Near Wilkes-Barre, Pennsylvania militiamen had even opened fire on Connecticut settlers.

From *The Wilson Quarterly*, Spring 1987, pp. 97-103. © 1987 by the Woodrow Wilson International Center for Scholars. Reprinted by permission.

Spain and Great Britain were poised to take advantage of the frontier's "anarchy." To the north, British troops still garrisoned forts along the Great Lakes, a violation of the Treaty of Paris. To the south, the Spaniards, who held New Orleans and claimed all the lands west of the Mississippi, had closed the great river to American shipping below Natchez. King Charles III's officers were actively encouraging American settlers in Kentucky to break away from the Union and establish political and commercial relations with Spain.

Washington worried about the nation's fragmentation and decline into a state of degrading neocolonial dependency.

Washington and his allies worried less about America's outright conquest by a foreign power than the nation's fragmentation and decline into a state of degrading neocolonial dependency. A postwar consumer spree deepened that concern. Samuel Adams, the austere Bostonian, fretted that his countrymen's hunger for "luxury" goods imported from England—glassware, clocks, rugs—was "prostituting all our glory, as people." Few of his peers shared Adams's vision of a future America reigning as a virtuous "Christian Sparta," but they worried that the expensive imports would drain the nation of scarce hard currency and hinder the growth of domestic industry.

The states themselves were badly divided over these and other issues. The merchants, farmers, and fishermen of the North regarded the slave-owning plantation proprietors of the South with deep suspicion. Geographically and culturally, great distances separated them. Thomas Jefferson once drew up a list comparing the people of the two regions, describing Northerners as "chicaning," "jealous of their liberties and those of others," and "hypocritical in their religion." Southerners, he said,

were "candid," "zealous for their own liberties but trampling on those of others," and devoted only to the religion "of the heart."

Economic issues were also divisive. Many Northern traders and politicians were angered by British laws that banned American merchantmen from the lucrative trade with the British West Indies, involving the exchange of Southern tobacco and rice for Caribbean sugar, molasses, and rum. But the Southerners feared a Northern monopoly on that traffic more than they did the relatively benign British one. Pierce Butler, later a South Carolina delegate to the Federal Convention, declared that the interests of North and South were "as different as the interests of Russia and Turkey."

DO-NOTHING CONGRESS

None of these challenges would have proved insurmountable for a strong national government. But the Continental Congress, operating under the Articles of Confederation, was ineffective. The Confederation was but "a firm league of friendship," as the 1781 document put it, that left the states their "sovereignty, freedom and independence, and every Power, Jurisdiction and right" not expressly delegated to the Continental Congress.

Among the many powers left to the states was that of taxing the citizenry. Congress received its revenues by levies on the state governments—"a timid kind of recommendation from Congress to the States," as George Washington described it. If a state chose not to pay, as often happened, Congress could do nothing.

Not only did the Articles grant Congress few powers, but they made it difficult for the legislature to exercise those that it did possess. There was no real executive, only a largely ceremonial president of Congress. The congressmen voted by states (there was thus no fixed number of legislators), and most important measures required the assent of nine of the 13 states to become law. Substantive amendments of the Articles could be adopted only by a unanimous vote in Congress and by the state legislatures.

Every effort to strengthen the Confederation failed.

The history of the Articles themselves illustrates the difficulty of organizing concerted action by the states. A year after the Declaration of Independence, the Continental Congress, assembled in Philadelphia, had finally endorsed a draft of the Articles and sent it to the new state legislatures for ratification. Each of the ex-Colonies had strong objections, but, amid the pressures of wartime, they all swallowed their misgivings—except Maryland. It held out for four years, until March 1781. Meanwhile, the Continental Congress was forced to carry on the war effort without any constitutional authority. Laboring under enormous handicaps, it gave George Washington's beleaguered forces in the field little in the way of coherent support.

THE 'DOGS OF WAR'

By the mid-1780s, Congress was hard-pressed even to muster a quorum, and it suffered numerous indignities. In June 1783, after the Treaty of Paris, a band of mutinous soldiers surrounded the Pennsylvania State House in Philadelphia, where Congress was meeting, holding the legislators captive for a day. After the Pennsylvania authorities refused to call out the militia and restore order, the legislators decamped for Princeton, New Jersey, then moved to Annapolis, Maryland, before settling in New York City in 1785. The *Boston Evening Post* mocked the politicians for "not being stars of the *first* magnitude, but rather partaking of the nature of *inferior* luminaries, or *wandering* comets."

Victory, in short, had shredded many of the old wartime bonds. Without a common enemy to fight, Americans seemed incapable of preserving their Union. "Lycurgus," a pseudonymous writer in the *New Haven Gazette*, complained that the Union under the Articles "is not a union of sentiment;—it is not a union of interest;—it is not a union to be seen—or felt—or in any manner perceived."

Many local politicians—Congressman Melancton Smith of New York, Luther Martin of Maryland, George Mason of Virginia—dismissed such worries. The Antifederalists, as they were later called, believed that the preservation of republican liberties won by the Revolution depended on maintaining the sovereignty and independence of the states. They held, with Montesquieu, the great French *philosophe,* that republican government could survive only in small countries, where citizens could be intimately involved in politics. Maryland planter John Francis Mercer spoke for the Antifederalists when he declared that he was "persuaded that the People of so large a Continent, so different in Interests, so distinct in habits," could not be adequately represented in a single legislature.

The weakness of the central government handicapped American diplomats.

With some justice, the Antifederalists could also claim that the states were managing quite well. Their citizens enjoyed the benefits of the most progressive constitutions the world had ever known and, by and large, they were prospering. Patrick Henry dismissed all the talk of trouble in the land. Had *Virginia* suffered, he asked?

But Washington, Virginia's James Madison, and other advocates of an "energetic" central government warned that the 13 states would not survive for long on their own, at least not as republics. These nationalists (later called Federalists) viewed the growing power of the states as a threat to peace. The state governments had begun to fill the vacuum left by Congress, adopting their own commercial policies, ignoring national treaties, and, at the behest of wealthy citizens who feared that they would never otherwise be repaid, even assuming some debts incurred by Congress. The nationalists feared that increasing conflicts among the states would un-

leash what the Old Dominion's Edmund Randolph called the "dogs of war."

WHISPERING REASON

Such warnings were not easily dismissed. In New York, Governor George Clinton was enriching the state treasury by taxing merchandise shipped through New York between New Jersey and Connecticut. Feelings ran so high that Congressman Nathaniel Gorham of Massachusetts worried that "bloodshed would very quickly be the consequence."

The weakness of the central government handicapped America diplomats. Britain had refused to abandon its outposts on U.S. soil, arguing (correctly) that Congress had failed to enforce some of *its* obligations under the Treaty of Paris, namely guarantees that prewar debts owed to British creditors would be repaid and that American loyalists would be reimbursed for their confiscated property.* Several states had simply ignored these provisions.

On the frontier, the threats from foreign powers were a constant worry. Rufus King, a Massachusetts congressman, observed that if the nation's disputes with Spain over the Mississippi and other matters were not settled, "we shall be obliged either wholly to give up the western settlers, or join *them* in an issue of force with the Catholic king." Both prospects, he concluded, were unthinkable.

More troubling still to the nationalists were the activities of the American frontiersmen themselves. From the Maine District of Massachusetts to western North Carolina, various separatists since the time of the Revolution had been petitioning Congress for admission to the Union as new states. But the older states refused to relinquish their claims. Vermont, legally a part of New York, was the most durable—and dangerous—of these rebellious territories. Rebuffed by Congress during the Revolution, the Vermonters, led by a group including Governor Thomas Chittenden and Ethan Allen, hero of the Green Mountain Boys, had entered into not-so-secret negotiations with London to rejoin the British empire.

The nationalists were dismayed when these talks resumed in 1786. Washington wrote that the Vermonters might "become a sore thorn in our sides," adding, "the western settlements without good and wise management . . . may be equally troublesome."**

The Westerners, in Kentucky and Tennessee, were understandably frustrated by the weakness of the central government. Chief among their complaints was the absence of congressional help in fending off constant attacks by marauding Indians, often instigated by the British and the Spaniards. Nor could the state governments, they argued, effectively govern distant territories. "Nature has separated us," wrote Judge David Campbell of the would-be state of Franklin in western North Carolina. The frontiersmen's anger grew during 1786 and 1787 as rumors circulated that Congress was negotiating with Spain, offering to relinquish American claims to free navigation of the Mississippi in exchange for trade advantages. (These suspicions were justified, but the talks collapsed.) Kentucky's General James Wilkinson and other Westerners talked openly about leaving the Union and forming alliances with the Old World.

A RAT AND A GAMBLE

All of the nationalists' apprehensions were dramatized by a shock in the summer of 1786: the outbreak of Shays's Rebellion.

The rebels were farmers in economically depressed western Massachusetts who faced ruinous new state taxes imposed to help retire the state's wartime debt. As distress turned to anger, Captain Daniel Shays, a veteran of the Revolution, emerged as the leader of a ragtag mob that gathered to close down the Massachusetts courthouses that oversaw farm foreclosures and sent debtors to jail.

Thomas Jefferson, serving abroad as the American minister to France, was

---

*During the Revolution, some 100,000 Loyalists fled to Britain, Canada, and the British West Indies. Many of the exiles were well-to-do farmers or merchants, and they claimed to have left behind more than $40 million worth of property, which the state governments seized.
**Vermont finally gained statehood in 1791.

unperturbed. "I like a little rebellion now and then," he wrote to Abigail Adams. "It is like a storm in the Atmosphere." But in the United States, the uprising could not be so airily dismissed. It sparked the first general alarm about the future of the Union. "I never saw so great a change in the public mind," observed Boston merchant Stephen Higginson that autumn.

Word of the insurrection spread quickly. In Annapolis, Maryland, the news came during the first week of September, just as delegates from five states were meeting to discuss the condition of the Confederation's commerce. Among them were two of the country's most ardent nationalists—James Madison and New York's Alexander Hamilton—who were desperately seeking ways to strengthen the central government.

The stage for the Annapolis Convention had been set two years earlier at Mount Vernon, at a meeting hosted by George Washington. There, in March 1785, commissioners from Virginia and Maryland had met to resolve their disputes over tolls and fishing rights on the Potomac River. The success of the meeting led the two state legislatures to call for a larger meeting of all the states, to be held at Annapolis, to consider granting Congress broader powers to regulate interstate commerce.

The Annapolis Convention was a failure. Eight of the 13 states sent no representatives. More out of desperation than careful forethought, Hamilton and Madison proposed yet another meeting to consider strengthening the Confederation, to be held in Philadelphia in May 1787.

So clear to the Annapolis delegates was the case for reform that they might well have agreed to the Philadelphia meeting even without the shocking news from Massachusetts. The six-month rebellion was effectively ended in January 1787, in a battle near the federal armory at Springfield. Four Shaysites lost their lives. But the insurrection had already persuaded many state and local leaders to put aside their doubts about the need for a stronger central government.

In February 1787, after several states had already elected delegates to the Philadelphia Convention, the Continental Congress in New York City endorsed the gathering, with the stipulation (added at the insistence of Massachusetts) that it meet "for the sole and express purpose of revising the Articles of Confederation."

Patrick Henry, the fierce opponent of a stronger Union, had already declined to be a delegate from Virginia, declaring that he "smelt a rat." Indeed, few of the American political leaders who recognized the need for reform harbored any illusions about merely patching up the Confederation. They did not know what would happen at Philadelphia, or even if, like the Annapolis meeting, it would prove to be a failure, but they were now prepared to gamble. As Madison put it one month before the Federal Convention, the hurdles confronting any reform were so great that they "would inspire despair in any case where the alternative was less formidable."

Constitutional Convention, Philadelphia, 1787:

...by the Unanimous Consent of the States

*'Something must be done, or we shall disappoint
not only America, but the whole world.'*

Elbridge Gerry

By Ezra Bowen

The author, Ezra Bowen, a Senior Writer at Time *magazine, is the son of historian Catherine Drinker Bowen.*

On Wednesday, June 27, a muggy afternoon pressed down upon Philadelphia. It was the summer of 1787. Flies droned through the high-ceilinged room of the State House where more than 40 Convention delegates from the quarrelsome American confederation of states, the New England men sweltering in their woolen suits, braced for yet another round of contention. They got it, this time from Maryland's Luther Martin, who enhanced a reputation for tiresome bombast with a three-hour speech. His subject was the rights of the thirteen sovereign states with which this Convention, said he ad infinitum, had neither legal power nor fair reason to tamper.

Already restive from five weeks of debate, his listeners could hardly bear it: Oliver Ellsworth of Connecticut later chided Martin, saying that the speech "might have continued two months, but for those marks of fatigue and disgust ... strongly expressed on whichever side of the house you turned your mortified eyes."

Two days later brilliant Alexander Hamilton, one of the men who at various times left the Convention to return or not, walked out. He might come back, he said, but only if persuaded it would not be a "mere waste of time." Hamilton's position was clear. His discourses, described by some as "logic on fire," presented the case for strong, central government—a near kin to the British monarchy, in fact—that the states felt most threatening.

And as it happened, Hamilton's vote didn't matter much to the Convention just then. He was one of three New York delegates and the other two hated the idea of federal government. Since Convention rules permitted each state only a single vote, they steadily overrode him. But soon it would be very much worth Hamilton's while to return. For during the first two weeks in July the proceedings dramatically neared complete collapse. And then, perhaps frightened by the possibility of total failure, the Convention finally hammered out a deal that not only held the delegates to the end but ultimately produced a daring blueprint for a federal constitution. It would, in time, substantially govern the most powerful nation on Earth.

From the viewpoint of high statesmanship, the pressure for compromise was strong. All the delegates knew they were laboring under the critical eye of history in the cause of as yet untried liberties. "What a triumph for our enemies. ... to find that we are incapable of governing ourselves," George Washington wrote, "and that systems founded on the basis of equal liberty are merely ideal and fallacious." No delegate doubted that stronger government of some sort was needed to replace the toothless Articles of Confederation. After the Revolution, national authority had become almost a joke. The Congress had no real power to tax, regulate commerce, enforce foreign treaties; and criminals who crossed state lines were likely to go scot-free, since extradition was almost unheard of.

Worse still, the beggar government had gone virtually broke. Seven of the states, and the Congress as well, had been churning out paper money until, as pamphleteer Tom Paine once memorably put it, their paper was worth less than hobnails and wampum. Delegates to the Philadelphia Convention, some of whom had to ride or sail as much as 600 miles through spring mud or tides

From *Smithsonian*, July 1987. © 1987 by Ezra Bowen. Reprinted by permission.

to get there, were obliged to change money into Pennsylvania shillings, the local coinage, as though entering a foreign country. Shipping states in the North wanted more laws to help them compete for world commerce against cut-rate British cargo rates. But most of the agricultural South was opposed to any protective ordinance that would drive up costs for its comfortable export trade in tobacco, indigo and rice.

Division and danger were everywhere. Beyond their economic squeeze the British were still a clear potential threat to American nationhood. The Union Jack still flew over the western posts where fur traders gathered pelts for London glove and hat makers. Former ally France desperately wanted to collect its wartime loans. Spain, another wartime friend, still controlled Florida, and was conniving for control of trade in the wild, fast-growing western reaches that stretched to the Mississippi, America's border under the terms of the 1783 Treaty of Paris. Spain had closed the Mississippi to American trade at New Orleans, and the river was the only shipping route from much of the western wilderness. Indeed, Georgia, which claimed land running from Savannah clear to the Mississippi, had just declared martial law in fear of Indians and Spaniards.

For more than a decade settlers had been flooding west over the mountains. Since early February 1787 alone, more than 1,000 flatboats had headed west on the Ohio carrying 18,000 pioneers, with 12,000 horses, cattle and sheep. These rude frontiersmen did not see eye to eye with the rich planters of Virginia or with the Eastern seaboard traders of New York, Philadelphia and Boston. Not at all. Would these immigrants to the west form into new states or, God forbid, new countries under the protection of some foreign power? If as states, would their votes be equal to those of the original thirteen? Would, say, Virginia's laws and contracts under the Confederation hold up in a separate, sovereign Kentucky, or separate, sovereign anywhere else, such as "Transylvania," part of what is now Kentucky and Tennessee, to name just one other would-be western state then

taking shape? And might these new states hold slaves or be free? "I dread the cold and sower temper of the back countries," said peg-legged, urbane lawyer and Pennsylvania delegate Gouverneur Morris, sounding very like any sober Briton contemplating the surly, separatist mood of colonial immigrants 15 years earlier.

Here was a set of time bombs that a young nation with huge, unorganized territories, whatever government it chose, must try to defuse as quickly as possible.

Some central control was crucial, but how much would be enough and yet not too much? Fear of an executive, or any central government for that matter, was strong in most delegates. They had fought for more than six years to throw off the distant, and not too onerous, rule of George III and his ministry. That helped explain both the toothlessness of the Articles of Confederation, and why they now defined each former colony represented at this Convention as a "sovereign and independent" state. James Madison, idealistic, politically relentless, the man who more than any other had brought the Convention into existence, spoke for all of them when he observed that "all men having power ought to be distrusted to a certain degree."

Almost as much, though, they feared the tyranny of the majority, any majority. And they knew that earlier attempts at creating anything like a democratic republic had failed. They had it from the much-admired Montesquieu, the world's leading authority on stable government, that democracies were unstable, that anything like a large republic was impossible to govern. Trying to regulate so vast and diverse a land as the United States (if there ever were to be a United States), as one Yankee wit put it, would be a bit like attempting "to rule Hell by prayer."

Besides, the small states wanted to know, what would happen to them when they were at the mercy of their large and populous neighbors? The same was true of the Southern states vis-à-vis the North. Beyond that lay the question of slavery, mentioned by name at the Convention as little as possible because the

delegates knew from the beginning that confrontation over it might wreck any chance they had of agreeing on *any* effective central power. They were there, after all, not to abolish slavery but to shape, against great odds, a stable government that could maintain democratic order as freedom evolved. Though slavery's existence contradicted the terms of the Declaration of Independence they did not seriously discuss abolition. However hotly individual delegates might inveigh against it, slavery was still legally practiced in all but one of the sovereign states; the obnoxious slave trade itself had been outlawed, or sharply discouraged, by only seven. Every delegate understood that slaves were legally private property and, in the South, worth millions. Every delegate understood that under English common law, the protection of property had served as the foundation of all political rights.

Yet at first the Convention moved swiftly, far faster than anyone had expected. Even when disagreements and contentious vote taking occurred (over the course of nearly four months there would be more than 569 votes taken), the proceedings, early on at least, did not bog down.

Mostly this was due to the advance lobbying and planning of Madison, a Virginia planter by birth, but by trade perhaps the most farsighted and perceptive politician and political analyst alive. From 1780 to 1783 he served as a hardworking delegate in the Continental Congress, and from bitter experience while confronting petty state rivalry as he tried to get the states to pay for the war against Britain, Madison had come to the conclusion that the country might not survive at all without a drastic change in the "partition of power" between the states and the nation. To save the tottering Union he had studied past attempts at democracy; made himself an expert economist; helped enlist the reluctant Washington's support for this Convention; and nurtured an outline, condensed into 15 "resolves," officially known as the Virginia Plan, for totally overhauling the Articles of Confederation.

Madison was small, some said no more than five feet tall, with a voice that could scarcely carry across a crowded room. So a friend and fellow Virginian, Edmund Randolph, was chosen to speak for the resolves—to be, as Madison later put it, the "organ on the occasion." Six feet tall, handsome, a man "of distinguished talents, and in the habit of public speaking," Randolph was already, at 33, the Governor of Virginia, the most important state for any such Convention, being as it was both large and at the same time Southern and agricultural and so able to influence states least likely to favor strong central government. Hardly had the Convention opened than Randolph had the floor, and variously shocked and delighted the delegates with Madison's distilled ideas.

The rough structure of what Madison (and Randolph) urged is familiar to us today—indeed, at the time, six of the states had constitutions roughly similar in shape. A government divided into three parts: executive, legislative and judicial, variously elected and appointed. And as a rough form the Convention swiftly agreed to it. Easy passage was also given to the idea of a bicameral legislature, a fixture everywhere but Georgia and Pennsylvania. The Virginia Plan's provision for popular election of the lower house also was accepted, though it would come up again for bitter dispute. So, in fact, would virtually everything else. The real trouble, though, lay in the proposals for what sort of power each house would have, and on what numerical (and voting) basis representatives would be chosen.

"An individual independence of the States," Madison had written, "is utterly irreconcilable. . . . Let national Government be armed with positive and complete authority." He wanted to extend his "national supremacy" to the judiciary as well, and noted that in order "to give the new system its proper energy," all this executive power should be "ratified by the authority of the people."

The words "national" and "supreme" exploded through the hall when Randolph read them, imperiling sacred creeds. During the war with Britain, New Jersey troops had refused to swear allegiance to the Confederation, declaring "New Jersey is our country." New York delegate John Lansing, dead set against a new constitution anyway, promptly

scalded this "triple-headed monster, as deep and wicked a conspiracy as ever was invented in the darkest ages against the liberties of a free people." Rising to challenge Randolph, South Carolina's Charles Pinckney, a dandy and later a Congressman, demanded: I wish to know if you "mean to abolish the State Governments altogether."

With characteristic mildness and courtesy, Randolph explained that he had merely "meant to introduce" some general propositions. And indeed, to others, this nationalist concept seemed exactly what anarchic America needed. Among them, Pennsylvania's James Wilson declared: "We must bury all local interests and distinctions."

The Convention might have broken down right there, except for two procedural devices that the delegates wisely adopted. The first was that no vote on any matter would be binding until a final vote was taken on a full, finished text of the Constitution. That way, no delegate would feel he was being pressured, and collectively, with a chance to reflect and reexamine, they all might produce a better document to place before the judgment of their countrymen.

Through another bit of cautious wisdom, they decided to keep the debates secret. Thomas Jefferson, in France as American Minister, protested in a letter "so abominable a precedent," yet not a single delegate objected. Guards were posted every day at the door. And at one point Washington, who hardly spoke in his role as President of the Convention, rose with a piece of paper in his hand. It was, he said sternly, a copy of their proceedings someone had dropped on the State House floor. If the newspapers ever got hold of such documents, the General scolded, their revelations could "disturb the public repose by premature speculations. I know not whose Paper it is," he continued, "but there it is." He tossed the paper on a table with the comment "let him who owns it take it," then bowed and walked out.

"It is something remarkable," delegate William Pierce of Georgia recalled, "that no Person ever owned that Paper."

As a result of what was essentially a gentleman's agreement about tight secu-

rity, no one but the delegates really knew what was said in the hall until 53 years later when Madison's widow released the meticulous notes he had copied out each night, a record of the debate that, translated into direct dialogue, has been used ever since in dramatic accounts of the Convention. Madison was convinced to the end that secrecy had given delegates freedom to speak with nearly complete candor, and even to change their minds, often several times, as they never would have done if each word had been shared with the press or with their volatile constituencies. "If the debates had been public," Madison later wrote, "no constitution would ever have been adopted."

Indeed the public might have erupted early over some of the arguments about the power and structure of the proposed executive branch. When Wilson put forward a motion for a single President, even Randolph boggled; he preferred an executive council. Of special concern, too, was the proposition that the President have veto power over laws written by the proposed National Legislature. "But why might not a Catiline or a Cromwell arise in this Country as well as in others?" South Carolina's Pierce Butler wanted to know. George Mason spoke darkly about "hereditary Monarchy."

Benjamin Franklin was worried too. Pennsylvania, after all, had an 11-man Executive Council. But everyone knew that if a national government were devised, George Washington would be elected the first President of the United States. They knew, too, that he had once been offered virtual dictatorship of the troubled country and steadfastly refused. With that in mind, though still distrustful of human nature, Franklin concluded, "The first man put at the helm will be a good one," but then added, "Nobody knows what sort may come afterwards." It took 60 different votes before the Convention finally agreed to a single President with a legislative veto—albeit a veto that two-thirds of the Congress could, as it still can, override.

Many men who arrived in Philadelphia fearful of executive power, and seeing states' rights as the best bulwark against an overreaching central government with a tendency to fall under the control of powerful interests, were impressed by Madison's reassurances. In a startling speech that contradicted Montesquieu's political theories, Madison refuted the argument that huge size and a large, diverse population were a hazard to stable democratic government. Quite the reverse. The unified Virginia Plan, he said, would so "enlarge the sphere and thereby divide the community into so great a number of interests ... that ... a majority will not be likely at the same moment to have a common interest ... and ... in case they should have such an interest, they may not be apt to unite in the pursuit of it."

Numerous standards were put forward as qualifications for serving as a national senator or representative. Many remain in the Constitution today. One that does not is the possession of property. If a man held property, it was estimated, the more substantial a citizen his interest would make him; he was likely to have a thoughtful, sober stake in stable government. After all, the delegates in the State House were mostly lawyers, bankers, merchants or plantation owners. Twenty-one of them had fought in the Revolution, 24 had served in the Continental Congress and, together with the leading figures from smaller states, they felt they had created the nation.

In June, debate began more and more to home in on the question over which the Convention soon almost foundered. Not only who would elect the representatives to the National Legislature, whatever their quality, but above all, how those representatives might be apportioned. According to the steadily evolving Virginia Plan, members of the first house (what we now call the House of Representatives) were to be chosen by the people for terms of three years.

For the other house (or Senate) representatives were to be chosen by the state legislatures for seven years. The aim was to create a lower house directly answerable to the people on a short-term basis, balanced by a less volatile, more elite body (a "House of Lords," opponents were to brand it) that did not need to worry about quick, popular complaint. Representation in both chambers would be portioned out

roughly according to the number of people in each state, the slaves included, but with each slave to be counted as three-fifths of a person—a bizarre bit of arithmetic that the Continental Congress had first settled on in 1783.

Many delegates were still a long way from swallowing such a radical direct-election principle. "[I am] opposed to the election by the people," said Roger Sherman of Connecticut bluntly. A lean, sharp-nosed man, "cunning as the devil" (even his friends put it that way), Sherman was born poor but had risen by shrewd industry as a farmer and lawyer. The people, he continued, "want information and are constantly liable to be misled." Delaware's John Dickinson scornfully defined the people as "those multitudes without property and without principle, with which our Country like all others, will in time abound."

Present-day politicians would not dare say such things, even if they believed them. But in 1787 these views were widespread. The debates were secret, and to many men interested in stable government they seemed the essence of common sense. It was a time, after all, when not a single government in the world received its power directly from the people; two years later, in the name of "the people," the uncontrolled power of the mob in France would eventually lead to a bloodbath, followed by an emperor. Elbridge Gerry, the man who would one day give his name to the word gerrymander, had been a firebrand during America's struggle against George III. Now, he told the delegates, he was convinced that "The evils we experience flow from the excess of democracy."

Many delegates disagreed. Whatever they may have felt about the mob, it was clear to them that the power of any just government must derive from the people, however much they and all other contending political forces needed to be hedged around with checks and balances. Along with Madison, one apparently surprising proponent of power to the people turned out to be James Wilson of Philadelphia, a rich businessman and lawyer to the monied interests, including, during the

Revolution, men accused of still being loyal to George III. George Mason of Virginia was another. Born to the privilege and responsibility of a 5,000-acre plantation, with more slaves than any delegate, he not only espoused abolition but now observed that since the "people will be represented; they ought therefore to choose the Representatives."

Gouverneur Morris, of course, disagreed. Other tempers were rising, along with the thermometer, as delegates fixed on points of conflict. Gunning Bedford of Delaware continued to denounce population-based representation as disastrous to the interest of small states. Virginia's population of 750,000 was almost 13 times that of Delaware; Pennsylvania, second largest of the original thirteen, had 430,000. How could the rights of a small state survive in such a government? "It seems as if Pennsylvania and Virginia ... wished to provide a system in which they would have an enormous and monstrous influence," Bedford asserted. And later he thundered at the large-state delegates, "*I do not, gentlemen, trust you.*"

But the Delaware delegate really jolted the Convention when he said, the "small [states] will find some foreign ally of more honor and good faith, who will take them by the hand and do them justice."

This dangerous turn in the arguments, raising the specter of a separate American confederacy under the thumb of Britain, Spain or France, brought the proceedings to their most desperate impasse. Madison said that the small states could depart if so inclined; they would have to join later, anyway. Wilson, equally out of patience, derided states, large and small, as "imaginary creatures," divisive, obsolescent. George Read, of Bedford's own delegation, grandly declared, "The State Governments must be swept away."

Small wonder, in the face of such wrangling, that delegates were all but ready to give up. Hamilton's conscience later brought him back. Mason, who stayed through to the end, declared that if he were doing this for money, a thousand pounds a day would not be enough pay. Even George Washington admitted, "I *almost* despair of seeing a favourable issue to the proceedings of the Convention, and do therefore repent having had any agency in the business."

Yet those days in early July, the worst times for the delegates, turned out to be the best times for the future United States of America. From them came a political compromise that saved the Convention and led to a Constitution that could be presented to the country with more than a fighting chance of ratification.

As the hot words flew, and proposals and counterproposals were voted on, one of the blows struck in the direction of possible compromise came from an unexpected quarter, Roger Sherman, who seemed to be changing his mind about the direct vote of the people.

According to Madison's notes, "Mr. Sherman proposed that the proportion of suffrage in the 1st branch should be according to the respective number of free inhabitants [a clear advantage for the large states]; and that in the second branch or Senate, each State should have one vote and no more." Thus could small states retain power beyond the size of their electorates. Like most useful ideas, the one Sherman presented was both simple and functional. But like all compromises it contained elements that each major faction—small states, large states, nationalists and states-righters—regarded either as imperfect or outright distasteful.

Also proposed by John Dickinson of Delaware and Oliver Ellsworth of Connecticut, the compromise was voted down. But the idea that "in *one* branch the *people,* ought to be represented; in the *other,* the *States*" did not disappear. Wilson and most other nationalists still wanted as little significant residue of state sovereignty as possible. Some delegates were outraged by the very idea that, say, tiny Rhode Island, which had boycotted the Convention and had been heavily engaged in smuggling before the Revolution, could vote with the august weight of Virginia or Massachusetts.

Like Wilson and Read, Madison was out of patience with state rivalries and petty fears of being dominated by neighbors. Such things seemed likely to destroy the dream of shaping the birth of a great republic. In his direct and prescient way he now let the delegates know where the real historic peril lay. "The great danger to our general government," said Madison, "is the great southern and northern interests of the continent being opposed to each other." The states, he also pointed out, are "divided into different interests not by their difference of size . . . but principally from their having or not having slaves."

It was true. Even with the help of a three-fifths count on slaves, if a National Congress based on proportional representation were put together right now, the North would have 31 votes to 25 for the South. Furthermore, during the same summer up in New York, the Confederation Congress was trying to put the finishing touches on an ordinance for the newly won Northwest Territories (previously claimed by Virginia, among others, and extending to the headwaters of the Mississippi) by which slavery was forbidden, currently and in the future, when these territories might become states.

Pierce Butler of South Carolina now offered an astonishing proposal—to add to the South's voting power by counting slaves equally with whites in apportioning the number of national delegates each state had. Gouverneur Morris riposted that Pennsylvanians, anyway, would not stand for "being put on a footing with slaves." Crusty Elbridge Gerry had already observed that property should not be involved in rules for political representation. Otherwise why should not horses and cattle in the North, like slaves in the South, count toward voting totals.

As the floor debate sank to the level of bitter farce, Wilson turned the discussion skillfully, in a slightly different direction. He spoke of taxation, but, as had been proposed earlier, taxation used as a way of measuring voting powers. Taxes came from property. Slaves were property. America had been founded on the principle that there be no taxation without representation.

The argument moved the debate forward. Delegates began working on various ratios whereby representatives of the South in the legislature would not be at the immediate mercy of the North. They sought ways of expanding the number of representatives in the future so as to preserve political balance as the country grew—and populous western states came in. And it was, indeed, this vision of a threatening future, when the large and powerful Eastern states might find themselves in the minority, that made them see there was merit in having at least one house in which all states had the same number of representatives regardless of population.

And at last, with the main issue so clearly defined, but with the regional voting blocks now slightly divided among themselves, the Convention gained momentum once more under the rising banner of compromise. When the strongest nationalists, including Madison and Wilson, clung to their objections about the proposed arrangement for the Senate, delegates thought of something Ben Franklin, ever the conciliator, had raised earlier—an idea made to order for propertied men. Why not have the first house control all money bills?

For the populous states this appeared to be a nice trade-off—dollars, and the power of appropriating public funds, against a loss of political clout in the Senate—and it became part of a package that was moving toward a floor vote.

Madison still did not like it. The dispute "ended in the compromise," Madison later wrote Jefferson, "but very much to the dissatisfaction of several members from the large States." The deal left the national government far weaker than Hamilton would have wanted, too, but he took a non-utopian view. It was not hard, he would suggest, to choose "between anarchy and Convulsion on one side," and the chance of good on the other. South Carolina's John Rutledge eventually voiced the changing mood toward accommodation when, noting that the delegates could not do what they all thought best, he added, "we ought to do something."

And they did. On Monday, July 16, by the narrow vote of five states to four, with one state divided, the Convention passed the Connecticut delegation's much-amended measure, which would soon become known as the Great Compromise. A strong, central government had been agreed upon, but the small states were protected from the large in the Senate, while in the House, the South, with slaves counted as part of population, could not easily be overborne by the North. It was clear that no other arrangement would be acceptable to a majority. Even so, Madison was openly angry. He had always insisted the supremacy of the central government in the proposed federation must be unequivocal. Beyond that the idea of Delaware as Virginia's equal in the Senate seemed antirepublican to him. But what could he do? The very fact of the Compromise seemed to prove his perception that in an enormous country only the free play of diverse and contending interests could lead to an acceptably balanced decision.

As a final concession, Southerners agreed that, after 1808, the slave trade could be prohibited by Congress. Sherman had noted that the "abolition of slavery seemed to be going on in the United States, and that the good sense of the several States would probably by degrees compleat it." Some conscience-troubled northern Southerns, like Washington, who hated slavery but lived off its production, agreed. They hoped that in 20 years the practice might fade away, a hope made somewhat more reasonable to them because their kind of mixed farming depended less on slaves than did the deep South's. Southerners may have been somewhat reassured by a clause in the Northwest Ordinances mandating the return of fugitive slaves who entered free territory.

Two more exhausting months would pass before their work was finished, but after July 16 the delegates were clearly minded to get the job done. Members of the House, they agreed, would serve two years, not three. There would be two Senators per state, with six-year terms. And they would, indeed, be elected by the state legislators. It was not until 1913 that the 17th Amendment conveyed their election directly to the people.

Though the Convention established a national judiciary, it never gave the courts specific authority to review legislative acts, or to strike them down as unconstitutional. That famous precedent was set in 1803, with the celebrated Marbury v. Madison case, when archfederalist John Marshall, Chief Justice during the presidency of anti-federalist Thomas Jefferson, broadly interpreted the new Constitution's breadth and power by declaring an act of Congress unconstitutional. So doing, he balanced for all time the three branches of government. He also opened the debate that rages today on how far judges may properly go in interpreting the original text and intent of the Constitution.

In 1787 some delegates believed they had done well to lay down broad principles rather than an interminable list of strict instructions. Others felt the document they were completing was far too vague and would fail to be ratified. "I'll be hanged if ever the people of Maryland agree to it," declared Luther Martin.

Martin had company. George Mason had become seriously alienated. Now at the eleventh hour he chose to ask why the document had no Bill of Rights. Mason was the spokesman on the point, though he surely had taken his sweet time about bringing it up. He would sooner chop off his right hand, Mason said, "than put it to the Constitution as it now stands." If some things were not changed or added, he wanted "to bring the whole subject before another general Convention." Eager to be finished, the other delegates disagreed and the Convention hurried on.

On September 17, 1787, the day the document was signed, Gouverneur Morris, a master of style to whom the final polishing of prose had been assigned, listened proudly as the finished work was read aloud to the 41 delegates who had stayed for the last act. It began with the ringing phrase, "We the People." With Franklin's special blessing, Morris had also fashioned a particular ending to the Constitution: "Done in Convention by the Unanimous Consent of the States present this Seventeenth Day of September."

It was a neat device, with a double purpose. Once signed, the Constitution would go to the Congress and then to state ratifying conventions. To carry the country, it needed all the help it could get and preferably should emerge from the State House with unanimous approval. For, as one Philadelphian, not in the Convention but clearly in the know, had lately noted, "no sooner will the chicken be hatch'd, but every one will be for plucking a feather." Franklin hoped the insertion of the words "the States" would keep the bird whole. As state delegates, he purred, gentlemen could approve the Constitution with their signatures while as individuals they retained personal reservations.

The artful measure nearly succeeded. Delegate after delegate stepped forward to sign. But some, most notably George Mason and Randolph, refused their signatures. They held firm though warned both of the "infinite mischief" the lack of their names might do at the ratifying conventions, where nine of the thirteen states would have to approve the document, and of the "anarchy and Convulsions" that might well ensue if the Constitution were rejected.

Predictably, it was in Virginia that one key ratification fight took place. In Richmond, Madison spearheaded one side, Mason and states' rightist Patrick ("give me liberty or give me death") Henry the other. "Who authorized them to speak the language of *We the People*," Henry roared, "instead of, *We the States*?"

If a bare majority of Congress could make laws, he argued, the "situation of our western citizens is dreadful. You have a bill of rights to defend you against state government [yet] you have none against Congress. . . . May they not pronounce all slaves free . . . ?" The torrent of Henry's words, steadily rebutted by Madison, lasted 23 days. Sometimes he made five speeches a day, and his list of proposed rights and amendments that must be added to the Constitution grew to 40. But eventually, though he didn't vote aye, he ceased fire, partly yielding to the promise that a Bill of Rights would be added after ratification.

Within two years, the national Congress under the new Constitution proposed the first ten amendments that make up the present Bill of Rights. But the historic issue of whether a young nation, so dedicated and so constituted, could long endure, was anything but settled.

The Founding Fathers, Conditional Antislavery, and the Nonradicalism of the American Revolution

William W. Freehling

By 1972, two years after publishing "The Editorial Revolution," I more clearly understood that the story of the events of 1860 must begin with the Founding Fathers. But I still hoped that my narrative of disunion could begin in 1850. I thus decided to publish my thoughts on the earlier history separately. The resulting first version of this essay, entitled "The Founding Fathers and Slavery," appeared in the American Historical Review in 1972.[1] "Founding Fathers" has been widely republished. I nevertheless regret its overemphasis on antislavery accomplishment. My changed title reflects my partial disenchantment. I am grateful to the American Historical Review for permission to republish some of the previous essay in this much-altered form.

When I wrote the original essay, historians were increasingly scoffing that the Founding Fathers ignored the Declaration of Independence's antislavery imperatives.[2] That denunciation has continued to swell despite my countervailing emphasis, indeed partly because of my overstated argument.[3] My original essay, as David Brion Davis pointed out, too much conflated Thomas Jefferson

and the Founding Fathers.[4] The essay also erroneously portrayed the Founding Fathers as pragmatic reformers, eager to assault slavery whenever political realities permitted. They were in truth skittish abolitionists, chary of pouncing on antislavery opportunity. The Founding Fathers freed some slaves but erected obstacles against freeing others. They also sometimes moved past those obstacles for crass rather than ideological reasons. Thus historians who dismissed the Founding Fathers as antislavery reformers could easily dismiss my argument.

I have come to be more unhappy about the historians who appropriated "Founding Fathers." They have used my contention that the Founding Fathers chipped away at slavery to support their contention that the Declaration of Independence inspired a true American social revolution.[5] I find that argument unpersuasive, even about the white male minority. The notion is still less persuasive about African Americans and about other members of the nonwhite and nonmale majority, which means that the contention mischaracterizes American society writ large. Neither women nor African Americans nor Native Ameri-

cans conceived that the American Revolution revolutionized their lives. Their position is relevant if we are to widen American history beyond Anglo-Saxon males, to write the story of a multicultural civilization.

Some historians answer that the majority's definition of a proper social revolution is irrelevant for judging the American Revolution, since only the white male minority had the power to define the event and the society. Such positions tend to narrow American history into solely a history of the white male power structure. But in the specific case of slavery, the elite's standard for judgment widens perspectives. Wealthy revolutionaries' criterion, no less than poorer Americans' criterion and posterity's criterion, required a proper American Revolution to include the slaves. By that universal yardstick, the Founding Fathers achieved no social revolution.

The Founding Fathers instead set us on our nonrevolutionary social history. Despite their dismay at slavery, America's worst multicultural dislocation, they both timidly reformed and established towering bulwarks against reform, not least because many of them *preferred a monoracial America. I have revised this essay to include more of the bulwarks against antislavery, in company with those who think the Founding Fathers did nothing to further abolition. But I hope the revision will yield more tolerance for my continued belief, and latter-day slaveholders' worried conviction, that the Founding Fathers also did a most nonrevolutionary something to weaken slaveholders' defenses. For without that ambivalent perspective on the nation's founders, we can understand neither the subsequent meandering road toward emancipation nor America's persistently nonradical road toward a radically new multicultural social order, based on the ethics of the Declaration of Independence.*

The American Revolutionaries intended to achieve a political revolution. They brilliantly succeeded. They split the British Empire, mightiest of the world's powers. They destroyed monarchical government in what became the United States. They recast the nature of republican ideology and structure with the federal Constitution of 1787. Over the next generation, their revolution helped undermine their own aristocratic conception of republicanism, leading to Andrew Jackson's very different egalitarian republicanism.

With a single exception, the men of 1776 intended no parallel revolution in the culture's social institutions. The Founders had no desire to confiscate property from the rich and give it to the poor. They gave no thought to appropriating familial power from males and giving it to females, or seizing land from whites and returning it to Native Americans. They embraced the entire colonial white male system of social power—except for slave holders' despotism over slaves. That they would abolish. To judge them by their standards, posterity must ask whether this, their sole desired social revolution, was secured.

The Founding Fathers partially lived up to their revolutionary imperative: They barred the African slave trade from American ports; they banned slavery from midwestern territories; they dis-

solved the institution in northern states; and they diluted slavery in the Border South. Yet the Founding Fathers also backed away from their revolutionary imperative: They delayed emancipation in the North; they left antislavery half accomplished in the Border South; they rejected abolition in the Middle South; and they expanded slaveholder power in the Lower South. These retreats both inhibited final emancipation where slavery had been damaged and augmented slave holders' resources where slavery had been untouched. The advances and retreats set off both an antislavery process and a proslavery counteroffensive. Slavery would eventually be abolished, partly because the Founding Fathers shackled the slaveholders. But emancipation would be so long delayed—partly because the Founders rearmed the slavocracy—that the slavery issue would epitomize the social nonradicalism of the American Revolution.

1

Since every generation rewrites history, most historians achieve only fading influence. One twentieth-century American historical insight, however, seems unlikely to fade. In his multivolume history of slavery as a recognized problem, David Brion Davis demonstrated that throughout most of history, humankind failed to recognize any problem in slavery.[6] Then around the time of the American Revolution, Americans suddenly, almost universally, saw the institution as a distressing problem. Davis showed that throughout the Western world, a changed Enlightenment mentality and a changing industrial order helped revolutionize sensibility about slavery. The American political revolution quickened the pace of ideological revolution. Slavery, as the world's most antirepublican social system, seemed particularly hypocritical in the world's most republican nation. Most American Revolutionaries called King George's enslavement of colonists and whites' enslavement of blacks parallel tyrannies. "Let us either cease to enslave our fellow-men," wrote the New England cleric Nathaniel Niles,

"or else let us cease to complain of those that would enslave us."[7]

Yet the Founding Fathers' awareness of slavery as a problem never deepened into the perception that slavery's foundations were a problem. A slaveholder's claim to slaves was first of all founded on property rights; and the men of 1776 never conceived of redistributing private property or private power to ensure that all men (or women!) were created equal. They believed that governments, to secure slaves' natural right to liberty, must pay slaveholders to surrender the natural right to property. That conviction put a forbidding price tag on emancipation.

The price escalated because these discoverers of slavery as a problem (and nondiscoverers of maldistributed property as a problem) also failed to see that other foundation of slavery, racism, as problematic.[8] Thomas Jefferson, like most of his countrymen, suspected that blacks were created different, inferior in intellectual talents and excessive in sexual ardency. Jefferson also worried that freed blacks would precipitate racial warfare. He shrank from abolition, as did most Americans who lived amidst significant concentrations of slaves, unless the freedmen could be resettled outside the republic.[9]

That race removal condition, like the condition that seized property required compensation, placed roadblocks before emancipation. To colonize blacks in foreign lands would have added 25 percent to the already heavy cost of compensated abolition. To coerce a million enslaved humans to leave a republic as a condition for ending coercive slavery could also seem to be a dubious step toward government by consent.

The Founding Fathers' conditional aspiration to free black slaves furthermore had to compete with their unconditional aspiration to build white republics. It was no contest. The American Revolutionaries appreciated all the problems in establishing free government; but that appreciation energized them, inspired them, led to sustained bursts of imaginative remedies. In contrast, these propertied racists exaggerated all the problems in freeing blacks; and that exaggeration paralyzed them, turned them into procrastinators, led to infrequent stabs at limited reforms.

The inhibitions built into the conditional antislavery mentality could be seen even in the Virginia abolitionist who scorned the supposedly necessary conditions. Edward Coles, James Madison's occasional secretary, intruded on Thomas Jefferson's mailbox with demands that the ex-President crusade for emancipation without waiting for slaveholder opposition to relent. Coles himself acted on antislavery imperatives without waiting for action on deportation imperatives. He migrated with his Virginia slaves to almost entirely freesoil Illinois, manumitted all of them, gave each family a 160-acre farm, and provided for the education of those who were underage. After that rare demonstration of how to turn conditional antislavery into unconditional freedom, Coles advised his ex-slaves to return to Africa! The black race, said Coles, might never prosper in the bigoted white republic. That message, coming from that messenger, well conveyed the national mentality that rendered an antislavery revolution impossible.[10]

2

In conditionally antislavery post-Revolutionary America, the more blacks in a local area, the less possibility of emancipation. Where blacks formed a high percentage of the labor force, as in the original Middle South states of North Carolina and Virginia (35 percent enslaved in 1790) and in the original Lower South states of Georgia and South Carolina (41 percent enslaved in 1970), whites' economic aspirations and race phobias overwhelmed conditional antislavery.[11] In contrast, where blacks were less dense and the slavebased economy was noncrucial, as in the original northern states (all under 5 percent enslaved in 1790) and in the original Border South states of Delaware and Maryland (25 percent enslaved in 1790), the inhibiting conditions for antislavery could be overcome—but after revealing difficulties.

In northern states, the sparse numbers of blacks made slavery seem especially unimportant, both economically and racially, to the huge majority of nonslaveholders. The low percentage of blacks, however, made abolition equally unimportant, economically and racially, to most northern citizens. For the Founders to secure emancipation in the North, an unimportant set of economic/racial antislavery imperatives and a conditional strategy for solving the newly perceived slavery problem had to supplement each other, for neither tepid crass motives nor a compromised ideological awakening could, by itself, overwhelm a vigorous proslavery minority.[12]

That vigor will come as a shock to those who think slavery was peculiar to the South. Yet northern slaveholders fought long and hard to save the institution in temperate climes. Although neither slavery nor emancipation significantly influenced the northern economy, the ownership of humans vitally influenced northern slaveholders' cash flow. Slaveholders made money using slavery up North, and they could always sell slaves for several hundred dollars down South. These crass motives of a few could never have held back an ideological surge of the many had a disinterested majority passionately believed that illegitimate property in humans must be unconditionally seized. But since northern nonslaveholders conceded that this morally suspect property had legal sanction, the struggle for emancipation in the North was long a stalemate.

The only exception was far northward, in New Hampshire, Vermont, and Massachusetts. In those upper parts of New England, the extreme paucity of blacks, a few hundred in each state, led to the phenomenon conspicuously absent elsewhere: total abolition, achieved with revolutionary swiftness, soon after the Revolution. But in the more southerly New England states of Connecticut and Rhode Island, and in the mid-Atlantic states of Pennsylvania, New Jersey, and New York, where percentages of blacks were in the 1 to 5 percent range, emancipation came exceedingly gradually, with antirevolutionary evasions.

Blacks' creeping path to northern freedom commenced in Pennsylvania in 1780, where the Western Hemisphere's first so-called post-nati emancipation law was passed.[13] Post-nati abolition meant freedom for only those born after the law was enacted and only many years after their birth. The formula enabled liberty-loving property holders to split the difference between property rights and human rights. A post-nati law required that no then-held slave property be seized. Only a property not yet on earth was to be freed, and only on some distant day. Accordingly, under the Pennsylvania formula, emancipation would eventually arrive only for slaves thereafter born and only when they reached twenty-eight years of age. Slaveholders thus could keep their previously born slaves forever and their future-born slaves throughout the best years for physical labor. That compromised emancipation was the best a conditional abolition mentality could secure, even in a northern Quaker state where only 2.4 percent of the population was enslaved.

Connecticut and Rhode Island passed post-nati edicts soon after Pennsylvania set the precedent. New York and New Jersey, the northern states with the most slaves, delayed decades longer. New York slaveholders managed to stave off laws freeing the future-born until 1799, and New Jersey slaveholders, until 1804. So it took a quarter century after the revolution for these northern states to enact post-nati antislavery—in decrees that would free no one for another quarter century.

Slaves themselves injected a little revolutionary speed into this nonrevolutionary process. Everywhere in the Americas, slaves sensed when mastery was waning and shrewdly stepped up their resistance, especially by running away. An increase of fugitive slaves often led to informal bargains between northern masters and slaves. Many northern slaveholders promised their slaves liberty sooner than post-nati laws required if slaves provided good service in the interim. Thus did perpetual servitude sometimes shade gradually into fixed-time servitude and more gradually still into wage labor, with masters retaining years of forced labor and slaves gaining liberty at a snail's pace. In 1817, New York's legislature declared that the weakening system must end by 1827.[14]

Although New Jersey and Pennsylvania never followed suit, by 1840 only a few slaves remained in the North. By 1860, thirteen New Jersey slaves were the last vestige of northern slavery.

For thousands of northern slaves, however, the incremental post-nati process led not to postponed freedom in the North but to perpetual servitude in the South. When New York and New Jersey masters faced state laws that would free slaves on a future date, they could beat the deadline. They could sell a victimized black to a state down south, which had no post-nati law. One historian estimates that as many as two-thirds of New York slaves may never have been freed.[15]

Despite this reactionary outcome for some northern slaves and the long delay in liberation of others, the post-nati tradition might still be seen as a quasi-revolutionary movement if it had spread to the South. But every southern state rejected post-nati conceptions, even Delaware, and even when President Abraham Lincoln offered extra federal inducements in 1861. Instead of state-imposed gradual reform, the two original Border South states, Delaware and Maryland, experimented with an even less revolutionary process: voluntary manumission by individual masters. Delaware, which contained 9,000 slaves and 4,000 free blacks in 1790, contained 1,800 slaves and 20,000 free blacks in 1860. Maryland, with 103,000 slaves and 8,000 free blacks in 1790, contained 87,000 slaves and 84,000 free blacks in 1860. The two states' proportions of black freedmen to black slaves came to exceed those of Brazil and Cuba, countries that supposedly had a monopoly on Western Hemisphere voluntary emancipation.

Just as fugitive slaves accelerated post-nati emancipation in Pennsylvania, New York, and New Jersey, so the threat of runaways sometimes speeded manumissions in Delaware and Maryland. Especially in border cities such as Baltimore and Wilmington, masters could profitably agree to liberate slaves at some future date if good labor was thereby secured before manumission. A hard-working slave for seven years was a bargain compared to a slave who might run

away the next day, especially since the slavemaster as republican, upon offering a favorite bondsman future freedom, won himself a good conscience as well as a better short-term worker. This combination of altruism and greed, however, ultimately lost the slaveholder a long-term slave. That result, portending a day when no slaves would remain in northern Maryland, was deplored in southern Maryland tobacco belts, where manumission slowed and blacks usually remained enslaved.[16]

The Maryland-Delaware never-completed manumission movement failed to spread south of the Border South, just as the long-delayed northern post-nati movement never spread south of the mid-Atlantic. True, in Virginia, George Washington freed all his many slaves. But that uncharacteristically extensive Middle South manumission came at a characteristic time. President Washington profited from his slaves while living and then freed them in his last will and testament. President Thomas Jefferson freed a more characteristic proportion of his many Middle South slaves—10 percent. Meanwhile, Jefferson's luxurious life-style piled up huge debts, which prevented the rest of his slaves from being manumitted even after his death.

South of Virginia, Jefferson's 10 percent manumission rate exceeded the norm. A master who worked huge gangs of slaves in the pestilential Georgia and South Carolina lowlands rarely freed his bondsmen before or after he died. By 1830, only 2 percent of the South Carolina/Georgia blacks were free, compared to 8.5 percent of the Virginia/North Carolina blacks and 39 percent of the Maryland/Delaware blacks. The revolutionary U.S. sensibility about slavery had, with nonrevolutionary speed, emancipated the North over a half century and compromised slavery in the original two Border South states. But the institution remained stubbornly persistent in the Border South and largely intact in the Middle South; and Lower South states had been left unharmed, defiant, and determined to confine the Founding Fathers' only desired social revolution to the American locales with the lowest percentages of slaves.

3

National considerations of slavery in the Age of the Founding Fathers repeated the pattern of the various states' considerations. During national debates on slavery, many South Carolina and Georgia Revolutionary leaders denounced the new conception that slavery was a problem. Their arguments included every element of the later proslavery polemic: that the Bible sanctioned slavery, that blacks needed a master, that antislavery invited social chaos. They warned that they would not join or continue in an antislavery Union. They sought to retain the option of reopening the African slave trade. In the first Congress after the Constitution was ratified, they demanded that Congress never debate abolition, even if silence meant that representatives must gag their constituents' antislavery petitions.[17]

The Georgians and South Carolinians achieved congressional silence, even though other Southerners and all Northerners winced at such antirepublican intransigence. North of South Carolina, almost every Founding Father called slavery a deplorable problem, an evil necessary only until the conditions for abolition could be secured. The conditions included perpetuating the Union (and thus appeasing the Lower South), protecting property rights (and thus not seizing presently owned slave property), and removing freed blacks (and thus keeping blacks enslaved until they could be deported). The first step in removing blacks from the United States was to stop Africans from coming, and the last step was to deport those already in the nation. In between, conditional antislavery steps were more debatable, and the Upper South's position changed.

The change involved whether slavery should be allowed to spread from old states to new territories. In the eighteenth century, Virginians presumed, to the displeasure of South Carolinians and Georgians, that the evil should be barred from new territories. In 1784, Thomas Jefferson's proposed Southwest Ordinance would have banned slavery from Alabama and Mississippi Territories after 1800. The bill would theoretically have prevented much of the nineteenth-century Cotton Kingdom from importing slaves. The proposal lost in the Continental Congress by a single vote, that of a New Jerseyite who lay ill at home. "The fate of millions unborn," Jefferson later wrote, was "hanging on the tongue of one man, and heaven was silent in that awful moment."[18]

The bill, however, would not necessarily have been awful for future Mississippi and Alabama cotton planters. Jefferson's bill would have allowed planters in these areas to import slaves until 1800. The proposed delay in banning imports into Mississippi and Alabama stemmed from the same mentality, North and South, that delayed emancipation in Pennsylvania, New York, and New Jersey for decades. In Mississippi and Alabama, delay would have likely killed antislavery. Eli Whitney invented the cotton gin in 1793. By 1800, thousands of slaves would likely have been picking cotton in these southwestern areas. Then the property-respecting Founding Fathers probably would not have passed the administrative laws to confiscate Mississippi and Alabama slaves, since the conditional antislavery mentality always backed away from seizing slaves who were legally on the ground. Probabilities aside, the certainty about the proposed Southwestern Ordinance of 1784 remains. The Founding Fathers defeated its antislavery provisions. Nationally no less than locally, they preserved slavery in Lower South climes.

They also retained their perfect record, nationally no less than locally, in very gradually removing slavery from northern habitats. Just as state legislators abolished slavery in northern states, with nonrevolutionary slowness, so congressmen prevented the institution from spreading into the nation's Northwest Territories, with yet more nonradical caution. Although the Continental Congress removed Jefferson's antislavery provisions from the Southwest Ordinance of 1784, congressmen attached antislavery clauses to the Northwest Ordinance of 1787. Slavery was declared barred from the area of the future states of Illinois, Indiana, Michigan, Wisconsin, and Ohio. Antislavery consciousness helped inspire the ban, as did capitalistic consciousness. Upper South tobacco planters in the Continental Congress explicitly declared that they did not wish rival tobacco planters to develop the Northwest.[19]

The history of the Northwest Ordinance exemplified not only the usual combination of selfishness and selflessness, always present whenever the Founders passed an antislavery reform, but also the usual limited and slow antislavery action whenever conditional antislavery scored a triumph. Just as northern post-nati laws freed slaves born in the future, so the national Northwest Ordinance barred the *future* spread of slavery into the Midwest. But had the Northwest Ordinance emancipated the few slaves who presently lived in the area? Only if congressmen passed a supplemental law providing administrative mechanisms to seize present property. That a property-protecting Congress, led by James Madison, conspicuously failed to do, just as property-protecting northern legislatures usually freed only future-born slaves. Congressmen's failure to enforce seizure of the few midwestern slaves indicates again the probability that they would have shunned mechanisms to confiscate the many slaves in Alabama and Mississippi in 1800 had the Southwest Ordinance of 1784 passed.

The few midwestern slaveholders, their human property intact, proceeded to demonstrate, as did New York slaveholders, that slavery could be profitably used on northern farms. Slaveholding farmers soon found allies in midwestern land speculators, who thought more farmers would come to the prairies if more slaves could be brought along. These land speculators, led by the future president William Henry Harrison of Indiana, repeatedly petitioned Congress in the early nineteenth century to repeal the Northwest Ordinance's prohibition on slave imports. But though congressmen would not confiscate present slave property, they refused to remove the ban on future slaves.

Although frustrated, a few stubborn Illinois slaveholders imported black so-called indentured servants who were slaves in all but name. Once again, Congress did nothing to remove these de facto slaves, despite the de jure declaration of the Northwest Ordinance. So when Illinois entered the Union in 1818, Congress had massively discouraged slavery but had not totally ended it. The congressional discouragement kept the number of indentured black servants in Illinois to about nine hundred, compared to the over ten thousand slaves in neighboring Missouri Territory, where Congress had not barred slavery. But those nine hundred victims of the loopholes in the Northwest Ordinance kept the reality of slavery alive in the Midwest until Illinois was admitted to the Union and Congress no longer had jurisdiction over the midwestern labor system.

Then slaveholders sought to make Illinois an official slave state. In 1824, a historic battle occurred in the prairies over a statewide referendum on legalizing slavery. The leader of Illinois's antislavery forces was none other than now-Governor Edward Coles, that ex-Virginian who had moved northward to free his slaves. Coles emphasized that slavery was antithetical to republicanism, while some of his compatriots pointed out that enforced servitude was antithetical to free laborers' economic interests. Once again, as in the Baltimore masters' decisions to manumit slaves and in the congressional decision to ban slavery from the Midwest, economic and moral motives fused. The fusion of selfish and unselfish antislavery sentiments secured 58 percent of Illinois electorate. That too-close-for-comfort margin indicated how much conditional antislavery congressmen had risked when they failed to close those indentured servant loopholes. But in the Midwest as in the North, the new vision of slavery as a problem had finally helped secure abolition—half a century after the American Revolution.

4

While the Founding Fathers belatedly contained slavery from expanding into the Midwest, Thomas Jefferson and his fellow Virginians ultimately abandoned the principle of containment. In 1819–20, when Northerners sought to impose post-nati antislavery on the proposed new slave state of Missouri, Jefferson called the containment of slavery wrong. Slaves should not be restricted to old areas, he explained, for whites would never free thickly concentrated slaves. Only if slaves were thinly spread over new areas would racist whites free them.[20]

Given many Founding Fathers' conviction that emancipation must be conditional on the removal of concentrations of blacks, their latter-day argument that slaves should be diffusely scattered made more sense than their earlier argument that slaves must be prevented from diffusing. Still, the Upper South's retreat from containment of slavery illuminates the forbidding power of that race removal condition. If Upper South Founding Fathers had opted for diffusion of blacks rather than containment in 1787, as they did in 1819–20, even the diluted antislavery provision in the Northwest Ordinance probably would not have passed. Then the already almost-triumphant Illinois slaveholders probably would have prevailed, and slavery would have had a permanent toehold in the North. On the subject of the expansion of slavery into new areas, as in the matter of the abolition of slavery in old states, the Founding Fathers had suffered a total loss in the South, had scored a difficult victory in the North, and had everywhere displayed the tentativeness of so conditional a reform mentality.

5

To posterity, the Virginians' switch from containing slavery in old American areas to diffusing slavery over new American areas adds up to a sellout of antislavery. The Thomas Jeffersons, however, considered the question of whether slavery should be contained or diffused in America to be a relatively minor matter. The major issues were whether blacks should be prevented from coming to America and whether slaves should be deported from America. On these matters, conditional antislavery men never wavered.

In the letter Jefferson wrote at the time of the Missouri Controversy in which he first urged diffusion of blacks within America, he repeated that blacks should eventually be diffused outside the white

republic. Four years later, in his final statement on antislavery, Jefferson stressed again his persistent conditional antislavery solution. His "reflections on the subject" of emancipation, Jefferson wrote a northern Federalist, had not changed for "five and forty years." He would emancipate the "afterborn" and deport them at "a proper age," with the federal government selling federal lands to pay for the deportations. Federal emancipation/colonization raises "some constitutional scruples," conceded this advocate of strict construction of the government's constitutional powers. "But a liberal construction of the Constitution," he affirmed, may go "the whole length."[21]

Jefferson's "whole length" required not only federal funding but also an organization that would resettle blacks outside the United States. That need found fruition in the Upper South's favorite conditional antislavery institution, the American Colonization Society, founded in 1817.[22] William Lloyd Garrison would soon denounce the society as not antislavery at all. But to Jefferson's entire Virginia generation, and to most mainstream Americans in all parts of the country in the 1817–60 period, the American Colonization Society was the best hope to secure an altogether liberated (and lily-white) American populace.

The only significant southern opponent of the society concurred that colonization of blacks could undermine slavery. South Carolinians doubted that the American Colonization Society would remove millions of blacks to its Liberian colony. (The society, in fact, rarely resettled a thousand in one year and only ten thousand in forty-five years.) But South Carolina extremists conceded that an Upper South-North national majority coalition could be rallied for colonization. They also realized that once Congress voted for an emancipation plan, whatever the absurdity of the scheme, abolition might be near. Capitalists would never invest in the property. Slaves would sense that liberation was imminent. Only a suicidal slaveholding class, warned the Carolinians, would take such a chance. Carolinians threatened to secede if Congress so much as discussed the heresy. So con-

gressional colonization discussion halted in the late 1820s, just as South Carolina's disunion threats had halted antislavery discussions in the First Congress.[23]

A few historians have pronounced these South Carolinians to be but bluffers, cynical blusterers who never meant to carry out their early disunion threats.[24] The charge, based solely on the opinion of the few Founding Fathers who wished to defy the Carolinians, does not ring true. Many South Carolina coastal planters lived among 8:1 concentrations of blacks to whites, a racial concentration unheard of elsewhere. The Carolinians farmed expensive miasmic swamplands, unlike the cheaper, healthier slaveholding areas everywhere else. Unless black slaves could be forced to endure the pestilential Carolina jungle, the lushest area for entrepreneurial profits in North America would become economically useless. So enormous a percentage of blacks might also be racially dangerous if freed. South Carolinians' special stake in slavery engendered understandable worry when Northerners and Southerners called slavery an evil that must be removed.

So South Carolinians threatened disunion. Posterity cannot say whether they would have had the nerve to secede if an early national Congress had enacted, for example, Jefferson's conditional antislavery plan of using federal land proceeds to deport slaves. South Carolinians might have early found, as they later discovered, that their nerves were not up to the requirements of bringing off a revolution against every other state. But though they might not have been able to carry out their threats, that hardly means they were bluffing. Their threats were credible because these sincere warriors intended to act, if the nation defied their non-bluff.

Still, the larger point is that so conditional an antislavery mentality was not equipped to test South Carolinians' capacity to carry out their threats, any more than that mentality's compromised worldview was equipped to seize presently owned property from recalcitrant slaveholders. The master spirit of the age was a passion to build white republics, not an inclination to deport black slaves; and South Carolinians threatened to splinter the Union unless congressmen ceased to talk of deporting blacks. The Founding Fathers' priorities prevailed. South Carolina's threats effectively shut off congressional speculation about removing slaves from America. That left only the other major conditional antislavery aspiration still viable: shutting off the flow of Africans to America.

6

South Carolinians long opposed closure of the African slave trade, too. But their opposition to stopping future slaves from traveling to America was mild compared to their opposition to deporting slaves from America. Like the northern slaveholders who could accept emancipation if they had fifty more years to use slaves, South Carolinians could accept the end of the African slave trade if they had twenty more years to import Africans.

Their potential interest in more African imports first surfaced at the beginning of the American national experience. When drafting the Declaration of Independence and cataloging King George's sins, Thomas Jefferson proposed condemning the tyrant for supposedly foisting Africans on his allegedly slavery-hating colonies. South Carolinians bridled at the language. Jefferson deleted the draft paragraph. Although Jefferson was not present at the 1787 Philadelphia Constitutional Convention, history repeated itself. When northern and Upper South delegates proposed that Congress be empowered to end the African slave trade immediately, South Carolinians warned that they would then refuse to join the Union. The issue was compromised. Congress was given authority to close the overseas trade only after 1807. South Carolinians had a guaranteed twenty-year-long opportunity to import African slaves.

In the early nineteenth century, with the emerging Cotton Kingdom avid for more slaves, Carolinians seized their expiring opportunity. In 1803, the state officially opened its ports for the importation of Africans. Some 40,000 Africans landed in the next four years. Assuming the normal course of black natural increase in the Old South, these latest arrivals in the land of liberty multiplied to 150,000 slaves by 1860, or almost 4 percent of the southern total.

Jefferson was President at the moment when Congress could shutter South Carolina's twenty-year window of opportunity. "I congratulate you, fellow-citizens," Jefferson wrote in his annual message of December 2, 1806, "on the approach of the period when you may interpose your authority constitutionally" to stop Americans "from all further participation in those violations of human rights which have been so long continued on the unoffending inhabitants of Africa, and which the morality, the reputation, and the best interests of our country have long been eager to proscribe.[25] Closure of the African slave trade could not take effect until January 1, 1808, conceded Jefferson. Yet the reform, if passed in 1807, could ensure that no extra African could legally land in a U.S. port. In 1807 Congress enacted Jefferson's proposal.

Prompt enactment came in part because almost all Americans beyond South Carolina shared Jefferson's ideological distaste for slavery. The African slave trade seemed especially loathsome to most white republicans. But neither the loathing nor the enactment came wholly because of disinterested republican ideology. Jefferson and fellow racists hated the African slave trade partly because it brought more *blacks* to America. So too South Carolina planters were now willing to acquiesce in the prohibition partly because they considered their forty thousand imports to be enough so-called African barbarians. So too Upper South slave sellers could gain more dollars for their slaves if Cotton South purchasers could buy no more blacks from Africa. With the closure of the African slave trade—as with the Northwest Ordinance and as with the abolition of northern slavery and as with the manumission of Baltimore slaves—republican selflessness came entwined with racist selfishness; and no historian can say whether the beautiful or the ugly contributed the stronger strand.

The closure of the African slave trade emerges in the textbooks as a nonevent, worthy of no more than a sentence. Whole books have been written on the Founding Fathers and slavery without a word devoted to the reform.[26] Yet this law was the jewel of the Founding Fathers' antislavery effort, and no viable assessment of that effort can ignore this far-reaching accomplishment. The federal closure's impact reached as far as Africa. Brazil and Cuba imported over 1.5 million Africans between 1815 and 1860, largely to stock sugar and coffee plantations.[27] Slaveholders in the United States could have productively paid the then-prevailing price for at least that many black imports to stock southwestern sugar and cotton plantations.

The effect of the closure of the African slave trade also reached deep into the slaves' huts and the masters' Big Houses. If the South had contained a million newly landed "raw Africans," as Southerners called those human folk, southern slaveholders would have deployed more savage terror and less caring paternalism to control the strangers. The contest between the United States, where the nineteenth-century overseas slave trade was closed, and Cuba and Brazil, where it was wide open, makes the point. Wherever Latin Americans imported cheap Africans, they drove down slave life expectancies. In the United States, alone among the large nineteenth-century slavocracies, slaves naturally increased in numbers, thanks to less fearful, more kindly masters and to more acculturated, more irreplaceable blacks.

The closure of the African trade also changed the demographical configuration of the South and the nation, to the detriment of slaveholders' political power. When white immigrants shunned the Slave South and voyaged to the free-labor North, the South could not import Africans to compensate. The North grew faster in population, faster in labor supply, faster in industrialization, faster in the ability to seize agricultural territories such as Kansas, and faster in the ability to control congressional majorities. Worse, after African slave trade closure, the Cotton South could race after the free-labor North only by draining slaves from the Border South. The combination of manumissions and African slave trade closure doubly hindered slavery in the most geographically northern slave states. In 1790 almost 20 percent of

American slaves had lived in this Border South tier. By 1860 the figure was down to 11 percent. On the other hand, in 1790 the Lower South states had 21 percent of American slaves, but by 1860, the figure was up to 59 percent. From 1830 to 1860 the percentage of slaves in the total population declined in Delaware from 4 to 1 percent; in Maryland from 23 to 13 percent; in Kentucky from 24 to 19 percent; in Missouri from 18 to 10 percent; and in the counties that would become West Virginia from 10 to 5 percent. By 1860 Delaware, Maryland, Missouri, and the area that would become West Virginia had a lower percentage of slaves than New York had possessed at the time of the Revolution, and Kentucky did not have a much higher percentage. The goal of abolition had become almost as practicable in these border states as it had been in New York in 1776, twenty-five years before the state passed a post-nati law and fifty years before the New York slave was freed. Had no Civil War occurred, fifty years after 1860 is a good estimate for when the last Border South slave might have been freed. Then slavery would have remained in only eleven of the fifteen slave states.

To sum up the antislavery accomplishments in the first American age that considered slavery a problem: When the Founding Fathers were growing up, slavery existed throughout Great Britain's North American colonies. The African slave trade was open. Even in the North, as John Jay of New York reported, "very few . . . doubted the propriety and rectitude" of slavery.[28] When the Founders left the national stage, slavery had been abolished in the North, kept out of the Midwest, and placed on the defensive in the South. A conditional antislavery mentality, looking for ways to ease slavery and blacks out of the country, prevailed everywhere except in the Lower South. If the Founders had done none of this—if slavery had continued in the North and expanded into the Northwest; if a million Africans had been imported to strengthen slavery in the Lower South, to retain it in New York and Illinois, to spread it to Kansas, and to preserve it in the Border South; if no free black population had devel-

oped in Delaware and Maryland; if no conditional antislavery ideology had left Southerners on shaky moral grounds; if, in short, Jefferson and his contemporaries had lifted not one antislavery finger—everything would have been different and far less worrisome for the Lower South slavocracy.

7

But the Founding Fathers also inadvertently empowered a worried Low South to wage its coming struggle. "Inadvertent" is the word, for most American Revolutionaries did not wish to strengthen an intransigent slavocracy, any more than they wished to delay African slave trade closure or to silence congressional consideration of colonization. The problem, again, was that these architects of republicanism cared more about building white republics than about securing antislavery. So opportunities to consolidate a republican Union counted for much and the side effects on slavery counted for little—when side effects on slavery where even noticed.

Thus at the Constitutional Convention, Lower South slaveholders, by threatening not to join the Union unless their power was strengthened, secured another Union-saving compromise. Slaves were to be counted as three-fifths of a white man, when the national House of Representatives was apportioned. This constitutional clause gave Southerners around 20 percent more congressmen than their white numbers justified. Since the numbers of members in the president-electing electoral college were based on the numbers of congressmen, the South also gained 20 percent more power over the choice of chief executive. An unappetizing number illustrates the point. The South received one extra congressman and presidential elector throughout the antebellum years as a result of South Carolina's 1803–07 importation of Africans.

The Founding Fathers also augmented Lower South territory. In 1803, Thomas Jefferson's Louisiana Purchase from France added the areas of Louisiana, Arkansas, and Missouri to the Union. In 1819, James Monroe's treaty with Spain secured the areas of Florida,

Southern Alabama, and Southern Mississippi. A desire to protect slavery was only marginally involved in the Florida purchase and not at all involved in the Louisiana Purchase. Presidents Jefferson and Monroe primarily sought to protect national frontiers. But they were so determined to bolster national power and gave so little thought to the consequences for slaveholder power that their calculations about blacks could not offset their diplomatic imperatives. Their successful diplomacy yielded territories already containing slaves. Then their antislavery mentality was too conditional to conceive of confiscating slave property. The net result: The Founding Fathers contributed four new slave states and parts of two others to the eventual fifteen slave states in the Union. That increased the South's power in the U.S. Senate 27 percent and the Lower South's economic power enormously.

If the Founding Fathers had done none of this—if they had not awarded the South the extra congressmen and presidential electors garnered from the three-fifths clause; if they had not allowed South Carolina to import forty thousand more Africans; if they had not acquired Florida, Louisiana, Arkansas, Missouri, southern Mississippi, and southern Alabama; if in short they had restricted the slavocracy to its pre-1787 power and possessions—the situation would have been far bleaker for the Cotton Kingdom. Indeed, without the Founding Fathers' bolstering of slaveholder power, their antislavery reforms, however guarded, might have been lethal. As it was, the American Revolutionaries made the slave system stronger in the South, where it was already strongest, and weaker in the North, where it was weakest. That contradictory amalgam of increased slaveholder vulnerabilities and increased slaveholder armor established the pattern for everything that was to come.

8

In the 1820–60 period, and on the 1861–65 battlefields, the slaveholders fought their added vulnerabilities with their added power. By 1860, the slaveholders had fifteen states against the North's sixteen. But if the four Border South states fell away, the North's margin would widen to twenty against eleven. Then all sorts of dangers would loom for a once-national institution, which in the wake of the Founding Fathers was slowly becoming more defensively and peculiarly southern.

Southern proslavery campaigns, ideological and political, could be summed up as one long campaign to reverse the Founding Fathers' conditional antislavery drift. The conditional antislavery ideology, declaring emancipation desirable *if* blacks could be removed and *if* the Union could be preserved, persisted in the North and the Upper South throughout the antebellum period. That predominant national apologetic attitude toward slavery, Lower South zealots persistently feared, could inspire a national political movement aimed at removing blacks and slaves from the nation unless the Lower South deterred it.

Deterrence began with a determined proslavery campaign aimed at showing Southerners that slavery was no problem after all. In its extreme manifestations in the 1850s, proslavery visionaries, led by Virginia's George Fitzhugh, called wage slavery the unrecognized problem. The impolitic implication (although Fitzhugh disavowed it): Even white wage earners should be enslaved.[29] Proslavery polemicists more commonly called freedom for blacks the unrecognized problem. The common message: Black slaves should never be freed to starve as free workers in or out of America.

While proslavery intellectuals took aim at the Founding Fathers' revolutionary awareness that slavery was a problem, proslavery politicians sought to counter the waning of slavery in the Border South. With the Fugitive Slave Law of 1850, particularly aimed at stopping border slaves from fleeing to permanent liberty in the North, and the Kansas-Nebraska Act of 1854, originally urged by its southern advocates to protect slavery in Missouri, Southerners endeavored to fortify the border regime which the Fathers had somewhat weakened. So too the most dramatic (although unsuccessful) Lower South political movement of the 1850s, the

campaign to reopen the African slave trade, sought to reverse the Fathers' greatest debilitation of the slavocracy.

The minority's persistent proslavery campaigns and frequent congressional victories eventually convinced most Northerners that appeasement of a slaveholding minority damaged rather than saved white men's highest priority: majority rule in a white men's republic. That determination to rescue majority rule from the Slavepower minority underrode Abraham Lincoln's election in 1860; and with Lincoln's election came the secession of the Lower South minority. Secessionists feared not least that the President-elect might build that long-feared North-Upper South movement to end slavery by deporting blacks, especially from the compromised Border South.

The ensuing Civil War would prove that latter-day Southerners had been right to worry about slavery's incremental erosion in the borderlands. The four Border South states would fight for the Union, tipping the balance of power against the Confederacy. Abraham Lincoln would allegedly say that though he hoped to have God on his side, he *had* to have Kentucky. He would retain his native Kentucky and all the borderlands, including his adopted Illinois, which the Founders had at long last emancipated.

He would also obtain, against his initial objections, black soldiers, who would again sense an opportunity to read themselves into the Declaration of Independence. Just as fugitive slaves had pushed reluctant Pennsylvania, New York, and Maryland slaveholders into faster manumissions, so fugitive blacks should push a reluctant Great Emancipator to let them in his army and thereby make his victory theirs. Black soldiers would help win the war, secure emancipation, and thus finally defeat the slaveholders' long attempt to reverse the Founding Fathers' conditional antislavery drift.

To omit the Fathers' guarded contributions to America's drift toward the Civil War and emancipation in the name of condemning them as hypocrites is to miss the tortuous way black freedom came to the United States. But to omit the Fathers' contributions to Lower

South proslavery power in the name of calling them social revolutionaries is to deny the very meaning of the word *revolution*.

9

More broadly and more significantly, the American Revolutionaries' stance on blacks illuminated their ambivalent approach to the one truly radical social implication of the Revolution. As the historian Jack P. Greene has brilliantly shown, nothing was radical about the Declaration's affirmation of an American right to life, liberty, and the pursuit of happiness, so long as only white males' pursuits counted as American.[30] Whatever the poverty in urban slums and tenants' shacks, American colonials had long since developed a radically modern social order, dedicated to white males' pursuit of happiness and rooted in unprecedented capitalist opportunity. The Revolution, while expanding political opportunity and political mobility, only a little further widened an economic doorway already unprecedentedly open—but labeled "white males only."

For the others who peopled America—the women, the Native Americans, the blacks, in short, the majority—opportunity was closed. To include these dispossessed groups in the American Revolution—to open up a world where all men and women were at liberty to pursue their happiness—was the Declaration's truly radical social implication. No such color-blind, ethnically blind, gender-blind social order had ever existed, not on these shores, not anywhere else.

The Founding Fathers caught an uneasy glimpse of this potential social revolution. Despite their obsession with white republics and white property, they recognized that the Declaration applied to blacks, too. But their racism led them to take a step backward from the revolutionary promise of the Declaration of Independence. Most of them were no advocates of an egalitarian multicultural society *in* America. The Virginia Dynasty especially would extend quality to black Americans by moving them *out* of America. That reactionary black-removal foundation of antislavery statecraft, peculiar among all the New World slavocracies to these North Americans, did not a progressive social revolution portend.

Thomas Jefferson had captured the nonradicalism of the American Revolution in one of the great American phrases. "We have the wolf by the ears," he wrote at the time of the Missouri Controversy, "and we can neither hold him, nor safely let him go."[31] The Founding Fathers had more wolves by the ears than Jefferson had in mind: blacks, slaves, their own antislavery hopes, their implication, that *all* people must be included in the Declaration of Independence. They propounded those ideals, but they quailed before their own creation. Someday, the ideals may prevail and Americans may cease to recoil from the Declaration's implications. But it would not happen to the Founders, not with revolutionary speed, not to men who equipped a nation to hang on to slavery's slippery ears for almost a century.

Notes

1. William W. Freehling, "The Founding Fathers and Slavery," *American Historical Review, 77* (1972): 81–93.

2. See, for example, Robert McColley, *Slavery and Jeffersonian Virginia* (Urbana, Ill., 1964); Donald L. Robinson, *Slavery in the Structure of American Politics, 1765–1820* (New York, 1971); William Cohen, "Thomas Jefferson and the Problem of Slavery," *Journal of American History, 56* (1969): 503–26.

3. Later writers have also extended the blame for failure to emancipate to encompass Northerners as well as Southerners. See, for example, Larry E. Tise, *Proslavery: A History of the Defense of Slavery in America, 1701–1840* (Athens, Ga., 1987), and Gary B. Nash, *Race and Revolution* (Madison, Wisc., 1990).

4. David Brion Davis, *The Problem of Slavery in the Age of Revolution, 177–1823* (Ithaca, N.Y., 1975), 168.

5. Most recently and notably in Gordon S. Wood, *The Radicalism of the American Revolution* (New York, 1992), 186–87, 401 *n* 43. For an estimate of this matter very close to my own,

6. see Drew R. McCoy in *Journal of American History, 79* (1993): 1563–64.

6. David Brion Davis, *The Problem of Slavery in Western Culture* (Ithaca, N.Y., 1966), and Davis, *The Problem of Slavery in the Age of Revolution.*

7. Quoted in ibid., 292.

8. A phenomenon splendidly illustrated in Winthrop D. Jordan, *White over Black: American Attitudes toward the Negro, 1550–1812* (Chapel Hill, N.C., 1968).

9. For further discussion of Jefferson's conditional antislavery position, see William W. Freehling, *The Road to Disunion,* Vol. 1, *Secessionists at Bay, 1776–1854* (New York, 1990), 123–31. For further discussion of the black-removal condition, see below, ch. 7.

10. For an excellent discussion of this episode, see Drew R. McCoy, *The Last of the Fathers: James Madison and the Republican Legacy* (New York, 1989), 310–16.

11. All demographic statistics in this essay derive from *The Statistics of the Population of the United Sates,* comp. Francis A. Walker (Washington, D.C., 1872), 11–74, and U.S. Bureau of the Census, *A Century of Population Growth; From the First Census of the United States to the Twelfth, 1790–1900* (Washington, D.C., 1909).

12. The classic study of emancipation in the North is Arthur Zilversmit, *The First Emancipation: The Abolition of Slavery in the North* (Chicago, 1967).

13. For an excellent discussion of the Pennsylvania episode, see Gary B. Nash and Jean R. Soderlund, *Freedom by Degrees: Emancipation and Its Aftermath in Pennsylvania* (New York, 1991).

14. For a fine recent study of the New York phase, see Shane White, *Somewhat More Independent: the End of Slavery in New York City, 1770–1810* (Athens, Ga., 1991).

15. Claudia Dale Golden, "The Economics of Emancipation," *Journal of Economic History, 33* (1973): 70.

16. Torrey Stephen Whitman, "Slavery, Manumission, and Free Black Workers in Early National Baltimore," Ph.D. diss., Johns Hopkins University, 1993, expertly develops these themes. On the broader Maryland milieu, see Barbara J. Fields, *Slavery and Freedom on the Middle Ground: Maryland during the Nineteenth Century* (New Haven, Conn., 1985).

17. Joseph C. Burke, "The Pro-Slavery Argument in the First Congress," *Duquesne Review, 16* (1969): 3–15; Howard Ohline, "Slavery, Economics, and Congressional Politics," *Journal of Southern History, 46* (1980): 335–60; Richard Newman, "The First Gag Rule," forthcoming. I am grateful to Mr. Newman for allowing me to use his excellent essay before its publication.

18. Quoted in Merrill D. Peterson, *Thomas Jefferson and the New Nation: A Biography* (New York, 1970), 283.

19. William Grayson to James Monroe, August 8, 1787, in *Letters of Members of the Continental Congress,* ed. Edmund C. Burnett, 8 vols. (Washington, D.C., 1921–36), 8:631–33. The following account of the Northwest Ordinance and its Illinois aftermath has been much influenced by the salutary notes of cynicism in Peter Onuf's fine *Statehood and Union: A History of the Northwest Ordinance* (Indianapolis, Ind., 1987) and in Paul Finkelman's several illuminating essays, especially "Slavery and the Northwest Ordinance: A Study in Ambiguity," *Journal of the Early Republic, 6* (1986): 343–70, and "Evading the Ordinance: The Persistence of Bondage in Indiana and Illinois," *Journal of the Early Republic, 9* (1989): 21–51. But for a cautionary note, see David Brion Davis's judicious "The Significance of Excluding Slavery from the Old Northwest in 1787," *Indiana Magazine of History, 84* (1988); 75–89.

20. Jefferson to John Holmes, April 22, 1820, in *The Writings of Thomas Jefferson,* ed. Paul Leicester Ford, 10 vols. (New York, 1892–99), 10:157–58.

21. Jefferson to Jared Sparks, February 24, 1824, ibid., 10:289–92.

22. Phillip J. Staudenraus, *The African Colonization Movement, 1816–1865* (New York, 1961).

23. The theme is discussed at length in William W. Freehling, *Prelude to Civil War: The Nullification Controversy in South Carolina, 1816–1836* (New York, 1966).

24. See, for example, Paul Finkelman's otherwise illuminating "Slavery and the Constitutional Convention: Making a Covenant with Death," in *Beyond Confederation: Origins of the Constitution and National Identity,* ed. Richard Beeman et al. (Chapel Hill, N.C., 1987), 188–225.

25. A *Compilation of the Messages and Papers of the Presidents,* comp. James D. Richardson, 10 vols. (Washington, D.C., 1900), 1:408.

26. See, for example, Nash, *Race and Revolution.*

27. David Eltis, *Economic Growth and the Ending of the Transatlantic Slave Trade* (New York, 1987).

28. John Jay to the English Anti-Slavery Society, [1788], in *The Correspondence and Public Papers of John Jay,* ed. Henry P. Johnston, 4 vols. (New York, 1890–93), 3:342.

29. See below, pp. 98–100.

30. Jack P. Greene, *Pursuits of Happiness: The Social Development of Early Modern British Colonies and the Formation of American Culture* (Chapel Hill, N.C., 1988).

31. Jefferson to John Holmes, April 22, 1820, in *Jefferson's Writings,* ed. Ford, 10:157–58.

Unit 3

Unit Selections

15. **The Greatness of George Washington,** Gordon S. Wood
16. **1796: The First Real Election,** John Ferling
17. **Lewis and Clark: Trailblazers Who Opened the Continent,** Gerald F. Kreyche
18. **Indians in the Land,** William Cronon and Richard White
19. **Jefferson's Retreat,** Joseph J. Ellis
20. **Before the "Trail of Tears,"** Teresa Amott and Julie Matthaei
21. **"All We Want Is Make Us Free!"** Howard Jones
22. **Mountain Legend,** Michael Martin
23. **James K. Polk and the Expansionist Spirit,** Harlan Hague
24. **All That Glittered,** Richard Reinhardt
25. **The Lives of Slave Women,** Deborah Gray White
26. **Eden Ravished,** Harlan Hague

Key Points to Consider

❖ George Washington presided over the formative years of government under the new Constitution. What were his strengths? His weaknesses? In what ways did the election of 1796 mark the beginning of a new era?

❖ Discuss James Polk with regard to his role in acquiring new territories for the United States. Who benefited and who suffered from American expansion?

❖ The question of slavery bedeviled Americans from the debates during the Constitutional Convention to the Civil War. How can one account for the contradictions of those, such as Thomas Jefferson, who extolled the virtues of freedom but who refused to emancipate their own slaves? How did the *Amistad* mutiny become a national issue?

 **Links** www.dushkin.com/online/

19. **Consortium for Political and Social Research**
   http://icg.fas.harvard.edu/~census/
20. **Department of State**
   http://www.state.gov/
21. **The Mexican-American War Memorial Homepage**
   http://sunsite.unam.mx/revistas/1847/
22. **Mystic Seaport**
   http://amistad.mysticseaport.org/main/welcome.html
23. **Social Influence Website**
   http://www.public.asu.edu/~kelton/
24. **University of Virginia Library**
   http://www.lib.virginia.edu/exhibits/lewis_clark/
25. **Women in America**
   http://xroads.virginia.edu/~HYPER/DETOC/FEM/
26. **Women in the West**
   ftp://history.cc.ukans.edu/pub/history/general/articles/prater1.art/

These sites are annotated on pages 4 and 5.

The first elections under the Constitution were held in 1788 and the new government got under way the following year. The Constitution provided only the framework within which the system would function, but did not contain instructions on day-to-day matters for which there were no precedents. By what title should one address the president, for instance, or what was the precise relationship between the executive office and Congress? When there were differing interpretations of specific articles in the Constitution, who should decide the one that should prevail? And finally, should governmental powers be limited to those expressly granted in the document, or were there "implied" powers that could be utilized as long as they were not specifically prohibited? Various individuals and groups jockeyed to promote programs that would benefit the interests they represented.

Two definable factions emerged during the early years of George Washington's first administration. One, located mostly in the northeast, represented commercial and manufacturing interests and was led by Alexander Hamilton. The other, concentrated in the South and West, favored agricultural and rural interests and was represented by Thomas Jefferson and James Madison. These two groups differed strongly over what the federal government could or should not do under the Constitution, which sources of revenue should be tapped, and a number of other matters. Washington loathed the growth of factions, but actually contributed to it by accepting Hamilton's views most of the time.

The first essay in this section, "The Greatness of George Washington," evaluates his conduct as president and as an individual. Author Gordon Wood gives Washington high marks for helping to lay the foundation of a system that has endured to this day. In "1796: The First Real Election," John Ferling carries the story up to Washington's refusal to serve a third term, even though it would have been his for the taking. The removal of this towering figure led to the first "real" election, one contested by two formal political parties.

Americans knew little about the vast, uncharted territories that extended from the Mississippi River to the Pacific Ocean. Thomas Jefferson had for years shown an interest in exploring this area, and when he became president he requested funds from Congress to form an expeditionary group that became known as the Corps of Discovery. Headed by Meriwether Lewis and William Clark, the Corps, in 1804, embarked on an arduous journey that eventually brought it to the shores of the Pacific. In "Lewis and Clark: Trailblazers Who Opened the Continent" Gerald Kreyche describes this lengthy expedition as well as the performance of its two leaders.

Three selections deal with different aspects of westward expansion. "James K. Polk and the Expansion Spirit" analyzes Polk's efforts to acquire Texas and the Oregon territory. According to author Harlan Hague, Polk compromised with the British over Oregon but went to war with Mexico over Texas. "Mountain Legend," by Michael Martin, tells the story of a legendary mountain man who helped "open up the American West for the settlers who followed." "All that Glittered" provides an account of the California Gold Rush, which occurred after the discovery of gold at Sutter's mill. Author Richard Reinhardt describes the lives of the "forty-niners" who flocked to the area in search of wealth.

Native Americans are the subject of two essays. "Indians in the Land," by William Cronon and Richard White, emphasizes the vast differences between the ways that whites and Native Americans regarded and treated the environment. "Before the 'Trail of Tears' " summarizes recent research on the rights and privileges that Native American women enjoyed within their communities. According to authors Teresa Amott and Julie Matthaei, the westward movement of European settlers helped to undermine their status.

In "Jefferson's Retreat," Joseph Ellis discusses the paradox of a man who fervently believed in human freedom and yet died a slaveowner. "All We Want Is Make Us Free!" concerns a slave mutiny aboard the Spanish vessel Amistad. Author Howard Jones describes the fate of the mutineers in a case that ultimately was heard by the Supreme Court. In "The Lives of Slave Women" Deborah Gray White examines the kinds of work that slave women did and their relationships with one another, with male slaves, and with whites.

The last selection, "Eden Ravished," concerns the environment. Author Harlan Hague tells us that despite warnings to the contrary, Americans tended to treat the lands, rivers, and forests as though they were inexhaustible resources that could be exploited without regard for the future.

The Greatness of George Washington

By Gordon S. Wood

George Washington may still be first in war and first in peace, but he no longer seems to be first in the hearts of his countrymen. Or at least in the hearts of American historians. A recent poll of 900 American historians shows that Washington has dropped to third place in presidential greatness behind Lincoln and FDR. Which only goes to show how little American historians know about American history.

Polls of historians about presidential greatness are probably silly things, but, if they are to be taken seriously, then Washington fully deserved the first place he has traditionally held. He certainly deserved the accolades his contemporaries gave him. And as long as this republic endures he ought to be first in the hearts of his countrymen. Washington was truly a great man and the greatest president we have ever had.

But he was a great man who is not easy to understand. He became very quickly, as has often been pointed out, more a monument than a man, statuesque and impenetrable. Even his contemporaries realized that he was not an ordinary accessible human being. He was deified in his own lifetime. "O Washington," declared Ezra Stiles, president of Yale, in 1783. "How I do love thy name! How have I often adored and blessed thy God, for creating and forming thee, the great ornament of human kind! . . . Thy fame is of sweeter perfume than Arabian spices. Listening angels shall catch the odor, waft it to heaven and perfume the universe!"

One scholar has said that Washington has been "the object of the most intense display of hero worship this nation has ever seen." Which helps explain the continuing efforts to humanize him—even at the beginning of our history. Parson Mason Weems, his most famous biographer, was less of a churchman than he was a hustling entrepreneur. He was ready when Washington died in 1799: "I've something to whisper in your lug," Weems wrote to his publisher Matthew Carey a month after the great man's death. "Washington you know, is gone! Millions are gaping to read something about him. I am very nearly primed and cocked for 'em." Weems had his book out within the year.

The most famous anecdotes about Washington's early life come from Weems. He wanted to capture the inner private man—to show the early events that shaped Washington's character, even if he had to make them up. Weems presumed that the source of Washington's reputation for truthfulness lay in his youth. He tells a story that he said he had heard from Washington's nurse. It was, he says, "too valuable to be lost, too true to be doubted." This was, of course, the story of the cherry tree about whose chopping down Washington could not tell a lie.

Despite the continued popularity of Parson Weems' attempt to humanize him, Washington remained distant and unapproachable, almost unreal and unhuman. There have been periodic efforts to bring him down to earth, to expose his foibles, to debunk his fame, but he remained, and remains, massively monumental. By our time in the late 20th century he seems so far removed from us as to be virtually incomprehensible. He seems to come from another time and another place—from another world.

And that's the whole point about him: he does come from another world. And his countrymen realized it even before he died in 1799. He is the only truly classical hero we have ever had. He acquired at once a world-wide reputation as a great patriot-hero.

And he knew it. He was well aware of his reputation and his fame earned as the commander-in-chief of the American revolutionary forces. That awareness of his heroic stature and his character as a republican leader was crucial to Washington. It affected nearly everything he did for the rest of his life.

Washington was a thoroughly 18th-century figure. So much so, that he quickly became an anachronism. He belonged to the pre-democratic and pre-egalitarian world of the 18th century, to a world very different from the world that would follow. No wonder then that he seems to us so remote and so distant. He really is. He belonged to a world we have lost and we were losing even as Washington lived.

II

In many respects Washington was a very unlikely hero. To be sure, he had all the physical attributes of a classical hero. He was very tall by contemporary standards, and was heavily built and a superb athlete. Physically he had what both men and women admired. He was both a splendid horseman at a time when that skill really counted and an extraordinarily graceful dancer. And naturally he loved both riding and dancing. He always moved with dignity and looked the leader.

Yet those who knew him well and talked with him were often disappointed. He never seemed to have very much to say. He was most certainly *not* what we would today call an "intellectual." We cannot imagine him, say, expressing his views on Plato in the way Jefferson and John Adams did in their old age. Adams was especially contemptuous of Washington's intellectual abilities. It was certain, said Adams, that Washington was not a scholar. "That he was too illiterate, unread for his station and reputation is equally past dispute."

Adam's judgment is surely too harsh. Great men in the 18th century did not have to be scholars or intellectuals. But there is no doubt that Washington was not a learned man, especially in comparison with the other Founding Fathers. He was very ill at ease in abstract discussions. Even Jefferson, who was usually generous in his estimates of his friends, said that Washington's "colloquial talents were not above mediocrity." He had "neither copiousness of ideas nor fluency of words."

Washington was not an intellectual, but he was a man of affairs. He knew how to run his plantation and make it pay. He certainly ran Mount Vernon better than Jefferson ran Monticello. Washington's heart was always at Mount Vernon. He thought about it all the time. Even when he was president he devoted a great amount of his energy worrying about the fence posts of his plantation, and his letters dealing with the details of running Mount Vernon were longer than those dealing with the running of the federal government.

But being a man of affairs and running his plantation or even the federal government efficiently were not what made him a world-renowned hero. What was it that lay behind his extraordinary reputation, his greatness?

His military exploits were of course crucial. But Washington was not really a traditional military hero. He did not resemble Alexander, Caesar, Cromwell, or Marlborough; his military achievements were nothing compared to those Napoleon would soon have. Washington had no smashing, stunning victories. He was not a military genius, and his tactical and strategic maneuvers were not the sort that awed men. Military glory was *not* the source of his reputation. Something else was involved.

Washington's genius, his greatness, lay in his character. He was, as Chateaubriand said, a "hero of an unprecedented kind." There had never been a great man quite like Washington before. Washington became a great man and was acclaimed as a classical hero because of the way he conducted himself during times of temptation. It was his moral character that set him off from other men.

Washington fit the 18th-century image of a great man, of a man of virtue. This virtue was not given to him by nature. He had to work for it, to cultivate it, and everyone sensed that. Washington was a self-made hero, and this impressed an 18th-century enlightened world that put great stock in men controlling both their passions and their destinies. Washington seemed to possess a self-cultivated nobility.

He was in fact a child of the 18th-century Enlightenment. He was very much a man of his age, and he took its

moral standards more seriously than most of his contemporaries. Washington's Enlightenment, however, was not quite that of Jefferson or Franklin. Although he was conventionally enlightened about religion, "being no bigot myself to any mode of worship," he had no passionate dislike of the clergy and organized Christianity, as Jefferson did. And although he admired learning, he was not a man of science like Franklin. Like many other 18th-century Englishmen, he did *not* believe, as he put it, that "becoming a mere scholar is a desirable education for a gentleman."

Washington's Enlightenment was a much more down-to-earth affair, concerned with behavior and with living in the everyday-world of people. His Enlightenment involved what eventually came to be called cultivation and civilization. He lived his life by the book—not the book of military rules but the book of gentility. He was as keenly aware as any of his fellow Americans of the 18th-century conventions that defined what a proper gentleman was.

Such conventions were expressed in much of the writing of the Enlightenment. The thousands of etiquette books, didactic stories, *Spectator* papers, Hogarth prints, gentlemanly magazines, classical histories—all were designed to teach Englishmen manners, civility, politeness, and virtue. Out of all this writing and art emerged an ideal of what it was to be both enlightened and civilized, and a virtuous leader. Our perpetuation of a liberal arts education in our colleges and universities is a present-day reminder of the origins of this ideal; for the English conception of a liberally educated gentleman had its modern beginnings in the 18th century.

An enlightened, civilized man was disinterested and impartial, not swayed by self-interest and self-profit. He was cosmopolitan; he stood above all local and parochial considerations and was willing to sacrifice his personal desires for the greater good of his community or his country. He was a man of reason who resisted the passions most likely to afflict great men, that is, ambition and avarice. Such a liberal, enlightened gentleman avoided enthusiasms and fanaticisms of all sorts, especially those of religion. Tolerance and liberality were his watchwords. Politeness and compassion toward his fellow man were his manners. Behaving in this way was what constituted being civilized.

Washington was thoroughly caught up in this enlightened promotion of gentility and civility, this rational rolling back of parochialism, fanaticism, and barbarism. He may have gone to church regularly, but he was not an emotionally religious person. In all of his writings there is no mention of Christ, and God is generally referred to as "the great disposer of human events." Washington loved Addison's play *Cato* and saw it over and over and incorporated its lines into his correspondence. The play, very much an Enlightenment tract, helped to teach him what it meant to be liberal and virtuous, what it meant to be a stoical classical hero. He had the play put on for his troops during the terrible winter at Valley Forge in 1778.

One of the key documents of Washington's life is his "Rules of Civility and Decent Behaviour in Company and Conversation," a collection of 110 maxims that Washington wrote down sometime before his 16th birthday. The maxims were originally drawn from a 17th-century etiquette book and were copied by the young autodidact. They dealt with everything from how to treat one's betters ("In speaking to men of Quality do not lean nor Look them full in the Face") to how the present one's countenance ("Do not Puff up the Cheeks, Do not Loll out the tongue, rub the Hands, or beard, thrust out the lips, or bite them or keep the Lips too open or too Close").

All the Founding Fathers were aware of these enlightened conventions, and all in varying degrees tried to live up to them. But no one was more serious in following them than Washington. It is this purposefulness that gave his behavior such a copybook character. He was obsessed with having things in fashion and was fastidious about his appearance to the world. It was as if he were always on stage, acting a part. He was very desirous not to offend, and he exquisitely shaped his remarks to fit the person to whom he was writing—so much so that some historians have accused him of deceit. "So anxious was he to appear neat

and correct in his letters," recalled Benjamin Rush, that he was known to "copy over a letter of 2 or 3 sheets of paper because there were a few erasures on it." He wanted desperately to know what were the proper rules of behavior for a liberal gentleman, and when he discovered those rules he stuck by them with an earnestness that awed his contemporaries. His remarkable formality and stiffness in company came from his very self-conscious cultivation of what he considered proper, genteel, classical behavior.

Washington and Franklin, both children of the Enlightenment, had very different personalities, but among the Founding Fathers they shared one important thing. Neither of them went to college; neither had a formal liberal arts education. This deficiency deeply affected both of them, but Washington let it show. Washington always remained profoundly respectful of formal education. Colleges like William and Mary were always an "Object of Veneration" to him. His lack of a formal liberal arts education gave him a modesty he never lost. He repeatedly expressed his "consciousness of a defective education," and he remained quiet in the presence of sharp and sparkling minds. He was forever embarrassed that he had never learned any foreign languages. In the 1780's he refused invitations to visit France because he felt it would be humiliating for someone of his standing to have to converse through an interpreter. He said that it was his lack of a formal education that kept him from setting down on paper his recollections of the Revolution. It was widely rumored that his aides composed his best letters as commander-in-chief. If so, it is not surprising that he was diffident in company. Some even called it "shyness," but whatever the source, this reticence was certainly not the usual characteristic of a great man. "His modesty is astonishing, particularly to a Frenchman," noted Brissot de Warville. "He speaks of the American War as if he had *not* been its leader." This modesty only added to his gravity and severity. "Most people say and do too much," one friend recalled. "Washington . . . never fell into this common error."

III

Yet it was in the political world that Washington made his most theatrical gesture, his most moral mark, and there the results were monumental. The greatest act of his life, the one that made him famous, was his resignation as commander-in-chief of the American forces. This act, together with his 1783 circular letter to the states in which he promised to retire from public life, was his "legacy" to his countrymen. No American leader has ever left a more important legacy.

Following the signing of the peace treaty and British recognition of American independence, Washington stunned the world when he surrendered his sword to the Congress on Dec. 23, 1783 and retired to his farm at Mount Vernon. This was a highly symbolic act, a very self-conscious and unconditional withdrawal from the world of politics. Here was the commander in chief of the victorious army putting down his sword and promising not to take "any share in public business hereafter." Washington even resigned from his local vestry in Virginia in order to make his separation from the political world complete.

His retirement from power had a profound effect everywhere in the Western world. It was extraordinary, it was unprecedented in modern times—a victorious general surrendering his arms and returning to his farm. Cromwell, William of Orange, Marlborough—all had sought political rewards commensurate with their military achievements. Though it was widely thought that Washington could have become king or dictator, he wanted nothing of the kind. He was sincere in his desire for all the soldiers "to return to our Private Stations in the bosom of a free, peaceful and happy Country," and everyone recognized his sincerity. It filled them with awe. Washington's retirement, said the painter John Trumbull writing from London in 1784, "excites the astonishment and admiration of this part of the world. 'Tis a Conduct so novel, so unconceivable to People, who, far from giving up powers they possess, are willing to convulse the empire to acquire more." King George III supposedly predicted that if

Washington retired from public life and returned to his farm, "he will be the greatest man in the world."

Washington was not naïve. He was well aware of the effect his resignation would have. He was trying to live up to the age's image of a classical disinterested patriot who devotes his life to his country, and he knew at once that he had acquired instant fame as a modern Cincinnatus. His reputation in the 1780's as a great classical hero was international, and it was virtually unrivaled. Franklin was his only competitor, but Franklin's greatness still lay in his being a scientist, not a man of public affairs. Washington was a living embodiment of all that classical republican virtue the age was eagerly striving to recover.

Despite his outward modesty, Washington realized he was an extraordinary man, and he was not ashamed of it. He lived in an era where distinctions of rank and talent were not only accepted but celebrated. He took for granted the differences between himself and more ordinary men. And when he could not take those differences for granted he cultivated them. He used his natural reticence to reinforce the image of a stern and forbidding classical hero. His aloofness was notorious, and he worked at it. When the painter Gilbert Stuart had uncharacteristic difficulty in putting Washington at ease during a sitting for a portrait, Stuart in exasperation finally pleaded, "Now sir, you must let me forget that you are General Washington and that I am Stuart, the painter," Washington's reply chilled the air: "Mr. Stuart need never feel the need of forgetting who he is or who General Washington is." No wonder the portraits look stiff.

Washington had earned his reputation, his "character," as a moral hero, and he did not want to dissipate it. He spent the rest of his life guarding and protecting his reputation, and worrying about it. He believed Franklin made a mistake going back into public life in Pennsylvania in the 1780's. Such involvement in politics, he thought, could only endanger Franklin's already achieved international standing. In modern eyes Washington's concern for his reputation is embarrassing; it seems obsessive and egotistical. But his contemporaries understood. All gentlemen tried scrupulously to guard their reputations, which is what they meant by their honor. Honor was the esteem in which they were held, and they prized it. To have honor across space and time was to have fame, and fame, "the ruling passion of the noblest minds," was what the Founding Fathers were after, Washington above all. And he got it, sooner and in greater degree than any other of his contemporaries. And naturally, having achieved what all his fellow Revolutionaries still anxiously sought, he was reluctant to risk it.

Many of his actions after 1783 can be understood only in terms of this deep concern for his reputation as a virtuous leader. He was constantly on guard and very sensitive to any criticism. Jefferson said no one was more sensitive. He judged all his actions by what people might think of them. This sometimes makes him seem silly to modern minds, but not to those of the 18th century. In that very suspicious age where people were acutely "jealous" of what great men were up to, Washington thought it important that people understand his motives. The reality was not enough; he had to *appear* virtuous. He was obsessed that he not seem base, mean, avaricious, or unduly ambitious. No one, said Jefferson, worked harder than Washington in keeping "motives of interest of consanguinity, of friendship or hatred" from influencing him. He had a lifelong preoccupation with his reputation for "disinterestedness" and how best to use that reputation for the good of his country. This preoccupation explains the seemingly odd fastidiousness and the caution of his behavior in the 1780's.

One of the most revealing incidents occurred in the winter of 1784–85. Washington was led into temptation, and it was agony. The Virginia General Assembly presented him with 150 shares in the James River and Potomac canal companies in recognition of his services to the state and the cause of canal-building. What should he do? He did not feel he could accept the shares. Acceptance might be "considered in the same light as a pension" and might compromise his reputation for virtue. Yet he believed passionately in what the canal compa-

nies were doing and had long dreamed of making a fortune from such canals. Moreover, he did not want to show "disrespect" to the Assembly or to appear "ostentatiously disinterested" by refusing this gift.

Few decisions in Washington's career caused more distress than this one. He wrote to everyone he knew—to Jefferson, to Governor Patrick Henry, to William Grayson, to Benjamin Harrison, to George William Fairfax, to Nathanael Greene, even to Lafayette—seeking "the best information and advice" on the disposition of the shares. "How would this matter be viewed by the eyes of the world?" he asked. Would not his reputation for virtue be harmed? Would not accepting the shares "deprive me of the principal thing which is laudable in my conduct?"

The situation is humorous today, but it was not to Washington. He suffered real anguish. Jefferson eventually found the key to Washington's anxieties and told him that declining to accept the shares would only add to his reputation for disinterestedness. So Washington gave them away to the college that eventually became Washington and Lee.

Washington suffered even more anguish over the decision to attend the Philadelphia Convention in 1787. Many believed that his presence was absolutely necessary for the effectiveness of the Convention, but the situation was tricky. He wrote to friends imploring them to tell him "confidentially what the public expectation is on this head, that is, whether I will or ought to be there?" How would his presence be seen, how would his motives be viewed? If he attended, would he be thought to have violated his pledge to withdraw from public life? But, if he did not attend, would his staying away be thought to be a "dereliction to Republicanism"? Should he squander his reputation on something that might not work?

What if the Convention should fail? The delegates would have to return home, he said, "chagrined at their ill success and disappointment. This would be a disagreeable circumstance for any one of them to be in; but more particularly so, for a person in my situation." Even James Madison had second thoughts about the possibility of misusing such a precious asset as Washington's reputation. What finally convinced Washington to attend the Convention was the fear that people might think he wanted the federal government to fail so that he could manage a miliary takeover. So in the end he decided, as Madison put it, "to forsake the honorable retreat to which he had retired, and risk the reputation he had so deservedly acquired." No action could be more virtuous. "Secure as he was in his fame," wrote Henry Knox with some awe, "he has again committed it to the mercy of events. Nothing but the critical situation of his country would have induced him to so hazardous a conduct."

IV

When the Convention met, Washington was at once elected its president. His presence and his leadership undoubtedly gave the Convention and the proposed Constitution a prestige that they otherwise could not have had. His backing of the Constitution was essential to its eventual ratification. "Be assured," James Monroe told Jefferson, "his influence carried this government." Washington, once committed to the Constitution, worked hard for its acceptance. He wrote letters to friends and let his enthusiasm for the new federal government be known. Once he had identified himself publicly with the new Constitution he became very anxious to have it accepted. Its ratification was a kind of ratification of himself.

After the Constitution was established, Washington still thought he could retire to the domestic tranquility of Mount Vernon. But everyone else expected that he would become president of the new national government. He was already identified with the country. People said he was denied children in his private life so he could be the father of his country. He had to be the president. Indeed, the Convention had made the new chief executive so strong, so kinglike, precisely because the delegates expected Washington to be the first president.

Once again this widespread expectation aroused all his old anxieties about his reputation for disinterestedness and the proper role for a former military leader. Had he not promised the country that he would permanently retire from public life? How could he then now assume the presidency without being "chargeable with levity and inconsistency; if not with rashness and ambition?" His protests were sincere. He had so much to lose, yet he did not want to appear "too solicitous for my reputation."

Washington's apparent egotism and his excessive coyness, his extreme reluctance to get involved in public affairs and endanger his reputation, have not usually been well received by historians. Douglas Southall Freeman, his great biographer, thought that Washington in the late 1780's was "too zealously attentive to his prestige, his reputation and his popularity—too much the self-conscious national hero and too little the daring patriot." Historians might not understand his behavior, but his contemporaries certainly did. They rarely doubted that Washington was trying *always* to act in a disinterested and patriotic way. His anxious queries about how this or that would look to the world, his hesitations about serving or not serving, his expressions of scruples and qualms—all were part of his strenuous effort to live up to the classical idea of a virtuous leader.

He seemed to epitomize public virtue and the proper character of a republican ruler. Even if John Adams was not all that impressed with George Washington, Adam's wife Abigail was certainly taken with him. She admired his restraint and trusted him. "If he was not really one of the best-intentioned men in the world," she wrote, "he might be a very dangerous one." As Gary Wills has so nicely put it, Washington gained his power by his readiness to give it up.

As president he continued to try to play the role he thought circumstances demanded. He knew that the new government was fragile and needed dignity. People found that dignity in his person. Madison believed that Washington was the only part of the new government that captured the minds of the people. He fleshed out the executive, established its independence, and gave the new government the pomp and ceremony many thought it needed.

Sometimes it had more pomp than even he enjoyed. His formal levees, complete with silver buckles and powdered hair, were painful affairs for everyone. These receptions, held at first on Tuesday and Friday afternoons and later on only Tuesdays, were an opportunity for prominent men to meet the president. The invited guests, all men, entered the president's residence at three o'clock, where they found the president standing before the fireplace. Fifteen minutes were allowed for the guests to assemble in a circle. As each guest entered the room he walked to the President, bowed, and without speaking backed to his place in the circle. The only voice heard was that of a presidential aide softly announcing the names. Promptly on the quarter hour the doors were shut; the President then walked around the circle, addressed each man by name, and made some brief remark to him. He bowed but never shook hands. Washington thought that handshaking was much too familiar for the president to engage in; consequently he kept one hand occupied holding a fake hat and the other resting on his dress sword. When the president had rounded the circle, he returned to the fireplace and stood until, at a signal from an aide, each guest one by one went to him, bowed without saying anything, and left the room. However excruciatingly formal these levees were, Washington thought they would continue. He thus designed the bowed shaped of the Blue Room to accommodate them.

Although many critics thought that the levees smacked of the court life of kings of Europe, Washington was not a crypto-monarchist. He was a devoted republican, at heart just a country gentleman. Martha used to break up tea parties at 9:30 p.m. by saying that it was past the President's bedtime.

As president he tried to refuse accepting any salary just as he had as commander-in-chief. Still, he wanted to make the presidency "respectable," and he spared few expenses in doing so; he spent 7 percent of his $25,000 salary on liquor and wine for entertaining. He was especially interested in the size and character of the White House and of the capital city that was named after him. The scale and grandeur of Washington, D.C., owe much to his vision and his backing of Pierre L'Enfant as architect. If Secretary of State Thomas Jefferson had had his way, L'Enfant would never have kept his job as long as he did, and the capital would have been smaller and less magnificent—perhaps something on the order of a college campus, like Jefferson's University of Virginia.

V

Washington was keenly aware that everything he did would set precedents for the future. "We are a young nation," he said, "and have a character to establish. It behoves us therefore to set out right, for first impressions will be lasting." It was an awesome responsibility. More than any of his contemporaries, he thought constantly of future generations, of "millions unborn," as he called them.

He created an independent role for the president and made the chief executive the dominant figure in the government.

He established crucial precedents, especially in limiting the Senate's role in advising the president in the making of treaties and the appointing of officials. In August 1789 he went to the Senate to get its advice and consent to a treaty he was negotiating with the Creek Indians. Vice President John Adams who presided read each section of the treaty and then asked the senators, How do you advise and consent? After a long silence, the senators, being senators, began debating each section, with Washington impatiently glaring down at them. Finally, one senator moved that the treaty and all the accompanying documents that the president had brought with him be submitted to a committee for study. Washington started up in what one senator called "a violent fret." In exasperation he cried, "This defeats every purpose of my coming here." He calmed down, but when he finally left the Senate chamber, he was overheard to say he would "be damned if he ever went there again." He never did. The advice part of the Senate's role in treaty making was dropped.

The presidency is the powerful office it is in large part because of Washington's initial behavior. He understood power and how to use it. But as in the case of his career as commander-in-chief, his most important act as president was his giving up of the office.

The significance of his retirement from the presidency is easy for us to overlook, but his contemporaries knew what it meant. Most people assumed that Washington might be president as long as he lived, that he would be a kind of elective monarch—something not out of the question in the 18th century. Some people even expressed relief that he had no heirs. Thus his persistent efforts to retire from the presidency enhanced his moral authority and helped fix the republican character of the Constitution.

He very much wanted to retire in 1792, but his advisors and friends talked him into staying on for a second term. Madison admitted that when he had first urged Washington to accept the presidency he had told him that he could protect himself from accusations of overweening ambition by "a voluntary return to public life as soon as the state of the Government would permit." But the state of the government, said Madison, was not yet secure. So Washington reluctantly stayed on.

But in 1796 he was so determined to retire that no one could dissuade him, and his voluntary leaving of the office set a precedent that was not broken until FDR secured a third term in 1940. So strong was the sentiment for a two-term limit, however, that the tradition was written into the Constitution in the 22nd amendment in 1951. Washington's action in 1796 was of great significance. That the chief executive of a state should willingly relinquish his office was an object lesson in republicanism at a time when the republican experiment throughout the Atlantic world was very much in doubt.

Washington's final years in retirement were not happy ones. The American political world was changing, becoming more partisan, and Washington struggled to comprehend these changes. During President Adams' administration he watched with dismay what he believed was the growing inter-ference of the French government in American politics. For him the Jeffersonian Republican party had become "the French Party." It was, he said, "the curse of this country," threatening the stability and independence of the United States. He saw plots and enemies everywhere and became as much of a high-toned Federalist as Hamilton.

His fear was real; his sense of crisis was deep. He and other Federalists thought that the French might invade the country and together with "the French Party" overthrow the government. "Having Struggled for Eight or nine Years against the invasion of our rights by one power, and to establish an Independence of it," he wrote in 1798, "I could not remain an unconcerned spectator of the attempt of another Power to accomplish the same object, though in a different way." He thus listened attentively to all the urgent Federalist calls that he come out of retirement and head the army that the Congress had created to meet the French invasion.

Again he expressed reluctance, and asked whether becoming commander-in-chief would not be considered "a restless Act—evidence of my discontent in retirement." Yet in 1798 he was far more eager to step back into the breach and do his duty than he ever had been before. It was a measure of his despair with this "Age of Wonders"!

Before he could actually commit himself, however, President John Adams acted and, without his permission, appointed him commander of all the military forces of the United States. He accepted, but scarcely comprehended how it had all come about. The next thing he knew he was on his way to Philadelphia to organize the army. Events were outrunning his ability to control them or even to comprehend them, and he more and more saw himself caught up in "the designs of Providence." His command was a disaster. He wrangled over the appointments of the second in command, intrigued against Adams, and interfered with his cabinet. When neither the French invasion nor the American army materialized, Washington crept back to Mount Vernon thoroughly disillusioned with the new ways of American politics.

In July 1799 Governor Jonathan Trumbull of Connecticut with the backing of many Federalists urged Washington once again to stand for the presidency in 1800. Only Washington, Trumbull said, could unite the Federalists and save the country from "a French President." Finally Washington had had enough. In his reply he no longer bothered with references to his reputation for disinterestedness and his desire to play the role of Cincinnatus. Instead he talked about the new political conditions that made his candidacy irrelevant. In this new democratic era of party politics, he said, "personal influence," distinctions of character, no longer mattered. If the members of the Jeffersonian Republican party "set up a broomstick" as candidate and called it "a true son of Liberty" or "a Democrat" or "any other epithet that will suit their purpose," it still would "command their votes in toto!" But, even worse, he said,

the same was true of the Federalists. Party spirit now ruled all, and people voted only for their party candidate. Even if he were the Federalist candidate, Washington was "thoroughly convinced I should not draw a *single* vote from the anti-Federal side." Therefore his standing for election made no sense; he would "stand upon no stronger ground than any other Federal character well supported."

Washington wrote all this in anger and despair, but, though he exaggerated, he was essentially right. The political world was changing, becoming democratic, and parties, not great men, would soon become the objects of contention. To be sure, the American people continued to long for great heroes as leaders, and from Jackson through Eisenhower they have periodically elected Washington-*manqués* to the presidency.

But democracy made such great heroes no longer essential to the workings

of American government. And Washington, more than any other single individual, was the one who made that democracy possible. As Jefferson said "the moderation and virtue of a single character . . . probably prevented this revolution from being closed, as most others have been, by a subversion of that liberty it was intended to establish."

Washington was an extraordinary heroic man who made rule by more ordinary mortals possible. He virtually created the presidency, and gave it a dignity that through the years it has never lost. But, more important, he established the standard by which all subsequent presidents have been ultimately measured—not by the size of their electoral victories, not by their legislative programs, and not by the number of their vetoes, but by their moral character. Although we live in another world than his, his great legacy is still with us.

1796: The First Real Election

BY JOHN FERLING *When George Washington announced that he would retire from office, he set the stage for the nation's first two-party presidential campaign.*

ON THE DAY in April 1789 that he took the oath of office at Federal Hall in New York City as the first president of the United States, George Washington noted in his diary: "I bade adieu to Mount Vernon, to private life, and to domestic felicity and with a mind oppressed with more anxious and painful sensations than I have words to express.

THE BETTMANN ARCHIVE

Throughout the Revolutionary War and the new United States' formative years, John Adams gave tireless service to his country, including eight years as its first vice president. Although he felt entitled to the presidency, Adams, the Federalist candidate, refused to campaign for the office.

Washington, who embodied the virtues exalted by his generation, had been given the unanimous vote of the new na-

tion's electors. He had done nothing to promote himself as a candidate for the presidency and had agreed to undertake the mammoth task with the utmost reluctance. Whatever his personal misgivings, Washington's first term in office went smoothly. It was so successful, in fact, that in 1792 he once again received the electors' unanimous endorsement.

Such smooth sailing of the ship of state could not be expected to last, however, and during President Washington's second term, the United States—and thus its chief executive—began to experience the kinds of problems that plague any government. Relations with the former "mother country" deteriorated until it seemed that another war with Great Britain might be inevitable. And on the domestic front, groups of farmers, especially those in the westernmost counties of Pennsylvania, protested and rebelled against the Washington administration's excise tax on the whiskey that they distilled from their grain, eventually rioting in the summer of 1794.

The hero of America's revolution also suffered personal attacks on his character. Rumors had it that Washington was given to "gambling, reveling, horseracing and horse whipping" and that he had even taken British bribes while he was commanding American troops.

During the last weeks of 1795, reports spread through Philadelphia—then the national capital—that Washington

planned to retire at the conclusion of his second term. It was true that similar ru-

THE GRANGER COLLECTION

Republican candidate Aaron Burr of New York, who later gained notoriety by killing political opponent Alexander Hamilton in a duel, ran fourth in the 1796 presidential race.

mors had circulated three years before, as the end of his first term drew near, but this time it appeared that he was determined to step down. Nearing his mid-sixties—a normal life span for a man in the eighteenth century—the president longed to retire to the tranquility of Mount Vernon, his beloved home in Virginia.

Although Washington said nothing to John Adams regarding his plans for retirement, his wife Martha hinted to the

From *American History*, December 1996, pp. 24-28, 66-68. © 1996 by Cowles Magazines, Inc. Reprinted through the courtesy of Cowles Magazines, publishers of *American History*.

vice president near Christmas 1795 that her husband would be leaving office. Ten days later, Adams learned that the president had informed his cabinet that he would step down in March 1797.* "You know the Consequences of this, to me and to yourself," Adams, aware that he might become the second president of the United States, wrote to his wife Abigail that same evening.

Adams's ascension to the presidency would be neither automatic nor unanimous. Before achieving that high office, he would have to emerge victorious from America's first contested presidential election.

Eight years earlier, in September 1787, the delegates to the Constitutional Convention had considered numerous plans for choosing a president. They had rejected direct election by qualified voters because, as Roger Sherman of Connecticut remarked, a scattered population could never "be informed of the characters of the leading candidates." The delegates also ruled out election by Congress. Such a procedure, Gouverneur Morris stated, would inevitably be "the work of intrigue, cabal and of faction."

Finally, the convention agreed to an electoral college scheme, whereby "Each state shall appoint in such manner as the Legislature thereof may direct, a Number of Electors, equal to the whole Number of Senators and Representatives to which the State may be entitled in the Congress." Presidential selection, therefore, would be decided through a state-by-state, rather than a national, referendum.

Each elector chosen by the voters or the legislature of his state would cast votes for two candidates, one of whom had to come from outside his state. The electors' ballots would be opened in the presence of both houses of Congress. If no one received a majority of the votes, or if two or more individuals tied with a majority of the electoral college votes, the members of the House of Representatives would cast ballots to elect the president.* Once the president had been decided upon, the candidate from among those remaining who had received the second largest number of electoral votes became the vice president.

The framers of the Constitution believed that most electors would judiciously cast their two ballots for persons of "real merit," as Morris put it. Alexander Hamilton argued in *Federalist 68*—one of a series of essays penned by Hamilton, James Madison, and John Jay to encourage ratification of the Constitution in New York State—that it was a "moral certainty" that the electoral college scheme would result in the election of the most qualified man. Someone skilled in the art of intrigue might win a high state office, he wrote, but only a man nationally known for his "ability and virtue" could gain the support of electors from throughout the United States.

Indeed, the "electoral college" plan worked well during the first two presidential elections in 1788 and 1792, when every elector had cast one of his ballots for Washington. But by 1796, something unforeseen by the delegates to the Constitutional Convention had occurred; men of different points of view had begun to form themselves into political parties.

The first signs of such factionalism appeared early in Washington's presidency On one side were the Federalists who yearned for an American society and national government established on the British model. Skeptical of the growing democratization of the new nation, the Federalists desired a centralized national government that would have the strength both to aid merchants and manufacturers and to safeguard America's traditional hierarchical society

By 1792, Secretary of State Thomas Jefferson and Congressman James Madison—both, like Washington, from Virginia—had taken steps to fashion an opposition party. Jefferson became the acknowledged leader of the new Anti-Federalists, a group soon known as the Democratic-Republican Party because of its empathy for the struggling republic that had emerged from the French Revolution of 1789. This party looked irreverently upon the past, was devoted to republican institutions, sought to give property-owning citizens greater control over their lives, and dreamt of an agrarian nation in which government would be small and weak.

Members of both parties ran candidates in congressional and state races in 1792, but they did not challenge President Washington. Partisanship, however, did surface that year in the contest for the vice presidency. Some Republicans acted behind the scenes in "support . . . of removing Mr. A," as the clerk of the House noted, mainly because Adams's writings on government included positive statements about the British monarchy. The movement came to naught because it did not have the support of Jefferson, who had known and liked Adams for nearly twenty years. Other Republicans rallied behind George Clinton, the newly elected governor of New York.

The activity of the Republicans threw a scare into the Federalists. Secretary of the Treasury Alexander Hamilton, the acknowledged leader of the Federalists, was so worried that he urged Adams to cut short a vacation and campaign openly against those who were—as he said—"ill disposed" toward him. Adams, who regarded electioneering with contempt, refused to do so and remained on his farm in Quincy, Massachusetts, until after the electors had cast their ballots.

By March 1796, when Washington finally told his vice president that he would not seek reelection, Adams had decided to run for the office of president. His decision was "no light thing," he said, since he knew that as president he would be subjected to "obloquy, contempt, and insult." He even told Abigail that he believed every chief executive was "almost sure of disgrace and ruin." While she had mixed emotions about his decision, she did not discourage him from running. In fact, she told him that the presidency would be a "flattering

---

*The March 4 date for the beginning of new terms of office went back to tradition begun under the Articles of Confederation and codified by Congressional legislation in 1792. The Twentieth Amendment to the Constitution, ratified in 1933, specified that henceforth Congressional terms would begin on January 3 and that an incoming president and vice president would take their oaths of office at noon on January 20 of the year following their election.

*Not since 1824 has the winner of a presidential contest been decided by the House of Representatives. In that year, John Quincy Adams gained the presidency when one more than half of the members of the House cast their ballots in his favor, giving him the necessary majority.

THE GRANGER COLLECTION

As a South Carolinian, Thomas Pinckney enjoyed Southern support. Although he was a Federalist, he suffered from rumors of political maneuvering by Alexander Hamilton, the leader of that party, and failed to get the New England votes that would have enabled him to serve as Adams's vice president.

and Glorious Reward" for his long years of service. Ultimately Adams decided to seek the office because, he asserted, "I love my country too well to shrink from danger in her service."

As he began his quest, Adams expected formidable opposition, especially from Jefferson. He foresaw three possible outcomes to the election: he might garner the most votes, with Jefferson running second; Jefferson might win and John Jay of New York, long a congressman and diplomat, could finish second; or Jefferson might be elected president, while he was himself reelected vice president. That last scenario was not one Adams was prepared to accept. He decided that he would not serve another term as vice president; if he finished second again, he declared, he would either retire or seek election to the House of Representatives.

Adams considered himself the "heir apparent to President Washington, having languished in the vice presidency—which he described as "the most insignificant office that ever the invention of man contrived or his imagination conceived"—for eight years, awaiting his turn. Furthermore, he believed that

no man had made greater sacrifices for the nation during the American Revolution than he. In addition to risking his legal career to protest British policies, he sat as a member of the First Continental Congress for three years and served abroad from 1778–88, making two perilous Atlantic crossings to carry out his diplomatic assignments. During that ten years, his public service had forced him to live apart from his wife and five children nearly ninety percent of the time.

Jefferson often proclaimed his disdain for politics, even though he held political office almost continuously for forty years. As 1796 unfolded, he neither made an effort to gain the presidency nor rebuffed the Republican maneuvers to elect him to that office. When he resigned as secretary of state in 1793, Jefferson had said that he did not plan to hold public office again and would happily remain at Monticello, his Virginia estate. But, while he did not seek office in 1796, neither did he say that he would not accept the presidential nomination. Adams—and most Republicans—interpreted Jefferson's behavior as indicating that he wanted to be president.

The Constitution said nothing about how to select presidential nominees. In 1800, the Republican Party would choose its candidates in a congressional nominating caucus; in 1812, the first nominating conventions were held in several states; and the first national nominating convention took place in 1832. But in 1796, the nominees seemed to materialize out of thin air, as if by magic. In actuality the party leaders decided on the candidates and attempted to herd their followers into line.

The Federalists' support centered on Adams and Thomas Pinckney of South Carolina. Pinckney who had recently negotiated a successful treaty with Spain that established territorial and traffic rights for the United States on the Mississippi River, was chosen for the second slot on the ticket by the party moguls—without consulting Adams—in part because as a Southerner, he might siphon Southern votes from Jefferson.

On the Republican side, Madison confided to James Monroe in February that "Jefferson alone can be started with

hope of success, [and we] mean to push him. The Republicans also endorsed Senator Aaron Burr of New York.

All this transpired quietly for Washington did not publicly announce his intention of retiring until the very end of the summer. Not that the parties' plans were a mystery. Before Washington finally informed the nation of his decision on September 19, 1796, in his "Farewell Address"—which was not delivered orally but was printed in Philadelphia's *American Daily Advertiser*—the keenly partisan *Philadelphia Aurora* declared that it "requires no talent at divination to decide who will be candidates.... Thomas Jefferson & John Adams will be the men."

But Washington's address, said congressman Fisher Ames of Massachusetts, was "a signal, like dropping a hat, for the party racers to start." During the next ten

THE GRANGER COLLECTION

The author of the Declaration of Independence, Thomas Jefferson, became the leader of the Anti-Federalists—otherwise known as the Democratic-Republicans—who opposed ties with Great Britain and admired the ideals of the French Revolution of 1789. He gained the second highest number of electoral votes in 1796, thus becoming the nation's second vice president.

weeks, the presidential campaign of 1796 was waged, as Federalists and Republicans—with the exception, for the most part, of the candidates themselves—worked feverishly for victory.

Adams, Jefferson, and Pinckney never left home. While their parties took stands on the major issues of the day these men embraced the classical model of politics, refusing to campaign. They believed that a man should not pursue an office; rather, the office should seek out the man. They agreed that the most talented men—what some called an aristocracy of merit—should govern, but also that ultimate power rested with the people. The qualified voters, or the

electioneering took place through handbills, pamphlets, and newspapers.

The campaign was a rough and tumble affair. The Republicans sought to convince the electorate that their opponents longed to establish a titled nobility in America and that Adams—whom they caricatured as "His Rotundity" because of his small, portly stature—was a pro-British monarchist. President Wash-

puppet who would plunge the United States into another war with Great Britain. They also charged that he was indecisive and a visionary. A "philosopher makes the worst politician," one Federalist advised, while another counseled that Jefferson was "fit to be a professor in a college . . . but certainly not the first magistrate of a great nation." Newspapers such as the *Gazette of the United States* and *Porcupine's Gazette* asserted that Jefferson's election would result in domestic disorder.

Behind-the-scenes maneuvering included a plan by Hamilton, who felt that Pinckney could be more easily manipulated than Adams, to have one or two Federalist electors withhold their votes for Adams. Hearing rumors of the ploy, several New England electors conferred and agreed not to cast a ballot for Pinckney.

Even the French minister to the United States, Pierre Adet, became involved in the election by seeking to convey the impression that a victory for Jefferson would result in improved relations with France. As one historian has noted: "Never before or since has a foreign power acted so openly in an American election."

THE GRANGER COLLECTION

Although he was not himself a candidate in the 1796 election, Alexander Hamilton (second from right, above), secretary of the treasury in Washington's first cabinet, played an influential role, supporting John Adams and actively campaigning against Thomas Jefferson.

Sixteen states took part in the balloting. The 138 electors were chosen by popular vote in six states and by the state legislatures of the remaining ten. Seventy votes were required to win a majority.

Adams expected to receive all of New England's 39 votes, but he also had to win all 12 of New York's votes and 19 from the other middle and southern states to win. He concluded that was impossible, especially after learning of Hamilton's machinations. On the eve of the electoral college vote, Adams remarked privately that Hamilton had "outgeneraled" all the other politicians and stolen the election for Pinckney.

The electors voted in their respective state capitals on the first Wednesday in December, but the law stipulated that the ballots could not be opened and counted until the second Wednesday in February And so for nearly seventy days, every conceivable rumor circulated regarding the outcome of the elec-

elected representatives of the people, were capable of selecting the best men from among the candidates on the basis of what Adams called the "pure Principles of Merit, Virtue, and public Spirit."

Burr alone actively campaigned. Although he did not make any speeches, he visited every New England state and spoke with several presidential electors. Many Federalist and Republican officeholders and supporters spoke at rallies, but most of the

ington was assailed for supporting Hamilton's aggressive economic program, as well as for the Jay Treaty of 1795, which had settled outstanding differences between the United States and Britain. The *Philadelphia Aurora* went so far as to insist that the president was the "source of all the misfortunes of our country."

The Federalists responded by portraying Jefferson as an atheist and French tion. By the third week in December, however, one thing was clear, Jefferson could not get seventy votes. Although 63 electors were Southerners, the South was a two-party region, and it was known that Jefferson had not received a vote from every Southern elector. In addition, because the Federalists controlled the legislatures in New York, New Jersey and Delaware, it was presumed that Jefferson would be shut out in those states.

Beyond that, nothing was certain. Many believed that Pinckney would win, either because of Hamilton's supposed chicanery or because all "the Jeffs," as Ames called the Southern Republican electors, supposedly had cast their second ballot for the South Carolinian in order to ensure that a Southerner succeed Washington. A good number of Americans fully expected that no candidate would get a majority of the votes, thus sending the election to the House of Representatives.

By the end of December, better information arrived in Philadelphia when Ames informed Adams that he had at least 71 electoral votes. On December 28, Jefferson wrote Adams a congratulatory letter and at Washington's final levee in 1796, the First Lady told the vice president of her husband's delight at his victory. Persuaded that he was indeed the victor, an ebullient Adams wrote his wife at year's end that he had "never felt more serene" in his life.

Finally on February 8, 1797, the sealed ballots were opened and counted before a joint session of Congress. Ironically, it was Vice President Adams, in his capacity as president of the Senate, who read aloud the results. The tabulation showed that Adams had indeed garnered 71 votes. Every New England and New York elector had voted for him. The tales about Hamilton's treachery had been untrue; ultimately the former treasury secretary found the prospect of a Jefferson administration too distasteful to risk the subterfuge necessary to defeat Adams, who also got, as expected, all ten votes from New Jersey

and Delaware. And in a sense, Adams won the election in the South, having secured nine votes in Maryland, North Carolina, and Virginia.

Jefferson, who finished second with 68 votes, automatically became the new vice president.* One Federalist elector in Virginia, the representative of a western district that long had exhibited hostility toward the planter aristocracy voted for Adams and Pinckney as did four electors from commercial, Federalist enclaves in Maryland and North Carolina. Whereas Adams secured enough votes in the South to push him over the top, Jefferson did not receive a single electoral vote in New England or in New York, New Jersey or Delaware.

Pinckney, not Adams, was the real victim of Hamilton's rumored duplicity. To ensure that the South Carolinian did not obtain more votes than Adams, 18 Federalist electors in New England refused to give him their vote. Had Pinckney received 12 of those votes, the election would have been thrown into the House of Representatives. Instead, he finished third with 59 electoral votes.

Burr polled only thirty votes. Southern Republicans—perhaps sharing the sentiment of the Virginia elector who remarked that there were "traits of character" in Burr which "sooner or later will give us much trouble"—rejected him.

Even among the enfranchised citizens, few bothered to cast ballots in this election. In Pennsylvania, a state in which the electors were popularly chosen, only about one-quarter of the eligi-

---

*This first contested presidential election demonstrated a flaw in the Constitution's electoral college scheme since the country now had a Federalist president and a Republican vice president. Four years later, the two Republican candidates, Jefferson and Burr, each received 73 electoral votes. Although it was clear during the election campaign that Jefferson was the presidential candidate and Burr the vice presidential, Burr refused to concede, forcing a vote in the House of Representatives that brought Jefferson into office. To correct these defects the Twelfth Amendment, which provided for separate balloting for president and vice president, was adopted in 1804.

ble voters went to the polls. But the contest in Pennsylvania was an augury of the political changes soon to come. The Republicans swept 14 of the state's 15 electoral votes, winning in part because they "outpoliticked" their opponents by running better-known candidates for the electoral college and because Minister Adet's intrusive comments helped Jefferson among Quakers and Philadelphia merchants who longed for peace. Many voters had rejected the Federalist Party because they thought of it as a pro-British, pro-aristocratic party committed to an economic program designed to benefit primarily the wealthiest citizens.

And what occurred in Pennsylvania was not unique. Jefferson won more than eighty percent of the electoral college votes in states outside New England that chose their electors by popular vote. In an increasingly democratic United States, the election of 1796 represented the last great hurrah for the Federalist Party.

On March 4, 1797, America's first orderly transferal of power occurred in Philadelphia when George Washington stepped down and John Adams took the oath as the second president of the United States. Many spectators were moved to tears during this emotional affair, not only because Washington's departure brought an era to a close, but because the ceremony represented a triumph for the republic. Adams remarked that this peaceful event was the sublimist thing ever exhibited in America." He also noted Washington's joy at surrendering the burdens of the presidency. In fact, Adams believed that Washington's countenance seemed to say: "Ay! I am fairly out and you fairly in! See which of us will be the happiest."

Historian John Ferling is the author of the recently re-released John Adams: A Life *(An Owl Book, Henry Holt and Company, 1996, $17.95 paper).*

Lewis and Clark

Trailblazers Who Opened the Continent

Few Americans better embodied the spirit of adventure and dedication that led 19th-century explorers to brave the perils of an unknown land.

by Gerald F. Kreyche

EVERY SOCIETY has a need for heroes who serve as role models. The U.S. is no exception and has produced its share of them—Pres. Abraham Lincoln, aviator Charles Lindbergh, civil rights leader Martin Luther King, Jr., and the astronauts, to name a few. Heroes belong to the ages, and we can refresh our pride and patriotism by recalling their deeds.

In the early 19th century, two relatively unsung heroes, Meriwether Lewis and William Clark, braved the perils of a vast unknown territory to enlarge knowledge, increase commerce, and establish a relationship with unknown Indians. Their journals produced eight detailed volumes of data ranging from maps, climate, geography, and ethnic observations to the discovery of new species of plants and animals.

In the late 18th century, America's western border was constituted first by the Allegheny Mountains and later the Mississippi River. Little was known of the geography immediately beyond the Father of Waters, and less yet of what lay west of the Missouri River. This was to change, however, for Pres. Thomas Jefferson had an unquenchable yearning for such knowledge and did something about it.

Dr. Kreyche, American Thought Editor of USA Today, *is emeritus professor of philosophy, DePaul University, Chicago, Ill.*

As early as 1784, he conferred with George Rogers Clark about exploring this uncharted area. In 1786 he hired John Ledyard, a former marine associate of British explorer James Cook, to walk from west to east, beginning in Stockholm, Sweden. The intent was to traverse Russia, Alaska, the western Canadian coast, and thence across the Louisiana Territory. Ledyard walked from Stockholm to St. Petersburg, Russia, in two weeks. The Russians stopped him at Irkutsk, Siberia, and Jefferson was disappointed again. Undaunted, Jefferson made plans for Andre Michael to explore the area, but this, too, failed.

After being inaugurated in 1801, Jefferson had the power to make his pet project a reality. He appointed as his private secretary Meriwether Lewis, a wellborn young army captain. In January, 1803, in a secret message to Congress, the President asked for funding to realize his exploratory project of what lay between the Missouri River and the Pacific Ocean. The sum of $2,500 was appropriated. (The project eventually was to cost $38,000, an early case of a governmental cost overrun.)

Jefferson asked Lewis to head the project. Lewis had served under William Clark (younger brother of George Rogers Clark) in earlier times and offered him co-leadership of the expedition, designated The Corps of Discovery. Clark accepted Lewis' offer to "participate with him in its fatiegues its dangers and its honors." Clark, no longer on active army status, was told he would receive a regular army captaincy, but Congress refused to grant it. Nevertheless, Lewis designated Clark as captain and co-commander; the expedition's men so regarded him and the journals so record it.

Lewis and Clark were scientist-explorers and singularly complementary. Although both were leaders of men and strict disciplinarians, Lewis was somewhat aloof, with a family background of bouts of despondency; Clark was more the extrovert and father figure. Lewis had great scientific interests in flora, fauna, and minerals, and Clark's surveying and engineering skills fit well with the demands of the expedition. While Lewis tended to view Indians fundamentally as savages, Clark, like Jefferson, saw the Indian as a full member of the human race and child of nature. At all times, the two soldiers were a team, each leading the expedition every other day. No known quarrel between them ever was recorded, although on a few occasions they thought it expedient to separate, probably to cool off and get out of each other's hair.

To prepare for their journey into the unknown, Lewis stayed in the East to study astronomy, plant taxonomy, practical medicine, etc., and to gather equipment from the armory at Harper's Ferry,

From *USA Today* magazine, January 1998, pp. 46-51. © 1998 by the Society for the Advancement of Education, Inc. Reprinted by permission.

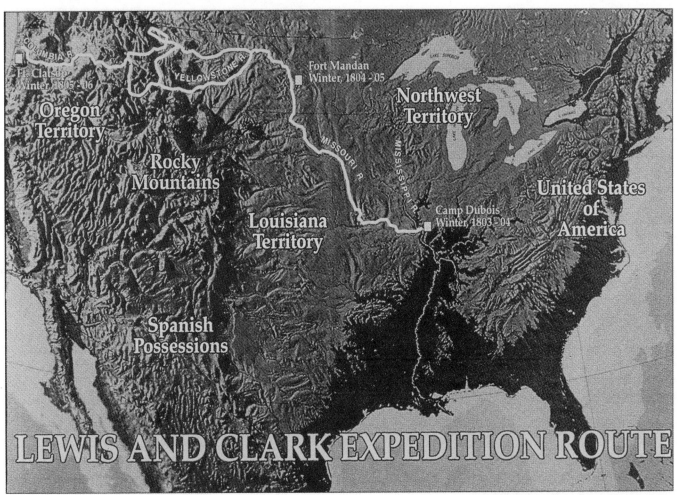

Map courtesy of National Park Service, Department of the Interior

The Lewis and Clark expedition started off from Wood River, Ill., opposite St. Louis, and headed northwest, concluding at Fort Clatsop at the mouth of the Columbia River in Oregon.

Va. The supplies would include trading goods such as awls, fishhooks, paints, tobacco twists, Jefferson medals, whiskey, and a generous amount of laudanum (a morphine-like drug). Lewis supervised the building of a 22-foot keelboat needed to take them up the Missouri to a winter quartering place. Additionally, he had his eye out for recruits for the expedition.

Clark went to St. Louis to recruit "robust, helthy, hardy" young, experienced, and versatile backwoodsmen. All were single. The captains needed interpreters, river experts, and hunters able to live under the most demanding conditions. Also sought were men with multiple skills who could do carpentry and blacksmith work and follow orders. With the exception of a hunter-interpreter, George Drouillard, if they were not already in the army, they enrolled in it. Privates re-

ceived five dollars a month; sergeants, eight dollars. Both leaders and the sergeants kept journals.

On May 14, 1804, the regular group of 29 men, plus a temporary complement of 16 others, set off from the St. Louis area for Mandan, in what is now North Dakota, the site of their winter quarters. With them came Lewis' Newfoundland dog, Scannon, and Clark's body-servant, a black man named York. Clark's journal entry reads, "I set out at 4 o'clock P.M. in the presence of many of the neighboring inhabitants, and proceeded under a jentle brease up the Missourie." Little did they know it would be some 7,200 miles and nearly two and a half years before their return.

The trip upriver was backbreaking, as spring floods pushed the water downstream in torrents. Hunters walked the shores, while the keelboat men alter-

nately rowed, poled, sailed, and rope-pulled the boat against the current. Wind, rain, and hail seemed to meet them at every turn in the serpentine Missouri. Snags and sandbars were everywhere. Bloated, gangrenous buffalo carcasses floated downstream, witnesses to the treachery of thin ice ahead. Often, for security reasons, the expedition party docked at night on small islands, some of which floated away as they embarked in the morning.

Ambassadors of goodwill, they stopped at major Indian villages, counseling peace instead of internecine warfare as well as distributing gifts. At the same time, they questioned the Indians about what lay ahead. Generally, such information was reliable. Tragedy struck at Council Bluffs (now Iowa), where Sgt. Charles Floyd died, probably of a ruptured appendix. He was the only member of the Corps to lose his life. After a proper eulogy, the captains wrote in their journals, as they were to do many times, "We proceeded on." Today, an obelisk marks the general location.

THE MYTH OF SACAJAWEA

On Nov. 2, 1804, they reached a river confluence about 30 miles north of present-day Bismarck, N.D., and settled in with the Mandan Indians, who welcomed them as security against Sioux attacks. They met Toussaint Charbonneau, a 40-year-old trapper wintering there, who, although ignorant of English, spoke a number of Indian languages. Equally important, he had a teenage wife, Sacajawea, a Shoshone who had been captured and traded by the Hidatsa (Minitari). Her tribe were horse-people and lived near the headwaters of the Missouri, two facts that enticed Lewis and Clark to hire Charbonneau and, as part of the deal, arrange for her to accompany them to the area. It would prove burdensome, though, for she delivered a baby boy, Baptiste, who would go with them. Clark took a liking to him and nicknamed him Pompey, even naming and autographing a river cliff prominence (Pompey's Pillar) after him. Later, Clark was to adopt the boy.

A myth of political correctness tells of Sacajawea being the guide for the expedition. Nothing could be further from the truth, as she was six years removed from her people and, when kidnapped, had been taken on a completely different route than that followed by the explorers. She did know Indian herbs, food, and medicine, though, and her presence and that of her child assured others that this was no war party.

Various factors of luck augured the party's success, such as Clark's flaming red hair and York's black skin and "buffalo hair." These would be items of curiosity to up-river Indians. The Corps also had an acrobat who walked on his hands, a one-eyed fiddler, and an air gun that made no explosion when fired. Some Indians previously thought that sound, not the rifle ball, killed, and

could not understand this magic. Lewis' dog always was viewed with larcenous eyes, as Indians used dogs for hauling, camp guards, and eating.

On April 7, 1805, the now seasoned expeditionary force left the village and went northwest for parts unknown. Their vehicles were six small canoes and two large perogues. The extras who accompanied them to the fort returned home with the keelboat. Aboard it were samples of flora and minerals, as well as "barking squirrels" (prairie dogs) and other hides and stuffed animals unknown to the East, such as "beardless goats" (pronghorn antelope). Lewis noted, "I could but esteem this moment of departure as among the most happy of my life."

They entered country that was increasingly wild and where white men had not penetrated. Grizzly bears proved to be a considerable threat, but food was plentiful as buffalo abounded. Frequent entries record that "Musquetoes were troublesum." For a time, they were plagued by the ague, dysentery, and boils. Clark drained a half-pint of fluid from one carbuncle on his ankle. The change of diet from meat to camas bulbs to fish didn't help. They laboriously portaged about 16-miles around Great Falls (now Montana), and reached the three forks of the Missouri River, which they named the Jefferson, Madison, and Gallatin. They were but a short distance northwest of what is now Yellowstone National Park.

Lewis followed the Jefferson fork, as Clark and Sacajawea lingered behind. Seeing some Indians, Lewis tried to entice them with presents to meet him, rolling up his sleeves and pointing to his white skin, calling out, "Tabba-bone." Supposedly, this was Shoshone for "white man," but a mispronunciation could render it as the equivalent of "enemy."

The Shoshone feared this was a trick of their hereditary enemies, the Blackfeet, as they never had seen white men. They scarcely were reassured when Clark, Sacajawea, and the rest of the party caught up with Lewis. However, Sacajawea began to suck furiously on her fingers, indicating she was suckled by these people. She also recognized another woman who had been kidnapped

with her, but had escaped. When a council was called, she recognized her brother, Cameawhait, a Shoshone chief. This helped the Corps in trading for needed horses to cross the Continental Divide.

The explorers were disappointed, for they had hoped that, by now, they would be close to the Pacific. This could not be so, though as these Indians knew no white men, and the salmon (a saltwater fish) they had were from trade, not the Indians' own fishing. Staying with the Shoshone for about a week, during which his 31st birthday occurred, Lewis wrote introspectively that he regretted his "many hours . . . of indolence [and now] would live for mankind, as I have hitherto lived for myself."

They hired a Shoshone guide known as "Old Toby" and his sons to cross the treacherous Bitterroot Mountains, the Continental Divide. After doing yeoman's service, the Indians deserted the party without collecting pay near the Clearwater and Snake rivers. The reason was the intention of the explorers to run ferocious rapids that seemed to swallow up everything in their fury. The Corps were able to run them without serious consequence, though. They proceeded on and came upon the Flathead Indians. One Flathead boy knew Shoshone, and a roundabout process of translation was established. Clark spoke English, and an army man translated it to French for Charbonneau. He, in turn, changed it to Minitari, and Sacajawea converted it to Shoshone, which the Flathead boy rendered in his language.

The group pursued the Clearwater River, which met the Snake River. This flowed into the Columbia, which emptied into the Pacific Ocean. Numerous Indian tribes inhabited the Columbia—Clatsop, Chinook, Salish, to name a few. Most were poverty-stricken and a far cry from the healthy Plains Indians. Many were blinded by age 30, as the sun reflecting off the water while they were fishing took its toll. Clark administered ointments and laudanum. Most didn't improve healthwise, but the Indians felt better for the drug and any placebo effects.

Lewis and Clark were overjoyed to find some Columbia River Indians using white men's curse words and wearing metal trinkets. Both only could be from ships' crews that plied the Pacific shores. The Corps were nearing the western end of their journey and, on Nov. 7, 1805, Lewis declared, "Great joy in camp we are in view of the Ocian." They constructed a rude Fort Clatsop (now rebuilt) by the Columbia River estuary near Astoria, in what today is Oregon, and sent parties in all directions to gather information. There was great excitement when reports of a beached whale reached the fort. Sacajawea, who continued with the expedition, insisted on seeing this leviathan, and she was accommodated. The men busied themselves hunting, making salt, and preparing for the journey home. (The salt cairn is reconstructed and preserved not many miles from the fort.)

THE JOURNEY HOME

The Corps entertained the hope that they might make contact with a coastal ship to return them home, and one ship, the *Lydia,* did arrive, but, through a communication failure or lying by the Indians, the captain believed the Corps already had left over land.

On March 23, 1806, after a rainy and miserable winter, the expedition left Fort Clatsop and, along the way, split into three groups hoping to explore more territory. They felt duty-bound to learn as much as they could and agreed to meet at the confluence of the Yellowstone and Missouri rivers. They traded beads and boats for horses and faced the worst kind of pilfering, even Scannon being nearly dog-napped.

Lewis, whose route took him through the territory of the fierce Blackfeet, in-vited a small party into his camp. One of them tried to steal soldier Reuben Field's gun and was stabbed for his efforts; another stole a horse and, losing all patience, Lewis "at a distance of thirty steps shot him in the belly." Fearing a large war party might be nearby, they traveled the next 60 miles nearly non-stop.

On the way to meet Clark, Lewis and a one-eyed hunter, Peter Cruzatte—both dressed in elkskin—went into the brush to hunt. Lewis was shot in the buttocks by Cruzatte, who apparently mistook him for an elk. The wound was painful, but no vital parts were damaged, although Lewis privately wondered if the shooting was deliberate.

Downriver, Lewis' party met two Illinois trappers searching for beaver. When they learned about the Blackfeet incident, they backtracked and accompanied Lewis to the rendezvous. There, with the captains' permission, they persuaded John Colter, who later discovered Yellowstone, to leave the party and to show them the beaver areas.

Having rendezvoused with the others, all stopped at the Mandan village in which they had spent the previous winter. Here, Toussaint Charbonneau, Sacajawea, and Baptiste (Pompey) parted company. The trapper was paid about $400–500 for his services.

Upon their return home, all the men received double pay and land grants from a grateful Congress. Several of the men went back to trap the area from which they had come, commencing the era of the mountain men. One became a judge and U.S. Senator, and another a district attorney. Others returned to farming. Clark had some sort of fallout with York, and the latter was reduced to a hired-out slave, a considerable fall from the prestigious body-servant status. Eventually, though, he was freed by Clark.

Lewis was appointed governor of the Louisiana Territory, but ran into personal and political problems. He suffered severe bouts of depression, began to drink heavily, and had to dose himself with drugs more frequently. To clear his name, he set off for Washington, but grew increasingly suicidal. He attempted to kill himself several times and finally succeeded on the Natchez Trace, at Grinder's Stand in Tennessee in 1809. Nevertheless, Meriwether Lewis should be remembered not for the circumstances of his death, but for his life of duty, leadership, and love of country.

Clark was appointed governor and Indian agent of the Missouri Territory. He also was given the rank of brigadier general in the militia—not bad for a bogus captain! He married Julia Hancock, a childhood friend, and named one of their children after Lewis, his comrade-in-arms. After Julia's death, Clark married her cousin, Harriet Kennerly.

Sacajawea died a young woman around 1812 at Ft. Union near the Missouri-Yellowstone confluence. Although she was rumored to die an old lady at Ft. Washakie in Wyoming—indeed, a large gravestone with her name is engraved there on the Shoshone Arapaho Reservation—the evidence for the Ft. Union death is more compelling. Clark adopted young Pompey, who later became a famous linguist and toured Europe in the company of royalty. Eventually, he became a mountain man.

William Clark died in 1838, a good friend of the Indians and, like Meriwether Lewis, a genuine American hero.

Indians in the Land

Did the Indians have a special, almost noble, affinity with the American environment—or were they despoilers of it? Two historians of the environment explain the profound clash of cultures between Indians and whites that has made each group almost incomprehensible to the other.

A conversation between William Cronon and Richard White

When the historian Richard White wrote his first scholarly article about Indian environmental history in the mid-1970s, he knew he was taking a new approach to an old field, but he did not realize just how new it was. "I sent it to a historical journal," he reports, "and I never realized the U.S. mail could move so fast. It was back in three days. The editor told me it wasn't history."

Times have changed. The history of how American Indians have lived in, used, and altered the environment of North America has emerged as one of the most exciting new fields in historical scholarship. It has changed our understanding not only of American Indians but of the American landscape itself. To learn more about what historians in the field have been discovering, American Heritage asked two of its leading practitioners, Richard White and William Cronon, to meet and talk about their subject.

White, who is thirty-nine, teaches at the University of Utah. While earning his B.A. from the University of California at Santa Cruz in the late 1960s, he became involved in Indian politics. He wrote his doctoral dissertation at the University of Washington on the environmental history of Island County, Washington. That work, which became his first book—*Land Use, Environment, and Social Change*—earned him the Forest History Society's prize for the

best book published in 1979–1980. This was followed by *The Roots of Dependency,* an environmental history of three Indian tribes: the Choctaws of the Southeast, the Pawnees of the Great Plains, and the Navajos of the Southwest. In it he showed how each had gradually been forced into economic dependency on the now-dominant white society.

William Cronon, thirty-two, teaches history at Yale University. His first book, *Changes in the Land: Indians, Colonists, and the Ecology of New England,* examined the different ways Indians and colonists had used the New England landscape. It won the Francis Parkman Prize in 1984. Cronon recently became a MacArthur Fellow, and is working on several projects in environmental history and the history of the American West.

This conversation, which was arranged and edited by William Cronon, took place late last year at Richard White's home in Salt Lake City.

William Cronon If historians thought about the environment at all up until a few years ago, they thought of it in terms of an older school of American historians who are often called "environmental determinists." People like Frederick Jackson Turner argued that Europeans came to North America, settled on the frontier, and began to be changed by the environment.

Richard White In a delayed reaction to Turner, historians in the late 1960s and early 1970s reversed this. They began to emphasize a series of horror stories when they wrote about the environment. The standard metaphor of the time was "the rape of the earth," but what they were really describing was the way Americans moving west cut down the forests, ploughed the land, destroyed the grasslands, harnessed the rivers—how they in effect transformed the whole appearance of the North American landscape.

WC Since then, I think, we've realized that both positions are true, but incomplete. The real problem is that human beings reshape the earth as they live upon it, but as they reshape it, the new form of the earth has an influence on the way those people can live. The two reshape each other. This is as true of Indians as it is of European settlers.

RW My first connections with Indians in the environment was very immediate. I became interested because of fishing-rights controversies in the Northwest, in which the Indians' leading opponents included several major environmental organizations. They argued that Indians were destroying the fisheries. What made this odd was that these same groups also held up Indians as sort of primal ecologists. I remember reading a Sierra Club book which claimed that In-

From *American Heritage*, August/September 1986, pp. 19-25. © 1986 by Forbes, Inc. Reprinted by permission of *American Heritage* magazine, a division of Forbes, Inc.

dians had moved over the face of the land and when they left you couldn't tell they'd ever been there. Actually, this

---

To regard Indians as primal ecologists is a crude view.

---

idea demeans Indians. It makes them seem simply like an animal species, and thus deprives them of culture. It also demeans the environment by so simplifying it that all changes come to seem negative—as if somehow the ideal is never to have been here at all. It's a crude view of the environment, and it's a crude view of Indians.

WC Fundamentally, it's a historical view. It says not only that the land never changed—" wilderness" was always in this condition—but that the people who lived upon it had no history, and existed outside of time. They were "natural."

RW That word *natural* is the key. Many of these concepts of Indians are quite old, and they all picture Indians as people without culture. Depending on your view of human nature, there are two versions. If human beings are inherently evil in a Calvinistic sense, then you see Indians as inherently violent and cruel. They're identified with nature, but it's the nature of the howling wilderness, which is full of Indians. But if you believe in a beneficent nature, and a basically good human nature, then you see Indians as noble savages, people at one with their environment.

WC To understand how Indians really did view and use their environment, we have to move beyond these notions of "noble savages" and "Indians as the original ecologists." We have to look instead at how they actually lived.

RW Well, take the case of fire. Fire transformed environments all over the continent. It was a basic tool used by Indians to reshape landscape, enabling them to clear forests to create grasslands for hunting and fields for planting. Hoe agriculture—as opposed to the plow agriculture of the Europeans—is another.

WC There's also the Indians' use of "wild" animals—animals that were not

domesticated, not owned in ways Europeans recognized. Virtually all North American Indians were intimately linked to the animals around them, but they had no cattle or pigs or horses.

RW What's hardest for us to understand, I think, is the Indians' different way of making sense of species and the natural world in general. I'm currently writing about the Indians of the Great Lakes region. Most of them thought of animals as a species of *persons*. Until you grasp that fact, you can't really understand the way they treated animals. This is easy to romanticize—it's easy to turn it into a "my brother the buffalo" sort of thing. But it wasn't. The Indians *killed* animals. They often overhunted animals. But when they overhunted, they did so within the context of a moral universe that both they and the animals inhabited. They conceived of animals as having, not rights—that's the wrong word—but *powers*. To kill an animal was to be involved in a social relationship with the animal. One thing that has impressed me about Indians I've known is their realization that this is a harsh planet, that they survive by the deaths of other creatures. There's no attempt to gloss over that or romanticize it.

WC There's a kind of debt implied by killing animals.

RW Yes. You incur an obligation. And even more than the obligation is your sense that those animals have somehow surrendered themselves to you.

WC There's a gift relationship implied . . .

RW . . . which is also a *social* relationship. This is where it becomes almost impossible to compare Indian environmentalism and modern white environmentalism. You cannot take an American forester or an American wildlife manager and expect him to think that he has a special social relationship with the species he's working on.

WC Or that he owes the forest some kind of gift in return for the gift of wood he's taking from it.

RW Exactly. And it seems to me hopeless to try to impose that attitude onto Western culture. We distort Indian reality when we say Indians were conservationists—that's not what conservation

means. We don't give them full credit for their view, and so we falsify history.

Another thing that made Indians different from modern Euro-Americans was their commitment to producing for *security* rather than for maximum yield. Indians didn't try to maximize the production of any single commodity. Most tried to attain security by diversifying their diet, by following the seasonal cycles: they ate what was most abundant. What always confused Europeans was why Indians didn't simply concentrate on the most productive part of the cycle: agriculture, say. They could have grown more crops and neglected something else. But once you've done that, you lose a certain amount of security.

WC I like to think of Indian communities having a whole series of ecological nets under them. When one net failed, there was always another underneath it. If the corn died, they could always hunt deer or gather wild roots. In hard times—during an extended drought, for instance—those nets became crucial.

All of this was linked to seasonal cycles. For me, one of the best ways of understanding the great diversity of environmental practices among Indian peoples is to think about the different ways they moved across the seasons of the year. Because the seasons of North America differ markedly between, say, the Eastern forests and the Great Plains and the Southwestern deserts, Indian groups devised quite different ways of life to match different natural cycles.

New England is the region I know best. For Indians there, spring started with hunting groups drawing together to plant their crops after having been relatively dispersed for the winter. While women planted beans, squash, and corn, men hunted the migrating fish and birds. They dispersed for summer hunting and gathering while the crops matured, and then reassembled in the fall. The corn was harvested and great celebrations took place. Then, once the harvest was done and the corn stored in the ground, people broke up their villages and fanned out in small bands for the fall hunt, when deer and other animals were at their fattest. The hunt went on until winter faded and the season of agriculture began again. What they had was agriculture during one part of the year, gathering going on continuously, and hunting concentrated in special seasons. That was typical not just of the Indians of New England but of eastern Indians in general.

RW For me the most dramatic example of seasonal changes among Indian peoples would be the horticulturists of the eastern Great Plains. The Pawnees are the example I know best. Depending on when you saw the Pawnees, you might not recognize them as the same people. If you came upon them in the spring or early fall, when they were planting or harvesting crops, you would have found a people living in large, semisubterranean earth lodges and surrounded by scattered fields of corn and beans and squash. They looked like horticultural people. If you encountered the Pawnees in early summer or late fall, you would have thought you were seeing Plains nomads—because then they followed the buffalo, and their whole economy revolved around the buffalo. They lived in tepees and were very similar, at least in outward appearance, to the Plains nomads who surrounded them.

For the Pawnees, these cycles of hunting and farming were intimately connected. One of my favorite examples is a conversation in the 1870s between the Pawnee Petalesharo and a Quaker Indian agent who was trying to explain to him why he should no longer hunt buffalo. Suddenly a cultural chasm opens between them, because Petalesharo is trying to explain that the corn will not grow without the buffalo hunt. Without buffalo to sacrifice at the ceremonies, corn will not come up and the Pawnee world will cease. You see them talking, but there's no communication.

WC It's difficult for a modern American hearing this to see Petalesharo's point of view as anything other than alien and wrong. This notion of sacrificing buffalo so corn will grow is fundamental to his view of nature, even though it's utterly different from what *we* mean when we call him a conservationist.

RW And yet, if you want to understand people's actions historically, you have to take Petalesharo seriously.

WC Environmental historians have not only been reconstructing the ways

Indians used and thought about the land, they've also been analyzing how those things changed when the Europeans invaded. A key discovery of the last couple of decades had been our radically changed sense of how important European disease was in changing Indian lives.

RW It was appalling. Two worlds that had been largely isolated suddenly came into contact. The Europeans brought with them diseases the Indians had never experienced. The resulting death rates are almost impossible to imagine: 90 to 95 percent in some places.

WC The ancestors of the Indians came to North America from ten to forty thousand years ago. They traveled through an Arctic environment in which many of the diseases common to temperate and tropical climates simply couldn't survive. They came in groups that were biologically too small to sustain those diseases. And they came without the domesticated animals with which we share several of our important illnesses. Those three circumstances meant that Indians shed many of the most common diseases of Europe and Asia. Measles, chicken pox, smallpox, and many of the venereal diseases vanished during migration. For over twenty thousand years, Indians lived without encountering these illnesses, and so lost the antibodies that would ordinarily have protected them.

RW Most historians would now agree that when the Europeans arrived, the Indian population of North America was between ten and twelve million (the old estimate was about one million). By the early twentieth century it had fallen to less than five hundred thousand. At the same time, Indian populations were also under stress from warfare. Their seasonal cycles were being broken up, and they were inadequately nourished as a result. All these things contributed to the tremendous mortality they suffered.

WC Part of the problem was biological; part of it was cultural. If a disease arrived in mid-summer, it had quite different effects from one that arrived in the middle of the winter, when people's nutrition levels were low and they were more susceptible to disease. A disease that arrived in spring, when crops had to be planted, could disrupt the food

supply for the entire year. Nutrition levels would be down for the whole subsequent year, and new diseases would find readier victims as a result.

RW The effects extended well beyond the original epidemic—a whole series of changes occurred. If Indian peoples in fact shaped the North American landscape, this enormous drop in their population changed the way the land looked. For example, as the Indians of the Southeast died in what had once been a densely populated region with a lot of farmland, cleared areas reverted to grassy woodland. Deer and other animal populations increased in response. When whites arrived, they saw the abundance of animals as somehow natural, but it was nothing of the sort.

Disease also dramatically altered relationships among Indian peoples. In the 1780s and 1790s the most powerful and prosperous peoples on the Great Plains margins were the Mandans, the Arikaras, the Hidatsas, the Pawnees, all of whom raised corn as part of their subsistence cycles. Nomadic, nonagricultural groups like the Sioux were small and poor. Smallpox changed all that. Those peoples living in large, populous farming villages were precisely those who suffered the greatest death rates. So the group that had once controlled the region went into decline, while another fairly marginal group rose to historical prominence.

WC That's a perfect example of biological and cultural interaction, of how complex it is. A dense population is more susceptible to disease than a less dense one: that's a biological observation true of any animal species. But which Indian communities are dense and which are not, which ones are living in clustered settlements and which ones are scattered thinly on the ground—these aren't biological phenomena but *cultural* ones.

RW Perhaps the best example of this is the way different Plains Indians responded to the horse, which, along with disease, actually preceded the arrival of significant numbers of Europeans in the region. The older conception of what happened is that when the horse arrived, it transformed the world. That may have been true for the Sioux, but not for the

Pawnees. The Sioux became horse nomads; the Pawnees didn't. They were not willing to give up the security of raising crops. For them, the horse provided an ability to hunt buffalo more efficiently, but they were not about to rely solely on buffalo. If the buffalo hunt failed, and they had neglected their crops, they would be in great trouble. As far as I know, there is no agricultural group, with the exception of the Crows and perhaps the Cheyennes, that *willingly* gave up agriculture to rely solely on the buffalo. The people like the Sioux who became Plains nomads had always been hunters and gatherers, and for them horses represented a *more* secure subsistence, not a less secure one.

WC It's the ecological safety net again. People who practiced agriculture were reluctant to abandon it, because it was one of their strongest nets.

RW And they didn't. When given a choice, even under harsh circumstances, people tried to integrate the horse into their existing economy, not transform themselves.

The horse came to the Sioux at a time when they were in trouble. Their subsistence base had grown precarious: the buffalo and beavers they'd hunted farther east were declining, and the decline of the farming villages from disease meant the Sioux could no longer raid or trade with them for food. The horse was a godsend: buffalo hunting became more efficient, and the buffalo began to replace other food sources. Having adopted the horse, the Sioux moved farther out onto the Plains. By the time they had their famous conflicts with the United States in the 1860s and 1870s, they were the dominant people of the Great Plains. Their way of life was unimaginable without the horse and buffalo.

WC The result was that the Sioux reduced the number of ecological nets that sustained their economy and way of life. And although the bison were present in enormous numbers when the Sioux began to adopt the horse, by the 1860s the bison were disappearing from the Plains; by the early eighties they were virtually gone. That meant the Sioux's main ecological net was gone, and there wasn't much left to replace it.

RW To destroy the buffalo was to destroy the Sioux. Of course, given time, they might have been able to replace the buffalo with cattle and become a pastoral people. That seems well within the realm of historical possibility. But they were never allowed that option.

WC Disease and the horse are obviously important factors in Indian history. But there's a deeper theme underlying these things. All North American Indian peoples eventually found themselves in a relationship of dependency with the dominant Euro-American culture. At some point, in various ways, they ceased to be entirely autonomous peoples, controlling their own resources and their own political and cultural life. Is environmental history fundamental to explaining how this happened?

RW I think it's absolutely crucial. Compare the history of European settlement in North America with what happened in Asia and Africa. Colonialism in Asia and Africa was very important, but it was a passing phase. It has left a strong legacy, but Africa is nonetheless a continent inhabited by Africans, Asia a continent inhabited by Asians. American Indian peoples, on the other hand, are a small minority in North America. Part of what happened was simply the decline in population, but as we've said, that decline was not simple at all. To understand it, we have to understand environmental history.

Many Indians were never militarily conquered.

Many Indians were never militarily conquered. They nonetheless became dependent on whites, partly because their subsistence economy was systematically undercut. Virtually every American Indian community eventually had to face the fact that it could no longer feed or shelter itself without outside aid. A key aspect of this was the arrival of a market economy in which certain resources came to be overexploited. The fur trade is the clearest example of this.

WC No question. The traditional picture of the fur trade is that Europeans arrive, wave a few guns and kettles and blankets in the air, and Indians come rushing forward to trade. What do they have to trade? They have beaver pelts, deerskins, bison robes. As soon as the incentive is present, as soon as those European goods are there to be had, the Indians sweep across the continent, wipe out the furbearing animals, and destroy their own subsistence. That's the classic myth of the fur trade.

RW It simply didn't happen that way. European goods often penetrated Indian communities slowly; Indian technologies held on for a long time. Indians wanted European goods, but for reasons that could be very different from why *we* think they wanted them.

WC One of my favorite examples is the kettle trade. Indians wanted kettles partly because you can put them on a fire and boil water and they won't break. That's nice. But many of those kettles didn't stay kettles for long. They got cut up and turned into arrowheads that were then used in the hunt. Or they got turned into high-status jewelry. Indians valued kettles because they were such an extraordinarily flexible resource.

RW The numbers of kettles that have turned up in Indian graves proves that their value was not simply utilitarian.

WC The basic facts of the fur trade are uncontestable. Europeans sought to acquire Indian furs, food, and land; Indians sought to acquire European textiles, alcohol, guns, and other metal goods. Indians began to hunt greater numbers of furbearing animals, until finally several species, especially the beaver, were eliminated. Those are the two end points of the fur-trade story. But understanding how to get from one to the other is very complicated. Why did Indians engage in the fur trade in the first place? That's the question.

RW We tend to assume that exchange is straightforward, that it's simply giving one thing in return for another. That is not how it appeared to Indian peoples.

WC Think of the different ways goods are exchanged. One is how we usually perceive exchange today: we go into the local supermarket, lay down a dollar, and get a candy bar in return. Many

Europeans in the fur trade thought that was what they were doing—giving a gun, or a blanket, or a kettle and receiving a number of furs in return. But for the Indians the exchange looked very different.

RW To see how Indians perceived this, consider two things we all know, but which we don't ordinarily label as "trade." One is gifts. There's no need to romanticize the giving of gifts. Contemporary Americans exchange gifts at Christmas or at weddings, and when those gifts are exchanged, as anybody who has received one knows, you incur an obligation. You often have relatives who never let you forget the gift they've given you, and what you owe in return. There's no *price* set on the exchange, it's a gift, but the obligation is very real. That's one way Indians saw exchange. To exchange goods that way, the two parties at least had to pretend to be friends.

At the other extreme, if friendship hadn't been established, goods could still change hands, but here the basis of exchange was often simple theft. If you had enemies, you could rob them. So if traders failed to establish some friendship, kinship, or alliance, Indians felt perfectly justified in attacking them and taking their goods. In the fur trade there was a fine line between people who sometimes traded with each other and sometimes stole from each other.

WC To make that more concrete, when the Indian handed a beaver skin to the trader, who gave a gun in return, it wasn't simply two goods that were moving back and forth. There were *symbols* passing between them as well. The trader might not have been aware of all those symbols, but for the Indian the exchange represented a statement about their friendship. The Indian might expect to rely on the trader for military support, and to support him in return. Even promises about marriage, about linking two communities together, might be expressed as goods passed from hand to hand. It was almost as if a language was being spoken when goods were exchanged. It took a long time for the two sides to realize they weren't speaking the same language.

RW Right. But for Indians the basic meanings of exchange were clear. You gave generously to friends; you stole from enemies. Indians also recognized that not everybody could be classified simply as a friend or an enemy, and this middle ground is where trade took place.

The concepts of price and market bewildered Indians.

But even in that middle ground, trade always began with an exchange of gifts. And to fail to be generous in your gifts, to push too hard on the price—Indians read that as hostility. When Europeans tried to explain the concept of a "market" to Indians, it bewildered them. The notion that demand for furs in London could affect how many blankets they would receive for a beaver skin in Canada was quite alien to them. How on earth could events taking place an ocean away have anything to do with the relationship between two people standing right here who were supposed to act as friends and brothers toward each other?

WC So one thing Indian peoples had trouble comprehending at certain stages in this dialogue was the concept of *price:* the price of a good fluctuating because of its abundance in the market. Indian notions were much closer to the medieval "just price." This much gunpowder is always worth this many beaver skins. If somebody tells me they want twice as many skins for the same gunpowder I bought last year at half the price, suddenly they're being treacherous. They're beginning to act as an enemy.

RW Or in the words Algonquians often used, "This must mean my father doesn't love me any more." To Europeans that kind of language seems ludicrous. What in the world does love have to do with giving a beaver skin for gunpowder? But for Indians it's absolutely critical.

Of course, exchange became more commercial with time. Early in the fur trade, Indians had received European goods as gifts, because they were allies against other Indians or other Europeans. But increasingly they found that the only way to receive those goods was through direct economic exchange. Gift giving became less important, and trading goods for set prices became more important. As part of these commercial dealings, traders often advanced loans to Indians before they actually had furs to trade. By that mechanism, gifts were transformed into debts. Debts could in turn be used to coerce greater and greater hunting from Indians.

WC As exchange became more commercial, the Indians' relationship to animals became more commercial as well. Hunting increased with the rise in trade, and animal populations declined in response. First the beaver, then the deer, then the bison disappeared from large stretches of North America. As that happened, Indians found themselves in the peculiar position of relying more and more on European goods but no longer having the furs they needed to acquire them. Worse, they could no longer even *make* those same goods as they once had, in the form of skin garments, wild meat, and so on. That's the trap they fell into.

RW And that becomes dependency. That's what Thomas Jefferson correctly and cynically realized when he argued that the best way for the United States to acquire Indian lands was to encourage trade and have government storehouses assume Indian debts. Indians would have no choice but to cede their lands to pay their debts, and they couldn't even renounce those debts because they now needed the resources the United States offered them in order to survive. Not all tribes became involved in this, but most who relied on the fur trade eventually did.

Of course, the effects go both ways. As whites eliminated Indians and Indian control, they were also, without realizing it, eliminating the forces that had shaped the landscape itself. The things they took as natural—why there were trees, why there weren't trees, the species of plants that grew there—were really the results of Indian practices. As whites changed the practices, those things vanished. Trees began to reinvade the grassland, and forests that had once been open became closed.

WC Once the wild animals that had been part of the Indians' spiritual and ecological universe began to disappear, Europeans acquired the land and began to transform it to match their assumptions about what a "civilized" landscape should look like. With native animals disappearing, other animals could be brought in to use the same food supply that the deer, the moose, and the bison had previously used. And so the cow, the horse, the pig—the animals so central to European notions of what an animal universe looks like—began to move across the continent like a kind of animal frontier. In many instances the Indians turned to these domesticated European species to replace their own decreasing food supply and so adopted a more pastoral way of life. As they lost their lands, they were then stuck with the problem of feeding their animals as well as themselves.

RW The Navajos are a good example of this. We tend to forget that Indians don't simply vanish when we enter the twentieth century. The Navajos are perhaps the group who maintained control over their own lands for the longest time, but their control was increasingly subject to outside pressures. They very early adopted European sheep, which became more and more important to their economy, both because wild foods were eliminated and because the government strongly encouraged the Navajos to raise more sheep. They built up prosperous herds but were gradually forced to confine them to the reservation instead of the wider regions they had grazed before.

The result was a crisis on the Navajo reservation. The land began to erode. By the 1920s and 1930s the Navajos had far more sheep than could be sustained during dry years. And here's where one of the more interesting confrontations between Indians and conservationists took place. The government sought to reduce Navajo stock, but its own motives were mixed. There was a genuine fear for the Navajos, but the main concern had to do with Boulder Dam. Conservationists feared Lake Mead was going to silt up, and that the economic development of the Southwest would be badly inhibited.

What they didn't understand were the causes of erosion. They blamed it all on Navajo sheep, but it now appears that there was a natural gullying cycle going on in the Southwest. Anybody familiar with the Southwest knows that its terrain is shaped by more than sheep and horses, no matter how badly it is overgrazed. So the result of government conservation policy for the Navajos was deeply ironic. Having adjusted to the European presence, having prospered with their sheep, they found their herds being undercut by the government for the good of the larger economy. It's a classic case of Indians—as the poorest and least powerful people in a region—forced to bear the brunt of economic development costs. So the Navajo economy was again transformed. As the Navajos became poorer and poorer, they grew more willing to lease out oil and allow strip mining on the reservation. They found themselves in the familiar situation of being forced to agree to practices that were harmful, even in their view, to the land. They had to do it in order to survive, but they were then attacked by white conservationists for abandoning their own values.

WC A real no-win situation.

RW There are lessons in all this. We can't copy Indian ways of understanding nature, we're too different. But studying them throws our own assumptions into starker relief and suggests shortcomings in our relationships with nature that could cost us dearly in the long run.

WC I think environmental history may be capable of transforming our perspective, not just on Indian history, but on all human history. The great arrogance of Western civilization in the industrial and postindustrial eras has been to imagine human beings existing somehow apart from the earth. Often the history of the industrial era has been written as if technology has liberated human beings so that the earth has become increasingly irrelevant to modern civilization—when in fact all history is a long-standing dialogue between human beings and the earth. It's as if people are constantly speaking to the earth, and the earth is speaking to them. That's a way of putting it that Indians would be far more capable of understanding than most modern Americans. But this dialogue, this conversation between earth and the inhabitants of earth, is fundamental to environmental history. With it we can try to draw together all these pieces—human population changes, cultural changes, economic changes, environmental changes—into a complicated but unified history of humanity upon the earth. That, in rather ambitious terms, is what environmental historians are seeking to do.

Jefferson's Retreat

Of all the gaps between his words and his actions, Jefferson's ownership of slaves is the most troubling. How did he manage the contradiction?

Joseph J. Ellis

Thomas Jefferson was many things, but mostly he was a creature of paradox: the wealthy Virginia aristocrat who wrote the most famous statement of equality in American history; the sincere advocate of agrarian simplicity who worshiped the art of architecture of Paris; above all, the fervent believer in human freedom who lived his entire life as a slave owner. This last paradox has always seemed the most poignant, in part because Jefferson himself acknowledged the massive gap between his principled ideals and his personal reality, and in part because the paradox Jefferson lived was emblematic of the larger disjunction in American society—now generally regarded as the central dilemma of American history—between the promise of liberty and the fact of racial discrimination.

Jefferson never resolved the paradox. He went to his grave owning almost 200 slaves and just after drafting a last letter in which he paid tribute to the egalitarian principles of the Declaration of In-

dependence. The question has always been: How did he manage this glaring contradiction? Granted, we all live lives that require us to straddle the space between our fondest hopes and our imperfect actions. But in Jefferson's life that space was a yawning chasm that seemed to defy the customary internal compromises. How did he do it?

If we had access to a time machine, and were also allowed to bring along a tape recorder and lie detector, the obvious place to interrogate Jefferson would be at Monticello, preferably as he strolled along Mulberry Row, where his household slaves were quartered. We could walk alongside the master of Monticello, reading for the record several of his most uplifting public statements about human rights and individual freedom, then ask him to comment on the apparent contradictions between the lyrical rhetoric and the sordid reality of the scene.

Since we obviously can't interview Jefferson, the next best course is to recover as much of the surviving historical

evidence as possible, acknowledge that it is unavoidably incomplete and fragile, then do all we can to interrogate that evidence with disciplined empathy. We must not be merely accusatory (i.e., how could you do it?). We shouldn't search the past for trophies that satisfy our political agenda in the present. We must show, as Jefferson so famously put it, "a decent respect to the opinions of mankind"—including those of dead men whose opinions, shaped by conditions two centuries ago, differ from our own. We also need to be canny about the place and time from which we extract our historical sample. The obvious place is Monticello. The most revealing moment is the three-year period between 1794 and 1797:

Jefferson has retired to Monticello after serving four years as America's first secretary of state. His evolving attitude toward slavery is just reaching a crucial stage of its development. And, most helpfully for our purposes, he is surrounded by his slaves. We even have an

 From *Civilization*, December 1996/January 1997, pp. 46-53. © 1996 by Joseph T. Ellis. Reprinted by permission of the author.

intriguing historical clue to confirm we are looking in the right place, for Jefferson tells us what is in his mind at the time: "I have my house to build, my fields to farm, and"—here is the clue—"to watch for the happiness of those who labor for mine."

Precisely because Jefferson's most inspiring utterances about humankind's prospects seem capable of levitating out of any specific social context, floating above messy realities like balloons at a political convention, we need to bring our recovered Jefferson back to earth. That means Monticello.

CONTEXT IS CRUCIAL TO OUR PURSUIT. The most elemental fact confronting Jefferson upon his return to Monticello in 1794 was that he was heavily in debt. He owed about £4,500 to English creditors and another £2,000 to bankers in Glasgow. (Comparisons in modern-day terms are notoriously tricky to calculate, but can conservatively be estimated at several hundred thousand dollars.) He was not, as he liked to describe himself, an independent yeoman farmer but an indebted Virginia planter. His many statements about returning to the bucolic splendors of the agrarian life were unquestionably sincere, but they masked the more pressing reality that farming for Jefferson, now more than ever before, meant making money.

His landed assets were impressive, but deceptively so. Jefferson owned nearly 11,000 acres, about equally divided between estates surrounding Monticello in Albemarle County and western lands concentrated in Bedford County, about 90 miles away. This made him one of the largest landowners in the state. One of the reasons he found it difficult to accept the full implications of his indebtedness was that he thought of wealth like an old-style Virginia aristocrat, in terms of land rather than money. For Jefferson, land was the best measure of a man's worth and, as he put it, "that of which I am the most tenacious." Despite the haunting presence of his English and Scottish creditors, he thought of himself as a landed and therefore a wealthy man.

Although Jefferson never fully grasped the intractability of his economic predicament, he had a sharp sense of the need to generate income. He described his thinking in a letter to a French correspondent in the spring of 1795:

On returning home after an absence often years, I found my farms so much deranged that I saw evidently ... that it was necessary for me to find some other resource in the meantime. ... I concluded at length ... to begin a manufacture of nails, which needs little or no capital, and I now employ a dozen little boys from 10 to 16 years of age, overlooking all the details of their business myself and drawing from it a profit on which I can get along till I can put my farms into a course of yielding profit.

Every morning except Sunday he walked over to the nailery soon after dawn to weigh out the nail rod for each worker, then returned at dusk to weigh the nails each had made and calculate how much iron had been wasted by the most and least efficient workers. Isaac Jefferson, a young slave at Monticello at the time, later recalled that his master made it clear that the nailery was a personal priority and that special privileges would be accorded the best nailmakers: "[He] gave the boys in the nail factory a pound of meat a week. ... Give them that wukked the best a suit of red or blue; encouraged them mightily." Jefferson even added the nailery to his familiar refrain in the pastoral mode: "I am so much immersed in farming and nailmaking," he reported in the fall of 1794, "that politicks are entirely banished from my mind."

From a financial perspective the nailery made perfect sense. But seen in the context of Jefferson's eloquent hymn to

the bucolic beauties of the pastoral life, it was a massive incongruity. Jefferson himself gave no sign that he was aware of any contradiction: At times his obliviousness seemed almost calculated. There is no evidence that it ever occurred to him that his daily visits to the nail factory, with its blazing forges and sweating black boys arranged along an assembly line of hammers and anvils, offered a graphic preview of precisely the kind of industrial world he devoutly wished America to avoid.

At a more mundane level, Jefferson's dedication to the meticulous management of the nailery illustrates what compelled his fullest energies as master of Monticello. Both Madison Hemings, son of Sally Hemings, and Edmund Bacon, who was Jefferson's overseer for 16 years, recalled that Jefferson never showed much enthusiasm for agricultural pursuits. "It was his mechanics he seemed mostly to direct, and in their operations he took great interest," Hem-

---

He spent no time at all behind a plow and almost no time watching his slaves perform the arduous tasks of farming

---

ings remembered. Jefferson spent little time in his fields, preferring to leave their cultivation to his overseers except at harvest time. He spent no time at all behind a plow and almost no time watching his slaves perform the arduous tasks of farming. What most fascinated him and commanded his fullest attention were new projects that demanded mechanical or artisanal skill of his laborers and that allowed him to design and superintend the entire operation. The nailery was the first of such projects, but it was followed by construction of a new threshing machine, plans for a flour mill, and an expensive canal along the Rivanna River.

But the biggest project of all was Monticello itself. He had been contemplating a major overhaul of his mansion ever since his return from France in

1789. From a financial point of view the idea of renovating Monticello, unlike his plans for the nailery, made no sense at all. But when it came to the elegance and comfort of his personal living space, Jefferson's lifelong habit was to ignore cost altogether, often going so far as to make expensive architectural changes in houses or hotels where he was only a temporary resident. His much grander plans for Monticello followed naturally from two idealistic impulses that seized his imagination with all the force of first principles: First, he needed more space, more than twice the space of the original house, in order to accommodate his domestic dream of living out his life surrounded by his children and grandchildren; second, his revised version of Monticello needed to embody the neoclassical principles of the Palladian style that his European travels had allowed him to study firsthand. Since the expansion had to occur within severely constrained conceptions of symmetry and proportion, the new structure could not just spread out like a series of boxcars; but neither could it rise vertically, since Palladian buildings must present at least the appearance of a one-story horizontal line, preferably capped by a dome. What this meant, in effect, was that the original house needed to be almost completely torn down and rebuilt from the cellar up.

Monticello became a congested construction site replete with broken bricks, roofless rooms, lumber piles and, if some reports are to be believed, over 100 workmen digging, tearing and hammering away The millions of 20th-century visitors to the mansion are the real beneficiaries of Jefferson's irrational decision to redesign and rebuild Monticello in the 1790s, though they would be mistaken to think the house in which Jefferson lived looked as it does now. It was in some state of repair or improvement throughout most of Jefferson's lifetime. More to our purposes, from 1794 to 1797 Monticello was part-ruin, part-shell and mostly still a dream.

ALMOST ALL THE WORK, WHETHER IN the fields, the nailery or at the construction site for Monticello itself, was done by slaves. The total slave population on Jefferson's several plantations was a fluctuating figure, oscillating above and below 200 and divided between Albemarle and Bedford counties at the ratio of roughly three to two. Between 1784 and 1794, as Jefferson attempted to consolidate his landholdings and reduce his mounting debts, he had disposed of 161 slaves by sale or outright gift. But natural increase had raised the slave population on all his estates to 167 by 1796, and that number would grow gradually over the ensuing years. On his plantations in Albemarle County it would seem safe to estimate that Jefferson was surrounded by about 100 slaves during his three-year retirement. African-American slaves constituted the overwhelming majority of residents at Monticello.

If Jefferson had a discernible public position on slavery in the mid-1790s, it was that the subject should be allowed to retire gracefully from the field of political warfare, much as he himself was doing by retiring to Monticello. He wanted the whole controversy over slavery to disappear. This represented a decided shift from his position as a younger man, when he had assumed a leadership role in pushing slavery onto the agenda in the Virginia legislature and the federal Congress. His most famous antislavery formulations, it is true, were rhetorical: blaming the slave trade and the establishment of slavery itself on George III in the Declaration of Independence; denouncing slavery as a morally bankrupt institution that was doomed to extinction in *Notes on the State of Virginia*. His most practical proposals, all of which were made in the early 1780s, envisioned a program of gradual abolition that featured an end to the slave trade, the prohibition of slavery in all the western territories, and the establishment of a fixed date (he suggested 1800) after which all newborn children of slaves would be emancipated. Throughout this early phase of his life it would have been unfair to accuse him of hypocrisy for owning slaves or to berate him for failing to provide moral leadership on America's most sensitive political subject. It would, indeed, have been much fairer to wonder admiringly how this product of Virginia's planter class had managed to develop such liberal convictions.

Dating the onset of a long silence is an inherently imprecise business, but Jefferson's more evasive posture toward slavery seemed to congeal in the 1780s with the publication of *Notes on the State of Virginia*. It was written in 1781 and 1782, when he was still reeling from charges of cowardice for fleeing a marauding British army in his last days as governor. *Notes* contained the most ringing denunciation of slavery Jefferson had yet composed, including an apocalyptic vision of racial war if emancipation were postponed too long. But these unquestionably sincere sentiments, written when he was emotionally exhausted and his customary protective shield was down, were not intended for public consumption. Jefferson never authorized the initial publication of *Notes,* which appeared in a French edition in 1785, and only grudgingly agreed to an English edition two years later, when it was clear there was nothing he could do to stop it.

Notes, in fact, was the only book that Jefferson published in his lifetime, for he much preferred to convey his opinions on controversial issues in private conversations and personal letters, where he could tailor his views to fit his particular audience. The publication *of Notes* put him "out there" on the most controversial subject of the day without the capacity to modulate or manipulate his language to fit different constituencies in France and England or, most worrisome to Jefferson, his fellow slave owners in Virginia. From the moment that *Notes* began to circulate within the planter class of the South, Jefferson began to back away from his leadership role in the debate over slavery. His more passive and fatalistic position, which he maintained for the rest of his life, was that public opinion was not prepared for emancipation at present and must await enactment at some unspecified time in the future. In effect, he was abdicating his position as the uncrowned king of Virginia's most progressive planters.

Moreover, the more pessimistic racial implications of the argument he had made in *Notes* began to settle in and cause him to realize, for the first time, that he had no workable answer to the unavoidable question: What happens once the slaves are freed? This was the kind of practical question that Jefferson had demonstrated great ingenuity in avoiding on a host of other major political issues. Indeed, one of the most seductive features of his political thinking in general was its beguiling faith that the

were sufficiently inferior to whites in mental aptitude that any emancipation policy permitting racial interaction was a criminal injustice to the freed slaves as well as a biological travesty against "the real distinctions which nature has made." The unavoidable conclusion, then, was that slavery was morally

The net result of all these influences was a somewhat tortured position on slavery that combined unequivocal condemnation of the institution in the abstract with blatant procrastination whenever specific emancipation schemes were suggested. The Duc de La Rochefoucauld-Liancourt, a French aristocrat fleeing the revolutionary bloodbath in Paris, captured the essential features and general flavor of Jefferson's slavery stance during his visit to Monticello in June of 1796:

Jefferson's fundamental conviction was that white and black Americans could not live together in harmony

---

future could take care of itself. Slavery, however, proved to be the exception to this larger pattern of inherent optimism. For one brief moment, in 1788, he seemed to entertain a bold if somewhat bizarre scheme whereby emancipated slaves would be "intermingled" with imported German peasants on 50-acre farms where both groups could learn proper work habits. But even this short-lived proposal only served to expose the inherent intractability of the postemancipation world as Jefferson tried to imagine it.

His fundamental conviction, one that he never questioned, was that white and black Americans could not live together in harmony. He had already explained why in *Notes:*

Deep rooted prejudices entertained by the whites; ten thousand recollections, by the blacks, of the injuries they have sustained; new provocations; the real distinctions which nature has made; and many other circumstances, will divide us into parties, and produce convulsions which will probably never end but in the extermination of the one or the other race.

Here was the single instance, with the most singularly significant consequences, when Jefferson was incapable of believing in the inevitability of human progress. Blacks and whites were inherently different, and, though he was careful to advance the view "as a suspicion only," he believed people of African descent

wrong, but racial segregation was morally right. And until a practical solution to the problem of what to do with the freed slaves could be found, it made no sense to press for emancipation.

Finally, during the 1780s Jefferson became more intensely aware how much his own financial well-being depended upon the monetary value and labor of his slaves. As the depth of his own indebtedness began to sink in, there seemed to be three ways to raise large amounts of capital to appease his creditors: He could sell off land; he could sell slaves outright; and he could rent or lease the labor of his slaves to neighboring planters. He expressed considerable guilt about pursuing the latter two options, suggesting they betrayed his paternal obligations to the black members of his extended "family." He gave specific instructions to his overseers that particular slaves who had been with him for some time should not be sold or hired out unless they wished it. But much as he disliked selling his slaves or temporarily transferring control over them to others, he recognized that such a course constituted his only salvation. In short, once he grasped the full measure of his personal economic predicament, the larger question of emancipation appeared in a new and decidedly less favorable light. It was now a matter on which he could literally not afford to be open-minded; nor, as it turned out, were the exigencies of this debt-induced predicament to change over his lifetime, except to grow worse.

The generous and enlightened Mr. Jefferson cannot but demonstrate a desire to see these negroes emancipated. But he sees so many difficulties in their emancipation even postponed, he adds so many conditions to render it practicable, that it is thus reduced to the impossible. He keeps, for example, the opinion he advanced in his notes, that the negroes of Virginia can only be emancipated all at once, and by exporting to a distance the whole of the black race. He bases this opinion on the certain danger, if there were nothing else, of seeing blood mixed without means of preventing it.

If his position on slavery as a young man merits a salute for its forthright and progressive character, his position as a mature man invites a skeptical shaking of the head for its self-serving paralysis and questionable integrity. He saw himself, even more than his slaves, as the victim of history's stubborn refusal to proceed along the path that all enlightened observers regarded as inevitable. In that sense, he and his African-American charges were trapped together in a lingering moment, a historical backwater in which nature's laws would be sorely tested as both sides waited together for the larger story of human liberation to proceed with freed blacks finding a more suitable location with people of their own kind in Africa or the Caribbean. In this overly extended transitional moment, his primary obligation, as he saw it, was to serve as a steward for those temporarily entrusted to his care and to think of his slaves, *as he* listed them in his *Farm Book,* as members of "my family," to be cared for as foster children until more permanent and geographically distant accommodations could be found.

Jefferson's sophisticated network of interior defenses allowed him to sustain this paternalistic self-image by blocking out incongruous evidence. For example, when forced by his creditors to sell 11 slaves in 1792, he ordered that they all be selected from his more remote Bedford plantations and that the sale itself be carried out in a distant location, explaining that he "[did] not like to have my name annexed in the public papers to the sale of property." Or, to take another example, in 1792 he approved the sale of Mary Hemings to Thomas Bell, a local Charlottesville merchant, claiming that the sale was justifiable "according to her desire." What he did not say was that Bell, a white man, was the father of Mary's two youngest children. The sale permitted the couple to live as common-law husband and wife.

Part by geographic accident, part by his own design, the organization of slave labor at Jefferson's plantations reinforced this shielding mentality in several crucial ways. Recall, first of all, that Jefferson's cultivated lands were widely distributed, half of them at Bedford several days' ride away. Until he completed his second house at Poplar Forest during his final retirement, Jefferson seldom visited those distant estates. Recall, too, that he seldom ventured into his fields at Monticello or Shadwell, leaving daily management of routine farming tasks to overseers. While he kept elaborate records of his entire slave population in his *Farm Book,* including the names and ages of all hands, his direct exposure to field laborers was limited. His cryptic notation on the division of slave labor is also revealing in this regard: "Children till 10 years of age to serve as nurses. From 10 to 16 the boys make nails, the girls spin. At 16 go into the ground or learn trades." The ominous phrase "go into the ground" accurately conveyed Jefferson's personal contact with that considerable majority of adult slaves who worked his fields. Except as names in his record books, they practically disappeared.

When Jefferson did encounter them, they were usually working on one of his several construction projects or apprenticing in the nailery. Most of his face-to-face contact with laboring slaves occurred in nonagrarian setting—the nailery, the sawmill, the construction site around the mansion—where he supervised them doing skilled and semi-skilled jobs. Even the nailery, with its overtones of assembly-line monotony and Dickensian drudgery, allowed him to think about the work of the slave boys as an apprentice experience providing them with a marketable trade. In explaining Jefferson's compulsive tendency to launch so many mechanical and construction projects at Monticello, it is possible that they not only served as outlets for his personal energies, but also allowed him to design a more palatable context for interacting with his slaves as hired employees rather than as chattel.

All the slaves working in the household, and most of the slaves living along Mulberry Row on the mountaintop, were members of two families that had been with Jefferson for over two decades. They enjoyed a privileged status within the slave hierarchy at Monticello, were given larger food and clothing rations, considerably greater latitude of movement, and even the discretion to choose jobs or reject them on occasion. Great George and his wife, Ursula, referred to as King George (a joke on George III) and Queen Ursula, were slaves in name only and effectively exercised control over management of the household. The other and larger slave family were all Hemingses, headed by the matriarch, Betty Hemings, whom Jefferson had inherited from his father-in-law, John Wayles, along with 10 of her 12 children in 1774.

It was an open secret within the slave community at Monticello that the privileged status enjoyed by the Hemings family derived from its mixed blood. Several of Betty's children, perhaps as many as six, had most probably been fathered by John Wayles. In the literal, not just the figurative sense of the term, they were part of Jefferson's extended family. All of the slaves that Jefferson eventually freed were descendants of Betty Hemings. If what struck the other slaves at Monticello was the quasi-independent character of the Hemings clan with its blood claim on Jefferson's paternal instincts, what most visitors tended to notice was their color. The Frenchman Liancourt left this account in 1796: "In Virginia mongrel negroes are found in greater number than in Carolina and Georgia; and I have even seen, especially at Mr. Jefferson's, slaves, who, neither in point of colour nor features, shewed the least trace of their original descent; but their mothers being slaves, they retain, of consequence, the same condition."

Since the members of the Hemings family were the front-and-center slaves at Monticello, most guests and visitors to the mountaintop experienced the Jeffersonian version of slavery primarily as a less black and less oppressive phenomenon than it actually was. And, as

Books of Interest

White over Black: American Attitudes Toward the Negro, 1580–1812
by Winthrop Jordan (University of North Carolina Press, 1968)
The best study of racism in early America with a penetrating assessment of Jefferson's psychological makeup

The Wolf by the Ears: Thomas Jefferson and Slavery
by John Chester Miller (University Press of Virginia, 1991)
The standard account of Jefferson's shifting position on slavery

American Slavery, American Freedom
by Edmund S. Morgan (W. W. Norton, 1976)
The story of the origins of slavery in Virginia and Jefferson's complicity in its preservation

overseer Edmund Bacon recalled, "there were no Negro and other outhouses around the mansion, as you generally see on [other] plantations," so the physical arrangement of appearances also disguised the full meaning of the slave experience. In short, Jefferson had so designed his slave community that his most frequent interactions occurred with African-Americans who were not treated like full-fledged slaves and who did not even look like full-blooded Africans because, in fact, they were not. In terms of daily encounters and routine interactions, his sense of himself as less a slave master than a paternalistic employer and guardian received constant reinforcement.

By the same token, if slavery was a doomed institution whose only practical justification was to preserve the separation of the races until the day of deliverance arrived at some unspecified time in the future, Jefferson was surrounded by rather dramatic evidence that it was failing miserably at that task. Racial mixing at Monticello was obviously a flourishing enterprise, much more so than his wheat fields. Several of Betty Hemings's grandchildren looked almost completely white, graphic testimony that whatever had begun with John Wayles had certainly not stopped back then. Jefferson's stated aversion to racial mixture had somehow to negotiate its visible examples all around him. In a sense, what he saw only confirmed his

---

In his declining years, Jefferson retreated even further from the progressive views he had held as a young man

---

deepest fears about an amalgamation of the races, though his code of silence dictated that no mention of the matter be permitted in public. Despite his remarkable powers of avoidance, this is one topic we can be sure he brooded about, even if he never talked about it for the record. The eloquence of his silence provides the best evidence of what Monticello was like as a real place rather than an imagined ideal. If literary allusions afford the best mode of description, we need to dispense with Virgil's pastoral odes and begin to contemplate William Faulkner's fiction.

OF COURSE, THE STORY OF JEFFERSON and his slaves at Monticello does not end in 1797. Twelve years later, after four years as vice president and eight years as president, he returned for his final encampment. During his declining years, especially after the Missouri crisis of 1820, Jefferson's public stance on slavery retreated even further from the leadership position of his youth. As a young revolutionary he had opposed the extension of slavery into the western territories. Now he reversed himself, advocating what he called "diffusion," the rather preposterous idea that the best way to end slavery was by allowing it to spread beyond the South. At the public level, diffusion was the most poignant and pathetic expression of his avoidance mentality, envisioning as it did the unpalatable evil of slavery conveniently disappearing in the misty expanses of the vast and uncharted lands of the West.

At the personal level, Jefferson's providential demise on July 4, 1826, spared him from witnessing the tragic end of the story. Only his spirit was present six months later when Monticello and all its possessions, including "130 valuable negroes," were put on the auction block and sold to the highest bidders. Jefferson was the invisible man that cold January day when his surviving daughter and grandchildren cried as the slave families were split up and dispersed. His grandson "Jeffy" never forgot the sad scene, which he compared to "a captured village in ancient times when all were sold as slaves." The auction lasted five days, and when it was over the proceeds covered only a portion of Jefferson's monumental debt—by then, in modern terms, several million dollars—and the slaves he had vowed to protect disappeared "down the river."

His life had always been about promise. And his enduring legacy became the most resonant version of the American promise in the national mythology. But in his life, if not his legacy, there were some promises he could not keep, because there were some facts he had chosen never to face.

Before the "Trail of Tears"

In "Race, Gender, and Work: A Multicultural Economic History of Women in the United States," Teresa Amott and Julie Matthaei tackle both the macro and the micro. Building upon the work of feminist scholars from various cultural backgrounds and areas of study, the authors reconstruct separate histories for different racial and ethnic groups, creating a truly multicultural picture. Here, an excerpt from their chapter on American Indian women.

By Teresa Amott and Julie Matthaei

"i am the fire of time./i am an Indian woman!"

—Niki Paulzine

American Indian women have kept the fire of the Indian spirit alive through five centuries of European colonization. Until recently, what we knew about Native American ways of life came from male European explorers and missionaries. For instance, in the early years of contact, Europeans described American Indian women as beasts of burden for their men. They were horrified by the hard work these women performed because, in upper-class European society, women were viewed as too fragile for such labor. American Indian men's work—hunting, fishing, and fighting—resembled the pastimes of upper-class European men, so European observers saw American Indian men as idle.

New research, much of it by Native American women, has revealed that American Indian societies practiced a degree of sexual freedom and equality

unknown by and hence unrecognizable to European colonists.

Like all known societies, American Indians maintained sexual divisions of labor. For the Blackfoot, for example, as Alice Kehoe explains: "the tipi, its furnishings, the food in it, clothing and other manufactures belonged to the woman, hers to give as she pleased. The marriage ceremony consisted of the woman inviting her intended to participate of food she had prepared.... Women ridiculed men who attempted to perform

---

Among the Ojibwa, women built the lodges, and they decided who could sleep there.

---

sustenance activities." The particular division of labor varied greatly. Among the Plains Indians, wooden bowls were carved by Pawnee women and by Omaha men, while for the Blackfoot, Cheyenne, and Hidatsa, both men and women made bowls. Cheyenne men crafted saddles; women covered them with hides.

These sexual divisions of labor, however, did not always translate into sexual inequality—unlike in most known societies. Each sex had control over its own work and over resources that were essential to the other sex. Among the Ojibwa, women were responsible for building the lodges, and they decided who could sleep there. Ojibwa women also processed furs for trading and negotiated directly with Europeans in the Great Lakes area. Among the Iroquois, women withheld corn and moccasins from warriors when they wanted to prevent them from forming a raiding party. In the different Plains societies, women maintained a monopoly on the skills of quill-working (necessary to decorate buffalo robes, tents, and cradle-covers), tipi-making, and tipi-decorating.

The more agricultural, settled societies were more likely to be matrilineal (inheritance and name were passed through females)—and/or matrilocal (upon marriage, the bride and groom resided in the household of the bride's mother)—which, as Maryann Oshana, a Chippewa, explains, "provided the greatest opportunities for women: women in these tribes owned houses, furnishings,

From *Ms.* magazine, November/December 1990, pp. 82-83. © 1990 by Teresa Amott and Julie Matthaei. Reprinted by permission.

fields, gardens, agricultural tools, art objects, livestock, and horses.... The woman had control of her children and if marital problems developed the man would leave the home."

Among the nomadic Plains peoples, the central activities of buffalo-hunting and war-making were dominated by men, leading most researchers to conclude that the Plains women were politically subordinate. However, some Blackfoot, Cheyenne, and eastern Dakota women also participated in warfare. Famous women warriors included Yellow Haired Calf Woman of the Cheyenne, who fought against the Shoshoni in 1869, the Other Magpie of the Crow, and Woman Chief of the Crow, whose accomplishments in war elevated her to the rank of third warrior among the chiefs.

At the same time, women often acted as peacemakers, a role formalized among the Shawnee in the "peace woman," responsible for dissuading the war chief from waging unnecessary or unpopular wars by reminding him of the pain wars brought to Shawnee mothers and wives, and to the women and children of the enemy.

Many American Indian religions accorded women and men their own, equally important, religious rituals. In many of the creation myths, woman was created simultaneously with man. The Laguna Pueblo described their creator deity as the spirit of intelligence: "In the beginning . . . Thought Woman finished everything, thoughts, and the names of all things. She finished also all the languages."

Some American Indian societies separated sex roles (or gender) from biological sex, and females could take up men's roles. Among the Mohave, for instance, a young female who felt strongly that she wanted to live as a man would go through a special ritual, the members of the nation would accept her/him as a man, and she would do men's work. Becoming a man also meant taking on a man's sexual practices—in other words, marrying women, and parenting children. Woman Chief, for example, had four wives.

Among the Mohave, lesbians, known as *hwame,* would undertake all masculine activities, including marriage, riding, and hunting. Navajos considered lesbians valuable assets; since their stories depicted homosexuals as wealthy, they usually put lesbians in charge of the household and its property. Among the Canadian Kaska, parents with more daughters than sons would encourage a daughter to "become a man"; such women married other women, and were often considered outstanding hunters. Many nations accepted a range of sexual practices—heterosexual, homosexual, and bisexual—and allowed youths to experiment sexually before marriage.

The European invasion, which began in the late fifteenth century, not only killed, displaced, and subordinated American Indians, but also undermined much of the equality and independence of American Indian women. In the early nineteenth century, for example, Quaker missionaries were shocked by the Allegheny Seneca women's predominance in agriculture, which was considered men's work among whites, and taught only men to plow. But Seneca women continued to farm, taking the new skill for their own use, and were instrumental in resisting the Quakers' plan to divide land into individual plots.

In other cases, skills were lost. Before the forced exile from Georgia and the Carolinas to land west of the Mississippi in the 1830s (known as the "Trail of Tears"), Cherokee women had been skilled botanists, using over 800 plants found in the Southeast for food, medicine, and crafts. The completely different Oklahoma lands deprived them of their skills and their people of valuable products.

Between the 1850s and the 1880s, western nations fought a losing battle to retain their lands. American Indian women were an important part of this resistance fighting. Buffalo Calf Robe (Cheyenne), who distinguished herself in battles against General George Crook and General Custer, was given the honorary name "Brave Woman" by her people.

Under the reservation system some nations, like the Iroquois, Pueblo, and Papago, were able to retain enough land to preserve their economic and cultural ways of life. Nomads, like the Sioux and Cheyenne, lost their hunting lands and were forced by whites into unsuccessful agricultural efforts in the semi-arid Indian territory. Sarah Winnemucca, a great orator who spoke at least five languages, organized her people to resist relocation from Oregon to the Washington territory, collecting thousands of names on a petition for Paiute land, which the U.S. Secretary of the Interior at first agreed to grant, but then never acted upon.

The U.S. government retained ultimate authority as "trustee" over reservation life, but in the 1870s, 13 religious denominations (from the Baptists to the Presbyterians to the Quakers) persuaded the government to give them control, and divided up the reservations among themselves.

A central part of whites' efforts to "domesticate" Native Americans was to deprive them of the right to raise and educate their own children. Beginning in the late 1870s, Native American children were placed in boarding schools away from the reservations, where they were forced to speak English and wear European American clothing. To further acquaint them with white ways, children spent one-half of their time working for nearby white families—boys at farming and blacksmithing, girls at domestic work.

We have little information on how the reservation system affected sex roles. "If a generalization may be made," American Indian anthropologist Beatrice Medicine points out, "it is that the female roles of mother, sister, and wife were ongoing because of the continued care they were supposed to provide for the family." But, she asks, what were the women's roles in dealing with soldiers and physical deprivation? "The strategies adopted for cultural survival and the means of transmitting these to daughters and nieces are valuable adaptive mechanisms that cannot even partially be reconstructed."

Teresa Amott and Julie Matthaei are feminist economists and activists who teach at Bucknell University and Wellesley College. This book grew out of work by the Economic Literacy Project of Women for Economic Justice, based in Boston.

"All we want is make us free!"

An 1839 mutiny aboard a Spanish ship in Cuban waters raised basic questions about freedom and slavery in the United States

By Howard Jones

Around 4:00 A.M. on July 2, 1839, Joseph Cinqué led a slave mutiny on board the Spanish schooner *Amistad* some 20 miles off northern Cuba. The revolt set off a remarkable series of events and became the basis of a court case that ultimately reached the U.S. Supreme Court. The civil rights issues involved in the affair made it the most famous case to appear in American courts before the landmark Dred Scott decision of 1857.

The saga began two months earlier when slave trade merchants captured Cinqué, a 26-year-old man from Mende, Sierra Leone, and hundreds of others from different West African tribes. The captives were then taken to the Caribbean, with up to 500 of them chained hand and foot, on board the Portuguese slaver *Teçora*. After a nightmarish voyage in which approximately a third of the captives died, the journey ended with the clandestine, nighttime entry of

THE NEW HAVEN COLONY HISTORICAL SOCIETY

Sengbe Pieh—given the name Joseph Cinqué in Cuba—who is depicted in a painting by Nathaniel Jocelyn.

the ship into Cuba—in violation of the Anglo-Spanish treaties of 1817 and 1835 that made the African slave trade a capital crime. Slavery itself was legal in Cuba, meaning that once smuggled

ashore, the captives became "slaves" suitable for auction at the Havana barracoons.

In Havana, two Spaniards, José Ruiz and Pedro Montes, bought 53 of the Africans—including Cinqué and four children, three of them girls—and chartered the *Amistad*. The ship, named after the Spanish word for friendship, was a small black schooner built in Baltimore for the coastal slave trade. It was to transport its human cargo 300 miles to two plantations on another part of Cuba at Puerto Principe.

The spark for the mutiny was provided by Celestino, the *Amistad*'s mulatto cook. In a cruel jest, he drew his hand past his throat and pointed to barrels of beef, indicating to Cinqué that, on reaching Puerto Principe, the 53 black captives aboard would be killed and eaten. Stunned by this revelation, Cinqué found a nail to pick the locks on the captives' chains and made a strike for freedom.

In the small, hot, and humid room beneath the Senate chamber, [John Quincy] Adams challenged the Court to grant liberty on the basis of natural rights doctrines found in the Declaration of Independence.

ALL: NEW HAVEN COLONY HISTORICAL SOCIETY

In this painting by an unknown artist (above, left), the badly weather-beaten schooner Amistad is at anchor in Long Island Sound, while several of the mutineers head for shore in search of provisions. In two of a series of murals painted in 1939 by Hale Woodruff (above, right) for the Amistad centennial, the Africans are depicted during the pre-dawn revolt and on their return home, almost three years later.

On their third night at sea, Cinqué and a fellow captive named Grabeau freed their comrades and searched the dark hold for weapons. They found them in boxes: sugar cane knives with machete-like blades, two feet in length, attached to inch-thick steel handles. Weapons in hand, Cinqué and his cohorts stormed the shadowy, pitching deck and, in a brief and bloody struggle that led to the death of one of their own, killed the cook and captain and severely wounded Ruiz and Montes. Two sailors who were aboard disappeared in the melee and were probably drowned in a desperate attempt to swim the long distance to shore. Grabeau convinced Cinqué to spare the lives of the two Spaniards, since only they possessed the navigational skills necessary to sail the *Amistad* to Africa. Instead of making it home, however, the former

captives eventually ended up off the coast of New York.

Cinqué, the acknowledged leader of the mutineers, recalled that the slave ship that he and the others had traveled on during their passage from Africa to Cuba had sailed away from the rising sun; therefore to return home, he ordered Montes, who had once been a sea captain, to sail the *Amistad* into the sun. The two Spaniards deceived their captors by sailing back and forth in the Caribbean Sea, toward the sun during the day and, by the stars, back toward Havana at night, hoping for rescue by British anti-slave-trade patrol vessels.

When that failed, Ruiz and Montes took the schooner on a long and erratic trek northward up the Atlantic coast.

Some 60 days after the mutiny, under a hot afternoon sun in late August 1839, Lieutenant Commander Thomas Gedney of the USS *Washington* sighted the ves-

sel just off Long Island, where several of the schooner's inhabitants were on shore bartering for food. He immediately dispatched an armed party who captured the men ashore and then boarded the vessel. They found a shocking sight: cargo strewn all over the deck; perhaps 50 men nearly starved and destitute, their skeletal bodies naked or barely clothed in rags; a black corpse lying in decay on the deck, its face frozen as if in terror; another black with a maniacal gaze in his eyes; and two wounded Spaniards in the hold who claimed to be the owners of the Africans who, as slaves, had mutinied and murdered the ship's captain.

Gedney seized the vessel and cargo and reported the shocking episode to authorities in New London, Connecticut. Only 43 of the Africans were still alive, including the four children. In addition to the one killed during the mutiny, nine

YALE UNIVERSITY LIBRARY

Margru was one of the three female captives on board the Amistad. After her return home, she was educated at the American mission school and sent back to the United States to study. She then returned to Africa, where she became principal of the mission's school.

had died of disease and exposure or from consuming medicine on board in an effort to quench their thirst.

The affair might have come to a quiet end at this point had it not been for a group of abolitionists. Evangelical Christians led by Lewis Tappan, a prominent New York businessman, Joshua Leavitt, a lawyer and journalist who edited the *Emancipator* in New York, and Simeon Jocelyn, a Congregational minister in New Haven, Connecticut, learned of the *Amistad's* arrival and decided to publicize the incident to expose the brutalities of slavery and the slave trade. Through evangelical arguments, appeals to higher law and "moral suasion," Tappan and his colleagues hoped to launch a massive assault on slavery.

The *Amistad* incident, Tappan happily proclaimed, was a "providential occurrence." In his view slavery was a deep moral wrong and not subject to compromise. Both those who advocated its practice and those who quietly condoned it by inaction deserved condemnation. Slavery was a sin, he declared, because it obstructed a person's free will inherent by birth, therefore constituting a rebellion against God. Slavery was also, Tappan wrote to his brother, "the

worm at the root of the tree of Liberty. Unless killed the tree will die."

Tappan first organized the "Amistad Committee" to coordinate efforts on behalf of the captives, who had been moved to the New Haven jail. Tappan preached impromptu sermons to the mutineers, who were impressed by his sincerity though unable to understand his language. He wrote detailed newspaper accounts of their daily activities in jail, always careful to emphasize their humanity and civilized backgrounds for a fascinated public, many of whom had never seen a black person. And he secured the services of Josiah Gibbs, a professor of religion and linguistics at Yale College, who searched the docks of New York for native Africans capable of translating Cinqué's Mende language. Gibbs eventually discovered two Africans familiar with Mende—James Covey from Sierra Leone and Charles Pratt from Mende itself. At last the *Amistad* mutineers could tell their side of the story.

Meanwhile, Ruiz and Montes had initiated trial proceedings seeking return of their "property." They had also secured their government's support under Pinckney's Treaty of 1795, which stipulated the return of merchandise lost for reasons beyond human control. To fend off what many observers feared would be a "judicial massacre," the abolitionists hired attorney Roger S. Baldwin of Connecticut, who had a reputation as an eloquent defender of the weak and downtrodden.

Baldwin intended to prove that the captives were "kidnapped Africans," illegally taken from their homeland and imported into Cuba and thus entitled to resist their captors by any means necessary. He argued that the ownership papers carried by Ruiz and Montes were fraudulent and that the blacks were not slaves indigenous to Cuba. He and his defense team first filed a claim for the *Amistad* and cargo as the Africans' property in preparation for charging the Spaniards with piracy. Then they filed suit for the captives' freedom on the grounds of humanity and justice: slavery violated natural law, providing its victims with the inherent right of self-defense.

The case then entered the world of politics. It posed such a serious problem

for President Martin Van Buren that he decided to intervene. A public dispute over slavery would divide his Democratic party, which rested on a tenuous North-South alliance, and could cost him reelection to the presidency in 1840. Working through his secretary of state, slaveholder John Forsyth from Georgia, Van Buren sought to quietly solve the problem by complying with Spanish demands.

Van Buren also faced serious diplomatic issues. Failure to return the Africans to their owners would be a violation of Pinckney's Treaty with Spain. In addition, revealing Spain's infringement of treaties against the African slave trade could provide the British, who were pioneers in the crusade against slavery, with a pretext for intervening in Cuba, which was a longtime American interest.

The White House position was transparently weak. Officials refused to question the validity of the certificates of ownership, which had assigned Spanish names to each of the captives even though none of them spoke that language. Presidential spokesmen blandly asserted that the captives had been slaves in Cuba, despite the fact that the international slave trade had been out-

YALE UNIVERSITY LIBRARY

Grabeau, drawn here from life by William H. Townsend in 1839, had been a blacksmith in his Mende homeland before he was seized by slave dealers and sent to Cuba for sale on the slave market.

lawed some 20 years earlier and the children were no more than nine years old and spoke an African dialect.

The court proceedings opened on September 19, 1839, amid a carnival atmosphere in the state capitol building in Hartford, Connecticut. To some observers, Cinqué was a black folk hero; to others he was a barbarian who deserved execution for murder. Poet William Cullen Bryant extolled Cinqué's virtues, numerous Americans sympathized with the "noble savages," and pseudo-scientists concluded that the shape of Cinqués skull suggested leadership, intelligence, and nobility. The New York *Morning Herald,* however, derided the "poor Africans," "who have nothing to do, but eat, drink, and turn somersaults."

To establish the mutineers as human beings rather than property, Baldwin sought a writ of habeas corpus aimed at freeing them unless the prosecution filed charges of murder. Issuance of the writ would recognize the Africans as persons with natural rights and thus undermine the claim by both the Spanish and American governments that the captives were property. If the prosecution brought charges, the Africans would have the right of self-defense against unlawful captivity; if it filed no charges, they would go free. In the meantime, the abolitionists could explore in open court the entire range of human and property rights relating to slavery. As Leavitt later told the General Antislavery Convention in London, the purpose of the writ was "to test their right to personality."

Despite Baldwin's impassioned pleas for justice, the public's openly expressed sympathy for the captives, and the prosecution's ill-advised attempt to use the four black children as witnesses against their own countrymen, Associate Justice Smith Thompson of the U.S. Supreme Court denied the writ. Thompson was a strong-willed judge who opposed slavery, but he even more ardently supported the laws of the land. Under those laws, he declared, slaves were property. He could not simply assert that the Af-

ricans were human beings and grant freedom on the basis of natural rights. Only the law could dispense justice, and the law did not authorize their freedom. It was up to the district court to decide whether the mutineers were slaves and, therefore, property.

Prospects before the district court in Connecticut were equally dismal. The presiding judge was Andrew T. Judson, a well-known white supremacist and staunch opponent of abolition. Baldwin attempted to move the case to the free state of New York on the grounds that Gedney had seized the Africans in that state's waters and not on the high seas. He hoped, if successful, to prove that they were already free upon entering New York and that the Van Buren administration was actually trying to enslave them. But Baldwin's effort failed; the confrontation with Judson was unavoidable.

Judson's verdict in the case only appeared preordained; as a politically ambitious man, he had to find a middle ground. Whereas many Americans wanted the captives freed, the White House pressured him to send them back to Cuba. Cinqué himself drew great sympathy by recounting his capture in Mende and then graphically illustrating the horrors of the journey from Africa by sitting on the floor with hands and feet pulled together to show how the captives had been "packed" into the hot and unsanitary hold of the slave vessel.

The Spanish government further confused matters by declaring that the Africans were both property and persons. In addition to calling for their return as property under Pinckney's Treaty, it demanded their surrender as "slaves who are assassins." The real concern of the Spanish government became clear when its minister to the United States, Pedro Alcántara de Argaiz, proclaimed that "The public vengeance of the African Slave Traders in Cuba had not been satisfied." If the mutineers went unpunished, he feared, slave rebellions would erupt all over Cuba.

Argaiz's demands led the Van Buren administration to adopt measures that constituted an obstruction of justice. To

facilitate the Africans' rapid departure to Cuba after an expected guilty verdict, Argaiz convinced the White House to dispatch an American naval vessel to New Haven to transport them out of the country *before* they could exercise the constitutional right of appeal. By agreeing to this, the president had authorized executive interference in the judicial process that violated the due-process guarantees contained in the Constitution.

Judson finally reached what he thought was a politically safe decision. On January 13, 1840, he ruled that the Africans had been kidnapped, and, offering no sound legal justification, ordered their return to Africa, hoping to appease the president by removing them from the United States. Six long months after the mutiny, it appeared that the captives were going home.

But the ordeal was not over. The White House was stunned by the decision: Judson had ignored the "great [and] important political bearing" of the case, complained the president's son, John Van Buren. The Van Buren administration immediately filed an appeal with the circuit court. The court upheld the decision, however, meaning that the case would now go before the U.S. Supreme Court, where five of the justices, including Chief Justice Roger Taney, were southerners who were or had been slaveowners.

Meanwhile, the Africans had become a public spectacle. Curious townspeople and visitors watched them exercise daily on the New Haven green, while many others paid the jailer for a peek at the foreigners in their cells. Some of the most poignant newspaper stories came from professors and students from Yale College and the Theological Seminary who instructed the captives in English and Christianity. But the most compelling attraction was Cinqué. In his midtwenties, he was taller than most Mende people, married with three children, and, according to the contemporary portrait by New England abolitionist Nathaniel Jocelyn, majestic, lightly bronzed, and strikingly handsome. Then there were the children, including Kale, who learned enough English to become the spokesperson for the group.

The supreme court began hearing arguments on February 22, 1841. Van Buren had already lost the election, partly and somewhat ironically because his *Amistad* policy was so blatantly pro-South that it alienated northern Democrats. The abolitionists wanted someone of national stature to join Baldwin in the defense and finally persuaded former President John Quincy Adams to take the case even though he was 73 years old, nearly deaf, and had been absent from the courtroom for three decades. Now a congressman from Massachusetts, Adams was irascible and hard-nosed, politically independent, and self-righteous to the point of martyrdom. He was fervently antislavery though not an abolitionist, and had been advising Baldwin on the case since its inception. His effort became a personal crusade when the young Kale wrote him a witty and touching letter, which appeared in the *Emancipator* and con-

cluded with the ringing words, "All we want is make us free."

Baldwin opened the defense before the Supreme Court with another lengthy appeal to natural law then gave way to Adams, who delivered an emotional eight-hour argument that stretched over two days. In the small, hot, and humid room beneath the Senate chamber, Adams challenged the Court to grant liberty on the basis of natural rights doctrines found in the Declaration of Independence. Pointing to a copy of the document mounted on a huge pillar, he proclaimed that, "I know of no other law that reaches the case of my clients, but the law of Nature and of Nature's God on which our fathers placed our own national existence." The Africans, he proclaimed, were victims of a monstrous conspiracy led by the executive branch in Washington that denied their rights as human beings.

Adams and Baldwin were eloquent in their pleas for justice based on higher

principles. As Justice Joseph Story wrote to his wife, Adams's argument was "extraordinary . . . for its power, for its bitter sarcasm, and its dealing with topics far beyond the records and points of discussion."

On March 9, Story read a decision that could not have surprised those who knew anything about the man. An eminent scholar and jurist, Story was rigidly conservative and strongly nationalistic, but he was as sensitive to an individual's rights as he was a strict adherent to the law. Although he found slavery repugnant and contrary to Christian morality, he supported the laws protecting its existence and opposed the abolitionists as threats to ordered society. Property rights, he believed, were the basis of civilization.

Even so, Story handed down a decision that freed the mutineers on the grounds argued by the defense. The ownership papers were fraudulent, making the captives "kidnapped Africans" who had the inherent right of self-de-

The court proceedings shown above in the Woodruff mural panel, "Trial of the Captive Slaves," proved to be long and tumultuous.

fense in accordance with the "eternal principles of justice." Furthermore, Story reversed Judson's decision ordering the captives' return to Africa because there was no American legislation authorizing such an act. The outcome drew Leavitt's caustic remark that Van Buren's executive order attempting to return the Africans to Cuba as slaves should be "engraved on his tomb, to rot only with his memory."

The abolitionists pronounced the decision a milestone in their long and bitter fight against the "peculiar institution." To them, and to the interested public, Story's "eternal principles of justice" were the same as those advocated by Adams. Although Story had focused on self-defense, the victorious abolitionists broadened the meaning of his words to condemn the immorality of slavery. They reprinted thousands of copies of the defense argument in pamphlet form, hoping to awaken a larger segment of the public to the sordid and inhumane char-

acter of slavery and the slave trade. In the highest public forum in the land, the abolitionists had brought national attention to a great social injustice. For the first and only time in history, African blacks seized by slave dealers and brought to the New World won their freedom in American courts.

The final chapter in the saga was the captives' return to Africa. The abolitionists first sought damage compensation for them, but even Adams had to agree with Baldwin that, despite months of captivity because bail had been denied, the "regular" judicial process had detained the Africans, and liability for false imprisonment hinged only on whether the officials' acts were *malicious* and without probable *cause*." To achieve equity Adams suggested that the federal government finance the captives' return to Africa. But President John Tyler, himself a Virginia slaveholder, refused on the grounds that, as Judge Story had ruled, no law authorized such action.

To charter a vessel for the long trip to Sierra Leone, the abolitionists raised money from private donations, public exhibitions of the Africans, and contributions from the Union Missionary' Society, which black Americans had formed in Hartford to found a Christian mission in Africa. On November 25, 1841, the remaining 35 *Amistad* captives, accompanied by James Covey and five missionaries, departed from New York for Africa on a small sailing vessel named the *Gentleman*. The British governor of Sierra Leone welcomed them the following January—almost three years after their initial incarceration by slave traders.

The aftermath of the *Amistad* affair is hazy. One of the girls, Margru, returned to the United States and entered Oberlin College, in Ohio, to prepare for mission work among her people. She was educated at the expense of the American Missionary Association (AMA), established in 1846 as an outgrowth of the Amistad Committee and the first of

its kind in Africa. Cinqué returned to his home, where tribal wars had scattered or perhaps killed his family. Some scholars insist that he remained in Africa, working for some time as an interpreter at the AMA mission in Kaw-Mende before his death around 1879. No conclusive evidence has surfaced to determine whether Cinqué was reunited with his wife and three children, and for that same reason there is no justification for the oft-made assertion that he himself engaged in the slave trade.

The importance of the *Amistad* case lies in the act that Cinqué and his fellow captives, in collaboration with white abolitionists, had won their freedom and thereby encouraged others to continue the struggle. Positive law had come into conflict with natural law, exposing the great need to change the Constitution

and American laws in compliance with the moral principles underlying the Declaration of Independence. In that sense the incident contributed to the fight against slavery by helping to lay the basis for its abolition through the Thirteenth Amendment to the Constitution in 1865.

NEW HAVEN COLONY HISTORICAL SOCIETY

This letter to Lewis Tappan from John Quincy Adams was in response to the gift of a Bible that had been sent to Adams by Cinqué and his comrades after they had been freed by the court and allowed to return home.

Howard Jones is University Research Professor and Chair of the Department of History at the University of Alabama. He is the author of numerous books, including Mutiny on the Amistad: The Saga of a Slave Revolt and Its Impact on American Abolition, Law, and Diplomacy, *published by Oxford University Press.*

Mountain Legend

By MICHAEL MARTIN *Born to a slave & a Virginia aristocrat, Jim Beckwourth became a legend in the American west as a rugged mountain man, a teller of tall tales, & an indian war chief.*

STANDING MORE THAN six feet tall, dressed in buckskins and beads, and sporting earrings and waist-length black hair braided into rolls, Jim Beckwourth must have cut a striking figure. Although stories of the bold escapades of this "larger than life" character spread throughout the West, making him a legend in his own lifetime, early chroniclers of the region generally agreed that the famed frontiersman was absolutely untrustworthy and a notorious liar to boot. Beckwourth's deeds were celebrated among fellow mountain men, but the harsh judgments of those who never knew him prevailed long after his death.

A closer look at Beckwourth's life today however, reveals a strikingly different picture. Almost everyone who met him remarked on his intelligence, good humor, and kindly open nature. According to one of his peers, Beckwourth was one of only three men known to have always dealt fairly with the Indians—the other two being Kit Carson and Daniel Boone.

James (Jim) Pierson Beckwith* was born around 1800. His father was Jennings Beckwith, grandson of Sir Marmaduke Beckwith of Richmond County Virginia; his mother was a black woman and almost certainly a slave. Wealthy, influential Virginians, the Beckwiths traced their ancestry back to English nobility.

Jennings, however, found the aristocratic life lacking. Disinterested in acquiring more land or money he doted on his several mixed-blood children and indulged the major passion in his life, the outdoors. He fished and hunted year-round and was quite content to live with Indians for weeks at a time while taking pleasure in those pursuits.

When Jim was about eight years old, the family moved to near St. Charles, Missouri, which was then on the very edge of the western frontier. The relocation, which provided Jennings with new hunting and fishing opportunities, probably was undertaken because the frontier offered a more tolerant atmosphere for a white man living openly with a black woman.

Little is known of Jim's childhood, although he obviously inherited his father's independent spirit and love of the wild. Children of slaves rarely received schooling, yet Jim did attend classes and learned how to read and write. Years later, after he had become well known, people were usually surprised to find him not only literate, but, in fact, quite articulate.

Although not raised a slave, Jim remained one in the eyes of the law and legal records show that Jennings had to go to court three times to swear out his son's Deed of Manumission. When Jim left for the Rocky Mountains in the early 1820s, he went as a free man.

Beckwourth and other young men who joined trapping expeditions heading out across the Plains were seeking adventure and personal financial gain. Few ever became wealthy but some—those who would come to be known as "mountain men"—fell in love with life in the wild. Hired by General William Henry Ashley's Rocky Mountain Fur Company, Beckwourth learned how to use a gun, bowie knife, and tomahawk and soon became a tough wilderness fighter.

For those who, like Beckwourth, possessed the skills and the courage needed to meet the considerable challenge of survival, the Western mountains during the mid-nineteenth century represented what has been called the ultimate opportunity for personal freedom. With the constraints of their own culture several hundred miles behind them, the mountain men made their way in the vast

---

*The spelling of his name was changed by T. D. Bonner, to whom Beckwourth dictated his life story.

From *American History,* September/October 1996, pp. 36-40, 72-73. © 1996 by Cowles Magazines, Inc. Reprinted through the courtesy of Cowles Magazines, publishers of *American History.*

unspoiled wilderness of seemingly unlimited expanse. As Beckwourth put it, there was "room to wander without any man to call your steps in question."

Wandering apparently suited him very well; except for one brief visit, 12 years passed before he returned to the settlements. Unlike some who were attracted to the mountains, Beckwourth was not a loner or a misfit. He exhibited a talent for storytelling and had a natural flair for languages. In addition to speaking fluent French and Spanish, he eventually mastered most Indian dialects.

The spinning of tall tales was of considerable importance to mountain men. While ensconced in some snowbound valley awaiting spring's arrival, they greatly appreciated a man who could entertainingly embellish a story. As a noted Western scholar has commented: "To be a gifted liar was as much a part of mountain honor as hard drinking or straight shooting."

Beckwourth and Jim Bridger, a fur trader and scout from Richmond, Virginia, became the champion tall-story tellers of the mountains. Within the context of Beckwourth's place and time that label was a source of pride. But taken out of that context—as it would be years later when his autobiography was published—it would severely harm his reputation.

Part of the problem lay in the types of stories the two men told. Bridger's were outlandish. He used to relate, for example, how he once shot at an elk that refused to move. Eventually he determined that a mountain of glass, acting as a giant magnifier, stood between him and his prey which was actually 25 miles away.

Beckwourth, on the other hand, tended to embellish true—or conceivably true—events. A typical story told of Beckwourth and a companion escaping on foot from several hundred Blackfoot Indians. As his partner was a poor runner, Beckwourth told him to hide in a creek while he led their pursuers on a marathon chase. "A thousand ideas peopled my feverish brain," he said, and, as the day wore on, he began to suffer from hunger and thirst. With the sun setting and bullets whizzing all around, Beckwourth stumbled into the safety of camp

at the last possible moment. The story ended with his claim that "According to the closest calculations, I ran that day ninety-five miles." Such tales, spun with mounting suspense and the proper degree of solemnity provided wonderful entertainment for fellow mountaineers. Committed to paper, however, they came across as lies and braggadocio.

Strangely enough, another man's tall tale led Beckwourth to his most talked about adventure. During the summer of 1828, Caleb Greenwood, a fellow trapper, "invented a fiction" by telling a group of Crow Indians that Beckwourth had been born a Crow but had been kidnapped by Cheyenne and sold to the whites. Believing the story, the Crow were very eager for their long lost "son" to return to them. Later that year, Beckwourth obliged.

His recollection of how that move came about sounds highly suspicious, but the story must have been great fun for him and his audiences. Supposedly Beckwourth and Bridger were out hunting when Bridger witnessed his comrade being taken captive by a large group of Indians. Not recognizing them as Crow—a tribe friendly toward whites—Bridger returned to camp and announced to a forlorn group the certain death of their companion.

As Beckwourth told it: "The faithful fellows little thought that, while they were lamenting my untimely fall, I was being hugged and kissed to death by a whole lodgeful of near and dear crow relatives—and that I was being welcomed with a public reception fully equal in intensity though not in extravagance, to that accorded to the victor of Waterloo on his triumphal entry into Paris."

All of the old women whose sons had been captured by the Cheyenne years earlier were summoned to the lodge. The women " . . . breathless with excitement, their eyes wild and protruding, and their nostrils dilated, arrived in squads, until the lodge was filled to overflowing. I believe never was [a] mortal gazed at with such intense and sustained interest as I was on that occasion. . . . At length one old woman, after having scanned my visage with the utmost intentness, came forward and said,

'If this is my son, he has a mole over one of his eyes.' My eyelids were immediately pulled down to the utmost stretch of their elasticity when, sure enough, she discovered a mole just over my left eye . . . such shouts of joy as were uttered by that honest-hearted woman were seldom before heard, while all the crow took part in her rejoicing."

Regardless of the actual circumstances, Beckwourth did remain with the Crow until 1836. During that time, the American Fur Company paid him to supply his "relatives" with trade goods in exchange for furs and buffalo robes. In theory a trader living with the Crow could make more money since there would be less danger of ambush by hostile Indians. Beckwourth, however, seems to have belonged to that breed of men who continually seek out danger; certainly he embraced Crow ways too enthusiastically for financial gain or personal safety to have been considerations.

Beckwourth adopted the Crow manner of dress so convincingly that, on occasion, he would startle unsuspecting whites by addressing them in English. He accepted the customs of the Crow and conformed to their ways very easily taking a succession of Indian wives and eventually rising to prominence as a war chief; a title that did not necessarily connote leadership, but was conferred on those who performed certain heroic feats in battle. The evidence, however, suggests that Beckwourth did have great influence within the tribe.

His autobiography has been called one of the goriest American books ever written. Readers must wade through an endless string of battle narratives that detail the taking of ludicrous numbers of enemy scalps. However, when allowances are made for numerical exaggeration and Beckwourth's natural sense of theater, the picture that emerges from his account is reasonably accurate. The Crow after all, were a military society in which personal prestige depended solely on success in battle.

Still, it was lucky for Beckwourth that his most famous exploit had independent verification. The battle of Blackfoot Fortress was witnessed by several white men, among them, a trapper named Zenas Leonard. On November 21, 1833, a group of Blackfoot were discovered deep in Crow territory. Outnumbered, they took refuge in a natural stone "fortress" on the brow of a hill. Attempts by some five to seven hundred Crow warriors to dislodge them ended with heavy loss of life on their side.

Losing heart, the Crow were about to retreat when Beckwourth climbed up on a rock and addressed the gathering. During a long, impassioned speech, he reminded the Crow warriors that "If we get killed, our friends who love us here will mourn our loss, while those in the spirit land will sing and rejoice to welcome us there, if we ascend to them dying like braves." Then, asserting that he was not afraid, Beckwourth jumped from the rock and ran alone toward the Blackfoot. His judgment of Crow psychology proved sound, as his "brothers" followed right behind. It was an exceptionally bloody assault, and when the carnage ended, all the Blackfoot were dead. The accounts of Beckwourth and Leonard differ on only one detail: Beckwourth's version of the story gives the number of scalps taken as 166, but Leonard counted 69.

After eight years with the Crow, Beckwourth began to grow weary of the relentless warring. "In good truth," he wrote, "I was tired of savage life under any aspect." So, in the summer of 1836, he left for St. Louis only to return briefly the following year. When an outbreak of smallpox struck the Indians, it was suggested that Beckwourth had returned for the purpose of intentionally introducing the disease into their midst. Since few men liked or respected Indians as Beckwourth did—and since he had not traveled near the area where the outbreak began—the charge was ridiculous. Nonetheless, the slander found its way into print and circulated throughout the West.

Beckwourth's next adventure took him to an unlikely setting for a mountain man. For several months during 1837–38, he served with distinction fighting Indians during the Second Seminole War in Florida and undertook the dangerous job of carrying military dispatches. Pay records reveal that, as a civilian employee of the Army Beckwourth received fifty dollars per month,

A Man's World

According to Beckwourth's autobiography in addition to living with the Crow, he also spent time with the Blackfoot, fitting easily into their way of life. However given his background, he found their practice of acquiring scalps during attacks on white settlers difficult to accept. One day a group of Indians rode into the camp carrying three white-men's scalps. Beckwourth was disgusted at the sight but dared not express his true feelings. Later as was their practice, the Blackfoot held a celebratory scalp dance that featured singing and dancing. When Beckwourth's Blackfoot wife wanted to join the merrymaking, he forbade her saying that "these scalps belonged to my people; my heart is crying for their death; you must not rejoice when my heart cries; you must not dance when I mourn."

Expecting that his wife would obey him, Beckwourth was shocked to hear that she "out-dances them all" at the festivities. He ran toward the ring of dancers, infuriated by her insubordination and "struck my disobedient wife a heavy blow in the head with the side of my battle-axe, which dropped her as if a ball had pierced her heart." Then he "dragged her through the crowd, and left her..." Amid cries of "Kill him: burn him" from the Indians, Beckwourth went back to his tent, anticipating retaliation at any moment.

To Beckwourth's amazement, As-as-to—his wife's father and the head chief— calmed the angry mob by reminding them that "When your wives disobey your command, you kill them; that is your right. . . . He did as you all would have done, and you shall neither kill or harm him." Having restored order the chief then offered Beckwourth another of his daughters, who, he assured his son-in-law, "is more beautiful; she has good sense and good ears. You may have her in the place of the bad one; she will hearken to all you say to her."

During the night, as Beckwourth and his new wife were sleeping, his first wife, weeping bitterly crept into his tent. Presumed dead by everyone, she had lain senseless on the ground for several hours before regaining consciousness and crawling back to Beckwourth's lodge. He called to her: "Go away . . . you have no business here; I have a new wife now, one who has sense." But she pleaded with him until he decided to adopt another Blackfoot custom, that of polygamy.

more than six times the pay of an enlisted man. But the war's pace proved too slow for Beckwourth's taste, so he returned the following summer to St. Louis. For the next ten years, he roamed the Southwest, trading with the Indians or carrying mail for the government.

Since his exploits while with the Crow had become common knowledge, Beckwourth could have experienced difficulty in dealing with their mortal enemies, the Cheyenne. But Beckwourth met the problem head-on with typical audacity: "I have killed a great Crow Chief, and am obliged to run away or be killed by them. I have come to the Cheyennes, who are the bravest people in the mountains, as I do not wish to be killed by any of the inferior tribes. I have come here to be killed by the Cheyennes, cut up and thrown out for their dogs to eat, so that they may say they have killed a great Crow chief."

Such talk shocked Beckwourth's less-experienced companions. As he expected, however, the Cheyenne were flattered and became his friends. That friendship would cause Beckwourth sadness later on, but, in the meantime, he exercised an uncanny knack for being present as history was being made.

During the 1840s, Beckwourth helped found the city of Pueblo, Colorado; traveled to California; and then participated in the insurrection in what is now New Mexico. He also ran the most famous saloon in Santa Fe, a "grand resort for liquor-imbibing, monte-playing, and fandango-disposed American officers and men."

Like his comrade Kit Carson, Beckwourth rode many dangerous miles carrying military dispatches along the Santa Fe Trail. Lewis Garrard, author of *Wah-to-Yah and the Taos Trail*, one of the best books ever written on the West, came across Beckwourth one night on the trail. "A mile beyond," he recounted, "we came upon a group of three men cooking, the leader of whom was a man known from Yellowstone to El Rio Bravo, from Salt Lake to Sangre Cristo, from Santa Fe to Missouri—the shrewd, independent Jim Beckwith. . . . He was a large, good-humored fellow: and while listening to the characteristic colloquy I almost forgot that he was of a race who, in the much boasted land of liberty, are an inferior, degraded people."

John Letts, a storekeeper at Mormon Bar, provided a description of Beckwourth, the forty-niner: "About nine in the morning, I saw, approaching the store, a strange looking being, mounted on a gray horse, a poncho thrown over his shoulder, over which was slung a huge rifle, skins wrapped around his legs, a pair of Mexican spurs on, and a slouched hat which partially obscured his copper complexion." Beckwourth, who supplied miners with trade goods,

in Beckwourth Valley dictating his memoirs to Thomas D. Bonner, a sometime temperance advocate who occasionally yielded to the temptation of the demon rum. Some suspect that, during the writing of the book, Bonner and Beckwourth were occasionally under the influence of more than cold mountain air, a fact that, if true, would help explain why the work reads more like a mountain man's yarn than a true autobiography.

Two years later, when Bonner published *The Life and Adventures of James P. Beckwourth, Mountaineer, Scout, and Pioneer and Chief of the Crow Nation of Indians,* the book was received as little more than a self-serving fantasy. More recently however, it has been seen in a different light. Although detail—particularly the number of scalps taken and horses stolen—are outrageously exaggerated, most events described actually did occur.

"BECKWOURTH ADOPTED *the Crow manner of dress so convincingly that he would startle unsuspecting whites by addressing them in English."*

Ironically the verbal skills that brought Jim Beckwourth early renown virtually guaranteed that the rest of his remarkable life would be regarded as fiction. The noted historian of the frontier, Francis Parkman, in a note scribbled in his own copy of Beckwourth's book, wrote: "Much of this narrative is probably false. . . . Beckwith is a fellow of bad character—a compound of white and black blood."

Having returned to California by 1848, Beckwourth carried mail along the lonely route between Monterey and Los Angeles. One of his stops on that route was the home of a wealthy Englishman named William Reed. When Beckwourth stopped there in December of that year, he found the bodies of Reed and his entire household—11 people in all—murdered by outlaws looking for gold. Given his record, it should be no surprise that Beckwourth was the first person to happen upon the scene of what became perhaps the most famous crime in early California history. The gruesome discovery spooked Beckwourth, who jumped back on his horse and rode the ninety miles to Monterey nonstop to report the crime to then-Lieutenant William Tecumseh Sherman. In later years, the future Civil War general remembered the old mountain man and warrior confessing to being about as scared as he had ever been. As it turned out, his fears were justified, the murderers were still in the house when Beckwourth entered and had intended to kill him when he walked into the room where they were hiding.

Beckwourth gave up the mail route when the Gold Rush of 1849 began.

was not averse to a little gambling on the side; among his other talents, he was reportedly one of the best monte players in the West. According to Letts, Beckwourth won $13,000 in just two nights.

In 1850, while roving Northern California, Beckwourth found a new route through the rocky Sierra Nevadas. With the help of some friends, he cleared a wagon road and, by 1851, was guiding the first of the tens of thousands of pioneers who would enter California from Nevada via the "Beckwourth Pass." Acclaimed California poet Ina Coolbrith was a child aboard the first wagon train to use the new route. In 1927, she recalled that Beckwourth rode bareback and wore his hair in two long braids tied with colored cord. "And when Jim Beckwourth said he would like to have my mother's little girls ride into California on his horse in front of him," Coolbrith added, "I was the happiest little girl in the world . . . we came at last in sight of California and there on the boundary Jim Beckwourth stopped, and pointing forward, said, 'Here is California, little girls, here is your kingdom.' "

During the winter of 1854, the man who had lived so much history stayed

During the 1850s, Beckwourth ran a combination trading post, ranch, and hotel in a valley on the California side of the Beckwourth Pass. Accounts from those days suggest that he was overly generous in lending money and in his hospitality to the often-destitute immigrants. Beckwourth Valley was, and still is, a pleasant place, one where a man nearing sixty might be content to finish out his days. Jim Beckwourth, however, had one more piece of history to witness firsthand.

By 1860, he was living in Denver, managing business interests for several friends who apparently held little stock in his reputation for dishonesty. He was also Acting Indian Agent. His old friends, the Cheyenne, often sought Beckwourth out concerning problems with the white man. Jim befriended the editor of the *Rocky Mountain News* and, on a number of occasions, used the paper to plead for justice for the Indians.

Unfortunately the mood of many whites at the time favored total annihilation of the Plains Indians. Those ugly sentiments found expression on November 29, 1864, at what became known as the Sand Creek Massacre, when 150 to 200 peaceful Cheyenne and Arapaho—more than half of them women and children—were slaughtered by the Third Regiment of the Colorado Volunteer Cavalry.

Beckwourth, then in the employ of the Army as a guide and interpreter (though probably not willingly), witnessed the massacre. At the hearings held afterward, he testified that he feared refusing to accompany the troops would have resulted in his being hanged.

His testimony—straightforward and accurate—must have required considerable courage, since the only officer to testify was later murdered on the streets of Denver.

Undoubtedly saddened, and ashamed of his participation in the massacre, Beckwourth left Denver soon after. He spent his last days as a guide and scout for the army. The West he had loved was changing irrevocably, yet Jim managed to find a final resting place particularly suited to an old mountain man.

In 1866, according to one story concerning Beckwourth's death, the Crow invited him to a tribal feast, during which they tried to persuade him to lead them again. When Beckwourth refused, they fed him poison in the conviction that if they could not have him as a live chief, they would keep him in the tribal burial ground. His body, in accordance with Crow custom, was wrapped in skins and placed on a platform in a tree. Even in death, Jim Beckwourth had a fine sense of the theatrical.

Although his real life story has been overshadowed by the tales that he and others fabricated, Beckwourth was, indeed, one of that rare breed of men whose daring exploits helped to conquer the wilderness and open up the American West for the settlers who followed.

Michael Martin is a freelance writer from Milwaukee, Wisconsin, whose articles have appeared previously in American History.

James K. Polk and the Expansionist Spirit

Harlan Hague

James K. Polk, 1795–1849. (Daguerreotype by Mathew B. Brady)

Only days after his inauguration in March 1845, President James K. Polk announced to Secretary of the Navy George Bancroft: "There are four great measures which are to be the measures of my administration: one, a reduction of the tariff; another, the independent treasury; a third, the settlement of the Oregon boundary question; and lastly, the acquisition of California."[1] It was the last two of his "great measures" that elected Polk, for he was swept into the White House by an expansionist fervor that peaked at his election. As President, Polk did not initiate a policy toward the West; he inherited one, based on the tenets of Manifest Destiny.

There was no doubt during the campaign where candidate Polk stood on the expansionist issue. In the spring of 1844, he called publicly for the annexation of both Texas and the Oregon country.[2] At the same time, Martin Van Buren, the assumed presidential candidate of the Democratic Party, announced his opposition to Texas annexation on grounds that it would mean war with Mexico.[3] Andrew Jackson, determined that the United States should have Texas, threw his support behind his fellow Tennessean for the Democratic Party nomination. In the end, Polk was nominated on the ninth ballot, as a compromise after the convention deadlocked on a choice between Van Buren, the lackluster ex-President whose political sun was setting, and Lewis Cass, an expansionist zealot who had won the support of many Westerners and Southerners and the enmity of multitudes. The Whig candidate, Henry Clay, had long opposed annexation of Texas, and the Whig platform ignored the issue. Polk's election assured the admission of Texas, and on 1 March 1845, the Lone Star Republic was invited into the Union by a joint resolution of Congress.

Upon his inauguration, the new President set to work on satisfying his campaign pledge. Polk was particularly concerned that the United States control important West Coast ports. He was not the first American leader to demand that a settlement of the Oregon question must give the United States control of Puget Sound, a region dominated by Britain's Hudson's Bay Company. A port on the Sound would be an Ameri-

can window on the Pacific, a jumping-off point for the Asian trade. Great Britain was just as determined that it would surrender no land north of the Columbia River. Logic seemed to support the British view. British settlement, chiefly the works and farms of the Hudson's Bay Company, was located north of the Columbia in present-day Washington, while American settlement was located south of the river, chiefly in Oregon's Willamette Valley.

Since 1818, the United States and Britain, by agreement, had jointly occupied the Oregon country. During the negotiations that had established joint occupancy, the United States had proposed a division of Oregon at the 49th parallel, but Britain, preferring the Columbia River as a boundary, rejected the offer. The American claim was subsequently pushed northward until it rested at 54°40', the southern limit of Russian claims which had been established by treaty between Russia and the United States in 1824.

By the early 1840s, interest in a settlement of the Oregon question had increased in both Great Britain and the United States. As presidential candidate in 1844, Polk accepted the demand of the Democratic Party leadership for a boundary at 5440° but only as a political expedient. Indeed in July 1845, after only a few months in office, he offered Richard Pakenham, the British minister in Washington, a boundary settlement at the 49th parallel. Privately, Polk acknowledged that American interests would be protected because the boundary would leave the United States in control of Puget Sound. Pakenham rejected the offer since it did not include free British navigation of the Columbia, a long-standing British condition. When London later showed interest, nevertheless, in the offer, Polk refused to renew it.[4]

The following December, the President explained rather weakly in a message to Congress that he had made the 49th parallel boundary offer only from respect for his predecessors, who had long favored that compromise. Perhaps, though unstated, he had also feared war with Britain. Now, in December, Polk vowed that he would make no other offer. Rather than accommodation, he recommended that notice of termination of joint occupancy be delivered to Britain. At the expiration of the agreement, he said, the United States would pursue its interests aggressively in the Oregon country. London favored accommodation and suggested that the issue be submitted to arbitration. Polk rejected arbitration on grounds that the British had no just claim to Oregon.[5]

The President's rhetoric was mostly bluff and bluster. It was directed as much at the British government and public as American. Polk's objective was more pacific than his words. He simply wanted to stimulate negotiations and to force the British to take the initiative. To Louis McLane, the American minister in London, Polk intimated that he would be receptive to a British restatement of his original proposal, that is, a 49th parallel boundary, though Britain could have all of Vancouver Island, but no free British navigation of the Columbia.[6] Polk expected that his belligerent posture would force the issue.

Many congressmen were alarmed at Polk's notice proposal, fearing that it could lead to war with Britain. Congress debated the proposal for over four months and finally, in April 1846, enacted a measure to give British notice to terminate joint occupancy.

In the end, the settlement of the Oregon question may be attributed less to belligerence than to a lack of zeal.[7] By the end of 1845, the British public and the larger part of the government were little interested in Oregon. They were preoccupied with the specter of famine at home because of the potato blight in Ireland and light harvests in Britain.

Great Britain now needed American wheat, and trade relations in general improved in early 1846, leading many, including Polk, to hope for a lowering of tariffs. Furthermore, the fur trade was declining in Oregon, and British leaders were hard pressed to justify defense of a claim to the region below the 49th parallel at the risk of war. Finally, British leaders were convinced that sufficient British access to the sea would be secured if an agreement on a 49th parallel boundary left Britain all of Vancouver Island.

Accordingly, London tendered a proposal to Washington, and a treaty was concluded on these terms in June 1846. Both sides breathed a great sigh of relief. The signing came none too soon, particularly for the United States. Fighting had already begun on the disputed Texas border.

Polk's views on Oregon were contradictory at best. His obligation as leader of a party that was committed to having all of Oregon often conflicted with his own view. His involvement stemmed from political necessity, not personal interest, and he did what he had to do.

A Southerner, Polk was more interested in Texas and California. He was personally and passionately committed to American domination in the Southwest. The Oregon question settled, Polk turned to the Texas question.

Trouble between Mexico and the United States had been brewing since 1836 when Mexico blamed the United States for its loss of Texas. Mexico had never acknowledged the loss and warned the United States not to interfere, a warning that Polk ignored. He had no more sympathy for the arguments of anti-imperialists and anti-slavery leaders who spoke out against Washington's growing interest in Texas.

Polk dispatched agents to the Lone Star Republic in early 1845 to gather information and encourage Texans to call for annexation.[8] Following annexation in March, he sent William S. Parrott to Mexico City with instructions to convince the Mexican leadership to accept the finality of the American annexation of Texas and to resume diplomatic ties with the United States, which the annexation had ruptured. The shaky government of José Joaquín Herrera, mindful of the growing public clamor in Mexico against the American annexation of Texas, was noncommittal. Herrera preferred a British plan that included Mexico's recognition of Texas in return for the Lone Star Republic's rejection of annexation.[9]

Polk applied pressure. His administration accepted the Texas claim to the Rio Grande River boundary, and he moved to reinforce the claim. In mid-June, he ordered Zachary Taylor to move his troops from Louisiana to Texas where they installed themselves on the south bank of the Nueces River, thus inside the disputed territory between that river and the Rio Grande. Polk vowed that no invading force would be allowed to cross the Rio Grande.[10] In spite of the belligerent tone, he considered the Army's deployment a defensive move. Polk was an expansionist, but he was no fool. He did not shrink from the necessity of war, but he sought none, at least not until other measures were exhausted.

Mexico indeed appeared prepared to settle differences amicably. In August from Mexico City, Parrott notified Polk that the government seemed prepared to receive an American emissary. Polk appointed John Slidell his secret agent—during his presidency, Polk would appoint an abundance of secret agents—and instructed him to secure Mexico's acceptance of the Rio Grande boundary and a promise to pay the claims of American citizens against Mexico. And the pièce de résistance: He was to offer Mexico as much as $40 million for California and New Mexico. At the same time, Polk warned Mexico—and Britain and France, as well—against any plan for a European protectorate for California. The Monroe Doctrine would be enforced. Polk's prohibition of European protectorates, a new factor in American hegemony, in time became called the "Polk doctrine."[11]

The Slidell mission was doomed from the start. The Herrera government fell on 2 January to a new revolutionary movement under General Paredes y Arrillaga. Anticipating that the new administration would be no more stable than the former, Polk toyed with the idea of asking Congress for a secret fund of $500,000 to a $1 million which he would transfer to Paredes to strengthen his government during negotiations. He abandoned the scheme when he could not win sufficient support among Democratic leaders.[12]

In early 1846, Polk was intrigued by the possibilities suggested to him by one Alexander J. Atocha. A naturalized American citizen, Atocha was a friend of ex-President Antonio Lòpez de Santa Anna who was overthrown in 1845. Atocha had recently visited General Santa Anna in Havana. He believed that Santa Anna would soon be once again in power and that the general favored a treaty in which Mexico would cede New Mexico and California to the United States. Santa Anna, he said, had told him that $30 million would be a satisfactory sum to conclude the deal, but that the United States must take action to pose such an armed threat that Mexican citizens would be convinced that the cession was the only alternative to destruction.[13] Polk concluded that Atocha was probably not reliable, but the President continued to pursue the diplomacy-by-bribery scheme off and on. Nothing came of it.[14]

Polk's fears for the stability of the new government were well founded. He learned in early April 1846 that Arrillaga, certain that he would be removed from office by an angry citizenry if he agreed to negotiations, had refused to receive Slidell. War now seemed likely. That same day, Polk had told his cabinet that if Mexico rejected his envoy, the American leaders must "take the remedy for the injuries and wrongs we had suffered into our own hands."[15] He now "saw no alternative but strong measures towards Mexico."[16] Slidell counseled Polk that war now was probably the best course.[17]

War was not long in coming. By early May, Polk had decided that war would be necessary to achieve his objectives, which included California and New Mexico and perhaps additional northern Mexican states. He prepared a message for delivery to Congress on 12 May, a delicately worded message, for he was asking Congress for authority to initiate war. Three days before the scheduled delivery date, Polk learned that a Mexican patrol had crossed the Rio Grande and fired on American troops. In Polk's view, Mexico had invaded American soil. He changed his message, and on 11 and 12 May, Congress, by huge majorities, declared war.

Polk soon clarified his war aims, privately at least. Shortly after the declaration of war, he read a dispatch that Secretary of State James Buchanan planned to send to European governments to notify them of the declaration. Polk was not pleased; he ordered the Secretary to strike from the message a statement that the United States had no intention "to dismember Mexico or make conquests . . . [and] that in going to war we did not do so with a view to acquire either California or New Mexico or any other portion of the Mexican territory." Polk told Buchanan that we would seek indemnities, and Mexico had no other way of indemnifying the United States, save in territory. Buchanan said that unless the assurance that he recommended was included in the message, both England and France would join the war on the side of Mexico. Polk replied testily that before he gave this assurance, he would "meet the war which either England or France or all the Powers of Christendom might wage. . . ." He would stand for no interference.[18] He had long since given his pledge to the American people, at least those of the public who counted, in Polk's estimation. Those who did not support his policy he branded as disloyal and hinted that such behavior was treasonous.

Polk had not forgotten that other prize that must come in a contest with Mexico: California. Polk's initial interest in the Mexican province was the same as his interest in Oregon; that is, its ports. For a while, it seemed that California might fall quietly to the United States. Thomas O. Larkin, American Consul to Mexican California, was making headway in convincing Californians that their destiny lay in an association, initiated by themselves, with the United States.[19] By the mid-1840s, however, there was reason for haste. American immigrants entering California overland were arguing belligerently for a "Texas solution" for California.

In 1845 affairs appeared to take an ominous turn in California. Larkin had written frequently to Washington from Monterrey during the past year, telling of the revolutionary ferment among *Californios*. Some *Californio* leaders, said Larkin, favored associating a liberated California with the United States. On the other hand, the Consul warned of apparent British and French intrigues in the province and the interest of some California leaders in seeking protection from a European country.[20] Polk was convinced that Britain wanted California, and he was determined that the United States would not permit Britain or any other foreign power to possess it.[21]

The President was impressed by Larkin's revelations. In October 1845, Polk appointed him his confidential agent with instructions to inform the Californians that though the United States would not interfere in any conflict between California and Mexico, Americans would not permit California's becoming a colony of Britain or France. The United States would not leave its neighbor unprotected. Indeed, Larkin was to assure the Californians that an application for admission into the American union by a free California would be most welcome.[22]

Acting on Larkin's information, members of Polk's cabinet, unquestionably at the President's direction, strengthened American preparedness. Secretary of War George Bancroft ordered Commodore John D. Sloat, commander of the American fleet off the Mexican coast, to be ready to blockade or seize California ports at the first sign of hostilities.[23] Secretary of State Buchanan alerted the American ambassador in London and briefed John Slidell on Larkin's correspondence.[24] Bancroft dispatched Commodore Robert F. Stockton to the West Coast to deliver the letters containing Sloat's new orders and Larkin's appointment. At the same time, Buchanan sent a copy of the appointment letter to Larkin by Marine Lieutenant Archibald H. Gillespie, who was to travel in disguise across Mexico. Gillespie, another of Polk's secret agents, also was ordered to deliver an informational copy of Larkin's letter to

Brevet Captain John D. Frémont, who was exploring in California.

Frémont's role in California affairs was stormy, controversial, and contradictory.[25] Frémont had arrived in California with an expedition of 60 well-armed mountain men early in 1846. He soon offended California authorities and was ordered to leave. Instead, in March he erected barricades atop Hawk's Peak in the Gavilan Mountains near Monterrey where he was besieged by a *Californio* force. Frémont soon withdrew, realizing that the affair was essentially personal and that his action could jeopardize Washington's plan to acquire California.[26]

Three months later in the Bear Flag affair, Frémont took a belligerent stance that angered *Californios* more than did the Hawk's Peak incident. He even arrested General Mariano Guadalupe Vallejo, who favored an association of California with the United States. By then, Frémont had seen the copy of Buchanan's letter to Larkin, and he was confident now that he was acting in the best interests of the United States. Questioned by Commodore Sloat in July 1846 about his part in the Bear Flag incident, Frémont replied that he "had acted solely on my own responsibility, and without any expressed authority from the Government to justify hostilities.' "[27]

Perhaps Frémont responded to a higher authority. "How fate pursues a man!" he had observed earlier, upon learning that Gillespie was on his trail.[28] Fate perhaps was on his side, but not his commander in chief. Polk later confided to his diary that Frémont had acted without authority.[29]

During the war in California, Frémont led his own men under the overall command of Commodore Stockton, who had replaced Sloat. When General Stephen Watts Kearny arrived from Santa Fé with an advance unit of his Army of the West, carrying orders that designated him governor of California, Frémont refused to recognize his authority.[30] A court-martial board in Washington the following January found Frémont guilty of mutiny and ordered him discharged from the service.

After a review of the court record and consultation with his cabinet, Polk con-cluded that the facts of the case did not prove mutiny. He dismissed that conviction, but let stand conviction on two lesser charges: disobedience of orders and conduct prejudicial to good order and military discipline. The President, influenced by the cabinet, also thought the sentence of dismissal from the Army too severe. Accordingly, he set aside the sentence and ordered Frémont to report for duty. The decision, he groaned, was "a painful and a responsible duty."[31] Frémont rejected Polk's clemency, for to accept would be to acknowledge guilt. He resigned from the Army and returned to California.

In the heated controversies between Kearny and Stockton and between Kearny and Frémont, Polk sided with Kearny. After a full examination of the correspondence in May 1847, Polk concluded that he was "fully satisfied that General Kearny was right, and that Commodore Stockton's course was wrong. Indeed, both he [Stockton] and Lieut.-Col. Frémont, in refusing to recognize the authority of General Kearny, acted insubordinately and in a manner that is censurable."[32]

At war's end, there was some concern in California that Washington would not assist in the peace treaty on retention of the province. Those that knew something of the origins of the New York Volunteer Regiment, which arrived in California in spring 1847, were less fearful. Polk had directed Colonel Jonathan D. Stevenson to recruit mechanics who would agree that they would, at war's end, accept their discharges and settle in California or the closest United States territory. The Eastern press, from the regiment's inception, guessed that its principal purpose was colonization rather than war.[33] Shortly before the end of the war, Polk confided in a letter to his brother that California indeed would be retained, and New Mexico as well, as war indemnifications. Furthermore, the longer Mexico continued hostilities by its "stubbornness," said Polk, the greater the indemnities.[34]

Publicly, Polk said little about California's destiny, for he did not wish to enter the debate on whether the United States intended to retain Mexican territory. He was no longer stating publicly, as he had before, that the United States had no intention to retain Mexican properties after the signing of a peace treaty.[35] His reluctance to make his position known baffled and angered the public. The public should have remembered that Polk at the outset of the war had similarly refused to clarify his war objectives.

At war's end, when it appeared that Polk might be forced to bow to powerful elements in the Democratic Party who were arguing for annexation of all of Mexico, Nicholas Trist signed the Treaty of Guadalupe Hidalgo for the United States, which established a boundary just south of San Diego Bay, virtually the same boundary that Polk had sought in the Slidell mission. The President's well-known quarrel with Trist would be overlooked, and the administration, according to the New Orleans *Picayune,* would be content to "swallow its disappointment, and California and New Mexico at the same time."[36]

Polk left to his successors the question of slavery which would become central to the issue of Westward Expansion for the next 15 years. During his presidency, Polk adopted a position that could have prevented sectional crisis if his successors had been so wise. He understood better than his contemporaries, and successors as well, the true nature of the issue of slavery in the Western territories. He assailed fellow Southerner John C. Calhoun for his extremist stance on the expansion of slavery. At the same time, he rejected the Wilmot Proviso which would have prevented slavery in any territory acquired from Mexico at the end of the war. Indeed, he favored the extension of the 1820 Missouri Compromise line of 36°30′ to the Pacific.

Polk saw no contradiction in his position. He was simply convinced that slavery would never exist in the territory south of the 36°30′ line.[37] A Southern man who wished to be president to all the people, he would permit slavery in the federal territories since he believed that it would never take hold there. If this view had prevailed, there might have been no Civil War.

Polk decided that he was going to enjoy retirement more than the presidency, and he left the office without regret. He was dismayed, however, to be succeeded by a Whig, especially by Zachary Taylor, whom he held in low regard. His opinion of Taylor undoubtedly reached rock-bottom during a coach ride to the Capitol on inauguration day. Polk was shocked when the President-elect, in the course of polite conversation, said that Oregon and California should not establish an independent government, since they were so far removed from the United States. Polk, for some time, had been anxious that Congress form a government for California, fearing that otherwise the territory could be lost to the Union by the formation of a separate government, precisely the course the new President seemed to advocate. Polk concluded that Taylor was a "well-meaning old man," though uneducated and politically ignorant.[38]

If Polk's election in 1844 can be traced at least partly to the American people's expansionist spirit, then it can be argued that the voters' rejection of the Democrats in 1848 can be interpreted as a repudiation of the siren song of Manifest Destiny.[39] Yet, Polk's contributions, the fruit of the expansionist spirit, were embraced and defended. His "Polk Doctrine," which warned Europe not to interfere in the affairs of the North American continent, was subsequently embraced by the American people. During the four-year tenure, over one-half million square miles of territory were added to the United States, a number second only to Jefferson's Louisiana Purchase.[40] Even ill-gotten gains, like horse thieves and harlots in the family tree, can be accepted with resignation or amusement, even some pride, when separated by a sufficient lapse of time.

Notes

1. James K. Polk, *Polk: The Diary of a President, 1845–1849,* Allan Nevins, ed. (New York, 1952), xvii.
2. See, for example, Polk to Chase *et al,* 23 Apr. 1844, in James K. Polk, *The Correspondence of James K. Polk,* Wayne Cutler and James P. Cooper, Jr., eds. (Nashville, TN, 1989), 105–106.
3. Polk, *Diary,* xxiii.
4. Frederick Merk, *The Oregon Question: Essays in Anglo-American Diplomacy and Politics* (Cambridge, MA, 1967), 410; Jesse S. Reeves, *American Diplomacy under Tyler and Polk* (Gloucester, MA, 1967, a reprint of the 1907 publication of The Johns Hopkins Press), 252–253.
5. Merk, *The Oregon Question,* 219–220.
6. *Ibid.,* 343.
7. For an elaboration of the view following, see Merk, *The Oregon Question,* 415–416, and Norman A. Graebner, *Empire on the Pacific: A Study in American Continental Expansion* (Santa Barbara, CA, reprint, 1983), 137–140.
8. Commodore Robert F. Stockton, the most energetic among the agents, appeared bent on provoking a war with Mexico. See, generally, Glenn W. Price, *Origins of the War with Mexico: The Polk-Stockton Intrigue* (Austin, TX, 1967). Texas President Anson Jones, who later wrote an account of the intrigues of Stockton and his Texan and American cohorts, charged that Polk secretly sought to provoke war at the point, 112.
9. Charles Sellers, *James K. Polk: Continentalist, 1843–1846* (Princeton, NJ, 1966), 259.
10. Neal Harlow, *California Conquered: War and Peace on the Pacific, 1846–1850* (Berkeley, 1982), 55; Paul H. Bergeron, *The Presidency of James K. Polk* (Lawrence, KS, 1987), 62.
11. Polk, *Diary,* 10; Bernard DeVoto, *Year of Decision: 1846* (Boston, 1942), 16–17. Slidell's mission was to be kept secret to prevent foreign powers, particularly Britain or France, from interfering with it. Polk, *Diary,* 10.
12. Graebner, *Empire on the Pacific,* 121.
13. Polk, *Diary,* 50–53; Sellers, *Polk: Continentalist,* 401.
14. Polk, *Diary,* 53; Bergeron, *Polk,* 70–71, 83, 103; Sellers, *Polk: Continentalist,* 427–428, 430–431.
15. Polk, *Diary* (4-7-1846), 69–70. Polk believed that the British ambassador had influenced the Mexican government to reject Slidell *Ibid.* (4-18-1846), 71–72], perhaps assuming that the Mexican issue would be sufficiently irritating to the United States to encourage the settlement of the Oregon question.
16. Polk, *Diary* (4-18-1846), 71.
17. Graebner, *Empire on the Pacific,* 152.
18. Polk, *Diary* (5-13-1846), 90–92.
19. For Larkin's role in trying to persuade Californians, see Harlan Hague and David J. Langum, *Thomas O. Larkin: A Life of Patriotism and Profit in Old California* (Norman, OK, 1990), especially chapter 7.
20. Larkin's role in the approach to war with Mexico is told in *Ibid.,* chapter 7.
21. Polk, *Diary* (10-14-1845), 19. Spence and Jackson indeed conclude that Polk's concern about British designs on California became "one of the cornerstones of his foreign policy." John Charles Frémont, *The Expeditions of John Charles Frémont: The Bear Flag Revolt and the Court-Martial,* Mary Lee Spence and Donald Jackson, eds., vol. 2 (Urbana, 1973), xxi. If that is true, then Larkin's influence on American foreign policy during Polk's presidency looms large. Polk's fear of European interference would extend to the end of the war. As late as December 1847, he argued that a premature withdrawal of the American Army from Mexico might open the way to European intervention. Robert W. Johannsen, *To the Halls of the Montezumas: The Mexican War in the American Imagination* (New York, 1985), 304.
22. Buchanan to Larkin, 17 Oct. 1845, in George P. Hammond, ed., *The Larkin Papers: Personal, Business, and Official Correspondence of Thomas Oliver Larkin, Merchant and United States Consul in California,* 10 vols. (Berkeley, 1951–1968), 4: 44–46.
23. Bancroft to Sloat, 17 Oct. 1845, in Robert E. Cowan, ed., "Documentary," *California Historical Society Quarterly,* 2 (July 1923): 167–170.
24. Buchanan to McLane, 14 Oct. 1845, cited in Robert Glass Cleland, "The Early Sentiment for the Annexation of California: An Account of the Growth of American Interest in California, 1835–1846," *The Southwestern Historical Quarterly* (Jan. 1915), 243; Buchanan to Slidell, 10 Nov. 1845, cited in Howard William Gross, "The Influence of Thomas O. Larkin Toward the Acquisition of California," M.A. thesis, University of California, Berkeley, 1937, 112.
25. For an overview, see: Harlow, *California Conquered,* principally chapters 6–8; Hague and Langum, *Thomas O. Larkin,* 120–130, 136–139.
26. John Charles Frémont, *Memoirs of My Life* (Chicago: Belford, Clarke & Company, 1887), 460.
27. Frémont, *Memoirs,* 534. In later life, Frémont, probably influenced by Jessie, his wife, claimed that the letter from Buchanan that was shown him in spring 1846 was actually meant for *himself* not Larkin, that *he,* not Larkin, had been appointed Polk's confidential agent. The record does not support his claim. See Hague and Langum, *Thomas O. Larkin,* 128–130.
28. Frémont, *Memoirs,* 486.
29. Frémont, *Expeditions,* 2: xxix.
30. This tangled story is best told in Harlow, *California Conquered,* chapters 14, 15.
31. Polk, *Diary* (2-16-1848), 303. See also Frémont, *Expeditions,* 468n, 469n.
32. Polk, *Diary* (5-4-1847), 226.
33. Graebner, *Empire on the Pacific,* 156.
34. *Ibid.,* 158–159.
35. *Ibid.,* 161–162.
36. Quoted in *Ibid.,* 213–214.
37. Polk, *Diary,* xvi, 189–190, 376.
38. *Ibid.,* 389.
39. This argument is suggested in Graebner, *Empire on the Pacific,* 227.
40. Polk, *Diary,* xvii.

Harlan Hague is the author, with David J. Langum, of Thomas O. Larkin: A Life of Patriotism and Profit in Old California *(1990), winner of the Caroline Bancroft Prize. He is currently editing a collection of unpublished Larkin letters and working on a biography of Stephen Watts Kearny for the University of Oklahoma Western Biographies series. Recipient of a number of grants, including NEH, the Huntington Library, and the Sourisseau Academy, Hague is particularly interested in Mexican California, exploration and travel, and environmental history.*

All That Glittered

SAVE FOR THE CIVIL WAR, what occurred after a carpenter glimpsed a flash of yellow 150 years ago was the biggest story of the nineteenth century. RICHARD REINHARDT examines what we think we know (and don't) about the people who made it happen.

IT WAS 150 YEARS AGO THIS JANUARY that Jim Marshall, the boss carpenter of a crew of Maidu Indians and transient Mormon settlers who were building a sawmill in the foothills of the Sierra Nevada, glimpsed a metallic twinkle in a freshly dug tailrace. Marshall took it to be the glint of gold, and he was right. From that moment—celebrated and debunked, distorted but unforgettable—Marshall's life and that of his patron, John Sutter, were effectively ruined; the state of California was prematurely delivered; the current of American history, which had been trickling leisurely westward for a couple of hundred years, surged abruptly across the continent to the Pacific Coast; a hundred thousand men and women left home and went to California to seek a pocketful of gold; and the world was changed.

AT THE VILLAGE OF COLOMA ON THE south fork of the American River, there are picnic grounds and a replica of John Sutter's mill to mark the spot where Marshall's exclamation (customarily rendered "Boys, I believe I've found a gold mine!") set off the greatest of all gold rushes. Busloads of schoolchildren swarm the site. Teachers dredge up everything they know about that chilly afternoon in 1848 and retell the story in all its debatable details: how Marshall took his chips of gleaming yellow gravel to the cabin of his foreman, Peter Wimmer, where

Wimmer's wife, Jane (or was her name Jennie?), boiled them in a pot of home-made soap to see if lye would dim their color; how Marshall carried his treasure in a knotted cloth to Sutter, an ambitious immigrant from Switzerland who had obtained a Mexican land grant and was building and fortifying a private empire he called New Helvetia; how Sutter, having bitten and hammered the grains

---

The current of history surged abruptly; a hundred thousand Americans went West; and the world was changed.

---

and doused them in nitric acid, concluded that they really *were* gold and then attempted (or possibly *did not attempt*) to keep the secret from the myriad outsiders who were certain to overrun his empire; and how, almost four months later, an enterprising Mormon colonist named Sam Brannan, having figured out what the fuss was all about, quickly built several supply stores to accommodate the anticipated invasion and then rambled through the streets of the village of San Francisco waving a little quinine bottle

and shouting, "Gold! Gold! Gold from the American River!"

More than thirty million people now live in California, and most of us, like the schoolchildren visiting Coloma, have a rough idea what happened after Sam Brannan's famous show-and-tell. In our collective mind the gold rush opens with a swift montage of banjos plinking "Oh, Susanna!" while wagon wheels creak westward. Next we cut to a black-and-white panorama of shack-town San Francisco, swollen from 850 motley adventurers to 85,000 motley adventurers. Abandoned ships from Baltimore and Bremen lie rotting under tangled hawsers on the tidal flats of Yerba Buena Cove. The waterfront is teeming with Tasmanian sheep farmers dressed in cabbage-tree hats and moleskin trousers and carrying bedrolls made of possum fur; Chinese in knee-length breeches and quilted jackets, with pigtails coiled up in hats that look like small, black beehives; Peruvians in chocolate brown ponchos; Malays with krises in their belts; and, of course, thousands of adolescent boys from the farms and towns of the East, dazzled by the noise, the smells, the opportunities for sudden wealth and reckless misbehavior. Picking their way along the rickety plank sidewalks slung among the scuttled ships, newcomers encounter peddlers hawking cakes and coffee at incredible prices, cheapjacks selling shirts and underdrawers from the sea chests of the recent dead, tinhorn gamblers rattling metal dice cups, thimbleriggers carrying trays on which to place your bet and guess the cup that hides a pea. Wharf rats from a hundred harbors dart along the rigging of the ships: the gray rats of Valparaiso, Canton, and Singapore; the long, white, pink-eyed rice rats of Batavia; the furtive brown rats of New York, Liverpool, and Boston; and the kangaroo rats of Sydney.

Up in the brick red foothills, under the oaks and cedars, in camps that bear such names as Whiskey Flat, Lousy Ravine, Petticoat Slide, and Piety Hill, thousands of other amateurs are hunkering in the creek beds, washing gravel in frying pans, looking for flakes that glitter. It is the outing of a lifetime. You may dine each day on salt pork, saleratus bread, and beans and dance the polka on Saturday night with a ripe-smelling man from across the ravine. You may die of scurvy, amoebic dysentery, diphtheria, or cholera. For entertainment there are pistol duels in canvas casinos, floozies singing hurdygurdy tunes, and impromptu vigilante hangings from the limbs of ponderosa pines. Occasionally someone shouts, "Boys, I believe I've found a gold mine!" or words to that effect.

AMONG THESE LANTERN FLASHES strides the bearded forty-niner, dressed in knee boots, denim trousers, red flannel shirt, and slouch hat, armed with a pistol or a bowie knife, hefting a shovel on his shoulder. Californians see him, persistently if incorrectly, as the father of their state, a fair-skinned Anglo-American lad from the Atlantic Coast, who came West searching for easy money, made his pile, and stayed on to plant grapevines and orange trees, build roads, plan cities, and found universities. He is an American icon, as familiar as the Cowboy, the Pathfinder, the Whaler, the Pilgrim, the Indian Chief, the Johnny Reb, the Pioneer Mother. He turns up in murals and friezes, statues, and beer labels, at costume parties, and in the municipal seal of the city and county of San Francisco. He is a dictionary entry in Webster's unabridged, a verse in a song about an awkward girl named Clementine, the mascot of San Francisco's professional football team.

As for the substance that lured the forty-niner here, it remains the metaphoric symbol of the West, although mining long ago declined into a minor industry in an urban, industrial state. California continues to call itself the Golden State. Its historic entrance is the Golden Gate. The colors of the state university are gold and blue; the state flower is the golden poppy. The motto of San Francisco is "Gold in Peace, Iron in War." The motto of the state is "Eureka!"—I have found it!

Like many archetypal figures, the forty-niner has no name, no heroic prototype. He is the composite of thousands of humble men, most of whom went home poorer than they came. As a prospector and placer miner, he was a failure and a fraud.

"Few goldseekers stuck with mining for more than a brief time," according to J. S. Holliday, whose bestseller *The World Rushed In* has become a standard reference work on the gold rush. Their experience in the diggings was "sickness, foul food, loneliness, the high cost of even the most miserable living, and mining claims that produced more disappointment than gold."

Most of the few who profited from the gold rush did so by selling barrels of whiskey, kegs of nails, cords of lumber, bags of flour, bottles of ipecac and liniment and India tonic, portable houses made in Baltimore, tombstones carved in Philadelphia, porter brewed in New York, sherry blended in Spain. They got rich by buying Mexican land cheap and selling it dear or by stealing it from Indians, by opening banks and stage lines and steamboat services, by running saloons, whorehouses, gambling halls, boardinghouses, beer gardens, or private mints.

BRIEFER AND LESS HAZARDOUS THAN a foreign war, the trek to California also was a splendid opportunity to make a literary reputation. Bayard Taylor, a sometime correspondent and editorial staffer for Horace Greeley's New York *Tribune,* seized the day in June 1849 and headed for California, dressed in stout hunter's boots and a suit of fustian and equipped with a pocket thermometer, barometer, compass, spyglass, sketchbook, journal, blanket, and "a good revolver." His detailed and candid reportage made *Eldorado,* published simultaneously in New York and London in 1850, a popular success and an enduring classic of Western Americana. Other correspondence, guidebooks, and memoirs rolled out of the presses of Britain, France, Germany, and the United States while mining companies were still recruiting members and chartering sailing vessels: E. Gould Buffum's *Six Months in the Gold Mines* (1850), William R. Ryan's *Personal Adventures in Upper and Lower California in 1848–49* (1851), and James Carson's *Recollections of the California Mines* (1852).

(It was two decades later when Samuel Clemens, Francis Bret Harte, Prentice Mulford, and Charles Warren Stoddard—all relative latecomers to California—found the forty-niner a ready-made character and installed him permanently in the gallery of American literary images, even inventing for him a language compounded of Down Eastern, Southwestern, and Sierra Nevada rustic. The resulting outburst of California color was exploited still later by the poet Joaquin Miller. Dressed in high boots, sombrero, and buckskin jacket, which his hostesses took to be characteristic California attire, Joaquin [whose real name was Cincinnatus] invaded the drawing rooms of New Orleans, New York, and London and claimed the entire Sierra Nevada as his spiritual territory.)

For more than a year after Marshall's discovery, most of the hunters—later styled the forty-eighters—came from the neighborhood, the underpopulated Pacific Coast, and most of the gold they found stayed in California. Reports of vast "discoveries" in the tributaries of the Sacramento were being published in newspapers on the East Coast and in Europe, but distance, indifference, and skepticism discouraged most people from leaving home to "see the elephant," as they put it. Meanwhile, most of the residents of the isolated province, blessed with proximity and exclusive information, took to the mountains. They hacked at the red clay along the American River, the Feather, the Tuolumne, and the Yuba with handpicks, trowels,

Perhaps the most enduring archetype of the gold-rush man was Levi Strauss, who never panned or dug for gold.

and knives. They washed their gravel in Indian baskets, dried it on bed sheets, and captured the metal with beads of quicksilver. Although the forty-eighters numbered only a few thousand, they carried off millions in free gold. They were among the few hunters who ever made significant money by mining placers, the visible deposits of fine gold that had been ground out of the quartz rock by centuries of erosion.

Neither in forty-eight nor in forty-nine, however, did a hero emerge to capture the world's affection—no Paul Revere, Ethan Allen, Davy Crockett, Geronimo, or Daniel Boone. James Marshall was a defective model, an irritable loner, obsessed by strange visions and pursued by demons. Squatters overran his claims, he drank away a pension from the state, and he died in bitter poverty. John Sutter, an exemplary land developer, was an opponent, not a champion, of the gold rush. His empire was invaded, as he had feared, and he lost his fortune in a legal struggle to uphold his property rights. Sam Brannan, a rich and noisy drunk, was disfellowshipped by the Mormon Church. San Francisco's gold-rush newspaper editor, Edward Gilbert, was killed in a duel; its gold-rush political leader, John Geary, who received every vote cast for mayor of San Francisco on August 1, 1849, saw more opportunity back East, where he became the territorial governor of Kansas, a Union general in the Civil War, and a two-term governor of Pennsylvania. John Frémont, the filibustering explorer, made a fortune in California land but had the good sense not to attack it with pick and shovel.

Perhaps the most enduring archetype of the gold-rush man was Levi Strauss, an immigrant from Bavaria, who never

panned or dug for gold but was an itinerant merchant, making and selling trousers of sailcloth, held together with copper rivets and known from that day to this as Levi's. A gold rush, after all, is a commercial enterprise, not an expedition of discovery, a crusade, or a military campaign. Its enduring marks in California were banks, roads, towns, and the manufacture of blue jeans.

Without a towering model to emulate, each of the so-called Argonauts cast himself as the hero of a personal saga. He saw himself as a member of an elite fraternity in a nation where the fellowship of language, religion, previous nationality, or shared experience was constantly dissolving in the great American melting pot. Those men (and those few women) who had gone to California before its admission to statehood in 1850 were eager to assert their kinship with other survivors, as do soldiers who have survived a war. To have "seen the elephant" left each of them with an ineradicable sense of his own importance.

In time, a sense of particularity began to infect all Californians, even those who had come long after '49.

TWENTY YEARS AFTER THE EVENT, two literate saloonkeeps in San Francisco, T. A. Barry and B. A. Patten, observing this kinship, looked back on the Days of Old, the Days of Gold, as "a time when the very sense of remoteness and isolation from the rest of the world brought men closer together; made men who knew each other merely by name, and men who had never spoken together, grasp each others hands and form life-long friendships, born of a sympathy in men so similarly circumstanced, drawn to one field by eager, adventurous enterprise, such a

long, weary way from home and loved ones, having something in common, so different from any experience known or read of by men."

In time this sense of particularity began to infect all Californians, even those who had entered the state long after the defining date. The forty-niner, with his recklessness, his youth, his optimism, became the state's defining figure, equivalent to Virginia's chivalrous planter and New England's puritan pilgrim.

Even those forty-niners who had eagerly rushed home continued to regard themselves as founders of California. Only a decade or two after the event, fraternities of gold-rush "pioneers" began gathering in cities far from San Francisco, the shrine of forty-niner worship. The New York Society of California Pioneers met in October 1869 for a twentieth-anniversary banquet to which they invited Mark Twain, whose recently published tale of the celebrated jumping frog of Calaveras County had instantly become a part of the gold-rush mythology. Twain declined. He bragged that he could "talk Pioneer like a native" but admitted he was neither a forty-niner nor a California pioneer.

THE SOCIETY OF CALIFORNIA PIONEERS of New England, formed in Boston in 1888, quickly enrolled 223 members and began planning an excursion to the scenes of the great adventure. Two years later 84 members of the society and 61 assorted wives, offspring, friends, and relatives set out from Fitchburg, Massachusetts, in a chartered train whose sponsors claimed it was the largest and heaviest ever to cross the continent. Two thousand well-wishers came down to the station to wave good-bye.

The excursion train carried six Pullman Palace sleeping cars with such inviting names as Etruria, Eurasia, and Servia, two dining cars, a baggage car, and a "combination car" with a library, barber's chair, smoking compartment, and bathroom. It rolled west by way of Niagara Falls to Chicago, dropped down to Kansas City, then took the tracks of the Atchison, Topeka & Santa Fe through Kansas, Colorado, New Mexico, and Arizona, a route that few forty-niners had fol-

The Price of Gold

OLNEY THAYER was just one of tens of thousands who rushed to California to seize the future. His experience is unique—and all too common.

Olney Thayer was born in 1825 in Mendon, Massachusetts. His forebears had helped found the community in the 1660s, and like most Americans of their time, successive generations had never strayed from their home. Then came the news from California, and Olney joined the throngs headed for the goldfields. What he found there is told in a series of letters that he wrote to his family "back in the States." They are eloquent both of the exhilaration that fueled a nation-making migration and of the cost that that exhilaration could exact. The letters, never before published, come to us through the courtesy of a great-grandnephew of Olney, Richard N. Thayer, of Cleveland.

New Yorke Jan. 23rd, 1852
Respected parents etc,

. . . I shall have to be on board the steamer tomorrow noon, we sail at 2 o'clocke. . . . The Steam ship company have raised again on the Steerage fare and those who buy now must pay $200, guess they will raise to $300, have not taken pains to ascertain but am told that they are all sold up to March 9th could take fifty dollars premium on my ticket tomorrow without any doubt but guess I shall see the elephant myself.

Think New England has taken an emetic and N Y is the slop pail, by the looks of the people here from that way there seems to be a perfect fever for California old gray headed men who were never before out of the limits of their native town may be seen thon[g]ing the ticket office and striding the streets with rapid steps, eager to catch the slightest intelligence from California, the yellow dust almost glowing on their wrinkled brow and El Dorado in letters of gold is written on every thing they behold. . . . What this immense em-

migration will do I cannot tell, give my best wishes to all inquiring friends.

Yours with esteem
Olney Thayer G.C.

Panama NC Feb. 10, 1852
Respected Parents
Brothers and Sisters

It is about three weeks since I was rubbing my fingers amid the snows of New England. Now the sweat is pouring out of me for good but I experience no inconvenience from it. I left N.Y on the 24th ult and had a pleasant passage to Havana in Cuba where we arrived on the following Friday, with the exception of 3 days on which I was seasick then I felt most disagreeable I assure you but have got entirely over it and can eat a raw dog now never felt so well all ways before in my life. . . . On Sunday we left for Chagres had beautiful weather all the way and arrived there Friday noon. . . . The scenery up the Chagres river is the most beautiful thing I ever saw. . . . I expect to leave here tomorrow at 4 o'clock I do not know how I shall succeed in my enterprise but mean to put the best foot forward and decide the matter as soon as possible if cannot succeed I shall be back as soon as I can. . . . You must take good care of my trees and get out all worms and borers and you shall lose nothing I am in a great hurry dont think of anything more so I will bid you good bye for the present.

Yours with esteem
Olney Thayer

Sacramento City Mr 16, 1852
Respected Parents,

. . . I had a pleasant voyage here, arrived safely here and am in good health got a short job the second day here at $75. per month got through yesterday and am just starting today for south fork of the American river about 50 miles to try my luck at gold digging times are

rather hard here at present and the emigration is so great I do not expect to make much out of California but must try to pay expenses. . . .

I subscrib myself
Your affectionate son
Olney Thayer

Placerville, June 10, 1852
Dear Brother.

I take this occasion to drop you a few lines from the eldorado of America and I might add of the world, for surely California is destined to exert a powerful influence, not only upon the destiny of this nation, but upon the whole civilized globe; the annals of history can furnish no parallel with the rapid rise and growth of this state. If you examine Olney's old school atlas you will see unexplored regions marked upon the map south of Oregon. Such was the state of the country where I now am, not more than five or six years ago, unexplored and unknown to the civilized world & inhabited only by a few miserable Indians; now it is crowded by men from every part of the world, and vocal with the hum of industry, even now within hearing there is a steam engine puffing away sawing up pine logs by night and day, in fact California is now in advance of some of the old states & at least a century in advance of all the Spanish countries south of us. I was a little surprised upon entering the harbor of San Francisco to see more shipping than I ever saw in Boston & then the city, containing 35,000 inhabitants, presented all the pomp and show of the eastern cities. . . . I am in good health and I have not seen a sick day since I left home, can eat like a hog and board myself in a log cabin for 50 cents a day. . . . I think I have written enough so give my best wishes to father, Mother, little Frank and everybody else so goodby

Yours sincerely
Olney Thayer

lowed but which led to some favored tourist destinations: the Hotel del Coronado in San Diego, the Hotel Raymond in Pasadena, the orange groves of Riverside County, and the obligatory Southern California ostrich farm.

Nostalgia overwhelmed the old men. At a banquet in San Bernardino, a re-

tired general from Norton, Massachusetts, tottered up to the head table to share his recollections of the day he had landed in San Francisco.

"It was on Sunday, and I heard there was to be preaching there, somewhere, in the hall devoted to justice—the courthouse, I think. I found it and went in,

and there were two ladies there, and I crowded my way up to them until I was within two feet of them, and that was as close as I dared to go, and oh! What a joy it was when one of them asked me to share her hymn book with her, and oh! how we did sing! Oh, such grand old hymns! Ladies were scarce in California

**Green Springs
Eldorado County
Oct. 10, 1852**

Respected Parents, Brothers & Sister,

As some time has elapsed since I wrote you from the Pacific shores, you might be led to suppose that I had forgotten my New England home; but far from it time may wing on its flight, mountain and seas interpose, but never will be erased from my mind the thousand fond appreciations that cling & cluster around my childhood home. Sometimes visions of the past will flit across my mind and in spite of myself will almost make me homesick, but I crush the rising spirit and all is well again; on the whole I am very well satisfied with my journey and new home, never have seen the moment when I regreted leaving home for when I did so I resolved to be content with any lot. . . . I shall go at mining again as soon as the rain comes. (We have had no rain since the 14th May) and try my luck if there is any for me. . . . I suppose when this letter reaches you, you will be poking in the snow but I shall be where the trees will be robed in living green & will be until near January. I would like to be with you at Thanksgiving but cannot make it convenient and will give you an invitation to come and spend the day with me I will give you a good dinner I will write again soon. . . . Accept my best wishes, give my respects to all inquiring friends and eat for me a piece of Christmas pie. . . .

Your affectionate son
O. Thayer

**San Francisco
Jan 30th 1853**

Mr. Thayer Dear Sir

I take an opportunity to write you a few lines to inform you of news that is hard to carry or write your Son Only Thayer came down from the Mines sick and was sick but a short time here before he was numbered with the spirits in the spirit land he was sick with the Typhoid Fever he Died Jan 19th at the states Hospital he was trying to get home he wanted to come the first of the month he had worked and not got his pay and had hard bad luck. . . . He was at a Hotell I was very

bisiy and did not see him for 2 or 3 days he was so as to be up round I went to se him and the Night before he was taken deranged and they was prepairing to carry him to the Hospital the loafers or some one had picked his pockets of money and papers I went to the Hospital with him he lived about twenty four ours

Yours in sorrow
Charles W Gates

Apr 16th 1853

Mr. Thayer

Dear Sir I just read your second letter & with plesher I answer it altho on a solom ocasion I will answer a few of your questions as my time is short I will answer but few I have got the No [number] of Onlys Grave I have not seen it but it is easy found I shall find tomorrow if nothing hapens there is great panes taken here in the burial of people they are buried in a good dry place & in a good Coffin & caried in a splendid herse the undertaker sits down the name and numbers & numbers the grave the care of Only was good he was able to take care of himself until the day but one before his death he had good care as could be he said nothing about anything at home. . . .

A set of Grave stones here are worth from fifty to two hundred plain cheap Marble $50,

Excuse me for this time
as I must close
Yours &c C W Gates

**U S Marine Hospital
San Francisco
Feb 27 1854**

Dear Wife

When I last wrote you I thought I should not be able to write you again for a month, but as I wish to get intelligence to Mr Thayer of the reception of his draft & what I have done I thought I would write the letter to you & so kill two birds with one stone I recieved a draft from Mr Thayer on Adams & company & made arrangements with Mr Gray to have Olney's remains taken up and sent home in the Clipper Ship Bald Eagle Mr Gray agreed to perform his post for $150,00 & as he

shiped home several at the same time the Capt, agreed to take the body for $52,50 I agreed to advance the money, that is fifty two dollars & a half & let Mr Thayer pay you the same, But the result of the disinterment of the remains will add another pang to the hearts of the distressed parents The remains disinterred under the No. of Olney's grave were those of a man about forty years of age, five feet nine inches in height with coarse red hair & whiskers It required but a glance of the eye to see they were not Olney's. A G C Bucklin was with me at the time, but I have never as yet been able to find Mr Gates. The body we reburied again Mr Gray says their were probably three or four bodies buried at the same time & a mistake made in numbering them. He thinks by taken up three or four bodies in the immediate neiborhood the right one might be found. We can ascertain how many were buried at the time & their numbers & stand a chance to find the right one so. Thus the matter stands at present. I shall deposite the $150.00 in Page Brecon & C Banking house & wait for further orders If Mr Thayer would wish to be at the expense of disentering the bodies I will do all that I can to assist and think from my knowledge of such things I should have no difficulty in recognizing the remains if we could find them. If he does not see fit to do anything more about it I will pay Mr G for his trouble & send the money back to him, or if we make further search & are unsuccessful will do the same. but tell him their is no use to try to do anything without paying the money down either for freight or anything else & that it is useless to try to get it done for less than we have written him & if we are obliged to dig up seven bodies it will add $50 more to the expense Tell him I will manage the business as though it were my own, but that Mr Haskel or any body else at home dont know anything about how such things are here.

The rest of the letter has been cut off with scissors. The Thayers never found Olney's body.

then, and you would have to run around two blocks to get a sight of one."

Bowing and smiling, he returned to his seat, slumped forward, and died. The pioneers shipped his body home, just as a fraternal order—the Masons, the Odd Fellows—would have done in 1849, and the tour pushed on to San Francisco.

O N April 28 the San Francisco *Examiner* reported that the Palace Hotel had been taken over by bald-headed, gray-bearded gentlemen wearing blue silk badges trimmed with gold fringe and inscribed with the totemic number, 49! Several, including one elderly Bosto-

nian who was later described by the historian John Walton Caughey as "an accomplished fictionist," gave epic interviews. Others were determined to seek out the tiny creek beds where they had painfully rinsed tons of red gravel in flat pans and long-tom washers.

Charles Stumcke, who had come west with a company of Boston boys in 1849, took a train from Sacramento to Auburn, a forty-mile jaunt that had taken him eight days to accomplish behind a four-yoke oxteam.

"When we left the cars, I looked for the spot where I pitched my tent, built a stone chimney at one end, made a mattress of fir boughs, and thought myself well fixed for the winter," Stumcke wrote in a letter to his son back East. "On the identical spot stood a nice, two-story house with a fine garden, neatly fenced.... It was hard to realize that this was the place where I had dug for gold, and that the hills of red clay we thought good for nothing were really the charming places now covered with grape vines, peach, apple and pear trees and other evidences of fertility.... I thought of all the hardy men who had helped build the place; but, by diligent inquiry, I could not find one of all who wintered here in '49 and '50. I suppose most of them have gone to their long home, and that the others are widely

The young Argonaut never ages as he pursues his endless search for gold under the blazing artificial sunset of Belasco's The Girl of the Golden West.

scattered. It makes me feel sad as I think of the old days."

The brevity of his great adventure, the moisture of his nostalgia, the crudeness of his manners often made the old Argonaut, the self-styled California Pioneer, a target of ridicule. Ambrose Bierce punched holes in his pretensions. Hubert Howe Bancroft, the voluminous and respected historian of early California, criticized his greed, prevarication, and profanity. Novelists discovered him, a parvenu whose red flannel shirt was visible under his starched white collar and black dinner jacket. He appears in Joseph Conrad (*Nostromo*), Ivan Bunin (*The Gentleman From San Francisco*), Robert Louis Stevenson (*The Wrecker*), and Bronson Howard (*Aristocracy*).

But the young Argonaut, the immortal forty-niner, never grows old. Fixed forever in time and place, he pursues his endless search for gold under the blazing artificial sunset of David Belasco's play *The Girl of the Golden West*. In the libretto of Giacomo Puccini's opera, the tenor speaks Italian, doubles as a bandit, and narrowly escapes lynching, but he wears red flannel and blue denim, his name is the impeccably Anglo-American Dick Johnson, and his heart is set on taking home his pocketful of gold.

Richard Reinhardt is a San Francisco novelist, writer of social history, and fourth-generation Californian, although his ancestors were not forty-niners. He is currently working on a novel set in the Nevada gold rush of 1907.

The Lives of Slave Women

Deborah Gray White

Deborah Gray White is associate professor of history and Africana studies at Rutgers University, New Brunswick, New Jersey. This chapter is adapted from her book, Ar'nt I a Woman? Female Slaves in the Plantation South, *published in 1985 by W. W. Norton.*

Slave women have often been characterized as self-reliant and self-sufficient, yet not every black woman was a Sojourner Truth or a Harriet Tubman. Strength had to be cultivated. It came no more naturally to them than to anyone else, slave or free, male or female, black or white. If slave women seemed exceptionally strong it was partly because they often functioned in groups and derived strength from their numbers.

Much of the work slaves did and the regimen they followed served to stratify slave society along sex lines. Consequently slave women had ample opportunity to develop a consciousness grounded in their identity as females. While close contact sometimes gave rise to strife, adult female cooperation and dependence of women on each other was a fact of female slave life. The self-reliance and self-sufficiency of slave women, therefore, must be viewed in the context not only of what the individual slave woman did for herself, but what slave women as a group were able to do for each other.

It is easy to overlook the separate world of female slaves because from colonial times through the Civil War black women often worked with black men at tasks considered by Europeans to be either too difficult or inappropriate for females. All women worked hard, but when white women consistently performed field labor it was considered temporary, irregular, or extraordinary, putting them on a par with slaves. Actress Fredericka Bremer, visiting the ante-bellum South, noted that usually only men and black women did field work; commenting on what another woman traveler sarcastically claimed to be a noble admission of female equality, Bremer observed that "black (women) are not considered to belong to the weaker sex."[1]

Bremer's comment reflects what former slaves and fugitive male slaves regarded as the defeminization of black women. Bonded women cut down trees to clear lands for cultivation. They hauled logs in leather straps attached to their shoulders. They plowed using mule and ox teams, and hoed, sometimes with the heaviest implements available. They dug ditches, spread manure fertilizer, and piled coarse fodder with their bare hands. They built and cleaned Southern roads, helped construct Southern railroads, and, of course, they picked cotton. In short, what fugitive slave Williamson Pease said regretfully of slave women was borne out in fact: "Women who do outdoor work are used as bad as men."[2] Almost a century later Green Wilbanks spoke less remorsefully than Pease in his remembrances of his Grandma Rose, where he implied that the work had a kind of neutering effect. Grandma Rose, he said, was a woman who could do any kind of job a man could do, a woman who "was some worker, a regular man-woman."[3]

It is hardly likely, though, that slave women, especially those on large plantations with sizable female populations, lost their female identity. Harvesting season on staple crop plantations may have found men and women gathering the crop in sex-integrated gangs, but at other times women often worked in exclusively or predominantly female gangs.[4] Thus women stayed in each other's company for most of the day. This meant that those they ate meals with, sang work songs with, and commiserated with during the work day were people who by virtue of their sex had the same kind of responsibilities and problems. As a result, slave women appeared to have developed their own female culture, a way of doing things and a way of assigning value that flowed from their perspective as slave women on Southern plantations. Rather than being squelched, their sense of womanhood was probably enhanced and their bonds to each other strengthened.

Since slaveowners and makers seemingly took little note of the slave woman's lesser physical strength, one wonders why they separated men and women at all. One answer appears to be that gender provided a natural and easy way to divide the labor force. Also probable is that despite their limited sensitivity regarding female slave labor, and the double standard they used when evaluating the uses of white and black

From *Southern Exposure,* November/December 1984, pp. 32-39. Adapted from *Ar'n't I a Woman? Female Slaves in the Plantation South* by Deborah Gray White. © 1984 by Deborah Gray White. Reprinted with permission of W. W. Norton & Company, Inc.

female labor, slave-owners did, using standards only they could explain, reluctantly acquiesce to female physiology. For instance, depending on their stage of pregnancy, pregnant women were considered half or quarter hands. Healthy nonpregnant women were considered three-quarter hands. Three-quarter hands were not necessarily exempt from some of the herculean tasks performed by men who were full hands, but usually, when labor was being parceled out and barring a shortage of male hands to do the very heavy work or a rush to get that work completed, men did the more physically demanding work. A case in point was the most common differentiation where men plowed and women hoed.[5]

A great deal of both field labor and nonfield labor was structured to promote cooperation among slave women.

Like much of the field labor, nonfield labor was structured to promote cooperation among women. In the Sea Islands, slave women sorted cotton lint according to color and fineness and removed cotton seeds crushed by the gin into the cotton and lint. Fence building often found men splitting rails in one area and women doing the actual construction in another. Men usually shelled corn, threshed peas, cut potatoes for planting, and platted shucks. Grinding corn into meal or hominy was women's work. So too were spinning, weaving, sewing, and washing.[6] On Captain Kinsler's South Carolina plantation, as on countless others, "old women and women bearin' chillun not yet born, did cardin' wid handcards." Some would spin, others would weave, but all would eventually learn from some skilled woman "how to make clothes for the family . . . knit coarse socks and stockins."[7]

"When the work in the fields was finished women were required to come home and spin one cut a night," reported a Georgian. "Those who were not successful in completing this work were punished the next morning."[8] Women had to work in the evenings partly because slaveowners bought them few ready-made clothes. On one South Carolina plantation each male slave received annually two cotton shirts, three pairs of pants, and one jacket. Slave women, on the other hand, received six yards of woolen cloth, six yards of cotton drilling, and six yards of cotton shirting a year, along with two needles and a dozen buttons.[9]

Perhaps a saving grace to this "double duty" was that women got a chance to interact with each other. On a Sedalia County, Missouri, plantation, women looked forward to Saturday afternoon washing because, as Mary Frances Webb explained, they "would get to talk and spend the day together."[10] Quiltings, referred to by former slaves as female "frolics" and "parties," were especially convivial. Anna Peek recalled that when slaves were allowed to relax, they gathered around a pine wood fire in Aunt Anna's cabin to tell stories. At that time "the old women with pipes in their mouths would sit and gossip for hours."[11] Missourian Alice Sewell noted that sometimes women would slip away and hold their own prayer meetings. They cemented their bonds to each other at the end of every meeting when they walked around shaking hands and singing, "fare you well my sisters, I am going home."[12]

The organization of female slave work and social activities tended not only to separate women and men, but also to generate female cooperation and interdependence. Slave women and their children could depend on midwives and "doctor women" to treat a variety of ailments. Menstrual cramps, for example, were sometimes treated with a tea made from the bark of the gum tree. Midwives and "doctor women" administered various other herb teas to ease the pains of many ailing slaves. Any number of broths—made from the leaves and barks of trees, from the branches and twigs of bushes, from turpentine, catnip, or tobacco—were used to treat whooping cough, diarrhea, toothaches, colds, fevers, headaches, and backaches.[13] According to a Georgia ex-slave, "One had to be mighty sick to have the services of a doctor." On his master's plantation "old women were . . . responsible for the care of the sick."[14] This was also the case on Rebecca Hooks's former Florida residence. "The doctor," she noted, "was not nearly as popular as the 'granny' or midwife, who brewed medicines for every ailment."[15]

Female cooperation in the realm of medical care helped foster bonding that led to collaboration in the area of resistance to abuses by slaveholders. Frances Kemble could attest to the concerted efforts of the black women on her husband's Sea Island plantations. More than once she was visited by groups of women imploring her to persuade her husband to extend the lying-in period for childbearing women. On one occasion the women had apparently prepared beforehand the approach they would take with the foreign-born and sympathetic Kemble, for their chosen spokeswoman took care to play on Kemble's own maternal sentiments, and pointedly argued that slave women deserved at least some of the care and tenderness that Kemble's own pregnancy had elicited.[16]

Usually, however, slave women could not be so outspoken about their needs, and covert cooperative resistance prevailed. Slaveowners suspected that midwives conspired with their female patients to bring about abortions and infanticides, and on Charles Colcock Jones's Georgia plantation, for example, this seems in fact to have been the case. A woman named Lucy gave birth in secret and then denied that she had ever been pregnant. Although the midwife attended her, she too claimed not to have delivered a child, as did Lucy's mother. Jones had a physician examine Lucy, and the doctor confirmed what Jones had suspected, that Lucy had indeed given birth. Twelve days later the decomposing body of a full-term infant was found, and Lucy, her mother, and the midwife were all hauled off to court. Another woman, a nurse, managed to avoid prosecution but not suspicion. Whether Lucy was guilty of murder, and whether the others were accessories, will never be known because the court could not shatter their collective defense that the child had been stillborn.[17]

The inability to penetrate the private world of female slaves is probably what kept many abortions and infanticides from becoming known to slaveowners. The secrets kept by a midwife named Mollie became too much for her to bear. When she accepted Christianity these were the first things for which she asked forgiveness. She recalled, "I was carried to the gates of hell and the devil pulled out a book showing me the things which I had committed and that they were all true. My life as a midwife was shown to me and I have certainly felt sorry for all the things I did, after I was converted."[18]

Health care is not the only example of how the organization of slave work and slave responsibilities led to female cooperation and bonding; slave women also depended on each other for childcare. Sometimes, especially on small farms or new plantations where there was no extra woman to superintend children, bondswomen took their offspring to the field with them and attended to them during prescheduled breaks. Usually, however, infants and older children were left in the charge of an elderly female or females. Josephine Bristow, for example, spent more time with Mary Novlin, the nursery keeper on Ferdinand Gibson's South Carolina plantation, than she spent with her mother and father, who came in from the fields after she was asleep: "De old lady, she looked after every blessed thing for us all day long en cooked for us right along wid de mindin'."[19] In their complementary role as nurses, they ministered to the hurts and illnesses of infants and children.[20] It was not at all uncommon for the children's weekly rations to be given to the "grannies" as opposed to the children's parents.[21] Neither the slaveowner nor slave society expected the biological mother of a child to fulfill all of her child's needs. Given the circumstances, the responsibilities of motherhood had to be shared, and this required close female cooperation.

Cooperation in this sphere helped slave women overcome one of the most difficult of predicaments—who would provide maternal care for a child whose mother had died or been sold away? Fathers sometimes served as both mother and father, but when slaves, as opposed to the master, determined maternal care, it was usually a woman who became a child's surrogate mother. Usually that woman was an aunt or a sister, but in the absence of female relatives, a non-kin woman assumed the responsibility.[22] In the case of Georgian Mollie Malone, for example, the nursery superintendent became the child's substitute mother.[23] When Julia Malone's mother was killed by another Texas slave, little Julia was raised by the woman with whom her mother had shared a cabin.[24] On Southern plantations the female community made sure that no child was truly motherless.

Because black women on a plantation spent so much time together, they inevitably developed some appreciation of each other's skills and talents. This intimacy enabled them to establish the criteria by which to rank and order themselves. The existence of certain "female jobs" that carried prestige created a yardstick by which bondswomen could measure each other's achievements. Some of these jobs allowed for growth and self-satisfaction, fringe benefits that were usually out of reach for the field laborer. A seamstress, for example, had unusual opportunities for self-expression and creativity. On very large plantations the seamstress usually did no field work, and a particularly good seamstress, or "mantua-maker," might be hired out to others and even allowed to keep a portion of the money she earned.[25] For obvious reasons cooks, midwives, and female folk doctors also commanded the respect of their peers. Midwives in particular often were able to travel to other plantations to practice their art. This gave them an enviable mobility and also enabled them to carry messages from one plantation to the next.

Apart from the seamstresses, cooks, and midwives, a few women were distinguished as work gang-leaders. On most farms and plantations where there were overseers, managers, foremen, and drivers, these positions were held by men, either black or white. Occasionally, however, a woman was given a measure of authority over slave work, or a particular aspect of it. For instance

Louis Hughes noted that each plantation he saw had a "forewoman who . . . had charge of the female slaves and also the boys and girls from twelve to sixteen years of age, and all the old people that were feeble."[26] Similarly, a Mississippi slave remembered that on his master's Osceola plantation there was a "colored woman as foreman."[27]

Clearly, a pecking order existed among bondswomen—one which they themselves helped to create. Because of age, occupation, association with the master class, or personal achievements, certain women were recognized by other women—and also by men—as important people, even as leaders. Laura Towne met an aged woman who commanded such a degree of respect that other slaves bowed to her and lowered their voices in her presence. The old woman, Maum Katie, was according to Towne a "spiritual mother" and a woman of "tremendous influence over her spiritual children."[28]

A slaveowner lamented that Big Lucy, one of his oldest slaves, had more control over his female workers than he did.

Sometimes two or three factors combined to distinguish a particular woman. Aunt Charlotte was the aged cook in John M. Booth's Georgia household. When Aunt Charlotte spoke, said Booth, "other colored people hastened to obey her."[29] Frederick Douglass's grandmother wielded influence because of her age and the skills she possessed. She made the best fishnets in Tuckahoe, Maryland, and she knew better than anyone else how to preserve sweet potato seedlings and how to plant them successfully. She enjoyed what Douglass called "high reputation," and accordingly "she was remembered by others."[30] In another example, when Elizabeth Botume went to the Sea Islands after the Civil War, she employed as a house servant a young woman named Amy who performed her tasks slowly and sullenly, until an older woman named Aunt Mary arrived from Beaufort. During slavery Amy and Aunt Mary had both worked in the house but Amy had learned to listen and obey Aunt Mary. After Aunt Mary arrived the once obstreperous Amy became "quiet, orderly, helpful and painstaking."[31]

The leadership of some women had a disruptive effect on plantation operations. Bennet H. Barrow repeatedly lamented the fact that Big Lucy, one of his oldest slaves, had more control over his female workers than he did: "Anica, Center, Cook Jane, the better you treat them the worse they are. Big Lucy the Leader corrupts every young negro in her power."[32] A self-proclaimed prophetess named Sinda was responsible for a cessation of all slave work for a considerable period on Butler Island in Georgia. According to a notation made by Frances Kemble in 1839, Sinda's prediction that the world would come to an end on a certain day caused the slaves to lay down their hoes and plows in the belief that their final emancipation was imminent. So sure were Sinda's fellow slaves of her prediction that even the lash failed to get them into the fields. When the appointed day of judgment passed uneventfully Sinda was whipped mercilessly. Yet, for a time, she had commanded more authority than either master or overseer.[33]

Bonded women did not have to go to such lengths in order to make a difference in each other's lives. The supportive atmosphere of the female community was considerable buffer against the depersonalizing regimen of plantation work and the general dehumanizing nature of slavery. When we consider that women were much more strictly confined to the plantation than men, that many women had husbands who visited only once or twice a week, and that slave women outlived slave men by an average of two years, we realize just how important the female community was to its members.

If we define a stable relationship as one of long duration, then it was probably easier for slave women to sustain stable emotional relationships with other bondswomen than with bondsmen. This is not to say that male-female relationships were unfulfilling or of no consequence. But they were generally fraught with more uncertainty about the future than female-to-female relationships, especially those existing between female blood kin. In her study of ex-slave interviews, Martha Goodson found that of all the relationships slaveowners disrupted, through either sale or dispersal, they were least likely to separate mothers and daughters.[34] Cody found that when South Carolina cotton planter Peter Gaillard divided his estate among his eight children, slave women in their twenties and thirties were twice as likely to have a sister with them, and women over 40 were four times more likely to have sisters with them than brothers. Similarly, daughters were less likely than sons to be separated from their mother. Over 60 percent of women aged 20 to 24 remained with their mothers when the estate was divided, as did 90 percent of those aged 25 to 29.[35] A slave song reflected the bonds between female siblings by indicating who took responsibility for the motherless female slave child. Interestingly enough, the one designated was neither the father nor the brother:

> A motherless chile see a hard time.
> Oh Lord, help her on de road.
> Er sister will do de bes' she kin,
> Dis is a hard world, Lord, fer a motherless chile.[36]

If female blood ties did indeed promote the most enduring relationships among slaves, then we should probably assume that like occupation, age, and personal achievement these relationships helped structure the female slave community. This assumption should not, however, obscure the fact that in friendships and dependency relationships women often treated non-relatives as if a consanguineous tie existed. This is why older women were called Aunt and Granny, and why unrelated women sometimes called each other Sister.[37]

While the focus here has been on those aspects of the bondswoman's life that fostered female bonding, female-to-female conflict was not uncommon. It was impossible for harmony always to prevail among women who saw so much of each other and who knew so much about one another. Lifelong friendships were founded in the hoe gangs and sewing groups, but the constant jockeying for occupational and social status created an atmosphere in which jealousies and antipathies smoldered. From Jesse Belflowers, the overseer of the Allston rice plantation in South Carolina, Adele Petigru Allston heard that "mostly amongst the Women" there was a "goodeal of quarling and disputing and telling lies."[38] The terms of a widely circulated overseer's contract advised rigorous punishment for "fighting, particularly amongst the women."[39] Some overseers followed this advice. According to Georgian Isaac Green, "Sometimes de women uster git whuppin's for fightin'."[40]

Occasionally, violence between women could and did get very ugly. Molly, the cook in James Chesnut's household, once took a red hot poker and attacked the woman to whom her husband had given one of her calico dresses.[41] Similarly, when she was a young woman in Arkansas, Lucretia Alexander came to blows with another woman over a pair of stockings that the master had given Lucretia.[42] In another incident on a Louisiana cotton plantation, the day's cotton chopping was interrupted when a feisty field worker named Betty lost her temper in the midst of a dispute with a fellow slave named Molly and struck her in the face with a hoe.[43]

The presence of conflict within interpersonal relationships between female slaves should not detract from the more important cooperation and dependence that prevailed among them. Conflict occurred *because* women were in close daily contact with each other and because the penalties for venting anger on other women were not as severe as those for striking out at men, either black or white. It is not difficult to understand how dependency relationships could become parasitical, how sewing and washing sessions could become "hanging courts," how one party could use knowledge gained in an intimate conversation against another.

Just how sisterhood could co-exist with discord is illustrated by the experience of some black women of the

South Carolina and Georgia Sea Islands between 1862 and 1865. On November 7, 1861, Commodore S. F. DuPont sailed into Port Royal Sound, quickly defeated the Confederates, and put Union troops ashore to occupy the islands. Almost before DuPont's guns ceased firing, the entire white population left the islands for the mainland. A few house servants were taken with the fleeing whites but most of the slaves remained on the islands. The following year they and the occupying army were joined by a host of government agents and Northern missionaries. Several interest groups were gathered in the islands and each had priorities. As Treasury agents concerned themselves with the cotton, and army officers recruited and drafted black soldiers, and missionaries went about "preparing" slaves for freedom, the black Sea Islanders' world was turned upside down. This was true for young and middle-aged men who served in the Union army, but also for the women who had to manage their families and do most of the planting and harvesting in the absence of the men.[44]

During the three years of upheaval, black female life conformed in many ways to that outlined here. Missionaries' comments indicate that certain women were perceived as leaders by their peers. Harriet Ware, for instance, identified a woman from Fripp Point on St. Helena Island named Old Peggy as "the leader." This woman was important because she, along with another woman named Binah, oversaw church membership. Ware's housekeeper Flora told her, "Old Peggy and Binah were the two whom all that came into the Church had to come through, and the Church supports them."[45]

On the Coffin's Point Plantation on St. Helena Island, a woman named Grace served her fellow women at least twice by acting as spokeswoman in disputes over wages paid for cotton production. On one occasion the women of the plantation complained to Mr. Philbrick, one of the plantation superintendents, that their wages were not high enough to permit them to purchase cloth at the local store. They were also upset because the molasses they bought from one of the other plantation superintendents was watered down. As Grace spoke

in their behalf, the women shouted words of approval. At least part of the reason for Grace's ascendancy stemmed from the fact that she was among the older women of the island. She was also a strong and diligent worker who was able despite her advanced age to plant, hoe, and harvest cotton along with the younger women.[46]

Ample evidence exists of dependency relationships and cooperation among Sea Island women throughout the war years. In slavery sick and "lying-in" women relied on their peers to help them, and the missionaries found this to be the case on the islands during the Union occupation as well. For instance, Philbrick observed that it was quite common for the blacks to hire each other to hoe their tasks when sickness or other inconveniences kept an individual from it. In 1862 some of the Coffin's Point men were recruited by government agents to pick cotton elsewhere in the Sea Islands. This left many of the women at Coffin's Point completely responsible for hoeing the land allotted to each. Women who were sick or pregnant stood to lose their family's allotment since neglected land was reassigned to others. However, the women saw to it, according to Philbrick, that "the tasks of the lying-in women [were] taken care of by sisters or other friends in the absence of their husbands." No doubt these "other friends" were women, since in the same letter Philbrick noted that the only men left on the plantation were those too old to work in the cotton.[47]

Another missionary, Elizabeth Hyde Botume, related similar episodes of female cooperation. Regardless of the circumstances surrounding a pregnancy, it was common for the women of Port Royal to care for, and keep company with, expectant and convalescing mothers. Several times Botume was approached by a spokeswoman seeking provisions for these mothers. Sometimes she gave them reluctantly because many of the women were not married. Usually, however, she was so impressed by the support that the pregnant women received from their peers that she suspended judgment and sent clothes and groceries for the mothers and infants. On one occasion she was approached by

several women who sought aid for a woman named Cumber. The women were so willing to assist one of their own that Botume remarked abashedly: " . . . their readiness to help the poor erring girl made me ashamed."[48] These were not the only instances of cooperation among the black women. Some moved in with each other and shared domestic duties; others looked after the sick together.[49] With so many of the men away, women found ways of surviving together and cooperating. Predictably, however, along with the "togetherness" went conflict.

Many situations held possibilities for discord. Charles P. Ware, a missionary from Boston, wrote that the work in the crops would go more smoothly if only he could get the women to stop fighting. At least some of the fights were caused by disputes over the distribution of the former mistress's wardrobe. According to Ware, when a woman said, "I free, I as much right to ole missus' things as you, a fight was sure to erupt.[50] Harriet Ware witnessed a fight in which the women "fired shells and tore each other's clothes in a most disgraceful way." The cause of the fight was unknown to her but she was sure it was the "tongues of the women." Jealousy, she noted, ran rampant among the women, and to her mind there was "much foundation for it."[51]

The experiences of the Sea Islands women in the early 1860s comprised a special episode in American history, but their behavior conformed to patterns that had been set previously by bonded women on large plantations. Historians have shown that the community of the quarters, the slave family, and slave religion shielded the slave from absolute dependence on the master and that parents, siblings, friends, and relatives served in different capacities as buffers against the internalization of degrading and dependent roles. The female slave network served as a similar buffer for black women, but it also had a larger significance. Treated by Southern whites as if they were anything but self-respecting women, many bonded females helped one another to forge their own independent definitions of womanhood, their own notions about what women should be and how they should act.

Notes

1. Fredericka Bremer, *Homes of the New World*, 2 vols. (New York, 1853), 2: 519; Frances Anne Kemble, *Journal of a Residence on a Georgian Plantation*, ed. John A. Scott (New York, 1961 [1863]), p. 66. See also: Harriet Martineau, *Society in America*, 3 vols. (London, 1837), 2: 243, 311–12.

2. Benjamin Drew, *The Refugees: A North Side View of Slavery*, in *Four Fugitive Slave Narratives* (Boston, 1969), p. 92.

3. George Rawick, ed., *The American Slave, A Complete Autobiography*, 19 vols. (Westport, CT, 1972), Ga., vol. 13, pt. 4: 139.

4. Frederick Olmsted, *A Journey in the Seaboard Slave States* (New York, 1856), pp. 430–32; Olmsted, *The Cotton Kingdom*, ed. David Freeman Hawke (New York, 1971), p. 176; William Howard Russell, *My Diary North and South (Canada, Its Defenses, Condition and Resources)*, 3 vols. (London, 1865), 1: 379–80; Solomon Northrup, *Twelve Years a Slave, Narrative of Solomon Northup* in Gilbert Osofsky, ed., *Puttin' on Ole Massa* (New York, 1969), pp. 308–309; Rawick, *American Slave*, Ark., vol 10, pt. 5: 54; Ala., vol. 6: 46, 336; Newstead Plantation Diary 1856–58, entry Wednesday, May 6, 1857, Southern Historical Collection (SHC), University of North Carolina at Chapel Hill; Adwon Adams Davis, *Plantation Life in the Florida Parishes of Louisiana 1836–1846 as Reflected in the Diary of Bennet H. Barrow* (New York, 1943), p. 127; Frederick Olmsted, *A Journey in the Back Country* (New York, 1907), p. 152; *Plantation Manual*, SHC, p. 4; Eugene Genovese, *The Political Economy of Slavery: Studies in the Economy and Society of the Slave South* (New York, 1961), p. 133; Stuart Bruchey, ed., *Cotton and the Growth of the American Economy: 1790–1860* (New York, 1967), pp. 176–80.

5. See note 4.

6. J. A. Turner, ed., *The Cotton Planters Manual* (New York, 1865), pp. 97–98; Guion B. Johnson, *A Social History of the Sea Islands* (Chapel Hill, NC, 1930), pp. 28–30; Jenkins Mikell, *Rumbling of the Chariot Wheels* (Columbia, SC, 1923), pp. 19–20; Bruchey, *Cotton and the Growth of the American Economy*, pp. 176–80.

7. Rawick, *American Slave*, S.C., vol. 2, pt. 2: 114.

8. Ibid., Ga., vol. 13, p. 3: 186.

9. *Plantation Manual*, SHC, p. 1.

10. Rawick, *American Slave*, Ok., vol. 7: 315.

11. George P. Rawick, Jan Hillegas, and Ken Lawrence, ed., *The American Slave: A Composite Autobiography, Supplement, Series 1*, 12 vols. (Westport, CT, 1978), Ga., Supp. 1, vol. 4: 479.

12. Rawick, *American Slave*, Mo., vol 11: 307.

13. For examples of cures see: Ibid., Ark., vol. 10, pt. 5: 21, 125; Ala., vol. 6: 256, 318; Ga., vol. 13, pt. 3: 106.

14. Ibid., Ga., vol. 12, pt. 1: 303.

15. Ibid., Fla., vol. 17: 175; see also: Rawick *et al.*, *American Slave, Supplement*, Miss. Supp. 1, vol. 6: 317; Ga. Supp. 1., vol. 4: 444; John Spencer Bassett, *The Southern Plantation Overseer, as Revealed in His Letters* (Northampton, MA, 1923), pp. 28, 31.

16. Kemble, *Journal of a Residence on a Georgian Plantation*, p. 222.

17. Robert Manson Myers, ed., *The Children of Pride: A True Story of Georgia and the Civil War* (New Haven, CT, 1972), pp. 528, 532, 542, 544, 546.

18. Charles S. Johnson, ed., *God Struck Me Dead: Religious Conversion Experiences and Autobiographies of Negro Ex-Slaves* in Rawick, *American Slave*, vol. 19: 74.

19. Rawick, *American Slave*, S.C., vol. 2, pt. 1: 99.

20. Ibid., Ga., vol. 12, pt. 2: 112; S.C., vol 2, pt. 2: 55; Fla., vol. 17: 174; see also Olmsted, *Back Country*, p. 76.

21. See, for instance, *Plantation Manual*, SHC, p. 1.

22. Rawick, *American Slave*, Ala., vol. 6: 73.

23. Rawick *et al.*, *American Slave, Supplement*, Ga. Supp. 1, vol. 4, pt. 3: 103.

24. Rawick, *American Slave*, Tex., vol. 5, pt. 3: 103.

25. Hughes, *Thirty Years a Slave*, p. 39; Rawick, *American Slave*, Fla., vol. 17: 158; S. C., vol. 2, pt. 1: 114; White Hill Plantation Books, SHC, p. 13.

26. Hughes, *Thirty Years a Slave*, p. 22.

27. Ophelia Settle Egypt, J. Masuoha, and Charles S. Johnson, eds., *Unwritten History of Slavery: Autobiographical Accounts of Negro Ex-Slaves* (Washington, 1968 [1945]), p. 41.

28. Laura M. Towne, *Letters and Diary of Laura M. Towne Written from the Sea Islands of South Carolina 1862–1884*, ed. Rupert Sargent Holland (New York, 1969 [1912]), pp. 144–45.

See also: Kemble, *Journal of a Residence on a Georgian Plantation*, p. 55.

29. Rawick, *American Slave*, Ga. vol. 13, pt. 3: 190.

30. Frederick Douglass, *My Bondage and My Freedom* (New York, 1968 [1855]), p. 36.

31. Elizabeth Hyde Botume, *First Days Amongst the Contrabands* (Boston, 1893), p. 132.

32. Davis, *Plantation Life in the Florida Parishes*, p. 191. See also pp. 168, 173.

33. Kemble, *Journal of a Residence on a Georgian Plantation*, pp. 118–19.

34. Martha Graham Goodson, "An Introductory Essay and Subject Index to Selected Interviews from the Slave Narrative Collection" (Ph.D. diss., Union Graduate School, 1977), p. 33.

35. Cheryll Ann Cody, "Naming, Kinship, and Estate Dispersal: Notes on Slave Family Life on a South Carolina Plantation, 1786 to 1833," *William and Mary Quarterly* 39 (1982): 207–09.

36. Rawick, *American Slave*, Ala., vol. 7: 73.

37. Herbert G. Gutman, *The Black Family in Slavery and Freedom, 1750–1925* (New York, 1976), pp. 216–22.

38. J. H. Easterby, ed., *The South Carolina Rice Plantations as Revealed in the Papers of Robert W. Allston* (Chicago, 1945), p. 291.

39. Bassett, *The Southern Plantation Overseer*, pp. 19–20, 32.

40. Rawick, *American Slave*, Ga., vol. 12, pt. 2: 57.

41. C. Vann Woodward, Ed., *Mary Chestnut's Civil War* (New Haven, CT, 1981), pp. 33–34.

42. Norman Yetman, *Voices from Slavery* (New York, 1970), p. 13.

43. J. Mason Brewer, *American Negro Folklore* (New York, 1968), p. 233.

44. Willie Lee Rose, *Rehearsal for Reconstruction: The Port Royal Experiment* (New York, 1964), p. 11.

45. Elizabeth Ware Pearson, ed., *Letters from Port Royal: Written at the Time of the Civil War* (New York, 1969 [1906]), p. 44.

46. Ibid., pp. 250, 303–04.

47. Ibid., p. 56.

48. Botume, *First Days Amongst the Contrabands*, p. 125.

49. See for instance: Ibid., pp. 55–56, 58, 80, 212.

50. Pearson, *Letters from Port Royal*, p. 1133.

51. Botume, *First Days Amongst the Contrabands*, pp. 210–11.

Eden Ravished

The Land, Pioneer Attitudes, and Conservation

Harlan Hague

Harlan Hague teaches history of the American West and American environmental history at San Joaquin Delta College, Stockton, California. He is the author of Road to California: The Search For a Southern Overland Route *and articles on western exploration and trails.*

In O. E. Rölvagg's *Giants in the Earth,* a small caravan of Norwegian immigrants stopped on the prairie, and the riders got down from their wagons. They scanned the landscape in all directions and liked what they saw. It was beautiful, all good plowland and clean of any sign of human habitation all the way to the horizon. After so much hoping and planning, they had finally found their place in the new land. One of the men, Per Hansa, still had difficulty comprehending what was happening:

"This vast stretch of beautiful land was to be his—yes, his. . . . His heart began to expand with a mighty exultation. An emotion he had never felt before filled him and made him walk erect. . . . 'Good God!' he panted. 'This kingdom is going to be mine!' "

Countless others who went to the West reacted like Rölvaag's Per Hansa. They entered the Promised Land with high expectations, possessed the land and were possessed by it. They changed the land and in time were changed by it.

The influence of the West on the American mind has interested historians ever since Frederick Jackson Turner read his momentous essay in 1893 to a meeting of the American Historical Association. In the essay, Turner concluded: "The existence of an area of free land, its continuous recession, and the advance of American settlement westward, explain American development." Turner went on to describe in some detail the various ways the western environment changed the frontiersman, molding him into the American. The processes and result of this evolution were in the end, by implication, favorable.

Writing in the early 1890s, Turner did not detect one of the most important themes, if not the most important, of the westward movement, a theme which would have immense impact on the shaping of the American character. This was the belief that the resources of the West were inexhaustible. Henry Nash Smith, in his influential *Virgin Land,* caught the point that Turner missed:

"The character of the American empire was defined not by streams of influence out of the past, not by a cultural tradition, nor by its place in a world community, but by a relation between man and nature—or rather, even more narrowly, between American man and the American West. This relation was thought of as unvaryingly fortunate."

This cornucopian view of the West was the basis of the frontiersman's attitude toward and his use of the land.

The typical trans-Mississippi emigrant in the last half of the nineteenth century accepted the assumption of inexhaustible resources. Yet the view of the West as an everlasting horn of plenty had been proven false long before the post–Civil War exodus. For example, commercial hunting of the sea otter along the California coast, which had begun in 1784, reached its peak around 1815; by the mid-1840s, the numbers of the animals had declined alarmingly, and the otter was soon hunted almost to extinction. The beaver's fate was similar. Soon after Lewis and Clark told about the teeming beaver populations in western streams, trappers moved westward to harvest the furs. They worked streams so relentlessly that the beaver began to disappear in areas where it had always been plentiful. By 1840, the beaver had been trapped virtually to oblivion. No mountain man in the 1820s would have dreamed there could ever be an end to the hardy little animal. Yet unbridled exploitation had nearly condemned the beaver to extinction. The lesson was lost on Westerners.

Pioneers were not noticeably swayed by the arguments of the naturalists, who publicized the wonders of nature or went further and pled for its preservation. William Bartram, a contemporary of Jefferson, wrote eloquently about the beauty of American nature in his *Travels.* Originally published in 1791, his book was more popular in Europe than in the United States, which had yet to discover its aesthetic environment. John James Audubon had more influence in this country upon publication of his *Birds of America* series (1827–1844) and his subsequent call for protection of wildlife. Francis Parkman, while not famed as a naturalist, wrote firsthand accounts about the scenic West and the Indian inhabitants who lived in harmony with nature. It is no wonder that Parkman, who was enthralled with the outdoors, admired Indians and mountain men more than the settlers he encountered during his western travels.

There was indeed a whole body of romantic literature and art during the first half of the nineteenth century that might have persuaded Americans that environmental values could be measured in terms other than economic. William Cullen Bryant wrote with such depth of feeling about the simple pleasures of the outdoors that he is still known as one of our foremost nature poets. The founding spirit of transcendentalism, Ralph Waldo Emerson, wrote in his first book, *Nature:*

"In the presence of nature, a wild delight runs through the man. . . . In the woods, is perpetual youth. . . . In the woods, we return to reason and faith. . . . The currents of the Universal Being circulate through me; I am part or particle of God. . . . In the wilderness, I find something more dear and connate than in streets or villages."

Emerson's contemporary, Henry David Thoreau, was even less restrained in his adoration of untamed nature when he wrote: "In Wildness is the preservation of the World." At the same time, Thomas Cole and the Hudson River school of landscape painters captured on canvas the essence of nature that the romantic writers had recorded in prose and poetry. And farther west, beyond the Mississippi River, George Catlin, Karl Bodmer, and Alfred Jacob Miller were painting the exotic wilderness that increasingly drew the attention of Americans.

Unmoved by praise of the aesthetic quality of the environment, frontiersmen were even less impressed by warnings that its resources were not without end. Every American generation since the colonial period had been told of the virtue of using natural resources wisely. An ordinance of Plymouth Colony had regulated the cutting of timber. William Penn had decreed that one acre of trees be left undisturbed for every five acres cleared. In 1864, only a moment before the beginning of the migration that would cover the West within one generation, George Perkins Marsh published his book *Man and Nature,* the most eloquent statement up to that time of the disastrous result that must follow care-

less stewardship of the land. "Man has too long forgotten," he wrote, "that the earth was given to him for usufruct alone, not for consumption, still less for profligate waste." That is, man could and should both cherish and use the land, but he should not use it up. The significance in Marsh's warning was the recognition that the land could be used up.

While American ambassador to Italy, Marsh had theorized that ancient Rome's fall could be traced to the depletion of the empire's forests. He predicted a like fate for the United States if its resources were similarly squandered. Marsh's book appears to have been widely read by American intellectuals and probably favorably influenced the movements for national parks and forestry management. In it, indeed, were the seeds of the conservation movement of the early twentieth century. Yet it is unlikely that many frontiersmen read or were aware of—or at least they did not heed—Marsh's advice.

Pioneers heard a different drummer. They read descriptions about the West written by people who had been there. Lansford W. Hastings's glowing picture of California and Oregon thrilled thousands:

"In view of their increasing population, accumulating wealth, and growing prosperity, I can not but believe, that the time is not distant, when those wild forests, trackless plains, untrodden valleys, and the unbounded ocean, will present one grand scene, of continuous improvements, universal enterprise, and unparalleled commerce: when those vast forests, shall have disappeared, before the hardy pioneer; those extensive plains, shall abound with innumerable herds, of domestic animals; those fertile valleys, shall groan under the immense weight of their abundant products: when those numerous rivers shall team [*sic*] with countless steam-boats, steam-ships, ships, barques and brigs; when the entire country, will be everywhere intersected, with turnpike roads, rail-roads and canals; and when, all the vastly numerous, and rich resources, of that now, almost unknown region, will be fully and advantageously developed."

Once developed, hopeful emigrants learned, the area would become the garden of the world. In the widely-distrib-

uted *Our Western Empire: or the New West Beyond the Mississippi,* Linus P. Brockett wrote that "in no part of the vast domain of the United States, and certainly in no other country under the sun, is there a body of land of equal extent, in which there are so few acres unfit for cultivation, or so many which, with irrigation or without it, will yield such bountiful crops."

Other books described the routes to the Promised Land. The way west was almost without exception easy and well-watered, with plenty of wood, game, and grass.

There was not just opportunity on the frontier. Walt Whitman also saw romance in the westward migration:

> Come my tan-faced children,
> Follow well in order, get your weapons ready,
> Have you your pistols? have you your sharp-edged axes?
> Pioneers! O pioneers!
> For we cannot tarry here,
> We must march my darlings, we must bear the brunt of danger,
> We the youthful sinewy races, all the rest on us depend,
> Pioneers! O pioneers! . . .
> We primeval forests felling,
> We the rivers stemming, vexing we and piercing deep the mines within,
> We the surface broad surveying, we the virgin soil upheaving
> Pioneers! O pioneers!.
> Swift! to the head of the army!-swift! spring to your places,
> Pioneers! O Pioneers!

The ingredients were all there: danger, youth, virgin soil. Well might frontiersmen agree with Mark Twain who wrote that the first question asked by the American, upon reaching heaven, was: "Which way West?" Thoreau also thought a westward course the natural one:

"When I go out of the house for a walk . . . my needle always settles between west and south-southwest. The future lies that way to me, and the earth seems more unexhausted and richer on that side. . . . westward I go free. I must walk toward Oregon."

Emigrants felt this same pull but for different reasons. Thoreau's West was a wild region to be enjoyed for itself and preserved untouched, while the West to the emigrants was a place for a new start.

The pioneers would conquer the wilderness and gather its immeasurable bounty. This did not imply that Westerners were oblivious to the beauty of the land. Many were aware of the West's scenic attractions but felt, with the influential artist Thomas Cole, that the wilderness, however beautiful, inevitably must give way to progress. In his "Essay on American Scenery," Cole described the sweet joys of nature—the mountains, lakes, rivers, waterfalls, and sky. The essay, dated 1835, is nostalgic. Cole closed his paean with an expression of "sorrow that the beauty of such landscapes are quickly passing away . . . desecrated by what is called improvement." But, after all, he added, "such is the road society has to travel!" Clearly, Cole, like most of his nineteenth-century readers, did not question the propriety of "improvement" or the definition of "progress."

The belief in the inexhaustability of western resources was superimposed on an attitude toward the land that Americans had inherited from generations past. In the Judeo-Christian view, God created the world for man. Man was the master of nature rather than a part of it. The resources of the earth—soil, water, plants, animals, insects, rocks, fish, birds, air—were there for his use, and his proper role was to dominate. It was natural then for God's children to harvest the rich garden provided for them by their Creator. They went into the West to do God's bidding, to use the land as he willed, to fulfill a destiny.

This attitude of man-over-nature was not universal. Like most primitive cultures throughout history, it was not held by the American Indian. The Indian saw himself as a part of nature, not its master. He felt a close kinship with the earth and all living things. Black Elk, a holy man of the Oglala Sioux, for example, believed that all living things were the children of the sky, their father, and the earth, their mother. He had special reverence for "the earth, from whence we came and at whose breast we suck as babies all our lives, along with all the animals and birds and trees and grasses." Creation legends of many tribes illustrate the Indian's familial attachment to the earth and his symbiotic relationship with other forms of life.

The land to Indians was more than merely a means of livelihood for the current generation. It belonged not only to them, the living, but to all generations of their people, those who came before and those who would come after. They could not separate themselves from the land. Of course, there were exceptions. Some Indians fell under the spell of the white trader who offered them goods that would make their lives easier, not to say better. As they became dependent on white man's goods, the land and its fruits began to assume for them an economic value that might be bartered for the conveniences produced by the white man's technology. This is not to say that the Indian attitude toward the land changed. Rather it illustrates that some Indians adopted the white man's view.

To European-Americans, the western Indians' use of the land was just another proof of their savagery. The pioneers had listened to the preachers of Manifest Destiny, and they knew that the nomadic tribes must stand aside for God's Chosen People who would use the land as God intended.

And so they returned to Eden. While some went to California and some to Oregon, the most coherent migration before the rush for California gold began in 1849 was the Mormon exodus to Salt Lake Valley. The latter was not typical of the westward movement. The persecuted saints entered the West not so much for its lure as because of its inaccessibility. In 1830, the same year that the Mormon Church was founded, Joseph Smith announced a revelation which would lead eventually to—or at least foresaw—the great migration:

"And ye are called to bring to pass the gathering of mine elect . . . unto one place upon the face of this land [which] . . . shall be on the borders by the Lamanites [Indians]. . . . The glory of the Lord shall be there, and it shall be called Zion. . . . The righteous shall be gathered out from among all nations, and shall come to Zion, singing with songs of everlasting joy!"

Mormons who trekked to the Utah settlements in the late 1840s and 1850s knew they were doing God's bidding.

Other emigrants were just as sure that the Lord had prepared a place for them.

"Truly the God in Heaven" wrote an Oregon-bound traveler in 1853, "has spread in rich profusion around us everything which could happily man and reveal the Wisdom and Benevolence of God to man." Oregon Trail travelers often noted in their journals that they were going to the "Promised Land." In A. B. Guthrie's *The Way West,* Fairman, who would be leaving Independence shortly for Oregon, proposed a toast "to a place where there's no fever." McBee, another emigrant, impatient to get started, responded:

" 'Y God, yes, . . . and to soil rich as anything. Plant a nail and it'll come up a spike. I heerd you don't never have to put up hay, the grass is that good, winter and all. And lambs come twice a year. Just set by and let the grass grow and the critters berth and get fat. That's my idee of farmin'.'"

It seems that most emigrants, in spite of the humor, did not expect their animals or themselves to wax fat in the new land without working. God would provide, but they must harvest.

Following close on the heels of the Oregon Trail farmers, and sometimes traveling in the same wagon trains, were the miners. This rough band of transients hardly thought of themselves as God's children, but they did nevertheless accept the horn-of-plenty image of the West. Granville Stuart wrote from the California mines that "no such enormous amounts of gold had been found anywhere before, and . . . they all believed that the supply was inexhaustible." Theirs was not an everflowing cornucopia, however, and each miner hoped to be in the right spot with an open sack when the horn tipped to release its wealth.

The typical miner wanted to get as rich as possible as quickly as possible so he could return home to family, friends, and a nabob's retirement. This condition is delightfully pictured in the frontispiece illustration in Mark Twain's *Roughing It.* A dozing miner is seated on a barrel in his cabin, his tools on the floor beside him. He is dreaming about the future: a country estate, yachting, carriage rides and walks in the park with a lady, an ocean voyage and a tour of Europe, viewing the pyramids. The dreams of other miners, while not so grand, still evoked pleasant images of home and an impatience to return there. This yearning is obvious in the lines of a miner's song of the 1850s:

> Home's dearest joys Time soon destroys,
> Their loss we all deplore;
> While they may last, we labor fast
> To dig the golden ore.

When the land has yielded its riches:

> Then home again, home again,
> From a foreign shore,
> We'll sing how sweet our heart's delight,
> With our dear friends once more.

Miners' diaries often reflected these same sentiments, perhaps with less honeyed phrases but with no less passion.

A practical-minded argonaut, writing in 1852 from California to his sister in Alabama, explained his reason for going to the mines: "I think in one year here I can make enough to clear me of debt and give me a pretty good start in the world. Then I will be a happy man." What then? He instructed his sister to tell all his friends that he would soon be "back whare (sic) I can enjoy there [sic] company." Other miners thought it would take a little longer, but the motives were the same. A California miner later reminisced:

"Five years was the longest period any one expected to stay. Five years at most was to be given to rifling California of her treasures, and then that country was to be thrown aside like a used-up newspaper and the rich adventurers would spend the remainder of their days in wealth, peace, and prosperity at their eastern homes. No one talked then of going out 'to build up the glorious State of California.'"

The fact that many belatedly found that California was more than worked-out diggings and stayed—pronouncing the state glorious and themselves founding fathers—does not change their motives for going there.

There was a substantial body of miners, perpetually on the move, rowdies usually, the frontier fraternity boys, whose home was the mining camp and whose friends were largely miners like themselves. They rushed around the West to every discovery of gold or silver

in a vain attempt to get rich without working. Though they had no visions of returning east to family and fireside, they did believe that the West was plentifully supplied with riches. It was just their bad luck that they had not found their shares. Their original reason for going to the mining camps and, though they might enjoy the camaraderie of their fellows, their reason for staying was the same as that of the more genteel sort of miner who had come to the western wilderness, fully expecting to return to the East. More than any other emigrant to the West, the miner's motive was unabashed exploitation. For the most part, he did not conserve, preserve, or enrich the land. His intention, far from honorable, was rape.

The cattleman was a transition figure between the miner who stripped the land and the farmer who, while stripping the land, also cherished it. The West to the cattleman meant grass and water, free or cheap. The earliest ranchers on the plains raised beef for the eastern markets and for the government, which had decreed that the cow replace the buffalo in the Plains Indians' life-style. The Indians, except for a few "renegades," complied, though they were never quite able to work the steer into their religion.

It was not long before word filtered back to the East that fortunes could be made in western stock raising. James Brisbin's *Beef Bonanza; or, How to Get Rich on the Plains,* first published in 1881, was widely read. Readers were dazzled by the author's minutely documented "proof" that an industrious man could more than double his investment in less than five years. Furthermore, there was almost no risk involved:

"In a climate so mild that horses, cattle, and sheep and goats can live in the open air through all the winter months, and fatten on the dry and apparently withered grasses of the soil, there would appear to be scarcely a limit to the number that could be raised."

Experienced and inexperienced alike responded. Getting rich, they thought, was only a matter of time, not expertise.

Entrepreneurs and capital, American and foreign, poured into the West. Most

of the rangeland was not in private ownership. Except for small tracts, generally homesteaded along water courses or as sites for home ranches, it was public property. Though a cattleman might claim rights to a certain range, and though an association of cattlemen might try to enforce the claims of its members, legally the land was open, free, and available.

By the mid-1880s, the range was grossly overstocked. The injury to the land was everywhere apparent. While some began to counsel restraint, most ranchers continued to ravish the country until the winter of 1886–1887 forced them to respect it. Following that most disastrous of winters, which in some areas killed as much as 85 percent of range stock, one chastened cattle king wrote that the cattle business "that had been fascinating to me before, suddenly became distasteful. . . . I never wanted to own again an animal that I could not feed and shelter." The industry gradually recovered, but it would never be the same. More land was fenced, wells dug, and windmills installed. Shelters for cattle were built, and hay was grown for winter feeding. Cattle raising became less an adventure and more a business.

In some cattlemen there grew an attachment, if not affection, for the land. Some, especially after the winter of 1886–1887, began to put down roots. Others who could afford it built luxurious homes in the towns to escape the deficiencies of the countryside, much as twentieth-century townsmen would build cabins in the country to escape the deficiencies of the cities. Probably most cattlemen after the winter of 1886–1887 still believed in the bounty of the West, but a bounty which they now recognized would be released to them only through husbandry.

Among all those who went into the West to seek their fortunes, the frontier farmers carried with them the highest hopes and greatest faith. Their forebears had been told for generations that they were the most valuable citizens, chosen of God, and that their destiny lay westward. John Filson, writing in 1784 about frontier Kentucky, described the mystique of the West that would be understood by post–Civil War emigrants:

"This fertile region, abounding with all the luxuries of nature, stored with all the principal materials for art and industry, inhabited by virtuous and ingenious citizens, must universally attract the attention of mankind." There, continued Filson, "like the land of promise, flowing with milk and honey, a land of brooks of water, . . . a land of wheat and barley, and all kinds of fruits, you shall eat bread without scarceness, and not lack any thing in it."

By 1865 the Civil War had settled the controversy between North and South that had hindered the westward movement, the Homestead Act had been passed, and the Myth of the Garden had replaced the Myth of the Desert. By the grace of God and with the blessing of Washington, the frontier farmer left the old land to claim his own in the new:

*Born of a free, world-wandering race,
Little we yearned o'er an oft-turned sod.
What did we care for the father's place,
Having ours fresh from the hand of God?*

Farmers were attracted to the plains by the glowing accounts distributed by railroads and western states. Newspapers in the frontier states added their accolades. The editor of the Kansas Farmer declared in 1867 that there were in his state "vast areas of unimproved land, rich as that on the banks of the far famed Nile, . . . acres, miles, leagues, townships, counties, oceans of land, all ready for the plough, good as the best in America, and yet lying without occupants." Would-be emigrants who believed this sort of propaganda could sing with conviction:

*Oh! give me a home where the buffalo roam,
Where the deer and the antelope play;
Where never is heard a discouraging word,
And the sky is not clouded all day.*

There was a reason for the sky's clarity, the emigrants learned when they arrived on the plains. It was not long before many had changed their song:

*We've reached the land of desert sweet.
Where nothing grows for man to eat;
I look across the plains
And wonder why it never rains.*

And, finally, sung to the cadence of a "slow sad march":

*We do not live, we only stay;
We are too poor to get away.*

It is difficult to generalize about the experience of pioneer farmers. Those who continued their journeys to the Pacific Coast regions were usually satisfied with what they found. It was those who settled on the plains who were most likely to be disillusioned. Their experience was particularly shattering since they had gone to the West not just to reap in it but also to live in it. Most found not the land of milk and honey they expected, but, it seems, a life of drudgery and isolation.

The most persistent theme in the literature of the period is disenchantment. This mood is caught best by Hamlin Garland. In *Main-Travelled Roads,* Garland acknowledged two views of the plains experience when he wrote that the main-travelled road in the West, hot and dusty in summer, muddy and dreary in fall and spring, and snowy in winter, "does sometimes cross a rich meadow where the songs of the larks and bobolinks and blackbirds are tangled." But Garland's literary road is less cluttered: "Mainly it is long and wearyful, and has a dull little town at one end and a home of toil at the other. Like the main-travelled road of life it is traversed by many classes of people, but the poor and the weary predominate."

The opposite responses to the plains are more pronounced in O. E. Rölvaag's *Giants in the Earth,* one of the most enduring novels of the agricultural West. Per Hansa meets the challenge of the new land, overcomes obstacles and rejoices in each success, however small. He accepts the prairie for what it is and loves it. Meanwhile, his wife, Beret, is gradually driven insane by that same prairie. Where Per Hansa saw hope and excitement in the land, Beret saw only despair and loneliness. "Oh, how quickly it grows dark out here!" she cries, to which Per Hansa replies, "The sooner the day's over, the sooner the next day comes!" In spite of her husband's optimistic outlook, Beret's growing insanity dominates the story as it moves with gloomy intensity to its tragic end. It is significant that Per Hansa dies, a victim of the nature that he did not fear but could not subdue.

Willa Cather, the best-known novelist of nineteenth-century prairie farm life, treated relationships between people and their environment more sensitively than most. While her earlier short stories often dwell on themes of man against the harsh land, her works thereafter, without glossing over the severity of farm life, reveal a certain harmony between the land and those who live on it and love it. Her characters work hard, and suffer; but they are not immune to the loveliness of the land.

The histories of plains farming dwell more on processes than suffering, but accounts that treat the responses of the settlers to their environment generally verify the novelists' interpretations. According to the histories, the picture of desperation painted by Garland and Rölvaag applies principally to the earliest years of any particular frontier region. By the time sod houses acquired board floors and women were able to visit with other women regularly, Cather's images are more accurate.

The fact that pioneer farmers were not completely satisfied with what they found in the Promised Land does not alter their reasons for going there. They had gone into the West for essentially the same reason as the trappers, miners, and cattlemen: economic exploitation. Unlike their predecessors, they also had been looking for homes. Yet, like them, they had believed fervently in the Myth of Superabundance.

The irrational belief that the West's resources were so great that they could never be used up was questioned by some at the very time that others considered it an article of faith. George Perkins Marsh in 1864 warned of the consequences of a too rapid consumption of the land's resources. In 1878, John Wesley Powell attacked the Myth of the Garden when he pointed out that a substantial portion of western land, previously thought to be cultivable by eastern methods, could be farmed successfully only by irrigation. Overgrazing of grasslands resulted in the intrusion of weeds and the erosion of soil, prompting many ranchers, especially after the devastating winter of 1886–1887, to contract their operations and practice range management. Plowing land where rainfall was inadequate for traditional farming methods resulted in wind and water erosion of the soil. Before the introduction of irrigation or dry farming techniques, many plains farmers gave up and returned eastward. The buffalo, which might have numbered fifty million or more at mid-century, were hunted almost to extinction by 1883. Passenger pigeons were estimated to number in the billions in the first half of the nineteenth century: around 1810, Alexander Wilson, an ornithologist, guessed that a single flock, a mile wide and 240 miles long, contained more than two billion birds. Yet before the end of the century, market hunting and the clearing of forest habitats had doomed the passenger pigeon to extinction. Examples of this sort led many people to the inescapable conclusion that the West's resources were not inexhaustible.

At the same time a growing number of people saw values other than economic in the West. Some plains farmers struggling with intermittent drought and mortgage could still see the beauty of the land. Alexandra in Cather's *O Pioneers!* could see it: "When the road began to climb the first long swells of the Divide, Alexandra hummed an old Swedish hymn. . . . Her face was so radiant" as she looked at the land "with love and yearning. It seemed beautiful to her, rich and strong and glorious. Her eyes drank in the breadth of it, until her tears blinded her."

Theodore Roosevelt wrote often of the "delicious" rides he took at his Badlands ranch during autumn and spring. He described the rolling, green grasslands; the prairie roses; the blacktail and white-tail deer; the songs of the skylark; the white-shouldered lark-bunting; and the sweet voice of the meadowlark, his favorite. Of a moonlight ride, he wrote that the "river gleams like running quick-silver, and the moonbeams play over the grassy stretches of the plateaus and glance off the wind-rippled blades as they would from water." Lincoln Lang, a neighbor of Roosevelt's, had the

same feeling for the land. He called the Badlands "a landscape masterpiece of the wild, . . . verdant valleys, teeming with wild life, with wild fruits and flowers, . . . with the God-given atmosphere of truth itself, over which unshackled Nature, alone, reigned queen."

Even miners were not immune to the loveliness of the countryside. Granville Stuart, working in the California mines, was struck by the majestic forests of sugar pine, yellow pine, fir, oak, and dogwood. He described the songs and coloration of the birds and the woodpeckers' habit of storing acorns in holes that they meticulously pecked in tree limbs. He delighted in watching a covey of quail near his cabin each day. "Never was I guilty of killing one," he added. Bret Harte lived among the California miners, and his stories often turn to descriptions of the picturesque foothills of the Sierra Nevada. After the birth of "The Luck" in Roaring Camp, the proud, self-appointed godfathers decorated the baby's "bower with flowers and sweetsmelling shrubs, . . . wild honey-suckles, azaleas, or the painted blossoms of Las Mariposas. The men had suddenly awakened to the fact that there were beauty and significance in these trifles, which they had so long trodden carelessly beneath their feet."

Success of some sort often broadened the frontiersman's viewpoint. The miner, cattleman, or farmer who had succeeded in some way in his struggle with the land had more time and inclination to think about his relationship with it. Viewing his environment less as an adversary, the Westerner began to see what was happening to it.

At times, concern for the environment led to action. The mounting protests of Californians whose homes and farms had been damaged by the silt-laden runoff from hydraulic mining finally led to the outlawing of this mindless destruction of the land. Frederick Law Olmsted, who had designed New York's Central Park, initiated an era in 1864 when he and some friends persuaded Congress to grant to the state of California a piece of land in California's Sierra Nevada for the creation of a park, merely because the land, which included Yosemite Valley and the

Mariposa Big Trees, was beautiful and the public would enjoy it. The idea took hold, and other parks soon followed, Yellowstone in 1872 being the first public "pleasuring ground" under federal management. The new art of landscape photography showed Easterners the wonders of the West, without the hardships of getting there, and revealed to many Westerners a land they inhabited but had never seen. With the improvement in transportation, principally railroads, more and more people ventured into the West to see these wonders firsthand.

A growing awareness that unrestrained exploitation was fast destroying the natural beauty of the West and that its resources, by the end of the nineteenth century widely acknowledged to be finite, were being consumed at an alarming pace led to considerable soul-searching. Frederick Jackson Turner, who had most eloquently described the influence that the great expanses of western land had on the shaping of American character, also hinted that the disappearance of available land was likely to cause some serious disruptions in American society. "The frontier has gone," he wrote, "and with its going has closed the first period of American history."

If the first phase of American history, in which a dominant theme was the advance of the frontier, ran from 1607 to 1890, the second phase began with the emergence of the conservation movement which would lead to the alteration of fundamental attitudes toward the land nurtured during the first phase. While based generally on concern for the environment, the movement split in the early twentieth century into two factions. One faction argued for wise management of the country's resources to prevent their being wasted. This "utilitarian conservation," was not a break with the frontier view of exploitation. It was a refinement. While the frontier view was one of rapid exploitation of inexhaustible resources, the utilitarian conservationists rejected the myth of inexhaustibility and advocated the careful use of finite resources, without rejecting the basic assumption that the resources were there to be exploited. This view of conservation led to the setting aside and management of forest reserves, soil and water conservation projects, and irrigation and hydroelectric programs.

The other faction, whose ideology has been called "aesthetic conservation," clearly broke with the frontier past when its members argued for the preservation of areas of natural beauty for public enjoyment. This group's efforts bore fruit in the establishment of national and state parks, monuments and wilderness areas. There are indications that the two factions are drawing closer together in the umbrella ecology movement of the 1970s, perhaps eventually to merge.

It is senseless to compare nineteenth-century frontier attitudes toward the land with today's more enlightened views. Faced seemingly with such plenty—billions of passenger pigeons, millions of buffalo, innumerable beaver, endless seas of grass, vast forests of giant trees, mines to shame King Solomon's—excess was understandable and probably inevitable. Excess in this case meant waste. Here the Turner thesis is most meaningful, for the belief in the inexhaustibility of resources in the West generated the unique American acceptance of waste as the fundamental tenet of a life-style. For this, the frontiersman is not entirely blameless. But certainly, he

is less blameworthy than the neo-pioneer who continues, against reason and history, to cling hopefully to the myth of inexhaustibility. Yet there were examples, however few, and voices, however dim, that the frontiersman might have heeded. It remains to be seen whether Americans today have learned the lesson their ancestors, four generations removed, failed to comprehend.

BIBLIOGRAPHIC NOTE

There are few comprehensive surveys of the evolution of American attitudes toward the environment. Three useful sources are Stewart L. Udall, *The Quiet Crisis* (New York: Holt, Rinehart, 1963); Hans Huth, *Nature and the American: Three Centuries of Changing Attitudes* (Berkeley: University of California, 1957); and Roderick Nash, *Wilderness and the American Mind,* rev. ed. (New Haven: Yale University, 1973), the last particularly concerned with the American response to wilderness. Frederick Jackson Turner's frontier thesis, which inevitably must be considered in any study of the relationship between Americans and their environment, is in his *The Frontier in American History* (New York: Henry Holt, 1921). Invaluable to an understanding of what Americans thought the West was is Henry Nash Smith, *Virgin Land: The American West as Symbol and Myth* (New York: Vintage Books, 1950). The most influential book of the twentieth century in the development of a land ethic is Aldo Leopold, *A Sand County Almanac* (New York: Oxford University, 1949).

Selections from historical materials and literature were blended in this study to illustrate western emigrants' expectations for and responses to the new country. In addition to titles listed in the text, literary impressions of nature are in Wilson O. Clough, *The Necessary Earth: Nature and Solitude in American Literature* (Austin: University of Texas, 1964) and John Conron, The *American Landscape: A Critical Anthology of Prose and Poetry* (New York: Oxford University, 1974). Useful bibliographies of the literature of the westward movement are Lucy Lockwood Hazard, The *Frontier in American Literature* (New York: Thomas Y. Crowell, 1927) and Richard W. Etulain, *Western American Literature* (Vermillion, S.D.: University of South Dakota, 1972). Bibliographies of historical materials are in Ray Allen Billington, *Westward Expansion, 4th* ed. (New York: Macmillan, 1974), and Nelson Klose, *A Concise Study Guide to the American Frontier* (Lincoln: University of Nebraska, 1964).

Unit 4

Unit Selections

27. **"The Doom of Slavery": Ulysses S. Grant, War Aims, and Emancipation, 1861–1863,** Brooks D. Simpson
28. **Lee's Greatest Victory,** Robert K. Krick
29. **Gallantry under Fire,** John E. Aliyetti
30. **The Struggle for Black Freedom before Emancipation,** Wayne K. Durrill
31. **The Northern Front,** Dara Horn
32. **The Man at the White House Window,** Stephen B. Oates
33. **Why the South Lost the Civil War,** Carl Zebrowski
34. **A War That Never Goes Away,** James M. McPherson
35. **The New View of Reconstruction,** Eric Foner

Key Points to Consider

❖ How and why did the Civil War change from a limited conflict to almost total war? What kept Abraham Lincoln from issuing the Emancipation Proclamation earlier, and why did he finally take the step?

❖ What went on in Boston before and during the Civil War that would justify entitling an article about the city "The Northern Front"?

❖ Discuss the views of historians as to why the South lost the Civil War. Which factors seem most important to you?

❖ Was Radical Reconstruction doomed to fail? What would it have taken on the part of the North to prevail over the opposition of white Southerners?

 **Links** **www.dushkin.com/online/**

27. **Anacostia Museum/Smithsonian Institution**
   http://www.si.edu/organiza/museums/anacost/
28. **Abraham Lincoln Online**
   http://www.netins.net/showcase/creative/lincoln.html
29. **Civil War**
   http://www.access.digex.net/~bdboyle/cw.html
30. **Gilder Lehrman Institute of American History**
   http://vi.uh.edu/pages/mintz/gilder.htm
31. **Secession Era Editorials Project**
   http://history.furman.edu/benson/docs/

These sites are annotated on pages 4 and 5.

As we have seen in preceding units, sectional disputes were commonplace in the decades following the adoption of the Constitution. Northerners tended to favor high tariffs and what were called "internal improvements" (construction of canals, turnpikes, and railroads), while most Southerners opposed them. These were manageable issues, however, and did not stir emotions as did the question of slavery. The acquisition of new territories was particularly divisive. Northerners wanted these lands reserved for free labor and Southerners were equally insistent that slavery be permitted to exist wherever it was profitable. Compromises over this question were hammered out in 1820 and 1850, but they really amounted only to truces that were unsatisfactory to both sides. The emergence in the North of abolitionists who demanded that the slave system be destroyed everywhere infuriated Southerners who responded by claiming that slavery benefited both blacks and whites.

Despite the efforts by moderates to keep the matter offstage, the struggle over slavery destroyed the Whig Party. The emergence of the Republican Party, which drew its strength almost exclusively from the North, appeared to Southerners to threaten their very way of life. Even though Abraham Lincoln denied that he intended to move against slavery where it already existed, he was regarded in the South as an abolitionist at heart. His victory in the 1860 presidential election caused Southern states to begin seceding from the Union, and his unwillingness to let them go led to the Civil War.

Two selections deal with the military aspects of the war. "The Doom of Slavery" describes how the struggle changed from a limited conflict to a concept of total war against Southern resources and morale. Author Brooks Simpson argues that General Ulysses S. Grant realized that at bottom the conflict was over slavery. "Lee's Greatest Victory," by Robert Krick, recounts General Robert E. Lee's masterly conduct of the battle of Chancellorsville. The victory was a costly one, however, as one of Lee's best generals, "Stonewall" Jackson, was accidentally killed by his own men.

There are two essays that treat the conduct of blacks during the war. "Gallantry under Fire" is an account by John Aliyetti of the bloody battle of New Market Heights. Of the 16 Medals of Honor awarded to black soldiers in the war, 14 of them were for this heroic assault. "The Struggle for Black Freedom before Emancipation" shows how blacks themselves sought freedom before the Emancipation Proclamation. Some simply fled the farms and plantations and made their way to free areas, while others stayed home but were able to redefine their conditions in the direction of greater rights and privileges.

Boston is a city usually associated with the Revolutionary War. Author Dara Horn, in "The Northern Front," describes the important role that Boston played prior to the Civil War and during the war itself. The vast majority of abolitionists resided in Boston, as did Frederick Douglass and the "Secret Six," a group that planned and financed John Brown's raid on Harper's Ferry. When the Northern army began recruiting for its first black regiment, volunteers were signed up in the basement of Boston's African Meeting House.

In "The Man at the White House Window," noted historian Stephen Oates evaluates Abraham Lincoln's presidency. He concludes that as the nature of the Civil War changed, Lincoln changed as well in pursuing his vision of national goals. To "win" the war the South did not have to conquer the North; all it had to do was hold out long enough so that Northerners would lose their will to go on fighting. This came close to happening during the early part of 1864. "Why the South Lost the Civil War" offers the views of 10 leading historians on why the North prevailed in the end. James McPherson's "A War That Never Goes Away" explains why the conflict has had such enduring interest for Americans.

Finally, a struggle took place after the war ended over how the South should be reintegrated into the Union. The most important issue was what status blacks would have in society. Moderates such as Lincoln wished to make Reconstruction as painless as possible, even though this meant white domination of the Southern states. "Radical" or "advanced" Republicans wished to guarantee freedpersons the full rights of citizenship, using force if necessary to achieve this goal. Southern whites resisted "Radical Reconstruction" any way they could and, when Northern will eroded, ultimately prevailed. Eric Foner's "The New View of Reconstruction" argues that even though Radical Reconstruction failed in the short run, it provided an "animating vision" for the future.

"The Doom of Slavery": Ulysses S. Grant, War Aims, and Emancipation, 1861–1863

Brooks D. Simpson

Like many northerners, Ulysses S. Grant went to war in 1861 to save the Union—and nothing more—in what he predicted would be a short conflict. By 1863, after two years of bloody struggle against a stubborn enemy, Grant came to understand that a war to preserve the Union must of necessity transform that Union. Central to that revolutionary transformation was the acceptance of emancipation as a war aim and the enrollment of ex-slaves in the bluecoat ranks. The intensity of Confederate resistance compelled Union commanders to accept this notion, while the influx of black refugees into Yankee camps helped to force a decision. In 1861 Grant believed that the Union should keep hands off slavery if a quick peace and rapid reconciliation was desired. By 1863 circumstances had changed. Notions of a limited conflict gave way to the concept of a total war waged against Southern resources and morale as well as manpower. New means were needed to attain victory. To save the Union one must destroy slavery. Grant's experiences as a field commander are illustrative of this process, suggesting the interaction between the progress of the war effort, the escalation of Southern

resistance, and the transformation of war aims to encompass emancipation.

From war's beginning Grant realized that at the core of the dispute was the institution of slavery. His position on the peculiar institution was ambiguous, and he left no detailed explanation of his feelings for historians to examine. Marriage to the daughter of a slaveholder entangled him in slavery: he worked alongside slaves, his wife owned four house servants, and he was a slaveholder for a short period. Yet family slaves heard him speak out against the institution, he did not succumb to the blatant prejudices of his age, and he freed the slave he owned at a time when the money a sale might have brought could have been a great boon. He showed no interest in protecting slavery, let alone perpetuating it.[1]

Moreover, Grant understood that the advent of war in the spring of 1861 would affect slavery, no matter the outcome. Southerners were risking the foundation of their society even as they defended it. "In all this I can but see the doom of Slavery," he told his father-in-law. "The North do not want, nor will they want, to interfere with the institution. But they will refuse for all time to give it protection unless the South shall return soon to their allegiance." The disruption of the Southern economy by war would render it vulnerable to international competition, reducing the worth of slaves "so much that they will never

be worth fighting over again." Slavery would be destroyed as a consequence of prolonged conflict, a casualty of events rather than the target of Union policy.[2]

Nevertheless, a quick Northern victory, achieved before hatred could become deep-seated, might minimize the impact of the conflict upon slavery. And Grant believed that such a rapid triumph was possible. Startled by the vigorous reaction of Northerners in Sumter's aftermath, he ventured that if Southerners ever discovered what they had wrought, "they would lay down their arms at once in humble submission." Confidently he predicted a Northern triumph in a conflict "of short duration." With "a few decisive victories" by the North the "howling" Confederates would flee the field. "All the states will then be loyal for a generation to come, negroes will depreciate so rapidly in value that no body will want to own them and their masters will be the loudest in their declamations against the institutions in a political and economic view." If slavery was to suffer, it would be as a byproduct of the conflict, not because of deliberate policy decisions to eradicate it. Indeed, to take such steps might only prolong the conflict by engendering resistance born of bitterness.[3]

In June, Grant was commissioned colonel of the 21st Illinois. Soon his regiment was dispatched to Missouri to hunt down scattered rebel detachments. Grant kept a close eye on his men, mak-

The author wishes to acknowledge the assistance provided by a research grant from Wofford College. He thanks Richard H. Sewell and Allan G. Bogue for their advice and counsel and John Y. Simon and David L. Wilson for their encouragement.

From *Civil War History*, Vol. 36, No. 1, March 1990, pp. 36-56. © 1990 by Kent State University Press. Reprinted by permission.

ing sure that they did not disturb citizens along the line of march. He reasoned that a well-behaved army would contradict rumors of a marauding bunch of Yankees bent upon plunder, eroding fears and enhancing the chances of a quick and easy peace. Such considerations were especially crucial in Missouri, where the population was nearly evenly divided between loyalists and secessionists. With the state still teetering on the edge of secession, it was of utmost importance that Grant maintain discipline among his new recruits. He did so, with good results. While there existed "a terrible state of fear among the people" when his troops arrived, he added that within a few weeks they discovered that the bluecoats "are not the desperate characters they took them for." He was convinced that "if orderly troops could be marched through this country . . . it would create a very different state of feeling from what exists now."[4]

Efforts to foster good feeling, however, met a serious obstacle in the stubborness of the local citizens. "You can't convince them but that the ultimate object is to extinguish, by force, slavery," he complained to his father. To his wife Julia he revealed concern that the war was getting out of hand. Not only were the citizens "great fools," but they "will never rest until they bring upon themselves all the horrors of war in its worst form. The people are inclined to carry on a guerilla Warfare that must eventuate in retaliation and when it does commence it will be hard to control."[5] Should the war transcend conventional limits, it would embitter both victor and vanquished, making it all the more difficult to achieve a lasting peace. Moreover, to abandon notions of a limited war fought between armies, in favor of a people's struggle, carried with it revolutionary implications. While both sides may have gone to war to preserve something—the North to save the Union, the South to protect a way of life—the resulting conflict, should it spill over its initial boundaries, promised to transform American society whatever the result.

Signs of Confederate determination caused Grant to reconsider his earlier notions about a short war. "I have changed my mind so much that I don't know what to think," he told his sister. While he still believed that the rebels could be crushed by spring, "they are so dogged that there is no telling when they may be subdued." As resistance stiffened, Grant adopted a tougher policy toward secessionist sympathizers, arresting several to prevent them from relaying information, seizing a prosouthern paper, and warning businessmen not to trade with Confederates. If Southerners wanted to broaden the scope of the war, Grant was willing to respond in kind.[6]

Inevitably such a struggle affected the institution of slavery. While Grant did not go to war to free the slaves, he had maintained that Northerners would not prop up slavery while the South continued to fight. Eventually Union field commanders found themselves confronted with the problem of what to do about slavery in the war zone. Despite Grant's avowed disinclination to become involved in political questions, his actions toward civilians, property, and fugitive slaves inescapably carried with them political overtones. In August, General John C. Frémont ordered Grant to take command of troops concentrating in southeast Missouri. Arriving at Cape Girardeau on August 30, Grant observed "Contrabands, in the shape of negroes," working on the fortifications. "I will make enquiries how they come here and if the fact has not been previously reported ask instructions," he informed Frémont's headquarters at St. Louis. Grant was trying to avoid initiating policies which interfered with slavery.[7]

Unknown to Grant, Frémont, tired of harassment by Confederate sympathizers, struck at slavery the same day. His abolitionism, bolstered by a visit from Owen Lovejoy, and his ambition combined to convince him to issue a proclamation which imposed martial law on Missouri, confiscated the property of active Confederate supporters, and declared their slaves free. Local commanders wired Grant for instructions. "Protect all loyal Citizens in all their right[s]," Grant replied, "but carry out the proclamation of Genl Fremont upon all subjects known to come under it." Frémont's order was soon countermanded by Lincoln, but it had alerted

Grant to the possibility that the war could assume a wider scope and thus involve him in the very political questions he wished to avoid.[8] Lincoln's removal of Frémont several weeks later also reminded the new brigadier of the cost of violating established policy.

Grant's decision to invade Kentucky in September 1861 provided him with an opportunity to issue a proclamation outlining war aims, and the contrast with Frémont's missive was marked. Through August, Kentucky had managed to preserve a precarious neutrality in the sectional conflict. Neither side had set foot in the state, although it was obvious that sooner or later Union troops would have to violate its neutrality if they intended to launch an offensive to recapture Tennessee. Grant had been sent to southeast Missouri to plan for just such an invasion, but Confederate forces conveniently relieved him of the onus of disrupting the status quo first by invading Kentucky on September 3. The Rebel commander, General Leonidias Polk, had made a serious error, one on which Grant seized in moving his troops across the Ohio River into Paducah, Kentucky, on September 6.

Once installed at Paducah, Grant issued his own proclamation. He had invaded Kentucky, "not to injure or annoy, . . . but to respect the rights, and to defend and enforce the rights of all loyal citizens." It was a purely defensive move. "I have nothing to do with opinions. I shall deal only with armed rebellion and its aiders and abetors." Nothing was said about slavery. Grant issued special instructions "to take special care and precaution that no harm is done to inoffensive citizens."[9]

Grant's proclamation was as much a political statement as that issued by Frémont. Both were issued in states still technically loyal to the Union, and both reflected the lack of a declaration of overall war aims from Washington. Frémont, anxious to make a name for himself, had sought to place the war effort on advanced ground; Grant's announcement reflected his own belief that the war was one for reunion, not revolution. In contrast to Frémont, who saw his handiwork annulled by Lincoln, Grant's statement stood. It still remained for the Lincoln administration to make known its policy in order to guide military commanders in their actions.

Although Lincoln's action in countermanding Frémont's proclamation helped people understand what his policy was not, Grant was unsure of what government policy was, especially as it applied to black refugees. Within two weeks of the occupation of Paducah, blacks began entering Union lines, intent on making good their escape from slavery. Like Grant, Kentucky blacks knew that the presence of Union troops meant the disruption of slavery, regardless of the unwillingness of Union commanders to play abolitionist. And, if the Yankee army would not come to the blacks, they would go to it. The slaveholders followed, demanding the return of their property. They were willing to overlook the irony that they were asking the assistance of a government that many of them were rebelling against to protect their right to own slaves, when many of them had justified secession precisely because they had no faith that the same government would protect that right. Grant wired Washington for instructions. None came.[10]

Left on his own, and aware that fugitive slave legislation was still in force, Grant ordered the return of at least one slave. Some two months later he finally received definite guidelines on what to do. Major General Henry W. Halleck succeeded Frémont in November with orders to convince civilians in his command that the sole purpose of the war was to uphold "the integrity of the Union." The day after he assumed command Halleck issued General Orders No. 3, which closed Union lines to black fugitives.[11]

Grant received the order with mixed feelings. To be sure, he still held fast to his belief that the sole object of the war was to restore the Union. "My inclination is to whip the rebellion into submission, preserving all constitutional rights," he told his father. But Grant was willing to admit the possibility that this might not be possible. "If it cannot be whipped in any other way than through a war against slavery," he continued, "let it come to that legitimately. If it is necessary that slavery should fall that the Republic may continue its existence, let slavery go." The general was willing to consider the possibility that slavery's demise might be a goal of Union war policy, instead of being merely the consequence of the disruptive impact of military operations. But he was not yet ready to take that step. Aware that many Northern newspapers had seized upon Halleck's order to renew their criticism of the narrow scope of Union war aims, Grant charged that such papers "are as great enemies to their country as if they were open and avowed secessionists." Adopting such broad goals would mean that the prospects for reunion and reconciliation would give way to a bitter struggle requiring the North to conquer the entire South.[12]

Despite his reaction to press criticism of Halleck's order, Grant was ambivalent about it. "I do not want the Army used as negro catchers," he explained in approving the return of a fugitive to a loyal master, "but still less do I want to see it used as a cloak to cover their escape. No matter what our private views may be on this subject there are in this Department positive orders on the subject, and these orders must be obeyed." While he still agreed that the army's mission did not include emancipation, he was not willing to endorse active support of slavery in all instances, especially in the face of growing resistance. Noting that it was not the military's policy "to ignore, or in any manner interfere with the Constitutional rights of loyal citizens," he denied the same protection to secessionist slaveholders when he refused to honor a Confederate master's demand for the return of a fugitive who had sought refuge in Grant's camp. "The slave, who is used to support the Master, who supported the rebellion, is not to be *restored* to the Master by Military Authority." The slaveholder might appeal to the civil authorities, but Grant did not "feel it his duty to feed the foe, or in any manner contribute to their comfort." This position, violating the letter of Halleck's order, went further in the direction of emancipation than existing congressional legislation outlining confiscation policy, which concerned only those slaves actively employed in support of the rebellion.[13]

Grant let slip his growing antislavery convictions on other occasions. During the fall of 1861 his forces sparred with Polk's units, and the two armies met once in a pitched battle at Belmont, Missouri. Inevitably, prisoners were taken at these clashes, and Grant met with Polk several times on a truce boat to arrange exchanges and discuss other issues. At the conclusion of one meeting, drinks were served, and Polk offered a toast: "George Washington!" No sooner had Grant tipped the glass to his lips, however, when Polk added, "the first rebel." Chagrined, Grant protested that such sharp practice was "scarcely fair" and vowed to get even. The opportunity came several weeks later, at another truce boat conference. This time Grant proposed a toast: "Equal rights to all." Heartily assenting, Polk began to down the contents of his glass, when Grant quickly added, "white and black." A sputtering Polk admitted that Grant had achieved his object.[14]

Nor was Grant willing to tolerate actions which exceeded the bounds of conventional warfare. In January 1862, upon receiving reports that several of his pickets had been shot by civilians, he ordered that the surrounding area "should be cleaned out, for six miles around, and word given that all citizens making their appearance in within those areas are liable to be shot," thus establishing the Civil War version of a free-fire zone. These orders restored stability. A week later, he instructed the local commander to release all civilians captured under these orders and to allow all slaves to return to their masters.[15]

During early 1862 Grant remained uncertain about the correct policy to pursue toward fugitives, and his capture of Fort Donelson on February 16 added to the problem. Halleck wanted to consolidate Grant's gains by erecting fortifications to hold Donelson and its twin, Fort Henry, and instructed Grant to use slaves owned by secessionsists to do the work. Grant sent division commander John A. McClernand out to capture slaves to increase the available work force. At least one expedition interpreted its orders liberally, seizing "mostly old men, women and children." The commander had violated Halleck's order, and the fugitives had to be returned. Grant finally halted McClernand, explaining, "It leads to constant mistakes and embarassment to have our men running through the country interpreting confiscation acts and only strengthens the enthusiasm against us whilst it has a demoralizing influence upon our own troops."[16]

The incident caused Grant a great deal of embarrassment. He reminded his troops that Halleck's order about returning fugitive slaves was still in force and must be observed. Union lines were flooded with slaveholders seeking to recover their slaves, proving that General Orders No. 3 continued to be a necessity. Halleck had issued a new order, reminding officers that civil courts, not military authorities, were empowered to rule on the status of slaves. Keeping fugitives out of camp would keep Grant out of trouble, or so he thought. But the image of Union soldiers returning "old men, women and children" to their masters was too much for many Northerners, and newspapers attacked Grant's action. "I have studiously tried to prevent the running off of negroes from all outside places," an exasperated Grant explained, "as I have tried to prevent all other marauding and plundering." It was not a matter of personal preference. "So long as I hold a commission in the Army I have no views of my own to carry out. Whatever may be the orders of my superiors, and law, I will execute." If Congress passed legislation "too odious for me to execute," he promised to resign. He enforced a strict observance of Halleck's order to avoid more trouble, including the arrest of any soldiers violating the order.[17]

Even when orders from Washington finally arrived, they did not ease Grant's mind. In March he received notification of new War Department guidelines which instructed soldiers not to return fugitives. One suspects that incidents in Grant's own command had contributed to the new directive. In response Grant pointed out the ramifications of such a policy. He had heard from former U.S. Representative J. M. Quarles that Confederate enlistments had risen around Clarksville, Tennessee, in reaction to the use of fugitives by a Union post com-

mander. The post commander told Grant that "the return of those two negroes would do more good, & go further to cultivate a union sentiment in & about Clarksville than any other act." Grant forwarded the case, uncertain how to respond in light of the new directives, but expressed his opinion that the blacks should be returned.[18]

As Grant realized, federal policy toward fugitive slaves was intertwined with efforts at reconciliation. After Fort Donelson, he believed that one more Union victory would end the conflict, an impression made plausible by circumstances in his command. Many Tennesseans were declaring their loyalty to the Union; others were enlisting in Grant's regiments. Confederate deserters reported great discontent in rebel ranks. "With one more great success I do not see how the rebellion is to be sustained," Grant told his wife. He thought that the question of fugitive slaves would simply disrupt the reconciliation process at a time when the end seemed so near. But the bloodbath at Shiloh in April disabused Grant of these hopes. He later claimed that the battle changed his thinking about the conduct of the war. After Shiloh, "I gave up all idea of saving the Union except by complete conquest." Previous policies to "protect the property of the citizens whose territory was invaded, without regard to their sentiments," went out the door, and Grant began to make war not only on Confederate armies but the resources which sustained the war effort.[19]

But Grant's change in attitude was a little slower in coming than he liked to recall later. "This war could be ended at once," he told his wife in June, two months after Shiloh, "if the whole Southern people could express their unbiased feeling untrammeled by leaders. The feeling is kept up however by crying out Abolitionest against us and this is unfortunately sustained by the acts of a very few among us." He detailed instances where Tennesseans "inclined to Union sentiments" watched as soldiers encouraged their slaves to escape. This did little to assist reconciliation. Still, as Grant took command of the District of West Tennessee in June, he expressed his confidence that as soon as his district

was "reduced to working order" its residents would "become loyal, or at least law-abiding." Others were not so sure. Dr. Edward Kittoe, a friend of Grant's patron Congressman Elihu B. Washburne, complained, "We curry favour of these secessionists, and real Union men do not fare as well as they: we are obsequious to them, we feed them, we guard their property, we humble ourselves to gain their favor, and in return we receive insult and injury." Unionists were "disgusted," and both officers and men "feel outraged . . . and very naturally ask is this the way to crush this rebellion." To Kittoe the answer was obvious: "The iron gauntlet must be used more than the silken glove to crush this serpent."[20]

Grant's early hopes for reconciliation were dashed when he observed the temper of the people. Far from anxiously awaiting reunion, most west Tennesseans remained defiantly loyal to the Confederate cause, chafing under occupied rule. They cheered on the small bands of guerrillas who sought to disrupt and disturb Grant's operations. As Grant struggled to secure his lines from raiders, he began to reassess his beliefs about limited war in the face of escalating Confederate resistance. The intensity of the Southern attack at Shiloh, while alarming, remained within the bounds of conventional warfare: but when resisting citizens and marauding guerrillas expanded the scope of conflict beyond these limits, Grant had to meet the challenge. It was combatting a restive populace in occupied territory, stalking guerrillas, and absorbing black refugees, not merely Shiloh, that persuaded Grant to abandon limited war for total war. He did so with surprising speed. On July 1, he ordered the *Memphis Avalanche* to shut down after the paper had complained about the behavior of Union troops. Within days a Unionist paper, the *Bulletin,* replaced it. Two days later he took steps to halt guerrilla activities by ordering that property losses sustained by his army would be made up by assessments on the property of Confederate sympathizers. All captured guerrillas would not be treated as prisoners of war, leaving open the possibility of execution. The order provoked one Mississippian to protest Grant's "infamous and fiendish proclamation . . . characteristic of your infernal policy. . . . Henceforth our motto shall be, Blood for blood, and blood for property."[21]

Grant also tired of dealing with Confederate sympathizers in Memphis. On July 10 he issued a special order directing families of Confederate officers and officeholders to move south. Although the order was later modified to allow such families to remain in Memphis upon taking a pledge not to aid enemy operations, it outraged Confederate General Jeff Thompson, who promised revenge. In contrast, a local Unionist applauded the order: "I would suggest that all persons who *uphold,* and *preach* Secession in our midst be required to 'skedaddle' to the land of *'secession'.*"[22]

As Federal units probed southward across the Tennessee-Mississippi border, blacks continued to flood into Union lines. Their sheer numbers negated any further attempts at exclusion. If whites were "sullen" at the sight of the bluecoats, Kittoe told Washburne, "the darkies seemed joyous at our presence." Grant's soldiers realized that their mere presence destroyed slavery, "Where the army of the Union goes, *there slavery ceases forever,*" wrote a Wisconsin captain. "It is astonishing how soon the blacks have learned this, and they are flocking in considerable numbers already in our lines." Another officer noted, "All that came within our lines were received and put to work and supplied with clothing and subsistence. This policy was viewed by the soldiers with very general approbation."[23]

Grant moved slowly at first in responding to these new circumstances. "It is hard to say what would be the most wise policy to pursue towards these people," he wrote Washburne. He put blacks to work fortifying Memphis from Confederate attack, much as he had used blacks at Donelson. But he remained unsure of his responsibilities in other cases, and, rather than invite more criticism by acting on his own, he asked for instructions. After arresting Confederate sympathizer Francis Whitfield on July 17, 1862, Grant had to decide what to do with Whitfield's slaves, who, since they were women and children, could not be used on fortifications. Whitfield, understandably, wanted the slaves sent south to relatives. Grant, preoccupied with enemy movements, asked Halleck what to do. The general-in-chief responded that if Grant had no use for or reason to detain the slaves, "let them go when they please."[24]

Halleck could have been more helpful to the befuddled Grant. On the day of Whitfield's arrest, Congress passed a second confiscation act which declared that slaves owned by rebels who came in contact with Union forces were free. Certainly Halleck should have been aware of this legislation, but he failed to pass policy directives down to his subordinates. Promulgation of a policy did not necessarily guarantee its immediate implementation and enforcement. Grant was not officially informed of the passage of the act for several weeks. Halleck finally instructed him to "clean out West Tennessee and North Mississippi of all organized enemies," eject civilian sympathizers, and confiscate rebel property. "It is time that they should begin to feel the presence of war on one side."[25]

Grant planned to make the war even more oppressive for Southern whites. He cracked down on the activities of Confederate sympathizers and guerrillas, following Halleck's advice to "handle that class without gloves." As William T. Sherman put it to Secretary of the Treasury Salmon P. Chase, "The Government of the United States may now safely proceed on the proper rule that all in the South are enemies of all in the North, and not only are they unfriendly, but all who can procure arms now bear them as organized regiments or as guerrillas." Grant also took steps to close down trade with the enemy, especially cotton speculators. To Chase he declared that such trade profited only "greedy" speculators and the enemy, failed to "abate [the] rancorous hostility" of Rebels, and hurt the war effort. Doubtless Grant's new toughness was due to his realization that the war had taken on a new character, but he was also frustrated with his present situation, holding territory while hunting down pesky guerrilla bands. If he could not attack the South in battle, he would find another way to strike back.[26]

Washburne apprised Grant of the new attitudes in Washington. "This matter of guarding rebel property, of protecting secessionists and of enforcing 'order No. 3' is 'played out' in public estimation. Your order in regard to the Secessionists of Memphis taking the oath or leaving, has been accepted as an earnest of vigorous and decided action on your part. . . . The administration has come up to what the people have long demanded—a vigorous prosecution of the war by all the means known to civilized warfare." Such measures included striking at slavery. "The negroes must now be made our auxiliaries in every possible way they can be, whether by working or fighting." The general "who takes the most decided step in this respect," Washburne hinted, "will be held in the highest estimation by the loyal and true men in the country."[27]

Grant followed Washburne's advice, freed of the responsibilities of playing slave catcher. "I have no hobby of my own with regard to the negro, either to effect his freedom or to continue his bondage," he told his father. "If Congress pass any law and the President approves, I am willing to execute it." His headquarters established guidelines for the enforcement of the new confiscation legislation. Blacks would no longer be turned away: instead, they would be put to work. Manpower needs would be met by impressing the slaves belonging to Confederate masters. Uncertain as to the scope of the legislation, Grant excluded unemployed blacks from the lines, and prohibited soldiers "from enticing Slaves to leave their masters." The order had an immediate impact. "If the niggers come into camp for a week as fast as they have been coming for two days past," a Wisconsin private noted some two days after Grant issued his order, "we will soon have a waiter for every man in the Regt."[28]

The result pleased Grant. "The war is evidently growing oppressive to the Southern people," he told his sister. "Their *institution* are beginning to have ideas of their own and every time an expedition goes out more or less of them follow in the wake of the army and come to camp." The general employed them as teamsters, cooks, and hospital attendants, but there was not enough work for all. "I don't know what is to become of these poor people in the end but it [is] weakening the enemy to take them from them."[29]

With the approach of fall the black refugee problem assumed serious dimensions. Grant's troops, busy repelling Confederate offensives near Corinth, found the flood of fugitives obstructing movements and causing health problems. They described the blacks coming by the hundreds each night, "bearing their bundles on their heads and their pickaninnies under their arms." Chaplain John Eaton of the 27th Ohio recalled that the influx of refugees resembled "the oncoming of cities": once in camp, the bedraggled blacks produced "a veritable moral chaos." Sherman wrote his senator brother that "if we are to take along and feed the negroes who flee to us for refuge" on top of clothing and transportation shortages, military movements would bog down. "A perfect stampede of contrabands" confronted William S. Rosecrans, who was preparing to advance against enemy positions. Rosecrans sent them behind his lines to shield them from guerillas, complaining, "But what a burden what shall be done with them then."[30]

At first Grant tried to make use of the refugees, putting them to work in the Corinth fortifications. He sent the women and children to campsites east of Corinth and asked Secretary of War Edwin M. Stanton what he should do next. Some people in Chicago thought they would make excellent servants, a practice Stanton permitted for nearly a month until an adverse reaction in the Midwest, encouraged by electioneering Democrats, forced him to rescind the order.[31] Grant then decided to establish camps for the blacks and to let them bring in the cotton and corn crops under his supervision. They would live off the land, receive wages for their work, and strive toward providing for themselves. The Union authorities would exercise a form of guardianship over the refugees, for Grant did not believe that blacks fresh from slavery were prepared to take on the responsibilities of freedom immediately. He sought to provide them with

some means of making the transition. His plan would allow him to provide for all blacks entering Union lines, not only the males able to work for the army.

Grant explained his reasoning to Chaplain Eaton, whom he had placed in charge of the project. Racial prejudice, Grant believed, was fundamentally a product of mistaken beliefs about behavior. One of those beliefs held by many whites was that blacks would not work of their own free will. Grant's plan would allow blacks to refute that stereotype. Once blacks assisting the military and working on the plantations had proved that they were responsible, whites would begin to accept the idea of handing a musket to a black man, and blacks could enlist in the Union army. And once blacks had fought for their freedom and demonstrated again that they were responsible and hard-working, whites could begin to entertain the idea of granting citizenship, even the ballot, to blacks. "Never before in those early and bewildering days had I heard the problem of the future of the Negro attacked so vigorously and with such humanity combined with practical good sense," Eaton recalled.[32]

Grant, who had once believed that the military should not interfere with slavery, now was pushing a plan of de facto emancipation, using military supervision to oversee the transition from slavery to freedom. It also reflected his belief that racial prejudice was best countered and conquered by actual demonstrations of its falsehoods. If his plan was paternalistic, at least it held out the prospect of progressive change. Of course, it also provided a solution to the problems of conducting military operations while disposing of a potential disaster by promising relief from the disease-ridden conditions currently confronting the freedmen. Grant took an active interest in Eaton's progress, ordering supplies and assistance whenever needed, and making sure that his subordinates followed suit.[33]

Perhaps the most notable aspects of Grant's solution to the refugee problem was that, for once, he acted without asking his superiors for advice. Not until four days after he had ordered Eaton's appointment did Grant tell Halleck what

he was doing and ask for instructions. Halleck, too busy to be bothered by these problems, approved of Grant's policy, although he had only a vague idea of what his subordinate was doing. In fact, the Lincoln administration seemed more interested in taking steps which would halt Grant's plans in their tracks. On September 22, 1862, Lincoln had made public a preliminary version of the Emancipation Proclamation, promising that he would put it into force on January 1, 1863. He sought to take advantage of those hundred days to encourage Tennesseans to reenter the Union on their own, holding out the prospect that if the Volunteer State returned it could do so with slavery intact, since the proclamation applied only to areas under Confederate control. On October 21, 1862, Lincoln informed both Grant and military governor Andrew Johnson of his plan. He wanted them to hold elections for congressmen wherever they could do so. The President hoped that Tennesseans would rejoin the Union "to avoid the unsatisfactory prospect before them."[34]

Grant, who once had held high hopes for the prospect of a speedy reunion, was skeptical of Lincoln's plan. Months before he had heard reports of Unionist speakers such as Emerson Etheridge being mobbed by Rebels; certainly the actions of Memphis's residents struck a telling blow against stories of latent Unionism. Now guerrilla bands were firing on Union steamers with civilians on board. Sherman suggested various ways to punish the guerrillas; Grant approved the expulsion of secessionist families as adequate retaliation. Other policies suggested an intensification of the war effort. With fall came reports of families suffering from a lack of food and shelter. Grant, convinced that those "not actively engaged in rebellion should not be allowed to suffer" amidst plenty, decided that "the burden of furnishing the necessary relief . . . should fall on those, who, by act, encouragement or sympathy have caused the want now experienced." Some of the troops agreed. They were tired of guarding secessionist property: one private wrote that it made his regiment "squirm like a Sarpent." He concluded that there were "few if any

Union men" in the area. Another veteran later remarked that the troops believed by now that "they did not go South to protect Confederate property."[35]

Nevertheless, Grant was not one to question presidential policy. On December 9, 1862, he issued a proclamation to the people of west Tennessee calling for elections in the 8th, 9th, and 10th Congressional districts. All "legal voters" as of 1860 were permitted to participate in the balloting, which would take place on Christmas Eve. Grant was more impressed with the sentiments displayed by the Mississippians, who "show more signs of being subdued than any we have heretofore come across." A reporter noted that many Mississippians wanted to reenter the Union "at whatever cost" before Lincoln's proclamation came into play.[36]

Confederate forces under Nathan Bedford Forrest and Earl Van Dorn had no intention of allowing the election to proceed. They launched an offensive that not only disrupted an attempt by Grant to take Vicksburg but also made it impossible to hold elections. Grant was too busy conducting military operations to take much notice. Attempts at reestablishing loyal governments were futile until military operations rendered territory secure from guerrillas. As the new year started, Grant instructed Brigadier General Stephen A. Hurlbut, commanding at Memphis, to transfer ten secessionist families to Confederate lines for every guerrilla raid launched by the enemy. The general's patience was wearing thin, and protecting his supply lines against cavalry thrusts and armed bands sapped too much energy, time, and men from offensive operations.[37]

But guerrillas proved to be only one of the problems disrupting Grant's control of his own lines. Despite Eaton's project, the flood of refugees threatened to overwhelm Union camps. As Grant reestablished his position around Corinth and Memphis, he sought help from Halleck. "Contraband question becoming serious one," he telegraphed the general-in-chief. "What will I do with surplus negroes?" He glimpsed one possible solution as he shifted his forces to the west bank of the Mississippi opposite Vicksburg in the aftermath of his

failed December offensive. It had long been a favorite belief of Union commanders that if the course of the river was diverted through the construction of a canal, Vicksburg, stripped of its western water barrier, would be rendered vulnerable. Grant, although somewhat skeptical, was willing to try the idea himself, using blacks to do the work. The project illustrated Grant's priorities. The problem presented by black refugees was first and foremost a military problem. Their presence obstructed military movements, disrupted camps, and promised to increase disease and disorder. Grant spared his soldiers of these risks as well as lessened the burden of digging trenches in the dirty swamps by employing black laborers. Military needs having been met, other concerns took over, as Grant worried about the conditions under which the blacks worked.[38]

But this solution was at best a stopgap measure. Nothing seemed to stop the influx of refugees. On February 12, 1863, Grant decided to issue an order excluding blacks from his lines. Soldiers were instructed to stop "enticing" blacks to enter Union camps; freedmen should remain on their plantations and work out a labor arrangement with the planters. "Humanity dictates this policy," he explained to Halleck. "Planters have mostly deserted their plantations taking with them all their able bodied negroes and leaving the old and very young. Here they could not have shelter nor assurances of transportation when we leave." The army was simply not equipped materially or mentally to take on any more freed men. As Grant told one subordinate, "the question is a troublesome one. I am not permitted to send them out of the department, and such numbers as we have it is hard to keep them in."[39]

Unfortunately for Grant, he was caught once more by a shift in administration policy. Halleck told Grant that reports had reached the War Department "that many of the officers of your command not only discourage the negroes from coming under our protection, but, by ill-treatment, force them to return to their masters." Obviously Grant's exclusion order had not gone over well with

the top brass. "This is not only bad policy in itself," Halleck continued, "but is directly opposed to the policy adopted by the government." In the wake of the Emancipation Proclamation, Washington decided to make war in earnest. Halleck—whose General Orders No. 3 in 1861 had epitomized the conservative attitude toward blacks—justified the new approach. "The character of the war has very much changed within the last year. There is now no possible hope of a reconciliation with the rebels. The union party in the south is virtually destroyed. There can be no peace but that which is enforced by the sword. We must conquer the rebels, or be conquered by them."[40]

With this acceptance of a total war approach against the Confederacy came new attitudes toward the treatment of black slaves by the Union army. It is the policy of the government to withdraw from the enemy as much productive labor as possible," Halleck explained, preaching with the passion of the recently converted. "Every slave withdrawn from the enemy, is equivalent to a white man put *hors de combat.*" Freedmen were to be used "so far as practicable as a military force for the defence of forts, depots, &c. . . . And it is the opinion of many who have examined the question without passion or prejudice, that they can also be used as a military force." Grant was instructed to assist this process by using his "official and personal influence to remove prejudices on this subject," and to assist General Lorenzo Thomas in efforts to organize black regiments."[41]

War had become revolution, taking the very path which Grant had outlined to Eaton the previous November. To arm ex-slaves was to make real the greatest fear of many a white Southerner by equipping blacks with the means to achieve revenge. Grant, who had grown weary of previous attempts at reconciliation, welcomed the change. "Rebellion has assumed that shape now that it can only terminate by the complete subjugation of the South or the overthrow of the Government," he informed Major General Frederick Steele, instructing him to provide for all the black refugees already in his lines and to "encourage all negroes, particularly middle aged males to come within our lines," obviously with an eye toward recruiting them. Then Grant welcomed Thomas to headquarters and did all he could to facilitate his mission. "At least three of my Army Corps Commanders take hold of the new policy of arming the negroes and using them against the rebels with a will," he told Halleck, adding: "You may rely on my carrying out any policy ordered by proper authority to the best of my ability." When several officers tendered their resignations over the new policy, Grant recommended that they be dismissed from the service instead.[42]

While Thomas proceeded with his mission, Grant embarked on yet another campaign against Vicksburg. Crossing the Mississippi below the city, Grant's army won five battles within three weeks, destroyed several factories at Jackson, and laid seige to Vicksburg itself in one of the most brilliant campaigns of the war. His troops took the war to the Southern people. Grant instructed commanders to make sure that their troops would "live as far as possible off the country through which they pass and destroy corn, wheat crops and everything that can be made use of by the enemy in prolonging the war. Mules and horses can be taken to supply all our wants and where it does not cause too much delay agricultural implements may be destroyed. In other words cripple the rebellion in every way."[43]

During the seige he received news that Thomas's recruits had engaged in their first battle at Milliken's Bend, some twenty miles upriver from Vicksburg. At first giving way, the blacks launched a vicious counterattack, spurred on in part by reports that Confederates were murdering blacks taken prisoner in the initial assault. Milliken's Bend proved blacks could fight, and many whites who were skeptical of black enlistment were won over when they heard accounts of the clash. Grant himself was pleased, endorsing the report of the Union commander at the battle with the comment that while the soldiers "had but little experience in the use of fire arms" they had been "most gallant and I doubt not but with good officers they will make good troops."[44]

But in the aftermath of the battle stories began to surface that the Confederates had executed captured black soldiers. Initially Grant was unsure whether such acts had official Confederate sanction, or if they had been perpetrated by "irresponsible persons"; but additional reports suggested that Confederate General Richard Taylor had approved the measures. Grant told Taylor that if the Confederates were initiating a policy, "I will accept the issue. It may be you propose a different line of policy towards Black troops and Officers commanding them to that practiced towards White troops? If so," Grant added, "I can assure you that these colored troops are regularly mustered into the service of the United States," and all Union authorities "are bound to give the same protection to these troops that they do to any other troops." Such a statement had revolutionary implications, for now Grant was demanding that prisoners in blue uniforms be treated equally, whether their skin was black or white. While Taylor denied the stories, he pointed out that all black prisoners would be turned over to state authorities in accordance with Confederate policy. Grant, accepting Taylor's denial of responsibility, was not so gracious about Confederate policy toward black POWs, commenting that "I cannot see the justice of permitting one treatment for them, and another for the white soldiers." But the exchange proved Grant's willingness to accept the notion that equal treatment followed naturally from emancipation, an idea which promised to transform American society.[45]

By the summer of 1863 Ulysses S. Grant's thoughts on the relationship between slavery, war, and reunion had undergone a drastic change from the ones he voiced during his early weeks of field command. He had always assumed that slavery would be a casualty of the war, but his initial passivity toward "the peculiar institution," fueled by a desire to achieve a quick and painless peace based on reconciliation, had given way in the face of fierce Confederate resistance. Once it had become obvious that the war would be long, Grant grasped that Union military operations would help turn it into a social and economic revolution by disturbing the very foundation of Southern society. Moreover, he now welcomed that challenge. To Lincoln he explained that he was giving "the subject of arming black troops my hearty support." The enlistment of blacks, "with the emancipation of the negro, is the heavyest blow yet given the Confederacy.... By arming the negro we have added a powerful ally. They will make good soldiers and taking them from the enemy weaken him in the same proportion they strengthen us."[46]

Such measures signalled the death of slavery. "The people of the North need not quarrel over the institution of Slavery," Grant reassured Washburne. "What Vice President Stevens [Alexander H. Stephens] acknowledges the corner stone of the Confederacy is already knocked out. Slavery is already dead and cannot be resurrected. It would take a Standing army to maintain slavery in the South" now. Then Grant injected a personal note. "I never was an Abolitionest, [not even what could be called anti slavery," he admitted, "but ... it became patent to my mind early in the rebellion that the North & South could never live at peace with each other except as one nation, and that without Slavery." To save the Union, one must first destroy slavery. Any other settlement would be flawed. With that in mind, he argued that no peace should be concluded "until this question is forever settled." War had become revolution, and Ulysses S. Grant had been both witness and participant in the process. As he told a committee of Memphis unionists, he, like they, had come to "acknowledge human liberty as the only true foundation of human government."[47]

Notes

1. On Grant and slavery see Brooks D. Simpson, "Butcher? Racist? An Examination of William S. McFeely's *Grant: A Biography,*" *Civil War History* 33 (March 1987), 63–83.
2. Ulysses S. Grant to Frederick Dent, April 19, 1861, in John Y. Simon, ed., *The Papers of Ulysses S. Grant,* 16 vols. to date (Carbondale, Ill.: Southern Illinois University Press, 1967–88), 2:3–4.
3. Ulysses S. Grant to Mary Grant, April 29, 1861, ibid., 2:13–14; Grant to Jesse Root Grant, May 6, 1861, ibid., 2:21–22. In fact,

Grant expressed some concern lest slaves rise up in insurrection against their masters.

4. Ulysses S. Grant to Julia Dent Grant, July 19, 1861, ibid., 2:72–73.

5. Ulysses S. Grant to Julia Dent Grant, August 3, 1861, ibid., 2:82–83; Grant to Jesse Root Grant, August 3, 1861, ibid., 2:80–81.

6. Ulysses S. Grant to Mary Grant, August 12, 1861, ibid., 2:105; Grant to John C. Kelton, August 14, 1861, ibid., 2:111; Grant to William H. Worthington, August 26, 1861, ibid., 2:139–40.

7. Ulysses S. Grant to John C. Kelton, August 30, 1861, ibid., 2:154–55.

8. Dudley Taylor Cornish, *The Sable Arm: Negro Troops in the Union Army, 1861–1865* (New York: Norton, 1966), 12–15; John Cook to Ulysses S. Grant, September 11, 1861, Simon, ed., *Grant Papers,* 2:220, and Grant to Cook, September 12, 1861, ibid., 2:243–44. Frémont issued a new proclamation on September 11 in line with Lincoln's policy.

9. Ulysses S. Grant, "Proclamation," September 6, 1861, and Grant to E. A. Paine, September 6, 1861. ibid., 194–95.

10. Ulysses S. Grant to Lorenzo Thomas, September 21, 1861, ibid., 2:291 and annotation.

11. Kenneth Williams, *Lincoln Finds A General,* 5 vols. (New York: Macmillan, 1949–59), 3:106–12.

12. Ulysses S. Grant to Jesse Root Grant, November 27, 1861, Simon, ed., *Grant Papers,* 3:227.

13. Ulysses S. Grant to John L. Cook, December 25, 1861, ibid., 3:342–43; William S. Hillyer (Grant staff officer) to L. F. Ross, January 5, 1862, ibid., 3:373–74; Charles F. Smith to Grant, January 4, 1862, ibid., 3:431.

14. James Grant Wilson, *Life and Public Services of Ulysses Simpson Grant* (New York: De Witt, 1885), 24.

15. Ulysses S. Grant to E. A. Paine, January 11, 19, 1862, Simon, ed., *Grant Papers,* 4:32, 68–69.

16. Henry W. Halleck to Ulysses S. Grant, February 8, 1862, and Grant to Halleck, February 11, 1862, ibid., 4:193–94; General orders No. 46, Department of the Missouri, February 22, 1862, ibid., 4:291; Grant to McClernand, February 18, 1862, ibid., 4:243; Grant to J. C. Kelton, February 22, 1862, ibid., 4:267–68; Grant to McClernand, February 22, 1862, ibid., 4:470.

17. General Orders No. 14, District of West Tennessee, February 26, 1862, ibid., 4:290–91; Grant to Elihu B. Washburne, March 22, 1862, ibid., 4:408; Grant to Philip B. Fouke, March 16, 1862, ibid., 4:377; Grant to Marcellus M. Crocker, March 17, 1862, ibid., 4:384; Grant to William T. Sherman, March 17, 1862, 4:382–83.

18. Ulysses S. Grant to Nathaniel H. McLean, March 31, 1862, ibid., 4:454; Philip B. Fouke to Grant, March 30, 1862, ibid., 4:454.

19. Ulysses S. Grant to George W. Cullum, February 23, 25, 1862, ibid., 4:276, 286; Grant to William T. Sherman, February 25, 1862, 4:289; Grant to Philip B. Fouke, March 16, 1862, ibid., 4:377; Grant to Nathaniel H. McLean, March 15, 30, 1862, ibid., 4:368, 447–48; Grant to Julia Dent Grant, March 18, 1862, ibid., 4:389; Ulysses S. Grant, *Personal Memoirs of U.S. Grant,* 2 vols. (New York: Charles L. Webster and Co., 1885–86), 1:368–69.

20. Ulysses S. Grant to Julia Dent Grant, June 12, 1862, Simon, ed., *Grant Papers,* 5:142–43; Kittoe to Washburne, June 24, 1862, Lloyd Lewis–Bruce Catton Research Notes, Ulysses S. Grant Association, Southern Illinois University.

21. Grant to Elihu B. Washburne, June 19, 1862, Simon, ed., *Grant Papers,* 5:146; Grant to William S. Hillyer, July 1, 1862, ibid., 5:181–82 and annotation; General Orders No. 60, District of West Tennessee, July 3, 1862, ibid., 5:190–91 and annotation.

22. "Union" to Grant, July 12, 1862, William S. Hillyer Papers, University of Virginia; see Simon, ed., *Grant Papers,* 5:192–94.

23. Seymour D. Thompson, *Recollections with the Third Iowa Regiment* (Cincinnati, 1864), 275; William P. Lyon, *Reminiscences of the Civil War* (San Jose, Calif.: Muirson and Wright, 1907), 53; Kittoe to Washburne, June 24, 1862, Lewis-Catton Research Notes, Ulysses S. Grant Association.

24. Ulysses S. Grant to Elihu B. Washburne, June 19, 1862, Simon, ed., *Grant Papers,* 5:146; Grant to Halleck, July 19, 1862, and Halleck to Grant, July 19, 1862, ibid., 5:218–19. See also Grant to Halleck, July 8[7], 1862, ibid., 5:199.

25. Herman Belz, *Emancipation and Equal Rights: Politics and Constitutionalism in the Civil War Era* (New York: Norton, 1978), 36–40; General Orders No. 72, District of West Tennessee, August 11, 1862, Simon, ed., *Grant Papers,* 5:273–74; Halleck to Grant, August 2, 1862, ibid., 5:243–44.

26. Grant to Halleck, July 28, 1862, and Halleck to Grant, August 2, 1862, ibid., 5:243–44; Grant to William W. Rosecrans, August 10, 1862, ibid., 5:282; Grant to Isaac F. Quinby, July 26, 1862, ibid., 5:238–41; Grant to Salmon P. Chase, July 31, 1862, ibid., 5:255–56; Grant to Rosecrans, August 7, 1862, ibid., 5:271; Sherman to Chase, August 11, 1862, quoted in John B. Walters, *Merchant of Terror: General Sherman and Total War* (Indianapolis: Bobbs-Merrill, 1973), 57–58.

27. Washburne to Grant, July 25, 1862, Simon, ed., *Grant Papers,* 5:226.

28. Grant to Jesse Root Grant, August 3, 1862, ibid., 5:264; General Orders No. 72, District of West Tennessee, August 11, 1862, ibid., 5:273–74; Stephen Ambrose, ed., *A Wisconsin Boy in Dixie: The Selected Letters of John K. Newton* (Madison. Wis.: The University of Wisconsin Press, 1961), 27–28.

29. Grant to Mary Grant, August 19, 1862, Simon, ed., *Grant Papers* 5:311.

30. Samuel H. M. Byers, *With Fire and Sword* (New York: Neale, 1911), 45; John Eaton, *Grant, Lincoln, and the Freedmen* (New York: Longmans, Green and Co., 1907), 2; William T. Sherman to John Sherman, September 3, 1862, William T. Sherman Papers, LC; Rosecrans to Grant, September 10, 1862, Simon, ed., *Grant Papers,* 6:32.

31. Grant to Thomas J. McKean, September 16, 1862, ibid., 6:54; James M. Tuttle to Edwin M. Stanton, September 18, 1862, ibid., 6:317; V. Jacque Voegeli, *Free But Not Equal: The Midwest and the Negro During the Civil War* (Chicago: University of Chicago Press, 1967), 60–61.

32. Eaton, *Grant, Lincoln, and the Freedmen,* 9–15.

33. Ibid., 18–32. For additional discussion about Grant, Eaton, and the development of this policy at Corinth and at Davis Bend, Mississippi, which Grant hoped would become "a negro paradise," see Cam Walker: "Corinth: The Story of a Contraband Camp," *Civil War History* 20 (March 1974), 5–22; Steven J. Ross, "Freed Soil, Freed Labor, Freed Men: John Eaton and the Davis Bend Experiment," *Journal of Southern History* 44 (May 1978), 213–32; Louis S. Gerteis, *From Contraband to Freedman: Federal Policy Toward Southern Blacks, 1861–1865* (Westport, Conn.: Greenwood Press, 1973); and Janet Sharp Hermann, *The Pursuit of a Dream* (New York: Oxford University Press, 1981), 37–60.

34. Grant to Halleck, November 15, 1862, and Halleck to Grant, November 16, 1862, Simon, ed., *Grant Papers,* 6:315; Lincoln to Johnson and Grant, October 21, 1862, ibid., 7:3.

35. General Orders No. 4, Department of the Tennessee, November 3, 1862, ibid., 6:252–53; William W. Lowe to John A. Rawlins, August 18, 1862, ibid., 5:314; John W. Brinsfield, "The Military Ethics of General William T. Sherman: A Reassessment," *Parameters,* Vol. 12, No. 2 (1980), 42; Fred A. Shannon, ed., *The Civil War Letters of Sergeant Onley Andrus* (Urbana: University of Illinois Press, 1947), 25–26; Bruce Catton, *Grant Moves South* (Boston: Little, Brown, 1960), 336.

36. Ulysses S. Grant, "Proclamation," December 9, 1862, Simon, ed., *Grant Papers* 7:3–4; Grant to Halleck, December 14, 1862, ibid., 7:31–32; Thomas W. Knox, *Camp-Fire and Cotton-Field* (New York: Blelock and Co., 1865), 233.

37. Grant to Steven A. Hurlbut, January 3, 1863, Simon, ed., *Grant Papers,* 7:167–68.

38. Grant to Halleck, January 6, 1863, ibid., 7:186; Grant to George W. Deitzler, February 2. 1863, ibid., 7:278; Eaton, *Grant, Lincoln and the Freedmen,* 44.

39. Special Field Orders No. 2, Department of the Tennessee, February 12, 1863, ibid., 7:339; Grant to Halleck, February 18, 1863, ibid., 7:338, Catton, *Grant Moves South,* 401–2.

40. Halleck to Grant, March 30, 1863, Simon, ed., *Grant Papers,* 8:93n.

41. Halleck to Grant, March 30, 1863, ibid., 8:93n.

42. Grant to Frederick Steele, April 11, 1863, ibid., 8:49; Grant to Halleck, April 19, 1863, ibid., 91–92.

43. Grant to Stephen A. Hurlbut, May 5, 1863, ibid., 8:159–60.

44. Cornish, *The Sable Arm,* 144–45; Grant to Lorenzo Thomas, June 16, 1863, Simon, ed., *Grant Papers* 8:328.

45. Grant to Richard Taylor, June 22, 1863, ibid., 400–401 and annotation; Grant to Taylor, July 4, 1863, ibid., 468–69 and annotation. [Grant was unaware of Federal policy on the treatment of black prisoners of war, expressed in General Orders No. 100, issued April 24. Lincoln, perhaps because of this incident, issued an executive order on July 30, promising to retaliate in kind if Confederate officials mistreated black prisoners.] Cornish, *The Sable Arm,* 165–68.

46. Grant to Lincoln, August 23, 1863, Simon, ed., *Grant Papers,* 9:196.

47. Grant to Washburne, August 30, 1863, ibid., 9:217–18; Grant to Rue Hough and others, August 26, 1863, ibid., 9:203.

Lee's Greatest Victory

*During three days in May 1863, the Confederate leader took astonishing
risks to win one of the most skillfully conducted battles in history.
But the cost turned out to be too steep.*

by Robert K. Krick

The ability of Robert E. Lee and Thomas J. ("Stonewall") Jackson never showed itself more vividly than during three days of battle in May 1863 around a rustic crossroads called Chancellorsville. At the battle's denouement, which might be considered the highest tide of the Confederacy, the two Virginians capped a reversal of fortunes as dramatic as any recorded in more than three centuries of American military affairs.

*Joseph Hooker had
stolen a march on Lee
as completely as
anyone did during the
entire war.*

During the last day of April the Federal commander Joseph Hooker had stolen a march on Lee as completely as anyone did during the entire war. In an amazing strategic initiative Hooker took his army far around Lee's left, across two rivers, and into an admirable position around Chancellorsville. His fellow general George G. Meade, a saturnine man and no admirer of Joseph Hooker when in the sunniest of moods, exclaimed jubilantly on April 30: "Hurrah for old Joe! We're on Lee's flank and he doesn't know it."

The army with which Joe Hooker stole his march on Lee was a tough, veteran aggregation that had suffered from ill use at the hands of a series of inadequate leaders. Most recently Ambrose E. Burnside had butchered more than twelve thousand of his brave men in a hopeless attack near Fredericksburg the preceding December. Earlier the Army of the Potomac had endured mishandling from a boastful bully named John Pope, whose tenure in command was numbered in days, not in months, and the brilliant but timid George B. McClellan had led the same regiments to the brink of victory—but never quite over the threshold—on famous fields in Virginia and Maryland.

General Hooker's rise to high rank during the war grew from a blend of training at West Point and experience in Mexico, with more than a tincture of political maneuvering. Bravery under fire in the 1862 campaigns won the general a name for valor and the nickname Fight-ing Joe. (According to some accounts the catchy name was coined by accident when two newspaper headlines—THE FIGHTING and JOE HOOKER—overlapped in some fashion.) Hooker had shamelessly schemed against Burnside, motivated in part by a wholesome distaste for Burnside's ineptitude but also by a powerful degree of personal ambition.

Abraham Lincoln concluded in January 1863 that Burnside must go and reluctantly identified Hooker as the officer to inherit the mantle. In a patient and appropriately famous letter the President bluntly informed Hooker that he was appointing him despite the "great wrong to the country" inherent in his behavior toward Burnside. "I have heard, in such way as to believe it," Lincoln continued, "of your recently saying that both the Army and the Government needed a Dictator. Of course it was not for this, but in spite of it, that I have given you the command. Only those generals who gain success, can set up dictators. What I now ask of you is military success, and I will risk the dictatorship."

During the three months between Hooker's appointment and the onset of the campaigning season, Lincoln must have been very much gratified by the accomplishments of his

From *American Heritage*, March 1990, pp. 66-79. © 1990 by Forbes, Inc. Reprinted by permission of *American Heritage* magazine, a division of Forbes, Inc.

new commander. A contemporary wrote that Hooker when young was a "very expert" baseball player, who could "take a ball from almost in front of the bat, so eager, active and dexterous were his movements." When applied to military administration, that same controlled zeal made the Army of the Potomac a much improved military implement. Joe Hooker ironed ineptitude and indolence out of the medical services, flogged quartermaster and commissary functions into a fine pitch of efficiency, revitalized the cavalry arm, and inaugurated an intelligence-gathering system far ahead of its time in that staff-poor era. The soldiers noticed the changes and took heart from them.

The men also relished their new commander's reputation as a profane, hard-drinking sort of fellow. "Our leader is Joe Hooker, he takes his whiskey strong," they sang in admiration of one of the general's two most widely mooted social traits. The other rumored trait resulted in a persistent tradition that remains in circulation to this day. General Hooker's campaign to tighten up the Army of the Potomac extended to controlling the prostitution that flourished on its fringes. Supposedly the general's name somehow became an appellation for the quarry of the overworked provost detachments enforcing his order. Joe Hooker's own reputation as a womanizer fed the story conveniently. Firm evidence that the etymology of the word hooker antedates 1863 by more than a decade has done little to check the legend.

Hooker's ranking subordinates by and large did not share the enthusiasm of the men in the ranks. The officer corps of the Old Army was a generally conservative body, both politically and morally. One immediate subordinate, the intensely pious O. O. Howard, doubtless felt particularly uneasy about Hooker, and Hooker reciprocated. Soon after the war he told an interviewer that Howard was "a good deal more" qualified to "command a prayer meeting" than an army corps. "He was always a woman among troops," said Hooker. "If he was not born in petticoats, he ought to have been, and ought to wear them. He was always taken up with Sunday Schools and the temperance cause."

Other corps commanders of note included George G. Meade and Daniel E. Sickles. General Meade, the snappish patrician who was destined to replace Hooker, seems in retrospect the most capable man who wore Union general's stars in the war's Eastern theater. Dan Sickles, by contrast, was a bawdy, rambunctious adventurer. Three years before Chancellorsville he escaped conviction for the public murder of his wife's lover on the then novel ground of temporary insanity. After the war he served as intermittent paramour to the queen of Spain.

Federal operations at Chancellorsville suffered dramatically from two absences. Much of Hooker's cavalry spent the crucial days on a largely irrelevant raid, leaving the main army bereft of its essential screening-and-reconnaissance function. Worse, the army's enormously capable chief of artillery, Henry J. Hunt, was off in a rear area, where Hooker had consigned him after the two had quarreled.

The men of the Army of Northern Virginia benefited from any number of subjective advantages over their familiar foemen of the Army of the Potomac, but no Southerner could help worrying over the apparent disparity of force. Although no one knew enemy strengths with precision—and, in fact, often neither side could firmly establish its own strength—Federals north of the Rappahannock clearly had a vast preponderance in numbers. The actual figures approximated 130,000 against 60,000.

The Northern army brought seven corps to the field of Chancellorsville. The Confederates countered with two, and one of the two was at less than one-half of its strength. The missing divisions had gone southeastward to the vicinity of Suffolk, Virginia, in quest of the foodstuffs that already dwindled at an alarming rate. The question now was whether the agrarian South could feed its armies on its own soil.

The two supporting arms that came up short for Hooker at Chancellorsville never looked better on Lee's side of the line than they did in that spring of 1863. The colorful Southern cavalry general James E. B. Stuart, universally called Jeb after his initials, stood at the height of his personal and professional powers,

tirelessly alert and active and energetic. As for the Southern artillery, it continued to labor under tremendous disadvantages in weaponry and ammunition but during the past winter had revolutionized its tactics by converting to a battalion system. Since the first whiff of gunpowder, cannon had suffered from the tendency of infantry officers to misuse the big guns simply as larger infantry weapons. In 1861 batteries assigned to brigades fought under infantry direction, often from positions at either end of the line. High ground, low ground, heavy enemy pressure, or no enemy pressure, it was all the same: Put the guns with the infantry. But now Confederate artillery would move and fight in clusters, usually of at least four four-gun batteries, and the higher-ranking artillerymen commanding these larger clusters would enjoy some degree of autonomy. Some of the South's brightest and best young men rode at the head of the reorganized guns.

Federal horsemen attempted to open the campaign that led to the Battle of Chancellorsville at the end of the second week in April. Gen. George Stoneman, commanding Hooker's cavalry, was to take the greater part of the available mounted force and cross the Rappahannock far upstream northwest of Fredericksburg, Virginia. The horse soldiers, Hooker hoped, would ricochet with deadly effect through Confederate rear areas, freeing Federal prisoners, tearing up railroads, breaking an aqueduct on the James River, and forcing a frightened Lee to fall back from Fredericksburg. In the event, heavy rains sluiced the bottoms out of Virginia's clay roads, and the raiding force did not cross the Rappahannock until April 29, after a substantial portion of Hooker's infantry had done so. Still, it is hard to avoid blaming the delay as much on Stoneman as on uncooperative weather.

Once launched, the cavalry raid caromed almost aimlessly about central Virginia, causing some localized discomfort but achieving not a thing of real military worth. Stuart detached just enough regiments to contain the raid within certain wide limits, harassing its rear and flanks and gathering in stragglers. One of the interesting reflections modern students draw from the Chancellorsville campaign is that the Federal cavalry raid, prudently checked by just the right number of Confederates, presaged in mirror image the cavalry situation a few weeks later at Gettysburg. There Stuart wasted his substance in a meaningless raid while his army fought blindly, and the Federals reacted prudently. It was as though the Federals had gone to school at Chancellorsville on the apt use of the mounted arm, with Stuart as teacher.

In the last two days of April, Hooker brought to a successful conclusion the huge turning maneuver that placed the center of his flanking element at the country crossroads of Chancellorsville. That polysyllabic name, whose ending suggests a busy settlement, actually belonged to a single building. The Chancellor kin who built the heart of the structure late in the eighteenth century expanded it into a wayside inn opened in 1815. By 1860 two additions had swelled the building into a really sizable structure, but dwindling traffic on the roads that met in the yard had reduced its function to that of a one-family residence. The Chancellors called their home Chancellorsville in the same fashion that other Southern homes were called Mount Vernon or Belle Hill. No one else lived within a half-mile of the crossroads, and only a few within several miles.

An environmental feature that contributed to Chancellorsville's meager dimensions also levied a heavy impact on military operations nearby. The land lay largely desolate under the dense, scrubby growth of a region known as the Wilderness of Spotsylvania. About seventy square miles of the Wilderness sprawled along the south bank of the Rapidan and Rappahannock rivers, stretching about three miles farther south than Chancellorsville and about two miles farther east. A numerically superior army ensnarled in those thickets, and confined to easy maneuver only on the few poor roads, would lose much of its advantage.

Joe Hooker pushed the head of his mighty army eastward to the edge of the Wilderness early on Friday, May 1, 1863. About three miles from the Chancellorsville crossroads the Federals came face-to-face with a commanding wrinkle of the earth's surface, atop which stood a little wooden Baptist church bearing the name of Zoan. The Zoan Church ridge represented about as succulent a military prize as Joe Hooker could have found just then in his zone of operations. It was high ground (none higher to the east, short of Europe); it straddled a key road; and most important, it rose on open ground just east of the entangling tendrils of the Wilderness.

Confederates on top of the prize ridge had been feverishly digging earthworks overnight on the orders of the division commander Richard H. Anderson. Despite the trenches, Hooker could have dislodged Anderson's relative handful of men and occupied Zoan Church without much exertion. Perhaps he would have, had not Stonewall Jackson ridden into the uncertain tableau and dominated the unfolding action with his force of personality. Stonewall ordered Anderson's men to pack their entrenching equipment and attack. Anderson left no account of his reaction, but he must have wondered how he and Jackson and a few assorted regiments could accomplish much.

As Jackson began pressing against the Northerners lapping around the western base of the ridge, he used two critically important parallel roads. The old Orange Turnpike came out of Fredericksburg past Zoan, through Spotsylvania County, and then on to Orange County and Orange Courthouse. About a decade before the Civil War local entrepreneurs had undertaken to supplant that century-old thoroughfare with a toll road paved on one of its lanes with planks. Elsewhere in the vicinity men of vision were putting their money into railroads; but trains and their trappings required vast capital outlay, and the plank-road people reasoned that everyone owned wheeled wagons already.

The brand-new Orange Plank Road proved to be a wretched idea economically, but in May 1863 it drew troops of both sides like a magnet because it formed a second usable corridor through the Wilderness. Hooker had moved east on both the Turnpike and the Plank Road, which near Zoan Church ran generally parallel to and a mile or so south of the older right-of-way. As the morning wore on, Confederates pushed west against both heads of Hooker's army on the two roads.

Hooker had collapsed within himself, and now he began inexorably pulling his mighty army down with him.

Jackson, soon joined by Lee in person, superintended an almost chaotic blend of Confederate regiments and brigades in the advance. Southern units arriving from various points funneled off into the Turnpike or the Plank Road at Jackson's whim and in response to unfolding exigencies, without much regard for command and control at levels below the corps commander in person. Their élan and their leader's determination were steadily reclaiming the ground of the earlier Federal advance when yet another transportation corridor swung the action entirely into the Confederate column.

Just before the war more prescient investors had founded and funded a railroad to run from Fredericksburg out to Orange and into fertile Piedmont Virginia. By the time the conflict halted work, the route had been surveyed and the line graded. The level stretch of cuts and fills and grades lay uncluttered by even the first stringers or rails, but it constituted a convenient third passage through the Wilderness. The unfinished railroad ran westward, parallel to the two wagon roads and about a mile south of the Plank Road. Gen. A. R. ("Rans") Wright's brigade, three regiments and a battalion of infantry from Georgia, sliced ahead along that convenient conduit and forced a reorientation of the

Federal line by ninety degrees. Contending lines that had stretched for miles from north to south readjusted to Wright's lunge. Hooker's right swung up away from Wright and left the Federals at the end of the first day of battle (and the first day of May) arrayed in a huge, irregular, shallow V. The apex of the broad V lay at or near Chancellorsville while one arm ran northeast toward the river and the other sprawled west toward Wilderness Church. (See map.)

Hooker hoped halting his advance would "embolden the enemy to attack him." His wish came true.

Before Jackson and Wright buffeted his right, Hooker himself had squandered a wonderful opportunity on his left. The V Corps of the Army of the Potomac, ably led by Meade, began May 1 by moving steadily eastward along the River Road. This fourth east-west route curled far north of the Turnpike and the Plank Road and led eventually past Banks Ford on the river into Fredericksburg. Meade moved vigorously ahead until his skirmishes reached the vicinity of Mott's Run, within hailing distance of Banks Ford. Federals holding the southern mouth of that ford would serve a number of highly desirable ends. By that hour, however, Joe Hooker had recoiled from the presence of the legendary Stonewall Jackson with such abruptness that he sought no opportunities, only shelter. Hooker had collapsed within himself, and now he began inexorably pulling his mighty and well-tempered army down with him.

General Hooker dished out bravado loudly and often during the Chancellorsville campaign, but his boasts seem in retrospect to have been feeble attempts to brace up his own wavering spirits. On

the evening before his advance of May 1, Hooker drummed out a staccato general order assuring his men "that the operations of the last three days have determined that our enemy must either ingloriously fly or come out from behind his defenses and give us battle on our own ground, where certain destruction awaits him." There can be little doubt that Hooker really meant that. Lee surely would react to Hooker's clever and successful movement to Chancellorsville, and to the Federal cavalry roaming in his rear, by sidling south away from the unhappy combination facing him. Good ground on the North Anna River would allow the Confederates a chance to regroup and start over. Even after a century and a quarter it is difficult to come to grips with Lee's daring choice. At the time Hooker clearly was flabbergasted.

With a difficult May 1 behind him, Hooker blustered anew. "It's all right . . . I've got Lee just where I want him," the Federal commander insisted to an incredulous subordinate. At headquarters Hooker declared, "The rebel army is now the legitimate property of the Army of the Potomac." To another audience he said, "The enemy is in my power, and God Almighty cannot deprive me of them." And he finally summarized his professed contentment in a written circular to his corps commanders. "The major general commanding trusts," he wrote incautiously, "that a suspension in the attack to-day will embolden the enemy to attack him." The first three boasts proved to be empty, but Hooker's written wish came true with a vengeance.

Across the lines that evening of May 1 the Confederate commanders weighed the situation somewhat more judiciously. Just about a mile from Hooker's headquarters at Chancellorsville, Lee and Jackson crouched together over a small fire on seats improvised from abandoned U.S. cracker boxes. R. E. Lee, who had ridden up toward the river on his right in a personal reconnaissance during the afternoon, told Jackson that poor roads, steeply cut stream beds, and Federals dense on the ground combined to deny the Confederates any opportunity there.

The two men sent their respective engineer officers on a moonlit scout directly toward the enemy center at Chancellorsville. T. M. R. Talcott of Lee's staff later wrote vividly of that tense experience. His companion, J. Keith Boswell of Jackson's staff, had no chance to record his impressions; Boswell fell dead from a volley that struck him as he rode at Stonewall's side a few hours later. The two capable young men came back convinced that the Federal center offered no opening whatsoever for an assault.

Jackson had a last quiet word with his chief, then rode away. The two men never saw each other again.

Other young men scouting through the darkness of the Wilderness sent back reports through the night that gradually suggested a way to get at Hooker. It would be horribly risky under the circumstances, but perhaps Lee and Jackson might be able to snake a column westward all the way across the enemy's front, around his right, and clear up behind him. Stonewall's favorite preacher, Beverly Tucker Lacy, knew some of the ground in the western reaches of the Wilderness because his brother lived there. Charles Beverly Wellford, a veteran of the army and now running the family iron furnace just down the road, knew more of the ground. Catharine Furnace (named for the matriarch of the Wellford clan) burned charcoal in enormous volume and owned thousands of acres nearby from which to harvest charcoal wood. Jackson's mapmaker Jedediah Hotchkiss, a converted New York Yankee now as zealously Southern as any native, wandered the woods roads with Wellford and Lacy and came back

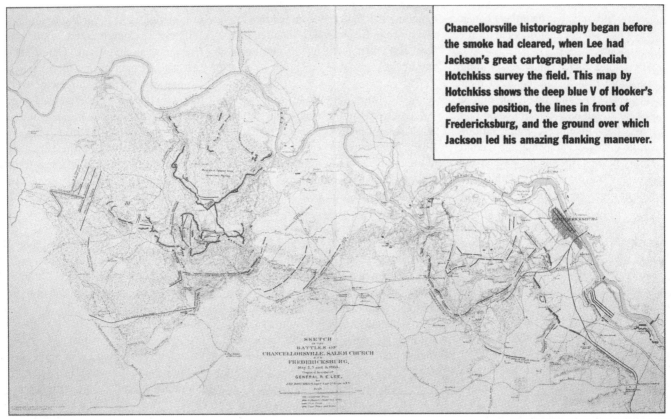

Chancellorsville historiography began before the smoke had cleared, when Lee had Jackson's great cartographer Jedediah Hotchkiss survey the field. This map by Hotchkiss shows the deep blue V of Hooker's defensive position, the lines in front of Fredericksburg, and the ground over which Jackson led his amazing flanking maneuver.

MAP DIVISION, NEW YORK PUBLIC LIBRARY

with some sketches. Jeb Stuart sent cavalry in the same direction under General Lee's boisterous twenty-seven-year-old nephew Fitzhugh Lee.

Very early on May 2 Lee reached his decision. Jackson would take two-thirds of the already heavily outnumbered Army of Northern Virginia and disappear on a daylong march over the horizon. With startling nonchalance the two commanders agreed that Lee would stand firm and act belligerent with no more than seventeen thousand men at his back while Jackson ventured far out on a limb with twice that many troops. An attack by Hooker of even moderate earnestness would simply destroy the Confederate army.

A rough pencil sketch of the roads showed that the desperate gamble might have a chance. Lee and Jackson and others pored over the map. At one point the army commander carefully arranged a handful of broomstraws on the edge of a box and then, by way of example to Jackson, swept them helter-skelter onto the ground. Jackson had a last quiet word with his chief, then rode away. R.

E. Lee and Stonewall Jackson never met again.

Lee at once set out upon the delicate mission of beguiling his opposite number. The tactical dogma of the day held that one or at most two companies of the ten that made up a regiment should go forward on skirmish or outpost duty. Those advance guards could give early warning of approaching enemy, fire a quick volley, and then scurry back to the

LIBRARY OF CONGRESS

Gen. Joseph Hooker, Lee's luckless adversary.

main line. Driving in hostile skirmishers was familiar business; so was finding their comrades behind them in a ratio of about nine to one. On May 2 Lee sent swarms of skirmishers toward the enemy, sometimes using all his men out in front, leaving no main line but creating the impression of great strength. Confederate units launched vigorous feints that Federals repulsed stoutly and with some smugness. Meanwhile, Jackson pushed on through the woods toward Hooker's rear, carrying a quiver full of thunderbolts.

Jackson's fabled flank march actually unfolded with far less stealth than any Confederate wanted. Barely one mile beyond the intersection where Lee and Jackson parted, the flanking column ran into its first taste of trouble. On high ground just before the road dropped into a bottom around Catharine Furnace, a gap in the woods allowed Federals a mile and a quarter away to see the Southerners moving steadily past the open space. Of course Northern artillery opened fire at the closely packed target; of course the Confederates double-timed past the hot spot. General Lee knew of this early difficulty, but then there began a long, tense silence that dragged on for endless hours.

The long-range shells spiraling across more than a mile annoyed their intended victims and no doubt hurt a few of them, but they constituted no real military impediment. A more serious threat gradually developed at the second milepost when Dan Sickles pushed his troops southward to the vicinity of Catharine Furnace to find out what all those moving Southerners were up to. Men of the 23d Georgia spread in an arc above the furnace as a flank guard fought against an increasing tide of Federals. The Georgians finally fell back to the cut of the same unfinished railroad that had played a role the day before in shaping the battle lines. By this time Jackson's entire infantry column had marched past. The Georgia regiment fell apart finally, and all but a handful of men became prisoners. Emory Fiske Best, the regiment's twenty-three-year-old colonel, was among those who escaped. A court-martial cashiered him just before Christmas, but his 23d Georgia had done well for a long time.

The bluecoats of Sickles's corps who captured the Georgians were pleased by their success, but in fact their prime quarry had eluded danger. The last two infantry brigades in Jackson's column turned back and easily repulsed any further advance by Sickles beyond the railroad. High open ground around the Wellford house, bisected by the narrow woods road climbing out of dense thickets, provided the Southern rear guard with a ready-made stronghold. The extensive trains of ambulances and ordnance wagons scheduled to follow Jackson's infantry avoided the furnace pressure point by detouring around it to the south and west on another set of primitive traces. Jackson was free to pursue his great adventure.

The narrowness of the wagon tracks Jackson followed toward his goal proved to be both a blessing and a curse. The Southern column needed secrecy, and the Wilderness that closed in all around provided it. But the column also needed to move fast, and that the primitive roads did not encourage. Even so,

Jackson's two-week-old circular about marching habits kept the march moving: two miles in fifty minutes, then ten minutes' rest, then do it again, and again, and again.

A little more than four miles from his starting point Stonewall Jackson reached the Brock Road. This was the main north-south route in the vicinity, and it led north around the enemy right. Jackson turned south. Someone attributed to Stonewall the military aphorism "Always mystify, mislead, and surprise the enemy." Moving the wrong way with almost thirty thousand men might accomplish that end, if anyone was watching. The wrong-way march lasted only long enough to cross two gentle ridgelines. Then Jackson turned off into the trees again on another set of woods tracks and angled northward parallel to the Brock Road.

Union men of the XI Corps whiled away their last moments of grace playing cards and writing letters.

Soldiers marching at the head of Jackson's corps rejoiced when, about two miles beyond the detour, they came to a small stream flowing across the road. Standing water dotted gullies throughout the Wilderness, but the stream supplied them with their first source of drinkable water along the route. It gurgled across the road at just about precisely the halfway point along the march. When Jackson's van reached the stream, the tail of his attenuated corps had not left the starting blocks six miles to the rear.

Officers prodded dusty and tired men through the enticing water and on their way. When Jackson reached the Brock Road again, he poured his troops onto it, and they surged northward. At the in-

tersection of the Plank Road he planned to turn right and cover the two miles to Wilderness Church, there to demolish Hooker's dangling flank. Gen. Fitzhugh Lee met Jackson at the intersection and led him east on the Plank Road to show him why that idea no longer made good sense. From a high plateau in the yard of a farmer named Burton, young Lee pointed out to Jackson the Federal line running west beyond Wilderness Church. To attack down the Plank Road would be to hit the enemy in front, canceling most of the advantages won by so much sweat and at such great risk.

Stonewall Jackson was about the most famous man on earth that spring; Fitz Lee knew he had served him well and prepared to bask in the glow of a deserved kudos. Instead, the dour Stonewall gazed intently across the intervening ground at his quarry without a glance at his disappointed benefactor. Turning without a word, Jackson hurried back to the head of his column on the Brock Road and pointed it up the road still farther north. Two extra miles of marching would complete the wider circuit now necessary. Good generals adapt to tactical verities, and Jackson was very good indeed at what he did. He paused long enough to scribble a four-sentence dispatch to Lee, then headed eagerly on with his men.

The Federals on whom Jackson planned to unleash his tidal wave belonged to the XI Corps under O. O. Howard. General Howard was new to his post, but the men in the ranks knew Jackson all too well. Stonewall had brought them to grief more than once in the past year while they served under Gen. Nathaniel Banks and Gen. Franz Sigel. That unhappy past, combined with the German origins of many of the men, left them the unpopular and misunderstood outcasts of the Army of the Potomac. After the battle many of them came to believe, or at least to claim, that they had known full well that Confederates by the tens of thousands lurked in the woods. But in the late afternoon of May 2, without access to hindsight, the infantrymen of the XI Corps whiled away their last moments of grace playing cards and writing letters and cooking food that they would never eat.

Several miles away Joe Hooker sat on the veranda of the pleasant Chancellorsville Inn and composed brash communiqués.

General Jackson could not wait for his entire column to snake through the narrow woods and uncoil across Howard's exposed flank. Despite all the risks he had successfully run and the superb opportunity that lay before him, Jackson knew that the inexorable slide of the sun toward the horizon had now become his greatest foe. The stern, devout Jackson was about as close to an Old Testament warrior as the Civil War produced, but he could not make the sun stand still. After pushing two-thirds of his men into three long, parallel lines, Jackson could wait no longer.

The two main Confederate lines, separated by only about one hundred yards, stretched for nearly a mile on either side of the Turnpike. They stood squarely at right angles to the unwitting Federal line strung out along the road and facing south. When the Southern avalanche struck, the bravest Northerner turning to confront this surprise attack from the rear would be outflanked by a mile to his right and a mile to his left. In naval parlance, Jackson had "crossed the T" on his quarry by forming the cap of the T and looking down its shank.

Sometime after 5:00 P.M. Stonewall Jackson reached under his coat and pulled his watch out of an inside pocket. Conflicting accounts place the moment at 5:15 or as late as 6:00. Jackson looked up from the watch at the handsome, capable Robert E. Rodes, a Virginian commanding the division waiting in the front line. "Are you ready, General Rodes?"

"Yes, sir."

"You can go forward then."

That quiet colloquy launched the II Corps and moved thousands of men through the brightest moment of the fabled Army of Northern Virginia. A nod from Rodes to a young officer named Blackford, who had grown up in nearby Fredericksburg but commanded Alabamians on this day, triggered the attack. Bugles told skirmishers to advance. About twenty thousand infantrymen followed close behind through dense brush that tugged at their tattered uniforms. As

the Rebels gained momentum, they broke into a hoarse, savage roar that escalated into the spine-chilling high-pitched shriek of the Rebel yell.

The dense two-mile line of Southern soldiers drove forest animals in front of its advance like beaters flushing game on an African safari, and many Northern troops got their first intimation that something was afoot in the woods behind them when animals scurried and fluttered past, hurrying eastward. Some Federals laughed and cheered the bizarre natural phenomenon. Then the paralyzing tremolo of the Rebel yell came floating after the wildlife.

An officer yelled, "You are firing into your own men!" The 18th N. Carolina's major cried, "It's a lie!"

Howard's unfortunate division and brigade commanders generally did their best in an impossible situation. No soldiers could have stood in the circumstances thrust upon the XI Corps—even had the Confederates been unarmed, and the Federals equipped with twentieth-century weapons not yet dreamed of. Troops simply do not stand when surprised from behind by hordes of screaming enemies. Leaders with those foreign names that made the rest of the army look askance encouraged brief rallies that inevitably spilled back in rout. Schurz, Krzyzanowski, Schimmelfennig, von Gilsa, von Einsiedel, and dozens more scrambled in vain to stem the wide and deep tide sweeping against and over them.

Capt. Hubert Dilger won a great name for himself by firing a piece of artillery with steadfast courage in the face of Jackson's legions. This freshly immigrated German, known as Leatherbreeches because of some doeskin pants

he wore, retired so stubbornly that Army legend held that he fell back only by reason of the recoil of his gun at each discharge.

Federals fleeing from the intolerable spot whence Jackson had erupted found little support as they ran eastward. Dan Sickles had taken most of his III Corps down toward the furnace to cope with Jackson's rear guard. The panicky fugitives ran back not onto a stalwart line of friends but into a comfortless vacuum.

Only the failure of one inept Confederate officer saved the Federal army from unmitigated disaster. Alfred H. Colquitt was a Georgia politician of starkly limited military attainments. Chance put this weak reed on the right end of Jackson's four-brigade frontline cutting edge. The spare fifth brigade of the front division fell in just behind Colquitt, ready to deploy into the first good seam popped open by the attack. Colquitt and his peers operated under strict orders to move straight and steadily ahead, ignoring matters on either side; they would exploit Jackson's strenuously won advantage while other troops tidied up around the edges and behind them.

Despite his unmistakable instructions, Colquitt came to a dead stop shortly after the attack began. One of the general's staff excitedly reported enemy off to the right. The highly capable young Stephen Dodson Ramseur of North Carolina, commanding the brigade just to the rear and stymied by Colquitt's halt, found to his immense disgust that "not a solitary Yankee was to be seen" in that direction. Colquitt had single-handedly obliterated the usefulness of two-fifths of Jackson's front line. Almost immediately after the battle Lee sent Colquitt into exile far away from the Army of Northern Virginia; by contrast, Georgians thought enough of Colquitt to elect him governor twice and then send him to the U.S. Senate.

Even without the 40 percent of his front line lost through incompetence, Jackson had enough men in place to sweep the field. His troops devoured more than two miles of the Federal line in about two hours. But near the end of

Mississippians on the Sunken Road: one of the starkest views of battle dead recorded during the war.

their triumphant plunge toward Chancellorsville the Southerners were themselves taken by surprise as the result of a bizarre accident. The 8th Pennsylvania Cavalry had spent that afternoon at the commanding artillery position known as Hazel Grove, about one mile south of the Turnpike at a point two miles east of where Jackson struck. An acoustical shadow kept those troopers and others around them from hearing, or at least clearly comprehending, the disaster that had befallen their friends far away to their right and rear. When the Pennsylvanians responded to a routine but outdated order to head north to the main road, then east to Hooker's headquarters at Chancellorsville, they stumbled into the midst of Jackson's columns. Surprised Southerners quickly dispersed the equally surprised Pennsylvania boys, who fought bravely but vainly in a sea

of gray. Gen. Alfred Pleasonton, who had command of the Federal cavalry, later wove the charge of the 8th into a vast panorama of self-serving lies that he concocted as his official report of the battle. Eventually Pleasonton won his well-earned reputation as the Civil War's Munchausen, but at the time the survivors could only fume impotently.

As darkness fell, the men of the Federal XI Corps completed a frantic run for shelter that in many instances took them all the way back to the river and across the pontoon bridges. One officer called these German fugitives the Flying Dutchmen; another, hoarse from his vain efforts to shout up a rally, said that "the damned Dutchmen ran away with my voice." To finish with these poor XI Corps fellows, it must be reported that they ran afoul of similarly grotesque bad luck a few weeks later at Gettysburg and

suffered an almost identical thrashing. Before year's end, though, many of the same men participated in the dramatic spontaneous charge that captured Missionary Ridge in Tennessee.

Dan Sickles's boys of the Federal III Corps blundered through their own personal nightmare after darkness fell. Thousands of them crashed about in the baffling Wilderness, far south of the position they had left when ordered to explore the area around Catharine Furnace and southwest of friendly lines still intact. When the III Corps troops groped back toward Chancellorsville in the darkness, they bumped into blazing muskets and thundering cannon, all fired by the Federal XII Corps. The number of men killed by friends in this hellish, confused pitch-black tangle cannot be ascertained with any certainty. Some Northern witnesses marveled that anyone survived, and Gen. Henry Warner Slocum, commanding the XII Corps, wrote that "the damage suffered by our troops from our own fire . . . must have been severe."

When this combat between bluecoats erupted, Confederates in the vicinity ducked for cover and expected the worst, only gradually coming to the soothing understanding that the storm excluded them. Meanwhile, a handful of Confederates as confused as were Slocum and Sickles inflicted a mortal wound on their own hero—and perhaps on the national prospects of their young country.

Stonewall Jackson's considerable military virtues did not include an intuitive grasp of terrain. Perhaps because of that, the general customarily worked hard and long in seeking understanding of ground where he would fight. In the smoke-smeared moonlight that evening of May 2, Jackson rode out before the amorphous tangle of troops that constituted his front line. The general and an entourage of staffers and couriers poked about in the Wilderness, looking for a route that would provide access to some point behind Chancellorsville, blocking the Federal retreat. When the little cavalcade headed back toward Confederate lines, it came athwart two North Carolina brigades. The noise of the horses prompted one of the brigades to fire a wild volley obliquely across the road from its southern edge. An officer with the general shouted a desperate plea to cease firing. "You are firing into your own men!" he yelled.

The major of the 18th North Carolina, just north of the road, bellowed: "It's a lie! Pour it into them, boys!"

This volley struck dead Jackson's faithful engineer officer, J. Keith Boswell, and inflicted mortal hurts on at least three others in the party. Three of its bullets hit Stonewall Jackson. Two shattered his left arm; the third pierced his right hand. Horrified subordinates gathered around the stricken leader, bound his wounds, and laboriously carried him from the field. At one point three young staff members lay around Jackson's litter in a hurricane of artillery fire, shielding him with their bodies as canister struck sparks from the road all around them. Twice men carrying a cor-

ner of the litter went down. The second time Jackson fell squarely on his mangled shoulder, renewing the arterial bleeding that already had cost him much of his vitality. Eventually the worried and sorrowful party delivered their general to a field hospital near Wilderness Tavern. There his medical director amputated Jackson's savaged arm just below the shoulder early on May 3. The bullet extracted from the general's right palm was round, one of the projectiles fired by the obsolete smoothbore muskets still carried by a surprising number of ordnance-poor Confederate units.

The steady rhythm of artillery at Hazel Grove built to a crescendo that won the battle for Lee.

By the time Jackson awakened from his anesthetic, artillery fire from the nearby battlefield was shaking the earth beneath him. During the night after Jackson's wounding, command of his corps passed to Jeb Stuart, who was dragooned into this unaccustomed temporary role because the only available infantry general of adequate rank had been wounded soon after Jackson went down. Col. Edward Porter Alexander, a fine young artillerist from Georgia, reported to Stuart that a high, open knoll called Hazel Grove offered a wonderful artillery vantage point and persuaded the general to capture it. At about 1:00 A.M. Stuart sent J. J. Archer's brigade of Tennessee and Alabama regiments to the vicinity, and at the first hint of dawn the Southern troops stormed out of the woods into the clearing. They reached the hilltop just in time to capture four guns and one hundred men of a Federal rear guard; Joe Hooker had decided during the night to abandon Hazel Grove, the key to the battlefield.

The newly installed battalion system of artillery, which ensured ready availability of ample guns in large, mobile masses, allowed Alexander to rush about fifty pieces of the right size and type to Hazel Grove. There they took under fire the Federal artillery some twelve hundred yards away at Fairview (still another Chancellor family farmhouse) and at the Chancellorsville crossroads itself. Although the gunners of the Army of Northern Virginia had achieved well-earned fame, they were accustomed to suffering under the fire of better-made and more modern Federal weapons that hurled far more reliable ammunition. The advantage of ground offered by Hazel Grove, however, combined with successful implementation of the battalion concept, resulted in a situation in which, said the army's leading historian, Douglas Southall Freeman, "the finest artillerists of the Army of Northern Virginia were having their greatest day."

One particularly noteworthy round fired from Hazel Grove spiraled over Fairview and headed unerringly for the Chancellorsville Inn. As the shell descended toward its target, General Hooker was leaning against one of the large white porch columns, looking out from the second-story veranda. The shell did not explode (an all-too-typical result from the Southern perspective; one officer on this day insisted that he kept track and only about every fifteenth round went off). The hurtling iron hit Hooker's pillar, though, and the impact knocked it and pieces of the porch in every direction. Lt. Col. Logan Henry Nathan Salyer of the 50th Virginia lay across the top of a piano in the inn's first-floor parlor, where Federal captors had taken him after he went down with a saber wound in the head. Salyer roused himself enough to ask scurrying staff officers what had happened, and they responded with an early and inaccurate report that Hooker had been killed. Salyer rejoiced quietly, but in fact Hooker was only stunned and paralyzed. He ostensibly conveyed to Gen. Darius N. Couch the command of the army, but as the day continued, it became apparent that he retained so many strings on Couch that the latter really wielded no substantial authority.

General Couch and his colleagues recognized that their army still enjoyed clear advantages in numbers and position. Could they commit the large body of unused men to action, they might still grind Lee's weak force to bits, Jackson's dazzling success of the previous day notwithstanding. But Hooker held his army passive and allowed Lee the luxury of choosing the time and place at which decisive actions developed.

Nevertheless, R. E. Lee experienced considerable difficulty on the morning of May 3. Almost all of the Federal infantry lines that Lee had to break that morning stood in the dense Wilderness. Southern brigades plunged into the brush and fought blindly against equally bemused Northern units, generally accomplishing little and ballooning the already dreadful casualty lists. Other brigades wandered through the storm without either doing much good or suffering much loss. "It would be useless to follow in detail the desperate fighting which now ensued. . . ." That admission by Edward Porter Alexander, a ranking Confederate officer who revisited the field after the war before writing a classic history, suggests the nature of the woods fighting on May 3.

Among the casualties of this hourslong brawl was Gen. Hiram G. Berry of Maine, shot down with a mortal wound as he crossed the road near Chancellorsville. But perhaps the most important Federal casualty, viewed from the long perspective of posterity, was Col. Nelson Appleton Miles of the 61st New York. Miles went down with a bullet in the abdomen, recovered, and went on to become commander in chief of the U.S. Army near the turn of the century. At about the time Miles gained his highest command, private citizens both North and South purchased huge chunks of the battlefield of Chancellorsville in hopes that the War Department would accept them as a donation to form a national military park on the order of those newly designated at Gettysburg and elsewhere. The Army chose not to accept the largess of those public-spirited preservationists. Gettysburg was one thing, but the scenes in which the U.S. Army had been humiliated in 1863 (and

where a rebellious Southerner punctured General Miles) certainly did not deserve protection. The portion of the battlefield preserved today, contains only a small fragment of what our forebears sought to protect almost a century ago.

Lee took the bad news with the same calm he always displayed, but his heart must have sunk.

Early during the woods fighting two Confederate generals became casualties of different sorts. Gen. John R. Jones of Virginia was one of Stonewall Jackson's special projects that turned out poorly. Jones had been accused of cowardice so blatant that it resulted in a formal court-martial, a shocking event in the general officer corps of an army fabled for its bravery. The court cautiously exonerated Jones two weeks before Chancellorsville. On May 3, however, the demands of combat among the bullets snapping through the trees proved to be too much for Jones. He left the field and resigned.

Another of Jackson's projects, E. F. Paxton, went into the morning's fight with the unshakable premonition that he would be killed at once. Paxton had known Jackson as a fellow communicant at Stonewall's beloved Presbyterian church before the war. When Paxton lost an election to be major of the 27th Virginia, Jackson calmly found means to promote him several ranks to brigadier general, out of reach of the whims of the electorate. Much of the army disdained this proceeding as another instance of Jackson's much mooted wretched judgment in selecting subordinates. Paxton had had little opportunity to confirm or disprove this conventional wisdom when he led his famous Stonewall Brigade into action on May 3. He knew he would not

survive the battle and prepared for death by studying his wife's photograph and reading his Bible by the scant predawn light. Moments after the action opened Paxton fell dead, surviving only long enough to reach for the pocket where he kept his treasured pictures.

Over all of the infantry chaos that morning there throbbed the steady rhythm of Confederate artillery at Hazel Grove, building to a crescendo that won the battle for Lee. The two divisions that had remained with Lee for the past day and a half pressed toward Chancellorsville from the south and east. Jackson's men under Stuart closed in from the west. Before the morning was far gone, the two Confederate wings reunited at last, ending that aspect of Lee's incredible gamble and providing the general with the chance to reassert direct control over his whole army. Gradually the consolidated Southern force swept Hooker's brave but poorly led legions back to the Chancellorsville intersection. A brief, confused stand there bought Hooker a few minutes. Then Confederates swarmed over the crossroads and around the burning inn in a frenzied victory celebration.

Into this animated scene rode R. E. Lee on his familiar gray horse. "His presence," wrote an officer who was there, "was the signal for one of those outbursts of enthusiasm which none can appreciate who have not witnessed them. The fierce soldiers with their faces blackened with the smoke of battle, the wounded crawling with feeble limbs from the fury of the devouring flames, all seemed possessed with a common impulse. One long, unbroken cheer, in which the feeble cry of those who lay helpless on the earth blended with the strong voices of those who still fought, rose high above the roar of battle, and hailed the presence of the victorious chief. He sat in the full realization of all that soldiers dream of—triumph; and as I looked upon him in the complete fruition of the success which his genius, courage, and confidence in his army had won, I thought that it must have been from such a scene that men in ancient days rose to the dignity of gods."

The impromptu celebration fizzled out when dreadful news arrived from Fredericksburg. Lee's eleven-thousand-

Federal wounded rest at Marye's Heights, where not long before Sedgwick's men had met Alabama regiments under Wilcox.

man rear guard there, under Gen. Jubal A. Early, had been facing twice as many Federals under Gen. John Sedgwick. When a Mississippi colonel named Thomas M. Griffin incautiously (and against regulations) accepted a flag of truce during the morning of May 3, Northern officers saw just how thin was the line opposing them. Adjusting their formations and tactics accordingly, the Federals pounded across the plain below Marye's Heights and burst over the stone wall and Sunken Road that had caused their army so much grief the previous December. This penetration of the rear guard opened a path to Lee's rear for Sedgwick's force. A government photographer accompanying the advancing Federals took some shots of the captured ground, among them one of freshly dead Mississippians in the Sunken Road that gave stark testimony

of the price of their colonel's impolitic behavior. The film captured one of the most graphic views of battle dead taken during the entire war.

Sedgwick's apparently wide-open opportunity to slice westward and do Lee some harm came to an abrupt obstacle about four miles west of Marye's Heights, at Salem Church. Gen. Cadmus Marcellus Wilcox and his brigade of five tough, veteran Alabama regiments began May 3 guarding Banks Ford on the Rappahannock River, two miles due north of Salem Church. Wilcox moved alertly toward Fredericksburg and the action developing there during the morning. When Early's line at Marye's Heights fell apart, Wilcox hurried across country and threw skirmishers in Sedgwick's path. The Alabama men retarded their enemy's advance from positions on each gentle crest and at fence rows perpen-

dicular to the road. Finally at Salem Church they made a stout stand.

Lee received the bad news from eastward with the same calm poise he always displayed, but his heart must have sunk within him. He turned Gen. Lafayette McLaws onto the Turnpike back toward Salem Church and later followed in person. Wilcox and his men stood at bay near the little brick building when McLaws arrived with reinforcements. The simple Southern Baptist sanctuary, built in 1844 by the farming brethren who worshiped in it, now served as a make-do fortification. Bluecoated infantry charged up to and around the building while Alabamians fired out the windows. Hundreds of men fell in the yard, in the church itself, and in the small log church school sixty yards to the east.

But McLaws and his men made the Salem Church ridge too strong to breach, and fighting flickered out late on May 3. The next day Confederates from the church and from Early's bypassed rear guard bottled Sedgwick up with his back to the Rappahannock. Soon after midnight of May 4–5, this Union detachment retreated back over the river under desultory shell fire and light infantry pressure.

Salem Church survives today, covered both inside and out with battle scars. All but a tiny fragment of the Salem Church ridge, however, disappeared during the past few years as gas stations and shopping centers destroyed the battlefield. Huge earth-moving machines chewed up and carried away the ground of the ridge itself, leaving the building a forlorn remnant of the historic past isolated on its little vestigial crest.

After Sedgwick headed for cover at the end of May 4, Lee could return his attention to Hooker's main army. The Federals had built a strong and deep line of earthworks shaped like an enormous capital V. The flanks were anchored on the river, and the apex stretched south to a point only one mile north of Chancellorsville. Within that sturdy fastness Joe Hooker continued to cooperate with Lee's objectives by holding his force quietly under the eyes of Southern detachments that he outnumbered by about four to one. When Lee was able to return to the Chancellorsville front on May 5, the men he brought back with him from around Salem Church improved the odds to some degree but not nearly enough to approach parity. Federal losses totaled about eighteen thousand during the campaign, but Lee had incurred some twelve thousand casualties as well and was still greatly overmatched. Even so, the Confederate commander was looking for some means to launch a renewed offensive against Hooker when, on the morning of May 6, his scouts reported that all the Federals had retreated north of the river during the night.

That same day, Joe Hooker announced in an order to the entire army: "The events of the last week may swell with pride the heart of every officer and soldier of this army. We have added new luster to its former renown . . . and filled [the enemy's] country with fear and con-

sternation." By contrast, Lee's congratulatory order to his troops, dated May 7, gave thanks to God "for the signal deliverance He has wrought" and encouraged divine services in the army to acknowledge that debt.

Historians continue to discuss many aspects of the campaign without any hint of unanimity. Was Joe Hooker drunk most of the weekend? After the war the general conclusion was that he had stopped drinking on accession to army command, leaving him unsettled after a lifetime of consistent bibulousness; new evidence suggests that he did indeed indulge his habit during the Chancellorsville weekend. Did R. E. Lee conclude from the evidence of his

---

Jackson's wife told him he was dying. "My wish is fulfilled," he said. "I have always desired to die on Sunday."

---

incredible victory that there was virtually nothing his battle-tested infantry could not do, leading to overconfidence at Gettysburg? The army had performed at an astoundingly high level during the first three days of May, and Lee soon did ask nearly impossible feats from it; on the other hand, the leaders of a tenuous revolutionary experiment could hardly afford to play conservatively against staggering negative odds.

Chancellorsville gave Lee the leverage to move the war out of torn and bleeding Virginia. His raid into Pennsylvania held the potential for great success, but it came to grief at Gettysburg, two months to the day after Chancellorsville.

The combination of bold strategy and even bolder tactics employed by the Confederate leaders at Chancellorsville turned an apparently impossible situation into a remarkable triumph. But the most important scenes in that tragic drama ultimately unfolded not around the old inn or at Hazel Grove but in an

outbuilding of a country house twenty-five miles to the southeast at Guinea Station. Stonewall Jackson seemed to be recovering favorably from the loss of his arm when an ambulance carried him to the Chandler place at Guinea on the hot fourth of May. His progress continued good for two more days at this new resting place farther from the dangers and distractions of the front. Then, early on the morning of May 7, Jackson awakened with a sharp pain in his side that his medical staff readily and worriedly diagnosed as pneumonia. The disease made rapid inroads on the general's weakened system, and doctors began to hint that he might not recover.

The grim news spread through the ranks. The loss of mighty Stonewall would transform the glorious name of Chancellorsville into the blackest of blots. Mrs. Jackson reached her husband's bedside on May 7, and three days later it was she who had to rouse Thomas Jackson from his delirium to warn him that he was dying. "I will be an infinite gainer to be translated," the fading man responded, and later: "My wish is fulfilled. I have always desired to die on Sunday."

In the early afternoon of a lovely spring Sunday, May 10, Stonewall Jackson called out for Gen. A. P. Hill and for Maj. Welles J. Hawks of his staff as his mind wandered to battles won and streams crossed at the head of his troops. At three o'clock a spell of calm intervened, broken only by the sobs of family and friends in the room and by the general's desperate gasping for breath. As the clock neared the quarter hour, Jackson spoke quietly from the bed: "Let us cross over the river, and rest under the shade of the trees." Then, as he so often had done during the year just past, Stonewall Jackson led the way.

Robert K. Krick is chief historian of Fredericksburg and Spotsylvania National Military Park, which preserves portions of Chancellorsville battlefield. He is the author of eight books; his Stonewall Jackson at Cedar Mountain *was published by the University of North Carolina Press.*

Gallantry under Fire

Could "colored" troops stand up to real combat? A charge at New Market Heights settled the question once and for all

John E. Aliyetti

IT WAS THE FALL OF 1864, AND THE CONfederacy was gasping for its final breaths. Earlier in the year, Lieutenant General Ulysses S. Grant had relentlessly pressed the Union Army of the Potomac against the Confederate Army of Northern Virginia in a series of battles at the Wilderness, Spotsylvania, North Anna, Cold Harbor, and the Crater at Petersburg. In August, Admiral David Farragut sailed into Mobile Bay and neutralized the last Confederate port in the Gulf of Mexico. On September 2, Union Major General William T. Sherman captured Atlanta. Virginia's precious Shenandoah Valley, the lifeblood of the Confederacy, was on its way to becoming little more than a charred wasteland.

Now, in mid-September, a deadly confrontation was about to occur, a struggle forgotten among the famous conflicts of the war, a battle that would provide a benchmark of valor, not only for the Civil War, but also for future generations of American soldiers. It was a fight that would convince some of the most stubborn skeptics that black men could rise to the call of battle as well as white men.

Major General Benjamin F. Butler, commander of the Army of the James, had convinced Grant to allow him to break out of his stalemated position in the Bermuda Hundred area, near the James River, south of Richmond, Virginia, to launch a two-pronged assault

LIBRARY OF CONGRESS

Most of the fighting in the engagement at New Market Heights was done by black regiments, including Fleetwood's 4th United States Colored Troops and the 22d U.S. Colored Troops.

From *Civil War Times Illustrated,* October 1996. © 1996 by Cowles Magazines, Inc. Reprinted through the courtesy of Cowles Magazines, Inc., publishers of *Civil War Times Illustrated.*

against key forts and possibly break through to Richmond itself. Butler's plan had Major General Edward Ord's XVIII Corps, less its 3d Division, crossing the James at Varina and attacking Fort Harrison. Major General David Bell Birney's X Corps would cross at Deep Bottom and attack the Confederate position along the New Market Road, with its main effort directed against Fort Gilmer.

The 3d Division of the XVIII Corps would lead the attack against the Confederate defense at an area along the New Market Road known as New Market Heights. For this assignment, Butler attached the division, under the command of Brigadier General Charles J. Paine, to Birney's X Corps, placing it on the left flank. The division faced a true test: the black troops who made up its nine regiments were freemen and former slaves who had never been in combat, and their commander, although a Butler favorite, had never led a division-size unit into battle.

Butler was an avowed abolitionist and was one of the first to encourage the acceptance of black men into the army. In May 1861 he had labeled a few black deserters of a Confederate labor battalion "contraband of war" and concluded that, as such, they could be "confiscated." In 1862, when he commanded the Union troops occupying New Or-

leans, he hurriedly recruited three regiments of liberated slaves from southern Louisiana and had them in the field by November of that year to face a threatened Confederate attack.

In the fall of 1864, there were more than 100,000 black troops in the Union forces in about 140 all-black regiments. At the war's end, almost 10 percent of the Yankees under arms would be black men. And while most people knew of the courage displayed by the black 54th Massachusetts Infantry the previous year at Fort Wagner, in South Carolina's Charleston Harbor, Butler sensed that some units still distrusted black regiments. In discussing his plan with Grant, he stated, "I want to convince myself, whether, under my own eye, the Negro troops will fight; and if I can take with the Negroes, a redoubt that turned Hancock's corps on a former occasion, that will settle the question."

On September 28, 1864, the 3d Division rested at Deep Bottom, Virginia, awaiting the arrival of the X Corps. Like most Union divisions, the 3d consisted of three brigades, each with three regiments. Although the strength of the regiments fluctuated daily, on this day the division had about 3,800 effectives. All the commissioned officers were white, and the enlisted men black. Colonel John H. Holman commanded the 1st Brigade, which consisted of the 1st, 22d,

and 37th United States Colored Troops (U.S.C.T.). Colonel Alonzo G. Draper led the 2d Brigade, with the 5th, 36th, and 38th U.S.C.T. The 3d Brigade, which was short one regiment (the 10th U.S.C.T. on detached duty) had Colonel Samuel A. Duncan in command of the 4th and 6th U.S.C.T. The 2d U.S.C.T. Cavalry would also take part in the action, but it was not attached to any brigade. Birney held in reserve the 7th, 8th, and 9th U.S.C.T., and the 29th Connecticut Colored Infantry, all of which had been assigned to the X Corps.

The next morning, the division was in a line of brigades, ready to commence the attack. From right to left they were Duncan's brigade (whose right flank tied in with the left flank of the X Corps' 1st Division, commanded by Brigadier General Alfred H. Terry), then Draper's brigade, and lastly, Holman's brigade. Holman's task was to keep the left flank secure. The division would advance in coordination with the general attack of the X Corps. Duncan's troops would lead, closely supported by Draper and, if necessary, some of Holman's troops.

The plan called for a swift attack against New Market Heights. Some unconfirmed accounts have the troops advancing with unloaded rifles so they would not stop to fire. The division expected to be going against inexperienced

At Deep Bottom, Virginia, along the James River, Federal soldiers rest at one foot of the pontoon bridge that Brigadier General Charles J. Paine crossed with his division of black regiments to reach New Market Heights.

a long time coming
The Medal of Honor

Long after the United States had declared itself independent from England, Americans still shared a general distaste for any lingering reminder of the British nobility. The thought of fancy dress uniforms decked with rows of colorful medals reminded them of the crusty aristocracy whose domination their forefathers had fought so hard to escape. So, except for one short-lived recognition program initiated by George Washington in 1782, the U.S. military never instituted a formal system of rewarding individual gallantry with medals.

At the start of the Civil War, that anti-medal bias pervaded the U.S. Army's high command. It required action by the navy to force the army to reconsider its position. When Navy Secretary Gideon Welles asked Congress to approve a medal for the navy, his request was granted, and President Abraham Lincoln signed the Navy Medal of Honor bill on December 21, 1861. Not to be outdone by the navy, the army developed its own program, and on July 12, 1862, the Army Medal of Honor bill became law. Although frequently referred to as the "Congressional Medal of Honor," the correct term is simply "Medal of Honor." Only enlisted men were eligible for the award initially, but the act was amended on March 3, 1863, to include officers.

The first black soldier to receive the medal was Sergeant William H. Carney of Company C of the 54th Massachusetts Infantry (Colored). Carney had grabbed his unit's flag after the bearer was shot down in the attack on Fort Wagner, South Carolina, on July 18, 1863. He led the advance to the wall of the fort under "intense musketry and cannon fire," and when he found himself surrounded by only dead or wounded troops, he returned to Union lines with the colors. He was wounded twice during the ordeal.

Through the course of the war, 2,438 Medals of Honor were awarded for "gallantry in action." That number seemed far too large to those scrutinizing the recognition program a few decades later. So an Army commission was formed to review

ABOVE AND BEYOND

The original army Medal of Honor. The engraving shows Minerva, the Roman goddess of wisdom and the arts, repulsing a male figure. Minerva represents the Union, and the male, the Confederacy.

the situation. On January 17, 1917, the commission ruled that many of the medals issued since the program's inception had been awarded outside the scope of the original intent. The ruling rescinded 911 of the medals, including the 864 given to all the members of one Civil War regiment.

Officially, then, the final tally of Medal of Honor winners during the Civil War was 1,200 soldiers, 310 sailors, and 17 Marines. The first medals were presented by Secretary of War Edwin M. Stanton to

six members of "Mitchel's Raiders," and the last was awarded more than 41 years after the war's end.

A total of 37 Medals of Honor were earned for gallantry during the engagement at New Market Heights, with 14 awarded to black troops. The final medal earned by a black soldier for gallantry in that battle was presented to Sergeant Major Thomas R. Hawkins, a veteran of the 6th U.S. Colored Troops, in 1870, about a month before he died.

The other 13 soldiers of the U.S. Colored Troops honored for gallantry in the battle were: Private William H. Barnes, Company D, 38th Regiment; 1st Sergeant Powhatan Beaty, Company G, 5th Regiment; 1st Sergeant James H. Bronson, Company D, 5th Regiment; Sergeant Major Christian A. Fleetwood, Company D, 4th Regiment; Private James Gardner, Company I, 36th Regiment; Sergeant James H. Harris, Company B, 38th Regiment; Sergeant Alfred B. Hilton, Company H, 4th Regiment; Sergeant Milton M. Holland, Company B, 56th Regiment; 1st Sergeant Alexander Kelly, Company F, 6th Regiment; Corporal Miles James, Company B, 36th Regiment; 1st Sergeant Robert A. Pinn, Company I, 5th Regiment; 1st Sergeant Edward Ratcliffe, Company C, 38th Regiment; and Corporal Charles Veal, Company D, 4th Regiment.

On July 9, 1918, Congress approved two "secondary medals": the Distinguished Service Cross and the Silver Star. Later, other medals were added to the so-called "Pyramid of Honor." The warrant for the Medal of Honor was clarified as "gallantry and intrepidity at the risk of life, above and beyond the call of duty." The clarification also specified that the gallant action should have been such that, if the nominee had not acted as he did, he could not have been criticized.

—John E. Aliyetti

militia, but they would soon find that the butternut-clad infantrymen defending the heights were the seasoned Texas veterans of Gregg's Brigade, under the command of Colonel Frederick S. Bass. Supporting the Texans were the 3d Richmond Howitzers; the 1st Rockbridge Artillery; and a cavalry brigade,

fighting dismounted, commanded by Brigadier General Martin W. Gary.

General Paine wanted to wait for Colonel Joseph C. Abbott's 2d Brigade of Terry's division, on his right, to move out and draw some attention from the Confederates before he committed his men, but there was no firing from that

area. In a letter to his father dated October 3, Paine wrote, "I waited a good while to hear Terry begin because I wanted him to draw some of the enemy away from me if he c'd, but after waiting a good while and not hearing from Terry I started my column. . . ." The two regiments of Duncan's brigade moved out with the three regiments of Draper's brigade close behind and slightly to the left. The troops formed a front about 400 hundred yards wide. Holman's brigade moved to cover the flank, and the 22d U.S.C.T. sent out skirmishers.

Rebel pickets began firing at the movement in their front and then fell back to a fortified line of rifle pits at the base of the heights. It was then they realized the size of the attacking force. Terry's three brigades and the rest of the X Corps finally began to advance, and the five-brigade front stretched to about 2,300 yards.

Duncan's brigade entered a ravine and came under a more intense fire. To Duncan's right, Terry's units were pinned down by an enfilade of artillery fire from the heights. In the ravine where Duncan's force struggled, men began to fall from the Texans' musket fire. "The enemy, in very heavy force, . . . were met with a terrific and galling fire," read an article in the *Richmond Enquirer* on November 22. "Texans, mounting the works, shot them like sheep." The artillery units on the heights were firing into the X Corps' lines, but the 3d Division continued to press ahead.

Casualties mounted in Duncan's brigade as it came to an abatis, a protruding line of sharpened loblolly pine. Axmen were called to the front to cut through the dense wood. As they worked, 16 cannon on the heights bombarded the stalled attackers. Many company commanders fell as they tried to rally the men. Duncan himself had been wounded four times and was down.

Paine sent Draper a message to move his brigade to the right, "as we are getting the worst of it over there." Draper's regiments now came on over the same ground Duncan's brigade had crossed. Through the dust and carnage, they surged through the first abatis only to encounter another line of obstacles the defenders had erected.

Meanwhile, except for the 22d U.S.C.T., which was still operating as skirmishers on the left flank, Holman's brigade moved in as reserve behind Draper and Duncan, but received no orders to engage. The 2d U.S.C.T. Cavalry was dismounted and deployed as skirmishers to Duncan's right. Effectively,

the division was now advancing on a one-brigade front, about 1,100 men, half of them skirmishers.

Fire poured down from a palisade of fortified rifle pits that formed the main Confederate line below the crest of the hill. Beyond the second barrier, Four Mile Creek formed a marshy area. The Federals had to wade the creek, and as they tried to reform on the other side, many commenced firing. Draper later reported the fire "made so much confusion that it was impossible to make the orders understood." Smoke and lead filled the air. A Lieutenant Bancroft of the 38th U.S.C.T. went down when a bullet passed through his hip as he slogged through the marsh. Unable to walk, he continued forward on his hands and knees, waving his sword and urging his men to follow. The leading units were now about 30 yards from the main enemy defense line, but the attacking force was in danger of collapse.

Draper tried to get his regimental commanders to rally around the colors and charge, but they and their men were falling all around him. The commander of the 5th Regiment, Lieutenant Colonel G. W. Shirtliff, fell mortally wounded. It was his third wound since the attack had begun. Elsewhere in the 5th, black soldiers rose from the ranks to replace lost junior officers. Sergeant Major Milton Holland, a 20-year-old from Austin, Texas, now led Company C; Richmond-born 1st Sergeant Powhatan Beaty commanded Company G; 1st Sergeant James Branson, a Virginia-born 19-year-old from Pennsylvania, led Company D; and 1st Sergeant Robert Pinn, an Ohio farmer, led Company I.

With disaster imminent, heroes of every rank snatched regimental colors and national standards from dying hands and led the bloodied mass into a smoking hell. Sergeant Major Christian Fleetwood of the 4th U.S.C.T. seized the national colors after a second bearer had fallen, and they ended up in the hands of Corporal Charles Veal. Corporal Miles James of the 36th U.S.C.T. was wounded so badly in the arm that the limb was immediately amputated. James, with blood from the mutilated stump soaking his tunic, kept moving forward, loading and firing with one arm.

As the momentum of Draper's attack deteriorated, the fire against his brigade roared in undiminished intensity. For 30 minutes chaos reigned on the battlefield. Then a few men from Duncan's brigade took up a yell, which caught on and swelled to a roar as the desperate force rallied to its colors. The screaming surge engulfed Draper's brigade, and with a rush, the 3d Division carried the Southerners' main line of defense. A Rebel officer mounted the parapet, and Private James Gardner of the 36th shot him down. Gardner charged the barrier and ran his bayonet through the man as the Confederate defenders fell back.

The din of cannon and musket fire to the right of the 3d Division rose in fury. Birney, aware that his flank was secure with Paine in control of the heights and with the subsequent easing of the enfilading fire against him, directed the X Corps to attack Fort Gilmer. But General Robert E. Lee, commander of the Army of Northern Virginia, was brilliant at maneuvering troops behind his own lines and managed to reinforce the defenders. Fort Gilmer held against a ferocious assault.

At the end of the battle, the Confederate line was pushed back. Ord's force captured and held Fort Harrison, subsequently renamed Fort Burnham for Brigadier General Hiram Burnham, who was killed at the head of his brigade, leading the attack. But the Richmond defense remained intact. Lee counterattacked the next day against troops armed with repeating rifles and was handed heavy casualties for his effort. He was forced to pull back and reconstruct his battered perimeter.

Butler's plan marked Grant's last serious effort to enter Richmond north of the James. The siege of Richmond continued another six months, until April 1, 1865, when Union forces broke through Lee's line at Petersburg. Eight days later Lee surrendered his army at Appomattox Court House.

By the war's end, more than 186,000 black men had served in the Union army. Their units had fought in 149 engagements and 39 major battles. During that time, 20 black men—16 soldiers and four sailors—were cited for valor and awarded the Medal of Honor. Fourteen of those medals were won on September 29, 1864, at New Market Heights, by men of General Paine's 3d Division. The 29th was truly a day of glory for the 3d Division soldiers, but they paid for that glory with the blood of hundreds of men.

Butler admitted years later that he had deliberately exposed his black units to risk far out of proportion to the value of their objective in the engagement at New Market Heights, but he had done it in order to establish confidence in their reliability. After the battle, he attempted to reward their heroic effort by ordering Tiffany's of New York to strike a solid silver medal known as the Army of the James Medal, which he later presented to more than 200 of his troops. His unique recognition program, however, created much controversy, and the army forbade the soldiers to wear the medal on their uniforms.

The 3d Division's performance, however, was not controversial, as more widely accepted tokens of appreciation attest. One such token is the highway historical marker on Virginia Route 5, near New Market Road, which reads: "On 28 September 1864, elements of Maj. Gen. Benjamin F. Butler's Army of the James crossed the James river to assault the Confederate defenses of Richmond. At dawn, on 29 September, 6 regiments of the U.S. Colored Troops fought with exceptional valor during their attack along New Market Road. Despite heavy casualties, they carried the earthworks and succeeded in capturing New Market Heights north of the road. Of the 16 Medals of Honor awarded to 'Negro' soldiers during the Civil War 14 were bestowed for this battle. 'The capacity of the Negro race for soldiers had then and there been fully settled forever.' "

John E. Aliyetti is a freelance writer living in Royal Oak, Maryland.

The Struggle
for Black Freedom
before Emancipation

Wayne K. Durrill

Wayne K. Durrill teaches American history at the University of Cincinnati.

The Civil War has recently become a hot ticket. The movie, *Glory,* the PBS series "The Civil War" by Ken Burns, and James McPherson's recent Pulitzer Prize-winning account of the conflict have all dramatized the continuing relevance of the war as a defining experience for a people and a nation. These stories, however, have often neglected an important part of that defining experience: the role of black people in securing their own emancipation. Most accounts of war date emancipation from Lincoln's famous proclamation and the military campaigns that followed. Even *Glory,* which traces the heroic deeds of black soldiers from Massachusetts, portrays slaves in the lowcountry of South Carolina as incompetent and ineffectual, persons who simply waited for Northern free black liberators to march South and rescue them from bondage.

However, even this relatively enlightened view of the role of black people in their own emancipation is historically inaccurate. As Ira Berlin and his colleagues have shown in their monumental multi-volume series, *Freedom: A Documentary History of Emancipation,* slaves throughout the South squeezed freedom in dribs and drabs from their own local situation as opportunities arose in wartime. In Kentucky, where blacks re-mained in bondage until after the Civil War, slaves fled to Tennessee where they could join the Union army as laborers and later as soldiers, and thereby free themselves and sometimes their families. Others stayed home, testing the limits of servitude in a volatile and dangerous situation, always with an eye toward establishing claims to property and place, as well as to their own humanity. These black struggles for freedom within slavery are sometimes difficult to visualize. Indeed, they seem to be a contradiction in terms. Yet they did occur, and with an intensity and regularity that historians have only just begun to uncover. As an example of such struggle, let us examine the story of how one group of North Carolina slaves redefined the rules of slavery in the crisis of war so as to create for themselves a larger space in which to carry on a life separate from their white masters.

In September of 1861, after the fall of federal forces off Hatteras Island on North Carolina's Outer Banks, Major General John Wool, Union commander of the island, reported that "negro slaves" were "almost daily arriving at this post from the interior." They came in small groups, many traveling over one hundred miles from the counties bordering the Albemarle Sound. At Columbia, on the eastern edge of the Sound and about five miles from William Pettigrew's plantation, a certain planter had brought his slaves to town for "safe-keeping." The militia had already mustered there and the town had a jail if he needed it. But shortly after their arrival, thirteen of the man's slaves quietly stole a boat and sailed for Hatteras, setting in motion a chain of events that quickly spread through counties all around the Sound. One planter complained that news of the escape had spread among slaves in the area, and he reasoned, "We may look for others to leave soon." In response, slave owners throughout the Sound region began to move to the upcountry, taking with them as many of their slaves as they could support on the land available to them.

William Pettigrew, one of the richest planters in Washington County, North Carolina, grasped the crisis early on and resolved to remove his slaves before planting began the following spring. On 4 March 1862, the planter arranged for twenty-five Confederate cavalrymen to descend upon Magnolia plantation. The move took the slaves by surprise, and all were captured. That day, men, women, and children were loaded onto wagons guarded by armed troopers, and began a long journey upcountry. After a nine-day forced march, Pettigrew and the slaves came to Haywood, a small crossroads community about fifty miles west of Raleigh where the planter had located a small farm for sale. He purchased the farm as his base camp in the

From *OAH Magazine of History* Vol. 8, No. 1, Fall 1993, pp. 7-10. Adapted from *War of Another Kind: A Southern Community in the Great Rebellion* by Wayne K. Durrill. © 1990 Oxford University Press, Inc. Reprinted by permission.

upcountry, but it was too small to support any but a handful of his slaves. The others he drove on foot fifty miles further west where he leased out eighty-seven of them in nineteen groups to fifteen different planters.

The exchange of slaves for promissory notes, however, signified more than simply a purchase of labor. It included a broader transfer of power from one planter to another. For this reason, William Pettigrew insisted that persons who hired his slaves provide them with certain goods in the coming year, mostly food, clothing, and shoes. The planter might have provided the goods himself and factored the cost into his asking price. But he did not. Instead, he included in the contract detailed directions specifying what each slave should receive. In doing so, Pettigrew ensured that his slaves' new master would become the sole source of some crucial goods for them, thus giving the new master enormous leverage over the hired-out slaves. By his actions, Pettigrew produced not merely new employers for his slaves, but new masters.

Such contracts, however, did not settle all questions of a planter's dominance and a slave's submission in the upcountry. Planters and slaves, in fact, had always created their own mutual expectations, in part by contesting the rules by which they lived. Before the war, this had not been a conflict among equals, to be sure. Instead, the struggle between planter and slave presumed an unequal resolution; the master would rule and the slave submit. But in 1862, the relations between planters and slaves had changed dramatically, even in the upcountry. Many of the Pettigrew slaves worked for new masters who might or might not be skilled in managing human property. Would these men have the wherewithal to nail the meat-house door shut, call in the slave patrol, or face down a personal challenge? No one knew. But William Pettigrew's slaves were determined to find out.

Mary Jane, for example, decided early on to see just what kind of master she had been assigned. William Pettigrew had hired her out as a cook to a planter named George Foushee, along with a slave named Dick Lake, his wife

Jenny, and their five children. Mary Jane complained "mostly of colick" during her first three weeks at Foushee's place. In that period, she rendered "very little service" in the planter's view. According to Foushee, "She don't seem to be very bad off, just sick enough to keep her from work." The planter further wondered if "a good deal of it is deception." To find out, Foushee asked Dick Lake about her, and the slave's answer confirmed the planter's suspicions. According to Lake, Mary Jane had "never done much the year she was in a family way." Mary Jane had a history of probing the limits of her master's power.

Similarly, Jenny took advantage of the change of masters to renew work rules she had known at Magnolia plantation. She had just borne a child and informed Foushee that she had "never been required to do any work until her child was eight weeks old." She also objected to Foushee's plan to put her to work in the fields. At Magnolia she always had labored as a cook and now complained that she "could not work out."

When members of the slave family initiated the same contest that took place on the Foushee plantation, Caveness could not comprehend their actions for what they were.

Mary Jane, Jenny, and their fellow slaves did not wish simply to avoid work by refusing to labor for their masters. Most, in fact, worked steadily and with a will. In late March, a friend of William Pettigrew's who saw some of the planter's slaves "most every Sunday" in church, reported them at work and "well satisfied" with their new circumstances. Therefore, the action taken by Mary Jane and Jenny must be inter-

preted as having some more specific purpose. Mary Jane had succeeded in making pregnancy a privileged status at their old plantation. Here, she renewed the rule by making a public event of her refusal to work while pregnant. Similarly, she served notice upon George Foushee that Pettigrew slaves could not be required to work when ill, no matter how slight the planter thought evidence of any malady appeared. Jenny, for her part, sought to reinforce two rules. The first would give women a special status when pregnant. The second would renew a longstanding division between housework and fieldwork that served as the basis for some very important and very sharp distinctions among the Pettigrew slaves themselves.

George Foushee understood all of this on a practical level. Doubtless, he could never admit publicly, or perhaps even to himself, that Mary Jane and Jenny's actions constituted a challenge to the local rules that governed relations between masters and slaves. But Foushee did have the presence of mind to remain calm. He reported by letter to William Pettigrew the two slaves' failure to work diligently. But Foushee did not propose that either he or Pettigrew take any action. The planter concluded his account of Mary Jane's behavior by saying simply, "I hope she will be better hereafter."

Mary Jane did become better. After she had made her point, she returned to work as usual. Other planters, however, did not fully appreciate the give-and-take that an exercise of a master's power required, particularly when the power of masters had been so undermined by Union military activity on the North Carolina coast. Or perhaps some planters sensed in small challenges larger issues that George Foushee had overlooked.

A. E. Caveness is a case in point. Caveness had hired one slave family from William Pettigrew—Jack, his pregnant wife, Venus, and their six young children. The children must have been young because the entire family hired out for twenty-five dollars, less than the cost of hiring a single prime male field hand. Caveness got a good deal more than he bargained for, however, when he paid his pittance to William Pettigrew. When members of the slave family initiated the same contest that took place on the Foushee plantation, Caveness could not comprehend their actions for what they were. In his view, the slaves attempted to "over-run" him. Finally, in a fit of ill-temper, the planter whipped the oldest child, a gal named Sarah, for what he considered her "laziness and disobedience."

The girl's parents objected violently to this. They "made a great ado about it," according to one account, so much so that Caveness felt compelled to "take Venus in hand." At that point, Venus "started off" down the plantation road and, as she walked, turned to the planter and told him off. What exactly she uttered that day remained a matter of dispute. Caveness claimed that she shouted, I am "going to the Yankees." Doubtless, she had no such intention—if she even spoke these words. Venus and her family had just made the nine-day trek from the coast on foot. She well knew that she needed food and extra clothing for such a journey, that Confederate troops blanketed eastern North Carolina and would demand a pass from her, and that William Pettigrew would hire a slave catcher to find her long before she reached federal lines. Later, Venus's husband claimed that she had said no such thing. By the slave's account, Venus told Caveness that she intended to walk to the plantation of William Campbell, Pettigrew's friend, presumably to lodge a complaint against her new master for his actions. Whatever the exact words, Venus had made her point in producing this small drama—pubicly and loudly She feared no man, planter or otherwise, and if she chose to oppose that man, she would make her claim a matter of public debate.

Caveness "ordered her to come back," but Venus refused and continued walking down the road. The planter then got his whip and followed her. Some distance from the house, he finally caught up with her. Again, Caveness commanded Venus to return to the plantation. Once more, the slave refused and voiced her intention to leave. At that point, the planter lost all patience and good sense. Caveness began to whip Venus, at which time Jack, who evidently had followed the two, "got in between them." The planter then "fell to

work on Jack, and drove both slaves back to the house."

But Venus had succeeded in her purpose even as she and her husband bore the lashes of the planter's whip. Caveness complained that "the fuss might have been heard all over the neighborhood." If he hoped to exercise any power over Pettigrew's slaves, Caveness now would have to submit to the scrutiny of his neighbors, both black and white. Each side in this conflict would mobilize its supporters. The battle between master and slave over who would rule the family, and particularly the children of Venus and Jack, became a public controversy.

In one sense, the customary rights of slaves acting within the rules of paternalism had been renewed. Yet, there was more to the story than a restoration of peaceable relations between masters and slaves.

The next day, Caveness traveled to William Campbell's plantation, where he hoped to make his case to the county's planters. To Campbell, he gave an account of the basic facts in the matter. But Caveness made no attempt to justify his actions. Instead he simply announced a solution. He demanded that Campbell, who had been charged with managing William Pettigrew's interest in Chatham and Moore counties, write to the slaves' owner seeking "permission to conquer them." If Pettigrew refused to grant him such authority, Caveness demanded that their master "take them away." By this ultimatum, Caveness cast the conflict in terms of fundamental is-

sues—in this case, the interest of planters in dominating their slaves. Essentially, Caveness argued that all planters must stand with him, no matter what the specifics of this case, in order to preserve their power over slaves as a whole.

Meanwhile, Venus and Jack also made their opinions known throughout the neighborhood. The couple communicated their interpretation of the conflict to slaves belonging to William Campbell who, in turn, approached their master after Caveness returned home. They told Campbell that Caveness had "not been good "to Pettigrew's slaves. They argued that Caveness was "a man of bad temper," and he acted "very ill" to Jack and his family. In particular Campbell's slaves charged that Caveness had refused to give Jack and his family "enough to eat," even though he had "plenty of meat and bread" to sell to other persons in the neighborhood.

During the next two weeks, Jack and Venus appealed directly to William Campbell. When Campbell visited the family, Jack accused Caveness of abusing them "without any just cause." To support the charge, the slave pointed out that recently Caveness had "knocked Edith [his youngest child] down with a handspike." The blow cut the little girl "severely on the head." And "since the first difficulty with Venus," Caveness had "knocked [her also] down with a chair." That piece of viciousness caused Venus to miscarry. On 10 June, she was reported "very bad off." Moreover, after he struck Venus, Caveness "threatened to kill her if she did not get up and go to work," according to Jack's account.

Jack therefore requested that Campbell write to William Pettigrew in order to give the planter the slaves' version of events. In the letter, Jack argued that he and his family had "worked harder" that spring than they had "ever worked in their lives," but Caveness could not be satisfied. Therefore, he implored William Pettigrew to remove them from Caveness's plantation. Jack declared his family "willing to live anywhere," even "on half feed," as long as they would "not be abused." We "did not want to put you to any trouble," Jack told his master, but we can not stand it."

In the end, Jack and his wife prevailed. Their story had a ring of truth that even Caveness himself made no attempt to deny. Moreover, Caveness's poor reputation in the area precluded his attempt to mobilize planter opinion in his cause. Campbell considered Caveness "very hard to please" and "a very passionate man." Finally, Caveness did not help his own case when he admitted to Campbell that if he had carried his gun along, he would have "killed some of them."

But all of this might have come to nothing if Venus had not made the dispute a public event. By mobilizing local opinion, both black and white, Jack and Venus forged a means by which the Pettigrew slaves could shape their own destiny, at least in some small part. William Campbell considered his slave's version of events "only negro news" and therefore, "only to be used as such." Yet, he recommended to William Pettigrew that Jack and his family be removed from Caveness' plantation to a place where they would be "well cared for." "If Caveness is not willing to keep them and treat them humanely as other negroes are treated in this part of the country," wrote Campbell, "I should take them away."

In one sense, the customary rights of slaves acting within the rules of paternalism had been renewed. Yet, there was more to the story than a restoration of peaceable relations between masters and slaves. The abuse by Caveness of Venus and her children provided an unprecedented opportunity to challenge a slaveholder. Caveness had made certain guarantees to Pettigrew—physical safety and an adequate subsistence for the slaves—that he failed to fulfill. And ironically, by insisting on Pettigrew's rights in his property, Venus advanced her own claim as a human being. Indeed, she used those double-edged claims to turn Caveness's own class against him; she forced Pettigrew and others to recognize not only her right to safety and subsistence but also her right to be heard and recognized as a person. In doing so, Venus and Jack and all the other Pettigrew slaves participated in a much larger defining moment, the self-emancipation of America's slaves in the crucible of the Civil War.

The Northern Front

***BOSTON IS SO BRIGHT** A beacon of Revolutionary history that it is easy to forget the city played an equally significant role in another civil war.* **Dara Horn,** *a Harvard junior, seeks out the moral engine of the Union cause.*

Time is a viscous fluid, and occasionally it sticks to places, leaving the residue of certain centuries attached to the edges of buildings, or to markers on the streets, or to the insides of tourists' heads. In Boston that clinging moment is the colonial period and the American Revolution. When tourists think of Boston, they think of Puritans and patriots, of minutemen and Paul Revere. The Freedom Trail, Boston's most famous historical tour route, takes visitors to pre-1776 spots: the site of the Boston Massacre, the Old North Church (of "one if by land, two if by sea" fame), and a half-dozen cemeteries filled with dead Mathers. The tourist business booms in the spring and summer, when visitors throng Faneuil Hall, a colonial city hall turned shopping center; Plimoth Plantation, where a "living museum" re-creates life in 1627; and Boston Harbor, where costumed interpreters re-enact the Tea Party several times a week. You don't even need to be a tourist to trip over the seventeenth-century milestones that poke out of the city's brick sidewalks.

This single-mindedness is unfortunate, however, because it obliterates the memory of the time when Boston last took the nation by storm, which was not the American Revolution but the Civil War. When I arrived in the city as a college student three years ago and took a few American history courses, I began to notice this omission in the way Boston bills its history. The more I read about the Civil War, the more of it seemed, contrary to what I had learned in high school history classes, to have

taken place in Boston. No battle was fought near the city, but Boston was the center of some of the most vocal protests against slavery and of the most enthusiastic support for the Union cause. Massachusetts freed its slaves in 1783, and it wasn't long before a large (and literate) free black community began to grow in Boston, offering support and lodging to fugitives headed for Canada.

The vast majority of abolitionists made their homes in Boston. Frederick Douglass lived here, as did the Secret Six, a cabal of businessmen and reformers who surreptitiously planned and financed John Brown's raid on Harpers Ferry, which gave the abolitionist cause its definitive martyr. Boston had long been America's "churchiest" city, and it was a Boston activist and reformer, Julia Ward Howe, who turned the soldiers' chant "John Brown's Body" into "The Battle Hymn of the Republic," a stirring and religiously inspired call to arms that proved to be the most influential song in American history. (Her husband, the reformer Samuel Gridley Howe, also had no small connection to "John Brown's Body"; he was one of the Secret Six.) Charles Sumner, the U.S. senator and hometown kid, got savagely beaten by a Southern representative when he dared to speak for abolition on the Senate floor. It was here in Boston that the first antislavery societies were formed; it was here that the abolitionist William Lloyd Garrison proclaimed "no union with slaveholders"; it was here that the Union Army recruited its first regiment of Northern blacks; it was here, more than anywhere else in Amer-

ica, where support of the Northern cause refused to be silenced. To call Boston the intellectual capital of the North, or even the moral engine of the Union, would not be an exaggeration.

So why is Boston so little associated with the Civil War? Maybe because its role in the conflict was one of mind rather than body, but that hardly seems an adequate excuse; there were plenty of actual fugitive slaves hiding out in Boston's basements. Maybe it's because only one moment can really cling to a place, and Boston's moment beat the Civil War to the punch. As a result, looking for traces of the Civil War past here is sort of like peeking into the little cracks in the city to find out where that extra century might have slipped through. But despite Boston's tendency to boast of itself only as the "cradle of the Revolution," you can still find traces of the cradle of the Union cause.

No real marks of the war scar the city, but you can feel its presence in buildings that once shook with passionate voices.

Boston is a town that carefully curates its memories. At the city's centennial celebration Boston's mayor writes a letter to be delivered to his yet unborn successor on the following centennial; it is stored in city hall for the next hundred

From *American Heritage,* April 1998, pp. 48-61. © 1998 by Forbes, Inc. Reprinted by permission of *American Heritage* magazine, a division of Forbes, Inc.

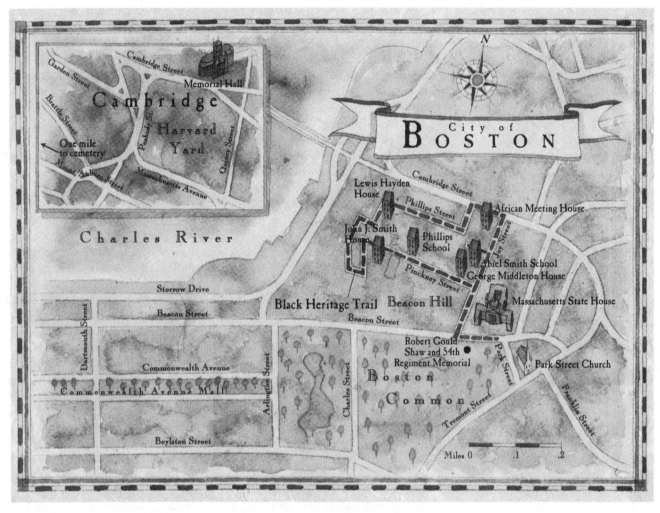

Except for Mount Auburn Cemetery and Memorial Hall (inset), Boston's Civil War sites are clustered on Beacon Hill.

years. There is a statue of some famous person you've never heard of approximately every sixteen feet. And since no real marks of the Civil War itself scar the city, Boston has built monument after monument in honor of its heroes, so many statues that after a while you stop looking at them, just as you eventually stop tripping on the colonial milestones. The Civil War appears in Boston in the form of statues and stone tablets, and in buildings that once shook with passionate voices. You just have to know what you're looking for.

A good place to begin searching, I discovered, is the city's Black Heritage Trail, which ends at the African Meeting House, a tiny brick building approachable by an alley grandly named Smith Court. Built in 1806, the Meeting House is the oldest standing black church building in the United States. It also served its congregants as far more than a place of worship. The building's cramped basement housed Boston's and perhaps America's first public school for black children, and when Massachusetts became the first Northern state to allow black soldiers to fight, the U.S. Army began recruiting soldiers for its first black combat regiment in that same basement room. It was a meeting place for Boston's black community, and the main sanctuary was among Frederick Douglass's most cherished public-speaking stops. And it was here that William Lloyd Garrison, perhaps the most effective of all abolitionists, created his New England Anti-Slavery Society.

In 1898 community migration led to the building's sale to a Jewish congregation, and it was used as a synagogue until it became a museum in 1972. Today it has been remodeled inside to resemble what it looked like as a church in 1855, which is to say very plain. The sanctuary is completely bare, with white-painted walls and unfinished wooden floors. But stand there in a moment when a school group isn't tramping through and read Garrison's words framed on the wall: "We have met tonight in this obscure schoolhouse, our numbers are few and our influence limited, but mark my prediction, Faneuil Hall shall long echo with the principles we have set forth. We shall shake the nation by their mighty power."

When I visited the African Meeting House, I read those words and felt the wooden room tremble, the first rumblings of Boston's great Civil War machine, the machine that would plow through eleven Rebel states and turn towns into smoldering ash and leave dead men in people's back yards, not to mention a dead President in its wake, the machine that would cause a nightmare of battle that Boston would be fortunate enough to see only through the eyes of its surviving sons. But those words would also tear into the hearts of thousands and give them strength, making people remember, as words do every now and then, that no one is doomed to anything, that right does, every few centuries or so, make might.

The Black Heritage Trail would be worth the walk even without its history, because it takes you on a wonderful tour.

And Garrison was right. Faneuil Hall, Boston's and America's oldest standing meetinghouse, which he claimed would one day "echo with the principles we have here set forth," now houses a sculpture of Frederick Douglass. More important, Boston really did "shake the nation" toward war, through the concerted efforts of its citizens to protect fugitive slaves. In the African Meeting House are all sorts of posters and pamphlets issued after the Fugitive Slave Act of 1850 put escaped bondsmen at risk of capture and return to slavery in the South. One poster permanently on display in the Meeting House urges people in the city to exercise what Henry David Thoreau had recently labeled "Civil Disobedience." "CAUTION!!" it screams in giant letters. "Colored People of Boston, One & All, You are hereby respectfully CAUTIONED and advised, to avoid conversing with the Watchmen and Police Officers of Boston, For since the recent ORDER OF THE MAYOR & ALDERMEN, they are empowered to act as KIDNAPPERS and Slave Catchers, And they have already been actually employed in KIDNAPPING, CATCHING, AND KEEPING SLAVES." As one of the more northern

of Northern cities, Boston represented for many fugitives the gateway to freedom in Canada, the final stop on the Underground Railroad. Scattered around Beacon Hill are the safe houses where escaped slaves once hid from kidnappers, and these sites are now marked on the Black Heritage Trail.

The Black Heritage Trail would be worth the walk even without its history, because it takes you on a wonderful tour of Beacon Hill, perhaps Boston's most rarefied and beautiful neighborhood. The tiny streets are almost always silent; the townhouses, while not large, are in impeccable condition; and the little brick sidewalks look almost as though they'd been polished to a shine. Today Beacon Hill represents Boston's new young professional class, but in the 1860s the neighborhood was a strange mix of elite white literati, business tycoons, free blacks, and former slaves. The trail leads you past the Phillips School, which in 1855 became the first school in Boston for both white and black children, as well as the Abiel Smith School, a home that was used as a school until the one in the African Meeting House was set up. You pass by three churches, each a center of abolitionist activity; one, the Park Street Church (a little bit off the trail but hard to miss), was the site of Garrison's first antislavery sermon ever. But the most memorable buildings are the homes of abolitionists, tidy little row houses where fugitives were welcomed and defended.

At 66 Phillips Street, for example, the brick townhouse, indistinguishable from the neighborhood's countless other townhouses, was well known to Boston's fugitives as an Underground Railroad station. Lewis Hayden, himself an escaped slave, turned his home into a safe house for runaways after the Fugitive Slave Act in 1850. While hiding runaways in their basement, Hayden and his wife, Harriet, kept two gunpowder kegs under their front stoop. Once, when bounty hunters arrived at their house, the Haydens came out holding lit candles, threatening to drop the flames and detonate their house, themselves—and their visitors—rather than turn over their hidden guests. A few blocks down on Pinckney Street lived George Middle-

ton, a black Revolutionary War veteran who appeared with a loaded musket and shouted down white children who were throwing rocks and clubs at black women and children outside his house. Farther down Pinckney is the home of John J. Smith, a local barber whose shop at the corner of Howard and Bulfinch served as a secret rendezvous place for abolitionists and fugitives.

The strange thing about all these houses, however, is that you can't actually go inside any of them. Each one of these beautiful townhouses is marked with a plaque on its side, but none has even so much as a gift shop, let alone an exhibit, inside. Instead, the houses remain just as they were in the nineteenth century; they are private homes. As I walked down the streets of Beacon Hill, I saw people going in and out of those Underground Railroad stations, not with candles but with groceries and briefcases. Occasionally I wished I could slip into one of them and find the secret compartments where people once hid, just to see what they looked like inside, as if I were a bounty hunter routing out fugitive slaves or a fugitive who knew that even living free in a broom closet would be better than living outdoors in bondage. Most of the time, though, the decision to keep these houses as homes seems a good one to me. It is as if the city were implying that the people bringing home their groceries today would make the same sacrifices that the earlier tenants did, should history call upon them.

Or would they? You have to be careful with Boston, because as a city obsessed with its own history, it tends to peddle only the most beautiful and morally blameless aspects of its past. You will hear about the generosity and virtue of the Puritans long before you hear about their penchant for executing innocent men and women. You will hear about the prominence of immigrants in local politics long before you hear about the once-prevalent signs reading NO IRISH NEED APPLY. Likewise, if you ever do hear about Boston's Civil War past, you will hear only of the city's passion for freedom and never of the distinct possibility that some of the city's most prominent citizens might have actually opposed abolition. How honest is Boston in portraying itself as the engine of liberation?

As I walked through Beacon Hill, I heard that question murmuring at me around each of the neighborhood's silent corners, but the only reason I could hear it was that I already knew the answer. I passed a house where an abolitionist published an underground newspaper, and another house where a family of fugitive slaves took refuge, and the half-dozen or so other sites like it on the specially marked trail, but while the neighborhood might have been teeming with hidden refugees, there are still all the houses in between, houses without any sort of plaque attached to an outer wall proudly proclaiming them to be the homes of abolitionists. Who lived in those? Lesser-known freedom fighters? Perhaps, although many of the abolitionists mentioned on the Black Heritage Trail are already rather obscure. Free blacks who went to church right around the corner? Yes, in some cases, although Boston's free black community, while it was one of the largest of its kind, still comprised only 2,261 people in 1860.

As the neighborhood climbs its way up the hill, the houses become gradually grander, and eventually the dynamic of the neighborhood becomes clear. Those living near the bottom of the hill were the servants of those who lived at its top, the Boston Brahmins, the first families of the city, who had lived there for as long as eight generations or more, the oldest and wealthiest families in town. Some of these Brahmins participated in the abolitionist movement, sometimes even with enough passion to lay down their lives. In fact, Boston's elite families were often the only ones with the capital and leisure time necessary to engage in activism. But by the middle of the nineteenth century, when the abolitionist movement emerged in full force, Boston's wealthiest class was making its money primarily through the city's largest industry, textiles. The Boston area had become famous for its textile mills in Lowell and other nearby towns, where young women were sent to work in the factories by day and to learn from church instructors about how to maintain Christian virtue in the evenings, a

pleasant arrangement including room, board, wages, and morality enough to ensure a young woman's situation until she found a man to marry. But while these mills played the typical Bostonian role of cities on the hill, they made their profits by churning out cotton fabric, made with raw material harvested on the cheap by slave labor in the South.

In one of the war's few moments of true racial equality, Shaw's body was thrown into a ditch along with his soldiers.

The people living down the street from where Garrison first spoke, while their city may have been the strongest pro-Union contingent in the country, still owed their fortunes to Southern slavery. In fact, Boston's abolitionists had such strong opponents that Garrison, who had publicly burned the Constitution, was later beaten in the streets of Beacon Hill, most likely by thugs sent out by the textile mafia.

At the beginning of the Black Heritage Trail is Boston's standing song to its greatest Civil War martyr, the monument to Col. Robert Gould Shaw and his 54th Massachusetts Regiment. Shaw, a Boston Brahmin and Harvard student, was a promising young soldier in the Army of the Potomac who could have ascended the ranks of the esteemed 2d Massachusetts Regiment. Instead he chose to serve as colonel of the 54th Massachusetts, one of the first black regiments to fight for the North. In one of his many letters home, Shaw told his family how happy he was with his decision: "I feel convinced I shall never regret having taken this step, as far as I myself am concerned; for while I was undecided I felt ashamed of myself, as if I were cowardly." In 1863, when Shaw was twenty-five, his regiment fought a brutal battle at Fort Wagner, on the South Carolina coast. One

quarter of the regiment died, including Shaw. In one of the few moments of true racial equality the Civil War ever saw, Shaw's body was thrown into a ditch with those of his soldiers, many of whom had escaped from slavery.

News of his death, and of the fate of the regiment, shocked the Boston Brahmins and also inspired them. As a friend wrote in a letter shortly after the regiment's defeat, "I have accepted it as a natural consequence when other good fellows have been killed, but Bob's death I can't get over. I don't think I ever knew any one who had everything so in his favor for a happy life." It was true. "Bob," brilliant, handsome, from a wealthy family, and most of all popular and well liked, had a shining career and had just gotten married. His death was a personal tragedy for many, but as time passed, Shaw became less a person than a symbol of the city. When the sculpture, by the artist Augustus Saint-Gaudens, was first unveiled in 1897, the orators at the dedication included Booker T. Washington and William James. Last year, at the memorial's hundredth anniversary, Gen. Colin Powell spoke in honor of Shaw and his soldiers.

When you look out at Boston Common from the street right below the gold-domed statehouse, the Saint-Gaudens memorial alters your view like a misplaced window in a Magritte painting, a rectangular window that looks out on a century-old moment in time. In high relief, surrounded by his soldiers, Colonel Shaw sits astride his horse, his back straighter than the rifles his troops are carrying. But while the rest of the sculpture's bronze men stare stoically ahead, Shaw's eyebrows strain at the corners of his face like those of a child trying not to cry. It must have been one of those anticipatory instants, this moment that the sculptor has framed in this marble window, a moment right before a tremendous change. In the monument he sits in bronze on his horse below an archaic angel as if uncomfortably trapped, frozen in the instant right before both he and the nation changed forever. The sculpture is a memorial to soldiers who died for the freedom of relatives and friends whom they had left behind in slavery, but it is also a memorial to Bob, the college boy who made a strange choice and ended up in a ditch, the twenty-five-year old kid who proved to the entire nation what Boston had been trying to prove for the previous two hundred years: that some things are right and some things are wrong.

I guess that's why I couldn't stop staring at that window on Boston Common. He was just a guy, just Bob, a college kid like me, but somehow he had succeeded in doing what everyone my age dreams of doing. He had proved to the world that he wasn't a kid anymore. When William James spoke at the monument's dedication, he described one of Shaw's final moments: "Walking up and down in front of his regiment, he briefly exhorted them to prove that they were men." Somehow they proved it, and I think that if they had lived, they would have proved it too. Bob has gone from being Bob to being Robert Gould Shaw, the man, not the boy, who despite his hesitations and personal prejudices still managed to shake the nation.

The Saint-Gaudens memorial is not the only shrine to Shaw in the city. Across the Charles River in Cambridge, around the corner from the statue of Charles Sumner in Harvard Square, is Memorial Hall, an imposing brick edifice that comes very close to being a secular cathedral, built both to honor knowledge and to remember the Union dead. If you enter Memorial Hall through its giant oaken portals, as most visitors do, you will find yourself inside Harvard's holiest site and its own private shrine for its Union soldiers, the sanctified Memorial Transept. Except for a few minutes on the hour each day when students come trooping out of Sanders Theatre, the lecture hall to the right, or out of Annenberg, the sprawling and stunning freshman dining hall to the left (take a peek inside to see the superb stained-glass restoration), the Memorial Transept stands empty and silent, and voices in this hallway, like voices in a cathedral, tend to evaporate into whispers toward the vaulted ceiling. The only light during the day comes from two stained-glass rose windows casting burgundy and blue shapes onto the marble floor. But the walls, lined with black walnut paneling and towering Latin inscriptions, are marked off at eye

level by slabs of white marble, each of which is carved and painted with the name of a Harvard graduate who died to preserve the Union.

The Memorial Transept was the center of a policy fight two years ago as Harvard tried to decide whether to add the names of those students who had fought and died for the Confederacy or to maintain the dark vessel of a room as a shrine to the Union dead. While Harvard's Civil War legacy is hardly impeccable by modern standards—a fair number of professors fought vehemently against the abolitionist line—the university has since chosen to leave the Memorial Transept alone, and I think rightly so. For many Bostonians the Civil War was less a senseless tragedy than an apocalyptic battle, a fight between the sinners and the saints. To record the names of the enemy, even if they were alumni, would mean compromising the idea that the war had been a matter of right versus wrong. And Boston has rarely been a place for moral ambiguity.

If you look in the middle of the names on the wall to the right, you'll find a plaque for Robert Gould Shaw, identical in size and shape to those of his classmates. All it gives is his name and the place and date of death (Fort Wagner, S.C., 1863), but this isn't the only mention of Shaw that was ever made here. Immediately to the right of the Memorial Transept is Sanders Theatre, Cambridge's largest auditorium, whose hard oaken pews can accommodate almost twelve hundred people. When the Saint-Gaudens memorial was dedicated, Henry Lee Higginson, a respected Boston public figure and philanthropist who was the first patron of the Boston Symphony Orchestra, gave an address to an entire class of Harvard students in this theater to honor his old friend and classmate Bob Shaw. But Higginson was less interested in mourning Shaw's death than he was in inspiring the students before him, and if you sit in the old Sanders Theatre seats, in front of the stern statue of Josiah Quincy and the giant Veritas seal, it is not hard to imagine Higginson's words resonating from the wooden stage: "Boys, your generation also in turn has its own fresh ideals, and its message to the world. . . .

We know that under stress of war you would prove yourselves brave and loyal soldiers, but your trial comes in the days of peace, and you as citizens are quite as much needed at the front as we were in '61 . . . In yonder cloister, on the tablet with his classmates of 1860, is engraved the name of Robert Gould Shaw. He will always be a heroic figure to you, while to us—his comrades—he will be all this, and furthermore the dear friend, respected and beloved. Harvard students! whenever you hear of Colonel Shaw, or of any officer or of any man of the Fifty-fourth Massachusetts Regiment, salute him in the name of Harvard University and Harvard men."

Mount Auburn is more like a park than a traditional cemetery; from its highest point you can look out and see the whole city.

Harvard men (and women) are still easy to find in Sanders Theatre, where students flock by the hundreds to Harvard's largest undergraduate lecture courses, two of which seem mystically linked to the city's past. Every other spring students crowd into Sanders for a course called "The Bible and Its Interpreters," and in the fall hundreds of them gather again for a course called, simply, "Justice." As one of those students, I pass through the Memorial Transept and into Sanders Theatre several times a week. Too often, as I stumble to and from class, thinking about what the professor in Justice just said or how I'll never finish that Bible paper due the next day, I am oblivious of the beauty of the cavernous theater and vestibule. But occasionally, when I am less preoccupied than usual, on my way out of the lecture, I pause in the hallway, look for Shaw's name on the wall, and silently salute him.

No matter how elusive a city's history may seem, every city in the world has a reservoir somewhere

where the drops of time collect, and that place is the local cemetery. Boston's dead lie beneath each square foot of the city, their gravestones breaking through the grass and concrete every few blocks, but Mount Auburn Cemetery in Cambridge is the city's great open museum of its past heroes.

Most cemeteries force a certain silence on their visitors, but Mount Auburn is more like a park than a traditional cemetery. In fact the place is so parklike that visitors have to be reminded that "bicycling, jogging, picnicking, skating and pets are prohibited since the Cemetery is still an active place of burial and visitation." Instead of hinting to those who walk through it that they too will someday die, the cemetery's endless garden of monuments brags about those who are already dead. Anyone searching here for signs and symbols of the Civil War, or of just about any other event in the past century and a half, will have no trouble finding the right address (this is a cemetery with named streets) of a particular grave by consulting one of the cemetery's many maps. Here rest the great families of nineteenth-century Boston, abolitionists and artists, crusaders and tycoons, poets and prophets, all in large family plots that would make any Cabot or Lowell feel right at home. Longfellow is buried here, as are Winslow Homer, Felix Frankfurter, Buckminster Fuller, and Oliver Wendell Holmes, to name only a few in this American pantheon. But for those in search of the residue of the Civil War, there are a few monuments especially worth seeing. The sphinx-shaped Memorial to the Preservation of the Union, with its wonderfully succinct slogan American Union Preserved—African Slavery destroyed," stands across from the large brownstone-and-marble monument to Robert Gould Shaw's grandfather, with its bronze plaque erected in honor of Colonel Shaw. The colonel's real grave is a ditch somewhere in South Carolina, but here he lies symbolically buried in his family's plot. Someone must have felt the way I felt about him, because there was a fresh flower resting beside the tombstone. Julia Ward Howe is also buried here, be-

TO PLAN A TRIP

The National Park Service offers a self-guided walking-tour map of the Black Heritage Trail as well as, in the summer, daily guided tours; the African Meeting House, at 46 Joy Street, is open Monday through Friday from 10:00 A.M. to 4:00 P.M. Call 617–742–5415 or see www.nps.gov/boaf/ for information. The Memorial Transept, at Harvard, is generally openm to the public on weekdays from 9:00 A.M. to 6:00 P.M.; call 617–496–4595 or see www.fas.harvard.edu/~memhall. Mount Auburn Cemetery (617–547–7105), at 580 Mt. Auburn Street in Cambridge, is open from 8:00 A.M. to 5:00 P.M.., seven days a week. For information on lodgings and more, contact the Grater Boston Convention and Visitors Bureau, at 888–SEE–BOSTON or www. bostonusa.com, or the Massachusetts Office of Travel & Tourism, at 1–800–227–6277 or www.mass-vacation.com.

neath a stone so plain and unassuming that you might easily miss it as you pass through Mount Auburn's sculpture garden of sepulchers. Set two rows back from the closest path, the grave of the woman whose eightieth-birthday tribute labeled her "Poet, Priestess, and Prophet" is inscribed with nothing but her name, her father's name, her husband's name, and the boundary years of her long life of activism, 1819–1910. But in Boston people remember her and the spiritual force that she saw within the great conflict. When I once visited the cemetery in the middle of winter, there were fresh flowers on her grave.

After passing by the graves of more reformers than I could remember the names of, I found myself climbing up toward the cemetery's highest point, marked by obelisks at the very top. From there I was able to look out and see the whole city, from my own university to the nine others beyond it, in a town where one out of every five people is a college student—just the sort of person to live in a place with a history of rallying to a cause.

There is far less to inspire us now. No obvious moral imperative looms on the national horizon, and religious passion, no longer associated with intellectual pursuit, now stands for ideas that don't match the city's liberal politics. Boston is no longer so much a city of ideas and activists as it is a city of students and of books. But as Higginson told Harvard students a century ago, our trial comes in the days of peace, and we are quite as much needed at the front as they were in "'61." The true spirit

of Boston comes not from what its citizens said about slavery or anything else but from the willingness of those citizens to say what they meant and mean what they said. You don't need a Civil War to do that.

As I looked down at the city, I noticed that my favorite moment in the day had arrived, the moment when the sun stops shining and starts glowing instead, when lines and edges are most pronounced and shadows yawn to their greatest lengths. It's not quite the moment of transition from day to night, but rather the moment just before that, the moment of anticipation of evening, when everything around you in both space and time—the trees, the shadows, where you've been, where you're going—becomes incredibly clear. The city has grown quiet in that strange omitted gap in time between day and night, but on these peaceful evenings, if you listen carefully, you can hear the mingled footsteps of the free and the freed, the living and the dead. On the other side of the river, a few miles and more than a century away, Robert Gould Shaw sits trapped on his bronze horse, surveying the future while wondering if anyone will discover that elusive residue of time that the nation, shaken by words' mighty power, once left behind. In the direction of Shaw's gaze, the sun is beginning to set behind the skyscrapers.

Dara Horn is majoring in literature and hopes to become a writer.

Why Lincoln Waged the Civil War

The Man at the White House Window

Stephen B. Oates

The Train of President-Elect Abraham Lincoln, trailing a plume of black smoke, roared southward through Pennsylvania at more than 30 miles per hour. Lincoln was on his way to Washington, D.C., by a circuitous route that had already taken him across several Northern states. In his carpeted, well-furnished coach with national flags draped at each end, he reflected on the crisis that threatened the federal government and on what he would say about it at his next stop, Philadelphia, the birthplace of the republic.

It was February 21, 1861, and seven states of the Deep South had already seceded from the Union and formed the slave-based Confederacy. Its provisional president, Jefferson Davis, had officially warned the Northern states to let the South go in peace or face "the final arbitrament of the sword." The pace of ominous events was almost too much to comprehend. Lincoln himself seemed bewildered by what was happening to the country. He found it hard to believe that his election to the presidency was causing the collapse of the very system of government that had enabled him to get there.

It was an excruciating irony, for in all the land he was perhaps the foremost champion of that government. Since his youth he had extolled the Founding Fathers for beginning a noble experiment

in popular government on these shores, to demonstrate to the world that a free people could govern themselves without hereditary monarchs and aristocracies. And the foundation of that experiment was the Declaration of independence, which in Lincoln's view proclaimed the highest political truths in history: all men are created equal and are entitled to liberty and the pursuit of happiness. The Declaration guaranteed all citizens the "right to rise," Lincoln said, to elevate themselves above the condition of their births, to go as far as their talent and toil would take them. To Lincoln, this equal start and equal opportunity was the "central idea" of the republic and the essence of his "American Dream."

Lincoln did not view this promise of America as limited to only the native-born. The frontier, he contended, should function as an outlet for people the world over who wanted to find a new home, a place to "better their conditions in life." In his eyes the American experiment was the way of the future for nations across the globe. It stood as a beacon of hope for the oppressed and for "the liberal party" throughout the world.

Yet, as Lincoln admitted, this beacon of hope harbored "a vast moral evil"— the institution of slavery. In his view bondage was the one "retrograde institution" that disfigured "the noblest political system the world ever saw." He

described it as a "cancer" in the body politic he could not but hate. "I hate it because of the monstrous injustice of slavery itself. I hate it because it deprives our republican example of its just influence in the world—enables the enemies of free institutions, with plausibility, to taunt us as hypocrites—causes the real friends of freedom to doubt our sincerity." Finally, he hated slavery because it violated the Declaration of Independence, denying black people the right to elevate themselves and thus threatening that right for everyone else. "I want every man to have a chance," he said in 1860, "and I believe a black man is entitled to it—in which he can better his condition—when he may look forward and hope to be a hired laborer this year and the next, work for himself afterward, and finally to hire men to work for him! That is the true system."

Yet he conceded that the peculiar institution, in the states where it already existed, was protected by the Constitution, a spate of national and state laws, and the grim dictates of "necessity." What he opposed was the spread of the evil. By keeping it out of the territories and hemming it in to "the narrowest limits of necessity," he and his party meant to place slavery on "the course of ultimate extinction." And therein, he contended, lay "the precise fact" upon which the entire sectional controversy depended. "You think slavery is *right* and ought to be extended," he told Southerners in 1860, "while we think it is *wrong* and ought to be restricted. . . . It certainly is the only substantial difference between us."

That was Lincoln's perception. In the eyes of Southerners, the differences between them and the Republicans were profound and irreconcilable. To them Lincoln and his party were violent abolitionists who intended to free the slaves at gunpoint, mongrelize the races, and put black people in power in Dixie. For those reasons the seven Deep South states, with their heavy concentration of slaves, left the Union even before Lincoln was inaugurated. "To remain in the Union is to lose all that white men hold dear in government," explained the editor of the Montgomery *Mail*. "We vote to get out."

On his way across the East, Lincoln could scarcely comprehend the magnitude of the disaster he faced. He kept insisting there was no real crisis, only "an *artificial one*" stirred up by "designing politicians." The devotion to the Constitution, he said, was "equally great on both sides of the [Ohio] River." If the people of the North and South would only keep their "self-possession," the crisis would clear up. But in moments of candor, he admitted wearily that upon his shoulders lay the awesome responsibility "of restoring peace to our distracted country."

When he reached Philadelphia on the afternoon of February 21, 1861, he intended to tell its citizens what he believed was at stake in the secession crisis; it was the principle that lay at the heart of his American Dream. He had tried to articulate this earlier in the day, at Trenton, New Jersey, saying he was "exceedingly anxious" to safeguard "that thing" for which the founders of the nation had struggled—"that something even more than National Independence; that *something* that held out a great promise to all the people of the world to all time to come." The next day, speaking with "deep emotion" in Philadelphia's Independence Hall, where the Declaration of Independence had been adopted, he explained what that "something" was. It was "that which

LLOYD OSTENDORF COLLECTION

As president-elect on his way to Washington, Lincoln (directly above the leftmost star on the flag) stopped at Independence Hall in Philadelphia to raise the American flag in honor of George Washington's birthday.

gave promise that in due time the weights should be lifted from the shoulders of all men, and that *all* should have an equal chance." Could the country "be saved upon that basis?" he asked. "If it can, I will consider myself one of the happiest men in the world if I can help to save it. . . . But, if this country cannot be saved without giving up that principle," he said and then paused for a moment. "I was about to say I would rather be assassinated on this spot than to surrender it."

Faced with assassination threats, Lincoln had to sneak through Baltimore and into Washington in disguise. On March 4, with reports circulating that there might be an assassination attempt or an attack by Rebel troops, he was inaugurated under heavy military and police protection. This was further evidence that the system that had allowed him to

gain the presidency was breaking down. As Lincoln spoke, plainclothes detectives eyed the crowd, and soldiers watched from the windows of the Capitol and the roofs of adjacent buildings. On a nearby hill, artillerymen manned a line of howitzers, ready to rake the streets at the first sign of assassins or Rebel troops.

Lincoln's address was conciliatory toward Southerners. "In *your* hands, my dissatisfied fellow countrymen, and not in *mine*, is the momentous issue of civil war. The government will not assail *you*. You can have no conflict, without being yourselves the aggressors. *You* have no oath registered in Heaven to destroy the government, while I shall have the most solemn one to 'preserve, protect and defend' it." He paused. "I am lo[a]th to close. We are not enemies, but friends. We must not be enemies. Though pas-

Lincoln: a photo essay . . .

1860, 1861: PRESIDENTIAL CANDIDATE, PRESIDENT-ELECT

CIVIL WAR TIMES FILES

At the time of his nomination for president, Lincoln had sat for only two dozen photographs, few of them handsome enough to serve as campaign portraits. So on June 3, Chicago photographer Alexander Hesler came to Springfield to pose the still largely unknown candidate in the State Capitol. Lincoln sported a handsome suit and freshly cut hair; only a stubbornly roving shirt collar hinted at the unkempt westerner of old. Hesler's flattering profile (above) was copied by painters and printmakers alike, and became a bestseller in its own right. But the Lincoln who arrived in Washington for his inauguration eight months later seemed transformed. A new beard had aged him, and posing for Alexander Gardner on February 24, 1861 (below), he seemed, an eyewitness remembered, "absorbed in deep thought"—barely aware of the camera. Not surprisingly, the resulting grim picture inspired few American artists. But Europeans admired it; it made America's incoming president look dignified.

CIVIL WAR TIMES FILES

sion may have strained, it must not break our bonds of affection. The mystic chords of memory, stretching from every battle-field, and patriot grave, to every living heart and hearthstone, all over this broad land, will yet swell the chorus of the Union, when again touched, as surely they will be, by the better angels of our nature."

The Confederates responded five weeks later by bombarding Fort Sumter in South Carolina's Charleston Harbor and plunging the country into civil war. Determined to "preserve, protect, and defend" the integrity of his people's government, Lincoln called for 75,000 volunteers to suppress the rebellion. That led to the mobilization of Rebel forces and the defection from the Union of four Upper South states. Initially envisioned by both sides as a 90-day conflict, the war swelled into a vast inferno of destruction that left scarcely a family on either side unscathed and that threat-

ened the very existence of "the noblest political system the world ever saw."

Through the first two years of the war, Lincoln was a deeply troubled president caught in a vortex of difficulties that would have unhinged a lesser man. He could often be seen standing at a White House window, a tall, melancholy figure looking out over his embattled capital and his divided and bleeding country beyond. When an old friend visited him early in the war, Lincoln confessed he was depressed and "not at all hopeful" he could ever suppress this "clear, flagrant, gigantic case of Rebellion" against his government. And the ravages of civil war—the spectacle of Americans killing and maiming one another, of wrecked homesteads and blasted towns, of uprooted families and endless funeral processions—took a terrible emotional toll on a man who sickened at the sight of blood, who abhorred stridency and physical violence, who

dreamed that "*mind,* all conquering *mind,*" would one day rule the world.

As the war continued, his hate mail grew vast and grotesque. "You are nothing but a goddamned Black Nigger," said one correspondent in 1861. Others related "stories of partisan bitterness and personal hatred," said presidential secretary William O. Stoddard. Still others resorted to "the wildest, the fiercest and the most obscene ravings of utter insanity." From all corners of the North came complaints that Lincoln was unfit to be president, that he was too inexperienced, too confused, too stupid and incompetent to reunite his distracted country. Even some of his cabinet secretaries feared that the war was too much for him.

Yet despite all his difficulties, despite his depression and self-doubt, Lincoln managed to see this sprawling and confusing conflict in a global dimension. He defined and fought it according to his core of unshakable convictions about America's experiment and historic mission in the progress of human liberty in the world. Historian Gabor Boritt has described the conflict as "Lincoln's war for the American Dream." The central idea of this struggle, Lincoln told his personal secretary John Hay, "is the necessity that is upon us, of proving that popular government is not an absurdity. We must settle this question now, whether in a free government the minority have the right to break up the government whenever they choose. If we fail it will go far to prove the incapability of the people to govern themselves."

He elaborated on that point in his Message to Congress on Independence Day of 1861. The principle of secession, he said, "is one of disintegration, and upon which no government can possibly endure. And this issue embraces more than the fate of these United States. It presents to the whole family of man, the question, whether a constitutional republic, or a democracy—a government of the people, by the same people—can, or cannot, maintain its territorial integrity, against its own domestic foes. It presents the question, whether discontented individuals . . . can always, upon the pretences made in this case, or on any other pretences, or arbitrarily, without any pretence, break up their Government, and thus practically put an end to free government upon the earth."

As Lincoln well knew, there were Europeans who argued that secession movements, anarchy, and civil war were inherent weaknesses of popular government and that a constitutional monarchy was the more stable form of government. When the Civil War began, British foes of popular government cheered "the trial of Democracy and its failure" in America and declared it good "riddance to a nightmare." In the American Civil War, popular government was indeed going through a fiery trial for its existence, and nobody saw that more clearly than the man at the White House window. To preserve democracy for this and all future generations, Lincoln said in his Independence Day message, the national government must meet force with force. It must teach Southern dissidents "the folly of being the beginners of

NATIONAL ARCHIVES

war." It must show the world that "those who can fairly carry an election, can also suppress a rebellion," and that popular government *was* a workable system, that people *could* rule themselves. "This is essentially a people's contest," Lincoln said. "On the side of the Union, it is a struggle for maintaining in the world, that form, and sub-

COURTESY OF HERB PECK, JR.

Former slave Frederick Douglass (left) used the pages of his newspaper, the *North Star,* to urge Lincoln to fight unabashedly for abolition. He breathed life into his appeal with vivid recollections of melancholy plantation scenes like those on the next page. One of the fruits of Douglass's labor was the eventual enlistment of free blacks into the Union army. Martin R. Delaney (below), commissioned a major by Lincoln, was the army's first black field-grade officer.

stance of government, whose leading object is, to elevate the condition of men—to lift artificial weights from all shoulders—to clear the paths of laudable pursuit for all—to afford all, an unfettered start, and a fair chance, in the race of life."

Yes, this was the central idea of the war. This was what Lincoln had in mind when he said, "I shall do nothing in malice. What I deal with is too vast for malicious dealing." Over the course of the war, he repeated the central idea to various audiences and visitors at the White House. They were fighting, he said, to preserve more than just the Union. They were fighting for what the Union represented—something that lay at the center of the American promise. "I happen temporarily to occupy this big White House," he told an Ohio regiment. "I am a living witness that one of your children may look to come here as my father's child has. It is in order that each of you may have through this free government which we have enjoyed, an open field and a fair chance for your industry, enterprise and intelligence, that you may all have equal privileges in the race of life, with all its desirable human aspirations. It is for this the struggle should be maintained, that we may not lose our birthright. . . . The nation is worth fighting for, to secure such an inestimable jewel."

Fighting for that "inestimable jewel," keeping the central idea foremost in his mind, Lincoln found the inner strength to surmount his multitude of wartime woes—the savage criticism he suffered throughout his presidency, the devastating loss of his cherished son Willie, the ensuing breakdown of his wife, Mary, and above all the endless, endless war. The war consumed him, demanding almost all his energy from dawn until late into the night. He had almost no time

LIBRARY OF CONGRESS

COURTESY OF THE NEW YORK HISTORICAL SOCIETY, NEW YORK CITY

harsh war measure after another to subdue the rebellion and save popular government. He declared martial law, suspended the writ of habeas corpus, and approved the arbitrary arrests of thousands of antiwar Democrats. "Must I shoot a simple-minded soldier boy who deserts," he said in defense of his policy, "while I must not touch a hair of a wily agitator who induces him to desert?" When Chief Justice of the Supreme Court Roger B. Taney rebuked Lincoln for suspending the writ and admonished him not to violate the laws he had sworn to uphold, Lincoln replied: "Are all the laws, but one, to go unexecuted, and the government itself go to pieces lest that one be violated?"

At the same time, Lincoln approved the confiscation of enemy property and saw to it that the two confiscation acts of 1861 and 1862 were faithfully enforced. He went on to em-

brace emancipation, the enlistment of black soldiers, conscription, and scorched-earth warfare. These measures turned the war into the very thing Lincoln had cautioned against: a remorseless revolutionary struggle. But it was a struggle that forged from the ashes of the old confederation a new, indestructible nation. And it became such a contest because of Lincoln's unswerving commitment to the war's central idea.

Nowhere was the struggle more evident than where it concerned the problem of slavery. At the beginning of hostilities, in deference to the loyal slave states and to his bipartisan war effort, Lincoln adopted a hands-off policy regarding slavery. He said he meant to put the old Union back together "as it was," with slavery intact and Southern society unaltered. But in little more than a year, the problems and pressures of civil war caused Lincoln to change his mind, convincing him that he had to "lay a strong hand on the colored element." There was no single reason why he changed his mind—certainly it was not political expediency. Rather, the pressures operating on Lincoln were many and complex.

First, from the summer of 1861 on, a group of so-called Radical Republicans led by Senators Charles Sumner, Benjamin Franklin Wade, and Zachariah Chandler pressed Lincoln to destroy slavery as a war measure. Since the institution was the cornerstone of the Confederacy, they said, emancipation would

for his family, for recreation beyond a daily carriage ride, for meals and leisurely jokes and laughter with old friends, for government matters unrelated to the conflict.

In short, the war and his response to it defined him as a president. As the war grew and changed, so Lincoln grew and changed. At first, he took pains to keep the war from degenerating, as he put it, "into a violent and remorseless revolutionary struggle." As a consequence, his initial war strategies were cautious and limited. But as the war ground on with no end in sight, Lincoln embraced one

NATIONAL ARCHIVES

LINCOLN ON SLAVERY

"As a nation, we began by declaring that 'all men are created equal.' We now practically read it 'all men are created equal except negroes'."

To Joshua F. Speed
August 24, 1855

"As I would not be a slave, so I would not be a master."

August 1, 1858(?)

"My first impulse would be to free all the slaves and send them to Liberia. . . ."

" . . . there is no reason in the world why the negro is not entitled to all the natural rights enumerated in the Declaration of Independence. . . . I hold that he is as much entitled to these as the white man."

" . . . I have no purpose to introduce political and social equality between the white and black races."

Debate with Douglas
Ottawa, Illinois
August 21, 1858

"If I could save the Union without freeing any slave I would do it. And if I could save it by freeing all the slaves, I would do it."

To Horace Greeley
August 22, 1862

cripple the Rebel war effort and hasten an end to the rebellion. They also reminded Lincoln that slavery had caused the war; it was the reason the Southern states had seceded. If the Rebel South returned to the Union with slavery intact, Southerners would start another war over slavery the next time they perceived a threat to the institution. In the end the current struggle would have accomplished nothing. If Lincoln really wanted to save the government, he must abolish slavery and smash the South's arrogant planter class, which the senators believed had masterminded secession and fomented war.

Beyond Washington, the great black abolitionist Frederick Douglass saw the end of slavery in this war, and he launched a one-man crusade to convert Lincoln to that idea. In his newspaper and on the platform, he thundered at the man in the White House, playing on the president's personal hatred of slavery and his commitment to the war's central idea. "The Negro is the key of the situation—the pivot upon which the whole rebellion turns," Douglas said. "Teach the rebels and traitors that the price they are to pay for the attempt to abolish this Government must be the abolition of slavery," he said. "Hence forth let the war cry be down with treason, and down with slavery, the cause of treason."

Douglas, Sumner, and members of Lincoln's own cabinet raised still another argument for emancipation. In 1862 his armies were short of troops in every theater. Thanks to repeated Union military failures and to a growing war-weariness across the North, volunteering had fallen off sharply, and Union generals bombarded Washington with shrill complaints, insisting that they faced an overwhelming Southern foe and must have reinforcements before they could win battles or even fight. "You need more men," Sumner told Lincoln. "You need the slaves."

Meanwhile the slaves themselves were putting pressure on Lincoln to emancipate them. Far from being passive recipients of freedom, as historian Vincent Harding has reminded us, the slaves were abandoning Rebel farms and plantations and escaping to Union lines by the thousands. This created a difficult legal problem for Lincoln's administration: what was the status of such "contraband of war," as Union Major General Benja-

min F. Butler designated them? Were they still slaves or were they free? For the most part, the administration allowed field commanders to solve the contraband problem as they wished. Some officers sent the fugitives back to their Rebel masters, while others turned them over to refugee camps to be cared for by charitable organizations. But with more and more slaves streaming into Union lines, Sumner, Douglass, several cabinet members, and many others urged Lincoln to grant them freedom and enlist the able-bodied men in the army. "Let the slaves and free colored people be called into service and formed into a liberating army," Douglass exhorted Lincoln, "to march into the South and raise the banner of Emancipation among the slaves."

At first Lincoln rejected a presidential move against slavery as "too big a lick." But by the summer of 1862, after

COURTESY OF LEBANON VALLEY COLLEGE

More than one calligrapher has tried to turn the poetic words of the 1863 Emancipation Proclamation into visual art in tribute to Lincoln and one of his boldest achievements.

failing to persuade the loyal border states to adopt voluntary, state-guided, compensated emancipation as the only alternative to Federal action, Lincoln realized that he had to abolish slavery himself. He could no longer avoid the responsibility. "Turn which way he would," Lincoln said, "this disturbing element which caused the war rose against him," compelling him to act. By invoking the war power, he would use the army to eradicate slavery as a military necessity to save the American system. How could he justify such a radical step? "By invoking the war power, he would use the army to eradicate slavery as a military necessity to save the American system. How could he justify such a radical step? "By general law life and limb must be protected," he explained, "yet often a limb must be amputated to save a life; but a life is never wisely given to save a limb. I felt that measures, otherwise unconstitutional might become lawful, by becoming indispensable to the preservation of the Constitution, through the preservation of the nation."

But there was a moral element in his decision, too. Emancipation would remove an evil institution Lincoln hated. "If slavery is not wrong," he kept declaring, "nothing is wrong." At the same time, emancipation would break the shackles of several million oppressed human beings to that they, too, could share in Lincoln's American Dream, so that they, too, could elevate themselves. With the central idea in mind, Lincoln struck at slavery because he realized that popular government and its promise of the right to rise could not survive so long as some people were denied that right, were denied "an unfettered start, and a fair chance, in the race of life." As he explained it to Congress that December: "In giving freedom to the slave, we assure freedom for the free—honorable alike in what we give, and what we preserve. We shall nobly save, or meanly lose, the last best, hope of earth."

The Emancipation Proclamation of January 1, 1863, was a powerful symbolic announcement to the world that Union *and* freedom, one and inseparable, were now Lincoln's war objectives. By issuing that decree, by striking at the

Lincoln: a photo essay . . .

1861: COMMANDER IN CHIEF

to my good friend, Mrs Fanny Speed.
A Lincoln.

For one of his first portraits as president, probably taken in the spring of 1861, Lincoln wore a well starched, round-tipped collar and exhibited a newly trimmed beard. He appeared vibrant and determined—a commander in chief exuding confidence on the eve of war. The melancholy that oozed from so many early photographs was gone—at least for now. But oddly, this flattering pose was not widely circulated to the public at the time. (Lincoln did autograph copies to two relatives of his closest friend, Joshua Fry Speed. The print above was sent to Speed's wife, Fanny.) The picture's rarity may be attributable to the fact that the photographer did such a poor job of concealing Lincoln's enormous ear, which juts out akimbo from his closely barbered hair. But while it enjoyed little public circulation, we know that Lincoln possessed several copies. Besides the two he gave to the Speed women, he probably provided yet another print to the artist Edward Dalton Marchant, who painted his portrait from life in the White House in 1863. Marchant found Lincoln "the most difficult subject who ever taxed" his skills as an artist, and Lincoln probably gave his this photograph to help him create his portrait. His finished oil painting bore an uncanny resemblance to the pose. The photo was probably made in Washington by C. D. Fredericks, to whom an engraver gave credit for the original in an 1864 print adaptation.

"cancerous" institution that violated the Declaration of Independence and endangered everyone's right to rise, Lincoln seized the high moral ground in this brutal war and promised a new birth of freedom for all Americans. The proclamation also admitted black Americans North and South into the Union's mili-

A political cartoon by Southern sympathizer Adalbert Volck suggests a demonic influence on Lincoln as he writes the Emancipation Proclamation. Note, for example, the cloven-hoofed [table] legs and devil inkstank.

tary forces to fight for their country, a major step toward full citizenship.

Lincoln understood perfectly well what forces he was unleashing. "The character of the war will be changed. It will be one of subjugation.... The South is to be destroyed and replaced by new propositions and ideas." The Emancipation Proclamation and the use of black soldiers, as historian James McPherson has said, "marked the transformation of a war to preserve the Union into a revolution to overthrow the old order." As Union forces drove across Rebel territory, they liberated all the slaves in the ares and states they conquered and recruited black men into the army. Senator Sumner described the process succinctly: "The glorious flag of the Union, wherever it floats, becomes the flag of Freedom." In this respect, as Lincoln said, the war brought on changes more fundamental and profound than either side had expected when the conflict began. Now slavery, and the planter class and social order based on it, would perish as the Confederacy perished, would die by degrees with every Union advance, every Union victory.

Even so, emancipation was the most explosive and unpopular act of Lincoln's presidency. By mid 1863, thousands of

Democrats were in open revolt against his administration, denouncing Lincoln as an abolitionist dictator out to mongrelize the white race. In the Midwest, dissident Democrats launched a peace movement to throw "the shrieking abolitionist faction" out of office and negotiate a peace with the Confederacy that would restore the old Union with slavery unharmed.

With all the public unrest behind the lines, conservative Republicans begged Lincoln to abandon emancipation and rescue his country "from the brink of ruin." But Lincoln was intractable. He had made up his mind to smash the slave society of the Rebel South, and no amount of public discontent was going to change his mind. He had given his promise of freedom to the slaves, he said, "and the promise being made, must be kept."

To the despair of his opponents, Lincoln also demanded unconditional surrender as his terms for peace: the Rebels must lay down their arms, disband their military forces, and recognize both "the restoration of the Union and the abandonment of slavery." Those terms and Lincoln's harsh war policy became the central issues of the election of 1864, when Lincoln ran for a second term against Democrat George B. McClellan,

whom Lincoln had relieved from command of the Army of the Potomac in 1862 because the general had "the slows." As historian David Long has pointed out, the election of 1864 was the most significant political canvass in American history. At stake was the fate of emancipation, the Union, and popular government itself. The Democratic platform contained a "war failure" plank, which made peace the first priority and reunion a distant second and which promised to leave slavery intact. True, McClellan repudiated the "peace" plank, saying he could not "look in the faces of gallant comrades of the army and navy" unless he did so. Nevertheless, as Long has persuasively argued, neither emancipation nor the Union could possibly have survived had McClellan and his party won control of the government.

For a time in the summer of 1864, it appeared that they would do just that. It was a time of unrelenting gloom for Lincoln, with his two major armies bogged down in sieges and with warweariness setting in across the land. Republicans across the North were in despair, contending that Lincoln's reelection campaign was hopeless. "I find everywhere a conviction that we need a change," said one Republican, "that the war languishes under Mr. Lincoln and that he *cannot* and *will* not give us peace." Another said flatly: "There are no Lincoln men."

Lincoln, too, thought he would be defeated. In the privacy of his office, he took out a sheet of stationery and dated it August 23, 1864. "This morning," he wrote, "as for some days past, it seems exceedingly probable that this Administration will not be re-elected. Then it will be my duty to so co-operate with the President elect, as to save the Union between the election and the inauguration; as he will have secured his election on such ground that he can not possibly save it afterward."

Some conservative Union men argued that there was only one way Lincoln could save his presidency. He must abandon emancipation and offer the Rebels peace conditions that promised to preserve their peculiar institution. Lincoln answered with a resounding no. The Union needed its thousands of

Southern black soldiers now more than ever. He would not, could not, throw them back to their former masters. He would be "damned in time and eternity" if he did.

But faced with what seemed massive opposition to his war policies, he wavered once. In late August he drew up terms in which he offered to end the fighting if the Rebels would return to the Union and recognize the national authority. Slavery and all other questions were to be left for "adjustment by peaceful means." But Lincoln changed his mind and with awakened resolution did not offer the terms. The cabinet supported him. A peace overture would be worse than losing the election, they decided; "it would be ignominiously surrendering it in advance."

Others begged Lincoln to cancel the election, even declare himself dictator, rather than let the government fall into McClellan's hands. But Lincoln adamantly refused because of his commitment to the war's central idea. "The election is a necessity," he insisted. "We can not have a free government without elections; and if the rebellion could force us to forego, or postpone a national election, it might fairly claim to have already conquered us."

There was no doubt in his voice now, no wavering in his resolve to stand his ground. To agree to an armistice, he insisted, would be "the end of the struggle" and the loss of all that Union men had fought and died for. "Keep my war policy, and you can save the Union. Throw it away, and the Union goes with it." There was an even greater reason to fight on to total victory. As he explained to the 148th Ohio: "I look upon [the war] as an attempt on the one hand to overwhelm and destroy the national existence, while, on our part, we are striving to maintain the government and institutions of our fathers, to enjoy them ourselves, and transmit them to our children and our children's children forever." This government, he went on, "is worthy [of] your every effort. Nowhere in the world is presented a government of so much liberty and equality. To the humblest and poorest amongst us are held out the highest privileges and positions. The present moment finds me at

LIBRARY OF CONGRESS

In this fictional illustration, Lincoln talks with the architect directing the building of a new dome for the U.S. Capital. The project was completed in early 1865.

the White House, yet there is as good a chance for your children as there was for my father's."

When Lincoln won the election that November, many contemporaries and most historians thereafter attributed it to the dramatic reversal in Northern military fortunes—Major General William T. Sheerman's capture of Atlanta and Major General Philip Sheridan's victory over a Rebel army in the Shenandoah Valley—which rallied the Northern electorate behind the administration. Yet Lincoln gave another reason. The election "shows that . . . he who is most devoted to the Union, and most opposed to treason, can receive most of the people's votes." And he interpreted his vic-

tory as a popular mandate for his policy of emancipation and reunion. "The voice of the people now, for the first time, [was] heard upon the question."

The election demonstrated something else, too. "It has long been a grave question, whether any Government not too strong for the liberties of its people can be strong enough to maintain its own existence in great emergencies," Lincoln told a group of serenaders. "On this point the present rebellion brought our republic to a severe test." Yet, he said, the election took place without a hitch, which proved "that a people's Government can sustain a national election in the midst of a great civil war. Until now, it has not been known to the world that this was a possibility. It shows, also, how sound and how strong we still are."

With his reelection mandate, Lincoln set about promoting a constitutional amendment that would guarantee the freedom of all slaves in America, including those in the loyal border states (which had been exempted from the Emancipation Proclamation). Since issuing that decree, Lincoln had worried it might be nullified in the courts or thrown out by a later Congress or a subsequent administration. A constitutional amendment, however, would safeguard the proclamation and prevent emancipation from ever being overturned.

As it happened, the Senate had passed an emancipation amendment—the present Thirteenth Amendment—back in April 1864, but the House had failed to approve it. After that, Lincoln had insisted that the Republican platform endorse the measure. Now, over the winter of 1864–1865, he put tremendous pressure on the House to pass the amendment, using all his powers of persuasion and patronage. He singled out "sinners" among the Democrats who were "on praying ground" and informed them that they had a better chance for the federal jobs they wanted if they voted for the amendment. Soon two Democrats crossed over to Lincoln's side. With the outcome still in doubt, Lincoln participated in secret negotiations never made public—negotiations that allegedly involved patronage, a New Jersey railroad monopoly, and the release of Rebels related to Congressional Democrats—to bring wavering opponents into line. "The greatest measure of the nineteenth century," said Republican Congressman Thaddeus

Stevens, "was passed by corruption, aided and abetted by the purest man in America." On January 31, 1865, the House finally adopted the Thirteenth Amendment by just three votes more than the required two-thirds majority.

Abolitionist William Lloyd Garrison credited Lincoln more than any other man "for this vital and saving amendment." Lincoln himself declared it "a great moral victory" and a "King's cure" for the evils of slavery. When ratified by the states, it would end human bondage everywhere in America and transform a Constitution that protected slavery into a charter of freedom under which no human being could be held as a slave. Lincoln pointed across the Potomac. "If the people over the river had behaved themselves, I could not have done what I have."

By January and February 1865 the end of the terrible war appeared near at hand. Lincoln's armies were mopping up the Confederacy in all directions, waging scorched-earth warfare against the Rebel economy and civilian morale with ruthless efficiency. Agreeing with Sherman's idea that war was "all hell" and should be ended as swiftly as possible, Lincoln fully endorsed Sheridan's burning of the Shenandoah Valley, Sherman's brutal March to the Sea through Georgia and the Carolinas, Brigadier General James H. Wilson's destructive raid across Alabama. Such warfare earned Lincoln and his generals undying hatred in Dixie, but it brought them victory: slightly less than five months after Sherman began his march, the war was over.

There was a moral purpose behind Lincoln's strategy of total war, of

pounding all his Rebel foes—soldiers and civilians alike—into total submission. It was the surest way he knew of ending the conflict, restoring the Union, and salvaging his American Dream. By annihilating the will and ability of the Rebels to wage war, he saw to it that they would never again be able to attempt the destruction of the government and all that it represented.

In the end, Lincoln did what he had told Congress must be done. He taught rebellious Southerners "the folly of being the beginners of war." He showed the world that "those who can fairly carry an election, can also suppress a rebellion." He demonstrated that popular government was strong enough to maintain its own existence without degenerating into a dictatorship. Adhering steadfastly to the war's central idea, he brought about a new birth of freedom for all Americans, so that "government of the *people,* by the *people,* for the *people*" would not perish from the earth. Then, in his hour of triumph, in the cruelest irony of all, he was assassinated by a Confederate sympathizer who thought him a despicable tyrant.

Stephen Oates, professor of history at the University of Massachusetts at Amherst, is the author of With Malice Toward None: The Life of Abraham Lincoln *(1977),* Our Fiery Trial: Abraham Lincoln, John Brown, and the Civil War Era *(1979),* Abraham Lincoln: The Man Behind the Myths *(1984), and other books. His most recent is* A Woman Of Valor: Clara Barton and the Civil War *(1994).*

Why the South Lost the Civil War

Interviews by Carl Zebrowski. Ten Civil War historians provide some contrasting—and probably controversial—views on how and why the Confederate cause ultimately ended in defeat.

Carl Zebrowski

Carl Zebrowski is associate editor of Civil War Times Illustrated, *another magazine published by Cowles.*

"The art of war is simple enough. Find out where your enemy is. Get at him as soon as you can. Strike at him as hard as you can and as often as you can, and keep moving on."

Put that way, the business of fighting and winning wars sounds simple enough. And perhaps it was simple in the mind of the man who so concisely described the complex art: General Ulysses S. Grant. After assuming command of all Union armies in March 1864, Grant crushed the Confederacy in about one year.

But the American Civil War, like any war, was not simple. The North and South engaged each other for four long years. More than half a million people were killed. Families were torn apart, towns destroyed. And in the end, the South lost.

For the past 130 years Americans have argued over the reasons for the Confederacy's downfall. Diverse opinions have appeared in hundreds of books, but the numerous possibilities have never adequately been summarized and gathered together in one place. So we decided to ask ten of the country's most

respected Civil War historians: "Why did the South lose the Civil War?" Here (edited for length) are their answers.
—Carl Zebrowski

WILLIAM C. DAVIS

Former editor of Civil War Times Illustrated *and author of more than thirty books about the war, including the recent* "A Government of Our Own": The Making of the Confederacy.

Why did the South lose? When the question is asked that way it kind of presupposes that the South lost the war all by itself and that it really could have won it. One answer is that *the North won it*. The South lost because the North outmanned and outclassed it at almost every point, militarily.

Despite the long-held notion that the South had all of the better generals, it really had only one good army commander and that was Lee. The rest were second-raters, at best. The North, on the other hand, had the good fortune of bringing along and nurturing people like Grant, William T. Sherman, Philip Sheridan, George H. Thomas, and others.

The South was way outclassed industrially. There was probably never any chance of it winning without European recognition and military aid. And we

can now see in retrospect what some, like Jefferson Davis, even saw at the time, which was that there was never any real hope of Europe intervening. It just never was in England or France's interests to get involved in a North American war that would inevitably have wound up doing great damage, especially to England's maritime trade.

"Despite the long-held notion that the South had all of the better generals, it really had only one good army commander and that was Lee. The rest were second-raters, at best."

Industrially the South couldn't keep up in output and in manpower. By the end of the war, the South had, more or less, plenty of weaponry still, but it just didn't have enough men to use the guns.

I don't agree with the theories that say the South lost because it lost its will to win. There's nothing more willful or stubborn than a groundhog, but whenever one of them runs into a Ford pick-up on the highway it's the groundhog that always loses, no matter how much willpower it has.

We can't fault the Southerners for thinking at the time that they could win when we can see in retrospect that there probably never was a time when they could have. The most important things they couldn't see was the determination of Abraham Lincoln to win, and the incredible staying power of the people of the North, who stuck by Lincoln and stuck by the war in spite of the first two years of almost unrelenting defeat. The only way the South could have won would have been for Lincoln to decide to lose. As long as Lincoln was determined to prosecute the war and as long as the North was behind him, inevitably superior manpower and resources just had to win out.

> "The South certainly did not lose for any lack of . . . bravery and skill on the battlefield. In those virtues the Confederate soldier was unexcelled."

The miracle is that the South held out as long as it did. That's an incredible testament to the courage and self-sacrifice of the people of the South—both the men in the armies and the people at home who sustained them, with nothing but continuing and expanding destruction all around them.

The South lost the war because the North and Abraham Lincoln were determined to win it.

ROBERT KRICK

Historian and author of ten books about the war.

The South lost because it had inferior resources in every aspect of military personnel and equipment. That's an old-fashioned answer. Lots of people will be scornful of

it. But a ratio of twenty-one million to seven million in population comes out the same any way you look at it.

The basic problem was numbers. Give Abraham Lincoln seven million men and give Jefferson Davis and Robert E. Lee twenty-one million, and cognitive dissonance doesn't matter, European recognition doesn't matter, the Emancipation Proclamation and its ripple effect don't matter. Twenty-one to seven is a very different thing than seven to twenty-one.

BRIAN POHANKA

Consultant for the weekly series "Civil War Journal" on the Arts and Entertainment network, on-set history advisor for the movie Gettysburg, *a staff writer and researcher for Time-Life Books'* The Civil War *series, and a founder of the Association for the Preservation of Civil War Sites.*

The South certainly did not lose for any lack of idealism, or dedication to its cause or beliefs, or bravery and skill on the battlefield. In those virtues the Confederate soldier was unexcelled, and it's my belief that man-for-man there was no finer army in the history of America than the Army of Northern Virginia.

But of course the factors that enter into the South's ultimate defeat are those things that you hear time and time again, and with a great amount of validity: the North's industrial base; the North's manpower resources; the fact that foreign recognition was denied the Confederacy. In time these things would tell on the battlefield, certainly on the broader level. The North was able to bring its industry and its manpower to bear in such a way that eventually through sheer numerical and material advantage, it gained and maintained the upper hand.

That's when you get into the whole truly tragic sense of the Lost Cause, because those men knew their cause was lost, they knew there was really no way they could possibly win, and yet they fought on with tremendous bravery and dedication. And that's, I think, one of the reasons why the Civil War was such a poignant and even heart-wrenching

(CIVIL WAR TIMES ILLUSTRATED COLLECTION)

time. Whether or not you agree with the Confederacy or with the justness of its cause, there's no way that you can question the idealism and the courage, the bravery, the dedication, the devotion of its soldiers—that they believed what they were fighting for was right. Even while it was happening, men like Union officer Joshua Chamberlain—who did all that he could to defeat the Confederacy—could not help but admire the dedication of those soldiers.

NOAH ANDRE TRUDEAU

Author of three books about the war's final year, including the recent Out of the Storm: The End of the Civil War *(April–June 1865).*

One main reason why the South lost (and this may seem offbeat because it flies in the face of the common wisdom) is that the South lacked the moral center that the North had in this conflict. Robert Kirby in his book on Florida's Edward Kirby Smith and the Trans-Mississippi suggests that the South's morale began to disintegrate in the Trans-Mississippi in about 1862.

The North had a fairly simple message that was binding it together, and that message was that the Union, *the idea of Union,* was important, and probably after 1863 you could add the crusade against slavery to that.

> *"One main reason why the South lost is that [it] lacked the moral center that the North had in this conflict."*

Ask the question, "What was the South fighting for; what was the Southern way of life that they were trying to protect?" and you will find that Southerners in Arkansas had a very different answer from Southerners in Georgia or Southerners in Virginia. And what you increasingly find as the war continued is that the dialogue got more and more confused. And you actually had state governors such as Joe Brown in Georgia identifying the needs of Georgia as being paramount and starting to withhold resources from the Confederacy and just protecting the basic infrastructure of the Georgia state government over the Confederacy. In the North you certainly had dialogue and debate on the war aims, but losing the Union was never really a part of that discussion. Preserving the Union was always the constant.

So, one key reason the South lost is that as time went on and the war got serious, Southerners began losing faith in the cause because it really did not speak to them directly.

JAMES M. MCPHERSON

Professor of history at Princeton University and author of nine books about the Civil War, including the Pulitzer Prize–winning Battle Cry of Freedom.

Historians have offered several explanations for the Confederate defeat in the Civil War. First, the North had a superiority in numbers and resources—but

superiority did not bring victory to the British Empire in its war against the American colonies that were fighting for their independence in 1776, nor did it bring victory to the United States in its war against North Vietnam in the 1960s and '70s. While Northern superiority in numbers and resources was a necessary condition for Union victory, it is not a sufficient explanation for that victory. Neither are the internal divisions within the Confederacy sufficient explanation for its defeat, because the North also suffered sharp internal divisions between those who supported a war for the abolition of slavery and those who resisted it, between Republicans and Democrats, between Unionists and Copperheads. And, in fact, the North probably suffered from greater internal disunity than the Confederacy.

Superior leadership is a possible explanation for Union victory. Abraham Lincoln was probably a better war president than Jefferson Davis and certainly offered a better explanation to his own people of what they were fighting for than Davis was able to offer. By the latter half of the war, Northern military leadership had evolved a coherent strategy for victory which involved the destruction of Confederate armies but went beyond that to the destruction of Confederate resources to wage war, including the resource of slavery, the South's labor power. By the time Grant had become general-in chief and Sherman his chief subordinate and Sheridan one of his hardest-hitting field commanders, the North had evolved a strategy that in the end completely destroyed the Confederacy's ability to wage war. And that combination of strategic leadership—both at the political level with Lincoln and the military level with Grant, Sherman, and Sheridan—is what in the end explains Northern victory.

GARY GALLAGHER

Professor of history at Pennsylvania State University and author, coauthor, or editor of eleven books about the war, including the recent Third Day at Gettysburg and Beyond *and* The Fredericksburg Campaign: Decision on the Rappahannock.

(CIVIL WAR TIMES ILLUSTRATED COLLECTION)

The principal cause of Confederate failure was the fact that the South's armies did not win enough victories in the field—especially enough victories in a row in the field—to both sustain Confederate morale behind the lines and depress Union morale behind the lines. In the end there was a waning of the will to resist on the part of Southern white people, but that was tied directly to the performance of the Confederate armies in the field; more than once they seemed to be on the brink of putting together enough successes to make Northern people behind the lines unwilling to pay the necessary price to subjugate the Confederacy.

The primary reason the Confederates did not have more success on the battlefield is that they developed only one really talented army commander, and that, of course, was Robert E. Lee. There never was a commander in the West who was fully competent to command an army—and I include Joseph E. Johnston and Albert Sidney Johnston and Braxton Bragg and the rest in that company. The almost unbroken string of failures in the West depressed Confederate morale. Lee's successes in the East were able to compensate for that for a good part of the war, but in the end there simply was too much bad news from the battlefield. And that bad news, together with Union advances into the South, the destruction of the Confederate infrastructure, and the problems of the Confederate economy that worked hardships on so many people, all came together to bring about Confederate defeat.

RICHARD MCMURRY

Historian and author of Two Great Rebel Armies, *which examines the Confederacy's defeat.*

If I had to pin the South's defeat down to one sentence, I would have to say it was due to very bad military commanders: Albert Sidney Johnston, P. G. T. Beauregard, Braxton Bragg, John C. Pemberton, Joseph E. Johnston, and John Bell Hood (and if you want to go down a notch or two in the command structure, Leonidas Polk, William J. Hardee, and Joseph Wheeler).

With people like Polk and Hardee you've got ranking generals in an army who deliberately sought to undermine their commanding general Braxton Bragg. With Wheeler you've got a subordinate general who on at least two occasions—in the fall of 1863 and the fall of 1864—went off joy-riding when he should have been obeying his orders from his army commander. With Beauregard and Johnston you had two generals who were unwilling to work with their government. With Hood and Bragg you had two generals who were basically incompetent as army commanders. And with Albert Sidney Johnston you had a general who underwent some kind of confidence crisis after Fort Donelson.

Let me point out that every one of those generals was in the West. Any explanation that does not account for the West is irrelevant to your question. The war was lost by the Confederates in the West and won by the Federals in the West. I don't see how you could even question that. In the crucial theater of the war, the Confederacy did not have a competent commanding general.

MARK GRIMSLEY

Professor of history at Ohio State University and author of Hard Hand of War *(1995), his first book about the war.*

There are really two interesting questions. One is: Why did the South fail to gain or maintain its independence? The other is: Why did the South not only lose its bid for independence but also its bid to influence the terms under which reunion would take place?

The answer to the second question seems to involve a combination of two things. First, the political culture in the South made it difficult for the many people (including those in leadership positions in the Confederacy) who wanted a negotiated settlement to make their will felt. Instead, Jefferson Davis, as president, was able to continue insisting on no peace short of independence. In a real two-party culture, Davis might have been pressured to compromise, or he might have been eased out, or the Congress might have been able to do something.

The other part of the answer is that while the key Confederate commanders—Beauregard, Lee, Joe Johnston—were trying to maximize their military position so as to influence any kind of peace negotiations and give the North an incentive to allow the South to reenter the Union on somewhat its own terms, military mistakes in the late winter and early spring of 1865 scuttled the Confederate military position in Virginia and the Carolinas. This precipitated a collapse sooner than might have happened, undermining any chance that the Confederate government might eventually pursue a negotiated settlement.

HERMAN HATTAWAY

Professor of history at the University of Missouri, Kansas City, and coauthor of Why the South Lost the Civil War.

My collaborators and I, in our book *Why the South Lost the Civil War,* laid out our theory, which is that the South lost the Civil War because it didn't really want to win badly enough. Defeat was ultimately due to a loss of collective will. But in other discussions with various learned groups, I've been induced to admit that in order for the Southern people to have a sufficient degree of will to win the war, they would have had to

be a different people than they were. And so, in that sense, victory for the South was ultimately an impossibility.

Now certainly the course of the war, the military events, had a lot to do with the loss of will. The Southerners hoped that they would win spectacular victories on Northern soil, and they didn't. They hoped that they would be able to exhaust the will of the Northern people, and they didn't. And I don't know that all of the Southern people put a great deal of stock in their hopes that Abraham Lincoln would not be reelected, but certainly the key Southern leaders did, and this was their great hope and great strategy toward the end.

With regard to military turning points, I'm not a fan of those, and I certainly don't think that Gettysburg and Vicksburg dictated the inevitable outcome of the war. We tend in *Why the South Lost* to imply that there was really still hope until March of 1865, but really I think the outcome of the war became inevitable in November 1864 with the reelection of Lincoln and that utter determination to see the thing through, and, of course, the finding of U.S. Grant by Lincoln and company. Grant was certainly the man to provide the leadership that the North needed.

EDWIN C. BEARSS

Former chief historian of the National Park Service and author of several books about the war.

The South lost the Civil War because of a number of factors. First, it was inherently weaker in the various essentials to win a military victory than the North. The North had a population of more than twenty-two million people to the South's nine-and-a-half million, of whom three-and-a-half million were slaves. While the slaves could be used to support the war effort through work on the plantations and in industries and as teamsters and pioneers with the army, they were not used as a combat arm in the war to any extent.

So if the South were to win, it had to win a short war by striking swiftly—in modern parlance, by an offensive *blitzkrieg* strategy. But the Confederates had established their military goals as fighting in defense of their homeland. In 1861, when enthusiasm was high in the South, it lacked the wherewithal and the resolution to follow up on its early victories, such as First Manassas in the East and at Wilson's Creek and Lexington in the West.

Despite the South's failure to capitalize on its successes in 1861, it came close to reversing the tide that ran against it beginning in February 1862. In the period between the fourth week of June 1862 and the last days of September and early days of October, the South did reverse the tide, sweeping forward on a broad front from the tidewater of Virginia to the Plains Indian territory. And abroad, the British were preparing to offer to mediate the conflict and, if the North refused, to recognize the Con-

federacy. But beginning at Antietam and ending at Perryville, all this unraveled, and the Confederates' true high water mark had passed.

In 1864, with the approach of the presidential election in the North, the Confederates had another opportunity to win the war. If the Confederate armies in Virginia, Georgia, and on the Gulf Coast could successfully resist the North and the war of attrition inaugurated by General Grant (with its particularly high casualties in Virginia), there was a good probability, as recognized by President Lincoln himself in the summer, that his administration would go down to defeat in November. But the success of Admiral David G. Farragut in Mobile Bay, the capture of Atlanta on the second of September by General Sherman, and the smashing success scored by General Sheridan at the expense of General Jubal

A. Early at Cedar Creek, Virginia on October 19 shattered this hope, and Lincoln was reelected by a landslide in the electoral vote. With Lincoln's reelection, the road to Southern defeat grew shorter.

Judging from these responses, it seems clear that the South could have won the war . . . if. If it had more and better-equipped men, led by more capable generals and a wiser president. If it had a more unified purpose and was more aggressive. If it faced a different opponent.

The last condition should not be underestimated. By the end of the war, Lincoln and his powerful army were remarkably proficient at prosecuting war according to Grant's simple strategy. As historian William C. Davis has succinctly put it, "the North won it."

A War That Never Goes Away

More than the Revolution, more than the Constitutional Convention, it was the crucial test of the American nation. The author of Battle Cry of Freedom, *a most successful book on the subject, explains why the issues that fired the Civil War are as urgent in 1990 as they were in 1861.*

James M. McPherson

James M. McPherson is the Edwards Professor of American History at Princeton University. His most recent book is Battle Cry of Freedom *(Oxford University Press).*

"Americans just can't get enough of the Civil War." So says a man who should know, Terry Winschel, historian of the Vicksburg National Military Park. Millions of visitors come to Vicksburg and to more than a dozen other Civil War national battlefield and military parks every year. More than forty thousand Civil War reenactors spend hundreds of dollars each on replica weapons, uniforms, and equipment; many of them travel thousands of miles to help restage Civil War battles. Another two hundred and fifty thousand Americans describe themselves as Civil War buffs or "hobbyists" and belong to one of the hundreds of Civil War round tables or societies, subscribe to at least one of the half-dozen magazines devoted to Civil War history; or buy and sell Civil War memorabilia.

Above all, Americans buy books on the Civil War. This has always been true. More than fifty thousand separate books or pamphlets on the war have been published since the guns ceased firing 125 years ago. In recent years some eight hundred titles, many of them reprints of

---

> *The war did in fact pit brother against brother, cousin against cousin, even father against son.*

---

out-of-print works, have come off the presses annually. Nearly every month a new Civil War book is offered by the History Book Club or the Book-of-the-Month Club, often as the main selection. Many bookstore owners echo the words of Jim Lawson, general manager of the Book 'N Card shop in Falls Church, Virginia. "For the last two years," he said

in 1988, "Civil War books have been flying out of here. It's not [just] the buffs who buy; it's the general public, from high school kids to retired people."

Although we are approaching the end of the 125th-anniversary commemorations of Civil War events, the boom shows no signs of fading. As a beneficiary of this popular interest in the Civil War, I am often asked to explain what accounts for it—in particular, to explain why my own recent contribution to the literature on the war and its causes, *Battle Cry of Freedom*, was on national best-seller lists for several months as a hardcover book in 1988 and again as a paperback in 1989. I have a few answers.

First, for Americans, the human cost of the Civil War was by far the most devastating in our history. The 620,000 Union and Confederate soldiers who lost their lives almost equaled the 680,000 American soldiers who died in all the other wars this country has fought combined. When we add the unknown but probably substantial number of civilian deaths—from disease, malnutrition, exposure, or injury—among the

From *American Heritage*, March 1990, pp. 41-44, 46-47, 49. © 1990 by Forbes, Inc. Reprinted by permission of *American Heritage* magazine, a division of Forbes, Inc.

hundreds of thousands of refugees in the Confederacy, the toll of Civil War dead may exceed war deaths in all the rest of American history. Consider two sobering facts about the Battle of Antietam, America's single bloodiest day. The 25,000 casualties there were nearly four times, the number of American casualties on, D-day; June 6, 1944. The 6,500 men killed and mortally wounded in one day near Sharpsburg were nearly double the number of Americans killed and mortally wounded in combat in all the rest of the country's nineteenth-century wars combined—the War of 1812, the Mexican War, and the Spanish-American War.

This ghastly toll gives the Civil War a kind of horrifying but hypnotic fascination. As Thomas Hardy once put it, "War makes rattling good history; but Peace is poor reading." The sound of drum and trumpet, the call to arms, the clashing of armies have stirred the blood of nations throughout history. As the horrors and the seamy side of a war recede into the misty past, the romance and honor and glory forge into the foreground. Of no war has this been more true than of the Civil War, with its dashing cavaliers, its generals leading infantry charges, its diamond-stacked locomotives and paddle-wheeled steamboats, its larger-than-life figures like Lincoln, Lee, Jackson, Grant, and Sherman, its heroic and romantic women like Clara Barton and "Mother" Bickerdyke and Rose O'Neal Greenhow, its countless real-life heroines and knaves and heroes capable of transmutation into a Scarlett O'Hara, Rhett Butler, or Ashley Wilkes. If romance is the other face of horror in our perception of the Civil War, the poignancy of a brothers' war is the other face of the tragedy of a civil war. In hundreds of individual cases the war did pit brother against brother, cousin against cousin, even father against son. This was especially true in border states like Kentucky, where the war divided such famous families as the Clays, Crittendens, and Breckinridges and where seven brothers and brothers-in-law of the wife of the United States President fought for the Confederate States. But it was also true of states like Virginia, where Jeb Stuart's father-in-law commanded Union cavalry, and even of South Carolina, where Thomas F. Drayton became a brigadier general in the Confederate army and

---

Civil War soldiers were the most literate up to that time. Their diaries and letters have had a lasting appeal.

---

fought against his brother Percival, a captain in the Union navy, at the Battle of Port Royal. Who can resist the painful human interest of stories like these— particularly when they are recounted in the letters and diaries of Civil War protagonists, preserved through generations and published for all to read as a part of the unending stream of Civil War books?

Indeed, the uncensored contemporary descriptions of that war by participants help explain its appeal to modern readers. There is nothing else in history to equal it. Civil War armies were the most literate that ever fought a war up to that time, and twentieth-century armies censored soldiers' mail and discouraged diary keeping. Thus we have an unparalleled view of the Civil War by the people who experienced it. This has kept the image of the war alive in the families of millions of Americans whose ancestors fought in it. When speaking to audiences as diverse as Civil War buffs, Princeton students and alumni, and local literary clubs, I have sometimes asked how many of them are aware of forebears who fought in the Civil War. I have been surprised by the large response, which demonstrates not only a great number of such people but also their consciousness of events that happened so long ago yet seem part of their family lore today.

This consciousness of the war, of the past as part of the present, continues to be more intense in the South than elsewhere. William Faulkner said of his native section that the past isn't dead; it isn't even past. As any reader of Faulkner's novels knows, the Civil War is central to that past that is present; it is the great watershed of Southern history; it is, as Mark Twain put it a century ago after a tour through the South, "what A.D. is elsewhere; they date from it." The symbols of that past-in-present surround Southerners as they grow up, from the Robert E. Lee Elementary School or Jefferson Davis High School they attend and the Confederate battle flag that flies over their statehouse to the Confederate soldier enshrined in bronze or granite on the town square and the family folklore about victimization by Sherman's bummers. Some of those symbols remain highly controversial and provoke as much passion today as in 1863: the song "Dixie," for example, and the Confederate flag, which for many Southern whites continue to represent courage, honor, or defiance while to blacks they represent racism and oppression.

This suggests the most important reason for the enduring fascination with the Civil War among professional historians as well as the general public: Great issues were at stake, issues about which Americans were willing to fight and die, issues whose resolution profoundly transformed and redefined the United States. The Civil War was a total war in three senses: It mobilized the total human and material resources of both sides; it ended not in a negotiated peace but in total victory by one side and unconditional surrender by the other; it destroyed the economy and social system of the loser and established those of the winner as the norm for the future.

The Civil War was fought mainly by volunteer soldiers who joined the colors before conscription went into effect. In fact, the Union and Confederate armies mobilized as volunteers a larger percentage of their societies' manpower than any other war in American history— probably in world history, with the possible exception of the French Revolution. And Civil War armies, like those of the French Revolution, were highly ideological in motivation. Most of the volunteers knew what they were fighting for, and why. What were they fighting for? If asked to define it in a single word, many soldiers on both sides would have answered: liberty. They fought for the heritage of freedom bequeathed to them by the Founding Fathers. North and South alike wrapped themselves in the mantle of 1776. But the two sides interpreted that heritage in opposite ways, and at first neither side included the slaves in the vision of liberty for which it fought. The slaves did, however, and by the time of Lincoln's Gettysburg Address in 1863, the North also fought for "a new birth of freedom. . . ." These multiple meanings of freedom, and how they dissolved and reformed in kaleidoscopic patterns during the war, provide the central meaning of the war for the American experience.

When the "Black Republican" Abraham Lincoln won the Presidency in 1860 on a platform of excluding slavery from the territories, Southerners compared him to George III and declared their independence from "oppressive Yankee rule." "The same spirit of freedom and independence that impelled our Fathers to the separation from the British Government," proclaimed secessionists, would impel the "liberty loving people of the South" to separation from the United States government. A Georgia secessionist declared that Southerners would be "either *slaves in the Union or freemen out of it.*" Young men from Texas to Virginia rushed to enlist in this "Holy Cause of Liberty and Independence" and to raise "the standard of Liberty and Equality for white men" against "our Abolition enemies who are pledged to prostrate the white freemen of the South down to equality with negroes." From "the high and solemn motive of defending and protecting the rights which our fathers bequeathed to us," declared Jefferson Davis at the outset of war, let us "renew such sacrifices as our fathers made to the holy cause of constitutional liberty."

But most northerners ridiculed these Southern professions to be fighting for the ideals of 1776. That was "a libel upon the whole character and conduct of the men of '76," said the antislavery poet and journalist

William Cullen Bryant. The Founding Fathers had fought "to establish the rights of man . . . and principles of universal liberty." The South, insisted Bryant, had seceded "not in the interest of general humanity, but of a domestic despotism. . . . Their motto is not liberty, but slavery." Northerners did not deny the right of revolution in principle; after all, the United States was founded on that right. But "the right of revolution," wrote Lincoln in 1861, "is never a legal right. . . . At most it is but a moral right, when exercised for a morally justifiable cause. When exercised without such a cause revolution is no right, but simply a wicked exercise of physical power." In Lincoln's judgment secession was just such a wicked exercise. The event that precipitated it was Lincoln's election by a constitutional majority. As Northerners saw it, the Southern states, having controlled the national government for most of the previous two generations through their domination of the Democratic party, now decided to leave the Union just because they had lost an election.

Civil War armies mobilized a larger percentage of volunteer manpower than any other war in our history.

For Lincoln and the Northern people, it was the Union that represented the ideals of 1776. The republic established by the Founding Fathers as a bulwark of liberty was a fragile experiment in a nineteenth-century world bestridden by kings, emperors, czars, and dictators. Most republics through history had eventually been overthrown. Some Americans still alive in 1861 had seen French republics succumb twice to emperors and once to the restoration of the Bourbon monarchy. Republics in Latin America came and went with bewildering rapidity. The United States in 1861 represented, in Lincoln's words, "the last, best hope" for the survival of re-

publican liberties in the world. Would that hope also collapse? "Our popular government has often been called an experiment," Lincoln told Congress on July 4, 1861. But if the Confederacy succeeded in splitting the country in two, it would set a fatal precedent that would destroy the experiment. By invoking this precedent, a minority in the future might secede from the Union whenever it did not like what the majority stood for, until the United States fragmented into a multitude of petty, squabbling autocracies. "The central idea pervading this struggle," said Lincoln, "is the necessity . . . of proving that popular government is not an absurdity. We must settle this question now, whether, in a free government, the minority have the right to break up the government whenever they choose."

Many soldiers who enlisted in the Union army felt the same way. A Missourian joined up as "a duty I owe my country and to my children to do what I can to preserve this government as I shudder to think what is ahead of them if this government should be overthrown." A New England soldier wrote to his wife on the eve of the First Battle of Bull Run: "I know . . . how great a debt we owe to those who went before us through the blood and sufferings of the Revolution. And I am willing—perfectly willing—to lay down all my joys in this life, to help maintain this government, and to pay that debt."

Freedom for the slaves was not part of the liberty for which the North fought in 1861. That was not because the Lincoln administration supported slavery; quite the contrary. Slavery was "an unqualified evil to the negro, to the white man . . . and to the State," said Lincoln on many occasions in words that expressed the sentiments of a Northern majority. "The monstrous injustice of slavery . . . deprives our republican example of its just influence in the world—enables the enemies of free institutions, with plausibility, to taunt us as hypocrites. . . ." Yet in his first inaugural address, Lincoln declared that he had "no purpose, directly or indirectly; to interfere with . . . slavery in the States where it exists." He reiterated this pledge in his first message to Con-

McPherson's Basic Reading List

Allan Nevins. **Ordeal of the Union,** 2 vols. (New York: Charles Scribner's Sons, 1947). **The Emergence of Lincoln,** 2 vols. (New York: Charles Scribner's Sons, 1950). **The War for the Union,** 4 vols. (New York: Charles Scribner's Sons, 1959–71). These eight volumes are a magisterial account of the crisis-laden years from the Mexican War to Appomattox, covering social, economic, political, and military events in compelling prose.

David M. Potter. **The Impending Crisis, 1848–1861** (New York: Harper & Row, 1976). The best single-volume survey of the political events that led to secession and war.

Shelby Foote. **The Civil War: A Narrative,** 3 vols. (New York: Random House, 1958–74). A superbly readable military history by a novelist who did a massive amount of historical research.

Bruce Catton. **The Centennial History of the Civil War,** 3 vols. (Garden City, N.Y: Doubleday and Co., 1961–65). Fast-paced chronicle of the fighting on the battlefield and the infighting in the political capitals of Washington and Richmond. **Mr. Lincoln's Army** (Garden City, N.Y: Doubleday and Co., 1951). **Glory Road** (Garden City, N.Y: Doubleday and Co., 1952). **A Stillness at Appomattox** (Garden City, N.Y. Doubleday and Co., 1953). Catton's superb trilogy on the Army of the Potomac emphasizes the gritty determination of private soldiers despite the incompetent commanders who led them so often to defeat until Grant finally took charge.

Douglas Southall Freeman. **R. E. Lee: A Biography,** 4 vols. (New York: Charles Scribner's Sons, 1934–35). A classic study in leadership and command. **Lee's Lieutenants,** 3 vols. (New York: Charles Scribner's Sons, 1942–44). The story of the Army of Northern Virginia seen through the eyes of its principal officers.

Bell Irvin Wiley. **The Life of Johnny Reb** (Indianapolis: Bobbs-Merrill Co., 1943). **The Life of Billy Yank** (Indianapolis: Bobbs-Merrill Co., 1952). Thoroughly researched and superbly written studies of the common soldiers in both armies.

---

gress, on July 4, 1861, when the Civil War was nearly three months old.

What explains this apparent inconsistency? The answer lies in the Constitution and in the Northern polity of 1861. Lincoln was bound by a constitution that protected slavery in any state where citizens wanted it. The republic of liberty for whose preservation the North was fighting had been a republic in which slavery was legal everywhere in 1776. That was the great American paradox—a land of freedom based on slavery. Even in 1861 four states that remained loyal to the Union were slave states, and the Democratic minority in free states opposed any move to make the war for the Union a war against slavery.

But as the war went on, the slaves themselves took the first step toward making it a war against slavery. Coming into Union lines by the thousands, they voted with their feet for freedom. As enemy property they could be confiscated by Union forces as "contraband of war." This was the thin edge of the wedge that finally broke apart the American paradox. By 1863 a series of congressional acts plus Lincoln's Emancipation Proclamation had radically enlarged Union war aims. The North henceforth fought not just to restore the old Union, not just to ensure that the nation born in 1776 "shall not perish from the earth," but to give that nation "a new birth of freedom."

Northern victory in the Civil War resolved two fundamental, festering issues left unresolved by the Revolution of 1776: whether this fragile republican experiment called the United States would survive and whether the house divided would continue to endure half slave and half free. Both these issues remained open questions until 1865. Many Americans doubted the Republic's survival; many European conservatives predicted its demise; some Americans advocated the right of secession and periodically threatened to invoke it; eleven states did invoke it in 1860 and 1861. But since 1865 no state or region has seriously threatened secession, not even during the "massive resistance" to desegregation from 1954 to 1964. Before 1865 the United States, land of liberty, was the largest slaveholding country in the world. Since 1865 that particular "monstrous injustice" and "hypocrisy" has existed no more.

In the process of preserving the Union of 1776 while purging it of slavery, the Civil War also transformed it. Before 1861 the words *United States* were a plural noun: "The United States *are* a large country." Since 1865 *United States* has been a singular noun. The North went to war to preserve the *Union;* it ended by creating a *nation.* This transformation can be traced in Lincoln's most important wartime addresses. The first inaugural address contained the word *Union* twenty times and the word *nation* not once. In Lincoln's first message to Congress, on July 4, 1861, he used *Union* forty-nine times and *nation* only three times. In his famous public letter to Horace Greeley of August 22, 1862, concerning slavery and the war, Lincoln spoke of the Union nine times and the nation not at all. But in the Gettysburg Address fifteen months later, he did not refer to the Union at all but used the word *nation* five times. And in the second inaugural address, looking back over the past four years, Lincoln spoke of one side's seeking to dissolve the Union in 1861 and the other side's accepting the challenge of war to preserve the nation. The old decentralized Republic, in which the post office was the only agency of national government that touched the average citizen, was transformed by the crucible of war into a centralized polity that taxed people directly and created an internal revenue bureau to collect the taxes, expanded the jurisdiction of federal courts, created a national currency and a federally chartered banking system, drafted men into the Army, and created the Freedman's Bureau as the first national agency for social welfare. Eleven of the first twelve amendments to the Constitution had limited the powers of the national government; six of the next seven, starting with the Thirteenth Amendment in 1865, radically expanded those powers at the expense of the states. The first three of these amendments converted four million slaves into citizens and voters within five years, the most rapid and fundamental social transformation in American history—even if the nation did back-slide on part of this commitment for three generations after 1877.

From 1789 to 1861 a Southern slaveholder was President of the United States two-thirds of the time, and two-thirds of the Speakers of the House and presidents pro tem of the Senate had also been Southerners. Twenty of the thirty-five Supreme Court justices during that period were from the South, which always had a majority on the Court before 1861. After the Civil War a century passed before another resident of a Southern state was elected President. For half a century after the war hardly any Southerners served as Speaker of the House or president pro tem of the Senate, and only nine of the thirty Supreme Court justices appointed during that half-century were Southerners. The institutions and ideology of a plantation society and a caste system that had dominated half of the country before 1861 and sought to dominate more went down with a great crash in 1865 and were replaced by the institutions and ideology of free-labor entrepreneurial capitalism. For better or for worse, the flames of Civil War forged the framework of modern America.

So even if the veneer of romance and myth that has attracted so many of the current Civil War camp followers were stripped away, leaving only the trauma of violence and suffering, the Civil War would remain the most dramatic and crucial experience in American history. That fact will ensure the persistence of its popularity and its importance as a historical subject so long as there is a United States.

The New View of Reconstruction

Whatever you were taught or thought you knew about the post–Civil War era is probably wrong in the light of recent study

Eric Foner

Eric Foner is Professor of History at Columbia University and author of Nothing but Freedom: Emancipation and Its Legacy.

In the past twenty years, no period of American history has been the subject of a more thoroughgoing reevaluation than Reconstruction—the violent, dramatic, and still controversial era following the Civil War. Race relations, politics, social life, and economic change during Reconstruction have all been reinterpreted in the light of changed attitudes toward the place of blacks within American society. If historians have not yet forged a fully satisfying portrait of Reconstruction as a whole, the traditional interpretation that dominated historical writing for much of this century has irrevocably been laid to rest.

Anyone who attended high school before 1960 learned that Reconstruction was a era of unrelieved sordidness in American political and social life. The martyred Lincoln, according to this view, had planned a quick and painless readmission of the Southern states as equal members of the national family. President Andrew Johnson, his successor, attempted to carry out Lincoln's policies but was foiled by the Radical Republicans (also known as Vindictives or Jacobins). Motivated by an irrational hatred of Rebels or by ties with Northern capitalists out to plunder the South,

the Radicals swept aside Johnson's lenient program and fastened black supremacy upon the defeated Confederacy. An orgy of corruption followed, presided over by unscrupulous carpetbaggers (Northerners who ventured south to reap the spoils of office), traitorous scalawags (Southern whites who cooperated with the new governments for personal gain), and the ignorant and childlike freedmen, who were incapable of properly exercising the political power that had been thrust upon them. After much needless suffering, the white community of the South banded together to overthrow these "black" governments and restore home rule (their euphemism for white supremacy). All told, Reconstruction was just about the darkest page in the American saga.

Originating in anti-Reconstruction propaganda of Southern Democrats during the 1870s, this traditional interpretation achieved scholarly legitimacy around the turn of the century through the work of William Dunning and his students at Columbia University. It reached the larger public through films like *Birth of a Nation* and *Gone With the Wind* and that best-selling work of myth-making masquerading as history, *The Tragic Era* by Claude G. Bowers. In language as exaggerated as it was colorful, Bowers told how Andrew Johnson "fought the bravest battle for constitutional liberty and for the preservation of

our institutions ever waged by an Executive" but was overwhelmed by the "poisonous propaganda" of the Radicals. Southern whites, as a result, "literally were put to the torture" by "emissaries of hate" who manipulated the "simple-minded" freedmen, inflaming the negroes' "egotism" and even inspiring "lustful assaults" by blacks upon white womanhood.

In a discipline that sometimes seems to pride itself on the rapid rise and fall of historical interpretations, this traditional portrait of Reconstruction enjoyed remarkable staying power. The long reign of the old interpretation is not difficult to explain. It presented a set of easily identifiable heroes and villains. It enjoyed the imprimatur of the nation's leading scholars. And it accorded with the political and social realities of the first half of this century. This image of Reconstruction helped freeze the mind of the white South in unalterable opposition to any movement for breaching the ascendancy of the Democratic party, eliminating segregation, or readmitting disfranchised blacks to the vote.

Nevertheless, the demise of the traditional interpretation was inevitable, for it ignored the testimony of the central participant in the drama of Reconstruction—the black freedman. Furthermore, it was grounded in the conviction that blacks were unfit to share in political power. As Dunning's Columbia colleague John W. Burgess put it, "A black skin means membership in a race of men which has never of itself succeeded in subjecting passion to reason, has never, therefore, created any civilization of any kind." Once objective scholarship and modern experience rendered that assumption untenable, the entire edifice was bound to fall.

The work of "revising" the history of Reconstruction began with the writings of a handful of survivors of the era, such as John R. Lynch, who had served as a black congressman from Mississippi af-

---

Black initiative established as many schools as did Northern religious societies and the Freedmen's Bureau. The right to vote was not simply thrust upon them by meddling outsiders, since blacks began agitating for the suffrage as soon as they were freed.

---

ter the Civil War. In the 1930s white scholars like Francis Simkins and Robert Woody carried the task forward. Then, in 1935, the black historian and activist W. E. B. Du Bois produced *Black Reconstruction in America,* a monumental revaluation that closed with an irrefutable indictment of a historical profession that had sacrificed scholarly objectivity on the altar of racial bias. "One fact and one alone," he wrote, "explains the attitude of most recent writers toward Reconstruction; they cannot conceive of Negroes as men." Du Bois's work, however, was ignored by most historians.

It was not until the 1960s that the full force of the revisionist wave broke over the field. Then, in rapid succession, virtu-

ally every assumption of the traditional viewpoint was systematically dismantled. A drastically different portrait emerged to take its place. President Lincoln did not have a coherent "plan" for Reconstruction, but at the time of his assassination he had been cautiously contemplating black suffrage. Andrew Johnson was a stubborn, racist politician who lacked the ability to compromise. By isolating himself from the broad currents of public opinion that had nourished Lincoln's career, Johnson created an impasse with Congress that Lincoln would certainly have avoided, thus throwing away his political power and destroying his own plans for reconstructing the South.

The Radicals in Congress were acquitted of both vindictive motives and the charge of serving as the stalking-horses of Northern capitalism. They emerged instead as idealists in the best nineteenth-century reform tradition. Radical leaders like Charles Sumner and Thaddeus Stevens had worked for the rights of blacks long before any conceivable political advantage flowed from such a commitment. Stevens refused to sign the Pennsylvania Constitution of 1838 because it disfranchised the state's black citizens; Sumner led a fight in the 1850s to integrate Boston's public schools. Their Reconstruction policies were based on principle, not petty po-

litical advantage, for the central issue dividing Johnson and these Radical Republicans was the civil rights of freedmen. Studies of congressional policy-making, such as Eric L. McKitrick's *Andrew Johnson and Reconstruction,* also revealed that Reconstruction legislation, ranging from the Civil Rights Act of 1866 to the Fourteenth and Fifteenth Amendments, enjoyed broad support from moderate and conservative Republicans. It was not simply the work of a narrow radical faction.

Even more startling was the revised portrait of Reconstruction in the South itself. Imbued with the spirit of the civil rights movement and rejecting entirely the racial assumptions that had underpinned the traditional interpretation, these historians evaluated Reconstruction from the black point of view. Works like Joel Williamson's *After Slavery* portrayed the period as a time of extraordinary political, social, and economic progress for blacks. The establishment of public school systems, the granting of equal citizenship to blacks, the effort to restore the devastated Southern economy, the attempt to construct an interracial political democracy from the ashes of slavery, all these were commendable achievements, not the elements of Bowers's "tragic era."

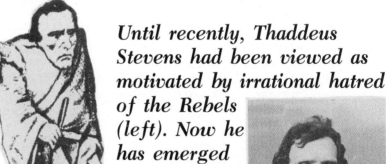

Until recently, Thaddeus Stevens had been viewed as motivated by irrational hatred of the Rebels (left). Now he has emerged as an idealist in the best reform tradition.

NEW YORK PUBLIC LIBRARY, PRINT ROOM

EDWARDS ELLIS, *The History of Our Country*, VOL. 5, 1900

Reconstruction governments were portrayed as disastrous failures (left) because elected blacks were ignorant or corrupt. In fact, postwar corruption cannot be blamed on former slaves.

Unlike earlier writers, the revisionists stressed the active role of the freedmen in shaping Reconstruction. Black initiative established as many schools as did Northern religious societies and the Freedmen's Bureau. The right to vote was not simply thrust upon them by meddling outsiders, since blacks began agitating for the suffrage as soon as they were freed. In 1865 black conventions throughout the South issued eloquent, though unheeded, appeals for equal civil and political rights.

With the advent of Radical Reconstruction in 1867, the freedmen did enjoy a real measure of political power. But black supremacy never existed. In most states blacks held only a small fraction of political offices, and even in South Carolina, where they comprised a majority of the state legislature's lower house, effective power remained in white hands. As for corruption, moral standards in both government and private enterprise were at low ebb throughout the nation in the postwar years—the era of Boss Tweed, the Credit Mobilier scandal, and the Whiskey Ring. Southern corruption could hardly be blamed on former slaves.

Other actors in the Reconstruction drama also came in for reevaluation. Most carpetbaggers were former Union soldiers seeking economic opportunity in the postwar South, not unscrupulous adventurers. Their motives, a typically American amalgam of humanitarianism and the pursuit of profit, were no more insidious than those of Western pioneers. Scalawags, previously seen as traitors to the white race, now emerged as "Old Line" Whig Unionists who had

opposed secession in the first place or as poor whites who had long resented planters' domination of Southern life and who saw in Reconstruction a chance to recast Southern society along more democratic lines. Strongholds of Southern white Republicanism like east Tennessee and western North Carolina had been the scene of resistance to Confederate rule throughout the civil War; now,

Under slavery most blacks had lived in nuclear family units, although they faced the constant threat of separation from loved ones by sale. Reconstruction provided the opportunity for blacks to solidify their preexisting family ties.

as one scalawag newspaper put it, the choice was "between salvation at the hand of the Negro or destruction at the hand of the rebels."

At the same time, the Ku Klux Klan and kindred groups, whose campaign of violence against black and white Repub-

licans had been minimized or excused in older writings, were portrayed as they really were. Earlier scholars had conveyed the impression that the Klan intimidated blacks mainly by dressing as ghosts and playing on the freedmen's superstitions. In fact, black fears were all too real: the Klan was a terrorist organization that beat and killed its political opponents to deprive blacks of their newly won rights. The complicity of the Democratic party and the silence of prominent whites in the face of such outrages stood as an indictment of the moral code the South had inherited from the days of slavery.

By the end of the 1960s, then, the old interpretation had been completely reversed. Southern freedmen were the heroes, the "Redeemers" who overthrew Reconstruction were the villains, and if the era was "tragic," it was because change did not go far enough. Reconstruction had been a time of real progress and its failure a lost opportunity for the South and the nation. But the legacy of Reconstruction—the Fourteenth and Fifteenth Amendments—endured to inspire future efforts for civil rights. As Kenneth Stampp wrote in *The Era of Reconstruction,* a superb summary of revisionist findings published in 1965, "if it was worth four years of civil war to save the Union, it was worth a few years of radical reconstruction to give the American Negro the ultimate promise of equal civil and political rights."

As Stampp's statement suggests, the reevaluation of the first Reconstruction was inspired in large measure by the impact of the second—the modern civil rights movement. And with the waning of that movement in recent years, writing on Reconstruction has undergone still another transformation. Instead of seeing the Civil War and its aftermath as a second American Revolution (as Charles Beard had), a regression into barbarism (as Bowers argued), or a golden opportunity squandered (as the revisionists saw it), recent writers argue that Radical Reconstruction was not really very radical. Since land was not distributed to the former slaves, the remained economically dependent upon their former owners. The planter class survived both the war and Reconstruction with its property (apart from slaves) and prestige more or less intact.

Not only changing times but also the changing concerns of historians have contributed to this latest reassessment of Reconstruction. The hallmark of the pst decade's historical writing has been an emphasis upon "social history"—the evocation of the past lives of ordinary Americans—and the downplaying of strictly political events. When applied to Reconstruction, this concern with the "social" suggested that black suffrage and officeholding, once seen as the most radical departures of the Reconstruction era, were relatively insignificant.

Recent historians have focused their investigations not upon the politics of Reconstruction but upon the social and economic aspects of the transition from slavery to freedom. Herbert Gutman's influential study of the black family during and after slavery found little change in family structure or relations between men and women resulting from emancipation. Under slavery most blacks had lived in nuclear family units, although they faced the constant threat of separation from loved ones by sale. Reconstruction provided the opportunity for blacks to solidify their preexisting family ties. Conflicts over whether black women should work in the cotton fields (planters said yes, many black families said no) and over white attempts to "apprentice" black children revealed that the autonomy of family life was a major preoccupation of the freedmen. Indeed, whether manifested in their withdrawal from churches controlled by whites, in the blossoming of black fraternal, be-

nevolent, and self-improvement organizations, or in the demise of the slave quarters and their replacement by small tenant farms occupied by individual families, the quest for independence from white authority and control over their own day-to-day lives shaped the black response to emancipation.

In the post–Civil War South the surest guarantee of economic autonomy, blacks believed, was land. To the freedmen the justice of a claim to land based on their years of unrequited labor appeared self-evident. As an Alabama black convention put it, "The property which they [the planters] hold was nearly all earned by the sweat of *our* brows." As Leon Litwack showed in *Been in the Storm So Long*, a Pulitzer Prize–winning account of the black response to emancipation, many freedmen in 1865 and 1866 refused to sign labor contracts, expecting the federal government to give them land. In some localities, as one Alabama overseer reported, they "set up claims to the plantation and all on it."

The Civil War raised the decisive questions of American's national existence: the relations between local and national authority, the definition of citizenship, the balance between force and consent in generating obedience to authority.

In the end, of course, the vast majority of Southern blacks remained propertyless and poor. But exactly why the South, and especially its black population, suffered from dire poverty and economic retardation in the decades following the Civil War is a matter of

much dispute. In *One Kind of Freedom* economists Roger Ransom and Richard Sutch indicted country merchants for monopolizing credit and charging usurious interest rates, forcing black tenants into debt and locking the South into a dependence on cotton production that impoverished the entire region. But Jonathan Wiener, in his study of postwar Alabama, argued that planters used their political power to compel blacks to remain on the plantations. Planters succeeded in stabilizing the plantation system, but only by blocking the growth of alternative enterprises, like factories, that might draw off black laborers, thus locking the region into a pattern of economic backwardness.

If the trust of recent writing has emphasized the social and economic aspects of Reconstruction, politics has not been entirely neglected. But political studies have also reflected the postrevisionist mood summarized by C. Vann Woodward when he observed "how essentially nonrevolutionary and conservative Reconstruction really was." Recent writers, unlike their revisionist predecessors, have found little to praise in federal policy toward the emancipated blacks.

A new sensitivity to the strength of prejudice and laissez-faire ideas in the nineteenth-century North has led many historians to doubt whether the Republican party ever made a genuine commitment to racial justice in the South. The granting of black suffrage was an alternative to a long-term federal responsibility for protecting the rights of the former slaves. Once enfranchised, blacks could be left to fend for themselves. With the exception of a few Radicals like Thaddeus Stevens, nearly all Northern policy-makers and educators are criticized today for assuming that, so long as the unfettered operations of the marketplace afforded blacks the opportunity to advance through diligent labor, federal efforts to assist them in acquiring land were unnecessary.

Probably the most innovative recent writing on Reconstruction politics has centered on a broad reassessment of black Republicanism, largely undertaken by a new generation of black historians. Scholars like Thomas Holt and

Some scholars exalted the motives of the Ku Klux Klan (left). Actually, its members were part of a terrorist organization that beat and killed its political opponents to deprive blacks of their rights.

Nell Painter insist that Reconstruction was not simply a matter of black and white. Conflicts within the black community, no less than divisions among whites, shaped Reconstruction politics. Where revisionist scholars, both black and white, had celebrated the accomplishments of black political leaders, Holt, Painter, and others charge that they failed to address the economic plight of the black masses. Painter criticized "representative colored men," as national black leaders were called, for failing to provide ordinary freedmen with effective political leadership. Holt found that black officeholders in South Carolina most emerged from the old free mulatto class of Charleston, which shared many assumptions with prominent whites. "Basically bourgeois in their origins and orientation," he wrote, they "failed to act in the interest of black peasants."

In emphasizing the persistence from slavery of divisions between free blacks and slaves, these writers reflect the increasing concern with continuity and conservatism in Reconstruction. Their work reflects a startling extension of revisionist premises. If, as has been argued for the past twenty years, blacks were active agents rather than mere victims of manipulation, then they could not be absolved of blame for the ultimate failure of Reconstruction.

Despite the excellence of recent writings and the continual expansion of our knowledge of the period, historians of

Reconstruction today face a unique dilemma. An old interpretation has been overthrown, but a coherent new synthesis has yet to take its place. The revisionists of the 1960s effectively established a series of negative points: the Reconstruction governments were not as bad as had been portrayed, black supremacy was a myth, the Radicals were not cynical manipulators of the freedmen. Yet no convincing overall portrait of the quality of political and social life emerged from their writings. More recent historians have rightly pointed to elements of continuity that spanned the nineteenth-century Southern experience, especially the survival, in modified form, of the plantation system. Nevertheless, by denying the real changes that did occur, they have failed to provide a convincing portrait of an era characterized above all by drama, turmoil, and social change.

Building upon the findings of the past twenty years of scholarship, a new portrait of Reconstruction ought to begin by viewing it not as a specific time period, bounded by the years 1865 and 1877, but as an episode in a prolonged historical process—American society's adjustment to the consequences of the Civil War and emancipation. The Civil War, of course, raised the decisive questions of America's national existence: the relations between local and national authority, the definition of citizenship, the balance between force and consent

in generating obedience to authority. The war and Reconstruction, as Allan Nevins observed over fifty years ago, marked the "emergence of modern America." This was the era of the completion of the national railroad network, the creation of the modern steel industry, the conquest of the West and final subduing of the Indians, and the expansion of the mining frontier. Lincoln's America—the world of the small farm and artisan shop—gave way to a rapidly industrializing economy. The issues that galvanized postwar Northern politics—from the question of the greenback currency to the mode of paying holders of the national debt—arose from the economic changes unleased by the Civil War.

Above all, the war irrevocably abolished slavery. Since 1619, when "twenty negars" disembarked from a Dutch ship in Virginia, racial injustice had haunted American life, mocking its professed ideals even as tobacco and cotton, the products of slave labor, helped finance the nation's economic development. Now the implications of the black presence could no longer be ignored. The Civil War resolved the problem of slavery but, as the Philadelphia diarist Sydney George Fisher observed in June 1865, it opened an even more intractable problem: "What shall we do with the Negro?" Indeed, he went on, this was a problem "*incapable* of any solution that will satisfy both North and South."

As Fisher realized, the focal point of Reconstruction was the social revolution known as emancipation. Plantation slavery was simultaneously a system of labor, a form of racial domination, and the foundation upon which arose a distinctive ruling class within the South. Its demise threw open the most fundamental questions of economy, society, and politics. A new system of labor, social, racial, and political relations had to be created to replace slavery.

The United States was not the only nation to experience emancipation in the nineteenth century. Neither plantation slavery nor abolition were unique to the United States. But Reconstruction was. In a comparative perspective Radical Reconstruction stands as a remarkable experiment, the only effort of a society experiencing abolition to bring the former slaves within the umbrella of equal citizenship. Because the Radicals did not achieve everything they wanted, historians have lately tended to play down the stunning departure represented by black suffrage and officeholding. Former slaves, most fewer than two years removed from bondage, debated the fundamental questions of the polity: what is a republican form of government? Should the state provide equal education for all? How could political equality be reconciled with a society in which property was so unequally distributed? There was something inspiring in the way such men met the challenge of Reconstruction. "I knew nothing more than to obey my master," James K. Greene, an Alabama black politician later recalled. "But the tocsin of freedom sounded and knocked at the door and we walked out like free men and we met the exigencies as they grew up, and shouldered the responsibilities."

Y ou never saw a people more excited on the subject of politics than are the negroes of the south," one planter observed in 1867. And there were more than a few Southern whites as well who in these years shook off the prejudices of the past to embrace the revision of a new South dedicated to the principles of equal citizenship and social justice. One ordinary South Carolinian expressed the new sense of possibility in 1868 to the Republican governor of the state: "I am sorry that I cannot write an elegant stiled letter to your excellency. But I rejoice to think that God almighty has given to the poor of S.C. a Gov. to hear to feel to protect the humble poor without distinction to race or color. . . . I am a native borned S.C. a poor man never owned a Negro in my life nor my father before me. . . . Remember the true and loyal are the poor of the whites and blacks, outside of these you can find none loyal."

Few modern scholars believe the Reconstruction governments established in the South in 1867 and 1868 fulfilled the aspirations of their humble constituents. While their achievements in such realms as education, civil rights, and the economic rebuilding of the South are now widely appreciated, historians today believe they failed to affect either the economic plight of the emancipated slave or the ongoing transformation of independent white farmers into cotton tenants. Yet their opponents did perceive the Reconstruction governments in precisely this way—as representatives of a revolution that had put the bottom rail, both racial and economic, on top. This perception helps explain the ferocity of the attacks leveled against them and the pervasiveness of violence in the postemancipation South.

The spectacle of black men voting and holding office was anathema to large numbers of Southern whites. Even more disturbing, at least in the view of those who still controlled the plantation regions of the South, was the emergence of local officials, black and white, who sympathized with the plight of the black laborer. Alabama's vagrancy law was a "dead letter" in 1870, "because those who are charged with its enforcement are indebted to the vagrant vote for their offices and emoluments." Political debates over the level and incidence of taxation, the control of crops, and the resolution of contract disputes revealed that a primary issue of Reconstruction was the role of government in a plantation society. During presidential Reconstruction, and after "Redemption," with planters and their allies in control of politics, the law emerged as a means of stabilizing and promoting the plantation system. If Radical Reconstruction failed to redistribute the land of the South, the ouster of the planter class from control of politics as least ensured that the sanctions of the criminal law would not be employed to discipline the black labor force.

A n understanding of this fundamental conflict over the relation between government and society helps explain the pervasive complaints concerning corruption and "extravagance" during Radical Reconstruction. Corruption there was aplenty; tax rates did rise sharply. More significant than the rate of taxation, however, was the change in its incidence. For the first time, planters and white farmers had to pay a significant portion of their income to the government, while propertyless blacks often escaped scot-free. Several states, moreover, enacted heavy taxes on uncultivated land to discourage land speculation and force land onto the market, benefiting, it was hoped, the freedmen.

In the end neither the abolition of slavery nor Reconstruction succeeded in resolving the debate over the meaning of freedom in American life.

As time passed, complaints about the "extravagance" and corruption of Southern governments found a sympathetic audience among influential Northerners. The Democratic charge that universal suffrage in the South was responsible for high taxes and governmental extravagance coincided with a rising conviction among the urban middle classes of the North that city government had to be taken out o the hands of the immigrant poor and returned to the "best men"—the educated, professional, financially independent citizens unable to exert much political influence at a time of mass parties and machine politics. Increasingly the "respectable" middle classes began to retreat from the very notion of universal suffrage. The poor were not longer perceived as honest producers, the backbone of the social order; now they became the "dangerous classes," the "mob." As the historian Francis Parkman put it, too much power rested with "masses of imported ignorance and hereditary ineptitude." To Parkman the Irish of the Northern cities and the blacks of the South were equally incapable of utilizing the ballot: "Witness the municipal corruptions of New York, and the monstrosities of negro rule in South Carolina." Such attitudes helped to justify Northern inaction as, one by one, the Reconstruction regimes of the South were overthrown by political violence.

In the end, then, neither the abolition of slavery nor Reconstruction succeeded in resolving the debate over the meaning of freedom in American life.

Twenty years before the American Civil War, writing about the prospect of abolition in France's colonies, Alexis de Tocqueville had written, "If the Negroes have the right to become free, the [planters] have the incontestable right not to be ruined by the Negroes' freedom." And in the United States, as in nearly every plantation society that experienced the end of slavery, a rigid social and political dichotomy between former master and former slave, an ideology of racism, and a dependent labor force with limited economic opportunities all survived abolition. Unless one means by freedom the simple fact of not being a slave, emancipation thrust blacks into a kind of no-man's land, a partial freedom that made a mockery of the American ideal of equal citizenship.

Yet by the same token the ultimate outcome underscores the uniqueness of Reconstruction itself. Alone among the societies that abolished slavery in the nineteenth century, the United States, for a moment, offered the freedmen a measure of political control over their own destinies. However brief its sway, Reconstruction allowed scope for a remarkable political and social mobilization of the black community. It opened doors of opportunity that could never be completely closed. Reconstruction transformed the lives of Southern blacks in ways unmeasurable by statistics and unreachable by law. It raised their expectations and aspirations, redefined their status in relation to the larger society, and allowed space for the creation of institutions that enabled them to survive the repression that followed. And it established constitutional principles of civil and political equality that, while flagrantly violated after Redemption, planted the seeds of future struggle.

Certainly, it terms of the sense of possibility with which it opened, Reconstruction failed. But as Du Bois observed, it was a "splendid failure." For its animating vision—a society in which social advancement would be open to all on the basis of individual merit, not inherited caste distinctions—is as old as America itself and remains relevant to a nation still grappling with the unresolved legacy of emancipation.

Index

A

abolition, of slavery, 83, 84, 87, 118, 129, 192, 195, 197, 199, 205
abstinence, sexual, of Native Americans, 18, 19
"Act Concerning Religion," 50
Adair, James, 19
Adams, John, 56, 57, 58, 59, 65–66, 68, 95, 99, 103, 104, 105
Adams, John Quincy, 59
Adams, Samuel, 56, 73
Adet, Pierre, 104, 105
aesthetic conservation, 159
African slave trade, closure of, 90–91
Allen, Ethan, 74
American Bottom, 9, 10, 14
American Colonialization Society, 87
American Dream, Lincoln's, 198, 199, 201, 204
American paradox, 216
Amistad mutiny, 124–128
anarchy, of the frontier, 73
Anglican Church, 53
animals, and American Indians, 111, 114–115
Annapolis Convention, 75
Annapolis, Maryland, 50, 52
Anti-Federalists, 74, 102
anti-party movements, 69
antislavery, 82–91
Archaic period, 9
Articles of Confederation, 73, 76, 77
Austen, Jane, 65

B

Beauregard, P. G. T., 211
beaver, near-extinction of, 153
Beckwourth, Jim 131–135
Black Elk, 155
Black Heritage Trail, 193, 194, 195, 197
Blackfoot Indians, 122, 123, 133
Bodmer, Karl, 154
Boston Brahmins, 195
Boston, Massachusetts, 192–197
Bragg, Braxton, 210, 211
Brannan, Sam, 141, 143
Bremer, Fredericka, 147
Brent, Margaret, 51
Brown, Joe, 210
Brown, John, 192
Bryant, William Cullen, 154, 215
Buchanan, James, 138
buffalo, 113, 158
Burr, Aaron, 67, 68, 103, 105
Butler, Benjamin F., 183, 203
Butler, Pierce, 73, 78, 80
Byrd, William, 18

C

Cabot, John, 21
Cabot, Sebastian, 21, 24
Cahokia, 8–14
Calhoun, John C., 61, 62, 139
California, 138, 139, 140, 158
Calvert, Cecil, 52
Calvert, Charles, 52
Calvert, George, 49
Calvert, Leonard, 51, 52
camino real, 26, 28
campaign, first presidential election, 104

carpetbaggers, 218, 220
Cass, Lewis, 136
Cather, Willa, 157
Catholicism, 31
Catholics, 53
Catlin, George, 154
cattlemen, 156
Chamberlain, Joshua, 209
Chancellorsville, Battle of, 172–173
Chandler, Zachariah, 202–203
Charleston Harbor, 200
Chase, Salmon P., 166
chastity, 17
Cheyenne Indians, 113, 122, 123, 133
childbirth, 46
Chittenden, Thomas, 74
Christianity, 31
Cinqué, 124, 125, 130
civil rights movement, modern, 220–221
civil rights, of freedmen, 219
Civil War, 63, 139, 171–191, 192, 193, 195, 196, 197, 199, 201, 202, 203, 204, 205, 206, 207, 208–217, 222
Clay, Henry, 136
Cole, Thomas, 154, 155
Coles, Edward, 84, 86
colonialism, 113
Colquitt, Alfred H., 177
Columbus, Christopher, 15, 20, 21
commercial society, 64, 66, 67, 69
Committee of the Whole, 56, 57
confiscation, of enemy property, in Civil War, 202
Connecticut, 84
conservation, and pioneers, 153–159
Constitution, U.S., 78, 79, 81, 103, 198, 199, 204, 207
Contact period, 34
Continental Congress, 58, 73, 79, 86
Coode, John, 52
Coode's Rebellion, 52
Cooke, John R., 61, 62, 63
cooperation, among female slaves, 151
corn, 32, 112
Crow Indians, 113, 133

D

Dakota Indians, 123
Davis, Jefferson, 198, 208, 209, 211, 215
Davis, William C., 212
Deane, Silas, 57
Declaration of the Rights of Man, 58, 61
Declaration of Independence, 56, 57–58, 60, 62, 63, 77, 82, 83, 88, 90, 118, 128, 198, 199, 204
Delaney, Martin R., 201
Delaware, 56, 57, 85, 89
deportation, of slaves, 85, 87–88
Dickenson, John, 79, 80
Digges, William, 52
Douglas, Stephen, 62, 63
Douglass, Frederick, 192, 193, 194, 201, 203
Drayton, Percival, 214
Drayton, Thomas F., 214
Dunning, William, 218

E

Early, Jubal A., 212
Eaton, Chaplain, 167, 168
economic royalists, 69
election: first contested presidential, 101–105; of 1864, 205, 206
electoral college system, early, 102
Elsworth, Oliver, 76, 80
emancipation, 188–191, 202, 203, 204, 205, 222, 223, 224
emancipation amendment. See Thirteenth Amendment
Emancipation Proclamation of January 1, 1863, 167, 204, 205, 207, 209, 216
Emergent Mississipian period, 10
England, 138
environmental determinists, 110
environmentalism, on the frontier, 153–159
epidemics, 30, 112
equality, sexual, of Native Americans, 122

F

family ties, of blacks, in Reconstruction, 221
"Farewell Address," George Washington's, 103
farming, 10; on the frontier, 156–157
Farragut, David G., 212
Faulkner, William, 214
Federalist Party, 58, 105
Federalists, 99, 102
fertilizer, use of by Native Americans, 39–43
Fifteenth Amendment, 63, 220
Fifty-fourth Massachusetts Regiment, 196
fish, use of, as fertilizer, 39, 40, 41, 42, 43
Fisher, Sydney George, 222–223
Fitzhugh, George, 90
Florida purchase, 89
Force, Peter, 59
Forrest, Nathan Bedford, 168
Fort Sumter, 200
forty-niners, 141–146, 156
Founding Fathers, 61, 68, 69, 82–91, 198, 215
Fourteenth Amendment, 63, 220
Fourth of July, 58, 63
France, 77, 99, 138
Franciscans, 32
Frankfurter, Felix, 197
Franklin, Benjamin, 57, 65, 78, 80, 96, 97
Fredericks, C. D., 204
Freedman's Bureau, 217, 220
freedmen, 168, 218, 219
Frémont, John D., 139, 143, 163, 164
French Revolution, 64, 214
frontier, 153–159
Fugitive Slave Act of 1850, 194
fur trade, 113, 114

G

Garden, Myth of the, 157
Gardiner, John, 72
Garrison, William Lloyd, 89, 192, 193, 194, 195, 207
Geary, John, 143

gentlemen, 65, 67, 95
George III, King, 77, 79, 96, 118, 215
Georgia, 57
Gerry, Elbridge, 79, 80
Gettysburg Address, 63, 215, 216
Gettysburg, Union victory at, 63
gifts, 114
Glorious Revolution, in Maryland, 52
Grant, Ulysses S., 162–170, 208, 211
Great Compromise, 80
Greeley, Horace, 203
Green Mountain Boys, 74
Greene, James K., 223
Guadelupe Hidalgo, Treaty of, 139

Halleck, Henry W., 164, 166, 167, 168, 169
Hamilton, Alexander, 67, 68, 72, 75, 76, 102, 104, 105
Hardee, William J., 211
Harding, Vincent, 203
Hardy, Thomas, 214
Harper's Ferry, 192
Harte, Bret, 158
Harvard University, 196, 197
harvest festival, 8
Hastings, Lansford W., 154
Hayden, Lewis, 194
Henry, Patrick, 74, 75, 81
Hidatsa Indians, 122
Higginson, Henry Lee, 196, 197
Holmes, Oliver Wendell, 197
Homer, Winslow, 197
Hood, John Bell, 211
Hooker, Joseph, 171, 172, 173, 174, 175, 178, 182
horses, 112, 113
Howe, Julia Ward, 192, 197
Howe, Samuel Gridley, 192
Hudson River school, of painting, 154
Hudson's Bay Company, 136
human rights, 90

incest, and Native Americans, 18
indentured servants, 86
Independence Day, 63
Indians, American, 9, 15–20, 74, 106, 110–115
inexhaustability of western resources, belief in, 155, 158, 159
internal revenue bureau, creation of an, 217
Iroquois Indians, 122
Iroquois nation, 123

Jackson, Andrew, 83, 136
Jackson, Thomas J. ("Stonewall"), 171, 173, 174, 175, 176, 179, 182
Jacksonians, 59
Jacobins. See Radical Republicans
James, William, 195, 196
Jamestown Archaeological Assessment, 33, 38
Jamestown, Virginia, 33, 35, 36, 37, 38
Jay, John, 72, 91, 102, 103

Jefferson, Thomas, 16, 56, 57, 58, 60, 62, 65, 67, 68, 73, 78, 82, 85, 87, 88, 91, 95, 98, 99, 102, 103, 104, 105, 106, 114, 116–121
Jews, 53, 193
Johnson, Andrew, 218, 219
Johnston, Albert Sidney, 210, 211
Johnston, Joseph E., 210, 211

Kansas, 62
Kansas-Nebraska Act, of 1854, 61, 62, 92
Kentucky, 89, 90, 156–157, 163, 214
King, Rufus, 74
Kittoe, Edward, 165
Ku Klux Klan, 220

La Cosa map, 24
labor, Native American, 26–32, 122; slave women's, 147–148; slave, 223
land, European challenge of Native American ownership of, 19
Lansing, John, 78
Larkin, Thomas O., 138
Late Mississippian period, 14
Late Woodland period, 34
Lee, Richard Henry, 56, 58
Lee, Robert E., 171–182, 208, 209, 210
L'Enfant, Pierre, 99
Lewis, Meriwether, 106–109
Lincoln, Abraham, 56, 61–62, 85, 90, 164, 167, 171, 198–202, 209, 212; and Reconstruction, 219
Livingston, Robert R., 56, 57
Locke's Essays (Locke), 58
Locke, John, 58
Long, David, 205
Lost Cause (Civil War as a), 209
Louisiana Purchase, 89, 140
Lowell, Massachusetts, 195
Lumbrozo, Jacob, 50

Madison, James, 67, 74, 75, 77, 79, 80, 81, 86, 102
majolica pottery, 28
manumission, of slaves, 84, 85, 86, 88, 90
Marbury v. Madison, 81
March to the Sea, Sherman's, 207
Marchant, Edward Dalton, 204
marriage: Native American, 17; American Puritan, 45
Marshall, James, 141, 143
Martin, Luther, 73, 76, 81
Maryland, 49–53, 56, 57, 73, 85, 89
Maryland Revolution, 52
Mason, George, 73–74, 78, 79, 81
Massachusetts, 60, 61, 86
Mather, Cotton, 44, 45, 48
matrilinearity, 17, 122
Mattapany, surrender at, 52–53
McClellan, George B., 205, 206
McClernand, John A., 164–165
McPherson, James, 205

Meade, George G., 172, 174
Mercer, John Francis, 74
merit, aristocracy of, 104
Mexico, 137, 138, 139
Michael, Andre, 106
Middle Woodland period, 34
Middleton, George, 194
Mill, John Stuart, 69
Miller, Joaquin, 142
Mississippi, 166
Mississippian period, 10
Missouri, 89, 103
Missouri Compromise, 139
Monks Mound, 9, 11, 12, 13, 14
Monroe, James, 89, 98, 103
Montesquieu, 74, 77, 79
Monticello, 60, 95, 116–118, 120–121
Mormon Church, 155
mounds, 9, 10, 11, 14
Mount Vernon, 95
mountain men, 131–135

Natchez Indians, 11
national currency, creation of a, 217
Navajo Indians, 115
Nebraska, 62
New Deal, 69
New Hampshire, 60, 84
New Jersey, 56, 57, 61, 84, 85
New Mexico, 133, 138, 139
New York, 56, 57, 61, 84, 85, 89
North Carolina, 57, 220
Northerners, 73, 90, 163, 215, 223
Northwest Ordinance of 1787, 86, 87, 88
Northwest Territories, 80, 86
nutritional deficiencies, 13

officeholding, black, 221, 223
Ojibwa Indians, 122
Olmstead, Frederick Law, 158
Omaha Indians, 122
Oregon, 136–137, 140
Oregon Trail, 155

Paine, Tom, 76
Pakenham, Richard, 136–137
palatinate, of Maryland, 50
Paleoindian period, 9, 34
Papago Indians, 123
Parkman, Francis, 153–154
parks, public, creation of, 158
passenger pigeon, 158
Pawnee Indians, 112, 113, 122
peace overture, in Civil War, 206
Pemberton, John C., 211
Penn, William, 154
Pennsylvania, 56, 57, 60, 78, 79, 84, 85, 105
Pennsylvania Constitution of 1838, 219
pensions, 71
Pettigrew, William, 189
Pettit, John, 61, 62
Philadelphia Convention, 76, 77, 78, 88
Philadelphia, Pennsylvania, 75
Pinckney, Charles, 78, 103, 104, 105

planter class, 203, 205, 221, 224
Pleistocene period, 34
Pocahontas, 15, 19
Polk Doctrine, 140
Polk, James K., 136–140, 164
Polk, Leonidas, 211
polygamy, 133
polygyny, 17
post-nati abolition, 84, 85, 86, 89
Powell, John Wesley, 157
Powhatan Indians, 15, 33
presidency, creation of the, 98, 100
price, and trade, 114
privacy, lack of, in Native American culture, 16–17
property, 79
prostitution, 17
Protestant Association, 52
Protestants, 49, 51, 52, 53
Protohistoric period, 34
Pueblo Indians, 123

Quincy, Josiah, 196

Radical Reconstruction, 220, 221, 223
Radical Republicans, 202, 218, 219
railroad network, national completion of, 222
Randolph, Edmund, 78
Randolph, John, 61
Reconstruction, 218–224; revised view of, 219–224
religion, 64–65, 67
religious liberty, 67
revisionist history, and Reconstruction, 219–224
Revolutionary War, 63–71, 76; and slavery, 64–93
Rhode Island, 51, 80, 84
Romans, Bernard, 17
Roosevelt, Franklin Delano, 99
Roosevelt, Theodore, 158
Rush, Benjamin, 16, 65
Rutledge, Edward, 56, 57
Rutledge, John, 80

Sacajawea, 108–109
Sampson, Deborah, 70–71
Sand Creek Massacre, 135
Sargeant, John, 60, 63
scalawags, 218, 220
scorched-earth warfare, 202, 207
Second Continental Congress, 56
Second Great Awakening, 65
Secret Six, 192
sexual freedom, of Native Americans, 122

sexuality, female, 16; Native American, 16–20
Shaw, Robert Gould, 195, 196, 197
Shays, Daniel, 74
Sheridan, Philip, 206, 207, 208, 212
Sherman, Roger, 57, 79, 80
Sherman, William T., 206, 207, 208
Shurtleff, Robert, 70–71
Sickles, Dan, 172, 176, 177
slavery, 61, 77, 81, 82–91, 118, 119–121, 147–152, 162–170, 195, 198, 199, 202, 203, 204, 205, 206, 215, 216; and Westward Expansion, 139
Slidell, John, 137, 138, 139
smallpox, 112
Smith, Adam, 67
Smith, Edward Kirby, 209
Smith, John, 15, 19, 20
Smith, John J., 194
Smith, Joseph, 155
Smith, Samuel Stanhope, 17
soil improvement, 39–43
South Carolina, 57, 87, 88
Southerners, 73, 81, 162, 163, 199, 201, 207, 211, 215, 217
Southwest Ordinance of 1784, 85, 86
Spain, 77
Sparks, Jared, 59
Sprague, Peleg, 60, 63
Squanto, 39–43
St. Augustine, Florida, 26, 29, 31
St. Mary's City, Maryland, 50, 51, 52, 53
Stevens, Thaddeus, 207, 219, 221
Stockton, Robert F., 138, 139
Stoddard, William O., 200
Strauss, Levi, 143
Stuart, Granville, 158
Stuart, James E. B., 172, 214
suffrage, black, 221, 223
Sumner, Charles, 196, 202–203, 205, 219
Superabundance, Myth of, 157
Sutter, John, 141, 143

tattooing, 16
taxation, 80; during Reconstruction, 223
Taylor, Richard, 169
Taylor, Zackary, 137, 140
Tennessee, 166, 168, 220
Texas, 137
Thayer, Olney, 144–145
Thirteenth Amendment, 63, 207, 217
Thoreau, Henry David, 154
tobacco, 35, 52, 222
Tocqueville, Alexis de, 66, 224
Toleration Act for Dissenting Protestants, 50
toleration, religious, 49

Tordesillas, Treaty of, 25
Trumbull, John, 59, 60, 96
Turner, Nat, 61
Twain, Mark, 143, 154, 214
Tyler, John, 61

Underground Railroad, 194
"Union," as a term, versus "nation," 216
Union landmarks in Boston, 192–197
Union, restoration of the, 205. See also Reconstruction
Upper South Founding Fathers, 87
Utah, 155

Van Buren, Martin, 136
Van Dorn, Earl, 168
Vermont, 60, 74, 84
Vespucci, Amerigo, 16
Vicksburg, Mississippi, 169
vindictives. See Radical Republicans
Virginia, 57, 61, 79
Virginia Plan, 77–79
Virginia, University of, 60
Volck, Adalbert, 205

Wade, Benjamin Franklin, 61, 63, 202–203
war failure plank, of Democratic platform, in election of 1864, 205
War of 1812, 58
war power, innovation of, by Lincoln, 204
Washington, Booker T., 195
Washington, George, 72, 73, 74, 76, 77, 79–80, 85, 103, 105; greatness of 94–100, 104
West Virginia, 91
Wheeler, Joseph, 211
Whigs, 59
Whiskey Ring, 220
Whitfield, Frances, 166
Whitman, Walt, 154
Wilkes, John, 58
William of Orange, 52
Wilmot Proviso, 139
Wilson, James, 56, 78, 79
women: moral authority of Puritan, 44–48; Native American, 15–16; slave, 147–152; violence against Native American, 18
"woodhenges," 11, 14
Woodland period, 9, 10
Woody, Robert, 219
workingmen, 67
Wythe, George, 56

AE Article Review Form

We encourage you to photocopy and use this page as a tool to assess how the articles in **Annual Editions** expand on the information in your textbook. By reflecting on the articles you will gain enhanced text information. You can also access this useful form on our Web site at **http://www.dushkin.annualeditions.com/**.

NAME:

DATE:

TITLE AND NUMBER OF ARTICLE:

BRIEFLY STATE THE MAIN IDEA OF THIS ARTICLE:

LIST THREE IMPORTANT FACTS THAT THE AUTHOR USES TO SUPPORT THE MAIN IDEA:

WHAT INFORMATION OR IDEAS DISCUSSED IN THIS ARTICLE ARE ALSO DISCUSSED IN YOUR TEXTBOOK OR OTHER READINGS THAT YOU HAVE DONE? LIST THE TEXTBOOK CHAPTERS AND PAGE NUMBERS:

LIST ANY EXAMPLES OF BIAS OR FAULTY REASONING THAT YOU FOUND IN THE ARTICLE:

LIST ANY NEW TERMS/CONCEPTS THAT WERE DISCUSSED IN THE ARTICLE, AND WRITE A SHORT DEFINITION:

ANNUAL EDITIONS revisions depend on two major opinion sources: one is our Advisory Board, listed in the front of this volume, which works with us in scanning the thousands of articles published in the public press each year; the other is you—the person actually using the book. Please help us and the users of the next edition by completing the prepaid article rating form on this page and returning it to us. Thank you for your help!

ANNUAL EDITIONS: American History, Volume I
Pre-Colonial through Reconstruction

ARTICLE RATING FORM

Here is an opportunity for you to have direct input into the next revision of this volume. We would like you to rate each of the 35 articles listed below, using the following scale:

1. **Excellent: should definitely be retained**
2. **Above average: should probably be retained**
3. **Below average: should probably be deleted**
4. **Poor: should definitely be deleted**

Your ratings will play a vital part in the next revision. So please mail this prepaid form to us just as soon as you complete it. Thanks for your help!

We Want Your Advice

RATING | ARTICLE

1. Mighty Cahokia
2. Columbus Meets Pocahontas in the American South
3. A "Newfounde Lande"
4. Laboring in the Fields of the Lord
5. Journey to Jamestown
6. Squanto and the Pilgrims
7. Bearing the Burden? Puritan Wives
8. America's First Experiment in Toleration
9. Making Sense of the Fourth of July
10. The *Radical* Revolution
11. "Pvt. Robert Shurtleff": An Unusual Revolutionary War Soldier
12. 'It Is Not a Union'
13. . . . by the Unanimous Consent of the States
14. The Founding Fathers, Conditional Antislavery, and the Nonradicalism of the American Revolution
15. The Greatness of George Washington
16. 1796: The First Real Election
17. Lewis and Clark: Trailblazers Who Opened the Continent

RATING | ARTICLE

18. Indians in the Land
19. Jefferson's Retreat
20. Before the "Trail of Tears"
21. "All We Want Is Make Us Free!"
22. Mountain Legend
23. James K. Polk and the Expansionist Spirit
24. All That Glittered
25. The Lives of Slave Women
26. Eden Ravished
27. "The Doom of Slavery": Ulysses S. Grant, War Aims, and Emancipation, 1861–1863
28. Lee's Greatest Victory
29. Gallantry under Fire
30. The Struggle for Black Freedom before Emancipation
31. The Northern Front
32. The Man at the White House Window
33. Why the South Lost the Civil War
34. A War That Never Goes Away
35. The New View of Reconstruction

(Continued on next page)

**ANNUAL EDITIONS: AMERICAN HISTORY, Volume I,
15th Edition**

BUSINESS REPLY MAIL
FIRST-CLASS MAIL PERMIT NO. 84 GUILFORD CT

POSTAGE WILL BE PAID BY ADDRESSEE

**Dushkin/McGraw-Hill
Sluice Dock
Guilford, CT 06437-9989**

IIʰﻬ.ﻬ.ﻫ.ﻫﻪﻫﻪﻫﻪﻫﻫﻫﻪﻫﻬﻫﻬﻫﻪﻫﻪﻫﻪﻫ

ABOUT YOU

Name _____ Date _____

Are you a teacher? ☐ A student? ☐
Your school's name _____

Department _____

Address _____ City _____ State ____ Zip ____

School telephone # _____

YOUR COMMENTS ARE IMPORTANT TO US !

Please fill in the following information:
For which course did you use this book?
_____

Did you use a text with this *ANNUAL EDITION*? ☐ yes ☐ no
What was the title of the text?
_____

What are your general reactions to the *Annual Editions* concept?
_____

Have you read any particular articles recently that you think should be included in the next edition?
_____

Are there any articles you feel should be replaced in the next edition? Why?
_____

Are there any World Wide Web sites you feel should be included in the next edition? Please annotate.
_____

May we contact you for editorial input? ☐ yes ☐ no
May we quote your comments? ☐ yes ☐ no